Return to an Address of the Honourable the House of Commons
dated 6 July 2016
for

The Report of the Iraq Inquiry

Report of a Committee of Privy Counsellors

Volume VI

Ordered by the House of Commons to be printed on 6 July 2016

HC 265-VI

Volume VI

CONTENTS

SECTION 6.3

MILITARY EQUIPMENT (PRE-CONFLICT)

Contents

Introduction and key findings

1. This Section addresses:

- the arrangements made to provide equipment to forces deploying for operations in Iraq;
- difficulties in the provision of Combat Identification (Combat ID), ammunition, Enhanced Combat Body Armour (ECBA), desert clothing, and equipment to protect against a chemical or biological attack; and
- asset tracking.

2. This Section does not address:

- the UK's military planning for the invasion of Iraq, which is addressed in Sections 6.1 and 6.2;
- the background to decisions made by the Treasury on equipment and Urgent Operational Requirement (UOR) funding, which is described in Section 13.1; and
- assessments of Iraq's capabilities and intent. Intelligence assessments relevant to military planning are addressed in Section 6.2 and the UK's assessment of Iraq's WMD programmes in Sections 4.1 to 4.4.

Key findings

- The decisions taken between mid-December 2002 and mid-January 2003 to increase combat forces and bring forward the date on which UK forces might participate in combat operations compressed the timescales available for preparation.
- The achievements made in preparing the forces in the time available were very considerable, but the deployment of forces more quickly than anticipated in the Defence Planning Assumptions meant that there were some serious equipment shortfalls when conflict began.
- Those shortfalls were exacerbated by the lack of an effective asset tracking system, a lesson from previous operations and exercises that the Ministry of Defence (MOD) had identified but not adequately addressed.
- Ministers were not fully aware of the risks inherent in the decisions and the MOD and Permanent Joint Headquarters (PJHQ) were not fully aware of the situation on the ground during the conflict.

Planning and readiness for expeditionary operations

3. **The Armed Forces' capacity to deploy and sustain expeditionary operations was determined by decisions in the 1998 *Strategic Defence Review* (SDR).**

4. **The SDR identified a major regional crisis, including in the Gulf, as the most demanding scenario against which the UK should plan for military operations.**

5. The SDR set out the UK's "defence requirements in the period to 2015".[1] That included the UK's defence priorities, the scenarios in which the Government envisaged deploying military forces, and what this meant for the UK's military force structure.

6. The SDR explained that, "in the post Cold War world", there was a greater need for the Armed Forces to build an expeditionary capability because "we must be prepared to go to the crisis, rather than have the crisis come to us".

7. A supporting essay to the SDR about future military capabilities listed those it considered "increasingly important", including:

- command, control, communications and computers and Intelligence, Surveillance, Target Acquisition and Reconnaissance (ISTAR);
- transport or lift capabilities because of "the trend towards force projections operations, for which we may need to deploy very rapidly in order to be successful";
- combat service support (logistics, equipment and medical support), which was "key to sustaining deployed operations, particularly those of significant duration"; and
- "protection against chemical and biological weapons" which was described as critically important in some of the regions in which we are likely to have to operate, such as the Gulf".[2]

8. The SDR was explicit in envisaging the UK operating in a number of areas, including the Gulf region. It stated:

"We have particularly important national interests and close friendships in the Gulf … There are already significant sources of instability in these regions – including the continuing threat represented by Saddam Hussein's Iraq … These dangers seem unlikely to diminish and may grow. Many of our Allies and Partners have similar important interests and friendships in these areas. We would therefore expect to work with them in responding to any future crises."[3]

9. The SDR continued:

"Outside Europe, the greatest risks to our national economic and political interest – and probably to international stability – will remain in the Gulf … this Mission may involve major combat operations … Such operations also impose demanding requirements, for example, in relation to strategic transport for deployment and supply, and to command and control … In operational terms, the most demanding individual scenario against which we must now plan is no longer all-out war in

---

[1] Ministry of Defence, *Strategic Defence Review*, July 1998.
[2] Ministry of Defence, *Strategic Defence Review: Supporting Essays*, July 1998.
[3] Ministry of Defence, *Strategic Defence Review*, July 1998.

Europe but a major regional crisis involving our national interest, perhaps on NATO's periphery or in the Gulf."

10. The SDR acknowledged that "major equipments take years to develop".

11. While the SDR identified no definitive timescales for its proposed changes, the MOD did publish a series of targets in December 1998 as part of its Public Service Agreement for 1999 to 2002.[4] Targets included achieving a "Full Joint Rapid Reaction Forces Capability by October 2001" and to "achieve reductions in book value of stocks of non-munitions of £2.2bn by April 2001".

12. The Public Service Agreement recognised that the plans set out in the SDR would "require substantial investment to improve inherited areas of weakness measured against future operational needs and to fund a continuing major equipment modernisation programme". The resources necessary to achieve this would be found "from making savings from rationalisation in other areas, a continuing programme of efficiency improvements and smarter procurement".

13. Decisions on the allocation of resources to the MOD, and within the MOD, were underpinned by a set of Defence Planning Assumptions (DPAs) about the totality of the commitments that the MOD would expect to meet and sustain at any one time and the time needed to prepare for operations.

14. The ability of the UK to deploy and sustain forces on operations was determined by the size of the Armed Forces and the readiness of units within the force structure. That is still the case today.

15. Decisions on those issues and the allocation of resources to and within the MOD were based on the DPAs. DPAs were developed by the MOD to convert policy into detailed guidance that could be used by military planners.[5] The DPAs outlined the levels of activity the Armed Forces were expected to be able to undertake, and the contexts in which they were expected to operate. They were (and are) used to identify and resource the planned force structure, capabilities and equipment of the Armed Forces.

16. The SDR "set some broad benchmarks for the scale of our planning" and said that the UK should be able to:

" – respond to a major international crisis which might require a military effort and combat operations of a similar scale and duration to the Gulf War when we deployed an armoured division, 26 major warships and over 80 combat aircraft.

"or

---

[4] *Public Services for the Future: Modernisation, Reform, Accountability*, December 1998, Cm 4181.
[5] Ministry of Defence, *Strategic Defence Review*, July 1998.

" – undertake a more extended deployment on a lesser scale (as over the last few years in Bosnia) while retaining the ability to mount a second substantial deployment – which might involve a combat brigade and appropriate naval and air forces – if this were made necessary by a second crisis. We would not, however, expect both deployments to involve war-fighting or to maintain them simultaneously for longer than six months."

17. The DPAs are addressed in more detail in Section 6.1.

18. The 'Defence Strategic Plan' was a confidential MOD document which included greater detail than was published in the SDR report.[6] The Plan identified some specific readiness criteria in relation to regional conflict outside NATO:

"… we need to maintain the ability to respond within short warning times to an Iraqi threat, and to build up forces thereafter. This again requires us to hold capabilities needed to mount a medium scale deployment at high readiness (30 days) … For a large scale deployment we need to plan on a framework division being ready within 90 days."

Scales of military operation

To inform the DPAs, the scales of military effort, over and above those required for day-to-day commitments, were defined in the SDR as:

- **small scale**: "a deployment of battalion size or equivalent";
- **medium scale**: "deployments of brigade size or equivalent", such as the UK's contribution to Bosnia in the mid-1990s;
- **large scale**: "deployments of division size or equivalent", such as the UK's contribution to the 1991 Gulf Conflict; and
- **very large scale and full scale**: forces needed "to meet significant aggression against an Ally", the difference between the two reflected the time available for preparation – "warning time" – and the size of the threat.[7]

Other factors to be considered included:

- **endurance** – the likely duration of any operation and the potential need to sustain a deployment for an indefinite period; and
- **concurrency** – the number of operations of a given scale of effort and duration that could be sustained by the force structure.

More detail on the planning assumptions for the scales of military operation is provided in Section 6.1.

---

[6] Ministry of Defence, 1998, 'Defence Strategic Plan 1998'.
[7] Ministry of Defence, *Strategic Defence Review: Supporting Essays,* July 1998.

Testing the UK's expeditionary capability: lessons learned?

19. The first Gulf Conflict had highlighted inadequacies in the UK's asset tracking and Combat ID equipment.

20. The UK deployed an armoured division during the Gulf Conflict in 1991, Operation GRANBY, comprising two combat brigades: 4 Brigade and 7 Armoured Brigade.[8]

21. The MOD identified a number of lessons relating to equipment following the 1991 Gulf Conflict in its *Statement on the Defence Estimates* in 1992.[9] It found that deficiencies in the reliability of older equipment had "considerable implications" for the UK's operational capability, and were "only overcome by a disproportionate application of maintenance effort and deployment of spares".

22. The MOD also found that the volume of stores and equipment that had to be moved to theatre, and the compressed timescales involved, led to problems with the visibility of stockholdings and items in transit.[10] A temporary system was devised for tracking operationally vital items but the MOD was examining "improved arrangements for the future". The system for allocating priorities in the movement of freight was "overloaded by the volume of high priority items" and a review had been commissioned to learn the lessons from the operation.

23. A secure and effective battlefield electronic identification system, which later became known as Combat ID,[11] "did not exist" during Op GRANBY. While practical steps were taken to avoid engagements between Coalition Forces, a number of incidents occurred.

24. The MOD stated that the UK was working with the US "to identify technical and operational options" to minimise the risk of further incidents. The Defence Research Agency was "also undertaking a research programme aimed at assessing both short term solutions and options for the longer term".

25. Concerns about progress on asset tracking systems were raised in Public Accounts Committee reports in 1993, 1997 and 2000.

26. A Public Accounts Committee report in 1993 on the first Gulf Conflict stated that it was "concerned the Department did not have a sound system for tracking freight".[12]

---

[8] Ministry of Defence, *Statement on the Defence Estimates – Britain's Defence for the 90s*, July 1991, Cm 1559.

[9] Ministry of Defence, *Statement on the Defence Estimates,* July 1992, Cm 1981.

[10] Ministry of Defence, *Statement on the Defence Estimates,* July 1992, Cm 1981.

[11] Combat ID enables military forces to distinguish friend from foe during operations, minimising the risk of accidental destruction of friendly or allied forces, otherwise known as fratricide or Blue-on-Blue incidents. The systems and procedures in place must be interoperable with those used by allied forces.

[12] Twenty-sixth Report from the Committee of Public Accounts, Session 1993-94, *Ministry of Defence: Movements of Personnel, Equipment and Stores to and from the Gulf*, HC 393, paras 18-19.

27. The Public Accounts Committee stated:

"We consider it unacceptable that the lack of elementary tracking led to some operationally critical items being 'lost to view', and note that 228 aircraft pallets worth £680,000 went missing completely during GRANBY. The failure to be able to locate some equipment also led to some duplicate requisitioning.

"We stress the importance of the Department taking urgent action to improve their management information systems relating to movements ... we recommend that the Department have regard to the best systems in operation in the commercial sector, in particular those used for keeping track of assets."

28. In 1997, the Public Accounts Committee report on the UK's operations in the former Yugoslavia found that it was "unsatisfactory" that asset tracking had "again proved to be a problem", despite assurances given by the MOD following the first Gulf Conflict.[13]

29. The Committee added:

"We suggest that some of the problems with the Department's asset tracking systems, particularly the strain on communications systems and the large volumes of data, could be regarded as foreseeable consequences of an operational environment. We note that the Department are considering what systems might be appropriate for the future. We recommend that, in doing this, they give particular attention to ensuring that they have systems robust enough to deal with operational conditions; it is at such times that large quantities of equipment and stores tend to be moving around, and it becomes easy to lose sight of them."

30. The Public Accounts Committee reported on operations in the former Yugoslavia again in 2000 and found that:

"The Department has little capacity to monitor the supply chain's performance in theatre, nor the condition and reliability of equipments in theatre. The Department do not expect to have IT systems fully operating to provide such information until 2003 ..."[14]

31. A military exercise in 2001 found that British equipment did not work well in hot and dusty conditions and needed to be improved, given the UK's focus on expeditionary operations.

32. The exercise also identified difficulties with clothing, boots and asset tracking.

---

[13] Twenty-third Report from the Committee of Public Accounts, Session 1996-97, *Ministry of Defence: Management of the Military Operations in the Former Yugoslavia*, HC 242, paras 45-46.
[14] Forty-sixth Report from the Committee of Public Accounts 1999-2000 – *Ministry of Defence: Kosovo – The Financial Management of Military Operations.*

33. In October 2001, the MOD conducted Exercise Saif Sareea II in Oman.[15] The exercise, which involved around 22,500 British Armed Forces personnel from all three services, aimed to test the Armed Forces' ability to conduct a medium scale operation over long distances, in the post-SDR expeditionary force structure. It tested the principle that the Joint Rapid Reaction Forces should be ready to conduct expeditionary operations in any area of the world at short notice.

34. In August 2002, the National Audit Office (NAO) published a report into the exercise, which included a number of recommendations and identified a number of problems to be addressed.[16]

35. Much equipment performed well, including Warrior Armoured Fighting Vehicles (AFVs) and the C17 strategic lift aircraft.

36. As a result of pre-exercise reconnaissance, 4 Armoured Brigade had made a number of recommendations for the modification of equipment, including 'desertisation'[17] of Challenger 2 tanks. Despite the recommendation, the Permanent Joint Headquarters (PJHQ) directed that the modifications would not be required given the predicted climatic conditions in Oman.

37. During the exercise, a number of Challenger 2 tanks experienced difficulties relating to the hot and dusty conditions. As a result, a much larger quantity of spare parts was required and equipment availability was lower than expected.

38. Sand filters were fitted to the engines of Lynx and Chinook helicopters, as a result of lessons learned from the 1991 Gulf Conflict. Overall helicopter availability, however, was 55 percent.

39. The MOD had insufficient desert combat suits and desert boots for all personnel. As a result, desert-specific clothing was issued only to personnel who would be in theatre for an extended period. Standard issue boots were unsuitable for the task; 4 Armoured Brigade's post-exercise report cited melting boots and foot rot as "a major issue".

40. The NAO reported that asset tracking systems remained weak. The Visibility In Transit Asset Logging (VITAL) system, introduced as a result of NAO recommendations following the first Gulf Conflict, had been operating "at 500 percent of its originally planned capacity" by 2001. It was slow during the exercise, taking 15 minutes to find the contents of a single ISO container. As VITAL was not available at the point of exiting the UK, there was no visibility of an item until it arrived in theatre.

---

[15] National Audit Office, *Exercise Saif Sareea II,* 1 August 2002, HC 1097.
[16] National Audit Office, *Exercise Saif Sareea II*, 1 August 2002, HC 1097.
[17] Modifications to equipment that enable it to operate in desert conditions.

41. On learning lessons, the NAO report stated:

"Some lessons identified during previous operations were re-learned, which illustrated the tendency that skills learned on medium size operations such as the Gulf War dissipate over time as people move on. There is a strong argument that exercises of the size of Saif Sareea need to be conducted regularly in order to keep skills and experience up to date and to check that lessons previously identified have been implemented."

42. In March 2002, the NAO considered the MOD's progress in implementing a Combat ID strategy following the 1998 SDR.

43. A report by the NAO on 7 March 2002 acknowledged the complexities surrounding Combat ID and recognised that the MOD had developed a clear strategy for finding a solution.[18]

44. The NAO did find, however, that there was more that could be done to move the issue forward. Amongst the projects it identified as a way of enhancing Combat ID work was Battlefield Target Identification (BTID). The NAO wrote that the MOD had spent £7m over the last 10 years on researching land solutions to Combat ID and there had been a successful trial of a BTID prototype in September 2001. Despite that, a proposal to fit an armoured brigade with BTID had not passed an Initial Gate Business Case.[19]

45. The MOD was confident that it would have integrated BTID equipment ready to participate in a US-led NATO demonstration in September 2005. That would provide an opportunity to show if its solution was compliant with the relevant NATO Standardisation Agreement. The MOD was confident that its solution was "already compliant".

46. A meeting in May 2002 highlighted concerns about whether the readiness levels specified in the SDR could be met.

47. On 21 May, Mr Blair attended a meeting with the Chiefs of Staff, Mr Geoff Hoon, Defence Secretary, and Sir Kevin Tebbit, MOD Permanent Secretary, to discuss current operations and resources.[20]

48. The note of the meeting recorded that Admiral Sir Michael Boyce, the Chief of the Defence Staff (CDS), said that the Armed Forces had "been under-resourced since the SDR" and they "could not continue to make do". From "each operation there was a lengthening list of inadequacies". In August the MOD "would reach a cliff edge, having to collapse operational capability to stay in budget".

---

[18] National Audit Office, *Ministry of Defence: Combat Identification*, 7 March 2002, HC 661.
[19] The procurement process, including the phases for business cases, is explained in Section 14.1.
[20] Note Rycroft, 21 May 2002, 'Prime Minister's Meeting with Chiefs of Staff'.

49. Adm Boyce also said that SDR readiness levels were not being met:

"For instance, a division should be capable of being produced in 90 days[21] but it would now be difficult to produce two thirds of a division in 6 months, with consequences on Iraq (US lead time by contrast would be 3 months)."

50. In addition, "resources were needed for new investment to secure information-dominance for the war on terrorism/asymmetric threats".

51. Mr Hoon described the three levels of funding that were required:

"(1) to deliver the SDR assumptions;

(2) to modernise equipment/training to deliver a modern Armed Forces; and

(3) to get the capabilities right post-11 September."

52. Sir Kevin "said the priority was filling gaps in capabilities".

53. In July 2002, the MOD published a follow-up to the 1998 SDR which confirmed that the shift towards expeditionary operations was likely to become more pronounced.

54. In July 2002, the MOD published *The Strategic Defence Review: A New Chapter*, an update on the SDR's progress and a consideration of the "UK's defence posture and plans" in light of the 9/11 attacks.[22]

55. The MOD stated it was likely that the trend towards expeditionary operations would "become even more pronounced". While the core regions identified in the SDR – Europe, the Gulf and the Mediterranean – were likely to remain "the primary focus" of UK interests, it was "increasingly clear that a coherent and effective campaign against international terrorism – and indeed other contingencies – may require engagement further afield more often than perhaps we had previously assumed".

56. On the Armed Forces' ability to conduct multiple, simultaneous operations, the MOD wrote:

"The capability of our forces is strained not just by the scale of operations, but by the number of simultaneous or near-simultaneous operations. Since the SDR we have assumed that we should plan to be able to undertake either a single major operation (of a similar scale and duration to our contribution to the Gulf War in 1990-91), or undertake a more extended overseas deployment on a lesser scale (as in the mid-1990s in Bosnia), while retaining the ability to mount a second substantial deployment – which might involve a combat brigade and appropriate naval and air

---

[21] This text reflects what is recorded in the note but is not what the SDR stated; it specified that a framework division should be ready within 90 days.
[22] Ministry of Defence, *Strategic Defence Review: A New Chapter*, July 2002.

forces – if this were made necessary by a second crisis. We would not, however, expect both deployments to involve war-fighting or to maintain them simultaneously for longer than 6 months."

57. The MOD had "analysed a set of plausible and realistic scenarios" to assess the demands potentially faced by the UK overseas. That work had taken account of lessons learned from operations, including in Afghanistan. The MOD recognised that the particular scenarios it had envisaged might not be "replicated precisely in real life", but they did allow the MOD to "draw general conclusions about the capabilities that may be particularly important".

The UK's expeditionary capability by 2002

58. By 2002, UK forces had not yet acquired the equipment envisaged by the SDR.

59. Mr Hoon's evidence to the Inquiry suggested that the time needed to deliver the changes envisaged by the SDR and the *New Chapter* was appreciated:

"[We] were moving the emphasis of the Ministry of Defence away from the kind of static territorial defence of the Cold War period to a much more flexible … expeditionary capability. But that sounds quite straightforward to describe. It actually … requires massive adjustments in capabilities."[23]

60. Asked if the SDR had "worked itself through satisfactorily" by the time of the invasion, Lord Walker, Chief of the Defence Staff from May 2003 to April 2006 said "No."[24] Asked to expand on that, Lord Walker stated that continuously operating outside the DPAs, and a shortfall in funding, were key reasons.

61. Air Chief Marshal Sir Jock Stirrup, Deputy Chief of the Defence Staff (Equipment Capability) (DCDS(EC)) from April 2002 to May 2003, told the Inquiry that some progress towards delivering the capabilities to support this expeditionary capability had been made by 2002 but the process was not complete: "We had moved some way, but we still had a fair distance to go."[25]

62. Sir Kevin Tebbit told the Inquiry that the SDR contained "big challenges for the Armed Forces and there were such a large number of actions for implementation for the SDR that it was inevitably going to take time to work through".[26]

---

[23] Public hearing, 19 January 2010, pages 124-125.
[24] Public hearing, 1 February 2010, page 40.
[25] Public hearing, 1 February 2010, page 3.
[26] Private hearing, 6 May 2010, page 44.

63. Lieutenant General Sir Robert Fulton, who succeeded ACM Stirrup as DCDS(EC), told the Inquiry:

> "My take on it would be that we went to Iraq with our Cold War capability, that there simply was not time between 1998 and 2002 to re-orientate a Capital Equipment Programme that stretched for 20 years."[27]

64. Lt Gen Fulton added:

> "… it was not possible in the time that I saw it from the time I was first engaged in the equipment area to be able to turn a Cold War-equipped military into a flexible, deployable, sustainable military within the life of the equipment plan."[28]

Equipment preparations for the invasion (2002 to 2003)

Planning begins

65. The MOD's initial thinking on options for military operations in Iraq focused on the deployment of an Army division. That would require a minimum of six months' lead time and ideally longer.

66. Consideration of the UK's options in the event of a US-led military invasion of Iraq began at the end of February 2002. That is addressed in detail in Section 6.1.

67. This Section considers the arrangements made for providing equipment to forces as part of the planning process for potential operations in Iraq.

68. On 6 March 2002, the Chiefs of Staff were informed that Iraq was "sliding rapidly up the scale of interest and a degree of strategic planning was essential at some point in the near future, given the lead times necessary to shape pol/mil thinking effectively".[29]

69. The Chiefs of Staff agreed that Air Chief Marshal Sir Anthony Bagnall, Vice Chief of the Defence Staff, who was chairing the meeting in CDS' absence, should "refresh" work on Urgent Operational Requirements (UORs)[30] to ensure that it was not left "too late".

70. On 3 April, Sir Kevin Tebbit asked Mr Trevor Woolley, MOD Director General Resources and Plans (DGRP), "just by way of prudent contingency planning you understand … what a deployment to Iraq of a Division minus (25-30,000 with enablers) would do to our SDR force structure and concurrency assumptions, assuming all other operations remained more or less as they are".[31] Sir Kevin asked Mr Woolley not to share the work with the Commitments area of the MOD.

---

[27] Public hearing, 27 July 2010, pages 8-9.
[28] Public hearing, 27 July 2010, page 19.
[29] Minutes, 6 March 2002, Chiefs of Staff meeting.
[30] An Urgent Operational Requirement (UOR) seeks to address a capability gap by rapidly procuring new or additional equipment or the enhancement of, or essential modification of, existing equipment. The procurement process is described in Section 14.1.
[31] Minute Tebbit to DG RP, 3 April 2002, 'Iraq Pre-Contingency Mind Clearing'.

71. On 8 April, following Mr Blair's talks with President Bush at Crawford, Texas (see Section 3.2), Mr Hoon instructed the MOD to undertake work on "the specific equipment requirements (UORs)" necessary to deliver the military options being considered as part of the initial discussions about possible UK participation in military action against Iraq.[32] This was because "equipment – rather than personnel – was likely to be on the critical path in terms of deployment timelines".

72. Following consultation with Sir Kevin Tebbit and Adm Boyce, Mr Simon Webb, MOD Policy Director, sent Mr Hoon a think piece entitled 'Bush and the War on Terrorism' on 12 April.[33] Mr Webb's minute provided formal advice on the possible scale of any UK military contribution and included a draft letter to Mr Blair.

73. Setting out the MOD's thinking on military issues, Mr Webb wrote:

- "The fundamental building block for a major US ground force operation is a division. Only on that scale (requiring 3 brigades as our planning base) would UK have significant influence over how the operation was developed and conducted: an independent brigade does not fit into the US structure and would in any case need substantial divisional scale enablers in order to be safe for high intensity operations ...

- "Such a deployment would be at the extreme end of the UK's capacity after the SDR: it was the scenario against which the 'large' option was scaled."

- The UK "should seek only to make a respectable large contribution that we can sustain properly ..."

74. On 9 May, Sir Kevin Tebbit was sent the first assessment of equipment lead times for potential operations in Iraq in response to his 3 April request.[34] The assessment noted that a minimum of six months lead time was "necessary to fill essential capability gaps before we could launch a Gulf War scale operation against Iraq". It also noted that the six months lead time was measured from "the point at which an unambiguous authorisation to spend the necessary money is given".

75. The MOD's assessment identified several "showstopping" equipment capability deficiencies with "the timelines for rectifying them", including:

- The desert environment modifications to the Challenger 2 tank would take six months, with a further three if air filtration was added.

- Chemical protection measures would require six months and biological protection measures would require between nine and 12 months.

- Aircraft secure communications.

---

[32] Minute Watkins to PSO/CDS, 8 April 2002, 'Iraq'.
[33] Minute Webb to PS/Secretary of State [MOD], 12 April 2002, 'Bush and the War on Terrorism'.
[34] Minute Witney to PS/PUS [MOD], 9 May 2002, 'Iraq – Equipment Lead Times'.

- Support helicopters were identified as "a clear pinch point". The eight Chinook Mk3 ordered in 1995 but not available for use would not be ready for another two years (see Box, 'The eight modified Chinooks', in Section 14.1).
- The UK had only enough tented accommodation for "some 2,500 personnel". The remainder of the stock was in use on other operations in Afghanistan, the Balkans and Oman. Acquiring more was identified as a high priority.

76. The assessment was sent to Adm Boyce and a limited number of senior MOD officials and military officers.

77. Adm Boyce instructed that the advice should be circulated to the Single Service Chiefs, who were not on the original distribution.[35]

78. In response to a suggestion from his Private Office that the work be shared with the Chief of Defence Logistics, Adm Boyce wrote: "No, not yet."[36]

79. Shortly afterwards, Sir Kevin Tebbit's Private Secretary sent a minute to Mr Webb and Lieutenant General Sir Anthony Pigott, Deputy Chief of the Defence Staff (Commitments) (DCDS(C)), proposing a limited core distribution list for Iraq contingency planning.[37] He wrote: "There may be occasions when you (or indeed the Spending Review team) feel that an even more limited distribution should apply but I would hope this would not be frequent."

80. The list did not include the Defence Logistics Organisation (DLO) or the Defence Procurement Agency (DPA). Neither organisation had been consulted on the 9 May advice.

81. The MOD established an informal inter-departmental group of senior officials for planning purposes, which became known as the "Pigott Group". The Pigott Group was supported by a Strategic Planning Group (SPG) and both are described in Section 6.1.

82. Lt Gen Pigott sent Mr Hoon an update on the SPG's work on 10 May.[38] Lt Gen Pigott stated:

> "Any thinking we do about joining the US in military operations against the Iraqi regime needs to be informed by our thinking in two key areas: the impact of potential courses of action open to a coalition and the capability the UK might contribute to such a coalition."

83. Work had been commissioned on the capabilities the UK might aim to provide within periods of three to four and six to eight months, setting out the key decision

---

[35] Manuscript comment Adm Boyce on Minute Witney to PS/PUS [MOD], 9 May 2002, 'Iraq – Equipment Lead Times'.
[36] Manuscript comment Adm Boyce on Minute Witney to PS/PUS [MOD], 9 May 2002, 'Iraq – Equipment Lead Times'.
[37] Minute PS/PUS [MOD] to Policy Director and DCDS(C), May 2002, 'Iraq'.
[38] Minute DCDS(C) to APS/Secretary of State [MOD], 10 May 2002, 'Iraq'.

and deployment points. Lt Gen Pigott suggested that this could lead to "a note to the Prime Minister setting out these and the financial implications of taking contingency action now".

84. General Sir Michael Walker was Chief of the General Staff (CGS) from 2000 to February 2003. His Private Office wrote to the Chiefs of Staff Secretariat on 13 June, referring to the 9 May advice on equipment lead times.[39] He stated that the advice highlighted "just a few of several areas where key deficiencies exist" if a medium or large scale operation were to be undertaken. Other areas included battlefield helicopters, the issue of stocks and the supply of items such as ammunition. Gen Walker would elaborate on these other areas at the Chiefs of Staff meeting on 18 June.[40]

85. The minutes from the weekly Chiefs of Staff meeting do not record any reference to a discussion on equipment planning for Iraq.[41]

86. As work on military options in the MOD progressed, it was recognised that, if a large scale option was pursued, not all of the essential UOR equipment required for operations in the Gulf could be procured and fitted within six months.

87. A paper produced by the SPG on 24 May, 'Contingency Thinking: Force Generation and Deployment for the Gulf', was sent to the Chiefs of Staff and a limited number of named MOD addressees.[42]

88. The SPG identified a number of key assumptions that included:

- Operations would not commence before autumn 2002.
- Decisions would not be taken incrementally because that would "add to timelines by making force generation increasingly complex and costly".
- Enhancements would be needed to enable units to operate in the Gulf. That would expose preparations from an early stage given the significant number of contracts that would be required with industry.

89. Three broad levels of effort in line with the MOD's planning assumptions were examined:

- the maximum the UK could provide (a large scale contribution);
- a "credible" medium scale package; and
- a small scale package.

90. Reflecting the UK's existing military commitments and the most recent MOD budgetary planning round, the SPG advised that the UK could realistically produce a

---

[39] Note MA1/CGS to COSSEC, 13 June 2002, 'Iraq – Equipment Lead Times'.
[40] It is believed that Gen Walker's Office was referring to the Think Tank discussion on 18 June referred to later in this Section, for which there was no record.
[41] Minutes, 18 June 2002, Chiefs of Staff meeting.
[42] Paper SPG, 24 May 2002, 'Contingency Thinking: Force Generation and Deployment for the Gulf'.

"maximum contribution … at the lower end of large scale … medium scale (minus) for maritime (about 10 major warships), and medium scale for air (about 60 fast jets)".

91. The force mix might not be evenly balanced (in terms of scale of effort) across the sea, land and air environments; but the UK would "always seek to achieve strategic influence across the three environments such that UK influence is in place throughout the joint environment".

92. Lt Gen Pigott presented the findings from the SPG analysis to Mr Hoon on 24 May.[43] He advised that "until there is greater visibility and clarity of US intent our work on potential approaches to an Iraq campaign remains speculative; this work is advancing but will lack definition until we engage with the US".

93. Three broad options ("force packages") had been identified, which were "illustrative of the maximum potential … contribution" that the UK might be able to make available for any offensive operations within given time periods:

a. **Three months' warning:** Deployment of medium scale joint force – 10 warships including a carrier, an armoured brigade, about 60 fast jets and associated support. That was described as at risk of being a "token contribution". The cost, including "essential" UORs for equipping the force was estimated at £500m to £800m.

b. **Six months' warning:** Deployment of a large scale, war-fighting force in addition to the medium scale maritime and air components, which would be "comparable to the 1990/1991 conflict" and "confer significant influence on the control of the campaign". Though the land element would be "capable of limited independent war-fighting", there would be sustainability issues. Large numbers of vehicles could become "unserviceable" and there would be reliance on others to supply ammunition and other stock. There would not be enough time for "the procurement and fitting of *all* UOR equipment considered to be essential for operations in the Gulf (such as the desertisation of all armoured vehicles)", which would generate further operational risks and result in the degradation of the "credibility of the UK's contribution as [the] campaign unfolded". That option would require the call out of 5,000-10,000 Reservists and cost £800m to £1.1bn. A decision would need to be taken immediately for operations to begin in December 2002.

c. **Nine months' warning:** The force package would be the same as (b) but would be better prepared and carry fewer risks, as a result of additional training and equipment. The package would have "enough capability and sustainability to be a credible contribution to any coalition". The cost would be £100m higher because of a greater volume of UORs.

94. The deployment and campaign costs would be additional to the costs identified for each option.

---

[43] Minute DCDS(C) to PS/Secretary of State [MOD], 24 May 2002, 'Iraq'.

95. Lt Gen Pigott explained that current commitments in Afghanistan[44] and subsequent recovery and deployment times would "limit the UK's ability to contribute significantly to any offensive operations in the region until November at the earliest".

96. If it was "likely that the UK would wish to contribute" to US action "when the call came", there was a "need to consider what action" was needed "now to reduce risks and as far as possible readiness times".

97. Mr Hoon was asked to agree further work to refine contingency planning, to be submitted in mid-June; and informed that "proper preparations" would require wider involvement in the MOD and discreet approaches to industry.

98. Mr Hoon wrote to Mr Blair on 31 May, explaining that UK contingency planning had concluded that, for the UK to have influence on US planning, a significant military contribution would be needed. That was defined as at "division level" for land forces.[45]

99. Mr Hoon suggested raising "in general terms, that our contingency planning has shown we need plenty of warning in order to be able to contribute to military action".

100. The SPG produced a paper in preparation for a "Strategic Think Tank on Iraq", to be held by the Chiefs of Staff on 18 June.[46]

101. While the paper was not designed to consider equipment in detail, a section on "UK enablers" briefly considered force capability requirements. It reiterated the analysis of 24 May about what would be possible with either three, six or nine months warning. The paper also identified additional requirements for force protection, including "NBC" [Nuclear, Biological and Chemical] protection.

102. The MOD has been unable to locate any record of the think tank discussion.

103. Subsequent revisions of the paper before the end of 2002 are addressed later in this Section and in Section 6.1.

104. Mr Tom McKane, Deputy Head of the Cabinet Office Overseas and Defence Secretariat (OD Sec), wrote to Sir David Manning, Mr Blair's Foreign Policy Adviser and Head of OD Sec, about the think tank discussion the same day.[47] He recognised that there was "a huge amount of work to be done if the UK is to be in a position to participate in any operation against Iraq".

---

[44] The UK had deployed 45 Commando Royal Marines from May to July 2002 as part of Operation JACANA that targeted Taliban and Al-Qaida fugitives in Afghanistan. *GOV.UK*, 14 January 2014, *The UK's work in Afghanistan: timeline*.
[45] Minute Hoon to Prime Minister, 31 May 2002, 'Iraq'.
[46] Minute Driver to PSO/CDS, 13 June 2002, 'Supporting Paper for COS Strategic Think Tank on Iraq – 18 Jun' attaching Paper [SPG], 12 June 2002, [untitled].
[47] Minute McKane to Manning, 18 June 2002, 'Iraq'.

105. Mr McKane recommended that Sir David should reply to Mr Hoon's letter of 31 May seeking "further and better particulars on the timelines and precisely what decisions incurring significant expenditure would be required now in order to keep open the possibility of a large scale deployment in six months time".

106. Sir David commented to Mr Jonathan Powell, Mr Blair's Chief of Staff: "We certainly need much greater precision from MOD."[48]

107. Mr Powell replied that he believed there was "a danger of getting ahead of ourselves here unless this is absolutely necessary to get us into detailed military planning with the US".[49] He recommended discussing the issue with Mr Blair.

108. Sir David Manning asked Mr McKane to "confirm that it is now absolutely necessary to get into the detailed planning with the US".[50] He added: "I suspect it is if we are to have a voice."

109. On 25 June, Sir David wrote to Mr Peter Watkins, Mr Hoon's Principal Private Secretary, referring to Mr Hoon's letter of 31 May.[51] He stated:

> "… the Prime Minister has asked for further advice on precisely what steps would have to be taken now, including financial commitments, in order to keep open the possibility of deploying a large scale force by the end of this year – bearing in mind we may not get six months warning …"

110. Mr Watkins replied on 26 June with an update on the MOD's understanding of US plans.[52] He wrote that a small MOD team would be going to Washington and Tampa "immediately" and that would inform whether the UK could "secure adequate influence for a large scale contribution". That would determine the need to commit resources, on which Mr Hoon would provide "specific advice" shortly.

111. Lt Gen Pigott, Air Marshal Joe French, Chief of Defence Intelligence, and Mr Desmond Bowen, MOD Director General Operational Policy, visited Washington and CENTCOM from 27 to 29 June 2002.[53]

112. Before they left, Major General Robert Fry, Deputy Chief of Joint Operations (Operations) (DCJO(Ops)) from May 2002 to July 2003, provided a paper commenting on US planning, which at that stage offered two basic approaches:

---

[48] Manuscript comment Manning on Minute McKane to Manning, 18 June 2002, 'Iraq'.
[49] Manuscript comment Powell on Minute McKane to Manning, 18 June 2002, 'Iraq'.
[50] Manuscript comment Manning on Minute McKane to Manning, 18 June 2002, 'Iraq'.
[51] Letter Manning to Watkins, 25 June 2002, 'Iraq'.
[52] Letter Watkins to Manning, 26 June 2002, 'Iraq'.
[53] Minute Fry to MA/DCDS(C), 26 June 2002, 'Comments on US Planning for Possible Military Action Against Iraq'.

- A "running start", with extra forces being deployed as the initial attacks were under way, which would have the advantage of surprise and allow for operations as early as October 2002.

- A "generated start", allowing full deployment before the beginning of operations, which was expected to require three months longer.[54]

113. Maj Gen Fry wrote that the "running start" option carried considerably more risk and would be "much more manoeuvrist" than the type of operations which had been conducted in 1991. A number of issues for the UK were identified including: the role and timing for a UK contribution; the need for very early decision making; how to integrate into a complex US plan; levels of risk; UK participation in US exercises; and the likely US expectations that would result from UK involvement in the planning process.

114. On 2 July, Mr Watkins wrote to Sir David Manning with the outcome of the US visit.[55] While a "de facto invitation to the UK and Australia to participate" was "now on the table", the extent of the desired UK contribution was "unclear".

115. In July, the Chiefs of Staff were informed that some stocks were sufficient to protect only a medium scale UK deployment from biological attack.

116. A revised version of the SPG paper 'UK Military Strategic Thinking on Iraq' was produced on 11 July for a "Strategic Think Tank" on Iraq the following week.[56]

117. The section on NBC force protection had been expanded to explain that the UK possessed "sufficient stocks" of Individual Protective Equipment for a large scale deployment. Taking UOR action ("in 3 months or less") could address "a number of shortfalls" but the "main shortfall" was in protection against a Biological Warfare (BW) attack, for which manufacturing time was needed for additional equipment. There were limited medical countermeasures to respond to a BW attack and the UK had "adequate stocks" only to support medium scale UK deployments.

118. The sustainment of operations beyond the level set out in the DPAs had "not been factored into calculations to date".

119. The key risks for UK capabilities included:

- preparation times for the desertisation of vehicles;
- not knowing whether there was sufficient industrial capacity available to satisfy the "likely UOR/preparation requirements" (and this could not be resolved until clearance had been given to engage industry); and
- BW medical countermeasures being restricted to a medium scale force package.

---

[54] Minute Fry to MA/DCDS(C), 26 June 2002, 'Comments on US Planning for Possible Military Action Against Iraq'.
[55] Letter Watkins to Manning, 2 July 2002, 'Iraq'.
[56] Paper [SPG], 11 July 2002, 'UK Military Strategic Thinking on Iraq'.

120. Lt Gen Pigott briefed Adm Boyce on 17 July that his view was that the UK should encourage thinking to move towards action in 2003 to 2004 rather than in 2002 to 2003, which "had a better chance of success" given the challenges "including political red cards".[57] That was: "Not a recipe for delay, indeed quite the reverse." It would be difficult for the UK to send land forces to participate in a "running start" but the UK thinking was "taking us towards a 'distinctive' (Package 3) role". For any significant contribution, force preparation would need to start "<u>now</u>".

121. The advice from Lt Gen Pigott and the SPG was discussed in a restricted Chiefs of Staff meeting on 17 July.[58]

122. In preparation for a meeting to be held on 18 July, Mr Bowen outlined the MOD's thinking in a minute to Mr Hoon on 17 July.[59] He drew attention to the US concepts of "running" and "generated" starts. He advised that the indications were that the US favoured the "running start" option (which could see US operations beginning during 2002).

123. Mr Bowen suggested that:

> "In the meantime, as we begin to explore possible UK contributions we need to identify what preparation – such as procurement for **urgent operational requirements** – could usefully begin now ... "

124. In mid-July, a Cabinet Office paper invited Ministers to "note" the potentially long lead times for equipping UK forces to undertake operations in Iraq and sought agreement that the MOD could bring forward proposals for procurement of equipment.

125. Although it was agreed that the UK should proceed on the assumption that the UK would participate in any military action, there was no decision on whether funds could be spent on preparations.

126. The Cabinet Office paper 'Iraq: Conditions for Military Action' was issued on 19 July to those attending a meeting to be chaired by Mr Blair on 23 July.[60] That meeting is addressed in Section 3.3.

127. Ministers were invited to "note the potentially long lead times involved in equipping UK Armed Forces to undertake operations in the Iraqi theatre"; and to "agree that MOD should bring forward proposals for the procurement of Urgent Operational Requirements under cover of the lessons learned from Afghanistan" and the "outcome" of the 2002 Spending Review.

---

[57] Minute DCDS(C) to DPSO/CDS, 17 July 2002, 'Iraq: Summary of Key Issues'.
[58] Minutes, 17 July 2002, Chiefs of Staff (Restricted) meeting.
[59] Minute DG Op Pol to PS/Secretary of State [MOD], 17 July 2002, 'Iraq'.
[60] Paper Cabinet Office, 19 July 2002, 'Iraq: Conditions for Military Action'.

128. In preparation for Mr Blair's meeting, Mr Bowen advised Mr Hoon that Adm Boyce had directed that UK planning should concentrate on two packages:

- a supporting/enabling package, including basing, maritime and air assets, in which the "the only land contribution would be Special Forces"; and
- a discrete land contribution of a division (minus) for operations in northern Iraq.[61]

129. Mr Bowen wrote that:

"Other options, such as providing land forces to integrate with the US main effort in the south have been discounted because [sic] the severe difficulties we would face due to interoperability, deployment time and geographic constraints affecting logistics in particular."

130. Mr Bowen provided "schematic timelines" showing decision dates and readiness which could be achieved.

131. Commenting on Mr Bowen's advice, Mr Watkins wrote that a division (minus) option "would require immediate action on UORs etc and early decisions (October) on reserves".[62] The latter would "definitely be visible".

132. Separate advice from Lt Gen Pigott to Adm Boyce stated that one of the issues to be covered in the "way forward" was that it should be agreed to implement "invisible" UORs now, and to be prepared to advise Ministers later on visible UORs.[63]

133. A record of the meeting on 23 July stated that Mr Hoon advised Mr Blair that, if he wanted UK military involvement, Mr Blair "would need to decide this early".[64]

134. The meeting concluded that work should proceed on the assumption that the UK would participate in any military action. Adm Boyce was to tell the US military that "we were considering a range of options".

135. Mr Blair stated that he would "revert on the question of whether funds could be spent on preparation for this operation".

136. The MOD identified three possible options for a UK contribution on 26 July but no recommendation was made about which option should be selected. The largest option comprised the deployment of a division but the MOD was also examining the possibility of deploying an additional light brigade and providing the framework for a UK-led Corps headquarters.

---

[61] Minute Bowen to PS/Secretary of State [MOD], 22 July 2002, 'Iraq: Meeting with the Prime Minister'.
[62] Manuscript comment Watkins on Minute Bowen to PS/Secretary of State [MOD], 22 July 2002, 'Iraq: Meeting with the Prime Minister'.
[63] Minute DCDS(C) to DPSO/CDS, 22 July 2002, 'Iraq: Update on Key Issues'.
[64] Letter Rycroft to Manning, 23 July 2002, 'Iraq: Prime Minister's Meeting, 23 July'.

137. Mr Hoon expressed caution about both the timescales required for a UK deployment and the impact of potential industrial action by the Fire Brigades Union in the autumn.

138. Mr Blair was advised that no decision was needed at that stage.

139. Following the 23 July meeting, No.10 asked the MOD to provide details of the proposed military campaign, and options for a UK contribution.[65]

140. Mr Bowen sent Mr Hoon a fuller analysis of the options for a UK contribution on 25 July.[66] He advised:

- It would take another couple of months to increase forces to medium scale.
- "To meet probable US timescales" it would "not be possible to deploy a fully prepared, fully sustainable armoured division for war-fighting". A fully prepared and sustained armoured division (one which could fight a significant Iraqi force) would take 10 months.
- Deployment of an armoured division (minus) would only be possible "within six months of a decision to deploy", and would have "limited sustainment and reach".

141. On 26 July, further MOD advice on options for a UK contribution to US-led military operations in Iraq was provided in a letter from Mr Watkins to Mr Matthew Rycroft, Mr Blair's Private Secretary for Foreign Affairs.[67]

142. Adm Boyce had recommended three options:

- **Package 1** – an "in-place support package" using forces already in the region.
- **Package 2** – an "enhanced support package" comprising Package 1 with additional air and maritime forces. While no conventional land forces could meet the timescales for the deployment of maritime and air forces: "Special Forces could be deployed very rapidly to match US timescales and priorities. This is likely to be very attractive to US planners, and their contribution to success would be significant …"
- **Package 3** – a "discrete UK package" based on deployment of an armoured division which the MOD envisaged would be used in northern Iraq, in addition to the forces in Package 2. The UK might consider providing an armoured division either as part of a US-led Corps or as part of a larger coalition force possibly led by the UK using the framework of the NATO Allied Rapid Reaction Corps [ARRC]."

---

[65] Minute Rycroft to McDonald, 23 July 2002 'Iraq: Prime Minister's meeting, 23 July: Follow Up'.
[66] Minute Bowen to PS/Secretary of State [MOD], 25 July 2002, 'Iraq – Potential UK Contribution'.
[67] Letter Watkins to Rycroft, 26 July 2002, 'Iraq'.

143. Mr Watkins stated "it would take **six months** for the whole division to be in place and then with limited sustainment and reach".

144. Mr Watkins cautioned that:

"… the timescales indicated are the best planning estimates we can make at this stage … they assume that, as soon as a decision in principle is reached to participate, funding will be available to improve sustainability … and implement urgent operational requirements … The ability of industry to respond to our demands can only be estimated at this stage."

145. Mr Hoon had:

"… commissioned more work in respect of sustainability and UORs with a view to expediting what would need to be done once a decision in principle was taken, with what visibility to the public eye and with what cost … It will involve widening the net of knowledge about this contingency planning within the MOD, although we will not yet contact industry who will have to be involved at some stage to determine actual lead times for procurement of UORs."

146. The advice was sent to Mr Blair on 31 July, as one of several "background papers" he had commissioned at his meeting on 23 July "for summer reading".[68]

147. Mr Rycroft commented to Mr Blair:

"The military are not yet ready to make a recommendation on which if any of the three options to go for. Nor can they yet judge whether the US have a winning concept. They are continuing to work with the US military. You do not need to take decisions yet."

148. The MOD advised Mr Hoon on 30 July that there was a shortfall in "essential" equipment enhancements for all three packages in respect of protection against an Iraqi biological attack. It had "low confidence" that those shortfalls could be addressed within six months.

149. The MOD sought approval to engage more widely to refine its work on lead times but Mr Hoon decided that would be premature.

150. On 30 July, an MOD official provided Mr Hoon with a "best estimate" of the equipment enhancements that might be necessary in order to deliver the potential UK force packages.[69]

151. In an attached annex, the enhancements had been categorised as either "essential now", "full operational capability enhancers", or "follow-on enhancements".

---

[68] Minute Rycroft to Prime Minister, 31 July 2002, 'Iraq: Background Papers'.
[69] Minute Sec(O)1a to PS/SofS [MOD], 30 July 2002, 'Iraq – Enhancements Required For Potential UK Contribution'.

152. The shortfall of essential items for Packages 1 and 2 was for NBC equipment that would be required to treat casualties in the event of an Iraqi biological attack. The MOD had "low confidence" that it could be obtained within six months. It could take "up to nine months" to procure certain stocks from industry but further work was needed to identify other possible sources.

153. For enhancements required to achieve full operational capability, the MOD had "a high degree of confidence" that work could be completed "within six months" for Packages 1 and 2. For those packages, "none of the enhancement items appear to be a showstopper".

154. For Package 3, the MOD had "lower confidence" in the ability to deliver desertisation for tanks "for the fully sustained war-fighting role", which it judged "would take around ten months". There would also be a shortfall in NBC protection and biological detectors if Package 3 were to be adopted. Further work was being done to see how quickly this could be acquired.

155. The purchase of ammunition and spares for land forces and support helicopters was listed in the annex of equipment which was "essential now" to sustain operations if Package 3 were to be adopted.

156. The official wrote that "the earlier decisions are taken to start Urgent Operational Requirements (UOR) and sustainability acquisition, the greater the UK's preparedness and choice".

157. The MOD official requested approval to engage the Front Line Commands, the DPA and the DLO to "refine" the MOD's work on lead times. This was "most pressing" where the MOD had "low confidence that activity or procurement deemed essential to the UK force packages" could be achieved within six months.

158. The official would seek further approval before the MOD made "any contact with industry to determine the actual lead-times" for procuring equipment.

159. On funding, Mr Hoon was advised that, as any UORs for a campaign in Iraq would fall outside the MOD's budget, it would need agreement from the Treasury to call on the Reserve and to secure funding for the UOR equipment and enhancement measures.

160. The Reserve is a fund held by the Treasury intended for genuinely unforeseen contingencies which departments cannot manage from their own resources and was used to pay for the net additional costs of military operations (NACMO). The NACMO included both UOR and non-UOR expenditure associated with operations in Iraq. The process behind this is explained in Section 13.1, where MOD's negotiations with the Treasury are also examined.

161. Mr Watkins replied on 31 July, explaining that Mr Hoon had decided "it would be premature to widen the net of knowledge"; and that:

> "... no costs should be incurred on UORs and sustainability enhancements for the purposes of a campaign in Iraq ... No estimates should be submitted to Treasury Officials."[70]

162. Mr Bowen wrote to Mr Watkins on 1 August, acknowledging Mr Hoon's clear directions but pressing "urgently" to take forward work on antitoxin[71] by widening the MOD planning circle.[72] Antitoxin was identified as an "essential" element in all three packages under consideration, "about whose potential availability we do not know nearly enough at present". Mr Bowen wrote:

> "In the event of any deployment, the proper preparations to enable British Forces to deal with the possible biological and chemical release would be essential ... It seems likely that decisions on the acquisition of antitoxin, when they come to be made, will be on the critical path for the deployment of a war fighting capability."

163. Mr Bowen recommended "strongly" that Mr Hoon should agree that "on a very limited, need-to-know basis further staffing should be conducted with the inclusion of nominated NBC and Porton Down[73] staff".

164. Mr Adam Ingram, Minister for the Armed Forces, responded on 7 August that, "exceptionally", staffing could be widened "on a strict need to know basis", including NBC and Porton Down staff as requested.[74]

DETAILED PLANNING FOR UORS BEGINS

165. The MOD had defined essential equipment needed "now" for potential operations in Iraq as "showstoppers". That became the benchmark for determining whether the unavailability of an item should halt the deployment of UK forces.

166. On 9 August, Lt Gen Pigott published lists of individuals within the MOD (the "Centurion" group) and PJHQ (the "Warrior" group) who were authorised to receive "the most sensitive material relating to US planning and UK scoping on Iraq" during the summer.[75] That is described in Section 6.1.

---

[70] Minute PS/SofS [MOD] to Sec(O)1a, 31 July 2002, 'Iraq – Enhancements Required For Potential UK Contribution'.
[71] An antibody with the ability to neutralise a particular toxin; used as a countermeasure in the event of chemical or biological attack.
[72] Minute DG Op Pol to PS/SofS [MOD], 1 August 2002, 'Iraq – Enhancements Required For Possible UK Contribution'.
[73] The headquarters for the Defence Science and Technology Laboratory (DSTL).
[74] Minute PS/Min(AF) to DG Op Pol, 7 August 2002, 'Iraq – Enhancements For Possible UK Contribution – Antitoxin'.
[75] Minute MA2/DCDS(C), 9 August 2002, 'Centurion Group'.

167. Air Vice Marshal Clive Loader, Assistant Chief of the Defence Staff (Operations), told Mr Bowen on 16 August that he had been directed to "drill down" on equipment issues in the planning phase and was setting up an Equipment and Sustainability Working Group.[76] Draft Terms of Reference for the Group were attached.

168. AVM Loader wrote that, in accordance with directions from Mr Hoon's Private Office, consultation would "be strictly limited to those on the Centurion and Warrior lists".

169. The Terms of Reference described the Working Group's purpose as "taking forward the analysis of equipment and sustainability issues" with a "particular emphasis" on equipment availability and support. Work would be based on all three possible packages. The Working Group would gather "all internal data" to place itself "in the best position to take these issues forward" when clearance was granted.

170. The Working Group's scope would be "medical equipment and sustainability issues", including the issue of antitoxins. Consultation would be limited to the Centurion Group, "though outsiders may be approached for specific detail in response to specific questions where no connection to specific planning for operations against Iraq within a defined timescale is inferred".

171. The Working Group would consider which force elements could be delivered in either two or four months, aligning to "potential key dates on the US timescale", from September 2002. Where it was not possible to deliver the force element, the Working Group would consider the implications upon force packages. That would "allow those firming up the package" to identify what the UK could provide and where any shortfalls lay.

172. "Single Service sustainability work" would be checked by the DLO to ensure that centrally provided commodities, such as fuel and rations, were included for the entire force package.

173. The Terms of Reference categorised equipment under the same headings provided in the MOD advice to Mr Hoon on 30 July. Those were defined as:

- "Essential now": items "without which the force cannot deploy – they are showstoppers".
- "Full operational capability enhancers": required to give the force "a fully generated operational capability for up to 30 days of combat".
- "Follow-on enhancements": items beyond the minimum required for up to 30 days of combat and those that would "achieve a substantial measure of risk reduction".

---

[76] Minute ACDS (Ops) to DG Op Pol, 16 August 2002, 'Equipment and Sustainability Working Group' attaching Paper, 16 August 2002, 'Equipment and Sustainability Working Group Terms of Reference'.

174. The questions for the Group to consider included:

- the equipment requirement – such as the effects required from each package, quantities, enhancements for particular geographical locations and an understanding of priorities;

- the justification for it – such as what would "the operational penalties" be for not providing the item and were there any "operational lessons" that reinforced the case, for example from the 1990/91 Gulf Conflict;

- alternative solutions;

- the management and timing of the requirement;

- potential risks and wider implications; and

- visibility and presentation – how to "cover" preparing or acquiring the requirement.

175. Detailed planning for UORs for potential operations against Iraq began on 22 August with the first weekly Equipment and Sustainability Working Group meeting.[77]

176. On 5 September, Mr Hoon requested detailed advice from Mr Ian Lee, who had replaced Mr Bowen as MOD Director General Operational Policy, on the UORs assumed within the "preparation cost figures" for the three packages, "covering the 'what', 'why' and 'when' for each UOR".[78]

177. Mr Blair and Mr Hoon agreed on 8 September that the UK should plan on the basis of a medium scale land contribution but there should be no visible preparations.

178. Mr Blair met President Bush at Camp David on 7 September. That meeting is described in Section 3.4. Before the meeting, Mr Watkins wrote to Sir David Manning on 6 September with an update on US military planning and "the factors informing decisions on any UK military contribution".[79] For Package 2, he wrote that "some" UORs would need to be raised at additional cost to the Reserve.

179. For Package 3, Mr Watkins stated that "even were [Operation] FRESCO[80] to end soon, we could not provide a self-standing division within US timescales". He continued:

"There would simply not be enough time to carry out the preparations we would need to make. We would not have enough time to engage industry in order to improve sustainability (ammunition, etc) and implement UORs to optimise forces for the theatre and interoperability with the US."

---

[77] Minute DCDS(EC) to PS/Minister(DP), 24 January 2003, 'Iraq: OP TELIC UORs'.
[78] Minute Watkins to DG Op Pol, 5 September 2002, 'Iraq'.
[79] Letter Watkins to Manning, 6 September 2002, 'Iraq: Military Planning'.
[80] The operation to address the fire fighters' strike.

180. The Chiefs of Staff were considering what the "maximum effort" UK contribution could be for a UK ground force operating as part of a larger US force in northern Iraq. The "illustrative" force package consisted of a divisional HQ, an armoured brigade, an air assault brigade and a logistics brigade. A decision to commit all those elements would comprise some 40,000 personnel (including up to 10,000 Reservists).[81]

181. Mr Hoon's Private Office wrote to Mr Lee on 9 September, reporting that Mr Hoon had spoken to Mr Blair on the evening of 8 September following Mr Blair's return from Camp David:

> "It was agreed that a full UK Divisional contribution was impracticable and the UK should play down our ability to take on an overall leadership role in the North. The UK should, however, remain involved, developing the enhanced support package with the addition of a land medium scale contribution."[82]

182. Mr Hoon requested that planning should continue. His Private Office added: "For now actions must remain invisible … and this situation is likely to last for about a month."

183. MOD officials continued to push for agreement to discuss UORs with a wider set of colleagues and the Treasury.

184. The MOD sought approval from Mr Hoon to progress 16 "showstoppers" but highlighted that there was also a number of urgent UORs that were necessary to bring a UK force up to full operational capacity.

185. On 4 September, in advance of a planned meeting with Mr Hoon, Mr William Nye, Head of the Treasury Defence, Diplomacy and Intelligence Team, briefed Mr Gordon Brown, Chancellor of the Exchequer, that MOD officials had done little work to refine the cost estimates for preparing a medium and large scale force, as they were under no pressure from Ministers to do so.[83] Neither had the MOD done any work to assess the cost of the campaign itself. Mr Nye said that it would be useful for Mr Brown to emphasise that the Treasury needed to be involved in some of the discussions on military planning, to enable it "to be kept informed of the context of financial and strategic decisions".

186. The Treasury informed the Inquiry that the meeting between Mr Brown and Mr Hoon was one-to-one and no record was taken.[84]

187. A minute from Mr Watkins to Mr Lee on 5 September summarised a series of discussions that Mr Hoon had had earlier that day.[85] In a meeting with Mr Brown,

---

[81] Letter Watkins to Manning, 6 September 2002, 'Iraq: Military Planning'.
[82] Minute APS/SofS [MOD] to DG Op Pol, 9 September 2002, 'Iraq – Defence Secretary's Conversation with the Prime Minister'.
[83] Minute Nye to Bowman, 4 September 2002, 'Meeting with Geoff Hoon: Iraq'.
[84] Email Treasury to Iraq Inquiry Secretariat, 26 February 2010, [untitled].
[85] Minute Watkins to DG Op Pol, 5 September 2002, 'Iraq'.

Mr Hoon had "again" run through the three options and "alerted Mr Brown to the likely broad order costs of Package 2".

188. Mr Hoon and Mr Brown had also agreed to "meet periodically thereafter so that Mr Hoon could keep Mr Brown in touch with our emerging thinking on the options for UK involvement in any military action and the implications for UORs".[86]

189. On 13 September, Dr Simon Cholerton, a junior official in Secretariat (Overseas) (Sec(O)), advised Mr Hoon on "the need to take forward essential UOR work" for potential operations in Iraq.[87] Mr Hoon was asked to:

- Note "that we have got as far as we can in defining urgent equipment and sustainability measures without consulting more widely" and the "very limited nature of our consultation and the broad scope of the packages on the table" meant that "we cannot have high confidence in the judgements we have made".

- Agree that the MOD should take forward "a limited package of 'ambiguous' tasks on 16 essential UORs" aimed at remaining "invisible" but with enough information to approach the Treasury.

- Note that "these tasks do not cover the full range of capability shortfalls which have been identified" and work was needed on a wider set of UORs "as soon as the 'invisibility' constraint was lifted" to inform the Treasury. It would require "a limited expansion" of the Centurion Group.

190. The 16 essential UOR "showstoppers" covered all three packages. That included NBC protection where there was a requirement to "improve" Individual Protective Equipment, Collective Protection (COLPRO) and NBC detection. Dr Cholerton explained that, for all three Services, the issue was "not so much that we do not hold equipment (capability exists), but whether we hold sufficient in the face of the risk".

191. Dr Cholerton wrote that six measures were essential for the land component, notwithstanding the uncertainty over which package would be adopted. That included desertisation of armoured vehicles and the procurement of additional Enhanced Combat Body Armour (ECBA), of which only 13,345 sets were available against a potential deployment of 47,000 personnel. Existing ECBA stocks would be sufficient to equip only the front line fighting troops. That would "leave support staff – who will nevertheless potentially face a high risk environment – less well protected".

192. On 16 September, Mr Hoon received advice on preparatory work to take forward "a small number of time-critical" UORs for Special Forces.[88]

---

[86] Minute Watkins to DG RP, 18 September 2002, 'Iraq: Meeting with the Chancellor: 23 September'.
[87] Minute Cholerton to PS/SofS [MOD], 13 September 2002, 'Iraq – Urgent Operational Requirements (UORs)'.
[88] Minute Sec(HSF)2 to PS/SofS [MOD], 16 September 2002, ' OP ROW: SF Urgent Operational Requirements'.

193. The MOD suggested it could use the cover of operations in Afghanistan "to handle these UORs in a discreet fashion", with costs being attributed to the same "ticket". Alternatively, there could be "some reprioritisation" of in-year resources: "Costs would then be claimed back retrospectively once a more general agreement has been reached with the Treasury on how to deal with the additional costs of any Iraq operations."

194. On 18 September, Mr McKane, now MOD DGRP, wrote he was "distinctly uneasy" about both options.[89] He proposed to either:

- urgently press for agreement to open up a dialogue with Treasury officials so that the funding of Iraq-related UORs was put "on to a sound footing"; or
- if AM Stirrup deemed the Special Forces' UORs "to be of such a high priority that he can re-prioritise the Equipment Plan, then he should do so". The Defence budget would have to absorb the costs.

195. On 19 September, Sir Kevin Tebbit's Private Office replied, agreeing with Mr McKane's advice that it would be "improper" to use the Afghanistan budget for Iraq and that it would, "in any case, be evident to Treasury in view of the 'item by item' requirement for scrutiny".[90]

196. Sir Kevin did not, however, agree Mr McKane's suggestion that the UORs could be met from the equipment budget through re-prioritisation "in view of the precedent this could set". Sir Kevin advised Mr Hoon to discuss the issue with Mr Brown "as soon as possible", which would be at their meeting scheduled for 23 September. Once that agreement was in place, the MOD could proceed, "either invisibly or otherwise".

197. Mr Hoon's Private Office decided not to show him the note from 16 September as a result of the comments from Mr McKane and Sir Kevin.[91] It requested further advice, "when appropriate".

198. Having seen Dr Cholerton's minute of 13 September, Air Chief Marshal Sir Peter Squire, Chief of the Air Staff, wrote to Adm Boyce on 16 September.[92] He believed that the situation had changed "considerably" since the Chiefs of Staff last discussed UORs. He wrote:

"Political statements from both London and Washington have confirmed that a UN resolution will, in the first instance be pursued but that, if this fails military action will follow. Under these circumstances, contingency action to prepare for the eventuality that the UN resolution is not effective would seem entirely appropriate."

---

[89] Minute McKane to Sec(HSF)2, 18 September 2002, 'Op ROW: SF Urgent Operational Requirements (UORs)'.
[90] Minute APS/PUS [MOD] to Sec(HSF)2, 18 September 2002, 'Op ROW: SF Urgent Operational Requirements (UORs)'. The MOD has confirmed that the date provided on the paper, 18 September, is incorrect and is content for the Inquiry to use 19 September.
[91] Minute APS/Secretary of State [MOD] to Sec(HSF)2, 18 September, 'Op ROW: SF Urgent Operational Requirements (UORs)'.
[92] Minute CAS to CDS, 16 September 2002, 'Iraq – Urgent Operational Requirements'.

199. ACM Squire wished to proceed with "not only those UORs classified as 'showstoppers' but also those that will secure within an appropriate timescale a significant enhancement to operational capability".

200. In response to ACM Squire's minute, Sir Kevin Tebbit wrote to Adm Boyce that he fully understood "the difficulty of possible timelines for military action, as long as the ban on overt preparations, including for UORs, has to remain in place".[93]

201. Sir Kevin added:

"I do not think the political situation has yet evolved sufficiently to be able to recommend to the Secretary of State that visible steps for contingency work or procurement action can go forward."

202. Sir Kevin concluded:

"I fear for the time being that we are still in a position of preparing and developing our UOR cases in readiness for detailed engagement with the Treasury, but stopping short of visible measures, or indeed, implementation, pending the political decision from the Secretary of State."

203. Mr Hoon's Private Office wrote to Dr Cholerton on 17 September.[94] Mr Hoon was content for work to "proceed on some of the UORs" identified in Dr Cholerton's minute, but "the potential profile of the remainder would be problematic at the present time". Mr Hoon would, "however, be willing to accept further advice in due course". In the meantime, "no funds should be committed to Iraq-related UORs" until the Treasury's agreement was secured.

204. An annex stated that Mr Hoon was content for MOD officials to proceed with 12 of Dr Cholerton's UORs, but the remaining four required further advice, including the desertisation of armoured vehicles and ECBA.

205. Mr Hoon was content for the Centurion Group to be expanded as requested, which he understood would be "an approximately 10 percent increase in the community aware of contingency planning work".

206. On 18 September, Lt Gen Pigott circulated draft advice for Mr Hoon on the UK's potential contribution for discussion at an operational Chiefs of Staff meeting the following day.[95] He stated:

"As Secretary of State is aware six essential equipment measures (Challenger II desertisation, fuel and water bowsers, enhanced combat body armour, SA80 and

---

[93] Minute PUS [MOD] to CDS, 17 September 2002, 'Iraq – UORs'.
[94] Minute APS/SofS [MOD] to Sec(O)1, 17 September 2002, 'Iraq – Urgent Operational Requirements'.
[95] Minute Warrior CPT Leader [junior officer] to MA/CJO, 19 September 2002, 'Warrior CPT – Update on planning' attaching Minute DCDS(C) to PS/Secretary of State [MOD], September 2002, 'Iraq: Potential UK contribution to US-led action'.

logistic vehicles) need to be taken forward. If we are to keep open our options on engaging, at or about the same time as the earliest potential US deployment in the North, work on *all* of these UORs plus others would need to be taken forward with the commitment of additional resources, and publicly visible placing of orders in early October."

207. The record of the Chiefs of Staff discussion on 19 September shows that Adm Boyce stated "there was still an embargo on discussing UORs with industry, and the issues could still not be discussed with a wider audience".[96]

208. The minutes from the meeting also recorded that Lt Gen Pigott's draft advice to Ministers was to be rewritten to include an explanation of the impact on future operations.

209. A note from Mr Watkins on 19 September stated that the draft advice was shown to Mr Hoon and Lord Bach, Parliamentary Under Secretary and Minister of State for Defence Procurement, that day.[97]

210. Lt Gen Pigott produced further advice on 26 September that did not contain the same level of detail on UORs.[98] The only reference to them stated:

"In MOD and PJHQ there is detailed work in hand on a range of force preparation issues. Those relating to the call-out of Reservists, training and Urgent Operational Requirements are the most pressing. The implications of this work will bear on our force options so we need to retain the necessary flexibility, until all this is clearer."

211. On 20 September, No.10 was informed that Package 2 comprised 13,000 personnel (Special Forces, Air and Maritime).[99] Consideration was also being given to including a Commando group of 1,700 Royal Marines personnel. Package 3 (comprising a Divisional HQ and an armoured brigade plus supporting elements), would comprise a further 28,000 personnel.

212. Mr Brown agreed proposals, in principle, for funding UORs on 23 September. The arrangements were confirmed on 4 October.

213. On 23 September, Mr Blair agreed with Mr Hoon that Package 2 could be offered as a potential UK contribution but there was a misunderstanding over whether the US should be informed that the UK was still considering a land option (Package 3). That issue is detailed in Section 6.1.

---

[96] Minutes, 19 September 2002, Chiefs of Staff (Operations) meeting.
[97] Minute Watkins to PSO/CDS, 19 September 2002, 'Iraq: Potential UK Contribution to Any US-led Action'.
[98] Minute DCDS(C) to CJO, 26 September 2002, 'Iraq – Potential Scale of UK Force Contribution For Use in UK/US Contingency Planning'.
[99] Minute Watkins to Manning, 20 September 2002, 'Iraq: Potential UK Contribution to any Military Action'.

214. Mr Brown and Mr Hoon met separately on 23 September to agree the process for funding UORs.[100] Mr Brown agreed the MOD's proposal to adopt a similar approach for managing Iraq UORs to that already in place for Afghanistan UORs, with an initial ceiling of £150m.

215. Mr Hoon undertook to provide "a broad breakdown of this sum", which he set out in a letter to Mr Brown on 25 September.[101] While he highlighted that "requirements and priorities may of course change" as US planning developed, Mr Hoon wrote that the first tranche of measures might include:

- strategic and theatre communications (approximately £25m to £35m);
- Special Forces, including communications and air support (approximately £40m to £60m);
- force protection measures, including items such as defensive aids for aircraft and NBC equipment (approximately £20m to £40m); and
- initial logistic support, campaign infrastructure and spares (£50m to £100m).

216. MOD and Treasury officials were tasked to work out the detailed arrangements. Mr Brown would write to Mr Hoon with proposals for handling UORs above the £150m ceiling.

217. On 26 September, Mr McKane met Mr Jonathan Stephens, Treasury Director Public Services, "to follow up" the meeting between Mr Hoon and Mr Brown.[102]

218. Mr McKane explained that the total volume of UORs was likely to cost more than £150m but the MOD was not yet in a position to say by how much.

219. Mr McKane also explained that the MOD might wish to use the £150m for "items that were not strictly speaking UORs" such as force generation costs.

220. The Treasury "did not demur" on either point.

221. Mr McKane reported that the Treasury asked when Mr Hoon:

" ... was likely to come forward with a firm recommendation on the overall scale of the British contribution. I said that this was likely to be within the next few weeks and that obviously the financial cost of the options would be one of the factors to be weighed in the balance."

222. Mr David Williams, MOD Director, Directorate Capabilities, Resources and Scrutiny (DCRS), wrote to the Treasury on 2 October, proposing a set of criteria for agreeing UORs against the Reserve.[103]

---

[100] Letter Hoon to Brown, 25 September 2002, 'Iraq: Urgent Operational Requirements'.
[101] Letter Hoon to Brown, 25 September 2002, 'Iraq: Urgent Operational Requirements'.
[102] Minute DG RP to Finance Director, 26 September 2002, 'Iraq: Urgent Operational Requirements'.
[103] Letter Williams to Treasury [junior official], 2 October 2002, 'UOR Criteria'.

223. On 4 October, Mr Williams advised Mr Hoon that the MOD had reached agreement with the Treasury on the UOR arrangements.[104] Work was "in hand" to prioritise the list of UORs, and to produce business cases for a range of "showstopper" UORs. He sought Mr Hoon's agreement for work to "now begin" on a wider range of UORs, "including discreet consultation with industry", and for resources to be committed as business cases were approved.

224. Mr Williams explained that Ministers were "not normally invited to approve individual UORs" unless project costs exceeded £400m; all UORs in this instance would cost less than £100m and fall "well within" the approval authority delegated to one-star officials.[105] Officials would, however, consult Mr Hoon separately where UORs could not be covered by the ambiguity of operations in Afghanistan, and on the four items where Mr Hoon had requested further advice in his 17 September note.

225. Mr Hoon's Assistant Private Secretary wrote a summary of the points on the minute, stating: "I believe this is now practical and appropriate. OK?"[106]

226. Mr Hoon replied: "I would like to see all of them first."[107]

227. Mr Hoon's Private Office replied to Mr Williams on 7 October:

"Before agreeing to the implementation process described in your minute … Mr Hoon wishes to see the UOR priority lists following consideration by the Chiefs of Staff."[108]

228. As work on UORs progressed, the capability shortfalls identified by Dr Cholerton on 13 September proved problematic.

229. On 8 October, Lt Gen Pigott prepared an update on the progress of UORs for the Chiefs of Staff to consider the following day.[109] It separated UORs into two tranches:

- Tranche 1 to "be implemented forthwith", funded from the first £150m agreed by the Treasury; and
- Tranche 2, which would "continue to be updated".

230. Lt Gen Pigott explained that the prioritisation had been governed by:

- "the need to provide individual and force protection";

---

[104] Minute DCRS to APS/SofS [MOD], 4 October 2002, 'Iraq: UORs – Update'.
[105] Brigadier or equivalent in the Armed Forces and Senior Civil Servant Level 1 for civilians.
[106] Manuscript comment MOD [junior official] on Minute DCRS to APS/SofS [MOD], 4 October 2002, 'Iraq: UORs – Update'.
[107] Manuscript comment Hoon on Minute DCRS to APS/SofS [MOD], 4 October 2002, 'Iraq: UORs – Update'.
[108] Minute APS/Secretary of State [MOD] to DCRS, 7 October 2002, 'Iraq: UORs – Update'.
[109] Minute DCDS(C) to PSO/CDS, 8 October 2002, 'Iraq Contingency Planning – Urgent Operational Requirements'.

- "the requirement to achieve maximum military effect at the strategic, operational and tactical levels";
- costs – including a consideration of whether the relative capability of a small number of more expensive enhancements was more valuable than a larger number of cheaper ones; and
- equipment lead times – those with long lead times had been given priority.

231. The difficulties of planning covertly and without wider consultation were reiterated. Lt Gen Pigott said that meant that there were "a number of particularly problematic capabilities" which were being addressed urgently by the MOD but "need to be drawn to the attention of COS and in some cases would benefit from higher level direction". Those included:

- NBC COLPRO – the majority of in-service equipment had been purchased for the 1991 Gulf Conflict but had not been fully taken into service, nor had its support been fully funded "so its effectiveness for future operations" was still to be determined.
- Antitoxin – work to address the current shortfall was "unlikely to meet the requirement in less than 6 to 8 months".
- ECBA – there were "about 20,000 complete sets of ECBA in-service which would be "sufficient to equip the Fighting Echelon of the Land Component, but not the whole Joint Force". The time taken to produce the shortfall could not be determined until industry was consulted but their current judgement was that "it may be very difficult to manufacture the amount of Kevlar armour plates in the amount required in time".

232. On visibility, Lt Gen Pigott wrote:

"… there will come a point where the presentational challenge will be not so much to ensure that UOR work remains veiled, but rather to demonstrate that we are taking action to address perceived capability shortfalls."

233. Lt Gen Pigott wrote that would include issues highlighted in recent NAO reports[110] on desertisation of armoured vehicles, Combat ID and Saif Sareea II.

234. When the Chiefs of Staff discussed the list of UORs on 9 October, it was advised that the Directorates of Equipment Capability (DECs) and Front Line Commands "were now engaged in the staffing of UORs".[111]

235. The minutes do not record any reference to specific UORs or equipment capabilities raised by Lt Gen Pigott.

---

[110] Looking at the NAO publications around this period, it appears that Lt Gen Pigott was referring to one report: the Saif Sareea report published on 1 August 2002 that dealt with all of the points to which he refers and that is detailed earlier in this Section.
[111] Minutes, 9 October 2002, Chiefs of Staff meeting.

236. Mr Williams wrote to Mr Hoon on the same day, informing him that the Chiefs of Staff had now endorsed the prioritised list of UORs for Iraq as requested.[112] He attached the list and asked Mr Hoon to agree that work should now be taken forward as recommended in his minute of 4 October.

237. Mr Williams added that Treasury officials had confirmed that the MOD's interpretation of access to the Reserve was shared by Mr Brown and they were ready to agree the commitment of resources.

238. The list of UORs covered all three Packages and included:

- communications equipment;
- force protection measures, including NBC equipment and defensive aid suites; and
- desertisation measures including clothing, hydration systems and sand filters.

239. Mr Hoon's Private Office commented:

"I suggest we have a system whereby we see the papers in parallel and draw any dodgy looking ones to your attention."[113]

240. Before agreeing Mr Williams' advice, Mr Hoon's Private Office wrote to Sir David Manning on 11 October with an update on the UOR process, explaining the approvals process and that wider consultation was necessary to ensure that cost information was "soundly based":

"This consultation will be carefully controlled but will inevitably increase the risk of wider disclosure. In the majority of cases, this is unlikely to excite public interest. But the nature of the work involved with some of the essential requirements ... will inevitably lead to comment and speculation that they are linked to preparation for Iraq. The Defence Secretary judges nevertheless that it is necessary to initiate this work now to meet likely timescales and has therefore authorised it to proceed".[114]

241. On 15 October, Mr Hoon's Private Office wrote to Mr Williams, agreeing that the necessary work should now be undertaken to progress the full range of the prioritised (Tranche 1) UORs.[115] Mr Hoon had asked for a copy of all approvals paperwork so that he could "maintain an awareness of progress, and be forewarned of any particularly contentious items". It would also be useful for Mr Williams to provide "the weekly summary of progress" he was understood to be producing.

---

[112] Minute DCRS to APS2/Secretary of State [MOD], 9 October 2002, 'Iraq: UORs'.
[113] Manuscript comment MOD [junior official] on Minute DCRS to APS2/Secretary of State [MOD], 9 October 2002, 'Iraq: UORs'.
[114] Letter Williams to Manning, 11 October 2002, 'Iraq: Potential UK Contributions – Urgent Operational Requirements'.
[115] Minute APS/SofS [MOD] to DCRS, 15 October 2002, 'Iraq: UORs'.

242. Lt Gen Pigott produced an update on UORs for the Chiefs of Staff on 21 October.[116] Tranche 1 UORs were being implemented: two UORs had been approved so far and a further 64 USURs[117] had been formally endorsed by PJHQ and the Director of Special Forces (DSF).

243. Lt Gen Pigott wrote that a working group had been established to inform the Chiefs on the risks associated of operating in a CBRN environment. The provision of COLPRO was being reviewed but detailed checks on armoured vehicle NBC filter packs was not possible under the current visibility guidelines. Routine appraisals were being carried out and checks were being incorporated into those.

244. Where there was no ambiguity about the purpose of the requirement, Mr Hoon was to be consulted before industry was approached. The measures that fell into this category included:

- weapons stocks;
- satellite communications technology;
- fuel distribution and water carriage systems;
- ECBA;
- COLPRO for NBC attacks, including antibiotics for all personnel which was considered essential; and
- desert clothing.

245. The Chiefs of Staff approved Lt Gen Pigott's paper at their meeting on 28 October and ACM Bagnall was directed to "take the work forward".[118]

246. The minutes do not record any reference to specific UORs or equipment capabilities raised in Lt Gen Pigott's minute.

247. On 29 October, Major General David Richards, Assistant Chief of the General Staff (ACGS), wrote to Lt Gen Pigott about his paper of 21 October, stating that he was:

"… content to endorse the recommendations within the paper subject to the requirement to increase the pace at which we address the UORs concerning NBC COLPRO and decontamination. There is a significant delta between current UORs and our anticipated requirement which needs urgent work."[119]

248. **Between 31 October and the middle of December 2002, Ministerial decisions and military planning and preparations were based on advice that the deployment**

---

[116] Minute DCDS(C) to COS, 21 October 2002, 'Iraq Contingency Planning – Urgent Operational Requirements and Related Funding Issues'.
[117] Urgent Statement of User Requests (USURs) are raised when there is a capability gap that needs addressing by the procurement of new equipment. That process is explained in detail in Section 14.1.
[118] Minutes, 28 October 2002, Chiefs of Staff meeting.
[119] Minute ACGS to MA1/DCDS(C), 29 October 2002, 'Iraq Contingency Planning – Urgent Operational Requirements and Related Funding Issues'.

of a divisional headquarters and a single combat brigade, with four battalions, in a northern option, and the possible deployment of a Royal Marines Commando Group to southern Iraq, were the maximum which could be deployed given the requirements of Op FRESCO and the timescale for military operations envisaged by the US.

249. The process for approving UORs continued against a deadline of the end of February for Packages 1 and 2, and the end of March for Package 3.

250. The difficulties surrounding desertisation measures, clothing, ECBA and NBC protection continued.

251. On 30 October, Mr Hoon's Private Office wrote to a DCRS official with a query raised by Mr Hoon while reading the UOR for Challenger 2 modifications:

> "He noted that the business case used a latest acceptable in-service date of April 2003. He wonders what in-service dates are currently being considered appropriate, given what we know of US planning."[120]

252. The DCRS official replied on 12 November.[121] He stated that the Challenger 2 In Service Date (ISD) was "used with 90% confidence" and would "almost certainly be brought forward". His understanding was that modifications would "be complete by early March" and did not require the vehicles to be returned to the factory; the modifications could be carried out in theatre "if necessary".

253. The official added that it was "not easy to align equipment ISDs with an operation, when the timing of the latter is moving constantly" but "rough timeframes" were necessary to negotiate delivery times and costs with industry, with the caveat that they were liable to change.

254. Adm Boyce's office added:

> "While this could add further flexibility to the time required for modifications, we should not lose sight of the implications for tank crewmen … Our experience in 1991 was that such modifications … were time-consuming and manpower-intensive. Planning should take account of this."[122]

255. Section 6.1 addresses Mr Blair's decision on 31 October that the MOD could offer Package 3 to the US for planning purposes.

256. Mr Hoon was advised on 1 November by a DCRS official that 88 USURs had been sent to DCRS, having been endorsed by PJHQ and DSF.[123] He wrote that 10 UOR

---

[120] Minute APS/SofS [MOD] to DCRS 1, 30 October 2002, 'Iraq: UORs'.
[121] Minute DCRS1 to APS/SofS [MOD], 12 November 2002, 'Iraq: UORs'.
[122] Minute PSO/CDS to DCRS 1, 19 November 2002, 'Iraq: UORs Challenger 2'.
[123] Minute DCRS 1 to APS/SofS [MOD], 1 November 2002, 'Possible Operations against Iraq UOR List, 1 November 2002'.

business cases had been approved internally and that Treasury officials were "actively considering" the AS90[124] and Challenger 2 desertisation cases. The approved business cases amounted to £20m, £800,000 of which was in the form of running costs that would be claimed against the Reserve.

257. The official added:

> "Most addressees will have seen the article that appeared in the Telegraph earlier this week alleging that contingency planning was being held up by HM Treasury. This assertion is entirely without foundation and serves only to complicate unnecessarily our excellent relationship with them."

258. On 6 November, the Chiefs of Staff considered a paper from Lieutenant General John Reith, Chief of Joint Operations (CJO), about the impact of "very hot weather" on the UK's war-fighting ability.[125] The points raised included:

- It was "well recognised" that weapon systems could be "degraded in hot weather".
- Ammunition storage was difficult and high risk.
- "Most" land vehicles required UOR action "to enable them to operate effectively in hot weather", some of which were "in hand". The lead time for modifications varied from one to 12 months.

259. The Chiefs of Staff noted the paper, which was to be revised and re-submitted "within one month".

260. On 12 November, a DCRS official sought Mr Hoon's approval to initiate discussions with industry for five equipment measures that would raise the visibility of planning for an invasion of Iraq:

- desert combat boots – an estimated 20,000 were required in particular sizes with a critical lead time of three to six months;
- ECBA – there was currently only sufficient stock for 15,000 personnel;
- water and fuel distribution; and
- medical equipment, including battlefield ambulance upgrades, COLPRO and field hospital infrastructure.[126]

261. Mr Hoon approved the request on the following day.[127]

---

[124] The AS90 is a self-propelled gun.
[125] Minute Reith to PSO/CDS and SECCOS, 5 November 2002, 'Warfighting in Iraq in the Summer'; Minutes, 6 November 2002, Chiefs of Staff meeting.
[126] Minute DCRS 1 to APS/SofS [MOD], 12 November 2002, 'Potential Operations in Iraq: Requirement to discuss Equipment Procurement with Industry'.
[127] Minute PS/SofS [MOD] to DCRS 1, 13 November 02, 'Potential Operations in Iraq: Discussions with Industry'.

262. The Chiefs of Staff had also considered a "CBRN Risk Paper" on 6 November and the key equipment issues arising were covered in Lt Gen Pigott's UOR update on 18 November.[128] The time needed to procure additional COLPRO under UOR action was "directly related to the amount of equipment required" and it was possible that the quantity which could be procured and fielded against "the most demanding timeframe may be insufficient to meet the full requirement". That could have an impact upon the UK's concept of operations (CONOPS). Options would be presented to the Chiefs of Staff "once the extent of the likely shortfall" was confirmed.

263. Lt Gen Pigott reported that 20 UORs had been approved to date, and a further 137 USURs endorsed. The latest ISD being used to gauge the delivery of UORs was the end of February for Packages 1 and 2 and the end of March for Package 3.

264. There were some key equipment gaps "that may not be fully addressed by the UOR process and for which Chiefs of Staff's direction on prioritisation and risk may be required", including:

- ECBA – " … it is possible we may not be able to procure sufficient numbers within the timeframe; this may necessitate differential levels of force protection".
- Desert clothing and boots – "It is likely that the numbers required will exceed the UK's manufacturing capability. There are operational, force health and presentational implications in not providing troops with appropriate clothing."

265. Options would be presented to the Chiefs of Staff once procurement timelines had been confirmed with industry.

266. Maj Gen Fry advised Adm Boyce on 22 November that it would take some four months from the order to deploy for the northern option (whether Package 2 or 3), and more than five months for the southern option.[129]

267. A DCRS official informed Mr Hoon on 22 November that contracts were shortly to be let for clothing, combat boots and body armour, and the procurement of these items would be highly visible.[130] The official wrote that the "continuing uncertainty over the size of the operation" meant that, initially, the procurement figures would be:

- clothing for 15,000 personnel;
- 20,000 pairs of desert boots; and
- 50,000 body armour plates.

---

[128] Minute DCDS(C) to COS, 18 November 2002, 'Iraq Contingency Planning – Urgent Operational Requirements and Related Issues'.
[129] Minute DCJO(Ops) to PSO/CDS, 22 November 2002, 'Potential Operations in Iraq – Northern and Southern Timelines'.
[130] Report DCRS 1 to APS/SofS [MOD], 22 November 2002, 'Potential Operations in Iraq: Letting of Contracts for Combat Clothing/Body Armour'.

268. On 29 November, a DCRS official provided a UOR update for Ministers, the Chiefs of Staff and various other senior personnel, recording that 35 UORs and 162 USURs had been approved.[131] Those included desert clothing, AS90 environmental enhancements, Challenger 2 dust mitigation and enhanced armour protection, battlefield ambulance upgrades and field hospital upgrades.

269. The combined cost of the 35 UORs was £115m, against the initial £150m allocated by the Treasury.

270. The same day, the DCRS official sought permission from Mr Hoon for the MOD to commence discussions with industry on the procurement of desert clothing, ECBA, water and fuel distribution and medical equipment.[132] The official explained that, although Mr Hoon had already given that permission on 13 November:

> "… there is a perception in other areas (including the DLO) that restrictions on consulting industry remain in place and the uncertainty needs to be removed."

271. The areas where "some concern had been expressed" included the build-up of sustainability commodities related to land forces and COLPRO.

272. Mr Hoon's Private Office replied on 2 December, agreeing that the MOD could discuss "any items of equipment relating to operations in Iraq" with industry "at the appropriate stage in the UOR process".[133] That was "on the understanding that appropriate confidentiality will be observed".

273. In December 2002, the MOD and the Treasury agreed how the MOD would claim the cost of military operations against Iraq from the Reserve.

274. On 28 November, Mr Hoon wrote to Mr Brown to request an increase in the UOR ceiling from £150m to £300m and to secure agreement that the MOD should begin to capture all non-UOR additional costs, with a view to repayment from the Reserve in due course.[134] He stated that the current UOR process was "working well".

275. Mr Blair agreed on 9 December that the MOD should plan on the basis that a political decision to commit land forces could be taken as early as 15 February 2003 (see Section 6.1).

276. A copy of the letter recording Mr Blair's decision was sent to Mr Mark Bowman, Mr Brown's Private Secretary.

---

[131] Minute DCRS 1 to APS/SofS [MOD], 29 November 2002, 'Possible Operations Against Iraq UOR List, 29 November 2002'.
[132] Minute DCRS 1 to APS/SofS [MOD], 29 November 2002, 'Potential Operations in Iraq: Requirement to Discuss Equipment Procurement with Industry'.
[133] Minute APS/SofS [MOD] to DCRS 1, 2 December 2002, 'Potential Operations in Iraq: Requirement to Discuss Equipment Procurement with Industry'.
[134] Letter Hoon to Brown, 28 November 2002, 'Iraq: Urgent Operational Requirements'.

277. Mr Brown agreed on the same day to increase the ceiling for UORs and that the MOD should begin to capture NACMO, but said that all such costs should be contained within the UOR ceiling "until any operation is initiated".[135]

278. On 11 December, Mr Rycroft confirmed that Mr Blair was "content that military preparations from January would become increasingly visible".[136]

279. Mr Hoon wrote to Mr Brown on 13 December, warning him that Mr Blair's decision on 9 December would increase the rate at which the MOD incurred additional costs.[137]

280. The recently agreed £150m tranche was "likely to be exhausted by 20 December". Mr Hoon requested an additional £200m for UORs, bringing the UOR total to £500m.

281. Mr Paul Boateng, Chief Secretary to the Treasury, agreed the request on 23 December.[138]

282. The discussions leading up to that decision are set out in greater detail in Section 13.1 which shows that the arrangement for reclaiming the NACMO worked as intended and did not constrain the military's ability to conduct operations against Iraq.

283. There was no delay or obstruction on the part of the Treasury that stifled the progress of UORs.

284. Mr McKane told the Inquiry that there had been no major obstacles to the preparations with the Treasury, although the need to return to the Treasury to increase the tranches of money available had been frustrating to some:

> "Inevitably in these kind of circumstances there is an anxiety and a concern on the part of the Ministry of Defence to get on with things and the – and it did take a month or so after my first engagement in this for the agreements to be reached to start to commit money to these Urgent Operational Requirements. But thereafter, the process operated smoothly. There were some, I think, who were probably frustrated at the fact that … we were given tranches of money … and I can remember that we would get quite quickly to the point where we had exhausted the first tranche and were then involved in the preparation of ministerial correspondence to secure the release of the next tranche, but I think … that was understandable in the circumstances."[139]

285. Lt Gen Pigott's UOR update for the Chiefs of Staff on 20 December stated that 79 UORs had been approved at a cost of £283m, 48 from Tranche 1 and 31 from

---

[135] Letter Brown to Hoon, 9 December 2002, 'Iraq: Urgent Operational Requirements'.
[136] Letter Rycroft to Watkins, 11 December 2002, 'Iraq: Military Preparations'.
[137] Letter Hoon to Brown, 13 December 2002, 'Iraq: Costs'.
[138] Letter Boateng to Hoon, 23 December 2002, 'Iraq: Costs'.
[139] Public hearing, 2 July 2010, pages 35-36.

Tranche 2.[140] There were nine Tranche 1 UORs outstanding. Additional sustainability measures of £44.75m had been approved.

286. The key issues included:

- Fuel and water distribution.

- COLPRO – the DLO was finalising its assessment of the consolidated requirement against serviceable holdings and was initiating UOR action for the balance. Early indications suggested "an initial delivery date of late Feb/Mar 03" although there may be a longer lead time for some components. As its delivery could affect the UK's ability to "field the required capability in the anticipated timescale", options for the prioritisation of the available equipment would continue to be refined.

- ECBA – contracts for an additional 37,400 ECBA plates were to be let the following week, to augment the 30,000 in stock. It was expected that the requirement would be "met in full by the end of March".

- Desert clothing – 10,000 sets of desert clothing were in stock and contracts had been placed for an additional 15,000 sets and 20,000 pairs of boots. Those would be available by the end of March. The MOD intended to procure a further 15,000 sets of clothing and 10,000 sets of boots but it would not be possible to confirm whether those would be available by the end of March until the contracts had been placed.

287. The difficulties in providing Combat ID were also highlighted. That is addressed later in this Section.

288. By 3 January 2003, a total of 242 USURs had been endorsed and 118 UOR business cases approved, totalling £340m.[141]

The decision to deploy ground forces to the South and its implications

289. **Between mid-December 2002 and mid-January 2003, the force to be deployed recommended by the MOD increased from an armoured brigade and a Commando Group to an armoured brigade and two light brigades.**

290. **The military recommendation to offer ground forces at large scale and to deploy for potential operations in southern Iraq was formally endorsed on 17 January, only two months before the possible start of military operations.**

291. **The only reference in the papers put to Mr Hoon and Mr Blair of the risks associated with deploying three combat brigades and committing them to earlier**

---

[140] Minute DCDS(C) to COS, 20 December 2002, 'Iraq Contingency Planning – Urgent Operational Requirements and Related Issues'.
[141] Minute from DCRS1d to APS/SofS [MOD], 3 January 2003, 'Possible Operations Against Iraq UOR List, 3 January 2003'.

operations was that some risk would have to be taken on fitting UOR equipment, but that risk was "considered acceptable".

292. The risk that some equipment might not be delivered in time for the start of operations does not appear to have been drawn to Ministers' attention or discussed.

293. The development of the military options between mid-December 2002 and mid-January 2003, the decision to offer 3 Commando Brigade for the amphibious assault, and the decision on 17 January to deploy two brigades for operations in southern Iraq rather than one brigade for the northern option, are addressed in detail in Sections 6.1 and 6.2.

294. Mr Hoon wrote to Mr Blair on 16 January seeking agreement to the "key role in southern Iraq" proposed by the US for the UK.[142]

295. Mr Hoon stated that the timescales for possible action would mean that some risk would have to be taken on the fitting of UOR equipment, but that risk was "considered acceptable".

296. Following a telephone conversation, Sir David Manning replied to Mr Watkins on 17 January that Mr Blair was "content to proceed on the basis of the Defence Secretary's recommendations".[143] The UK would proceed with Package 3.

297. Mr Hoon made a statement in Parliament on 20 January announcing that the Government had "reached a view" of the composition and deployment of a land force package for potential military action in Iraq.[144] That would include the Headquarters of 1st (UK) Armoured Division, comprising 7 Armoured Brigade, 16 Air Assault Brigade and 102 Logistics Brigade.

298. The total number of personnel would be "approximately 26,000 personnel" which was in addition to the "around 4,000 personnel" already being deployed with 3 Commando Brigade Royal Marines.

299. As Section 6.2 shows, it was envisaged that 3 Commando Brigade Royal Marines would have a combat role at the start of the land campaign in mid-March. The roles to be played by 16 Air Assault Brigade and 7 Armoured Brigade were less defined. It was envisaged that 16 Air Assault Brigade would relieve US forces in an area south of Basra approximately 10 days after the start of operations. 7 Armoured Brigade would protect the US flank.

---

[142] Letter Hoon to Blair, 16 January 2003, 'Iraq: UK Land Contribution'.
[143] Letter Manning to Watkins, 17 January 2003, 'Iraq: UK Land Contribution'.
[144] House of Commons, *Official Report*, 20 January 2003, columns 34-46.

300. To conduct those operations, 16 Air Assault Brigade would need to be deployed and ready in Kuwait by the beginning of March and 7 Armoured Brigade by mid-March. For the northern option, the UK had been planning for ground combat operations beginning in mid-April.

301. The implications for equipping three combat brigades and the plans for earlier operations were not explicitly acknowledged until late January.

302. Ministers were advised that there were "no showstoppers", but there is no record of formal advice on how the military had defined that term or the level of risk it entailed.

303. Following his statement on 20 January, Mr Hoon was asked by Mr Bernard Jenkin for an assurance that troops were "fully trained and fully equipped for whatever they may be asked to do".

304. Mr Hoon replied:

"As for preparations, I do not doubt that our forces are fully and thoroughly prepared to face this kind of operation. Indeed, the training exercise conducted in similar conditions in Oman just over a year ago was obvious preparation for this kind of deployment."

305. Lord Bach announced the composition and deployment of the UK's land force package in the House of Lords on 20 January.[145]

306. Asked whether the Challenger 2 tanks had now been desertised, if the lessons from Saif Sareea had been rectified, and if there was sufficient desert clothing for troops to be deployed, Lord Bach replied:

"As regards Challenger 2 and AS90 ... work is being carried out now to ensure that they are desertised sufficiently. That work is ongoing and will continue when forces are in transit and in theatre as required. I give the noble Lord the assurance he seeks as regards clothing ... We continue to work to ensure that our personnel are properly equipped to cope with the environmental conditions in which they may operate."

307. Pressed by Lord Elton for reassurance that "the work now being done will be completed before there is any question of any armoured vehicle moving in the desert – that they will be desertised before they are deployed", Lord Bach replied: "Of course the vehicles will be desertised by the time they are deployed."[146]

---

[145] House of Lords, *Official Report*, 20 January 2003, columns 492-497.
[146] House of Lords, *Official Report*, 20 January 2003, columns 499-500.

308. On 21 January, Gen Walker was advised that the delivery times for UORs had been refined to reflect the compressed timeframes and there were risks associated with the inability to deliver some key UORs within those.[147] Allowance had now been made to integrate UORs but no allowance had been made for any additional training required, or any delays in loading or transit to theatre. The tactical implications of the delivery shortfalls were "not yet well understood".

309. Gen Walker was advised that:

- The US commitment to loan Combat ID capability had so far proved inconclusive and there would be "**no guarantee of US support**".

- The DEC was "increasingly optimistic" they would have "full Target ID capability", but the necessary measures would have to be fitted in theatre.

- Confidence in the delivery of NBC protection was decreasing.

- The full capability of the Challenger 2 tank's dust mitigation and AS90's environmental enhancement were unlikely to be available until after 31 March and would have to be fitted in theatre.

- The fitting of ballistic protection enhancements for Combat Vehicle Reconnaissance (Tracked) vehicles[148] "may have to take place in theatre".

- There was "little visibility" of the amount of desert clothing "in the hands of soldiers" and the allocation of clothing had already been reduced from three sets per man to two sets per man to "try and prevent a shortfall at the start of operations". It was necessary to airlift clothing into theatre to meet operational timelines and "to have a favourable delivery of sizes". If both of these were achieved, it was "possible that all troops will have desert clothing and boots in time for the start of operations".

- 75 percent of the required unhardened COLPRO would be ready by the start of March, with the full requirement being met in theatre by 31 March.

- There was "insufficient stock" of COLPRO seals for Armoured Fighting Vehicles (AFVs) and more could not be procured in time. The lead time to procure seals was 12 to 36 months.

- The situation had improved "markedly" on ECBA, and Gen Walker could "be confident" that it would be delivered "to all troops in time for the committal of any ground troops".

- The full requirement for battlefield ambulances, however, would not be upgraded in time for the anticipated start of operations.

- The availability of sand filters for Lynx helicopters was driving the number of helicopters to be deployed.

---

[147] Minute DMO MO3 to MA1/CGS, 21 January 2003, 'Op TELIC UOR Delivery and Risks – Information Brief'.
[148] A type of Armoured Fighting Vehicle (AFV).

310. On 21 January, Lord Bach's Private Office wrote to AM Stirrup's Private Office, explaining that Lord Bach would be reviewing the progress of UORs, "with a view to highlighting potential risks and focusing on means of addressing them".[149] That was because, while Ministers were aware which UORs had been approved, they had less visibility of:

- how confident officials remained that equipment could be procured in the required timeframe; and
- the extent to which outstanding areas of concern about equipment capabilities were assessed as being "incapable of resolution" in the required timeframe.

311. Lord Bach agreed that the first step was to hold a meeting with key stakeholders to take stock of the position across all packages but he listed areas that were likely to be of particular concern, including desertisation of armoured vehicles, Combat ID, NBC capabilities and clothing and personal equipment. A short paper setting out the "key areas of shortfall or predicted risk" to assist discussions was requested.

312. The minutes from the Chiefs of Staff meeting on 22 January recorded that "unhelpful media coverage had exposed a UOR problem and it was clear that shortfalls would mean that FOC [Full Operating Capability] by some UK troops might not be achieved until 31 March".[150]

313. Adm Boyce directed that "immediate action" should be taken and for commands to be informed that "urgent action was underway". That included addressing "bad press" equipment stories and that UORs were to become a standing item on the agenda for operational Chiefs of Staff meetings.

314. On the same day, and in light of the brief provided to Gen Walker about equipment shortfalls, ACM Bagnall wrote to Lt Gen Pigott and AM Stirrup about Lord Bach's request.[151] He wrote:

"I have confirmed that DCDS(EC) [AM Stirrup] already has work in hand to respond. Clearly, this needs to include an operational assessment of the likely impact of any delays to particular UORs. It may be helpful to categorise UORs as low, medium, high and 'show stopper' under this heading, and I have asked DCDS(C) [Lt Gen Pigott] to provide the advice. There will also be a need to highlight any measures (for example a lack of camouflage paint) which may have a low operational impact but which would carry a very significant presentational and morale cost.

"As you are aware, CDS has asked me to retain oversight of the UOR process, and I would be grateful if your combined response to Min(DP) [Lord Bach] could be

---

[149] Minute PS/Min(DP) to MA/DCDS(EC), 21 January 2003, 'Iraq: Op TELIC – UORs'.
[150] Minutes, 22 January 2003, Chiefs of Staff meeting.
[151] Minute VCDS to DCDS(C) and DCDS(EC), 22 January 2003, ' Iraq: Op TELIC – UORs'.

copied to me. I would also intend, diaries permitting, to join any meeting which Min(DP) intends to hold on this topic."

315. In his witness statement ACM Bagnall told the Inquiry that Mr Hoon had asked Lord Bach:

" … to be his lead Minister for UORs and for DCDS(EC) to act as Senior Responsible Owner (SRO) for UORs. This led to regular and increasingly frequent meetings between the then Minister and his staffs and the then DCDS(EC) and his experts. For my part I monitored the UOR process on CDS' behalf and intervened if and when required."[152]

316. Lord Bach told the Inquiry:

"I was asked by the Secretary of State, in the second half of January 2003, to take temporary responsibility for UORs. This involved being briefed by DCDS(EC) [AM Stirrup] in writing, before chairing (for the most part) weekly meetings with senior officials in order to look at progress of UORs that had already been agreed between MOD and HMT. I played no part in determining what UORs should or should not be proceeded with. Those decisions were taken at a stage well before their progress was looked at by the Committee I chaired. I had played no role before the request in Jan 2003, nor should I have. UORs were not the responsibility of Min DP: they and the Defence Logistics Organisation were in the portfolio of Min AF [Mr Ingram]."[153]

317. Following his statement to the House of Lords on 20 January, Lord Bach was advised on 22 January by Mr Williams that there was "not only no need for him to clarify the statement made earlier this week about 'desertisation' but actual disadvantage in seeking to do so".[154]

318. Mr Williams confirmed that only one, "relatively minor", modification would be completed before the vehicles deployed. He stated:

"On that basis, if by 'deployed' the Minister meant the formal point at which units begin to leave their main bases and embark for the Gulf, then his statement on Monday would be misleading. I suspect, however, that Lord Bach meant the point at which UK forces were likely to become engaged on offensive operations. Given the context of the question and the fact that many Lords/MPs would not pick up on the formal military interpretation of the term 'deployed', that is probably a reasonable position to take. If that is the case, I do not judge that a public clarification of the use of the word 'deployed' is either necessary or would add much value."

---

[152] Statement, 6 January 2011, page 3.
[153] Statement, 22 December 2010, page 1.
[154] Minute Williams to PS/Minister(DP), 22 January 2003, 'Op TELIC – Challenge 2 'Desertisation' UOR Activity'.

319. In describing the modifications that the Challenger 2 was undergoing for Iraq, Mr Williams wrote that Lord Bach's comments were "reasonable: although the full planned upgrade may not be completed in time, Challenger 2s' desert performance should have been enhanced to a useful degree in the right timeframe".

320. Mr Williams added that, more generally, it was also "important to try and dampen down speculation" on when equipment modifications were likely to be completed because:

- the MOD's "general line" was that decisions about military action had "not yet been taken", and providing indications that it was "working to a hard and fast deadline" would "undermine that overall public position on the timing of possible action";
- the timeframes for delivery from industry were subject to change; and
- the MOD's own assumptions about the timeframe "may again change".

321. Mr Williams suggested that should be considered in light of the broader advice Lord Bach was expecting later that week.

322. Lord Bach received the advice, submitted on behalf of AM Stirrup, on 24 January.[155] He was invited to note that:

- 137 equipment UORs and 108 sustainability UORs had been approved, the "vast majority" of which remained "on track to deliver to the Front Line Commands in accordance with planned ISDs".
- "The compression of timescales for the Land Component, coupled with the late addition of 16 AA Bde [16 Air Assault Brigade] and the increase in the Amphibious Task Group to a Brigade(-) has meant that a number of UORs will not be delivered in full prior to the potential start date of operations."
- "None of the shortfalls is deemed to be a 'showstopper' and solutions for mitigating the potential operational risks involved are being developed by PJHQ and Front Line Commands."
- "Heavy pressure" would be placed on the supply and equipment support chains and advanced deployment dates had "added to the weight of UOR items which were always intended to be fitted in theatre".

323. The advice explained that the majority of UOR shortfalls affected ground forces. The key areas of concerns were the Challenger 2 desertisation, Combat ID and in-service stock items that could not be procured through UOR action, such as COLPRO filters for AFVs.

---

[155] Minute DCDS(EC) to PS/Minister(DP), 24 January 2003, 'Iraq: Op TELIC UORs'.

324. Lord Bach was advised:

"Whilst there are no showstoppers it should be understood that lack of some UOR capabilities … could require Commanders to make choices they might not otherwise have to make and could reduce operational effectiveness. Equally, delivery of the UOR capability cannot remove risks completely. The overall operational impact may be to constrain commanders' options, reduce the tempo of operations and risk the ability to operate in close conjunction with US forces."

325. In response to the high level of media and Parliamentary interest in the availability of equipment, as a general guideline, one of the points to emphasise was that:

"Our forces will have the equipment they need to undertake any tasks assigned to them as part of possible operations. The safety and well-being of our Service personnel are of paramount importance. Where appropriate, we should look to compare capabilities to those available in the 1991 Gulf War."

326. Details of the key shortfalls were provided in an annex, which largely reflected the advice to Gen Walker of 21 January. Additional information included:

- As 3 Commando Brigade and deploying RAF personnel had been fully equipped with desert clothing, there were "no remaining stocks". An additional 32,500 sets would be delivered on 7 March and the full requirement would be available on 28 March. It would need to be airlifted into theatre.
- Sufficient ECBA plates would be available "to equip the entire force" by 7 March and there was confidence that "the full ECBA capability" could be delivered "before the committal of any ground troops".
- The unavailability of COLPRO for AFVs remained the same, although the Defence Science and Technology Laboratory (DSTL) had provided advice that reduced the number of filter changes required "while maintaining sufficient protection for the crew". Even the reduced number could not be resourced and "the limited in-service stocks" would "therefore require prioritisation".

327. On the same day, as instructed at the Chiefs of Staff meeting on 22 January, Air Chief Marshal Sir Malcolm Pledger, Chief of Defence Logistics (CDL), wrote to Adm Boyce about which capability and sustainability UORs were unavailable within current timelines.[156] Those were listed in an annex which was consistent with other briefings on the shortfalls.

328. Referring to the inability to approach industry earlier and the constraint placed upon funds while arrangements were agreed with the Treasury, ACM Pledger stated that Adm Boyce should be aware of "the relative success" that had been achieved by the DLO.

---

[156] Minute CDL to PSO/CDS, 24 January 2003, 'UOR/Operational Sustainability Issues'.

329. ACM Pledger wrote:

"No strategic issues, that would deny UK the option to conduct a military campaign, arose within the UOR/Operational Sustainability staffing, hence it has not been raised at COS(O) by CDL or DCDS(EC). However, regular briefing has occurred through the established DCMO [Defence Crisis Management Organisation] process (Iraq Stocktakes and through SPG); PJHQ briefings (both at CJO's Jt Comd's Seminars and through the range of staff level planning meetings, which includes FLC representation). These briefings repeatedly flagged the consequences of defining force packages without the full knowledge of the impact of the associated logistic and capability enhancements on the basic plan."

330. ACM Pledger added that Adm Boyce "should feel assured" that the DLO was "wholly focused" on its delivery of UORs and would "continue to make every effort to synchronise the delivery of these equipments to theatre in a timely manner".

331. Lord Bach chaired his first meeting about UORs on 27 January.[157] The points recorded from the introductory discussion included:

- Given that "authority fully to engage industry had only been received on 2nd December, the time scales were challenging."

- The high priority requirements for Packages 0-2 were "capable of being met by 28th February". The "key risks" were now the UK's ability to "deliver, fit and train on UOR equipment whilst the force was deploying to or in theatre". In respect to Packages 0-2, these risks were considered "manageable".

- The compression of timescales and expansion of Package 3 meant an "increased risk that package 3 UORs would not be delivered before operations commenced". None of the resultant shortfalls were assessed as being a "showstopper" but "we would only be clear of the operational implications once detailed plans had been worked up".

- "[W]hatever the operational significance of delays in delivering UORs", it was expected that media would focus on "equipment shortcomings"; being well prepared to win the "presentational argument was vital". That was not just to preserve the MOD's reputation, but was "a key aspect of securing and preserving public support for the whole enterprise".

- A "key question for the future" was why the forces "were not better prepared for the kind of operations now in prospect", given the conclusions of the SDR about the likelihood of operations in the Middle East. The UK "needed to be more intelligent" about its holdings of certain long-term lead items such as desert clothing, NBC filters and COLPRO, and about "the extent to which equipment was capable of operating at a range of environmental conditions".

---

[157] Minute PS/Minister(DP) to MA/DCDS(EC), 27 January 2003, 'Iraq: Op TELIC UORs'.

332. The meeting discussed particular shortfalls, including:

- There was a need to "find a better way of explaining the improvements" being made to Challenger 2 tanks.

- There was still no assurance that the US would loan Combat ID assets – Lt Gen Reith was being briefed "to raise this personally" with General Tommy Franks, Commander US Central Command (CENTCOM).

- " …[I]nnovative measures were in place to acquire sufficient stocks of desert clothing and boots for at least two sets to be provided to all personnel in theatre by mid-March" and Lord Bach asked officials to review with industry the practicality of extending the number of personnel issued with three sets to cover all those deploying.

- There remained concerns about NBC capabilities – Lord Bach requested further advice on the operational risk within three days.

333. On 28 January, Mr Hoon asked Adm Boyce for "a clear recommendation from the Chiefs of Staff" as to whether UK forces could "participate in the operational plan as currently understood, particularly the potential start of major ground operations on 3 March".[158]

334. If this was not possible, Adm Boyce was asked on what date land forces could participate and what date would be the "implied start of initial combat operations". The advice was requested by 3pm the following day.

335. ACM Bagnall's Private Office replied on 29 January, stating:

"There are, in absolute terms, no showstoppers. In the case of maritime forces, all UORs should be in place by 28 February. Some contractual risk remains, but the systems involved carry a low operational risk. In the air environment, the force will be ready for operation by 28 February …

"The land environment carries the greatest risk in two areas: Challenger 2 and Combat Identification."[159]

336. The work in hand for Challenger 2 vehicles suggested that their availability and serviceability would "improve significantly" by 18 March when certain modifications were due to be completed. The situation would improve again after 7 April when new filters were fitted.

337. For Combat ID, systems to improve situational awareness within the UK and US forces were currently being evaluated in Germany. It was "not yet clear" whether they could "be integrated into a UK vehicle in the time available" but early indications were that the work was "proceeding well".

---

[158] Minute APS/SofS [MOD] to PSO/CDS, 28 January 2003, 'Iraq: UORs'.
[159] Minute MA/VCDS to PS/SofS [MOD], 29 January 2003, 'Iraq – UORs'.

338. ACM Bagnall's Private Office concluded:

> "In sum, if the start date for land operations is delayed, there will be greater time to embody the required land UORs. However, as I have noted earlier, there are no showstoppers."

339. The minutes of the Chiefs of Staff meeting on 29 January recorded that the "focus had shifted to what equipment was being delivered rather than what was being procured".[160] It was important that "all measures were taken" to ensure that equipment was fitted and not just made available. A "coherent plan was required with clear guidance on the division of responsibilities for ensuring equipment was available to units in theatre".

340. There was "a concern over the availability of desertised Challenger 2s" and, although the Land Component Commander was content with the current position, Adm Boyce "noted that it would clearly be better if availability was improved as a result of any slip in campaign timelines that allowed extra UOR work to be completed".

CONCERNS ABOUT COMBAT ID

341. Concerns about the provision of Combat ID and whether previous lessons had been learned were raised in both Houses of Parliament.

342. On 18 December 2002, Mr Hoon made a statement in the House of Commons on contingency preparations for possible military action in Iraq.[161]

343. Mr Hoon was asked by Mr Mark Prisk for an assurance that, "given the recent tragic incidents of friendly fire in different theatres of war", all deployed UK service personnel would have the equipment "they need to communicate speedily and effectively with friendly units".[162]

344. Mr Hoon replied:

> "I thank the hon. Gentleman for raising a serious and important point. I assure him that efforts are being made to ensure that that is the case."

345. Combat ID was raised as an issue on 20 December in Lt Gen Pigott's UOR update.[163] He stated that it was:

> " ... a vulnerable issue in presentational terms, particularly following the NAO report, but it is an issue that has not moved forward recently. Resolution has been thwarted while the UK awaits the formulation of US policy by CENTCOM."

---

[160] Minutes, 29 January 2003, Chiefs of Staff meeting.
[161] House of Commons, *Official Report,* 18 December 2002, columns 845-846.
[162] House of Commons, *Official Report,* 18 December 2002, column 854.
[163] Minute DCDS(C) to PSO/CDS, 20 December 2002, 'Iraq Contingency Planning – Urgent Operational Requirements and Related Issues'.

346. Gen Walker responded to Lt Gen Pigott the same day, stating that he remained "uneasy over Combat ID".[164] He continued:

"I understand that we are currently awaiting the formulation of coherent US policy … I am conscious that significant effort has been made at various levels to press this issue with CENTCOM but that, in the main, the bottom up approach has been adopted. Given the operational implication of not developing a coherent coalition policy and the presentational aspects of Combat ID, I believe that we can no longer afford to prevaricate. The issue now needs to be aired at the highest levels within CENTCOM."

347. Mr Watkins wrote on Mr Hoon's copy of the note: "He is right to focus on the presentational risks: this issue was raised in the House on Wednesday."[165]

348. On 7 January 2003, Mr Hoon was asked in the House of Commons what lessons had been learned from the past to ensure that British forces were equipped against the risk of friendly fire.[166] He replied:

"… we are engaged in a process of ensuring that combat identification is dealt with satisfactorily. There is no single technical solution to that difficult problem, but we will acquire new equipment that will be available in time for any potential conflict in the Gulf … I can assure the House that British troops will be able to work alongside American forces entirely safely and satisfactorily."

349. A junior MOD officer provided a DCRS official with a Combat ID update on the same day.[167] He first gave an overview of the work being done in NATO's development of a BTID which set "a basic technical requirement to be able to identify 'friend' or 'unknown' on the battlefield" and which had been endorsed by eight countries.

350. On Iraq, the officer stated that the Combat ID UOR was "still being scoped" and summarised what the requirement was likely to encompass.

351. A UOR was being developed to mirror "ad-hoc" US measures being considered for forthcoming operations:

"The UK has been anything but dilatory in developing a technological Combat ID capability. We have actually been a leading light in this area. That no solution is yet available anywhere in the world reflects merely the complexity of achieving a satisfactory technical solution to an extremely challenging requirement. The complexity is exacerbated by the need for international consensus on any solution.

---

[164] Minute CGS to DCDS(C), 20 December 2002, 'Combat ID'.
[165] Manuscript comment Watkins on Minute CGS to DCDS(C), 20 December 2002, 'Combat ID'.
[166] House of Commons, *Official Report*, 7 January 2003, columns 23-25.
[167] Minute MOD [junior officer] to DCRS 1, 7 January 2003, 'Combat Identification (CID)'.

"To meet the requirement in the short term, current UOR action will give the UK an identical Combat ID solution to that deployed by the US. In the circumstances, this is as close to the ideal as we could have hoped to achieve."

352. AVM Loader provided a summary note of work in progress on Combat ID for ACM Bagnall, recording that, "contrary to press speculation, progress continues to be made since the conflict in the Gulf", but that "notwithstanding any measures taken or currently under consideration, fratricide will always remain a real risk in the heat of conflict".[168]

353. AVM Loader explained that work continued but progress had been slow because measures could not be developed in isolation. The alignment of UK measures with those in the US had "been hampered by the lack of a coherent policy" but, to ensure that some capability could be delivered in time, UORs had been based upon assumptions agreed with key stakeholders and US Department of Defense and Army staff.

354. At the request of ACM Bagnall, the update was circulated to MOD Ministers and the Chiefs of Staff.

355. In the House of Lords on 9 January, Lord Bach was asked about the availability of satisfactory Combat ID equipment for British troops in any potential Gulf conflict.[169] He replied:

"... we take combat identification and the risk of friendly fire extremely seriously ... Lives depend on it. We believe that our combat identification procedures are effective. We have deployed successfully as a country on many operations since the tragedies in this field during the Gulf conflict. There have been no reported incidents of fratricide, or blue on blue, involving UK forces. I say that with caution because whatever technology one puts in, and however sophisticated it may be, these things sometimes happen.

"In the event of military action, British troops will be fully interoperable with United States troops for combat identification. That capability, including new equipment options, are [sic] currently being procured."

356. One of the questions put to Mr Hoon by Mr Jenkin in the House of Commons on 20 January (referred to earlier in this Section) was whether British troops would have access to electronic identification equipment, already fitted to US tanks and armour, to prevent the risk of fratricide.[170] Mr Hoon replied:

" ... a question I dealt with when I made my last statement, action is in hand to procure the necessary equipment to ensure that the equipment used by our forces is in every way compatible with the equipment that the United States is using."

---

[168] Minute MA/VCDS to PS/SofS [MOD], 9 January 2003, 'Combat Identification' attaching Minute ACDS(Ops) to MA/VCDS, 8 January, 'Combat Identification'.
[169] House of Lords, *Official Report,* 9 January 2003, columns 1144-1145.
[170] House of Commons, *Official Report,* 20 January 2003, columns 35-37.

357. Combat ID was raised at the House of Commons Liaison Committee by Mr Michael Mates on 21 January.[171] When asked by Mr Mates whether he was "happy" that British soldiers were most likely to be killed by "our own people rather than the enemy", Mr Blair answered:

> "We are looking at everything we can do for combat identification. I think the procedures are far better now than those that were in place at the time of the Gulf War. I have asked for discussions on this very issue so we can make sure we are doing everything we possibly and conceivably can. From previous conflicts we know it is a risk and we have got to do everything we can to provide against it. I know there has been a lot of work done on this and there have been joint operations carried out in order to test the effectiveness of it. Obviously it is something we have to carry on looking at carefully."

358. When pushed for further details by Mr Mates, Mr Blair added that the capability was:

> "… in a significantly better shape than it was back at the Gulf War ten years ago. The very reason I have asked to be kept closely informed as to what is happening on it is because this is one of the things we need to make sure of."

359. PJHQ confirmed on 29 January that the US had agreed to the loan of 43 Combat ID systems for use by British forces.[172]

PROGRESS ON UORS

360. As concerns over equipment shortfalls persisted, Ministers asked for industry "to be pressed again" on whether they could work faster to meet requirements.

361. They were told that industry was working to capacity and "any significant improvement" in delivery profiles should not be anticipated.

362. The risk of CW attacks was assessed as low, but the UK's NBC protective capability would be "initially fragile".

363. The update on UORs on 31 January informed Lord Bach that:

- 143 equipment UORs, at a value of £437m, and 108 sustainability UORs had been approved. A further 18 USURs had been endorsed by PJHQ and business cases were being developed.
- All personnel would be issued with three sets of desert clothing by the end of March and follow-on orders were being investigated to procure sustainment

---

[171] Select Committee on Liaison, *Official Report,* 21 January 2003, questions 82-83.
[172] Minute PJHQ to PS/Minister(DP), 29 January 2003, 'Iraq: Op TELIC – Combat Identification UOR'.

stocks for the summer. It was forecast that desert boots would be available for the whole force by "mid-March".

- The risks associated with a 30 percent shortfall in COLPRO filters for AFVs were being assessed.[173]

364. Lord Bach chaired a second UOR meeting on 3 February.[174] In addition to the points in the 31 January update, the record of the meeting stated:

- Lord Bach asked for the pressure on industry "to be kept up" on the delivery of desert clothing and had "stressed the need to work hard to rebut the idea" that troops were "ill-equipped" for the environmental conditions.
- The risk assessment for the shortfall of COLPRO filters "against the worst case requirement" was ongoing and expected by the end of the week; Lord Bach **"would be grateful for urgent sight of the headlines from this work, together with advice on the operational penalties"**.
- Based upon the current shipping plan of filters, a "two fold increase in the capability" of all deployed Challenger 2 tanks was expected by 18 March and a "four fold increase" by 7 April. Lord Bach sought confirmation that that remained the case.
- Concerns remained about "the ability of AS90 to operate in hot and dusty conditions". The necessary modifications were not expected to be delivered into theatre until the end of March and "would each take 63 man-hours to fit". Lord Bach asked for industry "to be pressed again on whether they cannot work faster to meet the requirement" and welcomed advice on the operational implications.
- The US was "being helpful" and the loan of Combat ID systems had been agreed with "the issue now being how they will be deployed".
- Aside from the timing of completing outstanding UORs ("which was tight"), the "key residual concerns related to Combat ID and NBC protection".

365. On 7 February, AM Stirrup advised Lord Bach that 156 business cases for equipment UORs and 108 sustainability UORs had been approved.[175]

366. AM Stirrup wrote that the operational risk associated with the lack of NBC filters for AFVs had been assessed as "minimal". The Directorate of Joint Warfare (DJW) had assessed the probability of a CW attack on all deployed AFVs as "low" and that filters could therefore "be managed on a theatre-wide basis". The UK's NBC capability would be "initially fragile" but would become "more robust by mid-March" as UORs were delivered, in-service equipment was refurbished and surge training completed.

367. There were "no major concerns" regarding the availability of desertisation filters for the Challenger 2 tanks but it was unlikely that industry would be able to advance the

---

[173] Minute DCDS(EC) to PS/Minister(DP), 31 January 2003, 'Iraq: Op TELIC UORs'.
[174] Minute PS/Min(DP) to MA/DCDS(EC), 3 February 2003, 'Iraq – Op TELIC – UORs'.
[175] Minute DCDS(EC) to PS/Minister(DP), 7 February 2003, 'Iraq: Op TELIC UORs'.

delivery of measures for the AS90. The level of operational risk would be determined by weather conditions but was "not deemed to be significant".

368. The Senior British Liaison Officer in theatre was examining when Combat ID systems would become available and was in discussions with the US. An initial operating capability for light forces was expected by late February, with a full operating capability "available not later than 18 March".

369. On the same day, Lt Gen Reith received a letter from Sir Robert Walmsley, the Chief of Defence Procurement, about the challenges created by an increase in the quantities of equipment to be delivered by air and sea as a result of the compressed timescales before military action.[176] He believed the DPA could deliver what was required and that those capabilities would reach the front line. He added:

"We continue to press Industry whom I am confident are doing all that they can to achieve early delivery. Industry is, however, now working to capacity and I would not anticipate any significant improvement in the currently projected delivery profiles."

370. In discussing AM Stirrup's update, Lord Bach's meeting on 10 February noted that while the UK's NBC capability was judged to be fragile:

" … all that could be done to improve NBC protection capabilities was being done … The bottom line was if the Iraqis launched repeated mass attacks, operational effectiveness would be impaired; but we did not believe that they could do so."[177]

371. The record of the meeting also stated:

"… it was noteworthy that a number of deficiencies with which we were currently grappling (Combat ID, DAS [Defensive Aid Suites] for transport aircraft, equipment readiness, desertisation) had been identified in post-GRANBY lessons learned reports …"

Reporting equipment issues from theatre

On 11 February 2003, Lord Bach requested advice by the end of that week on whether a direct link from theatre for reporting equipment issues should be established, and how the reporting might work.[178]

The advice had not been received by 17 February.[179] The record of the meeting stated:

"The Minister attached real importance to this and would like advice on what mechanism might be devised – presumably through the ECC [Equipment Capability Customer] organisation – for making it happen."

---

[176] Letter CDP to CJO, 7 February 2003, 'Op TELIC UOR Progress'.
[177] Minute PS/Min(DP) to MA/DCDS(EC), 11 February 2003, 'Iraq: Op TELIC – UORs'.
[178] Minute PS/Min(DP) to MA/DCDS(EC), 11 February 2003, 'Iraq: Op TELIC – UORs'.
[179] Minute PS/Min (DP) to MA/DCDS(EC), 17 February 2003, 'Iraq: Op TELIC UORs'.

> ACM Bagnall replied on 21 February:
>
> "... there is a need to avoid cutting across established and well understood command chains from theatre, through CJO, to CDS. Beyond that, given the large number of people who are at geographically remote locations in theatre – some of whom are still en route and many are in the process of acclimatisation and preparation for possible operations – it would be very difficult for an agent outside the command chain to keep an eye on the many equipment issues which may arise."[180]
>
> ACM Bagnall acknowledged "fully" the need for "a rapid and timely information flow" that could quickly alert Ministers to potential equipment issues and facilitate a swift response. He wrote that Lt Gen Reith had "taken steps to alert DCDS(EC) as a matter of urgency to any matters which require his attention" and similar arrangements were in place in terms of the interface with the DLO.
>
> A handwritten note on ACM Bagnall's minute from Lord Bach's Private Office stated:
>
> "Minister the predictable answer: VCDS agreed with Jock [Stirrup] but the COS wouldn't wear it. So I think we'll have to live with this."[181]

372. On 14 February, AM Stirrup reported that 161 equipment UORs, at a value of "some £472m", and 110 sustainability UORs at a value of £310m had been approved.[182] He stated:

- Combat ID equipment trials had been successful.
- There were "currently no major concerns regarding the availability of desert clothing".

373. At the meeting on 17 February, Lord Bach was advised that "the suite of Combat ID equipment had been delivered to contract" and would be fitted in theatre.[183]

374. It was also reported that there was "increased confidence in the DLO in the robustness of the timetable for the delivery of desert clothing to those that need it".

375. On NBC capabilities, the record stated:

"... concerns remain about the availability of various NBC consumables, on which advice will be submitted next week. Aside from operational implications, the Minister believes that we need very carefully to handle presentational aspects of this. He was particularly concerned to hear that stocks of time expired ComboPens[184] have recently re-lifed (following testing at Porton Down) and are being issued with revised

---

[180] Minute VCDS to MA/Min(DP), 21 February 2003, 'Operation TELIC – UORs'.
[181] Manuscript comment PS/Min(DP) on Minute VCDS to MA/Min(DP), 21 February 2003, 'Operation TELIC – UORs'.
[182] Minute DCDS(EC) to PS/Minister(DP), 14 February 2003, 'Iraq: Op TELIC UORs'.
[183] Minute PS/Min (DP) to MA/DCDS(EC), 17 February 2003, 'Iraq: Op TELIC UORs'.
[184] ComboPens are syringes containing an antidote to improve the chances of surviving a chemical attack.

documentation making clear that they are now assessed as being useable up until 2004."

376. The Chiefs of Staff meeting on 19 February was advised that:

"… the US definition of FOC [Full Operating Capability] was when a unit achieved 80% readiness. 7 Armd Bde would therefore be declared at FOC without its full suite of UORs. CDS directed that Ministers be informed of this interpretation of FOC so that they were not caught out on UOR issues."[185]

377. In mid-February, the MOD told Mr Blair that British troops would be adequately protected in the event of a BW or CW attack.

378. A Joint Intelligence Committee (JIC) Assessment on 19 February judged that southern Iraq was "the most likely area for the first use of CBW against both Coalition Forces and the local population" in the event of coalition military action.[186] It did not address the likelihood of a CBW attack.

379. On 20 February, Mr Blair asked the MOD for advice on a number of detailed questions following the publication of a report on Iraq by the International Institute of Strategic Studies.[187] That paper is addressed in detail in Section 6.5.

380. One question asked by Mr Blair was: "What is the prospect of a pre-emptive BW or CW attack on our troops in Kuwait, and are we certain we are adequately prepared and our troops protected?"

381. The MOD replied that Iraq retained the capability "(through a variety of means) to pre-emptively deliver CBW against Coalition Forces in Kuwait".[188] The question was "one of intent". In the MOD's view it remained "highly unlikely whilst Saddam believes war can be averted". If he was convinced that war was "inevitable and imminent" that "might make a pre-emptive move more attractive" but it was "more likely that Saddam would deploy CBW after the onset of the campaign".

382. The planned levels of NBC defence equipment "should enable all troops to withstand initial BW or CW attack".

383. The UOR update on 21 February informed Lord Bach that 167 business cases had been approved, accounting for "some £478m" of the £500m allocated by the Treasury.[189] Sustainability UORs, at a total cost of £318m, had also been approved.

---

[185] Minutes, 19 February 2003, Chiefs of Staff meeting.
[186] JIC Assessment, 19 February 2003, 'Southern Iraq: What's in Store?'.
[187] Dodge T & Simon S (eds). *Iraq at the Crossroads: State and Society in the Shadow of Regime Change.* Adelphi Paper 354 IIIS Oxford University Press January, 2003; Minute Rycroft to McDonald, 20 February 2003, 'Iraq: Political and Military Questions'.
[188] Letter Watkins to Rycroft, 24 February 2003, 'Iraq: Political and Military Questions'.
[189] Minute CM(SD) to PS/Minister(DP), 21 February 2003, 'Iraq: Op TELIC UORs'.

384. The update also stated:

- Further to ACM Bagnall's note earlier that day, PJHQ had set up a "comprehensive system to review, prioritise and then move UOR equipment into theatre" once delivery dates were known by industry.

- New respirator testing procedures had been introduced to ensure that deployed personnel would "be adequately protected" after trials found that a proportion of respirators did not fit properly.

- There was a shortfall of 15,000 ComboPens out of a total requirement for 135,000, but "every effort" was being made to procure more and "re-life existing stock".

- 1,000 additional Challenger 2 filters were being procured to support predicted operation activity.

- A plan had been produced for the installation of Combat ID equipment into selected vehicles.

- The 96 fully modified battlefield ambulances were expected to be available for shipping by "13/14 March". There were currently only 24 air conditioned ambulances in theatre.

- The delivery of desert clothing, including ECBA covers, was progressing well.

385. By the end of February, there were "significant" and "severe" shortfalls in parts of the UK's NBC protective capability.

386. The Chiefs of Staff were told that that reflected the compressed timescales for planning.

387. The Chiefs of Staff received an update on access to CBRN equipment and NBC protection on 28 February.[190] The paper reported "significant" and "severe" shortfalls in a number of NBC areas including the availability of Nerve Agent Immobilised Enzyme Alarm Detectors (NAIAD), Residual Vapour Detectors (RVD) and NBC water bottle tops. There was, however, a "marked improvement" in ComboPen availability.

388. The paper stated:

"The compressed timescales available to procure UORs necessarily introduced risk in achieving earliest possible delivery of all equipments … some shortfalls are now being exposed."

389. Lord Bach received the latest equipment update on the same day, reporting that 173 equipment UORs (totalling "some £487m") and £320m of operational sustainability requirements had been approved.[191]

---

[190] Minute DJW/NBC1 to COSSEC, 28 February 2003, 'Iraq Contingency Planning – Equipment Issues'.
[191] Minute DCDS(EC) to PS/Minister(DP), 28 February 2003, 'Iraq: Op TELIC UORs'.

390. On "CBRN Risks":

- The "most significant issue" was that the majority of RVDs had been found to be unserviceable, but that a "workaround" solution had been found. It had been agreed with DJW and PJHQ that this was "not a showstopper" although it would "impose a degree of operational degradation" which would increase as temperatures in theatre rose.

- New respirators were being procured and it was expected that this delivery would "enable 99.5% of personnel" to have a respirator that would fit them.

- Further investigation had revealed there were sufficient stocks of ComboPens.

- Further briefing would be provided to the Chiefs of Staff the following week.

391. An attached annex on the overall sustainability assessment of equipment stated that helicopter support remained fragile, despite a reduction in flying hours. That was attributed to long lead times for spare parts, and "historic levels of STP [Short Term Plan] funding".

392. On 3 March, Adm Boyce was advised by Lt Gen Reith that equipment procured through UORs was being prioritised for fitting and being carefully monitored, but it was "probable" that some equipment would not be in service as the UK crossed "the line of departure".[192] The "some" was referenced with a footnote stating: "The original RDD [Required Delivery Date] for the UORs was 31 March 03."

393. Priorities had been set by PJHQ based on four categories:

- Priority 1: "UORs with the potential to delay the start of operations", including Combat ID, Challenger 2 desertisation measures, NBC equipment and battlefield ambulances.

- Priority 2: UORs that enhance combat operations.

- Priority 3: "enablers" for aftermath operations.

- Priority 4: "Others".

394. Lt Gen Reith wrote that the late delivery of some UORs meant that deployment and prioritisation issues would become "more acute" as the date for operations approached. He added: "Any decision not to fit a UOR will be based on operational advice by theatre and recorded."

395. The record of Lord Bach's meeting on 3 March stated:

"… the major remaining area of concern was in NBC. Although things were not as bad as had been feared, with the respirator and ComboPen issues – for the time being – resolved, there were still outstanding concerns about some aspects of our CBRN 'layered defence.'"[193]

---

[192] Minute CJO to CDS, 3 March 2003, 'Fitting of Op TELIC Urgent Operational Requirements (UORs)'.
[193] Minute APS/Minister(DP) to MA/DCDS(EC), 3 March 2003, 'Iraq – Op TELIC – UORs'.

396. Those included NAIADS, RVDs and NBC water bottle tops. The replacement to NAIADs would not be available before April, RVDs should be delivered into theatre by 14 March and "industry was working flat out" to try and overcome the problem of water bottle tops. The Chiefs of Staff would discuss NBC at their next meeting.

397. The meeting also noted that the sustainability of helicopters was "a concern, including sand filters for Lynx" aircraft.

398. A 'CBRN Risk Overview' was circulated to the Chiefs of Staff on 3 March.[194] It stated:

> "For operations launched at 15th March 03 we believe that our overall CBRN defence remains fragile against a sustained CBRN attack … Against the more likely scenario of occasional limited short range attacks our defences are less fragile. The fragile assessment is based on a combination of the quality and quantity of some key equipment, the lack of priority to deploy equipment via AT [Air Transport] (PJHQ assessment is that these items are low priority assets) to front line personnel and on the estimated CBRN training state. Further equipment improvements will be limited even as at 15th April."

399. On 4 March, Lord Bach and Dr Lewis Moonie, Parliamentary Under Secretary of State for Defence and Minister for Veterans' Affairs, received a briefing about "a number of CBRN issues currently running" in the media.[195] It stated that, "given the WMD context of our case for confronting Saddam Hussein", it was important to "first emphasise our overall confidence in our NBC defence against any perceived threat".

400. If the UK's assessment that CBRN defences were fragile became more widely known, Ministers should adopt the line that they were not prepared to comment and that "the protection of our people is our top priority".

401. Internally, it was "imperative" that personnel had confidence in the CBRN protective measures in place and an "open and honest dialogue" about any shortfalls should be adopted, reassuring them about "the robustness of the overall system". The areas where progress had been made should be stressed.

402. A separate annex provided lines to take against each of the NBC equipment items that could raise concerns.

403. At the Chiefs of Staff meeting on 5 March, Rear Admiral Charles Style, Capability Manager (Strategic Development), said that CBRN risks were "attracting Ministerial attention".[196] Lord Bach had asked that "CBRN issues" be given priority for air transport, which was being done in conjunction with the Operational Command's priorities.

---

[194] Minute DJW and D CBW Pol to COSSEC, 3 March 2003, 'Iraq Contingency Planning – 4th CBRN Risk Overview'.
[195] Minute Howard to PS/Min(DP), 4 March 2003, 'Presentation Aspects of CBRN'.
[196] Minutes, Chiefs of Staff meeting, 5 March 2003.

404. Adm Boyce stated that "the provision of correctly fitted respirators continued to cause him considerable concern".

405. Maj Gen Fry reported that "there would be as few as 200 personnel who could not satisfactorily be protected through existing arrangements". Relocating those individuals "could ameliorate the problem, but there was a presentational issue".

406. ACM Bagnall was directed to lead on the issues and to ensure that Mr Tony Pawson, MOD Director General Corporate Communications, was engaged.

407. RAdm Style wrote to ACM Bagnall later that day reporting:

> "Sufficient equipment (the Respirator Test System and additional Respirators) and necessary support are available ... DCJO(Ops) has reported that he anticipates the majority of testing to be complete by about 10 March. I shall seek confirmation of their arrival and the expected testing timetable in time for Friday's Ministerial brief."[197]

408. ACM Bagnall wrote to the Directorate of Operational Capability (DOC), explaining that he was progressing the respirator issues as "a matter of urgency" but there was also a need to note the CBRN shortfalls in the wider Operation TELIC lesson process to "be clear about why we have got into this situation".[198] He raised several questions to illustrate his point including:

- "who is responsible for what aspects of the CBRN defence spectrum"; and
- "who is responsible for ensuring that individual units, ships etc are in date and properly equipped to operate in an NBC environment?"

409. A paper was circulated to the Chiefs of Staff on 7 March about respirator fit testing by the DJW, highlighting that it had raised issues "both in policy terms and dealing with the impact on the individual as the results are exposed".[199]

410. The DJW recommended the Chiefs of Staff agree that:

- Individuals who did not attain an optimum fit after testing were provided with the respirator that afforded "the best attainable level of protection, i.e. 'best fit'".
- Solutions for the residual 0.5 percent of individuals were being pursued: "At this stage it is impossible to predict whether a solution will be found in the time available."
- Advice to the Combined Joint Task Force should be "that individuals who cannot achieve an optimum fit should, where possible, only be deployed in areas where the NBC risk is assessed as lower".

---

[197] Minute Style to MA/VCDS, 5 March 2003, 'NBC Respirators'.
[198] Minute VCDS to DOC, 5 March 2003, 'Operation TELIC – CBRN Lessons Learned' attaching Minute Howard to PS/Min(DP), 'Presentation Aspects of CBRN'.
[199] Minute DJW and D CBW POL to COSSEC, 7 March 2003, 'Op TELIC – NBC Respirator Best Fit Policy'.

411. The UOR update for Lord Bach on 7 March highlighted:

- 176 business cases for equipment capability UORs had been approved at a cost of "some £488m".

- The list of UORs for the post-conflict phase, Phase IV, continued to be "urgently developed in parallel with the ongoing work" to develop more detailed planning guidance and CONOPS. It was likely to focus on potential shortfalls relating to force protection, infrastructure requirements and Intelligence, Surveillance, Target Acquisition and Reconnaissance (ISTAR).

- Agreement was being sought from the Treasury to increase the total UOR funding for Phase III by a further £60m. The funding for Phase IV had been discussed at official level.[200]

412. The update stated that the Integrated Project Team (IPT)[201] was "actively assessing" another source to assist in the production of desert pattern NBC suits. There was a requirement for 94,000 suits, but the contracted supplier could only produce 1,000 a week from the beginning of April (when the cloth to make the suits became available), and 4,000 plus a week by mid-June.

413. The DLO had issued sufficient ComboPens for the number of personnel deployed but "the precise location in theatre of approximately 4,000 [wa]s unconfirmed". Stocks had been withdrawn from UK-based warships to mitigate the risk. There would be sufficient water bottle tops to satisfy all demands by 10 March "and leave a reserve".

414. Two UOR sets of sand filters for Lynx helicopters would be delivered by 21 March with a further three refurbished sets. Further spares would be available from 31 March and the supplier was producing an additional four sets "at risk" which would be available from mid-April at a rate of one every two weeks. The MOD was not yet committed to a contract for these sets but the requirement was likely to be a "high priority" for Phase IV.

415. At a Chiefs of Staff meeting on 10 March, Lt Gen Reith reported that:

"A full check of in-theatre NBC equipment and redistribution had been completed, but respirator fitting had been slower than anticipated and was now expected to complete on 18 Mar."[202]

416. The record of Lord Bach's meeting on 10 March stated:

"CBRN was in a better position than thought last week … by 17 March all personnel would have their optimum fit of respirator. The testing was the most advanced in the world – *all* personnel had successfully been through the CS gas chamber in their respirator – we were now providing better still protection. The Commander in theatre

---

[200] Minute CM(SD) to PS/Minister(DP), 7 March 2003, 'Iraq: Op TELIC UORs'.
[201] Teams focused on delivering individual equipment programmes and projects. Their role is explained further in Section 14.1.
[202] Minutes, 10 March 2003, Chiefs of Staff meeting.

would have to decide how best to employ the 0.5% who did not have a perfect fit … NBC clothing and canisters were also no longer problem areas, although desert camouflage NBC suits were not yet available (but this was only a matter of their colour, not the materials). COLPRO was not being raised in theatre as a significant problem. The only outstanding issue on ComboPens was providing 600 to the BBC …"[203]

417. An updated paper on NBC respirator policy was sent to the Chiefs of Staff on 11 March.[204] It stated that alternative solutions to the fitting problem and the expected 0.5 percent of individuals who failed to achieve an optimum fit had been, and continued to be, "vigorously pursued" with DSTL and industry. Three possible solutions had emerged but it was impossible to predict whether or when these could be fielded, "but certainly not before 17th March".

418. The DJW intended to provide "a field commander's risk guide" to Lt Gen Reith by 13 March on deploying individuals who could not achieve an optimum fit.

419. The guide was circulated on 12 March.[205]

420. In his report following a visit to see the forces preparing for operations in Kuwait, General Sir Mike Jackson, Chief of the General Staff from February 2003 to August 2006, wrote on 10 March:

> "The one area of the media feeding frenzy that has some justification lies in the readiness of stocks for expeditionary operations. The introduction of resource accounting has created an imperative to drive down stockholdings. As a result, in the name of accounting orthodoxy we lack basic items such as desert clothing. I am unsure whether the cost of storing such items would really have been more than the inflated price we have no doubt paid by procurement under UOR action, but I am certain of the negative impact on the moral component that failure to provide these items has had."[206]

421. Gen Jackson wrote that the root of the problem was "partly financial, but also systemic" and there was no mechanism "within the Central Staff to safeguard the operational logistic interest". This had led to "a consistent lack of visibility" of the state of UK holdings.

The situation in the week before the invasion

422. Adm Boyce assured Mr Blair that there were "no serious equipment problems" on 13 March.

---

[203] Minute APS/Minister(DP) to CM(SD), 10 March 2003, 'Iraq: Op TELIC – UORs'.
[204] Minute DJW to COSSEC, 11 March 2003, 'OP TELIC – NBC Respirator Policy'.
[205] Minute DJW, 12 March 2003, 'Commanders' Guide to Respirator Best Fit Risk Assessment'.
[206] Minute CGS to CDS, 10 March 2003, 'CGS Visit to Op TELIC'.

423. Mr Blair held a meeting to discuss the military plan and timetable with Mr John Prescott, the Deputy Prime Minister, Mr Jack Straw, the Foreign Secretary, Mr Hoon and Adm Boyce on 13 March.[207] At the meeting, Adm Boyce "assured the Prime Minister that the Armed Forces faced no serious equipment problems".[208]

424. On 14 March, RAdm Style reported to Lord Bach that:

- 178 equipment UOR business cases had now been approved at a cost of "some £494m";
- 9 UORs had been accepted into service over the previous week;
- the manufacturer of desert NBC suits had revealed that production for the suits could not start "as early as we had hoped and will not deliver the first items until mid-April, a delay of 2 weeks";
- the delivery of RVD tickets to theatre had been delayed, and was expected to be complete by 19 March; and
- while the DLO was confident that sufficient ComboPens had been delivered to theatre, this could not be confirmed until the re-allocation exercise currently under way had been completed.[209]

425. On desert clothing, RAdm Style wrote:

"Sufficient desert clothing for the entire force was ordered in Dec 02 with an ISD of 31 March 03, with a small in-service reserve being available as a result of 3 Cdo Bde and 16 Air Asslt Bde personnel retaining their clothing from Op JACANA. Although pressed to advance their production and delivery schedules, few contractors have been successful … Across the desert clothing range, at least 70% of all deliveries are complete and in theatre, broadly equivalent to 2 sets per man, not counting those personnel already equipped before deployment. Providing contractor delivery profiles are met, we expect all outstanding demands to reach depots by 19 March and to be with personnel by the end of the month. There are some exceptions; desert helmet covers … and floppy hats … will not be delivered to depots until nearer the end of the month."

426. Lt Gen Reith provided Adm Boyce with an update on the redistribution of NBC equipment in theatre on the same day.[210] He wrote that "sufficient" NBC Individual Protective Equipment had been deployed, but "some stocks required redistribution to ensure that all personnel had their initial allocation of 3 suits". The redistribution of the maritime component was 100 percent complete, the land contingent 97 percent, and the air contingent 70 percent complete.

---

[207] Letter Manning to Watkins, 14 March 2003, 'Iraq: The Military Plan'.
[208] Minute Rycroft to Watkins, 13 March 2003, 'Iraq: Military Planning'.
[209] Minute CM(SD) to PS/Minister(DP), 14 March 2003, 'Iraq: Op TELIC UORs'.
[210] Minute Reith to PSO/CDS, 14 March 2003, 'Redistribution of NBC IPE and Respirator Testing'.

427. As part of the final battle preparations, the contingent was completing NBC respirator testing but, because 1 (UK) Div needed to move forward to assembly areas, its General Officer Commanding (GOC), Major General Robin Brims, had decided to suspend that process. Lt Gen Reith "strongly" supported this decision from an operational perspective and said he could restart the process of testing "if time allows". He added:

> "In terms of risk, his manoeuvre units would prove difficult targets, once battle begins. However the more static units in the Divisional Support Group and Joint Force Logistic Component would be at greater risk and thus I have directed that testing should continue for them. The Maritime and Air contingents will also complete the process."

428. Lt Gen Reith added: "Clearly Ministers will need to be informed."

429. In the record of Lord Bach's meeting on 17 March, the key points included:

- other than "the ongoing work on Phase IV", there were "no major outstanding UOR issues";
- a flexible approach was needed on whether to continue with undelivered UORs "as circumstances develop";
- there was "a 100 tonne backlog of equipment" waiting to be delivered to theatre;
- there were now "no significant outstanding NBC issues except on delivery of RVD tickets into theatre"; and
- "notwithstanding helmet covers and floppy hats, which were taking slightly longer than hoped for, 80% of clothing and boots ordered had been delivered and prioritised in theatre. The overall figure of 'desertised personnel' was higher, as it included those who had already been issued with desert kit for Op JACANA."[211]

430. At the Chiefs of Staff meeting on 19 March, it was reported that only 3 percent of the land component's respirators had been checked, "the work having been overtaken by other events in-theatre".[212]

431. On 21 March, AM Stirrup reported to Lord Bach that 183 business cases for UORs had been approved at a cost of £497m.[213]

432. Desertisation measures for the Challenger 2 vehicles had been delivered to theatre in the past week (the fitting process of which was ongoing), along with Combat ID equipment for all vehicles and ECBA, meaning that all unit demands for the latter had been met.

---

[211] Minute APS/Minister(DP) to MA/DCDS(EC), 17 March 2003, 'Iraq: Op TELIC – UORs'.
[212] Minutes, 19 March 2003, Chiefs of Staff meeting.
[213] Minute DCDS(EC) to PS/Minister(DP), 21 March 2003, 'Iraq: Op TELIC UORs'.

433. AM Stirrup also reported that "a problem with packaging" had led to a "small delay" in the provision of new books of RVD tickets. The last 450 were received on 20 March and should arrive in theatre that day.

Issues that emerged post-invasion

434. After the invasion began, it became clear that some personnel had not been equipped with desert clothing and body armour, there were difficulties with NBC equipment, and there were shortages of ammunition.

435. Lord Bach complained that he did not have visibility of equipment issues at the front line.

436. The reasons for the problems were not identified until 9 May.

437. On 4 April, Lt Gen Reith wrote to ACM Bagnall:

"I can assure DCDS(EC) that the chain of command is working well and that an embedded DPA LO [Liaison Officer] in theatre would have made no difference to the current situation. My staff monitor equipment availability on a daily basis and the DLO LO embedded in my Headquarters liaises regularly with relevant IPTs and other agencies concerning the flow of UORs from industry into theatre."[214]

438. On 8 April, Lord Bach's Private Office wrote to Brigadier Derek Jeffrey, MOD Director of Logistics Operations,[215] seeking clarity on the reliability of AFVs following a negative press article.[216]

439. The article had also suggested that there was a shortage of desert clothing and boots which sat "a little oddly with the assurances that the Minister has repeatedly been given about the availability of clothing and the arrangements for distributing it in theatre".

440. Lord Bach's Private Office wrote:

"The fact that there are continued rumblings about such basic requirements as this begs a wider question: are there other items that have been delivered by industry to the department but have yet to be distributed to all those that need them in theatre? Lord Bach has been briefed over recent weeks on the acceptance into service of a range of UORs. But he has very little visibility of the extent to which such items have actually reached the front line."

441. Brig Jeffrey replied on 10 April.[217]

---

[214] Minute CJO to MA/VCDS, 4 April 2003, 'Combat ID and ECBA'.
[215] Brigadier Jeffrey's name does not appear in the document but MOD has confirmed to the Inquiry that he was the post holder at that time.
[216] Minute PS/Minister(DP) to D Log Ops, 8 April 2003, 'Iraq: Op TELIC UORs – Delivery'.
[217] Minute D Logs Ops to PS/Minister(DP), 10 April 2003 'IRAQ: Op TELIC UORs – Delivery'.

442. Lord Bach was informed that there were "some unsatisfied demands due to sizing issues but new stock from contractors should clear these in the very near future". The full requirement for boots was "the greatest concern and may not be fully met until the end of April".

443. Brig Jeffrey added:

"Notwithstanding that sufficient clothing is now in theatre to meet demands … some individuals have not received any clothing. There are a number of reasons for this ranging from unit ordering errors to consignments being mis-located or being pushed down the priority list in theatre. The DLO in the UK and the JFLogC [Joint Force Logistic Component] in theatre are urgently carrying out an audit and progressively the problem is being ameliorated."

444. Brig Jeffrey wrote that the DLO, DPA, PJHQ, and National Contingent Headquarters (NCHQ) did "not have good visibility of the fast moving situation in the Division with regards to UOR fitting". That had meant "information on exactly what UORs had been fully fitted was not always available, nor was it prudent to press the Divisional staffs for this information at the height of battle".

445. Lord Bach's Private Office replied on 11 April, acknowledging the points raised and adding:

"But I think he [Lord Bach] will be interested to understand exactly which of the UORs on which he has been briefed over recent months were not in the event fitted despite having been available in theatre."[218]

446. The record of Lord Bach's meeting on 14 April highlighted his concern that he did not have "the visibility of equipment issues at the front line that he expected (and which he was reassured would be provided through the chain of command)".[219] His Private Office wrote:

"An example of the ad hoc nature of this reporting is on Combat ID: the first time Minister(DP) was made aware that CR2s [Challenger 2s] without it were being used operationally was following the blue on blue incident on 25 March. The presentational and moral repercussions had the CR2s in question not been fitted with Combat ID cannot be overstated."

447. Lord Bach sought advice on:

"(i) the extent to which shortfalls of key items (such as desert clothing) remain in theatre and what action is planned to ameliorate them; (ii) which UORs have been delivered to theatre but not – for whatever reason – passed on to the

---

[218] Minute PS/Minister(DP) to D Log Ops, 11 April 2003 'Iraq: Op TELIC UORs – Delivery'.
[219] Minute APS/Min(DP) to MA/DCDS(EC), 14 April 2003, 'Iraq: Op TELIC – UORs'.

front line – either in part or in total; and (iii) how the flow of information can be improved so that in future Ministers receive timely and accurate advice on these issues."

448. On 17 April, Maj Gen Fry replied to Lord Bach's request, on behalf of Lt Gen Reith, reporting that "other than the continuing saga of desert combat clothing, there [we]re no other key equipment shortfalls" in theatre.[220] As of 13 April, the "shortfall amounted to 18,300 suits and 12,500 boots". Additional clothing would arrive in theatre by 18 April, meeting the requirement for boots, and reducing the shortfall of suits to 3,275.

449. Maj Gen Fry confirmed that all UORs delivered to theatre were "forwarded to the front line". On Combat ID, he wrote that whilst its delivery into theatre was aligned with Challenger 2, "not all of it could be fitted within the compressed timeline before D-Day" because eight Challenger sets in a container "were temporarily misplaced within Kuwait". Maj Gen Fry stated that the decision to proceed without the full range of Combat ID fitted in some Challengers was the GOC's and implied that was necessary because of US timings.

450. Addressing the issues raised about the flow of information, Maj Gen Fry wrote that the weekly updates on UORs were "a significant staff burden" and that producing them "at any greater frequency would prove counter productive".

451. Commenting on the note to Lord Bach, his Private Office wrote:

> "This is, frankly, pretty dismissive of your concerns … [It] offers no explanation of why the 'desert clothing saga' arose and no guidance on how and when the shortfalls will be addressed … [It] contradicts the earlier advice from the DLO that some UORs had been delivered to theatre but not on to the front line."[221]

452. At his meeting on 28 April, Lord Bach noted that no more UORs for the invasion phase had been raised in the last fortnight, no more were expected, and all were expected to be delivered by 1 May.[222] He therefore agreed that the monitoring of Phase III UOR implementation should cease but perceived a continuing requirement, "for the time being at least", to keep track of the Phase IV UORs.

453. The "bulk of the discussion" focused on "the continuing difficulty experienced by the DLO, DPA and ECC in securing reliable information from theatre about equipment matters" and how best to present publicly what was understood to be "the generally positive news on this front". Lord Bach remained concerned about the flow of information on equipment matters.

---

[220] Minute Fry to PS/Min(DP), 17 April 2003, 'Iraq: Op TELIC: UORs'.
[221] Manuscript comment MOD [junior official] on Minute Fry to PS/Min(DP), 17 April 2003, 'Iraq: Op TELIC: UORs'.
[222] Minute PS/Minister(DP) to MA/DVCDS(EC), 28 April 2003, 'Iraq: Op TELIC UORs'.

454. The record of the meeting stated that Lord Bach believed work should be set in hand urgently "to develop a better handle on the facts of equipment performance (including the extent to which UORs reached users). Identifying and being able to account for potential vulnerabilities would be "vital" to address Parliamentary Questions (PQs) and reports of shortages in desert clothing, boots, ECBA and Combat ID equipment:

> "Ministers will need chapter and verse on these issues, and on any others yet to come to their attention; and they will need it whatever the conclusions of the lessons learned process."

455. Specific questions on desert clothing, boots and UOR delivery were set out in an Annex, including why the desert clothing "saga" came to light "so late in the day", given the attention it received in the run up to operations, and asking for clarification on whether all UORs delivered to theatre were fitted. Lord Bach also sought confirmation that all UORs had been received by the end user for whom they were intended. If not, he requested a list of those that had not been received, with an explanation in each case.

456. The record stated:

> "As I have tried to articulate previously, Minister(DP) is not seeking here to second guess decisions made by commanders in theatre, which he accepts will have been made for very good operational reasons. He simply wants to understand, and be able to defend as required, the facts and the arguments pertaining to these judgements."

457. Lord Bach also wanted to proactively "get the message across" publicly that, in general, equipment performance had "been impressive". He accepted that the MOD should be prepared to acknowledge that "not everything went exactly according to plan and that lessons are, of course, being learnt" but that this should not deter the MOD from highlighting positive news.

458. Mr Paul Flaherty, Head of Civilian Secretariat, PJHQ, replied on 9 May that Op TELIC had been "a great success both in terms of performance of equipment and the successful delivery of an enormous amount of equipment in a very short space of time".[223] He added:

> "… it is also becoming clear that there were problems in theatre, of which we were not aware, in relation to the fitting of UORs and the delivery of kit. At this stage contributory factors appear to include the sheer speed and scale of the deployment, the large number of UOR equipment, the significant advance of G day,[224] and the absence of an in theatre asset-tracking system with the consequent mismatch of people and equipment."

---

[223] Minute PJHQ Civ Sec to PS/Minister(DP), 9 May 2003, 'Iraq: Op TELIC UORs'.
[224] The date on which the ground operation commenced.

459. On the delivery of UORs to theatre Mr Flaherty wrote:

"The processes currently in place for tracking UORs only tracks them until they arrive to the original consignee in Theatre. There is therefore no means of tracking whether UORs reached the end user for whom they were intended. Work has been set in train to establish this and separate advice is being submitted by CJO to VCDS."

460. Mr Flaherty also covered the issues of desert clothing and Combat ID in separate annexes which are detailed later in this Section.

461. On Lord Bach's copy of the minute, his Private Secretary wrote:

"This is – at last – a serious attempt to respond to your concerns about equipment delivery/supply … and acknowledges the importance of providing Ministers with proper advice. The story it tells … about the flow of information from theatre which has obviously been lamentable – is pretty depressing."[225]

462. Mr Flaherty's note was discussed at Lord Bach's meeting on 12 May.[226] Lord Bach believed the note went "a long way to addressing some of the issues he raised about the availability of equipment at the front line". He accepted "the proffered explanation for this" but was "disappointed that a variety of factors" appeared to have undermined the efforts to equip troops as well as possible.

463. The note of the meeting recorded that Lord Bach:

"… regrets that – aside from the very practical consequence for our people, a number of whom might be expected to complain about having been sent into battle without relatively basic articles of key equipment – an unfortunate side effect has been that the advice provided to Ministers, albeit on the basis of advice from theatre, has turned out in retrospect to be less than wholly accurate. He agrees that these issues, particularly the lack of an effective asset tracking system, will need carefully to be examined during the lessons learned process."

464. In addition to ECBA, desert clothing and Combat ID kit, Lord Bach had heard at a meeting that morning that concerns had been expressed by commanders in theatre about shortages of morphine and NBC equipment. He sought advice on those points by the end of the week.

465. Lt Gen Reith provided a spreadsheet detailing when UORs had been delivered to theatre and an assessment on their effectiveness for ACM Bagnall on 15 May.[227] He explained that there had been "some inaccuracies in earlier reporting from theatre" but those had now been corrected.

---

[225] Manuscript comment PS/Min(DP) on Minute PJHQ Civ Sec to PS/Minister(DP), 9 May 2003, 'Iraq: Op TELIC UORs'.
[226] Minute APS/Minister(DP) to CM(M) and PJHQ-Civ Sec, 12 May 2003, 'Iraq: Op TELIC – UORs'.
[227] Minute CJO to PS/VCDS, 15 May 2003 'Operation TELIC – Equipment Performance'.

466. Lt Gen Reith provided specific briefing that:

- Combat availability of both Challenger 2 and AS90 tanks was "very high" and the desertisation and protection measures for Challenger 2 were fitted before war-fighting. The AS90 desertisation measure was not completed until 4 May "but was not required for war-fighting, although it would have been if hostilities had continued as had been expected".

- The supply of Combat ID was "over-taut" but 1 (UK) Div reported that "there was just enough for equipment in the direct fire zone". The late arrival was due to distribution problems but, where it was supplied, it had been effective.

- There had been a shortfall of ComboPens that was addressed by the issue of "out-of-date pens" as a "last resort". The shortfall was "traceable to enduring manufacturing difficulties, acknowledged in early 02". Alternative provision was being considered but was proving problematic.

- The respirator testing kits had arrived in theatre between 24 February and 7 March "but were subject to a delay in distribution because of the large amounts of higher priority stores, such as CR2 [Challenger 2] and Combat ID UOR equipment".

467. Lt Gen Reith wrote:

"I draw two valuable lessons from this work:

"(a) In future, we should try to be less reliant on UORs for operations; fitting these in the time available and in austere conditions further stretches an already over-loaded logistic organisation. Thus, there is a strong case for better resourcing and I hope this point now will be accepted where it perhaps has not been in the past.

"(b) 'Just enough just in time' is probably a flawed policy for military operations. SDR directed that the DLO should only hold that which could not be procured within readiness and preparation time. However, the stock levels held speak for themselves."

468. Lt Gen Reith added that both points had been "exacerbated by the understandable reluctance of Ministers to go early to industry … before formal committal to the operation". He also wrote that the military's commitment was, "as often happens, at a scale beyond that envisaged in the DPAs and thus not fully resourced".

469. Lt Gen Reith reiterated those points on 16 May when he produced a "Top 10 Lessons Identified" document for the DOC.[228]

---

[228] Minute CJO to DOC, 16 May 03, 'Operation TELIC –"Top 10" Lessons Identified – Pre-Deployment and Deployment Phases'.

470. On deployment processes, Lt Gen Reith wrote that it "went well" but "we should caution against too much reliance on chartered air and shipping assets". He stated:

"There were considerable challenges in tracking equipment, UORs, and stores particularly in theatre, because of inadequacies in the management of the deployed inventory systems, especially an 'end to end' tracking capability. This is an old chestnut which requires addressing urgently."

471. Lt Gen Reith continued:

"Stockholdings were inadequate for this scale of operation. Understandably Ministers will be reluctant to commit to operations until very late in the day, which means we cannot approach industry early and we will also often be required to do more than envisaged in defence planning assumptions. Thus, the policy of 'just enough just in time' needs urgent review."

472. Brigadier Shaun Cowlam, Commander of 102 Logistics Brigade, wrote in his post operational report in May 2003 that:

"Despite the success in getting the force into theatre in half the time taken for Op GRANBY, it was clear that poor personnel and equipment readiness across the force added significantly to both logistic and, subsequently, operational risk. Many personnel (particularly augmentees and Reservists) were poorly equipped and briefed for deployment, some arriving in theatre with no combat clothing, respirators, weapons or sleeping systems, and others not knowing which unit or location they were destined for … The lesson is that units should be equipped on deployment to the necessary scales. The argument that in many cases, broken readiness and preparation times explain the shortcomings, ignores the reality that readiness is simply an assumption. Op TELIC has shown that our current assumptions do not reflect operational reality and we are taking unseen risks that we are not managing."[229]

473. On 27 May, ACM Bagnall advised Lord Bach that he was "keen to establish the facts (rather than early anecdotal views) relating to UORs and equipment issues".[230] He wrote:

"Work on the lessons is well underway and I have taken steps to ensure that specific issues relating to UORs and equipment matters are properly captured. For now it is clear that the tight timeline from the decision to activate the UOR process; the need to properly balance the logistic push from the UK versus the Commander's pull requirement in theatre; asset tracking … will all feature prominently …"

---

[229] Report Cowlam, 12 May 2003, 'Operation TELIC – Joint Force Logistic Component (JFLOGC) Jan – May 2003 Post Operation Report'.
[230] Minute VCDS to PS/Minister(DP), 27 May 2003 'Iraq – Operation TELIC Equipment Performance/UORs'.

474. On 30 May, a list of all the equipment capability UORs approved for the pre-deployment and invasion phases was produced with an analysis of how they did or did not address equipment capability gaps.[231] It sought to determine where UOR activity was focused, "both in terms of the capability delivered and also in terms of the relationship between UORs and the Equipment Programme".

475. The capability shortfalls addressed by UORs were:

- network-enabled capability 31%;
- force protection 19%;
- force projection 12%;
- counter-terrorism/Special Forces 7%;
- precision strike 3%; and
- other 27%.

476. A breakdown of the UORs in terms of the relationship with capabilities being delivered in the Equipment Programme (EP) showed:

Table 1: The relationship between UORs for the start of Op TELIC and the Equipment Programme

Category of UOR	Number	UOR cost	% by number	% by cost
UORs to meet TELIC-specific requirements	21	£28.6m	11.5%	6%
UORs to fill a gap not previously identified	22	£28.8m	12%	6%
UORs to bring forward capability already in the EP	22	£138.5m	12%	27%
UORs providing a "patch" solution to bridge a gap until the introduction of an EP-funded solution	55	£154.9m	30%	31%
UORs to fill a previously identified capability gap not funded in the EP	63	£149.3m	34.5%	30%

477. A footnote set out that not all UORs "fell neatly into one of the categories and a degree of judgement was therefore required". The example provided was of desertisation measures for the Challenger 2 vehicles: "it was categorised as an EP bring-forward but could equally have been classed as a TELIC-specific requirement".

---

[231] Minute DEP and DCRS to DNO, 30 May 2003, 'Op TELIC UORs from DEP and DCRS'.

478. A report by the House of Commons Defence Committee produced a different categorisation of UORs:

Table 2: Categories of UORs for the start of Op TELIC

Category of UOR	% by value[232]
UORs that hastened existing programme	33
UORs that introduced new capabilities not previously programmed	20
UORs that topped up holdings of items already on MOD's inventory	30
UORs modifying existing equipment/infrastructure	17

479. The MOD's assessment of UOR availability for the start of operations was:

Table 3: Availability of UORs before the invasion[233]

Environment	% of UORs delivered on time[234]	% of UORs requested by this component fitted in time[235]	% of UORs considered effective/highly effective
Maritime	80%	70%	100%
Land	84%	79%	85%
Air	74%	57%	95%
Joint	45%	45%	76%
Joint Communications Infrastructure (J6)	75%	75%	86%
Overall	71%	65%	88%

Desert uniforms

480. Stocks for desert clothing were insufficient to support a large scale deployment in the time available.

481. In response to concerns raised with Adm Boyce during his visit to theatre, the DLO provided advice on desert combat clothing on 14 April.[236] It stated there was "an acknowledged maximum shortfall in theatre of 18,300 suits and 12,500 boots amongst the Land component, as of 13 Apr 03".

482. The DLO advised that the shortfall would reduce to 3,275 suits for 1 (UK) Div units within the next 72 hours as clothing and boots were pushed forward within theatre and further deliveries were received. The remaining items for the Division would be delivered by 22 April, and the Joint Force Logistic Component units by 28 April.

---

[232] Third Report of the House of Commons Defence Committee, Session 2003-04, *Lessons of Iraq*, HC 57-1, para 170.
[233] Minute VCDS to PS/Minister(DP), 27 May 2003, 'Iraq – Operation TELIC Equipment Performance/UORs'.
[234] Delivered into theatre by 15 March.
[235] On time is defined as the dates units crossed the start line for operations (19/20 March).
[236] Minute D Ops DLO to PSO/CDS, 14 April 2003, 'Op TELIC – Desert Combat Clothing'.

483. Clothing issued to 3 Commando and 16 Air Assault Brigades was deteriorating, so they would require an additional 10,000 replacement suits. Those would be dispatched to theatre at the beginning of May. Other formations would also require maintenance stocks.

484. Adm Boyce was advised that 12 months was "a realistic minimum lead time to allow for normal contracting processes" for desert clothing. Advice had been provided in September 2002 that the decision point for ordering clothing was 1 October with the "risk of shortages increasing thereafter". That risk had been "deemed to be acceptable" and permission was not given to approach industry until 4 December.

485. In Mr Flaherty's note to Lord Bach on 9 May addressing equipment performance, he summarised the position on desert clothing and boots as:

> "The shortage of desert clothing was caused primarily by the fact that the stocks held were insufficient for the speed and size of this deployment. The inability to equip even all fighting formations prior to the start of combat operations was caused by in theatre supply priorities. The weakness of the asset tracking system meant there was limited visibility outside theatre of these problems. During decisive combat operation the shortage of desert combats was not flagged up since it was not seen to have a serious operational impact. Sufficient desert combats have now been dispatched to theatre to meet previously declared shortfalls."[237]

486. Mr Flaherty added that after combat operations ended, the shortage of clothing was having "a negative impact on morale" and had therefore been flagged as a concern. He wrote that "excess stocks" were "now held centrally in theatre" and units could call on these stocks "as required to top up holdings".

487. Following the invasion, Brig Cowlam wrote:

> "… the saga of desert combat clothing where the UOR failed to meet the requirement indicates that risks that had been taken could not be recovered."[238]

488. On 31 August 2010, an analysis of the land operation in Iraq was published on behalf of the Chief of the General Staff by Brigadier Ben Barry. It was known as "the Barry Report".[239]

489. The report stated: "Desert boots, desert uniforms and body armour were all in short supply."

490. The NAO's report on 11 December 2003 stated that the procurement of desert clothing and boots was regarded as "of limited effectiveness because few troops

---

[237] Minute PJHQ Civ Sec to PS/Minister(DP), 9 May 2003, 'Iraq: Op TELIC UORs'.
[238] Report Cowlam, 12 May 2003, 'Operation TELIC – Joint Force Logistic Component (JFLOGC) Jan – May 2003 Post Operation Report'.
[239] Report Land Command, 31 August 2010, 'Operations in Iraq: An Analysis From a Land Perspective'.

received their full complement, and mismatches in sizing remained into the post-conflict phase of the Operation".[240]

491. The House of Commons Defence Committee report on Op TELIC found that:

"The issue of the availability of desert clothing and boots during Operation TELIC has been both a confusing and worrying story ... MOD clearly underestimated the impact on morale of failing to provide service personnel with the clothing and boots which they required and expected. We find it unacceptable that some two weeks after the start of the combat phase 60 percent of the additional clothing requirement that had been ordered was not available in theatre."[241]

492. In July 2003, the MOD published a *First Reflections* report on operations in Iraq.[242] It stated that the quantities of boots, clothing "and other personal equipment" routinely held was an area that it needed "to look at". While there was, "under SDR planning assumptions ... sufficient personal equipment" to equip a total of 9,000 personnel for desert operations, the MOD wrote:

"In the case of this operation, the numbers deployed were significantly higher, and whilst most materials were sent out in time, difficulties with in-theatre tracking meant that there were some problems with distribution."

493. The Inquiry asked the MOD for a statement on planned stockholdings of desert clothing and the actual stockholdings between July and September 2002. The MOD confirmed the planned stockholdings of desert clothing was 9,000 sets.[243] "Some stock" was being consumed by operations in Afghanistan over that period "but levels were being maintained by resupply from industry".

494. The MOD stated that between this period it was asked to examine the possibility of equipping a force of 30,000 personnel at three sets of clothing per person:

"Identification of lead times showed that contracts would need to be placed in November-December 2002 in order to receive delivery in time. Authority was given ... and agreement was reached with suppliers to provide 96,000 sets of clothing (3 sets per person) and 40,000 pairs of desert boots. This was to be delivered in tranches between January and April 2003. Deliveries started in January 2003 and were complete by the end of February 2003 (earlier than planned), with all deliveries to units designated to receive Desert Clothing complete by March 2003."

---

[240] National Audit Office, *Operation TELIC – United Kingdom Military Operations in Iraq,* 11 December 2003, HC 60.
[241] Third Report from the Defence Committee, Session 2003-04, *Lessons of Iraq*, HC57-I, para 257.
[242] Ministry of Defence, *Operations in Iraq: First Reflections*, July 2003.
[243] Paper [MOD], 21 December 2010, 'Equipment and Capability Issues (pre-invasion)'.

495. In his evidence to the Inquiry Mr Hoon stated:

"Desert combats were part of the UORs and I know some of the soldiers resented having to wear their green combats rather than their desert combats."[244]

496. Mr Hoon later added: "Some soldiers, I'm sure, did not have the right boots."[245]

497. ACM Stirrup told the Inquiry that extra time "would certainly have made a difference" to the provision of desert clothing and boots.[246] Although pressure on the manufacturers had delivered "just about sufficient sets", that was not enough in an operational environment where "a critical issue" was to get it to the right place on time.

498. Major General Graham Binns, Commander of 7 Armoured Brigade during the invasion, told the Inquiry:

"There were soldiers who didn't have desert combats, you know, we were asking them to go to war incorrectly dressed."[247]

499. Mr Ingram told the Inquiry that part of the reason behind Ministerial visits to Iraq during the operations was to investigate what he called the "urban myths" that were being reported in the media about equipment shortages.[248] He gave an example:

" ... I had one of my own constituents, a mother, on behalf of her son, complaining about the fact that her boy didn't have size 11 boots, and this went on for weeks and weeks, until the point I said, 'Well, is he running around barefoot?' to her. Of course he wasn't. He had bought his own boots, but she was annoyed that he – she was saying that he had not been issued with the size 11, and he had been."

Enhanced Combat Body Armour

500. Enough body armour was procured to equip only British fighting formations; that was insufficient to equip all British troops deployed.

501. Poor asset tracking meant that even fighting formations were not fully equipped, resulting in an urgent redistribution programme to the front line.

502. On 24 March 2003, Sergeant Steven Roberts was killed in Iraq as a result of a gunshot wound.[249] Sgt Roberts had been asked to relinquish his armour because of the shortfall in theatre.

---

[244] Public hearing, 19 January 2010, page 129.
[245] Public hearing, 19 January 2010, page 149.
[246] Public hearing, 1 February 2010, page 13.
[247] Private hearing, 2 June 2010, page 4.
[248] Public hearing, 16 July 2010, pages 26-27.
[249] *GOV.UK,* 24 March 2003, *Sergeant Steven Roberts*.

503. On 2 April, Lt Gen Fry advised Adm Boyce on the availability of ECBA:

"Despite the allocation of an increased baggage allowance, some units that had already been issued ECBA in the UK decided to load the plates in unit freight for surface shipping. Due to poor marking some of these containers were slow in being delivered to units, resulting [in] personnel crossing the LD [line of departure] without plates."[250]

504. Lt Gen Fry wrote that that was "mitigated by an urgent redistribution programme that ensured that forward troops were equipped at the expense of those in the rear". Following that programme, and subsequent deliveries, the NCHQ estimated that 60 percent of 1(UK) Div had been fitted with ECBA.

505. Following his requests, Mr Flaherty provided Lord Bach with further advice on the supply and distribution of ECBA on 16 May.[251] He wrote that "the majority of troops in the fighting formations had full combat body armour at the start of combat operations" but there were "some shortages of ceramic plates which meant that some elements of 7 Armoured Brigade and up to 50% of the Joint Force Logistics did not have ceramic plates at the outset of hostilities".

506. Mr Flaherty wrote that shortages were "exacerbated" by the fact that only ECBA sufficient to "equip the wartime establishment of units" had been procured. He estimated that "approximately 3,500 personnel, the majority of which were not in fighting formations, were affected by the shortage. About 500 sets of ECBA were withdrawn from rear units and redistributed to the front line".

507. The DOC's 17 October 2003 report stated that, before the invasion, the DLO "were not mandated to hold stocks of ECBA sufficient to meet the requirements of this operation".[252] It stated that 36,000 sets of ECBA were deployed to theatre which were "sufficient" to meet the total requirement but "late delivery, coupled with difficulties in consignment tracking and poor unit level control, led to localised shortfalls".

508. The Inquiry asked the MOD for a statement on planned stockholdings for ECBA and the actual levels of stockholdings between July and September 2002. The MOD advised that, on 1 July 2002, it had 25,754 plates in stock and by 30 September this figure was 30,482.[253]

509. The MOD's *Lessons for the Future* report in December 2003 stated:

"The decision (a change in policy) to equip all Service personnel whose role it required with Enhanced Combat Body Armour … posed a challenge because there were insufficient stocks to meet the needs of a large scale force. Through additional

---

[250] Minute DCJO(Ops) to PSO/CDS, 2 April 2003, 'Combat ID and ECBA'.
[251] Minute PJHQ Civ Sec to PS/Minister(DP), 16 May 2003, 'Iraq: Op TELIC UORs'.
[252] Report DOC, 17 October 2003, 'Operation TELIC Lessons Study'.
[253] Paper [MOD], 21 December 2010, 'Equipment and Capability Issues (pre-invasion)'.

purchases, over 38,000 complete sets of body armour were deployed to theatre. This should have met the total requirement, but late delivery against an advancing timescale, coupled with difficulties in equipment tracking and control of issue, led to localised shortfalls."[254]

510. The NAO's December 2003 report on Op TELIC stated:

" ... 21,759 [desert pattern] covers and 32,581 pairs of plates were issued into the supply chain by 24 March 2003. However, the Department's Defence Clothing Integrated Project Team estimated that approximately 200,000 sets had been issued since the Kosovo campaign in 1999, greatly exceeding the theoretical requirement, but these seem to have disappeared. The Team questioned whether items should, therefore, be issued as part of an individual's personal entitlement for which they would be held accountable."[255]

511. The NAO also reported that "insufficient numbers [of body armour] were distributed in theatre, largely as a result of difficulties with asset tracking and distribution."

512. The House of Commons Defence Committee concluded that:

"Body armour is another example of where MOD's in-theatre distribution and tracking led to shortages in critical equipment ... MOD should identify and implement solutions to address these shortcomings and ensure that service personnel receive the equipment they are entitled to."[256]

513. On 7 September, Mr Martin Howard, MOD Director General Operational Policy, wrote to Mr Ingram, asking him to note that, following scrutiny in recent House of Commons Defence Committee, Public Accounts Committee and NAO reports, a new policy had been endorsed by the Chiefs of Staff in June whereby "all entitled personnel" would deploy on operations with a full set of ECBA.[257] This policy had already been implemented and was being monitored.

514. The Board of Inquiry into Sgt Roberts' death concluded that he would not have been fatally injured if he had been wearing ECBA at the time.[258]

---

[254] Ministry of Defence, *Operations in Iraq: Lessons for the Future*, December 2003.
[255] National Audit Office, *Operation TELIC – United Kingdom Military Operations in Iraq*, 11 December 2003, HC 60.
[256] Third Report from the Defence Committee, Session 2003-04, *Lessons of Iraq*, HC 57-I, para 262.
[257] Minute DG Op Pol to PS/Minister(AF), 7 September 2004, 'Enhanced Combat Body Armour (ECBA) – An Update'.
[258] *BBC News*, 31 July 2006, *Iraq death due to kit shortage* attaching link to Report, [undated], 'Board of Inquiry into death of Sgt Steven Roberts'.

515. On 18 December 2006, Mr Andrew Walker, Oxfordshire Assistant Deputy Coroner, delivered a narrative verdict:

"Sgt Roberts' death was as a result of delay and serious failures in the acquisition and support chain that resulted in a significant shortage within his fighting unit of enhanced combat body armour, none being available for him to wear."[259]

516. Lieutenant General Robin Brims told the Inquiry:

"I was fully aware that there was a problem with the body armour and I ordered a redistribution of body armour to those people most in need, and similarly some other forms of equipment."[260]

517. ACM Stirrup told the Inquiry:

"… just before the start of operation, the clear message that we were receiving in the Ministry of Defence was that all unit demands for enhanced combat body armour had been met, but quite clearly not everybody who needed it in theatre got it when they needed it, and had it been – had that been two months earlier, then those sorts of issues I think could have been untangled."[261]

518. ACM Stirrup added:

"I think the area where we could have done better is in terms of enhanced combat body armour. We didn't have enough of that in theatre at the time, and I think, in part … the issue was it was all being done so rapidly at the last minute no one was quite sure who had what."

519. The process behind the prioritisation of the redistribution of body armour was described by Maj Gen Binns:

"We had insufficient body armour to equip all those who were likely to be coming into immediate contact with the fighting companies and squadrons and I took a decision to reallocate based on mitigating the risks to those who were most vulnerable to the dismounted troops and those who sat behind 70 tonnes of armour I was prepared to take a risk with …"[262]

520. ACM Bagnall told the Inquiry:

"I was not aware that, in some cases, all personnel did not have access to Enhanced Body Armour at the start of operations. That said, I heard anecdotal evidence of personnel being deployed on one ship whilst their body armour plates were on another vessel which went to a different port of disembarkation. Any shortfalls

---

[259] *BBC News,* 18 December 2006, *Kit delays led to soldier's death.*
[260] Public hearing, 15 January 2010, page 21.
[261] Public hearing, 1 February 2010, pages 12-13.
[262] Private hearing, 2 June 2010, page 7.

identified would have gone from theatre to CJO and, if required, onwards to DCDS(C) or DCDS(EC) and their staffs. I do not recall any shortfalls being identified to me at the start of the campaign although issues emerged later as the operation progressed."[263]

521. Lord Boyce told the Inquiry that he had not been told about the commanders' decisions to redistribute body armour:

"My understanding was everybody had body armour. Whether there was a sufficient number of enhanced body armour kits was something which didn't percolate out – and the need to redistribute such that appeared in theatre wasn't something which percolated up to the Chiefs of Staff."[264]

Biological and chemical warfare protection

522. Risks were taken with the levels of protection against the use of chemical or biological weapons.

523. In its *Lessons for the Future* report in December 2003, the MOD stated there had been "localised shortages" of NBC equipment, such as suits, "again caused by sizing difficulties or equipment distribution and tracking problems".[265] The MOD added:

"Other shortfalls were due to poor stock maintenance – for example the inspection regime for Residual Vapour Detectors had not been followed, leading to uncertainty over serviceability. Nevertheless, through a combination of purchasing spare parts and rigorous re-testing of the equipment, the operational requirement was met."

524. Rear Admiral Michael Wood, MOD DLO Director General Operations, visited Iraq between 10 and16 May to ascertain the logistic support issues that had emerged in theatre.[266] In his report to ACM Pledger on 20 May, he highlighted the shortage of NBC equipment:

"The one significant area of weakness and concern emphasised by all the senior Land Component commanders I met was NBC equipment and preparedness. Whilst … the threat did not manifest itself, the lack of crucial items of detection and protection equipment and consumables undermined the confidence of those preparing to go to war."

---

[263] Statement, 6 January 2011, page 5.
[264] Public hearing, 27 January 2011, page 44.
[265] Ministry of Defence, *Operations in Iraq: Lessons for the Future*, December 2003.
[266] Minute CDL to VCDS, 27 May 2003, 'Visit by DG Ops (DLO) to Op TELIC: 10-16 May 2003' attaching Minute Wood to Pledger, 20 May 2003, 'Op TELIC Trip Report – 10-16 May 2003'.

525. On 6 June, Mr Flaherty provided advice on the supply and delivery of NBC equipment to Lord Bach.[267] He stated:

> "Although the UOR system did produce some NBC equipment, the issues in this case relate more to the proper maintenance of existing stocks and the ability of our systems to cope with the delivery of very large surge requirements to personnel who are unfamiliar with the equipment in question, and may not easily be able to track its onward movement.

> "Although commanders will – rightly – place their priority on the out-load and delivery of battle-winning capability, and although the perceived NBC threat diminished with the collapse of the regime, there were occasions when our personnel perceived they were at high risk, due to the lack of NBC equipment."

526. On NBC suits, Mr Flaherty wrote that:

> "There were initially insufficient NBC suits in theatre to supply all personnel with three each at the outset of hostilities. In order to ensure all personnel had two suits each … suits were re-distributed … An additional 96,000 suits arrived from the UK on 19 March meaning there were sufficient suits in theatre to supply all personnel with four each. However due to a mismatch between the sizes of the suits and individuals a small number of troops crossed the Line of Departure with only one properly fitting suit …

> "Commanders assessed that the risk posed to the Force by these shortages was low … The effect on morale was judged to be more serious than the practical impact."

527. Mr Flaherty wrote that in order to alleviate shortages in NBC detectors, equipment held by 3 Commando Brigade and 16 Air Assault Brigade was redistributed, leaving them with "less than 50% of the required capability". All available NBC detection equipment, ancillaries and consumables were then flown out, "giving theatre a 50% capability by 13 March".

528. Mr Flaherty stated: "The shortage of NBC detection was assessed to pose a high risk to UK troops." This was "not fundamentally a 'UOR' issue but one of maintenance and supply of in-service equipment" exacerbated by the delayed in-service introduction of a new form of equipment.

529. There had also been a shortage of batteries for the NBC detection sets and for their remote alarms, "aggravated by the fact that some NAIAD arrived from stores without batteries or batteries for the remote". Commanders had assessed that this shortage "posed a high risk to UK Forces"; 1 (UK) Div had been ordered to turn off NBC detectors while in dispersal areas to preserve the batteries and to "only turn them back on if there were signs of an attack".

---

[267] Minute PJHQ J9 to PS/Minister(DP), 6 June 2003, 'Iraq: Op TELIC UORs'.

530. Lord Bach's Private Office wrote alongside this point: "<u>This is very serious.</u> It will be impossible to defend this adequately."[268]

531. On the front page of Mr Flaherty's advice, Lord Bach's Private Office wrote:

"This was not flagged up through the chain of command, despite (numerous) assurances that it would be, and it runs counter to the public lines Ministers were given. These were effectively – although there are some shortfalls (because NAIAD is no longer manufactured) – we have confidence in our NBC defence against any threat posed by Saddam. In fact, the point contradicts this and has, rather fittingly in my view, been described as 'playing Russian roulette with people's lives.'"

532. On 3 July, Lord Bach's Private Office replied to Mr Flaherty expressing alarm that there were occasions when personnel were assessed to be at high risk due to a lack of NBC equipment:

"[Lord Bach] recalls the assessments provided before the campaign that our NBC defence was 'fragile' but that nevertheless there was complete confidence in the NBC posture of UK forces – as reflected in Lord Bach's weekly UOR meetings and the Department's public line. In particular, whilst Lord Bach fully appreciates the right of Commanders to make decisions on the ground, he is concerned that Ministers were not made aware of this fact until it came to light through media questions."[269]

533. On 3 October, an MOD report to ACM Bagnall explained that, while the 'Defence Strategic Audit and Guidance for the 2004 Equipment Programme' had suggested that NBC capabilities constituted "vital ground" to be protected in the programme, its "high impact/low probability nature" had remained "an inhibiting factor regarding resource allocation".[270] However, a "quick estimate on what might have happened", on operations such as in Iraq, had been carried out and the issues raised had been addressed in its report.

534. The report stated:

"A recurrent theme emerging from our work is the need for culture change and an improved understanding of CBRN defence from Front Line to grand strategic; attitudes remain that CBRN is unlikely, too difficult, a Cold War issue, or only a problem for specialists."

535. The team recommended a number of "quick wins", including policy updates, more training, and preserving CBRN capabilities and research. In the longer term, the report advocated ensuring that CBRN stock holdings met Defence Planning Assumptions,

---

[268] Manuscript comment MOD [junior official] on Minute PJHQ J9 to PS/Minister(DP), 6 June 2003, 'Iraq: Op TELIC UORs'.
[269] Minute APS/Minister(DP) to PJHQ J9, 3 July 2003, 'Op TELIC UORs: NBC Equipment'.
[270] Minute ACNS to MA/VCDS, 3 October 2003, 'CBRN – Tiger Team Final Report'.

addressing CBRN defence capabilities for large scale deployments and ensuring wider force structure work took account of CBRN issues.

536. General Sir Michael Walker became Chief of the Defence Staff in May 2003. On 22 March 2004, his Private Office replied to questions from Mr Ingram about the availability of NBC filters for armoured vehicles prior to the invasion.[271] The advice confirmed that the distribution of NBC filter stocks was authorised on 27 January 2003, but that the filters were not dispatched until 13 March and arrived in theatre on 17 March. The operation commenced two days later and, as 1 (UK) Div was conducting its final battle preparation, the plans to move the stocks forward to units were not feasible: "NBC filters were a casualty of compressed planning and deployment timelines."

537. Mr Ingram's Private Office replied on 26 March that Mr Ingram's view was:

"... given the prominence of the NBC threat in the run up to Op TELIC and the understandable public attention and criticism [sic] the shortage of AFV NBC filters subsequently, his view is that a worrying picture is beginning to emerge. His perception that the shortages cannot be attributed solely to poor asset tracking appears to be well founded."[272]

538. A number of post-operation tour reports and lessons learned exercises found fault with the provision of NBC equipment.

539. The DOC Operation TELIC report on 17 October 2003 stated:

"Despite the lessons from Op GRANBY (the first Gulf War), much last minute work was required to achieve acceptable levels of preparedness for operations in a possible CBRN environment."[273]

540. In the 7 Armoured Brigade post-operation tour report, Brig Binns highlighted that NBC filters for the Challenger 2 tanks "simply never arrived".[274]

541. In an Army interview about lessons learned in Iraq on 8 January 2004, Maj Gen Brims said:

"...having to redistribute body armour and NBC kit amongst the troops... left a pretty sour taste."[275]

---

[271] Minute MA/CDS to MA/Min(AF), 22 March 2004, 'NBC Filters for Armoured Fighting Vehicles (AFVs) on Operation TELIC'.
[272] Minute MA/Min(AF) to MA/CDS, 26 March 2004, 'NBC filters for Armoured Fighting Vehicle (AFVs) on Operation TELIC'.
[273] Report DOC, 17 October 2003, 'Operation TELIC: Lessons Study'.
[274] Report, 6 June 2003, '7th Armoured Brigade Post Operation Report & Lessons Report Operation TELIC'.
[275] Report [unattributed], 8 January 2004, 'Interview Profoma'.

542. The Barry Report concluded that:

"No NBC filters for Challenger MBTs were received, leaving tanks with only six hours of NBC protection ... Insufficient NBC warning and monitoring equipment was available."[276]

543. In his post-operation tour report, Brigadier James Dutton, Commander 3 Commando Brigade, wrote:

"If the brigade had been subjected to a CBW attack we would at best have been 'fighting to survive' rather than 'surviving to fight' ... Inadequate stocks of the NBC consumables caused concern and uncertainty."[277]

544. In his post-operation tour report, Brig Cowlam wrote that the lack of NBC kit was "a major concern" and "unacceptable".[278]

545. The NAO's December 2003 Op TELIC report stated:

"Although overall protection against chemical agents was good, there was a 'significant shortfall' (some 40 percent) of Nerve Agent Immobilised Alarm and Detector units ... and a severe shortfall in Residual Vapour Detector kit availability ... While these shortfalls could be partially mitigated ... it made detection and therefore response to an attack inefficient.

"There were difficulties in providing Nuclear, Biological and Chemical protective suits for certain sizes in sufficient numbers. In addition ... some respirators did not fit as well as had been presumed ...

"A number of units reported shortages of necessary consumable items required for the effective operation of chemical agent detector systems ... The lack of these items prevented units from turning on these systems in order to preserve some reserve capability, amounting in some cases to between six and 24 hours worth of operation.

" ... On Operation TELIC, the war reserve of filters was issued from central holdings and dispatched to theatre. However, we found that these vehicle filters (for both Challenger 2 and other armoured vehicles) had not been delivered to the frontline units by the time of our field visit in late June 2003 ... "[279]

---

[276] Report Land Command, 31 August 2010, 'Operations in Iraq: An Analysis From a Land Perspective'.
[277] Report, 8 May 2003, 'Operation TELIC – 3 CDO Bde RM Post Operation Report'.
[278] Report Cowlam, 12 May 2003, 'Operation TELIC – Joint Force Logistic Component (JFLOGC) Jan – May 2003 Post Operation Report'.
[279] National Audit Office, *Operation TELIC – United Kingdom Military Operations in Iraq*, 11 December 2003, HC 60.

546. The House of Commons Defence Committee concluded:

"Given the potential threat posed by Iraqi armed forces, sufficient chemical warfare detection and protection were particularly important for this operation. However, there were serious shortcomings in the supply and distribution system and the required levels of detection and protection were not always available to everyone. Indeed, while MOD ideally would have liked each serviceman and woman to have had four suits available, only one suit per person was available, which MOD judged to be sufficient for this operation. Furthermore it is essential that personnel have confidence in the effectiveness of the equipment with which they are provided. It was fortuitous that service personnel did not suffer as a consequence, but had the Iraqis used chemical weapons systematically, as employed in the Iran-Iraq war, the operational consequences would have been severe. The lack of armoured vehicle filters seems to us to be a matter of the utmost seriousness. The lessons identified need to be implemented as a matter of urgency to ensure that servicemen and women serving on operations have complete and justified confidence that chemical warfare attacks will be detected in time, that their individual protection equipment will save their lives and that operational success will not be imperilled. This is particularly important given that UK service personnel are more likely to be operating in such environments in the future."[280]

547. Mr Hoon told the Inquiry: "I have to say I have not come across anything specific to suggest that NBC protection was not available to every soldier who needed it."[281]

548. When questioned about concerns that out-of-date kit had been issued, Mr Hoon replied:

"… I don't recall any suggestion that any of this kit was ineffective … I don't know whether there was a sell-by date on the kit. There may well have been but as far as I am aware, whenever this was tested, this equipment was fit for its purpose."

549. Lord Bach told the Inquiry in his witness statement that he was not aware of the level of respirator testing that was reported to the Chiefs of Staff on 19 March 2003:

"… we did not receive information that the Chiefs of Staff Committee apparently received on the eve of the invasion."[282]

550. When asked about the report provided to the Chiefs of Staff on 19 March 2003, which said that only 3 percent of the land component's respirators had been checked, ACM Bagnall told the Inquiry:

"I do not recognise the figure of 3 percent in relation to respirator fitting. I understood that all ground force personnel had been tested through what was described as the

---

[280] Third Report from the Defence Committee, Session 2003-04, *Lessons of Iraq*, HC 57-I, para 281.
[281] Public hearing, 19 January 2010, page 157.
[282] Statement, 22 December 2010, page 3.

most advanced testing facility in the world. Only 0.5 percent of all the personnel tested did not have a perfect fit ..."[283]

551. Asked about respirator testing, Lord Boyce told the Inquiry that he believed only 0.5 percent of personnel had not been tested.[284]

552. Lord Boyce told the Inquiry:

"The one area of equipment which did give me concern was our ability to cope with any biological or chemical threat and therefore the right kit for that, which is basically the suit you wear, the protection equipment you wear, and also a gas mask. That's something which did trouble me. That was our sort of worst case scenario – once we went over the line, of having chemical or biological weapons thrown at us; and a lot of effort was put into making sure those who would be going in the leading echelons did have the right IPE [Individual Protective Equipment], the right sort of protective equipment, and everybody had their gas mask checked which at the time I went out was a shortfall."

553. Lord Boyce added that, by 19-20 March, he thought "we had a satisfactory level of kitting out of gas masks and IPE".[285]

554. The Inquiry asked the MOD for further information regarding the level of stock holdings and provision of NBC clothing and equipment before the invasion and the lead times for providing additional provisions. The MOD responded:

"Sufficient stock of NBC suits and respirators were sent to theatre before the start of combat operations to provide two per person. Further deliveries to theatre increased this to four per person from 19 March 2003."[286]

Ammunition

555. Supplies of ammunition were insufficient for the size and speed of the British deployment.

556. The problem was exacerbated by poor asset tracking.

557. In analysing the options for a possible UK contribution, Mr Hoon had been advised on 25 July 2002 that an armoured division could be deployed within six months "but only with limited sustainment (eg 10 days ammunition)".[287]

---

[283] Statement, 6 January 2011, page 5.
[284] Public hearing, 27 January 2011, pages 42-43.
[285] Public hearing, 27 January 2011, page 46.
[286] Paper [MOD], 21 December 2010, 'Equipment and Capability Issues (pre-invasion)'.
[287] Minute Bowen to PS/SofS [MOD], 25 July 2002, 'Iraq – Potential UK Contribution'.

558. The Barry Report stated:

"Small arms ammunition was in such short supply that 1 DWR [Duke of Wellington's Regiment] had only 10% of its requirement until after G-day, and some Royal Engineers started the operation with only 10 rounds per man."[288]

559. In his post-operation report Brig Binns wrote: "Ammunition was a constant cause of concern throughout the deployment."[289]

560. The NAO's December 2003 Op TELIC report stated:

"Lack of consignment tracking led to inefficiencies ... There were difficulties in scheduling the delivery of some supplies due to mis-prioritisation of loading of stocks for transport. For example, the majority of the force's flat racks (required for the movement of ammunition by specialist vehicles) were on the penultimate deployment ship, arriving in Kuwait in 17 March. This significantly limited the ability of logistic units to move ammunition to the frontline and exacerbated a perception among troops that there were ammunition shortages."[290]

561. Brig Cowlam told the House of Commons Defence Select Committee that all units had been issued ammunition during the initial deployment to Iraq when stocks were very limited.[291]

562. The House of Commons Defence Committee concluded:

"Our examination suggests that there were problems with the supply of ammunition when the fighting echelon began operations. MOD accepts that in the very early stages there were some problems and not all service personnel had the right amount. We expect MOD to establish the scale of the problem, to investigate any specific cases identified, in particular the tragic incident involving the six Royal Military Policemen [See Section 9.2], and to implement the necessary action to avoid any re-occurrence in the future."[292]

563. Gen Reith told the Inquiry there was "a scrabble at the end to find certain items, particularly the ceramic plates for the flak jackets, and some natures of ammunition."[293]

---

[288] Report Land Command, 31 August 2010, 'Operations in Iraq: An Analysis From a Land Perspective'.
[289] Report, 6 June 2003, '7th Armoured Brigade Post Operation Report & Lessons Report Operation TELIC'.
[290] National Audit Office, *Operation TELIC – United Kingdom Military Operations in Iraq*, 11 December 2003, HC 60.
[291] Third Report from the Defence Committee, Session 2003-04, *Lessons of Iraq*, HC57-I, para 268.
[292] Third Report from the Defence Committee, Session 2003-04, *Lessons of Iraq*, HC 57-I, para 270.
[293] Private hearing, 15 January 2010, page 52.

564. Maj Gen Binns told the Inquiry that "there were some serious shortfalls" which were eventually "helped by a redistribution of ammunition across the division".[294] He described a particular problem with ammunition for Warrior vehicles:

> "We couldn't find the operational ammunition for the Warrior. We knew that it had left Bicester and there was evidence that it had arrived in Kuwait, and there was a risk, a real risk, that ammunition was in such short supply that we may have fired it in training. And because the ammunition had just been taken to the range, they naturally assumed that that was the ammunition, and I thought we had fired it. So there was a risk over ammunition."

565. With only four months' preparation, equipment had, in a number of cases, arrived a month or two after the operation started.

Combat ID

566. Despite the public assurances given prior to the invasion that previously identified problems had been resolved, Combat ID equipment was not fitted to all vehicles before the start of operations.

567. Nine blue-on-blue incidents, four of which resulted in the death[295] or injury of UK personnel, were reported during the combat phase of Op TELIC.[296]

568. At Lord Bach's UOR meeting on 1 April 2003, it was reported that "the story overall on equipment was positive" but despite having the same equipment as the US, "we were going to 'come in for a schlocking' on Combat ID".[297] The record of the meeting did not explain why.

569. A note from Maj Gen Fry to Adm Boyce on 2 April stated that only 1,861 sets of Combat ID had been provided for 1 (UK) Div vehicles, 30 percent of the total required.[298] By the date of the invasion, all vehicles had been fitted for the equipment, but "due to the mal-location of two containers two Squadrons were not fitted with the equipment". The containers "were subsequently found and sent forward so that units could be fitted with Combat ID when an appropriate moment occurred".

570. The minute from Mr Flaherty on 9 May detailed the extent of the problem:

> "Three ISO containers of Combat ID were temporarily misplaced in theatre meaning 32 Challenger 2s were not fitted with combat identification prior to the start of combat operations. All tanks in the two lead battle groups, were, however, fitted with Combat ID. GOC 1 Division assessed that proceeding with the advance without

---

[294] Private hearing, 2 June 2010, pages 4-5.
[295] Flight Lieutenant Kevin Barry Main, Flight Lieutenant David Rhys Williams, Corporal Stephen Allbutt, Trooper David Clarke and Lance Corporal of Horse Matty Hull were killed in these incidents.
[296] Report DOC, 17 October 2003, 'Operation TELIC Lessons Study'.
[297] Minute APS/Minister(DP) to MA/DCDS(EC), 1 April 2003, 'Iraq: Op TELIC – UORs'.
[298] Minute DCJO(Ops) to PSO/CDS, 2 April 2003, 'Combat ID and ECBA'.

Combat ID was preferable to delaying the advance. In both the UK blue-on-blue CR2 [Challenger 2] incident and the incident involving a US A-10 firing on 2 CVR(T)s, all UK vehicles were fitted with the appropriate Combat ID."[299]

571. The MOD's *First Reflections* report in July 2003 stated:

"By the start of operations, MOD had deployed 1,861 vehicle-mounted and 5,000 dismounted Combat ID sets. This was sufficient to meet the full requirement, although the scale of equipment modifications required in theatre meant that some formations were still being fitted as the first units crossed the line of departure."[300]

572. The 17 October 2003 DOC report stated that training packages, which were created to aid recognition of Coalition vehicles, arrived "too late and in too small a quantity to be made widely available" and that the packages were "inadequate for aircrew training".[301]

573. The DOC found that there were not enough Thermal ID and Combat ID panels, which formed part of the UK's Combat ID capability for all vehicles, and that they were not robust and proved to be inadequate aids for Coalition aircrew.

574. The House of Commons Defence Committee concluded that:

"We expect MOD to implement the lessons from Operation TELIC on Combat ID. MOD should push forward with the work with its allies to agree on a single system … We note MOD's view that the opportunities for fratricide in an increasingly complex battle space are likely to increase, but look to MOD to identify the required action and make the necessary investment to ensure that such incidents are reduced to a minimum."[302]

Asset tracking

575. The failures in asset tracking identified in the 1991 Gulf Conflict had not been rectified in 2003.

576. Until January 2003, the UK military plan was to enter Iraq through Turkey. The US, which was to manage the entry route, stipulated that UK forces should have an asset tracking system that was compatible with that in use by US forces.[303] As a result, the MOD approved a UOR for the purchase of a US asset tracking system, known as Total Asset Visibility (TAV). The new system was not in place until the end of February 2003; too late to be used in the early stages of the deployment.

---

[299] Minute PJHQ Civ Sec to PS/Minister(DP), 9 May 2003, 'Iraq: Op TELIC UORs'.
[300] Report Ministry of Defence, *Operations in Iraq: First Reflections*, July 2003.
[301] Report DOC, 17 October 2003, 'Operation TELIC Lessons Study'.
[302] Third Report from the Defence Committee, Session 2003-04, *Lessons of Iraq*, HC 57-I, para 233.
[303] National Audit Office, *Operation TELIC – United Kingdom Military Operations in Iraq*, 11 December 2003, HC 60.

577. On 31 January, Lt Gen Reith wrote to Adm Boyce that one of the areas that "may cause difficulty" as Op TELIC developed was asset tracking.[304] He wrote:

"All that can be achieved in the time available is being progressed. The integration of the current system (VITAL …) and UOR provision of TAV (Total Asset Visibility, a US System) offers considerable improvement, but is nonetheless a 'quick fix' which does not fully address the capability gap. Medium term work by DLO is in hand."

578. In his post-operation report, Brig Binns stated:

"An inability to track items … all contributed to a serious impact upon the morale of soldiers about to conduct operations."[305]

579. When Maj Gen Fry was interviewed by the NAO on 7 August, the report of the interview sent to Mr Lee stated he had cited poor asset tracking as a "negative aspect" of Op TELIC.[306] It "compounded the lack of availability of certain scarce resources" and was quoted as saying "we had it but couldn't find it!"

580. The MOD DOC report on 17 October 2003 stated:

"During Operation TELIC, the flow of logistic information up and down the supply chain and between all stakeholders was poor. For example it was difficult to track UORs through to the end user in order to match the equipment with relevant training packages …"[307]

581. On asset tracking it stated:

"Large amounts of equipment, stores and supplies were reportedly 'lost' in theatre, including ammunition, ECBA & NBC Defence equipment … It was not possible to track down high priority equipment that was arriving simultaneously with the sustainment flow. As a result UORs and other priority equipment could not be targeted for rapid processing. This inability to identify the exact location of equipment resulted in the degradation of operational capability."

582. In its *Lessons for the Future* report in December 2003, the MOD stated:

"… the flow of logistics information between theatre and the UK was poor, particularly affecting the tracking of UORs into theatre. It was difficult to monitor the rates at which supplies were consumed, making it hard to determine when re-supply would be required. The lack of available information also reduced commanders' confidence in the logistics system, causing units to over-prioritise their requests

---

[304] Minute CJO to PSO/CDS, 31 January 2003 'OP JACANA Lessons for Op TELIC'.
[305] Report, 6 June 2003, '7th Armoured Brigade Post Operation Report & Lessons Report – Operation TELIC'.
[306] Minute DCJO to DG Op Pol, 7 August 2003, 'Readout of NAO Interview with DCJO(Ops) – 7 Aug 03'.
[307] Report DOC, 17 October 2003, 'Operation TELIC Lessons Study'.

and re-order equipment already en route. This added to the burden on the already over-stretched system."[308]

583. The MOD stated that "these problems were caused by the continuing lack of a robust tri-Service inventory system, the ability to track equipment into and through theatre, and an information system capable of supporting this technology."

584. The NAO recommended in December 2003 that:

"The Department should, as a matter of urgency, continue to work to develop appropriate logistics systems to track materiel to theatre and ensure its timely delivery to frontline units."[309]

585. On 30 January 2004, Mr Hoon's Private Secretary wrote to No.10 with a summary of lessons learned from Op TELIC, drawing "heavily" on the lines Mr Hoon intended to use before the House of Commons Defence Committee the following week.[310] He wrote:

"We have consistently acknowledged that some things did not go as well as we would have wished. In evidence to HCDC last May Mr Hoon acknowledged that there were bound to be some problems in a logistics operation of this size, and that some of our personnel may have experienced shortages of equipment. Our subsequent work and that of the NAO has shown that these shortages were more widespread and in some respects more serious than we believed to be the case at that time.

"In general this was not the result of a failure to obtain and deploy the equipment required. There is room for debate about the balance between routinely holding items in our inventory and relying on our ability to generate operation-specific equipment in short timescales. But a major problem, in our analysis, was that there were serious shortcomings in our ability to track consignments and assets through theatre, and to distribute them in a timely fashion to the front line."

586. Mr Hoon's Private Secretary wrote that the MOD had "identified numerous other areas for further work" and had, for example, increased its stockholdings of desert clothing and boots and NBC Individual Protective Equipment sets by an additional 32,000.

587. The House of Commons Defence Committee concluded that:

"We are in no doubt that one of the key lessons to emerge from Operation TELIC concerns operational logistic support and specifically, the requirement for a robust

[308] Ministry of Defence, *Operations in Iraq: Lessons for the Future*, December 2003.
[309] National Audit Office, *Operation TELIC – United Kingdom Military Operations in Iraq*, 11 December 2003, HC 60.
[310] Minute PS/SofS [MOD] to No.10, 30 January 2004, 'Op TELIC – Readiness, Equipment, Logistics & Lessons Learned'.

system to track stock and equipment both into and within theatre – a requirement which was identified in the 1991 Gulf War."[311]

588. In May 2009, the NAO recognised that the MOD had "made a number of important changes" to its logistic support process since the end of combat operations in Iraq.[312]

589. The MOD's existing systems only provided "a limited tracking capability: a consignment is only visible once it passes through a specific point in the logistics chain, but cannot be tracked at all points along the course of its journey". The NAO stated that was "nonetheless" an improvement compared to the systems in place in 2003.

590. The NAO recommended that the MOD should:

" … further improve and integrate its logistics information systems, including consignment and asset tracking, so users on operations have visibility over the stock already available at different locations in theatre, can track the progress of deliveries throughout the supply pipeline and see stock availability back in the United Kingdom."

591. Sir Kevin Tebbit told the Inquiry:

"… I think the biggest problem we had was with the tracking systems to actually ensure we knew exactly what was where, when; and that consignments that were sent actually arrived in time to be fielded properly. That system was not fully effective."[313]

592. Gen Reith told the Inquiry:

"There wasn't a shortage of equipment in the end. What there was, was an inability to track it. We knew it was in theatre, but some of it we couldn't find."[314]

593. ACM Stirrup told the Inquiry:

" … I think it was clear that lack of visibility on what was actually happening in theatre was hampering us, but, of course, even if you have that visibility, you have got to identify what are the real substantive problems, and the real substantive problems were very much to do with asset tracking with knowing where things were, so you could get them to the right place at the right time. In a number of instances, the necessary equipment was in theatre, it just wasn't in the right place, and in some instances, people didn't know where it was in theatre."[315]

---

[311] Third Report from the Defence Committee, Session 2003-04, *Lessons of Iraq*, HC57-I, para 291.
[312] National Audit Office, *Support to High Intensity Operations*, 14 May 2009, HC 508.
[313] Public hearing, 3 December 2009, page 73.
[314] Private hearing, 15 January 2010, page 52.
[315] Public hearing, 1 February 2010, page 14.

594. ACM Stirrup also described the impact of the difficulties with asset tracking on the delivery of UORs:

"I was clear in my own mind that the Urgent Operational Requirement process was only complete when the particular item of equipment was in the hands of those in theatre who needed it and they were satisfied with it. I actually tried to get some of my senior staff deployed into theatre to check those specific issues, but it was decided that we shouldn't do that and that we should rely on the chain of command. That, I think, turned out to be the wrong decision and now we routinely have people deployed for those purposes."

595. Maj Gen Binns told the Inquiry that, in 2003, he had "one of those moments with my commanding officers in early March when they were saying, 'I don't think we can be ready'".[316] One of the examples he gave as to why they were saying that alluded to asset tracking:

"We lost a company of Warriors at one stage. We knew that it had been offloaded from the boats, but I didn't know where it was. There were a quarter of a million men in the desert and we couldn't find this company of Warriors – empty vehicles that had been taken off lowloaders."

596. In his statement, ACM Bagnall told the Inquiry that:

"The information which I saw indicated that equipments had arrived in theatre. I did not see (or at least I do not recall seeing) what became known as 'the final mile' once a particular bit of kit had been unloaded in theatre and moved to where it was needed. Indeed, this is arguably not information which is required in MOD unless problems were identified which could not be resolved in theatre by CJO and his staffs or by the staffs in MOD."[317]

597. When asked what steps he had taken to assure himself that the forces deployed had access to sufficient kit and equipment including whether he ever discussed the matter with Lt Gen Reith or Air Chief Marshal Sir Brian Burridge, Deputy Commander in Chief Strike Command and UK National Contingent Commander during the invasion of Iraq, or any other commander in the field, ACM Bagnall told the Inquiry:

"… it was CDS who would routinely contact CJO, the national component commanders, Tampa and others, and I was aware that he was doing so. I did not have any discussions with them other than on the occasions when I filled the role of Acting CDS."

---

[316] Private hearing, 2 June 2010, page 5.
[317] Statement, 6 January 2011, pages 4-5.

598. ACM Bagnall told the Inquiry:

"I was not aware of any concerns which were raised before the invasion about the quality and the accuracy of information available in MOD about equipment delivery to Iraq. I was subsequently told (I think by DCDS(EC)) about concerns relating to the availability of equipment delivered under the UOR process, and I recall that he asked for agreement to send some of his people into theatre to monitor progress. I also recall that I supported this request, but for reasons I cannot remember, the request was denied. What I was aware of were concerns relating to asset tracking. This was not a new issue, and it was a topic which we had been working on for some time."[318]

599. In his evidence to the Inquiry, Lord Boyce stated that he could not recall whether Ministers had ever been advised of the known weaknesses in asset tracking or the risks this entailed.[319]

600. Lord Boyce stated:

"It was absolutely correct that a lot of our stores problems in theatre come 2003 were as a result of poor asset tracking – and I wonder what the situation is today if we were to go and ask."

601. Problems with logistic support were identified soon after the campaign.

602. RAdm Wood's findings in his report to ACM Pledger on 20 May included:

"A combination of OP SEC and late definition of force elements and operational plans all exposed Defence's growing dependence on industry as a materiel provider as well as the fragility of some key planning assumptions. This was exacerbated by some less than adequate personnel and equipment readiness. In the event, this inevitably manifested itself as significant logistic risk which imposed operational risk."[320]

603. RAdm Wood also specified that he considered:

- "Inadequate asset tracking and visibility hindered material preparation for war."
- An "urgent review" of the provisioning policy, processes and requirements for land units was required because the supply chain was "under extreme strain and, at times, unable to cope" trying to meet equipment requirements.

604. In his post-operation report on 6 October 2003, Major General Peter Wall, GOC 1 (UK) Div May 2003 to January 2005, wrote that one of the "key areas" to note

---

[318] Statement, 6 January 2011, page 4.
[319] Public hearing, 27 January 2011, pages 40-41.
[320] Minute CDL to VCDS, 27 May 2003, 'Visit by DG Ops (DLO) to Op TELIC: 10-16 May 2003' attaching Minute Wood to Pledger, 20 May 2003, 'Op TELIC Trip Report – 10-16 May 2003'.

was "the breaking of LAND mandated and resourced readiness states and training in readiness assumptions".[321] He added:

> "OP TELIC demonstrated clearly that current readiness states are not in line with strategic reality ... The time given for deployment was significantly shorter than that defined in the Defence Planning Assumptions. This had many impacts in the manning, equipping and building the ... sustainability of the force."

MOD reflections on equipping the forces deployed for the conflict

605. Reports published in 2003 after the conflict suggested that land equipment performed well during the combat phase of operations.

606. In the MOD's *First Reflections* report on operations in Iraq in July 2003, it stated that the "success of operations in Iraq demonstrated the effectiveness and extensive capability of the modern equipment and logistics support available to our Armed Forces".[322]

607. The MOD's second report, *Lessons for the Future*, assessed that:

> "Overall, land equipment performed well and reliability levels were often exceptionally high despite the challenges of a very demanding environment."[323]

608. The DOC stated that during the deployment and invasion phases of Op TELIC, "UK equipment and maintenance regimes coped well with the environment and manoeuvre demands placed upon them".[324]

609. The NAO concluded in its report on 11 December 2003 that:

> "Throughout the war-fighting phase of Operation TELIC a number of both new and in service equipments operated effectively in the austere environment of Iraq."[325]

610. The late delivery of some UORs, however, meant that soldiers were not always able to be trained on equipment before its use.

611. The DOC report on 17 October 2003 stated:

> "A consequence of the compressed timescales for UOR delivery was that personnel did not always have time to train or become properly familiar with equipment, either before deployment or in theatre ... This undermined the rationale for delivering UOR equipment to improve operational effectiveness. Users did not have complete confidence in their ability to use equipment, and commanders were not always able

---

[321] Report Wall to HQ 3 Cdo Bde, 6 October 2003, 'Post Operation Report – Version 2 Operation TELIC'.
[322] Ministry of Defence, *Operations in Iraq: First Reflections*, July 2003.
[323] Ministry of Defence, *Operations in Iraq: Lessons for the Future*, December 2003.
[324] Report DOC, 17 October 2003, 'Operation TELIC Lessons Study'.
[325] National Audit Office, *Operation TELIC – United Kingdom Military Operations in Iraq*, 11 December 2003, HC 60.

to gain full appreciation of the additional capabilities available and how they might be used in combination to deliver an effect."[326]

612. The Barry Report published in August 2010 stated:

"The UOR process did not produce enough equipment to meet the training requirements. So some troops first encountered new equipments in theatre and commanders assessed that casualties resulted, particularly in the period immediately after a brigade relief in place."[327]

613. Lord Boyce told the Inquiry:

"There is no point being told 'Here is a UOR for a nice gizmo, a nice new piece of kit which you can only have, by the way, in theatre', if the person operating that kit doesn't see it for the first time until he actually gets to theatre, because he will die trying to learn how to use it."[328]

Training on equipment post-conflict

Before 2006, it was not possible to purchase equipment with a training margin with a UOR. One of the results of this was consistent reports from the field about the difficulties presented by the lack of training on equipment that personnel would use once deployed.

A DOC report in September 2007 stated:

"Combat Body Armour (CBA), protected vehicles, comms and ECM(FP) (Electronic Counter Measure Force Protection) equipment, particularly UOR procured equipment, were regularly unavailable for training/familiarisation at PDT [Pre-Deployment Training]."[329]

Major General William Rollo, GOC MND(SE) from July 2004 to December 2004, wrote in his post-operation tour report:

"More training on Snatch and other UOR equipments … must be factored into pre-deployment preparation."[330]

That point was reiterated in post-operation tour reports from the following two successors to his role, Major General Jonathon Riley and Major General James Dutton.[331]

---

[326] Report DOC, 17 October 2003, 'Operation TELIC Lessons Study'.

[327] Report Land Command, 31 August 2010, 'Operations in Iraq: An Analysis From a Land Perspective'.

[328] Public hearing, 27 January 2011, page 102.

[329] Report DOC, September 2007, 'Protection of the Deployed Force Operational Audit Report 1/07'.

[330] Report HQ MND(SE), 4 December 2004, 'Post Operation Report Operation TELIC 4/5 – 14 July – 1 December 2004'.

[331] Report HQ MND(SE), 10 June 2005, 'Progress Report – Operation TELIC'; Report HQ MND(SE), 18 January 2006, 'Progress Report – Operation TELIC'.

> The UOR rules were changed to include a training margin in 2006.[332] The September 2007 DOC report stated:
>
> > "The recent Treasury decision to permit UOR procured equipment to include an allocation for training is already having an effect…"
>
> Lieutenant General Andrew Figgures, Deputy Chief of Defence Staff (Equipment Capability) from June 2006, told the Inquiry that decision was "an important step forward".[333]

614. The restrictions until 15 October 2002 on discussions with industry about potential operations in Iraq did prevent early conversations with industry about the provision of equipment.

615. But it is clear that the most senior military officers and officials understood the reasons for that decision.

616. Sir Kevin Tebbit told the Inquiry:

"… some very contingent UOR work was authorised by Mr Hoon at the time under CDS' pressure … but those were very much ones which could be done invisibly."[334]

617. Asked if he had sensed some reluctance in the Government to agree preparatory steps, Maj Gen Fry replied that he thought there was, but that had to be qualified to reflect the fact that what he saw was determined by his role in the PJHQ. In his view it was understandable if Ministers had been "trying to reserve their positions for as long as they could".[335]

618. Mr Hoon told the Inquiry:

"All I know is that Mike [Boyce] and I went to meetings in September, where we argued the case and that we were both made very well aware of the attitude in Downing Street towards the requirement for minimising publicity and for avoiding the visibility of preparations. We were both there at these meetings. So there was no doubt of the fact that we could not go out, either of us, and overtly prepare, which is why we had to approach some of the UORs in a particular way …

"I think the judgement that I had to make and he had to make was the extent to which we could go on with preparations without affecting that diplomatic process in the United Nations."[336]

---

[332] Report DOC, September 2007, 'Protection of the Deployed Force Operational Audit Report 1/07'.
[333] Public hearing, 27 July 2010, page 43.
[334] Public hearing, 3 December 2009, page 36.
[335] Public hearing, 16 December 2009, pages 11-13.
[336] Public hearing, 19 January 2010, page 136.

619. The evidence given to the Inquiry demonstrates that senior military officers and officials in the MOD fully understood the limitations on the size and readiness of the forces available for deployment on expeditionary operations agreed in the 1998 Strategic Defence Review and set out in the Defence Planning Assumptions (DPAs).

620. Sir Kevin Tebbit stated that the scale of the deployment was consistent with the DPAs, and that: "It was the type of operation that we expected from time to time to be able to mount."[337]

621. Sir Kevin Tebbit was later asked what lessons had been learned from the earlier experience in Iraq.[338] One lesson he cited was:

"… we assumed that we would have stocks for six months, and that when we came to a major operation we would have preparation time to conduct a large scale operation by building up stocks in that period.

"… if we wanted to go for a large scale, we would need six months in order to acquire the necessary extra equipment, stores, personnel, clothing, ammunition, things like that."

622. On the SDR, Sir Kevin Tebbit told the Inquiry:

"… when we said that the SDR did involve the ability to move up to large scale from time to time, we hadn't got a precise view, but we were looking at once every 10 years we could gravitate up to large scale.[339]

623. Gen Jackson told the Inquiry that:

"… the Defence Planning Assumptions which had emerged from the Strategic Defence Review of 1997/98 allowed for, from time to time, a large commitment, which in land force terms was at the divisional level, this was not regarded as anything we could contemplate on an enduring basis, a one-off from time to time …

"More germanely we would be able to maintain a medium-sized commitment, i.e. brigade level, indefinitely and we could on a one-off basis add a second medium scale commitment.

"There was some small print about a small scale … but I think it is within the ability to produce a second brigade on a short-term basis."[340]

624. The MOD also understood that the deployment could not be sustained for more than six months.

---

[337] Public hearing, 3 February 2010, page 24.
[338] Private hearing, 6 May 2010, pages 48-49.
[339] Private hearing, 6 May 2010, page 51.
[340] Public hearing, 28 July 2010, page 7.

625. The impact on the UK's ability to continue to conduct military operations after the conflict phase of operations was never fully considered.

626. Lord Boyce told the Inquiry:

"The theoretical planning against the Defence Planning Assumptions is you don't do this sort of operation for an extended period longer than about six months. But it never seemed to me very likely that we would be out [of] there [Iraq] in six months."[341]

627. Sir Kevin later said: "Our assumptions never involve more than six months at that level."[342]

628. With regard to large scale deployments, Gen Jackson stated:

"… the large scale concept, in land component terms we are talking around 30,000 or 25,000 certainly, the concept is you put in that large commitment on a one-off basis and then you must downsize, because the Army cannot sustain a deployment of 25,000 to 30,000 indefinitely."[343]

629. The Inquiry was offered different perspectives on the degree to which exceeding the Planning Assumptions had put a strain on the system that it was not able to meet.

630. Lt Gen Fry told the Inquiry that:

"Over time the scale of ambition got larger and larger, so at the end of it we were looking at something which involved a full deployed joint force with … land, air and maritime forces, and in addition to that, special forces and logistic forces as well."[344]

631. Asked if he had thought there was sufficient time to prepare the force for battle, Lt Gen Fry stated that it was "a bit of a rush and there were inherent risks involved".[345]

632. Gen Reith told the Inquiry that he was "quite happy" in terms of readiness and training.[346] He said that 7 Armoured Brigade had been selected because it was "the most highly trained of all the armoured brigades". In addition, 3 Commando Brigade and 16 Air Assault Brigade were both part of the Joint Rapid Reaction Force and, therefore, "maintained a high standard of training and readiness on a permanent basis".

---

[341] Public hearing, 3 December 2009, page 101.
[342] Private hearing, 6 May 2010, page 53.
[343] Public hearing, 28 July 2010, page 42.
[344] Public hearing, 16 December 2009, page 5.
[345] Public hearing, 16 December 2009, page 40.
[346] Private hearing, 15 January 2010, page 50.

633. ACM Stirrup told the Inquiry:

"… we simply did not have enough time … to do everything that we needed to before the operation started."[347]

634. Sir Kevin Tebbit stated that:

"The timescale was slightly compressed, more than we would have wished, which we made very clear, so that we didn't have everything that we would have wanted at the right moment, but the shortfall was not operationally significant …"[348]

635. Sir Kevin Tebbit subsequently told the Inquiry that the switch to the South:

" … was not as difficult as I thought it was going to be … I think it was a great achievement … which surprised me … [T]he quality of the military effort was tremendous … because it wasn't just a question of moving to a different host nation support arrangements, it's a question of a differently configured force …

"I think the military had been running a slightly parallel option for a bit of time during December, actually."[349]

636. Sir Kevin Tebbit added:

"I think that to the extent that there were pressures and problems with the operation itself … those were more about the amount of time available to do the planning of the actual build-up itself, warning time, the switch from one area to another, the difficulty of doing overt military preparations as early as they needed to be done because of the desire not to disrupt the UN track.

"Those were the bigger problems in ensuring that we got the force structure ready when eventually the time came, and the fact that we would have preferred another month, in ideal circumstances, to do that build-up."[350]

637. Gen Jackson told the Inquiry that the "whole order of battle" had been "in a state of flux" until early 2003.[351] But he confirmed that he had been confident the UK could put a division into the field.

638. Gen Jackson subsequently described the forces deployed as "a very interesting divisional construct" which he did not think had been done before: "but it was the right construct for the task which confronted 1 (UK) Armoured Division."[352]

---

[347] Public hearing, 1 February 2010, page 11.
[348] Public hearing, 3 February 2010, page 28.
[349] Private hearing, 6 May 2010, page 19.
[350] Private hearing, 6 May 2010, pages 38-39.
[351] Public hearing, 28 July 2010, page 9.
[352] Public hearing, 28 July 2010, page 13.

639. Asked when the UK started looking at the South as an alternative, Lord Boyce told the Inquiry that the process had started "at least in December 2002".[353] He acknowledged that December was "quite late in the day" to start looking at options in the South.

640. The Inquiry asked Lord Boyce whether, as a result of the late changes to the military package, British troops had the necessary equipment.[354] Lord Boyce replied that while it "left us with some very short timelines", he was "confident" that the "front of the front line" were properly equipped on 20 March.

641. When asked whether he would have ideally deployed the land force sooner to allow for more training and time to acclimatise, or to ensure it had the right equipment, Lord Boyce replied:

"My advice was that they had had sufficient time to make themselves ready."[355]

642. In his later statement to the Inquiry, Lord Boyce wrote that the land forces for the South:

"… were largely based on what were already being prepared for the northern option. However, because of the change in plan, the US agreed to assist with some enabling and logistics assets in the south. Maritime (including amphibious) and air force levels were much the same. The thinking about a possible southern option had started in late autumn 2002 and so the concept was already well developed by the time the northern option was abandoned."[356]

643. Lord Boyce added:

"…the equipment being procured for the land forces previously designated for the northern option largely serviced them when they were re-roled south, although there was a need to recognise the more extensive desert environment."

644. Lord Boyce subsequently told the Inquiry:

"Although the final switch did happen around mid-January, really our minds in terms of planning and thinking about it and looking at all the potential pitfalls or difficulties or whatever had started, as you say, probably as far back as October; but during the course of December we really thought that was possibly where we were going to finish up …

---

[353] Public hearing, 3 December 2009, page 55.
[354] Public hearing, 3 December 2009, pages 64-68.
[355] Public hearing, 3 December 2009, page 69.
[356] Statement, 7 January 2011, page 1.

"… we could afford to take the decision quite late. It wasn't starting with a fresh plan in the middle of January. The southern plan was pretty well developed, in fact almost entirely developed, by then."[357]

645. Asked about the impact of the reduction in preparation time, Lord Boyce stated:

"… it meant everything was being done at a rush … some aspects of the full operational capability weren't achieved until literally the nth hour … I don't believe … that our capability at the end of the day was in any sense seriously degraded … but nonetheless it did make it a tight run thing."[358]

646. Describing the thinking which had led to the UK's original offer in Package 3 in October of a brigade and divisional headquarters, Lord Boyce stated that it was "not a huge move then … into a division minus, which is what we actually finished up with".[359]

647. Asked whether, when he had visited UK forces just before the start of operations, he had been given any indications that they were lacking equipment such as body armour and ammunition, Lord Boyce replied: "No". But he added that he had been concerned about the "ability to cope with any biological or chemical threat", and at the time of his visit, a "very small percentage" of the force had not had their gas masks checked.

Conclusions

648. **The achievements of the MOD and the Armed Forces in preparing the forces deployed for combat operations in Iraq against tight deadlines were very considerable.**

649. **But the evidence set out in this Section of the Report demonstrates that significant risks were taken as a result of decisions made in mid-January to deploy a larger combat force in a very compressed timescale. The difficulties were exacerbated by the absence of systems which could accurately track and report the situation on the ground.**

650. **The provision of additional funding from the Reserve for UORs worked well and there is no evidence of any delay or obstruction on the part of the Treasury.**

651. **A number of witnesses to the Inquiry stated, or implied, that the serious shortfalls of some equipment could have been mitigated if permission to discuss procurement with industry had been given earlier.**

652. **That claim is impossible to determine. It is clear that the restrictions on discussions with industry before 15 October did hinder planning and preparations and cause anxiety.**

---

[357] Public hearing, 27 January 2011, pages 17-18.
[358] Public hearing, 27 January 2011, page 28.
[359] Public hearing, 27 January 2011, page 30.

653. However, the most senior military officers and officials understood the political and diplomatic reasons for that decision and Ministers were not advised that the restrictions would have a direct adverse impact on capabilities.

654. The problems encountered by the forces deployed to Iraq in early 2003 do not appear to have been directly attributable to the absence of discussions with industry before 15 October.

655. The evidence suggests that most of the difficulties arose from the decisions to deploy a force more quickly than the Defence Planning Assumptions (DPAs) envisaged.

656. The 1998 Strategic Defence Review (SDR) and Defence Strategic Plan had set clear guidelines about the military resources required for potential operations of different scale and duration. The DPAs also set out the time likely to be necessary to adequately prepare UK forces for operations, including the time needed to procure and deploy equipment and train personnel on its use.

657. The DPAs determined the equipment procured for the Armed Forces and that the stocks held should be sufficient only to meet the readiness requirements specified in the DPAs.

658. The 1998 SDR had also concluded that the UK needed a better expeditionary capability to reflect the nature of future threats and the environments, such as the Gulf, in which the UK should plan to operate.

659. By 2002, when military planning for potential operations in Iraq commenced, that capability had not been fully achieved.

660. The policy underpinning the DPAs of relying on sufficient preparation time to procure UORs and additional stocks to meet identified shortfalls before a large scale deployment was explicitly acknowledged by the MOD in spring 2002.

661. In the second half of 2002, however, the MOD was already supporting two simultaneous medium scale operations, in the Balkans and Operation FRESCO, and a number of small scale operations, including in Afghanistan. The Armed Forces were thus already stretched to the maximum level envisaged under the DPAs, beyond which time would be needed to acquire additional stocks and equipment.

662. The decisions between mid-December 2002 and mid-January 2003, to increase the force deployed for ground operations to three combat brigades and the decisions to commit 16 Air Assault Brigade and 7 Armoured Brigade to military operations in southern Iraq in late March, had a significant impact on the scale of some UORs and compressed the time available for the provision and delivery of equipment to front line units.

663. The force deployed in 2003 was larger than the UK contribution in the Gulf Conflict in 1991 and the time to prepare was significantly shorter than the six to nine months assumed in the DPAs.

664. Lt Gen Reith acknowledged in May 2003 that the military commitment was, "as often happens, at a scale beyond that envisaged in the DPAs and thus not fully resourced".

665. When decisions were made in mid-January, the inherent risks for equipping the force to be deployed and its readiness were neither properly identified nor considered.

666. The military advice in late January 2003 that there were "no showstoppers" disguised the fact that risks had been accepted which had not been fully exposed to Ministers.

667. Adm Boyce had assured Mr Blair on 13 March 2003 that the Armed Forces faced "no serious equipment problems".

668. The context suggests he was referring to the invasion phase. As Section 8 shows, the US and UK did not expect Iraqi forces to be able effectively to resist Coalition Forces.

669. There may be circumstances in the future when a Government will feel it necessary to take decisions to commit the Armed Forces to military operations which exceed the planning assumptions on which they have been equipped and prepared. But they should not do so without an explicit acceptance of the risks being taken.

670. In addition, a number of lessons from previous conflicts and exercises had not been addressed before the deployment to Iraq.

671. In particular, poor asset tracking systems meant that an already over-burdened system was put under even greater pressure, and equipment that had been deployed to the forces in Kuwait did not reach the front line before military operations began.

672. ACM Stirrup accurately summarised the position when he told the Inquiry that "the issue was it was all being done so rapidly at the last minute no one was quite sure who had what".

673. The MOD's asset tracking system was still in need of improvement when the UK left Iraq in 2009.

674. The MOD had given assurances before the 2003 invasion that the necessary lessons had been learned since 1991. This proved not to be the case. In any future eventuality, the MOD has a responsibility to ensure that past mistakes are not repeated, and that its systems for asset tracking are robust.

675. The emergence after the conflict of the scale and nature of the problems encountered illuminated the extent to which Ministers had been unaware of risks being taken for which they would have been accountable. The shortfalls in individual equipment, protection against chemical and biological attack, and ammunition did not have an impact on the overall success of the invasion.

676. But they did have an impact on individuals.

677. In the case of Sgt Steven Roberts, it was judged that his death could have been prevented if he had still had his body armour.

678. As the evidence in this Section shows, reports about equipment shortfalls from the media and from members of the Armed Forces also had a negative impact on the perceptions of the morale of troops on the ground and on how the campaign was seen by the public and Parliament.

679. In addition, analysis of the events in 2003 shows that, until May, neither PJHQ nor MOD had a proper understanding of the problems with equipment that units were experiencing on the ground.

680. Lord Bach was right to have suggested on 11 February 2003 that a direct and robust system accurately to report on readiness and equipment issues from theatre to Ministers was needed.

681. During military operations, reporting to the MOD will always be constrained by the limitations of military operations and the pressures on those involved, and military commanders need the freedom to take operational decisions.

682. In any future operations, however, the MOD should ensure that it has robust systems in place to accurately report the situation on the ground without usurping the responsibilities of the chain of command.

SECTION 6.4

PLANNING AND PREPARATION FOR A POST-SADDAM HUSSEIN IRAQ, MID-2001 TO JANUARY 2003

Contents

Introduction and key findings

1. Sections 6.4 and 6.5 consider the UK's planning and preparation for a post-Saddam Hussein Iraq between late 2001 and March 2003.

2. Section 6.4 covers the period up to Mr Blair's decision on 17 January 2003 to deploy UK forces to support US military preparations.

3. Section 6.5 covers the 10 weeks between the decision to deploy UK forces and the first post-invasion meeting between Mr Blair and President Bush at Camp David on 26 and 27 March 2003.

4. The two parts address:

- the development of UK post-conflict strategy and objectives;
- planning and preparation to implement those objectives;
- UK civilian and military planning machinery;
- UK influence on US planning and preparation and the impact of US planning on the UK; and
- Parliamentary interest in post-conflict planning and preparation.

5. The two parts do not consider:

- military plans for the invasion, which are addressed in Sections 6.1 and 6.2;
- intelligence on weapons of mass destruction (WMD) or preparations for the post-invasion search for WMD, addressed in Section 4;
- the financial and human resources available for post-conflict administration and reconstruction, addressed in Sections 13 and 15; and
- the outcome in post-conflict Iraq, which is addressed in Sections 9 and 10.

6. Descriptions of US preparations for post-conflict Iraq in Sections 6.4 and 6.5 are mostly taken from *Hard Lessons*, Mr Stuart Bowen's account, as US Inspector General for Iraq Reconstruction, of the US experience of reconstruction between 2002 and 2008.

7. Key findings for Sections 6.4 and 6.5 are listed below.

8. The Inquiry's conclusions relating to Sections 6.4 and 6.5 are at the end of Section 6.5.

Key findings

- Before the invasion of Iraq, Ministers, senior officials and the UK military recognised that post-conflict civilian and military operations were likely to be the strategically decisive phase of the Coalition's engagement in Iraq.

- UK planning and preparation for the post-conflict phase of operations, which rested on the assumption that the UK would be able quickly to reduce its military presence in Iraq and deploy only a minimal number of civilians, were wholly inadequate.

- The information available to the Government before the invasion provided a clear indication of the potential scale of the post-conflict task and the significant risks associated with the UK's proposed approach.

- Foreseeable risks included post-conflict political disintegration and extremist violence in Iraq, the inadequacy of US plans, the UK's inability to exert significant influence on US planning and, in the absence of UN authorisation for the administration and reconstruction of post-conflict Iraq, the reluctance of potential international partners to contribute to the post-conflict effort.

- The Government, which lacked both clear Ministerial oversight of post-conflict strategy, planning and preparation, and effective co-ordination between government departments, failed to analyse or manage those risks adequately.

- Mr Blair, who recognised the significance of the post-conflict phase, did not press President Bush for definite assurances about US plans, did not consider or seek advice on whether the absence of a satisfactory plan called for reassessment of the terms of the UK's engagement and did not make agreement on such a plan a condition of UK participation in military action.

Pre-conflict management of information on Iraq

9. During 2002 and early 2003, a growing body of evidence on the state of Iraq under Saddam Hussein and on the potential impact of conflict was available to UK planners.

10. The evidence was fragmented and incomplete. Many of the sources were not reliable.

11. A number of departments shared responsibility for the gathering, analysis and dissemination of that information.

12. The principal sources of information potentially available to UK planners before March 2003 on social, political and economic conditions in Iraq included:

- the UN, including the UN-managed Oil-for-Food (OFF) programme;
- reports on visits to Iraq by diplomats at the British Embassy in Amman, Jordan;[1]

---

[1] Paper FCO, 17 November 2010, 'Note for the Iraq Inquiry on the FCO's diplomatic contacts in Baghdad, 1990-2003'.

- a humanitarian programme funded by the Department for International Development (DFID) focused on northern Iraq;[2]
- Assessments produced by the UK's Joint Intelligence Committee (JIC);
- the US State Department's Future of Iraq Project;[3] and
- other sources, including non-governmental organisations (NGOs), academics, journalists, Arabic media, Iraqi émigrés and allied countries with Embassies in Baghdad.[4]

13. The information available to the Government before the invasion on Iraq's weapons of mass destruction (WMD) is addressed in Section 4. Information on Iraq's other military capabilities is in Sections 6.1 to 6.3.

The Foreign and Commonwealth Office

14. In December 2003, the Foreign and Commonwealth Office (FCO) presented a *Strategy for the FCO* to Parliament, in which it listed the department's "key contributions" to government.[5] They included:

- "co-ordination and leadership of the UK's international policies";
- "expert foreign policy advice for Ministers and the Prime Minister, feeding into the wider policy process"; and
- "rapid gathering, analysis and targeting of information for the Government and others".

15. Within the FCO between 2001and 2003, prime responsibility for information on other countries fell to the relevant regional department. For Iraq, that was the Middle East Department (MED), under the supervision of the Director Middle East and North Africa.

16. The FCO Directorate of Strategy and Innovation (DSI) reported to the Permanent Under Secretary (PUS)[6] and the FCO Board. Its role was to review policy in areas of high priority and to supplement or challenge advice from the relevant department within the FCO. DSI was a significant contributor of strategy papers on Iraq in the second half of 2002.

---

[2] Minute Western Asia Department [junior official] to Private Secretary [DFID], 10 May 2002, 'Iraq: Proposed humanitarian activities 2002/03'.
[3] The National Security Archive, Electronic Briefing Book No. 198, 1 September 2006, *New State Department Releases on the "Future of Iraq" Project*.
[4] Public hearing Ricketts, Chaplin, 1 December 2009, pages 66-67; Statement Foreign and Commonwealth Office Research Analysts, 23 November 2009, page 1.
[5] Foreign and Commonwealth Office, *UK International Priorities: A Strategy for the FCO*, December 2003, Cm 6052.
[6] In keeping with variations in use within departments, the Inquiry refers to the most senior civil servant in the FCO and the MOD as the Permanent Under Secretary (PUS), but in all other departments as the Permanent Secretary. The Permanent Under Secretaries and Permanent Secretaries are referred to collectively as Permanent Secretaries.

17. The FCO Research Analysts (RA) provided expert support and background for the policy recommendations made by MED and the Iraq Planning Unit (IPU), which was established in February 2003.[7] The FCO told the Inquiry that one analyst worked full-time on Iraq during 2001, increasing to two from mid-2002.[8] RA also acted as the contact point within government for the US State Department's Future of Iraq Project.[9]

18. After the closure of the British Embassy Baghdad on 12 January 1992, the UK had no diplomatic relations with Iraq.

19. In other cases where diplomatic relations have been interrupted, the UK has often maintained a British Interests Section within a friendly Embassy. The FCO told the Inquiry it did not consider opening an Interests Section in Iraq staffed with permanent UK diplomatic staff.[10] Instead, Russia acted as the UK's Protecting Power in Baghdad from November 1992 until the invasion, but did not provide the UK with political reporting from Iraq.

20. The FCO told the Inquiry that, from the late 1990s, junior UK diplomats based in Amman visited Baghdad about every six months to check on UK property, in particular the Embassy building, deal with locally-employed staff, call on resident diplomats from other countries and glean what information they could on the situation in Iraq.[11] On return to Amman, the UK diplomats produced reports containing political and economic information, some of which are described later in this Section.

21. Initially, the reports from Amman had an administrative focus. The FCO explicitly advised visiting diplomats from Amman not to travel to Basra, as such visits would not be consistent with that purpose and might suggest the UK was increasing contact with Iraq.[12] Visiting diplomats were instructed to "avoid all political contacts".

22. In July 1998, FCO Economic Advisers asked the British Embassy Amman for help in monitoring Iraq's economy, explaining that basic economic indicators were unavailable and that those with an interest in the issue had to rely on "snippets of information, on anecdote, and on speculation".[13] The Embassy was asked to make a "modest effort" to gather economic information during routine administrative visits to Iraq, focusing on:

- living standards;
- employment/unemployment and the structure of economic activity;

---

[7] Briefing Wilson, November 2009.
[8] Email FCO to Iraq Inquiry, 3 June 2013, 'FCO Research Analysts'.
[9] Briefing Wilson, November 2009.
[10] Paper FCO, 17 November 2010, 'Note for the Iraq Inquiry on the FCO's diplomatic contacts in Baghdad, 1990-2003'.
[11] Paper FCO, 17 November 2010, 'Note for the Iraq Inquiry on the FCO's diplomatic contacts in Baghdad, 1990-2003'.
[12] Telegram 366 Amman to FCO London, 16 July 1997, 'Proposed visit to Iraq'; Telegram 390 FCO London to Amman, 18 July 1997, 'Iraq: proposed visit'.
[13] Letter Economic Advisers [junior official] to Amman [junior official], 15 July 1998, 'Reporting Economic Developments in Iraq'.

- inflation;
- trade and capital flows;
- public finances and monetary policy;
- structural policies and economic philosophy;
- northern Iraq; and
- long-term planning.

23. From early 2002, UK diplomats based in Amman began to visit Iraq more often. They produced reports on political and social developments, drawing on information gleaned from business and other travellers and monthly UN briefings in Baghdad.[14]

24. The FCO has not been able to provide the Inquiry with the complete series of reports between July 1998 and March 2003.

25. Dr Robert Wilson and Mr Mark Hetherington, the two research analysts working on Iraq before the invasion, explained to the Inquiry that the FCO drew on a range of sources for information about the social, economic and political situation in Iraq:

"These included Iraqi politicians and exiles from both Iraqi Kurdistan and the rest of the country, contact with whom was one of the core tasks of Research Analysts during this period. Amongst those were individuals who visited either Saddam-controlled Iraq or Northern Iraq (where Saddam had withdrawn his administration and which was under de facto control of the two main Kurdish parties) and those who had links to family or contacts within the country. Though the majority of those with whom we were in contact were opposed to Saddam Hussein's regime, their analysis was far from homogenous – religious organisations and NGOs in particular offering more nuanced analysis. Of course we were aware that many of these individuals had their own particular agenda – especially when it came to the question of what level of political support their parties or ideologies had within Iraq, and this was hard to assess independently. In addition there were many Iraqis who shied away from contact with the British Government …"[15]

26. Dr Wilson told the Inquiry that RA had "no shortage of information on Iraq of varying degrees of reliability".[16] In addition to Iraqi exiles, the FCO's network of Embassies in the region (particularly in Jordan and Turkey) kept in touch with local Iraqi officials and opinion formers. Though most contacts were opposed to Saddam Hussein's regime, their analysis was far from homogeneous.[17] Researchers were aware their contacts had their own agendas and it was hard to assess independently what support specific parties or ideologies had in Iraq.

---

[14] Teleletter Amman [junior official] to MED [junior official] 24 January 2002, 'Iraq: our interests'.
[15] Statement Foreign and Commonwealth Office Research Analysts, 23 November 2009.
[16] Briefing Wilson, November 2009.
[17] Statement Foreign and Commonwealth Office Research Analysts, 23 November 2009.

27. Dr Wilson told the Inquiry that academics, the UN and its agencies, NGOs and the Arabic media were also sources of information.

28. Lord Jay, the FCO PUS from 2002 to 2006, told the Inquiry that the FCO had only a "partial" picture of what was going on in Iraq.[18] He highlighted the critical role of an Embassy in understanding a country:

"… we did not have first-hand knowledge of what was going on inside Iraq, of how Saddam Hussein and his government operated.

"We had it second- or third-hand from other powers to whom we spoke … [W]hat we did not have was the … constant day-to-day contact between well-qualified, Arabic-speaking diplomats in Baghdad able to report back constantly on the ebb and flow of power and influence and what that meant for us.

"… [Y]ou really do need people on the ground feeding stuff back. If you don't have that, you are going to make mistakes."

29. Lord Jay agreed that, in the absence of first-hand information, No.10 looked to the UK's intelligence services to provide advice on a broader range of issues than normal.[19]

30. Lord Jay added:

"I don't think we had thought through as much as we should have done what the implications were going to be of an invasion of a country such as Iraq … I wished we had had a better understanding of what Iraq was like in the 1990s, early 2000s before a decision was taken to invade."[20]

31. Mr Edward Chaplin, FCO Director Middle East and North Africa from 2002 to 2004, characterised UK knowledge of what happened inside Iraq as "patchy".[21] He told the Inquiry he could, nevertheless, draw on a number of useful sources of information: the British Embassy Amman, which held a "watching brief"; contacts with exiled Iraqi groups in London and Washington; contacts with close allies, like the French, who had long experience of, and still had representation in, Iraq; contacts in a number of academic institutions; and contacts with journalists.

32. Mr Chaplin commented:

"… I don't think we lacked for sources of information, but I think one of the problems is that actually nobody outside Iraq, including Iraqi exiles, quite realised how broken Iraqi society had become … nobody really had that information."[22]

---

[18] Public hearing, 30 June 2010, pages 8-10.
[19] Public hearing, 30 June 2010, pages 12-13.
[20] Public hearing, 30 June 2010, page 67.
[21] Public hearing, 1 December 2009, page 39.
[22] Public hearing, 1 December 2009, page 67.

33. Mr Chaplin rejected the suggestion that he had made no attempt to fill gaps in the UK's knowledge base on Iraq, highlighting the multiple sources of information that were available.

34. Mr Simon Webb, Ministry of Defence (MOD) Policy Director from 2001 to 2004, told the Inquiry he felt he had a very good feel for Iraq's military capability, but not for what was happening within Saddam Hussein's administration, the state of Iraq's infrastructure, or the mood of the population in the South:

> "If we had thought that we were going to play a big role in reconstruction, and we'd been asked to gather that information, I suspect we could have had a better picture."[23]

35. Mr Webb agreed that the Government could have made more use of "open source" reporting and analysis, including from academia, think-tanks and NGOs.

The Iraq Planning Unit

36. In early February 2003, the Government established the Iraq Planning Unit (IPU) to focus on post-conflict Iraq. The IPU was an inter-departmental (FCO/MOD/DFID) unit, based in the FCO and headed by a former member of MED. In the FCO, the IPU reported to the Director Middle East and North Africa.

37. The origin and purpose of the IPU are addressed in more detail in Section 6.5.

38. Mr Dominick Chilcott, Head of the IPU from February to June 2003, told the Inquiry there was "a lot of expertise" he could draw on, in particular from FCO RA, Iraqi exiles and FCO posts in the region.[24]

The Joint Intelligence Committee

39. The JIC was (and continues to be) responsible for:

> "... providing Ministers and senior officials with co-ordinated intelligence assessments on a range of issues of immediate and long-range importance to national interests, primarily in the fields of security, defence and foreign affairs."[25]

40. The JIC is supported by Assessments Staff analysts seconded to the Cabinet Office from other departments. The Assessments Staff's draft assessments were (and still are) subject to formal inter-departmental scrutiny and challenge in Current Intelligence Groups (CIGs), which bring together working-level experts from a range of government departments and the intelligence agencies. In the case of Iraq between 2001and 2003, the CIG brought together the desk-level experts from the FCO (including MED and RA),

---

[23] Private hearing, 23 June 2010, pages 79-81.
[24] Public hearing, 8 December 2009, page 50.
[25] Cabinet Office, *National Intelligence Machinery*, November 2010, pages 23-24.

MOD (including the Defence Intelligence Staff (DIS)), Cabinet Office and the intelligence agencies, and any other department with an interest in the issue being considered.

41. The JIC agrees most assessments before they are sent to Ministers and senior officials, although some papers, including urgent updates on developing issues, are issued under the authority of the Chief of the Assessments Staff.

42. The current JIC Terms of Reference make clear that it is expected to draw on "secret intelligence, diplomatic reporting and open source material".[26]

43. Iraq was regularly considered by the JIC in 2000 and 2001, with the focus on weapons of mass destruction (WMD), sanctions and the implications of the No-Fly Zones (NFZs).[27]

44. Sir John Scarlett, JIC Chairman from 2001 to 2004, considered that Iraq had been one of the top priorities for the JIC for most of his time as Chairman.[28]

45. Sir John told the Inquiry that, with the limited resources available to the Assessments Staff, the breakdown, decay and decrepitude of Iraq's civilian infrastructure was "not a natural intelligence target".[29] He added:

> "That kind of information and that kind of understanding of the fragility of the structures of the State … could have been … presented or understood from a whole range of sources, not necessarily from intelligence."

46. Sir John later told the Inquiry that the JIC had not been asked to look at Iraqi civilian infrastructure and institutions, other than Saddam Hussein's power structures:

> "If we had been, I think almost certainly my response would be: that's not for us. Why should that be an intelligence issue? I wouldn't quite be able to understand how intelligence would help. I would see it as fundamentally something which in the first instance advice would need to come from the Foreign Office … Of course, if we had been asked, we would have said can you identify or can we between us work out what would be particularly susceptible to an intelligence view or consideration? And I think it would have been quite narrow. I don't quite see how secret intelligence would have particularly helped."[30]

47. Mr Julian Miller, Chief of the Assessments Staff from 2001 to 2003, told the Inquiry that intelligence available to the JIC gave some peripheral indications on issues such as Iraq's civilian infrastructure and the state of its institutions, but was not focused on those areas.[31] In retrospect, he believed that if the UK had wanted to find out more, it might

---

[26] Cabinet Office, *National Intelligence Machinery*, November 2010, page 26.
[27] Public hearing Webb, Ricketts, Patey, 24 November 2009, pages 51-54.
[28] Public hearing, 8 December 2009, page 10.
[29] Public hearing, 8 December 2009, page 51.
[30] Private hearing, 5 May 2010, pages 65-66.
[31] Private hearing, 5 May 2010, pages 63-64.

have been possible for the JIC to ask the agencies to make an effort in that direction. He had no recollection of any such request.

48. Mr Miller added that departments had shown interest in the internal politics of Iraq and the relationship between the Shia and the Kurds, but only very limited intelligence had been available on those subjects.

49. The majority of JIC assessments relevant to Iraq between 2002 and the start of the invasion on 19 March 2003 dealt with Saddam Hussein's military and diplomatic options, WMD, or regional attitudes to Iraq.[32]

50. The weekly Intelligence Updates issued by the Assessments Staff from November 2002 and more frequently from February 2003, concentrated on the same three themes.

The Defence Intelligence Staff

51. The principal task of the Defence Intelligence Staff (DIS)[33] was the provision of intelligence to inform MOD policy formulation and procurement decisions, and to support military operations.[34]

52. The DIS worked closely with other UK intelligence organisations and with overseas allies.[35] Its sources included human, signals and imagery intelligence, as well as open sources. The DIS produced a number of reports on the state of Iraq.

53. In late February 2003, the DIS established a Red Team to give key planners in Whitehall an independent view of intelligence assumptions and key judgements, to challenge those assumptions and judgements if appropriate and to identify areas where more work was needed (see Section 6.5).[36] Papers were copied to the Chiefs of Staff, the Permanent Joint Headquarters (PJHQ), the MOD, FCO, IPU and the JIC.

54. Mr Martin Howard, Deputy Chief of Defence Intelligence from February 2003 to May 2004, the senior civilian in the DIS, told the Inquiry:

"… at the strategic level the lead agency was the JIC. They are the ones who produced, as it were, the capstone intelligence assessments.

"What the DIS tried to do was do things at a level a little below that, to produce products which would be of interest to high level policy makers, but also extremely useful to planners, to commanders and so on and so forth. So I'm not sure we were necessarily the lead, but we probably did the bulk of the analytical work."[37]

---

[32] JIC Assessments on Iraq, 1 January 2002 to 18 March 2003.
[33] Now known as Defence Intelligence (DI).
[34] Letter Ministry of Defence to Iraq Inquiry, 29 April 2010, 'MOD Evidence – Submission on Defence Intelligence Staff (DIS)'.
[35] Ministry of Defence Website, 'Defence Intelligence'.
[36] Minute PS/CDI to APS2/SofS [MOD], 25 February 2003, 'Iraq: Red Teaming in the DIS'.
[37] Private hearing, 18 June 2010, page 20.

55. Mr Howard stated that the DIS produced "a mass of material, even in the short time we had available, and I'm not sure that there would have been a fundamental improvement in what we could have provided if we had had another few months".[38]

56. Mr Howard did not recall the Red Team having a huge impact on work done by DIS. It raised "some interesting points", but "in the end, although it had a senior level distribution list ... the practical impact would have been at the analytical level, rather than necessarily the policy making level".[39]

57. Mr Ian Lee, MOD Director General Operational Policy (DG OpPol) from September 2002 to May 2004, told the Inquiry that the MOD looked to the DIS for information about what the UK should expect to encounter in Iraq after a military campaign, including the state of the country, its sectarian, ethnic, political, and economic makeup.[40] There was not much detail available. Mr Lee described the written briefing as "a bit generalised".

58. Major General Michael Laurie, MOD Director General Intelligence Collection from 2000 to 2003, told the Inquiry he did not recall the DIS being tasked to look at the situation after the campaign, but did recall "a general feeling that we weren't paying as much attention to follow-on operations and what would happen as we should have done".[41] He agreed that it would have been within the DIS remit to consider the state of Iraq's infrastructure: the DIS had a number of teams working on infrastructure issues and had an established capability to collect open source information, including from the academic and scientific communities.

The Cabinet Office Overseas and Defence Secretariat

59. The Cabinet Office contains the Cabinet Secretariats, which support the Cabinet and Cabinet committees, and draw staff from across government.[42] Between 2001 and 2003 the Overseas and Defence Secretariat (OD Sec)[43] was responsible for foreign and defence policy issues, of which Iraq was one.[44]

60. The Head of OD Sec (Sir David Manning from September 2001) was also Mr Blair's Foreign Policy Adviser.[45] In 2001 and 2002, of about a dozen staff in OD Sec, just two had any responsibility for Iraq.[46] In both cases, Iraq was only part of their job.

---

[38] Private hearing, 18 June 2010, page 23.
[39] Private hearing, 18 June 2010, page 27.
[40] Private hearing, 22 June 2010, pages 42-52.
[41] Private hearing, 3 June 2010, pages 21-27.
[42] Statement McKane, 8 December 2010, page 1.
[43] Later renamed the Foreign and Defence Policy Secretariat (F&DP Sec) and now part of the National Security Secretariat).
[44] Public hearing Manning, 30 November 2009, pages 44-45.
[45] Public hearing Sheinwald, Sawers, Bowen, 16 December 2009, page 15.
[46] Public hearing McKane, 19 January 2011, pages 2-3.

The Ad Hoc Group on Iraq

61. OD Sec chaired the cross-Whitehall Ad Hoc Group on Iraq (AHGI), which met for the first time on 20 September 2002.[47] The AHGI was the principal Whitehall co-ordination mechanism for non-military Iraq planning until the creation of the inter-departmental IPU in February 2003.

62. The origin and purpose of the AHGI are addressed in greater detail later in this Section.

63. The MOD participated in the AHGI but its own post-conflict military planning was not part of the AHGI process.

The Department for International Development

64. Within DFID the Iraq Team in Middle East and North Africa Department included advisers with expertise on conflict, humanitarian assistance, governance, infrastructure, economics and social development who provided analysis to inform decisions.[48] The DFID Iraq Team worked closely with the FCO and drew on the FCO's Iraq-related research and analysis.

65. Advisers were drawn from the relevant DFID professional cadres with consultants brought in to provide advice on specific issues and projects where required.

66. In addition, DFID's Conflict and Humanitarian Affairs Department (CHAD) provided specific policy and operational advice on Iraq.

67. DFID's August 2002 review of northern Iraq drew on a combination of DFID papers and consultations with UN agencies, non-governmental organisations (NGOs) and western European donor countries.[49]

68. The DFID desktop analysis of central and southern Iraq, completed in October 2002, was produced without consulting the UN, NGOs or bilateral partners because of restrictions on external contacts by DFID officials, but did draw widely on external (including UN) publications.[50]

---

[47] Minute Drummond to Manning, 23 September 2002, 'Ad Hoc Group on Iraq'.
[48] Email DFID to Iraq Inquiry Secretariat, 19 June 2013, 'Iraq Inquiry new queries'.
[49] Minute CHAD Operations Team [junior official] to [DFID junior official], 8 August 2002, 'Northern Iraq Desktop Review and Background Briefing Document' attaching Paper Conflict and Humanitarian Affairs Department, July 2002, 'Northern Iraq Desktop Review and Background Briefing Document'.
[50] Email DFID [junior official] to Fernie, 17 October 2002, 'CSI analysis' attaching Paper Conflict and Humanitarian Affairs Department, October 2002, 'Central/southern Iraq humanitarian situation analysis'.

69. Sir Suma Chakrabarti, DFID Permanent Secretary from 2002 to 2008, told the Inquiry that DFID's knowledge of Iraq in 2002 was "pretty scanty". It had not itself implemented humanitarian programmes in Iraq in the period leading up to the invasion, working instead through the UN agencies, NGOs and the International Committee of the Red Cross (ICRC).[51]

UK international development policy and the Department for International Development

Between 1979 and 1997, the UK's international development programme was managed by the Overseas Development Administration (ODA), a "wing" of the FCO. The Overseas Development and Cooperation Act 1980 allowed aid funds to be used for a wide variety of purposes, including supporting political, industrial and commercial objectives.[52]

A separate Department for International Development (DFID), headed by a Cabinet Minister, replaced the ODA in 1997.[53] Its mission was to "refocus [UK] international development efforts on the elimination of poverty and encouragement of economic growth which benefits the poor". That was to be achieved by focusing on the eight Millennium Development Goals:

- eradicate extreme poverty and hunger;
- achieve universal primary education;
- promote gender equality and empower women;
- reduce child mortality;
- improve maternal health;
- combat HIV and AIDS, malaria and other diseases;
- ensure environmental sustainability;
- develop a global partnership for development.[54]

DFID's mission was enshrined in law through the International Development Act (IDA), which came into force in July 2002.[55] The IDA required that all programmes and projects must either further sustainable development or promote the welfare of people and be likely to contribute to the reduction of poverty.

In 2002, DFID adopted a target to increase the proportion of its bilateral aid going to low income countries from 78 percent to 90 percent (the so-called "90:10" target).[56]

In 2002/03 nearly half DFID's resources were spent through multilateral agencies. The largest parts were the UK's share of European Community development assistance and contributions to the World Bank, regional development banks and the UN agencies.[57]

---

[51] Public hearing, 8 December 2009, Page 9.
[52] Barder, Owen, *Reforming Development Assistance: Learning from the UK experience*. CGD Working Paper No.50, October 2005.
[53] UK Government, *White Paper on International Development*, 1997.
[54] DFID, *Departmental Report 2003*, page 141.
[55] DFID, *Departmental Report 2003*, page 9.
[56] DFID, *Departmental Report 2003*, page 105.
[57] DFID, *Departmental Report 2003*, page 106.

US and UK planning machinery

70. US planning machinery was reorganised a number of times during 2002 and 2003:

- Before August 2002, two separate planning processes operated in parallel in the State Department and the Department of Defense (DoD).

- Between August 2002 and January 2003, greater inter-agency co-ordination was loosely overseen by an Executive Steering Group of the National Security Council (NSC). The US Agency for International Development (USAID) was brought into the planning process for the first time.

- From January 2003, all post-conflict planning was consolidated under Mr Donald Rumsfeld, US Secretary of Defense.[58]

71. The UK introduced significant changes to its planning machinery in September 2002 and February 2003, in part to reflect US reorganisation:

- Until September 2002, a tightly held process was largely confined to No.10 and the MOD, with some work in the FCO and limited Whitehall co-ordination through the MOD-based Pigott Group (described later in this Section) and the Cabinet Office OD Sec.

- Between September 2002 and February 2003, the AHGI co-ordinated Whitehall planning at official level. DFID, the Treasury and other departments were brought into the planning process for the first time. The MOD attended the AHGI, but planning for military operations continued on a separate track.

- From February 2003, the inter-departmental Iraq Planning Unit (IPU), located in the FCO, but including staff from the MOD and DFID, was responsible for Whitehall planning for civilian aspects of post-conflict Iraq, with the MOD continuing to lead on military planning.

72. Those changes are described in more detail later in this Section and in Section 6.5.

The US approach to nation-building

73. The future President Bush expressed his opposition to US military involvement in post-conflict nation-building during the 2000 US presidential election.

74. In October 2000, Governor George W Bush cited the US military intervention in Somalia in 1992 and 1993 as an example of why the US military should not be involved in nation-building.[59] He said that what had started as a humanitarian mission:

"… changed into a nation-building mission, and that's where the mission went wrong. The mission was changed. And as a result, our nation paid a price. And so

---

[58] Bowen SW Jr. *Hard Lessons: The Iraq Reconstruction Experience.* U.S. Government Printing Office, 2009.
[59] Commission on Presidential Debates, 11 October 2000, *October 11, 2000 Debate Transcript: The Second Gore-Bush Presidential Debate.*

I don't think our troops ought to be used for what's called nation-building. I think our troops ought to be used to fight and win a war. I think our troops ought to be used to help overthrow the dictator when it's in our best interests. But in this case it was a nation-building exercise, and same with Haiti. I wouldn't have supported either."

75. Dr Condoleezza Rice, who was Governor Bush's adviser on national security before becoming President Bush's National Security Advisor, explained that Governor Bush was proposing a new division of labour in NATO:

"The United States is the only power that can handle a showdown in the Gulf, mount the kind of force that is needed to protect Saudi Arabia and deter a crisis in the Taiwan Straits. And extended peacekeeping detracts from our readiness for these kinds of missions."[60]

76. Dr Rice stated:

"Carrying out civil administration and police functions is simply going to degrade the American capability to do the things America has to do. We don't need to have the 82nd Airborne escorting kids to kindergarten."

77. Similar views were held by Mr Rumsfeld, US Secretary of Defense from 2001 to 2006.

78. In his memoir, Mr Rumsfeld described his views before the invasion of Iraq as "straightforward".[61] The US goal was:

"... to help the Iraqis put in place a government that did not threaten Iraq's neighbours, did not support terrorism, was respectful to the diverse elements of Iraqi society, and did not proliferate weapons of mass destruction. Period ...

"As soon as we had set in motion a process, I thought it important that we reduce the American military role in reconstruction and increase assistance from the United Nations and other willing coalition countries."

79. Mr Rumsfeld added:

"I recognized the Yankee can-do attitude by which American forces took on tasks that locals would be better off doing themselves. I did not think resolving other countries' internal political disputes, paving roads, erecting power lines, policing streets, building stock markets, and organizing democratic governmental bodies were missions for our men and women in uniform."

80. The US adopted the minimalist approach in Afghanistan, where military action began on 7 October 2001.

---

[60] *The New York Times*, 21 October 2000, *The 2000 Campaign: The Military; Bush Would Stop US Peacekeeping in Balkan Fights*.
[61] Rumsfeld D. *Known and Unknown: A Memoir.* Sentinel, 2011.

81. In April 2002, Sir Christopher Meyer, British Ambassador to the US, warned of the need to learn the lessons from Afghanistan, where "US fear of getting sucked into nation-building" and Secretary Rumsfeld's insistence on a "minimalist approach" threatened failure.[62]

82. In a speech in New York on 14 February 2003, described in more detail in Section 6.5, Secretary Rumsfeld drew lessons for Iraq from the US experience of nation-building in Afghanistan:

> "Afghanistan belongs to the Afghans. The objective is not to engage in what some call nation-building. Rather it is to help the Afghans so they can build their own nation. This is an important distinction. In some nation-building exercises well-intentioned foreigners … can create a dependency."[63]

83. Sir David Manning told the Inquiry:

> "… it's quite clear throughout 2002, and indeed throughout 2003, that it is the Pentagon, it's the military, who are running this thing …
>
> "… Bush had this vision of a new Middle East. You know, we are going to change Iraq, we are going to change Palestine, and it's all going to be a new Middle East.
>
> "But there were … big flaws in this argument. One is they won't do nation-building. They think this is a principle. So if you go into Iraq, how are you going to achieve this new Iraq? And the military certainly don't think it's their job."[64]

84. *Hard Lessons* characterised US planning for post-conflict Iraq between autumn 2001 and early 2003 as a "tense interplay" between the DoD and the State Department.[65] Many in the DoD anticipated US forces being greeted as liberators who would be able leave Iraq within months, with no need for the US to administer the functions of Iraq's government after major combat operations. The State Department judged that rebuilding Iraq would require "a US commitment of enormous scope" over several years.

Initial UK consideration of post-Saddam Hussein Iraq

85. In his Chicago speech of 22 April 1999, Mr Blair listed five considerations to guide decisions on military intervention in another country. Those included being prepared for the long term: "we cannot simply walk away once the fight is over".

---

[62] Telegram 451 Washington to FCO London, 1 April 2002, 'PM's Visit to Texas: Bush and the War on Terrorism'.
[63] US Department of Defense, 14 February 2003, *Speech: Beyond Nation Building*.
[64] Private hearing, 24 June 2010, pages 42-43.
[65] Bowen SW Jr. *Hard Lessons: The Iraq Reconstruction Experience.* U.S. Government Printing Office, 2009.

86. During 2001, UK officials began to consider the possible shape of Iraq after the departure of Saddam Hussein.

87. At that stage, the UK assumption was that the most likely successor to Saddam Hussein was another Sunni strongman.

88. A number of concerns emerged during initial exchanges:

- **the long-term implications of military action;**
- **US support for the Iraqi opposition;**
- **the dilapidated state of Iraq's infrastructure;**
- **the risks of de-Ba'athification; and**
- **the absence of obvious successors to Saddam Hussein.**

89. In his memoir, Mr Blair stated that the final part of his speech to the House of Commons on 18 March 2003, in which he set out the moral case for action against Saddam Hussein, echoed his Chicago speech of 22 April 1999.[66]

90. In the Chicago speech, described in more detail in Section 1.1, Mr Blair had raised the importance of being prepared for the long term after military intervention.[67]

91. In a reference to international security, Mr Blair identified "two dangerous and ruthless men" as the cause of "many of our problems": Saddam Hussein and Slobodan Milošević (President of the Federal Republic of Yugoslavia), both of whom had waged "vicious campaigns against sections of their own community". Instead of enjoying its oil wealth, Iraq had been "reduced to poverty, with political life stultified through fear".

92. Mr Blair set out "five major considerations" to guide a decision on when and whether the international community should intervene militarily in other countries, including:

"... are we prepared for the long term? In the past, we talked too much of exit strategies. But having made a commitment we cannot simply walk away once the fight is over; better to stay with moderate numbers of troops than return for repeat performances with large numbers."

93. Mr Blair sent a draft 'Contract with the Iraqi People' to President Bush in December 2001.

94. In autumn 2000, the Government began a review of the UK's Iraq policy. That process, which continued into 2001, is addressed in detail in Section 3.1.

---

[66] Blair T. *A Journey*. Hutchinson, 2010.
[67] Speech, 23 April 1999, Tony Blair, *Doctrine of the International Community*.

95. During 2001, on the initiative of Mr Robin Cook, the Foreign Secretary, the UK Government worked on a draft 'Contract with the Iraqi People' intended to deliver a clear statement on the steps the international community would take to restore and rehabilitate Iraq in the event of Saddam Hussein's departure (see Box below).[68]

The 'Contract with the Iraqi People'

The 'Contract with the Iraqi People' made clear that Iraq could not be re-integrated into the international community without fundamental change in the behaviour of Saddam Hussein's regime, but stopped short of calling directly for the regime's overthrow.[69] It was designed "to appeal to regional states and to signal to any successor regime the sort of relationship with the international community that would be in prospect".

The last (December 2001) version of the text seen by the Inquiry stated:

"We want to work with the International Community to enhance stability and security in the Gulf region. We are committed to maintenance of Iraq's sovereignty and territorial integrity within its current borders.

"We want to work with an Iraq which respects the rights of its people, lives at peace with its neighbours and which observes international law. We want to see Iraq's full integration into the International Community.

"The Iraqi people have a right to live in a society based on the rule of law, free from repression, murder, torture and arbitrary arrest; to enjoy respect for human rights, economic freedom and prosperity.

"For all this to happen the Iraqi regime must abide by its obligations under international law …

"The record of the current regime … suggests that its priorities remain elsewhere. The regime must end its mistreatment of the Iraqi people and be held to account for its war crimes. We must ensure that the Iraqi people have access to information not controlled by the regime. Those who wish to promote change in Iraq deserve our support.

"Until such time as Iraq is able to rejoin the international community we will continue to ensure that it is not in a position to threaten its neighbours and that there are tight controls on its ability to build up its military and WMD capability. We will also endeavour to minimise the impact of these controls on the Iraqi people."

The 'Contract' set out objectives to be pursued once Iraq rejoined the international community:

• support for an international reconstruction programme for Iraq;

• rebuilding political relations with the rest of the world;

---

[68] Minute MED [junior official] to Goulty, 7 June 2001, 'Iraq Basket III: The Opposition And Regime Change' attaching Paper Middle East Department, 7 June 2001, 'Iraq: Policy Towards The Opposition' and Annex, 'Contract with the Iraqi People'.
[69] Letter McDonald to Tatham, 3 December 2001, 'Iraq: Options' attaching Paper [unattributed and undated], 'Contract with the Iraqi People'.

- pursuit of growth-orientated economic policies with International Monetary Fund (IMF) and World Bank support;
- integration into the region and an application to join the World Trade Organization (WTO);
- promotion of investment in Iraq's oil industry;
- establishment of a comprehensive retraining programme for Iraqi professionals, academic exchanges and scholarships;
- promotion of an EU aid/trade package.

Many elements of the 'Contract' were incorporated into the first draft of the FCO's 'Vision for Iraq and the Iraqi People', produced in October 2002 and addressed later in this Section.

96. On 3 December 2001, in response to a request from Mr Blair for "a note on the options for dealing with Iraq", Mr Simon McDonald, Principal Private Secretary to Mr Jack Straw, the Foreign Secretary, advised No.10 that:

> "A strategy to deal with a WMD threat will require ratcheting up our present policy of containment … We should encourage and support the Iraqi opposition. We could mount a higher profile campaign on the issue of war crimes and consider the options for an international tribunal to try Saddam and his principal lieutenants. We could set out a vision of post-Saddam Iraq by deploying a 'Contract with the Iraqi People'."[70]

97. The other issues addressed in Mr McDonald's letter are considered in Section 3.1.

98. On 4 December, Mr Blair sent President Bush a paper, 'The War against Terrorism: The Second Phase', which was delivered by Sir David Manning (see Section 3.1).[71]

99. The key points relating to Iraq included the need for "a strategy for regime change which builds over time" and might include supporting opposition groups, and setting out an agenda for a post-Saddam Hussein Iraq (the FCO's 'Contract with the Iraqi People').

100. In December 2001, an attempt was made by a senior Republican close to the Pentagon to persuade Mr Kevin Tebbit, MOD PUS, that the opposition Iraqi National Congress (INC) could be a force to be reckoned with, "sufficient to cause an Iraqi response and enable the US to take supportive military action" (see Section 3.1).[72]

101. On 13 December, Mr Tebbit commissioned an analysis of that thesis, which he expected would "show it to be flawed".[73]

---

[70] Letter McDonald to Tatham, 3 December 2001, 'Iraq: Options' attaching Paper, 'Contract with the Iraqi People'.
[71] Note [Blair to Bush], 4 December 2001, 'The War against Terrorism: The Second Phase'.
[72] Minute PS/PUS [MOD] to PS/CDI, 13 December 2001, 'Iraq: is there a 'Northern Alliance'?'
[73] Minute PS/PUS [MOD] to PS/CDI, 13 December 2001, 'Iraq: is there a 'Northern Alliance'?'

102. In its response on 14 January 2002, the DIS concluded that the INC's weaknesses far outweighed its strengths and that it would have no chance of overthrowing the regime.[74]

103. On 21 December 2001, in the context of discussions on the sustainability of US/UK joint patrols to enforce the NFZs in Iraq, Mr Geoff Hoon, the Defence Secretary, asked MOD officials for advice on options for future military action against Iraq and their "political, legal and military implications" (see Section 6.1).[75]

104. Dr Simon Cholerton, a junior official in Overseas Secretariat (Sec(O)), replied on 24 January 2002.[76] He focused on options for patrolling the NFZs, but also addressed the issue of wider action against Iraq. Dr Cholerton emphasised that neither the MOD nor the FCO had seen any "detailed US planning". Work on policy options, at both military and political levels, was continuing in the US but "little, if anything has been shared with the UK". He advised that the "initial assessment of the efficacy (never mind the legality) of military action to effect regime change is that it is poor".

105. Dr Cholerton explained that work commissioned by Mr Tebbit in December 2001 had addressed the strengths and weaknesses of the INC. In the MOD's view:

> "There is no [Afghan] Northern Alliance equivalent in Iraq who could take advantage of precision bombing – nor is it obvious that a successor regime would be an improvement on the existing one. In the absence of any detailed US planning … it is very difficult to comment further."

106. In January and February 2002, the DIS in London and junior officials based at the British Embassy Amman produced a number of reports on the state of Iraq's politics, economy and society.

107. The DIS reports painted a bleak picture of the state of Iraq's infrastructure and highlighted the degree of inter-connectedness between the Ba'ath Party and Iraq's armed forces and civil bureaucracy.

108. The British Embassy Amman reported that foreign diplomats based in Baghdad were agreed that, without massive external commitment on the ground or the continuation of "the current system of order", there was a risk that regime change would destabilise Iraq.

109. In mid-January 2002, the DIS reported on Iraq's infrastructure.[77] With the exception of road and rail transport, the picture was comprehensively bleak. Services had been degraded substantially in the Iran-Iraq war and the 1991 Gulf Conflict. Repairs

---

[74] Minute PS/CDI to PS/PUS [MOD], 14 January 2002, 'Iraq: Regime Change and the Iraqi National Congress'.

[75] Minute Williams to Sec(O)1, 21 December 2001, 'Iraq'.

[76] Minute Cholerton to APS/Secretary of State [MOD], 24 January 2002, 'Iraq: No Fly Zones'.

[77] Paper DIS, 18 January 2002, 'Infrastructure Briefing Memorandum: Iraq'.

since then had been minimal. The DIS assessed that theoretical power generation capacity was about 10,000 megawatts (MW), but that the "practical limit" was about 5,000 MW, well below "even the most basic demand". Power cuts were widespread and prolonged. The report stated that the UN had begun extensive works to rehabilitate the transmission network.

110. The DIS cited "a recent UN report" which suggested the Iraqi oil industry had declined seriously over the previous 18 months and that "urgent measures" needed to be taken to avoid yet more deterioration of oil wells and petroleum infrastructure. Of 12 oil refineries in Iraq, only three were operating, inefficiently and unreliably. Pipelines in Iraq had not been repaired since 1991 and oil distribution was by road.

111. On Iraq's water and sewerage systems, the DIS assessed that:

"... despite recent heavy investment into modernisation and extension of municipal water systems, the water supply and sanitation sectors in Iraq are in a state of continuous deterioration."

112. The DIS reported that, across Iraq, power outages and damage to water pipes meant a substantial proportion of piped water was routinely lost and that the water supply was known to be affected by sewage leaks. There were marked differences between urban areas, where 96 percent of the population had access to safe, potable water, and rural areas, where the figure was 48 percent. In particular, Basra province was "chronically short" of drinkable water, with treatment plants working at less than 60 percent of capacity.

113. The sewerage system was in very poor condition. Sewage treatment, even in Baghdad, was "virtually non-existent", with the few treatment plants that were functioning operating at less than a third of capacity. Sanitary conditions were deteriorating because of indiscriminate dumping of sewage and industrial and medical waste.

114. The DIS warned that, throughout Iraq, water supplies were:

"... contaminated by pathogenic bacteria, parasites and viruses. Given the shortages of essential treatment chemicals, deployed forces could not rely on local water supplies as a source of safe, potable water."

115. A second DIS report, in late January, stated that the Ba'ath Party, the Iraqi civil bureaucracy and the armed forces were intertwined: "every government ministry (as well as state labour organisations, youth and student organisations and media organisations) has within it, at each level, a parallel Ba'ath Party structure".[78]

---

[78] Paper DIS, 1 February 2002, 'The Iraqi Ba'ath Party – its history, ideology and role in regime security'.

116. The second report concluded:

"… any 'regime insider' succeeding Saddam would find the functional roles of the Party indispensable in administering the state and controlling the populace. One can therefore assume that, unless a fundamental political change accompanies the succession to Saddam, the Ba'ath Party will continue in its present role. Were a figure outside the inner circle of the regime to take power (such as a senior military officer), the future of the party would be open to question."

117. The paper provided details of eight ranks in the Ba'ath Party. The three most senior, in ascending order, were: *Udw Firqa* (Division Leader); *Udw Shu'ba* (Section Leader); and *Udw Fara'* (Branch Leader). Party membership was estimated at between 600,000 and 700,000, four percent of the Iraqi population.

118. The earliest UK consideration of options for dealing with the Ba'ath Party in a post-Saddam Hussein Iraq seen by the Inquiry appeared in an MOD paper on UK military strategic thinking in mid-June 2002, described later in this Section.

119. The DIS papers on infrastructure and the Ba'ath Party were included in Mr Blair's summer reading pack at the end of July.

120. Much of the material in the infrastructure paper was incorporated into a DIS report on Basra in March 2003 (see Section 6.5).

121. In January 2002, the British Embassy Amman reported on the economic situation in Iraq, drawing on a seven-day visit to Iraq by an Embassy junior official.[79] Changes to the Oil-for-Food (OFF) programme had led to improvements to Baghdad's infrastructure and the provision of some essential services, although "underlying poverty" remained and power cuts continued. There were signs that the private sector was picking up. A "free market" was well established in the public sector: a nurse receiving only US$3 a month from the Iraqi government might expect to earn US$250 a month by charging patients. The situation was very different outside Baghdad, where the standard of living in the countryside did not seem to be improving: "Many people, particularly in the south, are dependent on the monthly ration."

122. In separate reports on Iraqi politics, religion and society, the official reported that:

- Unemployment in Iraq was believed to be more than 25 percent and underemployment affected almost half the population.[80]
- The Iraqi Christian community was concerned that it risked marginalisation, with some senior figures worrying about what would happen to their community if the current Iraqi regime fell or changed.

---

[79] Telegram 21 Amman to FCO London, 24 January 2002, 'Iraq: Economic'.
[80] Teleletter Amman [junior official] to MED [junior official], 24 January 2002, 'Iraq: Religion/Society'.

- There was "a large thriving diplomatic, UN and NGO community established in Baghdad". If the UK hoped to tap into that it would be necessary for officials to visit more frequently.[81]

123. A fourth report, on regime change, stated:

- Regime change was being discussed "frequently and openly by many diplomats, and by some Iraqis too".

- The assumption in the diplomatic community in Baghdad was that there would be military action and that, as a result, the regime would be toppled.

- It was agreed by "all" that there was a risk of destabilisation of the country if there were not either a "massive external commitment on the ground" or a continuation of the "current system of order" following regime change.

- "Concerns about an Arab or Islamic backlash against a large Western presence seem unfounded. The Iraqi society is already lapping up whatever American culture it can get – Coca Cola, Western clothes, Western music, Western films and British football ..."[82]

124. The February round-up from Amman stated that there had recently been a significant turnover of senior staff within the Iraqi Ministry of Foreign Affairs, with all under secretaries removed in the name of combating corruption.[83] It also reported:

"... continued apathy on the streets. Despite the feeling that something is really going to happen this time, those who can run have already done so. There is little to do except watch the space over Baghdad."

Preparations for Mr Blair's meeting with President Bush at Crawford, 6 April 2002

125. After President Bush's State of the Union address on 29 January 2002 (the "axis of evil" speech), UK policy makers began to consider more closely the objectives and possible consequences of military action in Iraq.

126. Mr Blair sought further advice on what might follow Saddam Hussein before meeting President Bush at Crawford on 6 April 2002.

127. On 19 February, the Cabinet Office commissioned papers for Mr Blair's planned meeting with President Bush after Easter (see Section 3.2).[84]

128. On 20 February, Mr Alan Goulty, FCO Director Middle East and North Africa, produced a paper on contingency planning in the event of military action against

---

[81] Teleletter Amman [junior official] to MED [junior official], 24 January 2002, 'Iraq: Political'.
[82] Teleletter Amman [junior official] to MED [junior official], 24 January 2002, 'Iraq: Regime Change'.
[83] Teleletter Amman [junior official] to MED [junior official], 5 March 2002, 'Iraq: Feb sitrep'.
[84] Minute McKane to Manning, 19 February 2002, 'Papers for the Prime Minister'.

Iraq.[85] He warned of the need for "a plan to address the humanitarian consequences" if military action were to force the withdrawal of UN and NGO staff and suggested that the information campaign to make the case for war should "highlight our commitment to helping the Iraqi people before, during and after any action".

129. Mr John Sawers, British Ambassador to Egypt, who had been closely associated with the development of the UK's policy on Iraq as Mr Blair's Private Secretary for Foreign Affairs, responded to Mr Goulty's minute with a teleletter to Sir Michael Jay and senior colleagues offering his views on the direction of policy.[86]

130. In Mr Sawers' view, the UK needed to say "clearly and consistently that our goal is Regime Change – for the sake of stability in the Middle East, for the Iraqi people, and for the goal of controlling the spread of WMD".

131. Mr Sawers argued that:

"... by associating ourselves with Bush's heartfelt objective of seeing Saddam removed, we will be given more houseroom in Washington to ask the awkward questions about how.

"And there are many such questions. What is the plan? How long would it take for a direct confrontation to succeed? How do we retain the support of our regional friends meanwhile? ... If we were to build up the Kurds and Shia as proxies, what assurances would we have to give them that we would not let them down yet again? How would we keep the Iranians from meddling? How do we preserve Iraq's territorial integrity ...? How would we provide for stability after Saddam and his cronies were killed?"

132. On 27 February, Mr Webb warned Mr Hoon of the importance of establishing clear strategic objectives before taking a decision on military action against Iraq.[87] In advice on possible responses to President Bush's State of the Union address, he cautioned against ruling out UK participation in military action against Iraq, "if that is the only way to stem the tide of WMD proliferation and a worthwhile and legal option exists at the time". Mr Webb added:

"Before assessing military options we should need to be clear about the strategic objectives ...

"It is not easy to see the satisfactory end states which should be the objective of military operations."

133. A JIC Assessment of 27 February reached the view that, without direct intervention on the ground, the Iraqi opposition would be unable to overthrow Saddam Hussein's regime (see Section 6.1).

---

[85] Minute Goulty to Fry, 20 February 2002, 'Military Action Against Iraq: Issues'.
[86] Teleletter Sawers to Jay, 21 February 2002, 'Iraq: Policy'.
[87] Minute Webb to PS/Secretary of State [MOD], 27 February 2002, 'Axis of Evil'.

134. The JIC produced its Assessment, 'Iraq: Saddam under the Spotlight', addressing "Saddam's threat perceptions and internal position: whether he is secure, what opposition he faces, and what he is doing to try and avoid the internal and international threats he faces", on 27 February.[88]

135. The JIC considered that it was "absolutely clear" that the Kurds and Shia "would not show their hand until US resolve to overthrow Saddam". There was "no obvious leader" among those groups who was "capable of unifying the opposition" and had "credibility and popular appeal inside Iraq". No likely replacement for Saddam Hussein from within the regime had been identified, but the JIC stated that, in the event of internal change, it was "likely that any successor would be autocratic and drawn from the Sunni military elite".

136. The DIS issued a paper on possible US military options for removing Saddam Hussein on 5 March.

137. The paper reiterated that the only viable, long-term successor to Saddam Hussein would come from within the Sunni security/military structure. A US attempt to create a more equitable long-term distribution of power in Iraq would require massive and lengthy commitment.

138. At the request of Air Marshal Joe French, Chief of Defence Intelligence (CDI), the DIS produced a paper on 5 March examining US military options for removing Saddam Hussein over the next 12 months.[89] The paper is described in more detail in Section 6.1.

139. In the list of key judgements, the paper stated:

"The UK intelligence community has consistently assessed that the only viable, long-term successor to Saddam will come from within the Sunni security/military structure. Such a figure is unlikely to command popular support among the Shia or Kurdish populations and would be forced (and probably inclined) to run Iraq along autocratic lines. Iraq will remain a unitary state, but many of the long-term problems of Iraq will not disappear with Saddam."

140. The paper described the Iraqi opposition in exile:

"The Iraqi National Congress (INC), based in London, remains the main umbrella opposition grouping. Both Kurdish factions (KDP [Kurdistan Democratic Party] and PUK [Patriotic Union of Kurdistan]) are represented along with various monarchist and independent Shia factions. SCIRI [Supreme Council for Islamic Revolution in Iraq] is not a member ... Current INC 'leader' Ahmad Chalabi is a London-based Iraqi Shia who is mistrusted by regional powers and many within his own movement – he has little credibility in Iraq. Chalabi's prominence owes much to his success in handling the US media. Republican politicians ... see him as a

---

[88] JIC Assessment, 27 February 2002, 'Iraq: Saddam under the Spotlight'.
[89] Paper DIS, 5 March 2002, 'Politico Military Memorandum, Removing Saddam'.

credible opposition figure and CIA have not been engaged with the INC since 1996. Indeed as it is currently organised the INC is less than the sum of its parts. **We assess that it would have a nugatory role in any regime change scenario** – US are well aware that the INC (and other exile groups) are completely penetrated by Iraqi intelligence."

141. The concluding section addressed Iraq after Saddam Hussein:

"We assess that despite potential instability Iraq will remain a unitary state. But many of Iraq's structural problems will remain. Sunni hegemony, the position of the Kurds and Shia, enmity with Kuwait, infighting among the elite, autocratic rule and anti-Israeli sentiment will not disappear with Saddam. We should also expect considerable anti-Western sentiment among a populace that has experienced ten years of sanctions.

"A US attempt to create a more equitable long-term distribution of power in Iraq would require massive and lengthy commitment. Modern Iraq has been dominated politically, militarily and socially by the Sunni. To alter that would entail re-creation of Iraq's civil, political and military structures. That would require a US-directed transition of power (ie US troops occupying Baghdad) and support thereafter. Ten years seems a not unrealistic time span for such a project."

142. The paper was sent to Mr Hoon, the Chiefs of Staff, Sir Kevin Tebbit, Mr Webb, Lieutenant General Sir Anthony Pigott (Deputy Chief of the Defence Staff (Commitments)) and a small number of other individuals. It was also sent to Mr Scarlett and the Assessments Staff, Mr Tom Dodd (OD Sec), Dr Amanda Tanfield (Head of Iraq Section in MED) and the Secret Intelligence Service (SIS).

143. The paper was later included in the pack of reading material on Iraq for Mr Blair sent to No.10 by Mr Scarlett on 1 August.

144. On 8 March, the Cabinet Office raised the potential long-term consequences of a full-scale military campaign in Iraq in a paper preparing the ground for the meeting between Mr Blair and President Bush in Crawford, Texas, on 6 April.

145. The 'Iraq: Options Paper', addressed in more detail in Section 3.2, was commissioned by Sir David Manning and co-ordinated by OD Sec.[90] It was sent to Mr Blair by Sir David Manning on 8 March, as part of the collection of "background briefs that you asked for" for the meeting with President Bush.

146. The paper was prepared as background. It did not represent agreed interdepartmental advice for Ministers.

---

[90] Minute Manning to Prime Minister, 8 March 2002, 'Briefing for the US'.

147. The 'Iraq: Options Paper' set out three options for bringing about regime change, including a full-scale ground campaign.[91] It identified two options for a successor regime: a Sunni military strongman or "a representative, broadly democratic government". The paper stated: "we need to wait and see which options or combination of options may be favoured by the US government". It warned that achieving a representative, broadly democratic successor government would require "the US and others to commit to nation-building for many years. This would entail a substantial international security force and help with reconstruction."

148. Throughout 2002 and early 2003, the UK remained sceptical about the capacity and credibility of the Iraqi opposition in exile and in Iraq, both as a force for change and as the potential core of a credible post-Saddam Hussein administration.

149. The 'Iraq: Options Paper' stated that:

"Unaided, the Iraqi opposition is incapable of overthrowing the regime. The **external opposition** is weak, divided and lacks domestic credibility. The predominant group is the Iraqi National Congress …

"The **internal opposition** is small and fractured on ethnic and sectarian grounds."

150. On 5 March 2002, Mr Ben Bradshaw, FCO Parliamentary Under Secretary of State, held a meeting with the "Group of Four" (G4) Iraqi opposition parties: the Iraqi National Accord (INA), represented by future Iraqi Prime Minister Dr Ayad Allawi, the KDP, the PUK and SCIRI.[92] The delegation told Mr Bradshaw that "things were moving in Iraq", the people supported regime change and the UK could play a role. Mr Bradshaw stated that the UK wanted to pursue the UN route first.

151. On 12 March, Mr Bradshaw met a delegation from the INC headed by Dr Ahmed Chalabi, at which Dr Chalabi suggested that the INC would like to hold a conference in London to garner international support for planning for a post-Saddam Hussein Iraq.[93]

152. The Inquiry has seen no evidence of any response from Mr Bradshaw.

---

[91] Paper Cabinet Office, 8 March 2002, 'Iraq: Options Paper'.
[92] Minute MED to APS/Mr Bradshaw, 5 March 2002, 'Iraq: Mr Bradshaw's meeting with Iraqi Opposition'.
[93] Minute MED to APS/Mr Bradshaw, 25 March 2002, 'Iraq: Mr Bradshaw's Meeting with Iraqi National Congress, 12 March'.

> ## Government contact with the Iraqi opposition
>
> The Inquiry has seen evidence of four meetings between UK Ministers and the Iraqi opposition in the year before the invasion of Iraq:
>
> - separate meetings with the "Group of Four" (G4) Iraqi opposition parties and the Iraqi National Conference (INC) in March 2002, hosted by Mr Ben Bradshaw, FCO Parliamentary Under Secretary of State;
> - a visit to No.10 by the two leaders of the Iraqi Kurds in December 2002, part of which was attended by Mr Blair;[94] and
> - a meeting between Mr Straw and "Iraqi exiles" in London on 21 February 2003.[95]
>
> At official level, by late 2002, it was UK policy "to stay in touch with the thinking of opposition groups who may have a role to play in shaping a post-Saddam Iraq".[96] "Regular, routine meetings" took place between opposition representatives and junior FCO officials. There were occasional meetings at senior official level.

153. On 15 March, Mr William Patey, Head of MED, sent Mr Straw a paper by Research Analysts on the "nature and role of the opposition to Saddam" commissioned by Sir David Manning.[97]

154. The paper cautioned that the UK's ability to influence or direct the Iraqi opposition was constrained by dependence on contacts with Iraqi exiles. Ten years without diplomatic representation in Iraq meant that the UK knew little about the internal opposition to Saddam Hussein.

155. The paper listed three main problems dealing with the external opposition:

- the absence of a coherent structure, with Western offers of financial support or political backing exacerbating rivalries between groups;
- the absence of Sunni representation in the INC, which was dominated by Kurds and Shia Arabs;
- lack of credibility. Regional governments had no faith in the INC's ability to achieve its goals and high-profile Western support left it open to charges of being a Western stooge.

156. Research Analysts reported few signs of co-ordinated opposition in Iraq, where most organisations were believed to be penetrated by agents of the regime. It concluded that Saddam Hussein's immediate successor was most likely to be a senior Sunni member or ex-member of the Iraqi military.

---

[94] Letter Rycroft to Sinclair, 19 December 2002, 'Iraqi Kurds: Meeting with Prime Minister, 19 December'.
[95] Minute Tanfield to PS/PUS [FCO], 21 February 2003, 'Iraq Morning Meeting: Key Points'.
[96] Telegram 104 FCO London to Amman, 20 November 2002, 'Iraqi Opposition Sitrep'.
[97] Minute Patey to PS [FCO], 15 March 2002, 'Iraq' attaching Paper Research Analysts, 14 March 2002, 'Iraq: the nature and role of the opposition to Saddam Hussein'.

157. US post-conflict planning began to take shape in spring 2002 at meetings of the NSC Deputies Committee[98] involving DoD, the State Department, the CIA and the Pentagon Joint Staff:

"The Deputies Committee focused on three concepts: a liberation model in which Iraqis would quickly take charge through a provisional government; a military administration led by CENTCOM [the US Central Command]; or a civilian transitional authority, perhaps run under UN auspices."[99]

158. What might replace Saddam Hussein's regime was one of the themes of talks between Mr Blair and Vice President Dick Cheney in London on 11 March.

159. The FCO briefing for Mr Blair's meeting with Vice President Cheney on 11 March covered a range of issues.[100] Iraq was highlighted as:

"… the main issue, including for the media given speculation that the US are moving towards early decisions on military action … This will … be an important opportunity … to get a feel for where the debate in Washington stands and what options are emerging."

160. The FCO suggested that the key messages for Mr Cheney on Iraq included:

"Issues arising from regime change on which I [Mr Blair] would welcome your thoughts:

- Assessment of Iraqi Opposition …;
- Require serious movement on MEPP to give us space in which to act;
- Day after issues loom large. Territorial integrity of Iraq important. Likely replacement for Saddam – another Sunni strongman. Establishing representative government would require long term commitment;
- Genuine consultation and construction of convincing legal basis will be important …"[101]

161. Mr Matthew Rycroft, Mr Blair's Private Secretary for Foreign Affairs, advised Mr Blair that he needed Vice President Cheney to give him Washington's latest views on a number of issues, including "what to do on the day after regime change".[102]

---

[98] A committee of the National Security Council (NSC), chaired by the Deputy National Security Advisor (Mr Stephen Hadley from 2001 to 2005) and including the deputies to the members of the NSC. The Deputies Committee is the senior sub-Cabinet inter-agency forum for consideration of policy issues relating to US national security.

[99] Bowen SW Jr. *Hard Lessons: The Iraq Reconstruction Experience.* U.S. Government Printing Office, 2009.

[100] Letter McDonald to Rycroft, 8 March 2002, 'US Vice President's call on the Prime Minister, 11 March'.

[101] Paper [unattributed and undated], 'Visit of US Vice President Dick Cheney 11 March: Iraq'.

[102] Minute Rycroft to Prime Minister, 8 March 2002, 'Lunch with Dick Cheney'.

162. The record of the meeting, described in more detail in Section 3.2, shows that Mr Blair raised several post-conflict issues:

- the need for "a proper strategy for dealing with the Iraqi opposition", one that was better than anything Mr Blair had seen so far;
- the need "to guard against the law of unintended consequences" by building support in the region;
- the need for "an acceptable successor government"; regime change was not enough.[103]

163. After the meeting, Mr Blair commented that he thought the US was still vague about the nature and role of the opposition inside and outside Iraq, and unclear about what would follow Saddam Hussein. He asked for further advice.

164. Sir David Manning raised the issue at a meeting with Dr Rice in Washington on 14 March (see Section 3.2).[104]

165. Sir David recorded that he had "made it clear that we would continue to give strong support to the idea of regime change, but were looking to the US to devise a convincing plan of action. This would also need to answer the question of who would follow Saddam."

166. Sir David Manning told Dr Rice that a series of issues would need to be addressed if the US decided on military action against Iraq. One was whether the US "wanted company". If it wanted the support of a coalition, it would have to address a number of concerns that would be critical in determining the attitude of potential partners:

"… the US would need to:

- mount a public information campaign explaining the nature of Saddam's regime and the threat he posed;
- describe the role that the US envisaged for the UN, and particularly for the weapons inspectors;
- provide a convincing plan setting out how a combination of outside military pressure, and external and internal opposition could topple Saddam; and
- provide an equally convincing blueprint for a post Saddam Iraq … acceptable to its neighbours as well as to its own population.

"… Preparing public opinion and deciding who and what might replace Saddam were tough propositions."

---

[103] Letter Manning to McDonald, 11 March 2002, 'Conversation between the Prime Minister and Vice President Cheney: 11 March 2002'.
[104] Letter Manning to McDonald, 14 March 2002, 'Discussions with Condi Rice on 12-13 March'.

167. Before Mr Blair's meeting with President Bush at Crawford, Mr Hoon, Mr Straw and Sir Christopher Meyer expressed concern about the potential longer-term implications of military action in Iraq.

168. On 22 March, Mr Hoon advised Mr Blair: "If a coalition takes control of Baghdad … it will probably have to stay there for many years."[105]

169. In evidence to the Inquiry, Mr Hoon recalled that he had pointed out that:

"… we had never successfully identified at that stage someone who might replace Saddam Hussein. There was real concern about what Iraq might look like in the aftermath of his regime being removed, and … that debate was a very live debate …"[106]

170. Mr Straw wrote to Mr Blair on 25 March, advising that the Government was a long way from convincing the Parliamentary Labour Party that "the consequence of military action really would be a compliant, law abiding replacement government".[107] On the "big question" of what military action would achieve, there was "a larger hole … than on anything". Mr Straw added: "Iraq has had <u>no</u> history of democracy so no-one has this habit or experience."

171. Sir Christopher Meyer advised on 1 April that President Bush had raised expectations that the US would take military action against Iraq in autumn 2002, but questions were beginning to be asked about the risks.[108]

172. Sir Christopher Meyer reported:

"There is no shortage of Bush insiders who tell us that the die is cast for a regime-change operation of some sort this autumn. But there is now a sense that the Administration are for the first time really staring the hard questions in the face: how much international support is needed: what smart options are available to topple Saddam: above all what happens afterwards. There is a doubt among some – no bigger than a fist sized cloud on the horizon – that Iraq might be too risky politically."

173. Sir Christopher also offered advice on the US approach in Afghanistan, where decisions had been taken:

"… in a very small circle of key officials around the President. Where Rumsfeld (and General [Tommy] Franks [Commander in Chief CENTCOM]) have not been fully engaged, little action has resulted. Many in the Administration recognise that, on the ground, there is a real danger of losing Afghanistan because of a US fear of getting sucked into nation-building. But Rumsfeld has, in effect, blocked all but a minimalist approach."

---

[105] Minute Hoon to Prime Minister, 22 March 2002, 'Iraq'.
[106] Public hearing 19 January 2010, pages 108-109.
[107] Minute Straw to Prime Minister, 25 March 2002, 'Crawford/Iraq'.
[108] Telegram 451 Washington to FCO London, 1 April 2002, 'PM's Visit to Texas: Bush and the War on Terrorism'.

174. Sir Christopher Meyer told the Inquiry that he had advised Mr Blair:

"'There are three things you really need to focus on when you get to Crawford. One is how to garner international support for a policy of regime change, if that is what it turns out to be. If it involves removing Saddam Hussein, how do you do it and when do you do it?' And the last thing I said, which became a kind of theme of virtually all the reporting I sent back to London in that year was, 'Above all … get them to focus on the aftermath, because, if it comes to war and Saddam Hussein is removed, and then …?'"[109]

175. On 2 April, Mr Blair held a meeting at Chequers to prepare for his meeting with President Bush at Crawford (see Section 3.2).

176. No formal record was made of the discussion or who was present.

177. Accounts given by participants suggest that Admiral Sir Michael Boyce (Chief of the Defence Staff (CDS)), Sir Kevin Tebbit (representing Mr Hoon, who was unable to attend), Lt Gen Pigott, Lieutenant General Cedric Delves (senior UK liaison officer at CENTCOM in Tampa, Florida), Sir Richard Dearlove (Chief of SIS), Mr Jonathan Powell (Mr Blair's Chief of Staff), Sir David Manning, Mr Alastair Campbell (Mr Blair's Director of Communications and Strategy) and Mr Scarlett were present.

178. The FCO was not represented.

179. In his diaries, Mr Campbell recorded that Lt Gen Pigott said at the meeting: "post-conflict had to be part of conflict preparation".[110] Mr Campbell added: "There was a discussion about who would replace Saddam and how could we guarantee it would be better. Scarlett said it couldn't be worse."

180. Mr Rycroft told the Inquiry that, around this time: "Undoubtedly the thought was in the Prime Minister's mind that if at the end of this we were going to go down the military intervention route … the aftermath would be many years."[111]

Post-conflict issues after Crawford

181. At Crawford, Texas, on 6 April 2002, Mr Blair and President Bush discussed who might replace Saddam Hussein.

182. There is no evidence that Mr Blair commissioned further work on post-conflict issues after Crawford, or that Mr Straw requested further work from FCO officials.

---

[109] Public hearing, 26 November 2009, pages 27-28.
[110] Campbell A & Hagerty B. *The Alastair Campbell Diaries. Volume 4. The Burden of Power: Countdown to Iraq.* Hutchinson, 2012.
[111] Private hearing, 10 September 2010, page 12.

183. **Mr Hoon commissioned work from MOD officials on military options, to be conducted "on very close hold".**

184. **Limited Whitehall co-ordination took place in the MOD-based Pigott Group.**

185. **In the absence of direction from No.10 after Crawford:**

- **the FCO was effectively sidelined from planning and preparation for possible military action in Iraq at a stage when policy remained fluid and FCO views on strategic direction might have been expected to have most influence;**

- **UK military planning dominated Whitehall consideration of Iraq, with the consequence that any potential UK involvement was considered principally in terms of the military role;**

- **DFID expertise on post-conflict issues was excluded from discussion as strategy took shape;**

- **the systematic research and analysis of post-conflict issues that was needed to underpin UK policy was not commissioned; and**

- **Mr Blair sought to influence US thinking on post-conflict issues with only a broad concept of the post-conflict task and no clearly defined UK negotiating position.**

186. **Many of the failings in UK planning and preparation over the coming year stemmed from those developments.**

187. Mr Blair discussed Iraq with President Bush at Crawford, Texas, on 6 April. The discussions are addressed in more detail in Section 3.2.

188. A three-page record of the discussions on Iraq was circulated on a secret and strictly personal basis by Sir David Manning.[112] Sir David recorded that, among other issues, Mr Blair and President Bush had discussed who might replace Saddam Hussein if action were taken to topple him.

189. Mr Powell told the Inquiry:

"… one of the things that is so interesting is that the Prime Minister was talking at that stage about the things that you would need to do to make this successful … He talked about what would happen on the day after. If you go into Iraq, are you going to be prepared for what happens thereafter? So I think he in many ways listed all the right questions at that stage when he was talking to Bush at Crawford."[113]

---

[112] Letter Manning to McDonald, 8 April 2002, 'Prime Minister's Visit to the United States: 5-7 April'.
[113] Public hearing, 18 January 2010, page 26.

190. In his speech at College Station on 7 April, Mr Blair argued:

"Prevention is better than cure. The reason it would be crazy for us to clear out of Afghanistan once we had finished militarily, is that if it drifts back into instability, the same old problems will re-emerge. Stick at it and we can show, eventually, as in the Balkans, the unstable starts to become stable."[114]

191. Immediately after Crawford, UK officials and the UK military began to define the possible end state after a military operation against Iraq.

192. Section 6.1 describes how consideration of UK military options intensified after Crawford.

193. On 8 April, Mr Hoon discussed Iraq with Adm Boyce and Sir Kevin Tebbit.[115] Afterwards he commissioned further work on potential military options, to be conducted "on very close hold".

194. On 12 April, Mr Webb sent Mr Hoon a "think piece", listing three possible US options for invasion and touching briefly on post-invasion commitments:

"To secure the country subsequently would depend critically on the extent of popular support: but without it how could we justify staying? It is possible that forces would be needed only sufficient to secure a new popular figure from being dislodged by dissident remnants. But we have to be ready for a longer job against an uncertain background of host nation support and regional instability."[116]

195. Mr Webb suggested that:

"… there could be advantage in the MOD doing some discreet internal strategic estimating. This should help us think through what would be the key strategic objectives and end states and the 'centre of gravity' of the situation we need to tackle; and give better shape to redefining potential force packages (within the large region).

…

"Actively to prepare for operations on Iraq would obviously attract interest and possibly reactions … There would come a point at which preparations could apply some valuable pressure on Saddam; or be seen as a natural reaction to prevarication over inspections. In general, however, until that point – say in the summer – we should keep a low profile, confining ourselves to the items that timeline analysis shows need to be got underway to preserve the ability to contribute on time later.

[114] The National Archives, 7 April 2002, *Prime Minister's speech at the George Bush Senior Presidential Library*.
[115] Minute Watkins to PSO/CDS & PS/PUS [MOD], 8 April 2002, 'Iraq'.
[116] Minute Webb to PS/Secretary of State [MOD], 12 April 2002, 'Bush and the War on Terrorism'.

"… The FCO are content for activity to be centred on MOD to preserve the best prospect for dialogue with US DoD. All scoping activity would be confined to the minimum number of named individuals."

196. Sir Kevin Tebbit explained to the Inquiry that: "At this early stage … April 2002, we did not know whether the Americans were going to go for a military option and, if so, which one. So this was very, very preliminary ground clearing."[117]

197. An MOD-led, inter-departmental group of senior officials, headed by Lt Gen Pigott, was established in April 2002. That body, which came to be known as the Pigott Group, considered issues related to UK participation in a US-led ground offensive in Iraq.

198. In spring 2002 the Pigott Group was the FCO's principal forum for contributions to cross-government consideration of post-conflict Iraq.

199. Mr Peter Ricketts, the FCO Political Director and FCO member of the Pigott Group, took responsibility for Whitehall consideration of the UK's desired "end state" for a post-Saddam Hussein Iraq.

200. On 25 April, Mr Peter Ricketts, the FCO Political Director, informed Mr Straw's Private Office, Sir Michael Jay and a small number of other senior FCO officials, that the MOD had established "a small group of senior officials and military planners [the Pigott Group] to think about the issues that would be involved in any military operation in Iraq, as the basis for initial contingency planning in the MOD".[118] Participants included the FCO, Cabinet Office, JIC and Intelligence Agencies.

201. Mr Ricketts described the Group's work as "a sensitive exercise". Participation was being tightly restricted and paperwork would be kept to a minimum, but it was "important that the FCO was involved from the ground floor with MOD thinking".

202. The first meeting of the Pigott Group took place in late April. Mr Ricketts reported that it had covered "mainly the political context, including the implications of the Arab/Israel crisis, attitudes in the Arab states, the risks of Iraq disintegrating and the consequences of that".

203. The meeting also considered how to define the objective, or "end state" of a military operation:

"As we found in the run-up to the Afghanistan operation, defining the objective of an operation is crucial since this defines the scope of the operations and hence the scale of military effort required. The MOD had tried their hand at a definition of the 'end state' which was discussed at length, and I undertook to produce a further version.

---

[117] Public hearing, 3 December 2009, page 15.
[118] Minute Ricketts to Private Secretary [FCO], 25 April 2002, 'Iraq: Contingency Planning'.

"I have now done so. Before feeding it in to the Whitehall [Pigott] group, it would be helpful to know whether the Foreign Secretary thinks we are on the right lines. At this stage, it is only to inform MOD contingency planning: at the right point, these issues would have to be negotiated carefully and at a high level with the Americans, who will have their own priorities. My proposal is as follows:

- 'A stable and law-abiding Iraq, within its present borders, co-operating with the international community, no longer posing a threat to global security or to its neighbours, and abiding by its international obligations on control of its WMD.'"

204. Mr Ricketts reported that the Pigott Group had debated a number of issues related to the end state, including:

"... should there be anything more explicit about a future regime abiding by international norms on the treatment of its own population? I have got 'law-abiding' which is designed to capture that. There is a risk in overloading a definition of the 'end state' with desirable outcomes which cannot be achieved by military means."

205. Mr Ricketts explained that the meeting had commissioned further work on a range of intelligence issues, which would be addressed by the JIC. The military would work on "the likely scale of effort required". He proposed that he or Mr Stephen Wright, Director General Defence and Intelligence, should represent the FCO at future meetings, accompanied by Mr Edward Chaplin (Mr Goulty's successor as Director Middle East and North Africa), who should remain the FCO "point man on Iraq issues".

206. Mr Ricketts made no reference to further contingency planning in the FCO.

207. On 3 May, Mr Ricketts sent a very slightly amended definition of the end state, agreed by Mr Straw, to Mr Webb:

"A stable and law-abiding Iraq, within its present borders, co-operating with the international community, no longer posing a threat to its neighbours or to international security, and abiding by its international obligations on control of its WMD."[119]

208. On 10 May, Lt Gen Pigott advised Mr Hoon that, although his Group was focused on military options, it needed to be supported by thinking on the end state.[120] He explained that the FCO was already engaged on the issue.

209. A revised version of the end state, agreed by Mr Straw and Mr Hoon, was sent to Mr Blair on 31 May and is described later in this Section.

---

[119] Letter Ricketts to Webb, 3 May 2002, 'Iraq: Contingency planning'.
[120] Minute DCDS(C) to APS/Secretary of State [MOD], 10 May 2002, 'Iraq'.

210. Sir Peter Ricketts told the Inquiry:

"We [the Pigott Group] didn't discuss military planning as such. We discussed the implications of military planning for other departments' activities … We worked up in that group an end state which was one of the political implications of any military plan."[121]

211. In early May 2002, the international effort to resolve the India/Pakistan crisis was the FCO's principal foreign policy concern and the major preoccupation for Mr Straw, Sir Michael Jay and Mr Ricketts.

212. Iraq policy was a lower priority and restricted to a small number of officials.

213. Despite those constraints, it fell to the FCO to ensure that the military contingency planning already under way in the MOD was placed in a wider strategic context, and that it took place alongside analysis of non-military options for achieving the desired end state in Iraq.

214. There is no indication that senior FCO officials commissioned such work during spring and early summer 2002.

215. Mr Tom McKane, Deputy Head of OD Sec, was asked by the Inquiry whether the Pigott Group had considered aftermath planning. He explained:

"There wasn't from my recollection much, if any, discussion about the aftermath in terms of infrastructure of the country, the security of the country, or humanitarian or development assistance. That wasn't the focus of these meetings, and I think that it's not really surprising, given that they were meetings being convened in the Ministry of Defence and had quite a defence focus.

"… [T]he focus of everybody at that point was … what is the military plan going to be? What is the form of the UK contribution likely to be? … [U]ntil one had … some resolution on those points the question of precisely what the aftermath was going to be was not something that could be settled."[122]

216. Mr McKane added:

"We had not got to the point at that stage of planning for an aftermath, because there wasn't yet an aftermath to be planned for."

217. In late May, the MOD Strategic Planning Group (SPG) advised that the post-conflict phase of operations had the potential to add significantly to the costs and scale of a UK military commitment in Iraq.

---

[121] Public hearing, 1 December 2009, page 20.
[122] Public hearing, 19 January 2011, pages 61 and 65.

218. On 24 May, the MOD Strategic Planning Group (SPG), headed by Brigadier James Dutton and reporting to Lt Gen Pigott, produced a paper for the Chiefs of Staff on potential UK military commitments.[123] 'Contingency Thinking: Force Generation and Deployment for the Gulf' (see Section 6.1) was circulated to a limited number of named MOD addressees. It aimed to provide sufficient information "to judge what the UK's maximum level of commitment could be in the event of a contingent operation against Iraq, together with appropriate costs and timings".

219. On the post-conflict phase, the paper stated that it might be necessary to maintain force elements in theatre for policing, stabilisation or humanitarian operations, which had the potential to add considerably to the cost and commitments, depending on the end state of the campaign.

220. The emerging findings from the SPG analysis were presented to Mr Hoon on 24 May to report to Mr Blair in advance of a planned meeting with Secretary Rumsfeld in early June.[124]

221. Mr Hoon sent Mr Blair an update on military contingency planning for Iraq on 31 May (see Section 6.1).[125]

222. Mr Hoon's minute was copied to Mr Gordon Brown (Chancellor of the Exchequer), Mr Straw and Sir Richard Wilson (Cabinet Secretary). The minute included a definition of the end state, which it described as "tentative objectives to guide" contingency planning. The definition, agreed with Mr Straw, envisaged:

> "A stable and law-abiding Iraq, within its present borders, co-operating with the international community, no longer posing a threat to its neighbours or international security, abiding by its international obligations on WMD."

223. Mr Hoon advised:

> "In order for us to plan properly we need to know what outcome in Iraq the US would wish to achieve … and when the US might wish to take action. It would also be useful to know how long the US see themselves as remaining engaged in Iraq. Further, we need to clarify the policy basis and legal justification for any action."

224. Mr William Nye, Head of the Treasury Defence, Diplomacy and Intelligence Team, provided a commentary for Mr Brown on 7 June.[126] He pointed out that the MOD had only provided costings for preparing for an operation, not for deploying a force, for a campaign, or for any "follow-up operation". He commented:

> "MOD have understandably given no thought to costs 'after the war' … But there must at least be the possibility of some medium-term deployment for peacekeeping or occupation. If on the scale of the Balkans, it would cost several £100m a year."

---

[123] Paper SPG, 24 May 2002, 'Contingency Thinking: Force Generation and deployment for the Gulf'.
[124] Minute DCDS(C) to PS/Secretary of State [MOD], 24 May 2002, 'Iraq'.
[125] Minute Hoon to Prime Minister, 31 May 2002, 'Iraq'.
[126] Minute Nye to Chancellor, 7 June 2002, 'Iraq: potential costs'.

225. **On 5 June, Mr Blair and Secretary Rumsfeld agreed that the future of Iraq would be an important issue for the international coalition.**

226. Secretary Rumsfeld visited London for talks with Mr Blair and Mr Hoon on 5 June. Mr Blair expressed concern about the possible unintended consequences of any military action. He and Secretary Rumsfeld agreed that the future of Iraq would be an important issue for the international coalition.[127]

227. On 14 June, Mr Chaplin visited Washington with Mr Charles Gray, the Head of MED.[128] The British Embassy reported that US interlocutors from the NSC and State Department had confirmed that the US was "pressing ahead with trying to prepare the Iraqi opposition for regime change" and that Congressional funding had been agreed for the State Department's Future of Iraq Project (see Box below), a series of working groups under Iraqi opposition ownership to look into issues of governance after Saddam Hussein's departure.

228. In response to a US suggestion that successful regime change depended on a clear strategy for the day after, Mr Chaplin proposed that the UK and US should "exchange views on scenarios".

229. That exchange took place in Washington on 6 November and is described later in this section.

The Future of Iraq Project

In October 2001, the US State Department began work on what became known as the Future of Iraq Project.[129] The project was launched publicly in early 2002. It involved a series of working groups of Iraqi exiles and officials from the State Department, each looking at an area of importance to Iraq's future, including justice, education, the economy, infrastructure, the environment and reform of government institutions.[130] The objective was to expand the scope of US post-war planning and provide a common focus for competing exile groups.

The Future of Iraq Project worked independently of the US inter-agency planning process. It developed parallel proposals for post-invasion Iraq that did not contribute to the official US planning effort. According to *Hard Lessons*:

> "The richly developed reports constitute the single most rigorous assessment conducted by the US Government before the war. Although the findings ... did not amount to an operational plan ... [they] contained facts and analysis that could – and in some cases did – inform operational planning."[131]

---

[127] Letter Rycroft to Watkins, 5 June 2002, 'Prime Minister's Meeting with Rumsfeld, 5 June: Iraq'.
[128] Telegram 802 Washington to FCO London, 14 June 2002, 'Iraq: UK/US Talks, 13 June'.
[129] The National Security Archive, Electronic Briefing Book No. 198, 1 September 2006, *New State Department Releases on the "Future of Iraq" Project*.
[130] Bowen SW Jr. *Hard Lessons: The Iraq Reconstruction Experience*. U.S. Government Printing Office, 2009.
[131] Bowen SW Jr. *Hard Lessons: The Iraq Reconstruction Experience*. U.S. Government Printing Office, 2009.

As a whole, the project failed to make a significant impact on US planning:

"... the project's reports did not capture the attention of the State Department's senior decision-makers ... Without a high-level patron, the ... reports lacked the visibility and clout to reach key decision-makers in time."

UK officials were aware of the project, but the Inquiry has seen very little evidence of UK engagement with the working groups or analysis of the final report.

The 1,500 page, 13 volume final report is publicly available in the US National Security Archives.[132] It is a compendium of papers prepared by the different working groups, some agreed by consensus, others not.

The US National Security Archive summary of the project highlights some prescient observations in the final report, including warnings that:

- the period after regime change might provide an opportunity for criminals "to engage in acts of killing, plunder looting, etc.";

- former Ba'athists not re-integrated into society "may present a destabilizing element", especially if unable to find employment;

- a decade of sanctions had resulted in the spread of "endemic corruption and black market activities into every sector of ... economic life" that would be difficult to reverse;

- the relationship between the new Iraqi state and religion was an intractable issue "which ultimately only the people of Iraq can decide on";

- repair of Iraq's electricity grid would be a key determinant of Iraqis' reaction to the presence of foreign forces.

The Economy and Infrastructure Working Group

The final report of the Economy and Infrastructure Working Group provides one example of the range of material generated by the Future of Iraq Project.[133]

Quoting data from the US Department of Energy, the Working Group reported that 85-90 percent of Iraq's national power grid and 20 power stations had been damaged or destroyed in 1991. The UN programme to restore electricity generation in central and southern Iraq to pre-1991 levels required US$10bn, of which $US4.7bn had been allocated from Oil-for-Food (OFF) funds since 1996. US$1.67bn of material had reached Iraq, but only 60 percent had been put to use. In northern Iraq, problems included:

- damage to transmission lines and substations in 1991;

- the need to replace major circuits constructed out of salvaged material after the region's disconnection from the Iraqi national grid in 1991;

---

[132] The National Security Archive, Electronic Briefing Book No. 198, 1 September 2006, *New State Department Releases on the "Future of Iraq" Project*.
[133] US State Department, The Future of Iraq Project, [undated], *Economy and Infrastructure (Public Finance) Working Group*.

- the poor state of repair of the two hydroelectric power stations supplying all the power to two northern governorates;
- lack of investment and maintenance since 1991.

Other issues of concern included:

- an "extremely poor" telecommunications infrastructure that had hindered humanitarian programmes under OFF;
- a water treatment system operating at 50 percent efficiency, resulting in an increase in water-borne disease;
- three years' drought between 1999 and 2001;
- 50 percent unemployment.

The report stated that "every Iraqi seeks new job opportunities that will enable them to provide their households with incomes and provide more food, better clothing, and improved healthcare for their families". It warned:

"Any new war or military confrontation in Iraq could cause further damage to the Iraqi infrastructure and existing weak economy. Furthermore, this would exasperate the high unemployment rates already existing in Iraq. The post-Saddam government has to immediately consider economic initiatives to create new jobs through labor intensive projects."

230. Between June and December 2002, the SPG produced six editions of a paper on UK military strategic thinking.

231. The first, issued on 13 June, identified a "spectrum" of possible post-conflict commitments, where the worst case was "a long period with a large bill" that would represent "a significant burden on defence resources".

232. The paper stated that the post-conflict commitment needed to be "planned and agreed before we embark on military action".

233. On 13 June, the SPG issued a paper on UK military strategic thinking on Iraq to a limited number of senior MOD addressees.[134] The paper was "part of ongoing work developed by a cross-Whitehall Group [the Pigott Group] that has met on a regular basis to exchange ideas and information, and undertake UK contingency thinking … in advance of any detailed consultations with the US."

234. The SPG paper was intended for discussion at a Strategic Think Tank on Iraq held by the Chiefs of Staff on 18 June, for which the MOD has been unable to find a record.[135]

---

[134] Minute Driver to PSO/CDS, 13 June 2002, 'Supporting Paper for COS Strategic Think Tank on Iraq – 18 June' attaching Paper [SPG], 12 June 2002, [untitled].
[135] Letter MOD to Iraq Inquiry Secretariat, 23 May 2012, [untitled].

235. Mr McKane described the 18 June discussion to Sir David Manning as "preparatory to military talks with the US ... at which Tony Pigott and Desmond Bowen [MOD Director General Operational Policy (DG Op Pol)] would represent the UK" (see Section 6.1).[136]

236. The SPG paper set out the desired end state for Iraq in two forms:

- A UK text, substantively unchanged from the version agreed by Mr Straw and Mr Hoon: "A stable and law-abiding Iraq, within present borders, co-operating with the IC [international community], no longer posing a threat to its neighbours or to international security, and abiding by its international obligations on WMD."

- A US version derived from the CENTCOM Iraq plan: "maintenance of Iraq as a viable nation state, disavowing the use of WMD but capable of defending its borders and contributing to the counter balance of Iran". The SPG paper added that US was "determined to achieve a more representative, non-tyrannical government".[137]

237. The SPG stated that the end state "cannot be achieved while the current Iraqi regime remains in power. Consequently, regime change is a necessary step and there is no point in pursuing any strategy that does not achieve this."

238. The paper listed a number of "military/strategic implications" of this approach, including:

"<u>Post-conflict</u>. Need to acknowledge that there will be a post-conflict phase with an associated commitment, manpower and finance bill. Depending on how the regime change is achieved, and the form of the replacement, there is a spectrum of commitment where the worst case is a long period with a large bill."

239. The SPG judged that domination of Iraq's state institutions, security organisations and the officer corps by Sunni Arabs, who constituted just 15 percent of the population, made the country "potentially fundamentally unstable". Iraq was held together by the strong security apparatus. It would require considerable force to break the security structure, but when that happened the regime would "shatter".

240. Three possibilities for regime change were presented:

- removal of Saddam Hussein and key advisers, including his sons, to be replaced by a Sunni strongman;

- removal of Saddam Hussein and "his wider security and governing regime" to be replaced by an "International Presence coupled with a bridging process leading eventually to a broad based coalition"; and

- removal of the entire Ba'athist regime to be replaced by a federated state.

---

[136] Minute McKane to Manning, 18 June 2002, 'Iraq'.
[137] Minute Driver to PSO/CDS, 13 June 2002, 'Supporting Paper for COS Strategic Think Tank on Iraq – 18 June' attaching Paper [SPG], 12 June 2002, [untitled].

241. The section of the paper on post-conflict tasks stated:

"This will depend on how regime change occurs, and what shape the campaign takes to bring about the change. However, key differences between Iraq and recent experience in Afghanistan and Balkans are:

- Iraq is naturally wealthy with significant oil reserves and potential revenue, therefore reconstruction should be self-sufficient, with cash from OFF escrow account providing significant pump priming as compared to Afghanistan or Balkans.
- Iraq has a sound agricultural base ('fertile crescent').
- Educated and able technical, industrial, and managerial population exists.
- Although ethnic suppression has occurred there is limited regional inter-ethnic mixing as compared to Afghanistan and Balkans.
- International intervention is not in tandem with ongoing, and in the case of Afghanistan, prolonged civil war."

242. The paper listed likely short-, medium- and long-term post-conflict military tasks:

"Immediate (0 – 6 months):

- Provide external and internal security, law and order to prevent any potential for inter-ethnic violence, or opportunity for organised crime
- Detention and processing of key regime figures …
- Confine and monitor remaining elements of Iraqi Armed Forces likely to rebel …
- Secure and account for WMD capability (materiel and intellectual)
- Enable humanitarian relief
- Assist in restoration of key infrastructure elements
- Secure oilfields and oil distribution/refining infrastructure
- Negotiate and secure alternative lines of communication (LoC) through Syria/Turkey/Jordan
- Scope of tasks likely to demand large numbers of ground troops, comprehensive C2 [command and control] and air mobility (circa 200,000 plus)

"Medium Term (6 months – 2 plus years)

- Continue to provide both external and internal security, law and order to prevent any potential for inter-ethnic violence, or opportunity for organised crime, but commence transfer of requirement to new Iraqi security structures
- Detention and processing of key regime figures

155

- Develop SSR [Security Sector Reform] model, with DDR [disarmament, demobilisation and reintegration] aimed at reducing size and scope of internal security forces
- Support SSR with training and equipment
- Begin transfer [of] security of oilfields and production facilities to Iraqi forces
- Provide international security guarantees
- Scope of tasks is likely to continue to demand large scale[138] forces.

"Long Term (2 – 10 years)

- Support SSR through training and presence on ground to effect gradual resumption of full responsibility for internal and external security by new regime
- Detention of key regime figures
- Exercises to underpin international security organisations."

243. There was no estimate of the scale of forces required for the long term, but the paper included the "key judgement" that: "In the worst case, we need to be prepared for a substantial long-term commitment."

244. The paper listed "sustainability" as one of a number of principles affecting campaign design. The post-conflict commitment needed to be "planned and agreed before we embark on military action". The paper advised that "sustainment beyond initial SDR [Strategic Defence Review] assumptions" had not yet been factored into calculations, and that prolonged post-conflict deployment would be a "significant burden on defence resources".

245. The paper also set out a list of actions required as "precursors" to shape the necessary conditions for whichever military option was selected. They included preparations "to support [a] new (post-conflict) regime, politically, militarily and economically".

246. The SPG paper was revised five times between June and December. The second edition was issued on 11 July.

247. **Between March and June 2002, the British Embassy Amman and the DIS in London continued to report on aspects of the political, social and economic situation in Iraq.**

---

[138] Defined in the 1998 Strategic Defence Review as deployments of division size or equivalent.

248. The March update from the British Embassy Amman, issued at the beginning of April, reported a number of demonstrations in Baghdad against recent Israeli incursions into Palestinian territory.[139] The Embassy commented that:

> "Iraqis no doubt are willing to demonstrate on this issue to vent anti-Western feeling and disgust at Israeli action against an Arab state. But they are unlikely to put their necks on the line by demonstrating out of turn. Support is also tempered by anger that so much Iraqi money is being given to the Palestinians instead of being used to address the problems at home ..."

249. The Embassy reported that there had been rumours Saddam Hussein was "threatening to use chemical weapons in Baghdad itself if necessary to quell any uprising. Stockpiling of food and enough fuel to get to the border is now standard amongst families in Baghdad."

250. In the April update, the Embassy reported "mixed stories" of the mood on the street in Baghdad: "Some say that Iraqis are used to American threats and simply do not believe that the regime will ever fall. Others report a freer atmosphere in Baghdad, encouraged by the possibility of change at the end of the year."[140]

251. The May update contained some insights into both social and infrastructure issues.[141] It highlighted Saddam Hussein's "scare tactics" over what would happen in the event of a coalition invasion of Iraq and the possibility of Iraqi and regional instability thereafter: "This line plays on real fears of the unknown and of religious instability. For all his faults, Saddam does, for now, mean stability and peace."

252. The May report also included a snapshot of communications infrastructure in Baghdad: a medical student had reported significant difficulty accessing the internet, both because of state controls on what could be viewed but also because of limited server access. Illegal access via satellite to both the internet and international news (copied onto CD and then sold) was becoming popular but was both expensive and risky.

253. On 6 June, the DIS assessed that, while there were undoubtedly divisions between Shia and Sunni groups in Iraq, these were not straightforward. The interaction between tribal allegiance, Arab identity, religious affiliation and political persuasion was highly complex.[142] The relationship between some tribes was characterised by "general lawlessness and brigandry ... and occasional incidents of inter-tribal conflict", leading the DIS to question whether the activities of southern tribal insurgents really represented a political challenge to Saddam Hussein's regime rather than simply traditional tribal activity that had always resented central government rule.

---

[139] Teleletter Amman [junior official] to MED [junior official], 4 April 2002, 'Iraq: March sitrep'.
[140] Teleletter Amman [junior official] to MED [junior official], 6 May 2002, 'Iraq: April sitrep'.
[141] Teleletter Amman [junior official] to MED [junior official], 9 June 2002, 'Iraq: May sitrep'.
[142] Paper DIS, 6 June 2002, 'The Iraqi tribes: their identity and role in internal security'.

254. On 19 June, Adm Boyce was informed that the US was ready for a UK input into US military planning.

255. Lt Gen Pigott warned that US military planning was taking place "in a policy void".

256. General Richard Myers, Chairman of the US Joint Chiefs of Staff, confirmed to Adm Boyce on 19 June, that he had a "green light to set up the necessary mechanism for a UK input into Iraq [military] planning" (see Section 6.1).[143]

257. On 26 June, in a paper summarising the state of US military planning, Major General Robert Fry, Deputy Chief of Joint Operations (Operations) (DCJO(O)), commented that, although US plans contained an implicit assumption that post-conflict nation-building was achievable, "this has not been addressed by US planning thus far".[144]

258. *Hard Lessons* stated that, by mid-2002:

"... differences [in Washington] among the three underlying policies for a post-war framework – rapid transfer to Iraqi control, military administration, or civilian transitional authority – had yet to be seriously addressed, much less resolved. Nor had officials reached consensus on the public order and reconstruction requirements for each scenario."[145]

259. A team from the MOD headed by Lt Gen Pigott visited the US to discuss military planning from 27 to 29 June.[146]

260. Mr Peter Watkins, Mr Hoon's Principal Private Secretary, reported the outcome to No.10 on 2 July: US planners' assumed mission was "to conduct offensive operations in Iraq to overthrow the regime, destroy the WMD capability, and reduce the threat to the Iraqi people, the region and the US". That was being discussed "in a policy void": "the end state to be achieved after conflict has not been defined and the identified military task currently runs out after the overthrow of the regime".

261. In early July, Mr Hoon and Mr Straw encouraged Mr Blair to try to influence US thinking on post-conflict objectives and the strategic framework for Iraq before President Bush was briefed on US military plans in August.

262. On 2 July, Mr Hoon proposed that Mr Blair convene a "small group of colleagues" specifically to consider "how best to get the US to address the strategic, as opposed to the narrowly military, dimension".[147]

---

[143] Minute Shireff to PS/SofS [MOD], 27 June 2002, 'Iraq Planning'.
[144] Minute Fry to MA/DCDS(C), 26 June 2002, 'US Planning for possible military action against Iraq'.
[145] Bowen SW Jr. *Hard Lessons: The Iraq Reconstruction Experience.* U.S. Government Printing Office, 2009.
[146] Minute Watkins to Manning, 2 July 2002, 'Iraq'.
[147] Minute Watkins to Manning, 2 July 2002, 'Iraq'.

263. Mr Hoon also recommended that officials from the MOD, FCO and Cabinet Office "do some more homework urgently" to put Mr Blair in a better position to influence President Bush and Dr Rice before they were briefed on an updated CENTCOM plan during August.

264. Sir Kevin Tebbit advised Mr Hoon on 3 July that Ministers who had not been exposed to the issues over the previous three months might "run a mile" from the picture of "a military plan being worked up in a policy vacuum, with no strategic framework" and "no clearly defined end state".[148] It might be that an Iraq campaign was unlikely to happen, but that was not certain. If it did happen, the UK might not be able to avoid being linked to a US military campaign. In those circumstances, it was not responsible for the UK "to let matters run without greater active engagement designed seriously to influence US conceptual as well as operational thinking". The UK needed "some early careful engagement with the US policy machine, rather than just with the Pentagon".

265. Mr Straw endorsed Mr Hoon's proposals on 8 July.[149] He advised Mr Blair:

"We are all agreed that we must act to remove the threat posed by Iraqi WMD. If the US decide that to do so requires military action then the UK will want to support them. But this will be harder for us to do without serious US action to address some of the lacunae in their plan, notably:

- no strategic concept for the military plan and, in particular, no thought apparently given to 'day after' scenarios. Although other parts of the US Administration have done some work on such aspects, US military planning so far has taken place in a vacuum."

266. Mr Straw added: "Regional states in particular will want assurance that the US has thought through the 'day after' questions before giving even tacit support."

267. Mr Straw concluded:

"The key point is how to get through to the Americans that the success of any military operation against Iraq – and protection of our fundamental interests in the region – depends on devising in advance a coherent strategy which assesses the political and economic as well as military implications. They must also understand that we are serious about our conditions for UK involvement."

268. The question of whether a satisfactory plan for post-conflict Iraq should have been a condition for UK involvement in military action is addressed later in this Section and in Section 6.5.

269. Mr Hoon's proposal prompted Mr Nye to advise Mr Brown to write to the MOD to propose that all options for UK participation in military operations (including smaller and

---

[148] Minute Tebbit to Secretary of State [MOD], 3 July 2002, 'Iraq'.
[149] Letter Straw to Prime Minister, 8 July 2002, 'Iraq: Contingency Planning'.

more specialised options) should be costed.[150] That would enable the Government to assess how much it wished to devote to securing a degree of influence over US policy and operations, in terms of risk to UK troops, the opportunity cost of withdrawing from other operations, and the financial cost.

270. The Treasury told the Inquiry that Mr Brown decided not to write to the MOD.[151]

271. On 4 July, the JIC assessed the cohesion of the Iraqi regime.[152] It acknowledged an absence of "detailed knowledge about the significance of particular motivators and alternative loyalties (eg to tribe versus State) for regime insiders", but judged that "real loyalty and support for Saddam Hussein's regime is confined to the top of the hierarchy".

272. The JIC reported, as had earlier DIS papers, that Ba'ath Party membership was compulsory for anyone holding an official position and that the "extensive party network provides all-pervasive oversight of Iraqi society, with representatives in most Iraqi social, government and military organisations". While the Sunni officer corps of the Iraqi military was likely to remain loyal, the Shia rank-and-file was less likely to, and mass desertions seemed likely.

273. On 11 July, Lt Gen Pigott sent a revised version of the SPG paper on UK military strategic thinking to a limited number of senior MOD addressees.[153]

274. The only change to the material on post-conflict planning in the June edition of the paper was the addition of references to the "weakness" of US planning, which needed "much greater definition".[154]

275. The advice from the SPG was discussed in a restricted Chiefs of Staff meeting on 17 July, described in more detail in Section 6.1.[155] At the meeting, Adm Boyce concluded that "the UK needed greater visibility of US intent in a number of areas".

276. **In his discussions with President Bush at Crawford in April, Mr Blair set out a number of considerations that were subsequently described by others as "conditions".**

277. **The Cabinet Office paper, 'Iraq: Conditions for Military Action', was issued on 19 July to inform Mr Blair's meeting with Mr Straw, Mr Hoon, Lord Goldsmith (the Attorney General) and key officials on 23 July.**

278. **The paper advised that an analysis of the post-conflict phase was among the preparations needed to fulfil Mr Blair's "conditions".**

---

[150] Minute Nye to Bowman, 5 July 2002, 'Iraq'.
[151] Email Treasury to Iraq Inquiry, 26 February 2010, [untitled].
[152] JIC Assessment, 4 July 2002, 'Iraq: regime cohesion'.
[153] Minute DCDS(C) to MA/CDS, 11 July 2002, 'UK Military Thinking on Iraq' attaching Paper [SPG], 11 July 2002, 'UK Military Strategic Thinking on Iraq'.
[154] Paper [SPG], 11 July 2002, 'UK Military Strategic Thinking on Iraq'.
[155] Minutes, 17 July 2002, Chiefs of Staff (Restricted) meeting.

279. Mr Jonathan Powell advised Mr Blair to avoid a repeat of the Afghanistan experience, where there had been a "scramble" to get post-conflict arrangements ready. He advised that post-conflict planning for Iraq needed to start immediately.

280. In his diaries, Mr Chris Mullin, Chairman of the Home Affairs Select Committee from 2001to 2003, recorded that he raised post-conflict issues with Mr Blair at a meeting of the Parliamentary Labour Party (PLP) on 17 July.[156] Mr Mullin stated that the UK needed to be thinking about a number of issues, including what Saddam Hussein would do if cornered, the extent of the collateral damage and "how much help would we get from the Americans when it came to clearing up afterwards?"

281. Mr Mullin recorded that Mr Blair had replied that those questions needed to be answered:

"'… if we can't answer them we won't do it.' He [Mr Blair] added that, contrary to what most people seemed to believe, the Americans had stayed engaged both in Kosovo and in Afghanistan."

282. On 19 July, OD Sec issued 'Iraq: Conditions for Military Action'.[157] The paper, described in more detail in Section 3.3, reminded Ministers that Mr Blair had discussed Iraq with President Bush at Crawford in April, where he had said the UK would support military action to bring about regime change, provided certain conditions were met.

283. The paper stated that the considerations and preparations that needed to be addressed to "fulfil the conditions" set out by Mr Blair included an analysis of whether the benefits of military action outweighed the risks, including whether a "post-war occupation of Iraq could lead to a protracted and costly nation-building exercise". US military plans were "virtually silent" on that point and Washington could look to the UK to "share a disproportionate share of the burden". Further work was needed on what form of government might replace Saddam Hussein's regime and the timescale for identifying a successor.

284. Mr Powell made a similar point in a note for Mr Blair on 19 July, in which he suggested points to put in writing to President Bush. Those included:

"… we need a plan for the day after. Loya Jirga[158] and peacekeeping in Afghanistan have worked well but we had to scramble to get them ready in time. We need to be working on this now for Iraq …"[159]

285. Sir Kevin Tebbit visited Washington from 17 to 20 July for talks with senior US officials, including Mr Paul Wolfowitz (Deputy Secretary of Defense), Mr Stephen Hadley

---

[156] Mullin C. *A View from the Foothills: The Diaries of Chris Mullin*. Profile Books, 2009.
[157] Paper Cabinet Office, 19 July 2002, 'Iraq: Conditions for Military Action'.
[158] A grand assembly of elders in Afghanistan or Pashtun areas of Pakistan.
[159] Minute Powell to Prime Minister, 19 July 2002, 'Iraq'.

(Deputy National Security Advisor), Mr Richard Armitage (Deputy Secretary of State) and Mr Frank Miller (NSC Senior Director for Defense Policy and Arms Control).[160]

286. The British Embassy reported that Sir Kevin emphasised the need for clarity on aftermath management and that Mr Wolfowitz, although he endorsed Sir Kevin's view, suggested that aftermath management was in many ways an easier issue than military planning.

287. Mr Wolfowitz restated that position in public later in the year.[161]

288. On his return, Sir Kevin Tebbit informed No.10 of growing US resolve on aftermath management and widespread recognition in Washington that the US would remain in Iraq for several years after military intervention. At the same time, he reported "an air of unreality, given the enormity of what is envisaged and the absence of planning detail or policy framework to credibly make it happen".[162]

289. On 23 July, Mr Blair discussed Iraq with Mr Straw, Mr Hoon, Lord Goldsmith, Sir Richard Wilson, Adm Boyce, Sir Richard Dearlove, Sir Francis Richards (Head of the Government Communications Headquarters (GCHQ)), Mr Scarlett, Mr Powell, Baroness Morgan (No.10 Director of Political and Government Relations), Mr Campbell and Sir David Manning (see Section 3.3).[163]

290. Sir David Manning's annotated agenda for Mr Blair indicated that there would be a lot of ground to cover in a short time. It made no reference to post-conflict issues.[164]

291. Mr Rycroft's record of the meeting said that there had been "little discussion in Washington of the aftermath" and that Mr Blair's meeting had concluded that the UK needed a fuller picture of US planning before taking any firm decisions on its own commitment.[165]

292. In a note commissioning further work from the FCO, MOD and Cabinet Office, Mr Rycroft recorded that Adm Boyce would send Mr Blair "full details of the proposed military campaign and options for a UK contribution".[166] No work was commissioned on post-conflict issues.

293. Maj Gen Fry raised post-conflict issues in a minute to Lt Gen Pigott on 25 July.[167] Maj Gen Fry commented that work on "post-operational" effects had focused so far

---

[160] Telegram 970 Washington to FCO London, 20 July 2002, 'Iraq: Sir K Tebbit's Visit to Washington, 18-19 July'.
[161] US Department of Defense News Transcript, 18 December 2002, *Deputy Secretary Wolfowitz Interview with Tom Ricks, Washington Post*.
[162] Letter Tebbit to Manning, 22 July 2002, 'Iraq'.
[163] Minute Rycroft to Manning, 23 July 2002, 'Iraq: Prime Minister's Meeting, 23 July'.
[164] Minute Manning to Prime Minister, 22 July 2002, 'Iraq Meeting: 23 July: Annotated Agenda'.
[165] Minute Rycroft to Manning, 23 July 2002, 'Iraq: Prime Minister's Meeting, 23 July'.
[166] Letter Rycroft to McDonald, 23 July 2002, 'Iraq: Prime Minister's Meeting, 23 July: follow up'.
[167] Minute Fry to MA/DCDS(C), 25 July 2002, 'Developing Work on UK Options for Operations Against Iraq.'

on the consequences for UK force-regeneration: "what is beginning to emerge in the development of our work is the need for a possible post-conflict stabilisation force in order to meet the grand strategic end state of a new acceptable government".

294. The concept of a stabilisation force does not re-emerge in the papers seen by the Inquiry until the second half of December.

295. Mr Watkins sent Mr Rycroft MOD advice on three options for a UK contribution to US-led military operations in Iraq on 26 July.[168] Mr Watkins reported that US "thinking about dealing with the aftermath of a successful attack remains sketchy".

296. The three options identified by the MOD, known as Packages 1, 2 and 3, made no explicit reference to possible post-conflict commitments. They remained the broad framework for discussions until the end of 2002.

297. Mr Rycroft commented to Mr Blair:

"The military are not yet ready to make a recommendation on which if any of the three options to go for. Nor can they yet judge whether the US have a winning concept. They are continuing to work with the US military. You do not need to take decisions yet."[169]

298. Mr Straw spoke to Mr Colin Powell, US Secretary of State, on 26 July. Reporting the outcome to Mr Blair, he explained that the "day after" was a shared anxiety: military action would work, but the US and UK would need "an army of occupation for many years afterwards. That was the only way. The dissidents would not run a government."[170]

299. As a contingency for a possible follow-up visit to the US by Mr Straw, Mr Ricketts commissioned briefing from Mr Chaplin on a number of issues, including "Prospects for post-war stability" on 30 July.[171] Questions for Mr Chaplin to consider included:

- was the US doing "serious work on how to hold Iraq together"?
- was the US military prepared to stay on in the numbers needed?
- where would an Iraqi Karzai[172] emerge from?
- would the UN lead reconstruction and nation-building?

300. Mr Chaplin provided answers to some of those questions in early September.

301. In his address to a CENTCOM conference on 2 August, described in more detail in Section 6.1, Major General David Wilson, Senior British Military Adviser (SBMA) at CENTCOM, made a number of observations about the US military plan, including that:

---

[168] Letter Watkins to Rycroft, 26 July 2002, 'Iraq'.
[169] Minute Rycroft to Prime Minister, 31 July 2002, 'Iraq: Background Papers'.
[170] Letter Straw to Blair, 26 July 2002, 'Iraq'.
[171] Minute Ricketts to Chaplin, 30 July 2002, 'Iraq'.
[172] Mr Hamid Karzai, Chairman of the Afghan Interim Administration, 2001-2002.

"it would be helpful for my colleagues in London to have a better feel for the 'post-conflict' thinking and aftermath management".[173] The experience of Afghanistan had shown:

> "… that it is every bit as important to win the peace as it is to win the war. That will be even truer in Iraq. I would not wish to over state the case, but it is undoubtedly true that both UK politicians and my military colleagues would like to know what we are getting ourselves into in the longer term."

302. Mr Blair raised post-conflict issues with President Bush at the end of July.

303. Mr Blair made clear that his own thinking on what might follow Saddam Hussein was still fluid.

304. Mr Blair sent a personal Note to President Bush on 28 July.[174] The 'Note on Iraq', which is addressed in detail in Section 3.3, stated that removing Saddam Hussein was the right thing to do, but that establishing a new regime would take time. The US and UK would need to commit to Iraq for the long term and, without coalition partners, there was a possibility the unintended consequences of removing Saddam Hussein would persist beyond the military phase. Part of the message to win round potential partners might be that regime change must protect Iraq's territorial integrity and provide security. That might involve another key military figure, but should lead in time to a democratic Iraq, governed by the people. Mr Blair would need advice on whether that approach was feasible, but just swapping one dictator for another seemed inconsistent with US and UK values.

305. Sir David Manning delivered the 'Note on Iraq' to Dr Rice on 29 July.[175]

306. Sir David told the Inquiry that he had a "pre-meeting" with Mr Armitage.[176] During that meeting, Mr Armitage said that the US was thinking through "day after" scenarios and that "it was better to be right than to hurry".[177]

307. The record of Mr Blair's conversation with President Bush on 31 July included a brief reference to post-conflict Iraq: that focusing on the end state of a democratic Iraq would give the US and UK the moral high ground.[178]

308. In his statement to the Inquiry, Mr Blair explained:

> "I did ask … President Bush in July 2002 whether it might be feasible to install a military leader then move to democracy in Iraq. I cannot recall specifically calling for formal advice, but the subject of what sort of Iraq we wanted to create was part

---

[173] Paper Wilson, [undated], 'CENTCOM Iraq Planning – A UK Perspective'.
[174] Note Blair [to Bush], 28 July 2002, 'Note on Iraq'.
[175] Minute Manning to Prime Minister, 31 July 2002, 'Iraq: Conversation with Condi Rice'.
[176] Public hearing, 30 November 2009, page 17.
[177] Minute Rycroft to Manning, 31 July 2002, 'Iraq: Armitage'.
[178] Minute Rycroft to Manning, 31 July 2002, 'Iraq: Prime Minister's Conversation with Bush, 31 July'.

of a perpetual discussion, interaction with various Iraqi opposition groups and the analysis of the country set out in the various FCO papers."[179]

309. On 12 September, Sir David Manning commissioned advice from the FCO on what a post-Saddam Hussein government might look like.[180]

310. **At his request, Mr Blair received a pack of reading material on Iraq at the beginning of August 2002, including on the extent of economic degradation in Iraq since 1991 and the complex interaction between tribal allegiance, ethnic identity, religious affiliation and political persuasion.**

311. In late July, Mr Blair asked his staff to assemble a pack of "summer reading material" on Iraq.[181]

312. The material supplied by the FCO, DIS and Mr Scarlett included the DIS papers on removing Saddam Hussein, Iraq's infrastructure, the role of the Ba'ath Party and the role of Iraq's tribes in internal security produced earlier in the year.

313. Mr Scarlett sent Mr Blair an assessment of the cohesiveness of the Iraqi regime, in which he stated:

> "Conditions inside Iraq are better now than they were immediately before the start of the Oil-for-Food (OFF) programme in late 1996. OFF rations guarantee that at least basic needs are met ... The 'winners' under sanctions are those with a hand in sanctions-busting trade ... The greatest losers under sanctions have been the middle classes ... The poorer, rural communities in the south may have suffered less. The agricultural economy may actually have benefited from the rise in prices ..."[182]

314. Mr Scarlett advised that the Kurds "would probably demand a reversal of the 'Arabisation' of the north" after Saddam Hussein's departure, leading to "a risk of inter-ethnic fighting and the expulsion of the Arab community from areas of the north".

315. **A JIC Assessment of 5 August on the attitudes of regional states to military action against Iraq stated that the US needed to convince them of its "determination and ability to remove Saddam Hussein quickly", and to offer "credible plans for the aftermath".**

316. **The Assessment also stated that, after a US attack began, "Iran would probably boost its support for Shia groups working against Saddam".**

---

[179] Statement, 14 January 2011, pages 15-16.
[180] Letter Manning to McDonald, 12 September 2002, 'Iraq'.
[181] Minute Rycroft to Blair, 31 July 2002, 'Iraq: background papers'; Minute Scarlett to Powell, 1 August 2002, 'Iraq: classified reading material'.
[182] Minute Scarlett to Manning, 31 July 2002, 'The Iraqi regime: risks and threats'.

317. On 5 August, at the request of the MOD, the JIC reviewed the likely attitude of regional states to military action against Iraq.[183] The JIC assessed that:

> "Most regional governments would be happy to see Saddam's demise. But they would be likely to have profound misgivings about a campaign without a well-constructed plan for a new Iraq. All agree that Iraq's territorial integrity must be maintained. But there are differing regional concerns about the place of the Kurds and Shia in any new regime, the type of government and its relationship with the West."

318. After a US attack began, "Iran would probably boost its support for Shia groups working against Saddam". The Islamic Revolutionary Guard Corps (IRGC) "would be likely to work directly to undermine US influence, eg by manipulating Iraqi groups through propaganda and the selective provision of money and arms, although it would not provoke anything that would provoke US military retaliation".

319. The JIC concluded that: "The US must continue to convince regional governments of its determination and ability to remove Saddam quickly and offer credible plans for the aftermath."

320. The Pigott Group discussed US and UK military planning on 8 August.[184] Although the MOD judged that progress had been made towards "a winning military concept", the Group expressed concern at the "absence of a clear strategy for the morning after".

321. The MOD reported on 12 August that President Bush had authorised preparatory military activities.

322. The British Embassy Washington described the "day after" as the "most vexed" issue.

323. Mr Straw warned Secretary Powell of the dangers of introducing democracy to a country with no democratic tradition.

324. A letter from Mr Hoon's Private Office to No.10 on 12 August reported that President Bush had authorised preparatory military activities costing $1bn and that an inter-agency process in Washington had been launched.[185]

325. Mr Tony Brenton, Deputy Head of Mission at the British Embassy Washington, advised Mr Straw's Private Office on 15 August that:

> "Despite repeated affirmations that no decisions have yet been taken, there is a general assumption that the [US] Administration is moving towards military action to

---

[183] JIC Assessment, 5 August 2002, 'Iraq: Regional Attitudes and Impact of Military Action'.
[184] Minute Drummond to McKane, 8 August 2002, 'Iraq'.
[185] Letter Davies to Wechsberg, 12 August 2002, 'Iraq: US contingency planning'.

remove Saddam … The private language of the vast majority of those to whom we speak is 'when rather than if'.

…

"But the most vexed issue is probably the 'day after' question – what does the US do with a conquered Iraq. [Mr William] Burns [State Department Assistant Secretary Near East] has told me that they are increasingly thinking in terms of some form of democracy, but recognised that this would need to be propped up by a long term international (i.e. almost certainly US) security presence. They have of course been working hard on their contacts with the Iraqi opposition … to prepare for this eventuality. However the opposition have made clear they want to be in charge – this should not be a 'foreign invasion'. And some Administration contacts are realistic about the democracy objective – the nature of the opposition groups and the political culture of Iraq; and the difficulty of justifying pursuing the conflict if a benign dictator overthrew Saddam."[186]

326. Mr Brenton's letter was seen by Mr Blair before a telephone call between Mr Blair and Mr Straw on 19 August in preparation for Mr Straw's meeting with Secretary Powell.[187]

327. On 19 August, Dr Michael Williams, Mr Straw's Special Adviser, sent Mr Straw a paper on the lessons for Iraq of other US military interventions since 1945.[188] Dr Williams advised that:

"… a UN mandate will be essential for post-war Iraq. It will simply not be possible for the US to do this alone as it found out after UK intervention in Afghanistan. Experience elsewhere – in Cambodia, Bosnia, Kosovo, East Timor – has underlined the necessity of the UN as the mechanism indispensable for the marshalling of global, political and economic support in the context of post-war construction."

328. At Mr Straw's request, Dr Williams' paper was copied to Sir Michael Jay and Sir David Manning.[189]

329. On 20 August, Mr Straw visited the US for talks on Iraq with Secretary Powell (see Section 3.4).[190]

---

[186] Letter Brenton to Private Secretary [FCO], 15 August 2002, 'Iraq'.
[187] Manuscript comment Wechsberg, 19 August 2002, on Letter Brenton to Private Secretary [FCO], 15 August 2002, 'Iraq'.
[188] Minute Williams to Secretary of State [FCO], 19 August 2002, 'The United States and Iraq: Historical Parallels'.
[189] Manuscript comment McDonald on Minute Williams to Secretary of State [FCO], 19 August 2002, 'The United States and Iraq: Historical Parallels'.
[190] Letter McDonald to Manning, 21 August 2002, 'Foreign Secretary's Visit to the US, 20 August 2002'.

330. Mr Straw told Secretary Powell that he had discussed the position with Mr Blair the previous day. Mr Straw explained that:

> "The key issue for the Prime Minister was whether the US wanted an international coalition or not. The US could go it alone if they wanted that, they only had to tell us."

331. Mr Straw's view was:

> "… that the case for an international coalition was overwhelming: first for basing and access, and then for what happened after getting rid of Saddam. But also, especially, if things went wrong. In such circumstances the US would need the international community at the scene of the crime …"

332. Commenting on the "day after", Mr Straw pointed out that Iraq had been an artificial creation of the UK in 1921. Iraq had "no experience of democracy and democracy could pull it apart".

333. Secretary Powell commented that: "Some of his colleagues did not want UN involvement in any shape: it might frustrate their purpose."

334. The record of the discussion was not to be seen by anyone other than Sir David Manning and Mr Blair.

335. On 30 August, Mr Blair set out his position on Iraq in a note to No.10 officials.[191] He stated that the basic strategy to deal with those arguing against any action should be to answer their questions and, in doing so, to set Iraq in a bigger context. That included working on a post-Saddam Hussein Iraqi regime:

> "The conundrum is: if it is merely changing Saddam for another military dictator, that hardly elicits support from the rest of Iraq, especially the Shia majority, and is in any event, not in line with our principles; on the other hand, if the whole nature of the regime changes, the Sunni minority in power may be less tempted to fold and acquiesce in Saddam's removal. But there are ways through this."

336. Mr Blair's note is addressed in more detail in Section 3.4.

The DFID Iraq programme

337. In August 2002, DFID completed a review of its programme in northern Iraq.

338. The review, which was not sent outside DFID, drew on a range of sources to present as clear a picture as possible of the humanitarian situation in northern Iraq.

---

[191] Note Blair [to No.10 officials], 30 August 2002, [extract 'Iraq'].

339. The authors stated that they were aware of MOD contingency planning for military action against Iraq, but not of its extent.

340. DFID was not involved in cross-Whitehall planning on Iraq until September 2002.

341. During the first half of 2002, DFID involvement in Whitehall discussion of Iraq was limited to the humanitarian impact of the proposed Goods Review List (GRL), addressed in more detail in Section 3.2. The GRL was adopted in May 2002 and introduced fast track procedures for the export to Iraq of all goods other than WMD- and military-related items of concern.[192] DFID did not participate in discussion of post-conflict issues or wider Iraq strategy.

342. On 10 May, DFID officials recommended to Ms Clare Short, International Development Secretary, that the department review its existing humanitarian programme for Iraq to inform its strategy for the next three years.[193]

343. In their advice of 10 May, officials described the purpose of DFID's existing (2002/03) programme for Iraq, as being: "to improve the provision of effective humanitarian support by UN agencies and NGOs for the poor affected by internal and regional conflict in Iraq".

344. Officials explained that there were problems assessing the humanitarian situation in Iraq: "The GoI's [Government of Iraq's] strict censorship policy of key data has inhibited comprehensive analyses from other [non-UN] sources … UN reports offer the most reliable means of reaching whatever information is available." Although DFID had conducted "informal consultations" with UN agencies, those agencies respected Iraqi Government conditions on sharing information.

345. The paper stated that, despite the shortage of reliable survey evidence assessing human development in Iraq, there was a consensus in the international development community that the situation had "deteriorated severely" since 1990. UN/Government of Iraq joint sectoral surveys showed a "general deterioration" in areas such as health, nutrition, and child and maternal mortality. UNICEF assessed that, while the food ration provided under OFF had arrested the rate of decline in the humanitarian situation, it had not reversed it, and interference by the Iraqi Government meant that the benefits had not been evenly distributed across Iraq. UNICEF was also concerned that there was a high level of dependency on the food ration.

---

[192] Minute DFID [junior official] to Private Secretary [DFID], 10 May 2002, 'Proposed humanitarian activities 2002/03'.
[193] Minute Western Asia Department [junior official] to Private Secretary [DFID], 10 May 2002, 'Proposed humanitarian activities 2002/03' attaching Paper Western Asia Department, May 2002, 'Iraq – Humanitarian Assistance Programme for 2002/03'.

The UN Oil-for-Food programme

The UN Oil-for-Food (OFF) programme was established by resolution 986 in April 1995. Implementation began in May 1996 after the signing of a Memorandum of Understanding between the UN and the Iraqi Government.[194]

The programme allowed Iraq to export its oil and use a portion of the proceeds to buy humanitarian supplies.[195] Revenue from the oil sales was allocated to different tasks:

- 72 percent for humanitarian supplies;
- 25 percent for the UN compensation fund for Kuwait;
- 2.2 percent for the UN's OFF administration costs;
- 0.8 percent for the UN's Monitoring, Verification and Inspection Commission (UNMOVIC).

Funds allocated for humanitarian supplies were used in accordance with a distribution plan approved by the UN.

The Iraqi Government implemented OFF in central and southern Iraq, with the UN in an observer role. UN agencies implemented OFF in northern Iraq, either directly or through contractors and local non-governmental organisations (NGOs).

Nine UN agencies operated in Iraq under the OFF: the Food and Agriculture Organization (FAO); the UN Settlements Programme (HABITAT); the International Telecommunications Union (ITU); the UN Development Programme (UNDP); the UN Educational, Scientific and Cultural Organization (UNESCO); the UN Children's Fund (UNICEF); the UN Office for Project Services (UNOPS); the World Food Programme (WFP); and the World Health Organization (WHO).

By 2002, OFF had been expanded to include infrastructure rehabilitation and 24 "sectors", including health, electricity, education, water and sanitation, and oil industry parts and spares.[196]

The UN published reports on its activities under OFF, both on the UN Office of the Iraq Programme (UNOIP) website[197] and on individual agency websites.[198]

The UN Secretary-General provided regular reports on the performance of the programme to the Security Council.[199]

346. According to the DFID report, the UN Children's Fund (UNICEF) assessed that about half of Iraq's schools were physically unsafe and unfit for teaching, and the UN Development Programme (UNDP) estimated that around a third of six-year-olds had no access to basic education. Adult literacy levels were estimated to have fallen from 89 percent in 1985 to 57 percent in 1997, and to have continued to decline thereafter. UNICEF also reported that infant and child mortality levels in central and southern Iraq

---

[194] UN Office of the Iraq Programme, *About the Programme: Oil-for-Food*.
[195] Paper DFID, 11 October 2002, 'Iraq: Potential Humanitarian Implications'.
[196] UN Office of the Iraq Programme, *About the Programme: Oil-for-Food*.
[197] UN Office of the Iraq Programme, *Oil-for-Food*.
[198] UNICEF.org.
[199] Report of the Secretary-General pursuant to paragraphs 7 and 8 of Security Council resolution 1409 (2002).

had increased by up to 160 percent since 1990, placing Iraq bottom of 188 countries assessed. Malnutrition problems were also on the increase. Problems were less acute in northern Iraq.

347. On 1 August, the Cabinet Office reported to Sir David Manning that Ms Short had agreed proposals to make the DFID bilateral programme in Iraq "more structured".[200] It also reported that a review of DFID activity in Iraq was under way, but that the focus of officials' concern was the need to improve the UK's understanding of the existing humanitarian situation in Iraq.

348. The first product of DFID's review of its Iraq programme, the 'Northern Iraq Desktop Review', was circulated within DFID on 8 August.[201] The Inquiry has seen no evidence that it was copied outside the department.

349. The 'Desktop Review' drew on a combination of DFID papers and consultations with UN agencies, NGOs and western European donor countries. It did not take account of UK military planning. The reviewers commented: "Although we are aware that the … MOD … is carrying out contingency planning for military action against Iraq, the extent of this planning is not known."

350. Among their conclusions, the DFID reviewers stated that:

- OFF had significantly improved the humanitarian situation in northern Iraq, but it could be argued that it "had served to undermine the viability of local economic initiatives and has been detrimental to coping mechanisms, contributing to a high degree of vulnerability now and for the foreseeable future".
- 60 percent of the population was dependent on the OFF food basket and "highly vulnerable to external shocks".
- Many civil servants had resorted to alternative sources of income or left the country in order to secure a stable income.
- Development projects aimed at building livelihoods were "significantly hampered" by the scale of OFF and its destructive effect on local markets, particularly in the agricultural sector.

351. In her memoir, Ms Short explained that:

"DFID had been involved over many years in supporting efforts to ease Iraqi suffering. It was easier to work in the north but we had some projects in central Iraq and were well aware of how bad things were."[202]

352. The Inquiry asked Sir William Patey what assessments the UK Government had made of the humanitarian situation in Iraq before 2003 and in particular the effect of sanctions. Sir William explained that the UK had great difficulty in establishing whether

---

[200] Minute Dodd to Manning, 1 August 2002, 'Iraq'.
[201] Minute CHAD Operations Team [junior official] to [DFID junior official], 8 August 2002, 'Northern Iraq Desktop Review and Background Briefing Document' attaching Paper, Conflict and Humanitarian Affairs Department, July 2002, 'Northern Iraq Desktop Review and Background Briefing Document'.
[202] Short C. *An Honourable Deception: New Labour, Iraq and the Misuse of Power*. The Free Press, 2004.

allegations made by Saddam Hussein's regime that sanctions were damaging the people of Iraq were true.[203] The UK had tried to get the World Health Organization (WHO) into Iraq to assess the situation, but Saddam Hussein had refused permission. Sir William judged that:

> "... it was in Iraq's interest not to have a reasonable assessment because, obviously, if the picture was left to them to tell, they would exploit that picture. So there wasn't a good assessment, mainly because UN agencies couldn't get in to do it, and the claims that were coming out of Iraq were pretty spurious at best."

353. Military and humanitarian planning began to converge in September, with DFID's partial integration into Whitehall's reorganised Iraq planning machinery. That change was reflected in a second DFID review, described later in this Section, which was produced in October and included material on the possible impact of military action on central and southern Iraq.[204]

UK and US organisational changes

354. President Bush signed the US national security document setting out US goals, objectives and strategy for Iraq on 29 August 2002.

355. The document stated that the US was prepared to play a sustained role in the reconstruction of post-Saddam Hussein Iraq with contributions from and the participation of the international community.

356. On 29 August 2002, President Bush signed the national security document 'Iraq: Goals, Objectives, Strategy'.[205] The stated goal of the US was to free Iraq in order to:

- eliminate WMD;
- end Iraqi threats to its neighbours;
- stop the Iraqi government tyrannising its own people;
- cut Iraqi links to terrorism; and
- "[l]iberate the Iraqi people from tyranny and assist them in creating a society based on moderation, pluralism and democracy."[206]

357. The document stated that the US was "prepared to play a sustained role in the reconstruction of post-Saddam Iraq with contribution from and participation of the international community", and that it would work closely with the Iraqi opposition to liberate and build a new Iraq.[207]

---

[203] Public hearing, 24 November 2009, pages 164-165.
[204] Paper Conflict & Humanitarian Affairs Department, October 2002, 'Central/southern Iraq humanitarian situation analysis'.
[205] Bowen SW Jr. *Hard Lessons: The Iraq Reconstruction Experience.* U.S. Government Printing Office, 2009.
[206] Feith DJ. *War and Decision.* Harper, 2008.
[207] Bowen SW Jr. *Hard Lessons: The Iraq Reconstruction Experience.* U.S. Government Printing Office, 2009.

358. A revised version, modified to reflect developments in US thinking on post-Saddam Hussein Iraq, was sent to Principals by Dr Rice on 29 October. The document, published in *War and Decision,* the memoir of Mr Douglas Feith, US Under Secretary of Defense for Policy 2001-2005, stated the need to:

> "Demonstrate that the US and Coalition partners are prepared to play a sustained role in providing security, humanitarian assistance, and reconstruction aid in support of this vision ..."[208]

359. The document was not shown to the UK until 31 January 2003 (see Section 6.5).

360. The US made a number of organisational changes to implement the goals approved by President Bush on 29 August.

361. *Hard Lessons* records that the US took a number of steps to help implement the goals approved by President Bush on 29 August:

- The Joint Staff in the Pentagon instructed CENTCOM to start planning to administer Iraq for an interim period after an invasion.
- Mr Feith enlarged the office in the Pentagon responsible for policy planning in Iraq in a new Office of Special Plans.
- Dr Rice established an NSC Executive Steering Group on Iraq, chaired by Mr Miller, to "jump-start" post-conflict planning across the US government.
- Inter-agency working groups responsible for energy, diplomacy, global communications and humanitarian issues were established under the umbrella of the Executive Steering Group.[209]

362. The inter-agency Humanitarian Working Group was set up in September.[210] It was headed by Mr Elliot Abrams, NSC Senior Director for Democracy, Human Rights and International Organizations, and Mr Robin Cleveland, Associate Director of the White House Office of Management and Budget. Membership included representatives of the Joint Staff and the Departments of Defense, State, Treasury, Justice and Commerce, and the US Agency for International Development (USAID). It was USAID's first formal involvement in the Iraq planning process.

363. The Humanitarian Working Group focused on the response to large-scale humanitarian contingencies, including the possible use of WMD by Saddam Hussein. It also considered the administration of revenue generated under OFF, liaised with the international aid community to identify critical civilian infrastructure for a military "no-strike" list and began to assess the demands of post-war reconstruction.

---

[208] Feith DJ. *War and Decision.* Harper, 2008.
[209] Bowen SW Jr. *Hard Lessons: The Iraq Reconstruction Experience.* U.S. Government Printing Office, 2009.
[210] Bowen SW Jr. *Hard Lessons: The Iraq Reconstruction Experience.* U.S. Government Printing Office, 2009.

364. *Hard Lessons* explained that the Working Group's task was hampered by the absence of detailed assessments of the state of Iraq's economy and infrastructure, and poor integration with other planning:

> "The few detailed reports reviewed by the Working Group suggested that sanctions had significantly limited Iraq's recovery from the first Gulf War ... In light of Iraq's substantial oil wealth, however, the scope of expected infrastructure repairs seemed manageable. The Group assumed that long-term repairs could be undertaken and funded by the Iraqis.

> "With military, political and democratization plans developed out of sight of the Humanitarian Working Group, its members could consider only in general terms how reconstruction might help legitimize a new Iraqi state. The Group asked for but never received a briefing on how public-order requirements would be met ... The Defense Department asserted that it had plans for post-war security well in hand ..."

365. The UK Government also made organisational changes.

366. Officials began to discuss changes to the Government's machinery for Iraq policy and planning in June 2002.

367. Recommendations to improve Whitehall co-ordination at official and Ministerial level were put to Mr Blair in mid-September.

368. At official level, the cross-Whitehall Ad Hoc Group on Iraq (AHGI) met for the first time on 20 September. It became the principal forum for co-ordination of planning and preparation for a post-Saddam Hussein or post-conflict Iraq.

369. Mr Blair put on hold proposals for the creation of a separate Ministerial Group.

370. On 26 June, Mr Webb informed Mr Hoon's office that MOD officials were encouraging the Cabinet Office to supplement the Pigott Group with a broader body involving a wider range of departments with a policy interest in Iraq and the region.[211]

371. Those ideas began to take shape on 8 August, when Mr Jim Drummond, Assistant Head (Foreign Affairs) OD Sec, informed Mr McKane that he had spoken to Sir David Manning about possible changes to Whitehall structures.[212] Mr Drummond explained that one consequence of existing Whitehall mechanisms for discussing Iraq, including in particular the Pigott Group's focus on military matters, was that "we are focusing a lot on military aspects and less on the alliance building, morning after, unintended consequences etc. Come September there may be a case for a tighter grip from the Centre."

---

[211] Minute Webb to PS/Secretary of State [MOD], 26 June 2002, 'Iraq'.
[212] Minute Drummond to McKane, 8 August 2002, 'Iraq'.

372. Mr Drummond raised the issue with Sir David Manning again on 30 August.[213] He recalled that Sir David had commented earlier in the summer that it was too soon to think about management of the unintended consequences of conflict, but that the issue would probably need to be discussed in the autumn.

373. Mr Drummond enclosed a "skeleton" paper on the subject prepared by a Cabinet Office junior official and suggested meeting to discuss the paper and Whitehall machinery for Iraq at the same time.

374. The Cabinet Office paper on unintended consequences focused on the possible impact of war on UK interests and on countries in the region, rather than on post-conflict Iraq.

375. The FCO produced a more substantial paper on the unintended consequences of conflict for the region and beyond on 20 September.[214] The paper is described later in this Section.

376. Also attached to Mr Drummond's minute was a "list of headings for future work" on unintended consequences, which included: "avoiding fragmentation of a failed state in Iraq".

377. Sir David Manning replied to Mr Drummond: "Let us discuss p[lea]se with Tom McKane before he goes. We need to do this work: there is a question about timing."[215]

378. Mr McKane sent Sir David Manning a note on possible machinery "for managing Iraq" on 2 September.[216] He recalled that he and Sir David had already agreed that, "following the pattern of Afghanistan", there should be two groups of officials; an "inner group" chaired by Sir David (or Mr Desmond Bowen who would shortly be taking over from Mr McKane as Sir David's Deputy in OD Sec) and a more junior "wider group", chaired by Mr Bowen or Mr Drummond.

379. Mr McKane proposed that the inner group "should begin work once you [Sir David Manning] decide that the time is right". It would comprise the Chair of the JIC or Chief of the Assessments Staff, the FCO Middle East Director, the Deputy Chief of the Defence Staff (Commitments) (DCDS(C)) and/or Mr Ian Lee (MOD Director General Operational Policy (DG OpPol)), and representatives of all three Intelligence Agencies and the Home Office. Mr McKane asked whether it should also include the DIS and a No.10 information specialist. He proposed that the wider group "should meet periodically from now on and, inter alia, address the issues set out in Jim Drummond's minute of 30 August".

---

[213] Minute Drummond to Manning, 30 August 2002, 'Iraq: Unintended Consequences' attaching Note Cabinet Office, 30 August 2002, 'Outline of a Paper: Iraq: Managing the Unintended Consequences' and Paper Cabinet Office, 28 August 2002, 'Unintended Consequences of War on Iraq: Skeleton of Paper'.
[214] Paper Directorate for Strategy and Innovation, [undated], 'Iraq – Consequences of Conflict for the Region and Beyond'.
[215] Manuscript comment Manning on Minute Drummond to Manning, 30 August 2002, 'Iraq: Unintended Consequences'.
[216] Minute McKane to Manning, 2 September 2002, 'Iraq'.

380. Mr McKane wrote that "we also need to consider the composition of a Ministerial Group". He recommended the creation of a separate Ad Hoc Sub-Committee of the Defence and Overseas Policy Committee (DOP), chaired by the Prime Minister, with the participation of the Foreign and Defence Secretaries and the Intelligence Chiefs. DOP "could meet less frequently and be the means of formalising decisions". Mr McKane also suggested that Lord Goldsmith, the Attorney General, be invited "to be in attendance at both these groups, as required" and Mr Robin Cook, the Leader of the House, "be invited to attend DOP".

381. Sir David Manning put the proposals to Mr Blair on 12 September.[217] At official level, Sir David recommended that he or Mr Bowen would chair an inner group, to include the JIC, FCO, MOD, SIS, Security Service, GCHQ, Home Office and Sir David Omand, the Cabinet Office Permanent Secretary.

382. A wider group, chaired by OD Sec, would be "tasked as necessary by the inner group".[218] The additional members would include DFID, the Metropolitan Police, the Treasury, the Department of Trade and Industry (DTI) and media specialists from No.10 and the FCO.

383. In his advice to Mr Blair, Sir David Manning adjusted Mr McKane's proposal for a Ministerial Group. He suggested:

> "If we follow the Afghan precedent, we would set up an Ad Hoc Group (perhaps technically a Sub-Committee of DOP under your chairmanship) to include Jack [Straw], Geoff [Hoon], CDS [Adm Boyce], C [Sir Richard Dearlove] and No.10. The idea would be to keep it tight with meetings in the Den. If we move to military action, we would, of course, need to widen this to include John Prescott [the Deputy Prime Minister], David Blunkett [the Home Secretary] and perhaps others.

> "This leaves the question of what to do about the Attorney. I assume that you would not want him to attend your Ad Hoc Group except by invitation on specific occasions."

384. Ms Clare Short, the International Development Secretary, was not on Sir David's list of recommended participants.

385. Mr Blair wrote on Sir David Manning's advice: "Yes but we can wait before setting up a key Cabinet Group."[219]

386. Mr Jonathan Powell, Mr Blair's Chief of Staff, instructed Sir David Manning: "to progress official groups and leave Minist[eria]l groups for now".[220]

387. Mr Blair's decision not to establish a Ministerial Group in September 2002, in the face of advice to the contrary from officials, limited the opportunities for

---

[217] Minute Manning to PM, 12 September 2002, 'Iraq'.
[218] Minute Manning to Prime Minister, 12 September 2002, 'Iraq'.
[219] Manuscript comment [unattributed] on Minute Manning to Prime Minister, 12 September 2002, 'Iraq'.
[220] Manuscript comment Powell on Minute Manning to Prime Minister, 12 September 2002, 'Iraq'.

Ministerial consideration, challenge and direction of post-conflict planning and preparation.

388. Asked by the Inquiry whether having more stress testing by very senior Ministers not directly involved with Iraq issues might have helped to highlight some of the weaknesses in areas such as post-conflict planning, Mr Blair replied:

"... in one sense I would like to say 'yes', because it would be in a way an easy enough concession to make. My frank belief is it would not have made a great deal of difference, no. The committee meetings that we had, small 'a', small 'h', ad hoc meetings, I think there were 28 of them, 14 of which were minuted. I had the right people there ... no-one was saying to me 'Do it a different way'. I mean, if someone had I would have listened to it, but I have to say to you in addition when I looked, for example, at Mrs Thatcher's War Cabinet, it didn't have the Chancellor of the Exchequer on it ... you have there the people that you need there."[221]

389. No Ministerial Group along the lines recommended by Sir David Manning was convened until the "War Cabinet" met on 19 March 2003, the day the invasion began (see Section 2).[222]

390. The inner group of officials, which discussed a range of issues including counter-terrorism and Afghanistan, was known as the Restricted COBR or COBR(R). Records of the meetings were not produced, although actions were recorded in some instances.

391. The Wider Group, known as the Ad Hoc Group on Iraq (AHGI), met for the first time on 20 September.

392. Sir Kevin Tebbit expressed concern to Mr Hoon about the new Whitehall arrangements.

393. Sir Kevin Tebbit set out his views to Mr Hoon on 17 September:

"Mindful of the difficulties (and frustrations) we have experienced in the past in establishing the right machinery and processes to run crucial politico/military campaigns, I saw David Manning yesterday to discuss the arrangements which might be presented to the Prime Minister, designed to help successful delivery of an Iraq campaign.

"I reminded David of the importance of a small 'core' Ministerial team, meeting very regularly to execute daily business (as distinct from less frequent policy meetings and Cabinet itself). I outlined the linkage needed with the wider COBR and DOP machinery that would pull in government departments and agencies as a whole ...

"David said that he had little influence over such matters as distinct from Jonathan [Powell]. However, he took the point, especially about the importance of acting

---

[221] Public hearing, 21 January 2011, pages 26-27.
[222] Minute Drummond to Rycroft, 19 March 2003, 'Iraq Ministerial Meeting'.

through key Ministers in small groups. The position at present was that the Prime Minister had decided over the weekend on the following:

"a. no Ministerial meetings at this stage;

b. a preference, when they became necessary, for the 'late Afghan' model to apply - ie PM; Defence Secretary; Foreign Secretary; CDS; C; Scarlett; Attorney General and Alastair Campbell as appropriate;

c. meanwhile for Restricted COBR meetings to begin on a twice weekly basis under Manning's chairmanship;

d. for a wider DOP Committee of officials to begin work, under Bowen's chairmanship, which would be the vehicle for bringing in OGDs [other government departments] – DFID, Customs etc."[223]

394. Sir Kevin commented:

"This seems satisfactory for the time being, although we shall need to watch to ensure that (b) does not begin without you being present and that (c) provides the framework we need to link effectively with the contingency planning in the MOD (and perhaps to begin to consider tricky issues of wider relevance, eg the effect on energy prices and oil aftermath management). I should have preferred Bowen to run a restricted officials forum, given the other pressures on Manning's time, the need to begin setting a regular rhythm, and some of the wider issues to be confronted. But I do not think we can do better for the present."

395. The clearest statement of the composition and remit of the AHGI seen by the Inquiry is in a letter from Mr Drummond to government departments on 18 September, in which he stated:

"Desmond Bowen here will be chairing a new committee, known as the Ad Hoc Group on Iraq (AHGI), which will pull together wider issues (both overseas and domestic), and some elements of contingency planning. The Group will have to consider both the inspection route, and the implications if that route failed and military action follows. I will be Desmond's alternate with Tom Dodd as secretary. The Group will comprise representatives of the FCO, MOD, Treasury, Home Office, DfT [Department for Transport], Intelligence Agencies, Cabinet Office, DTI, DFID and ACPO [Association of Chief Police Officers]. Other departments will be invited as and when they have an interest in the agenda. We will be looking to have a fairly settled membership at Head of Department level or above as much of the work will need to be conducted in a discreet manner. At this stage we envisage AHGI meeting on a weekly basis, with the first meeting later this week. Detailed pol/mil [politico-military] co-ordination will be handled separately.

---

[223] Minute Tebbit to Secretary of State [MOD], 17 September 2002, 'Iraq: Machinery of Government'.

"In parallel, the (Cabinet Office) Information Strategy Group (ISG) will be considering the information aspects. This will focus very much on the co-ordination of cross-government strategic messages relating to Iraq, rather than day-to-day media handling. It will meet on an ad hoc basis, and will be chaired by Alastair Campbell or, in his absence, Desmond Bowen."[224]

396. At the first meeting of the AHGI, departments agreed the proposed composition and remit, adding the Department for Environment, Food and Rural Affairs (DEFRA) to the list of participants "to cover environmental aspects".[225]

397. Asked by the Inquiry to explain the Whitehall arrangements, Sir David Manning said that the restricted group chaired by him or his deputy included "all those who had access to the most sensitive intelligence".[226] It was not focused solely on Iraq, and often had other pressing issues to deal with but:

"... it was an opportunity ... to report on the progress that different departments had made, on the latest assessment that may have come out of the agencies, the political issues that were being confronted by the Foreign Office, the difficulties that the Ministry of Defence might be encountering and so on and so forth."

398. Sir David explained that the AHGI drew in those with less or very little access to sensitive intelligence.

399. Mr Bowen told the Inquiry that, when the AHGI started its work in September 2002, the context was "a serious policy commitment to deal with weapons of mass destruction in Iraq". Conflict was just one of "any number of outcomes".[227]

400. At the end of August 2002, Sir Michael Jay identified the need to put the FCO's Iraq work on a new footing.

401. Mr Ricketts was put in charge of ensuring the FCO's approach was "suitably dynamic and coherent".

402. Between September and mid-November 2002, the FCO's principal preoccupation on Iraq was the negotiation of UN Security Council resolution (UNSCR) 1441.

403. Mr Straw and Mr Ricketts were heavily engaged in those negotiations.

404. On 30 August, Mr Gray sent Sir Michael Jay a draft minute from Sir Michael to Mr Straw, setting out the steps Sir Michael was taking to "draw together threads of activity on Iraq" in the FCO.[228] The draft explained that, in addition to intensifying work

---

[224] Letter Drummond to Wright, 18 September 2002, 'Iraq Co-ordination'.
[225] Minute Drummond to Manning, 23 September 2002, 'Ad Hoc Group on Iraq'.
[226] Public hearing, 30 November 2009, page 45.
[227] Public hearing, 7 December 2009, page 10.
[228] Minute Gray to PS/PUS [FCO], 30 August 2002, 'Iraq' attaching Minute [draft] PUS [FCO] to Secretary of State [FCO], 30 August 2002, 'Iraq'.

on a UN Security Council resolution (see Section 3.5), Sir Michael was setting up a "strategy group" reporting to Mr Ricketts to ensure FCO work on Iraq was "suitably dynamic and coherent". The group would meet weekly; more often if necessary.

405. The Inquiry has not seen a final version of that minute and it is not clear whether it was seen by Mr Straw, but Mr Gray's draft was seen by officials in No.10.

406. The Inquiry has seen no further reference to an FCO "strategy group", but Mr Ricketts did chair the first "FCO Iraq Co-ordination Meeting" on 6 September.[229] Among the issues discussed was a paper on the consequences of military action in the region and beyond being prepared by the Directorate of Strategy and Innovation (DSI).

407. It is not clear whether officials from outside the FCO attended the meeting, but the record was copied to the Cabinet Office Assessments Staff and to the MOD. It was not copied to OD Sec.

408. A second meeting was scheduled for 18 September, but the Inquiry has seen no record of it taking place.

409. From mid-September, Mr Ricketts was increasingly focused on the negotiations for what was to become resolution 1441.

410. In his witness statement, Mr Stephen Pattison, Head of FCO United Nations Department (UND), who was responsible for the formulation of policy on Security Council resolutions and provided instructions to the UK Permanent Mission to the UN in New York (UKMIS New York), explained that the key tactical decisions on how to handle negotiations on the text were taken at twice daily meetings chaired by Mr Ricketts.[230] The instructions were complemented by daily telephone conversations between Mr Ricketts and Sir Jeremy Greenstock, UK Permanent Representative to the UN, and by correspondence with other members of UKMIS New York.[231]

411. The first reference to Iraq in the minutes of the FCO Board during the period covered by the Inquiry was on 20 September 2002, when members observed that Iraq had risen up the agenda since August and asked whether the FCO was "prepared for a crisis".[232] The Board was informed by officials that work was in hand on how the FCO should handle concurrent crises and on the possible need to commit resources "in preparation for any need to move quickly into Baghdad".

412. Preparations for the reopening of an Embassy in Baghdad are described in Section 15.1.

---

[229] Minute [FCO junior official] to Gray, 6 September 2002, 'Iraq Coordination Meeting'.
[230] Statement, 6 January 2011.
[231] Public hearing, 31 January 2011, pages 22-23.
[232] Minutes, 20 September 2002, FCO Board.

The potential scale of the post-conflict task

413. During late August and early September, UK analysts advised on:

- **the likely need for sustained international commitment to Iraq's reconstruction;**
- **the importance of starting preparations early; and**
- **the need for greater clarity on US thinking.**

414. An FCO paper on the economic consequences of military action assessed that "an enormous task of reconstruction and economic and financial normalisation" lay ahead. If serious preparatory work did not begin many months before regime change, there was likely to be a "serious and politically embarrassing hiatus".

415. A paper by Treasury officials compared the reconstruction of Iraq with Yugoslavia, Afghanistan and East Timor. It concluded that reconstruction in Iraq could prove more expensive, but might also be less challenging.

FCO PAPER: 'REGIONAL ECONOMIC CONSEQUENCES OF MILITARY ACTION AGAINST IRAQ'

416. On 29 August, the FCO Economic Adviser for the Middle East and North Africa produced an assessment of short- and long-term economic consequences of military action for the region and for Iraq.[233] The paper identified a number of priorities for the UK, including mobilising the International Monetary Fund (IMF) and the World Bank as soon as possible to begin building up a picture of Iraq's economy:

> "An enormous task of reconstruction and economic and financial normalisation lies ahead. For all Iraq's oil wealth it will take many years before the country can get back to levels of prosperity seen in the 1990s.

> "... [T]here will be a huge job of reforming Iraqi economic policies and institutions: dismantling Ba'ath Party economic control and corruption and replacing it with competent, transparent market-orientated management will probably be akin to dismantling Communist Party control in Central and Eastern Europe. A strategy for reconstruction and long-term development will have to be worked out.

> "... [T]here is a desperate shortage of available information on Iraq's economy which will delay assessment of both the financial position and the requirement for institutional change/technical assistance. Unless serious preparatory work is put in hand many months before regime change there is likely to be a serious and politically embarrassing hiatus."

---

[233] Minute Economic Policy Department [junior official] to Gray, 29 August 2002, 'Iraq: economic issues raised by military action and regime change' attaching paper, undated, 'Regional economic consequences of military action against Iraq'.

417. The assessment was copied widely within the FCO, including to Mr Chaplin, and to Trade Partners UK (TPUK). The Inquiry has seen no evidence that it was copied to other departments.

418. Mr Creon Butler, the FCO Chief Economist, endorsed the economic adviser's analysis and the importance of thinking about economic issues "<u>at the same time</u>" as military options.[234] He advised that:

"… a few $bn spent on a Jordan safety net [to cushion the economic shock of conflict] and more rapid intervention in Iraq post-conflict is likely to be small beer vis-a-vis the total costs of military intervention and could do a great deal to ensure the ultimate success of the exercise."

419. Mr Butler added that:

- The Government would need to make special provision for the costs.
- It was important to learn the lessons of post-Milošević Yugoslavia, where a "first rate" economic team, largely from the Yugoslav diaspora, had made "a tremendously positive impact" on economic management. Did such people exist in Iraq's case?
- International financial institutions (IFIs) were unlikely to sanction any significant work on Iraq until there was a clear international mandate. If they did not, it could still make sense for the UK to do work in-house and start a dialogue with the US.

420. Mr Butler did not copy his email to Mr Chaplin, Mr Ricketts, or outside the FCO.

TREASURY PAPER: 'WHAT WOULD BE THE ECONOMIC IMPACT OF WAR IN IRAQ?'

421. On 6 September, Treasury officials sent Mr Brown a paper on the economic impact of military action on the global, regional and Iraqi economies.[235] The paper addressed three scenarios: a large-scale invasion leading to relatively quick regime change (identified as the most likely scenario); regime change through an internal uprising; and regime change after a prolonged campaign during which WMD had been used.

422. The paper assessed that oil prices could rise by $US10 per barrel. Over a year, that could reduce global growth by 0.5 percent and raise inflation by 0.4-0.8 percent. Investor and consumer confidence could fall and there was limited room for easing monetary and fiscal policy across the G7.[236]

423. In the region, "a small group of countries could lose out quite heavily" as a result of a range of factors from reduced tourism to disruption of trade with Iraq.

---

[234] Email Butler to Gray, 30 August 2002, 'Iraq: Economic Issues Raised by Military Action and Regime Change'.
[235] Email Crook to Bowman, 6 September 2002, 'What would be the economic impact of a war in Iraq?' attaching Paper, September 2002, 'What would be the economic impact of war in Iraq?'.
[236] The G7 group of industrialised countries: Canada, France, Germany, Italy, Japan, United Kingdom, United States.

424. The paper's analysis of the impact on Iraq drew on three recent precedents: the Federal Republic of Yugoslavia (FRY), Afghanistan and East Timor. The paper concluded that there were four reasons why reconstruction in Iraq might be "even more expensive" than in the FRY, which had already cost nearly US$10 billion:

- Iraq's infrastructure might be in a worse condition.
- Iraq's economy would need stabilising after years of sanctions, reckless spending and high inflation, and there was a huge external debt burden.
- A large peacekeeping force would be needed to "keep a lid on" ethnic and religious tensions.
- The UK should expect "heavy moral pressure" to make a generous contribution to the reconstruction effort.

425. The paper added that, although reconstruction in Iraq might be more expensive than in the FRY, it might be less challenging: Iraq already had "institutions of government", the private sector had not been completely destroyed, and Iraq was much richer.

426. That analysis informed a paper on Treasury policy towards post-conflict Iraq produced in February 2003 (see Section 6.5).

SPG PAPER, 4 SEPTEMBER 2002: 'UK MILITARY STRATEGIC THINKING ON IRAQ'

427. In the 4 September edition of its paper on UK military strategic thinking, the SPG stated:

> "Given fractious nature of Iraqi politics, broad regional concern on nature of new Iraqi government, and poor state of Iraqi infrastructure, delivery of stated post-conflict objectives will require lengthy engagement."

428. The SPG also stated that:

- **"lack of clarity in US on post-conflict Iraq means we do not yet have a winning concept";**
- **the "key military question" to be addressed was whether there was a winning military concept; and**
- **the absence of a clear post-conflict strategy would be a reason for not participating in the US plan.**

429. It is not clear who outside the MOD saw the SPG paper.

430. On 4 September, the SPG issued the third edition of its paper on military strategic thinking, previously updated on 11 July.[237]

---

[237] Paper [SPG], 4 September 2002, 'UK Military Strategic Thinking on Iraq'.

431. In a new list of "key deductions", the SPG advised:

"Given fractious nature of Iraqi politics, broad regional concern on nature of new Iraqi government, and poor state of Iraqi infrastructure, delivery of stated post-conflict objectives will require lengthy engagement.

"Successful post-conflict delivery of US support to a new, broad-based government will require co-operation and agreement of regional states on acceptability of the outcome, if its efforts are not to be undermined."

432. The SPG also listed strategic issues needing resolution before there could be a "winning concept". They included:

- the "likely model for Iraqi governance, security structures, and economy, to inform estimates of post-conflict engagement"; and
- the likely post-conflict role of the UN.

433. In the section on post-conflict tasks, the list of likely short-, medium- and long-term post-conflict military tasks from earlier versions was replaced with a briefer description of planning priorities. The SPG stated that US military planners were working on detailed post-conflict plans, but drawing on very broad assumptions about the nature of the new regime. The SPG recommended that:

"… clarity and broad agreement on [the] following is needed before coherent plans can be effectively delivered:

- **Political.** Nature of regime, extent of franchise, land tenure, and relations with other states.
- **Economic.** Ownership and redevelopment of oil resources and development of other economic activity.
- **Security.** Security structures and security sector reform (SSR). Purpose, size and nature of Iraqi Armed Forces and internal security forces."

434. The SPG continued:

"Planning will need to be undertaken with DFID in order to effectively manage [the] NGO response to humanitarian consequences. Saddam may well use mass movement of refugees as an operational tool to slow Coalition advance and as part of a strategic attack on Coalition … domestic public support …

"Without clear post-conflict plans potential scale … of UK military commitment remains an unknown."

435. The SPG stated that "lack of clarity in US on post-conflict Iraq means we do not yet have a winning concept", but:

> "US military planners are fully aware of the need to establish a strategic context and for an inter-agency approach, and considerable work has been done to address these concerns. Our analysis and judgements are now based on a sound knowledge of the CENTCOM plan and recent military developments to which we are privy, and our assessment of whether to engage or not is (now based on a much surer footing) predicated on this imperfect basis.

> "… The key **military** question to be addressed is:

> > 'Is there a winning military concept and plan?'"

436. The SPG set out two responses: a list of conditions to be met before the answer could be "yes" and a list of reasons why the answer should be "no":

- The list of conditions for participation included:
  - preparation of an acceptable post-conflict administration (US military planners were reported to have identified the military tasks to be addressed, but how those would be co-ordinated with other aspects of nation-building was not yet clear); and
  - UK post-conflict tasks to be "limited in scope and time".
- Reasons for not participating in the US plan included the absence of a clear post-conflict strategy, which would make it likely that the UK military commitment would become open-ended.

Mr Blair's commitment to post-conflict reconstruction

437. Before Mr Blair's meeting with President Bush at Camp David on 7 September, Sir Christopher Meyer advised that pacifying Iraq would make Afghanistan look like "child's play". Afghanistan had shown that the US was not good at consolidating politically what it had achieved militarily.

438. On 2 September, a few days before Mr Blair's visit to Camp David, Mr Rycroft showed Mr Blair, Mr Powell and Sir David Manning an article by *New York Times* columnist Mr Thomas L Friedman about the scale of the post-conflict task.[238] In the article, Mr Friedman commented:

> "… we are talking about nation-building from scratch. Iraq has … none of the civil society or rule of law roots that enabled the United States to quickly build democracies out of the ruins of Germany and Japan …

> …

---

[238] Manuscript comment Rycroft to Prime Minister on *International Herald Tribune,* 2 September 2002, *Remaking Iraq looks like a tall order.*

"This is not a reason for not taking Saddam out. It is a reason to prepare for a potentially long, costly nation-building operation and to enlist as many allies as possible to share the burden.

…

"My most knowledgeable Iraqi friend tells me he is confident that the morning after any US invasion, US troops would be welcomed by Iraqis and the regime would fold quickly. It is the morning after the morning after that we have to be prepared for.

"In the best case, a 'nice' strongman will emerge from the Iraq army to preside over a gradual transition to democracy, with America receding into a supporting role. In the worst case, Iraq falls apart, with all its historical internal tensions – particularly between its long-ruling Sunni minority and its long-frustrated Shia majority. In that case, George W Bush will have to become Iraq's strongman – the iron fist that holds the country together, gradually re-distributes the oil wealth and supervises a much longer transition to democracy.

"My Iraqi friend tells me that anyone who tells you he knows which scenario will unfold doesn't know Iraq."

439. Sir Christopher Meyer reported on 5 September that the US Government was considering starting to make the case against Saddam Hussein, including by using President Bush's speech at the UN General Assembly to indict him and circulating a draft resolution the following week.[239] Congressional resolutions authorising military action would be sought in early October.

440. On 6 September, Sir Christopher Meyer advised that, while President Bush's decision to take the UN route and to consult widely at home and abroad was welcome, it left "a raft of questions unanswered".[240]

441. Sir Christopher judged that a military invasion and its aftermath would be "less perilous [for the US] in company". On post-conflict issues, he wrote:

"The preconditions for military action are a focal point for Camp David. So are post-war Iraq and the MEPP [Middle East Peace Process] … The President seems to have bought the neo-con notion that with the overthrow of Saddam all will be sweetness and light in Iraq, with automatic benefits in the rest of the Middle East (which partly explains his inactivity on the latter). In reality, it will probably make pacifying Afghanistan look like child's play. The US is probably in greater need of coalition and UN support for what is likely to be a very protracted post-war phase, than for the attack itself. Afghanistan has shown that the US is not good at consolidating politically what it has achieved militarily."

---

[239] Telegram 1130 Washington to FCO London, 5 September 2002, 'Iraq: The US Diplomatic Game Plan'.
[240] Telegram 1140 Washington to FCO London, 6 September 2002, 'PM's visit to Camp David: Iraq'.

442. Mr Blair discussed options for a UK military contribution in Iraq with Mr Hoon on 5 September.[241] Mr Straw was also present.

443. There was no No.10 record of the discussion, but Mr Watkins recorded that no decisions were taken and Mr Blair "did not expect President Bush to commit himself imminently to a military campaign".

444. On 6 September, Mr Watkins sent No.10 an assessment of US military plans and factors informing a UK military contribution in Iraq. He cautioned that the assessment was "necessarily provisional", partly because the US plan was still evolving, and partly because there had not yet been "detailed joint planning with the US".[242]

445. Mr Watkins described three UK military options (Packages 1 to 3) ranging from minimum to maximum effort. He also drew attention to the "sketchy" post-conflict plans and the importance of keeping in mind the US timetable when identifying the contribution the UK might offer and the influence it was hoped to bring.

446. Copies of the letter were sent to Mr Straw's and Sir Andrew Turnbull's Private Secretaries, and to Mr Bowen in the Cabinet Office.

447. The letter is addressed in more detail in Section 6.1.

448. On 6 September, Mr Webb told Mr Lee that Mr Feith had asked for UK advice on post-Saddam Hussein regimes.[243] Mr Webb suggested that officials work on an FCO-led piece "to contribute to a key gap in US thinking".

449. The FCO produced papers on post-Saddam Hussein regimes during September and October and the subject was discussed at the first round of US/UK/Australia talks on post-conflict issues in Washington on 6 November. The papers and the Washington talks are described later in this Section.

450. Although it is likely that UK papers were shared with the US in the context of those talks, the Inquiry has seen no documentary evidence of a UK paper on post-Saddam Hussein administrations being shared with the US until 12 December.

451. At Camp David, Mr Blair told President Bush that an enormous amount of work would be needed to get post-Saddam Hussein Iraq right.

452. The meeting between President Bush and Mr Blair at Camp David on 7 September was in two parts, addressed in more detail in Section 3.4.

453. Mr Blair, supported only by Sir David Manning, discussed Iraq with President Bush, Vice President Cheney and Dr Rice from 1600 to 1745.[244] Sir David recorded that, during

---

[241] Minute Watkins to DG Op Pol, 5 September 2002, 'Iraq'.
[242] Letter Watkins to Manning, 6 September 2002, 'Iraq: Military Planning'.
[243] Minute Webb to DG Op Pol, 6 September 2002, 'Close Allies: Berlin 4 September: Iraq Margins'.
[244] Minute Manning to Prime Minister, 8 September 2002, 'Your Visit to Camp David on 7 September: Conversation with President Bush'.

the meeting, Mr Blair warned that, even if Saddam Hussein were overthrown relatively quickly, the big issue would remain of what followed his departure in a country that had never known democracy. There would be an enormous amount of work needed to get post-Saddam Hussein Iraq right, even if US troops were to remain in Iraq for up to 18 months after any conflict.

454. A plenary meeting between President Bush and Mr Blair and their teams followed the restricted discussion.[245] During the plenary meeting, Mr Hadley put forward three principles for post-Saddam Hussein Iraq: territorial integrity, democracy and a role for the UN.

455. Detailed consideration of the options for UK force contributions in Iraq began in September 2002.

456. Military planners advised that, in the event of the deployment of UK land forces, there was a judgement to be made on whether the UK military should be engaged in the conflict or post-conflict phase. Both would be difficult to sustain.

457. Adm Boyce described it as "inconceivable" that the UK military would not contribute "in some manner" to post-conflict tasks.

458. On 9 September, the MOD prepared advice for the meeting between Mr Hoon and Secretary Rumsfeld on 11 September, including some high level questions on post-conflict planning:

- "How does the military plan work" after regime change?
- What role would the US and others have in reconstruction?
- How long would military engagement last?[246]

459. There is no indication that those issues were raised during Mr Hoon's visit to Washington.[247]

460. On 19 September, the Chiefs of Staff discussed a commentary on options for UK force contributions in Iraq prepared by the SPG.[248]

461. The SPG paper presented four options for a UK military contribution and highlighted a number of continuing strategic uncertainties: the shape of the campaign, its timing, post-conflict commitments and the legal basis for military action.[249]

---

[245] Letter Rycroft to Sedwill, 8 September 2002, 'Prime Minister's Meeting with Bush, Camp David, 7 September: Public Presentation of Iraq Policy'.
[246] Minute Cholerton to APS/Secretary of State [MOD], 9 September 2002, 'Iraq – Defence Secretary's Meeting with Rumsfeld'.
[247] Telegram 1159 Washington to FCO London, 11 September 2002, 'Iraq: Mr Hoon's Visit to Washington, 11 September'.
[248] Minutes, 19 September 2002, Chiefs of Staff meeting.
[249] Paper SPG, 19 September 2002, 'Iraq Package Options – Military Strategic Commentary at 19 September 2002'.

462. On post-conflict commitments the paper stated:

"The likely post-conflict scenarios and demands have yet to be clearly articulated. Scenarios include immediate and catastrophic regime collapse, the mounting of an internal coup as the campaign commences, or at the opposite end of the spectrum an exhausted Iraq suing for peace. Each of these will require a different response. The infant US inter-agency process has just started to identify the means by which transition to a post-Saddam regime might take place. This commences with a CENTCOM-led military government."

463. In the section headed "Conflict vs Post-conflict", the SPG asked whether, if UK forces were to participate in the military campaign, "our effort should be against the need to meet US short-term planning for combat, or the equally demanding and pressing need for preparations for the post-conflict phase". It continued:

"Conflict phase. Commitment to this phase may carry with it inherent risks with regard to post-conflict engagement with little choice on role, timing, location, or future extraction. An alternative approach that offers a UK lead, or UK participation in the post-conflict phase may be equally attractive to the US as our commitment to a land role in the conflict phase.

"Post-Conflict. Given the wide range of possible post-conflict scenarios these forces would have to be combat capable forces at high readiness, and in all probability with key elements forward deployed during the conflict phase. The length and scale of our post-conflict commitment will determine our ability to fulfil a range of other operations, and most notably our Balkan commitment. An enduring medium scale[250] commitment in Iraq would preclude continued medium scale engagement in the Balkans.

"Strategic Balance. We are currently committed to two medium scale land operations (FRESCO[251] and the Balkans), and a land commitment to Iraq at anything above small scale[252] will commit us to **three medium scale** land operations. Although with a full Package 3[253] commitment to the conflict phase we retain the SLE [Spearhead Land Element], our ability to deploy and sustain even a small scale force package has yet to be determined, and anything above this Scale of Effort will be impossible … Recovery and recuperation will also be key to our judgements as to which phase to commit to. Hard and fast judgements are not possible, however, commitment of Package 3 will have an effect for at least two years."

---

[250] Defined in the 1998 Strategic Defence Review as "deployments of brigade size or equivalent" for war-fighting or other operations, such as the UK contribution in the mid-1990s to the NATO-led Implementation Force (IFOR) in Bosnia.

[251] The use of military forces to provide cover in the event of a strike by the Fire Brigades' Union.

[252] Defined in the 1998 Strategic Defence Review as "a deployment of battalion size or equivalent".

[253] The most ambitious of the four options and the only one involving the deployment of UK land forces (to northern Iraq).

464. The SPG concluded:

> **"Assuming that UK land participation is a requirement, there is a judgement to be made on whether we should be engaged in the conflict or post-conflict phases. Both would be difficult to sustain."**

465. Lt Gen Pigott and Lieutenant General John Reith, Chief of Joint Operations (CJO), briefed the Chiefs of Staff Committee on the options available, explaining that "Package 4 was being developed to address the inevitable post-conflict tasks".[254] Adm Boyce commented that it was "inconceivable that the UK would not contribute in some manner, to those tasks".

466. The Chiefs of Staff Committee on 19 September and subsequent correspondence and discussions involving No.10 and Mr Blair are covered in more detail in Section 6.1.

467. Post-conflict military operations were not addressed in Mr Watkins' letter of 20 September to Sir David Manning on the potential UK contribution to military action.[255]

468. Nor do they appear in the record of the discussion between Mr Blair and Mr Hoon on 23 September, at which it was decided that land forces, while not being ruled out altogether, should not be put forward as part of the potential UK contribution at the CENTCOM planning conference later that week (see Section 6.1).[256]

469. The Chiefs of Staff discussed Iraq planning on 25 September.[257] They recognised that the post-conflict phase of military operations (Phase IV) "would not have a clear-cut start" and that the UK should "guard against any accusation that the 'US does the war-fighting while the UK does the peacekeeping'". Not being involved in Package 3 at all "would be difficult to manage".

470. The Chiefs of Staff commissioned Lt Gen Pigott to: "Explore options for potential UK involvement in Phase IV", with a deadline of 2 October.

471. Lt Gen Pigott summarised the potential scale of the UK military contribution in Iraq in a minute to Lt Gen Reith on 26 September.[258] He explained that aftermath requirements were still to be addressed and "could impact on the final shape" of the force packages he was describing.

472. The 30 September edition of the SPG paper on UK military strategic thinking included more detail on post-conflict issues and is described later in this Section.

---

[254] Minutes, 19 September 2002, Chiefs of Staff meeting.
[255] Letter Watkins to Manning, 20 September 2002, 'Iraq: Potential UK Contribution To Any Military Action'.
[256] Minute Watkins to DG Op Pol, 23 September 2002, 'Iraq: Meeting with the Prime Minister: 23 September'.
[257] Minutes, 25 September 2002, Chiefs of Staff meeting.
[258] Minute DCDS(C) to CJO, 26 September 2002, 'Iraq – Potential Scale of UK Force Contribution for use in UK/US Contingency Planning'.

473. Mr Blair told Cabinet on 23 September that the international community had to be committed to Iraq's reconstruction.

474. Cabinet met on 23 September (see Section 3.5). Points made in discussion included:

> "… in the event of military action, a clear vision was required of the outcome we wanted in reconstructing Iraq: this would be a major task".[259]

475. Summing up the discussion, Mr Blair said that a "crunch point" had been reached:

> "The sanctions regime … was being eroded and Saddam Hussein was on the way to acquiring new capability in weapons of mass destruction. Iraq had to comply with the obligations placed on it by the United Nations. A tough line was required. If military action was required, the job could be done. There would be a discussion about the military options … civilian casualties should be kept to a minimum, but there could be no doubt that the main beneficiaries of the removal of Saddam Hussein would be the Iraqi people. Iraq was basically a wealthy country. The international community had to be committed to Iraq's reconstruction."

476. Mr Cook wrote in his memoir that he closed his contribution:

> "... by stressing the vital importance of getting approval for anything we do through the UN. 'What follows after Saddam will be the mother of all nation-building projects. We shouldn't attempt it on our own – if we want the rest of the international community with us at the end, we need them in at the start.'"[260]

477. Mr Campbell wrote in his diaries that Mr Brown had made "a few long-term points for the US, the need to think through post-Saddam, the importance of the MEPP".[261]

478. Late on 23 September, Mr Brenton reported that the US Administration was "starting to get to grips with 'Day After' questions – in [the] State [Department]'s case, with considerable trepidation".[262] A senior State Department official had suggested that anything other than an Iraqi General succeeding Saddam Hussein would be extremely challenging and involve the US in a massive presence for an indefinite period.

479. Parliament was recalled to discuss Iraq on 24 September. There was considerable concern in both Houses about arrangements to support Iraq after an invasion.

480. Mr Blair drew attention, in the context of Afghanistan, to the UK's commitment to "stick with" the Afghan people "until the job of reconstruction is

---

[259] Cabinet Conclusions, 23 September 2002.
[260] Cook R. *The Point of Departure*. Simon & Schuster UK, 2003.
[261] Campbell A & Hagerty B. *The Alastair Campbell Diaries. Volume 4. The Burden of Power: Countdown to Iraq*. Hutchinson, 2012.
[262] Telegram 1221 Washington to FCO London, 23 September 2002, 'US/Iraq'.

done". He maintained that the question of who might replace Saddam Hussein did not yet require a decision.

481. Parliament was recalled to discuss Iraq on 24 September (see Section 3.5).

482. In his statement to the House of Commons, Mr Blair drew attention to the UK's continuing commitment to Afghanistan:

> "Afghanistan is a country now freed from the Taliban but still suffering. This is a regime we changed, rightly. I want to make it clear, once again, that we are entirely committed to its reconstruction. We will not desert the Afghan people. We will stick with them until the job of reconstruction is done."[263]

483. During the adjournment debate that followed, Mr Charles Kennedy, Leader of the Liberal Democrats, observed that:

> "In his statement, the Prime Minister spoke about the need for Iraq to be led by someone who variously can abide by international law, bring Iraq back into the international community, make the country rich and successful, and make its government more representative of the country. However, he was silent on the question of who or where that person or set of people is. The Prime Minister, quite rightly, with our support and that of others, was able to point to the mobilisation of forces in Afghanistan, which could lead to an alternative, more acceptable government there. Is there capacity or potential for a similar mobilisation to take place within Iraq?

> "In the context of Afghanistan, the Prime Minister made it clear that, if such a course of action proved successful – which it did – the country and the international community would not walk away. Is a similar approach being identified for Iraq? Does such an approach encompass the mindset of the present American Administration? If we were not to walk away following the toppling of Saddam, who would provide the necessary presence to police and create the ongoing stability in Iraq that would be essential because of the shell-shocked nature of that country?

> "When the American Defense Secretary speaks of a 'decapitation strategy' with a view to Iraq does he reflect the mind processes of the British Government? Should we not instead be talking about the longer-term need for a rehabilitation strategy for Iraq, not least for its innocent, oppressed people with whom none of us has any argument whatever?"[264]

484. Mr Blair responded:

> "As for not walking away, we should not walk away from the situation in Afghanistan, and the US Administration themselves have made clear that should it come to

---

[263] House of Commons, *Official Report*, 24 September 2002, column 6.
[264] House of Commons, *Official Report*, 24 September 2002, column 10.

regime change in Iraq they will not walk away from that either. I simply emphasise this point. Of course all sorts of issues will have to be resolved, but the fact is, as I said a few weeks ago, that the first decision we must make is this: do we allow the situation to continue, with this weapons of mass destruction programme?"[265]

485. In response to a question from Mr Jon Owen Jones (Labour) about what threats would ensue if the Iraqi regime were replaced by force of arms, Mr Blair stated:

"Although some of these questions – if we get to the stage of regime change, what replaces Saddam – do not arise for decision now, as I have said throughout I of course agree that they are very serious questions, which we need to look at. The only thing that I would say to my honourable Friend about regime change is that it is hard to think of an Iraqi regime that would be worse than Saddam, but that said, it is obviously important that we deal with all these issues, including making it quite clear to the people of Iraq that should it come to the point of regime change, that has to be done while protecting the territorial integrity of Iraq. That is an important point."[266]

486. Mr Bruce George (Labour) proposed a number of criteria to be satisfied before any decision was taken on whether to go to war, including: "a credible military strategy with considerable thought given to what the consequences would be if war were undertaken and strong consideration given to post-operation peace support".[267]

487. Ms Glenda Jackson (Labour) and Mr Doug Henderson (Labour) both warned that, although the US and UK were certain to win a war in Iraq, there was no such certainty about who would win the peace.

488. Ms Jackson asked whether the UK was ready to commit itself to "a massive commitment of money, materials and personnel to bring about change".[268]

489. Mr Henderson warned: "If we do not start with a coalition of public support, it will be impossible to build any stable society in Iraq and neighbouring countries afterwards."[269]

490. Several speakers raised post-conflict issues in the House of Lords.

491. Lord Strathclyde (Conservative), in expressing support for the Government's position on Iraq, asked, among other questions:

"What vision do the Government have of a post-Saddam Iraq, which is surely in itself the most important question for those who want regime change?"[270]

---

[265] House of Commons, *Official Report*, 24 September 2002, column 12.
[266] House of Commons, *Official Report*, 24 September 2002, column 20.
[267] House of Commons, *Official Report*, 24 September 2002, columns 47-48.
[268] House of Commons, *Official Report*, 24 September 2002, column 96.
[269] House of Commons, *Official Report*, 24 September 2002, column 112.
[270] House of Lords, *Official Report*, 24 September 2002, column 865.

492. Baroness Williams (Liberal Democrat), spoke of "facing up to the necessity of force should that prove inevitable", but expressed:

> "… grave concerns about the exit strategy that was followed in Afghanistan, a country that appears to be sliding back to anarchy rather rapidly … In some ways Afghanistan represents a failure of the international community to build upon the military victory that it claimed would open the door to a democratic and just Afghanistan".[271]

What assurance could be given that the UK and US would "turn their minds more seriously to the matter of the exit strategy and what follows victory"? Without that, it remained unclear what the strategy was or how to ensure it "will not enrage and unite the Muslim world against us".

493. Baroness Symons, joint FCO/DTI Minister of State for International Trade and Investment, set out the Government's position:

> "Many will ask what will happen next if there is armed intervention. How will it be done? When and how would those undertaking such action withdraw from Iraq? What is the exit strategy? The truth is that discussion of those questions in detail is not for today."[272]

494. Lord Howell (Conservative), expressing full support for Mr Blair's approach on Iraq, asked:

> "What will happen later? Do we have a vision – I do – of a federal, democratic Iraq … Is there a possibility of a benign Iraq; a force for stability in the Middle East, instead of a force for evil and the culture of death? Is that wider vision in the Government's mind? We have not heard much about that, but it is important we should have such a wider vision. If we do, how is it to be secured? Should US troops, thousands of whom are already in the region, stay there for a long time and occupy the whole area? Are they ready to go into other areas that might be at risk?

> "Those questions hang in the air. We must have from the Government some indication of where we are going. As Clausewitz said, you should not take the first step … towards war unless you have thought about the last step as well."[273]

495. Lord Hurd (Conservative), warned of the scale of the reconstruction task:

> "We must not delude ourselves. The process of nation rebuilding in Iraq will be a slow and strenuous one. We have to consider – it will be difficult; it will be the problems of Afghanistan on a much bigger scale – whether we and the Americans are prepared to keep troops after an immediate military victory to support and prop

---

[271] House of Lords, *Official Report*, 24 September 2002, column 868.
[272] House of Lords, *Official Report*, 24 September 2002, column 875.
[273] House of Lords, *Official Report*, 24 September 2002, column 879.

up whatever government emerges until it establishes its own authority against a background where such occupation would inevitably soon become unpopular."[274]

496. The Earl of Onslow (Conservative) called on the Government to plan for the worst. If force were used and the Iraqi Government collapsed, "what is the worst-case scenario, are we thinking about it and do we know what to do?"[275]

Initial analysis of the issues and the Ad Hoc Group on Iraq

497. From 20 September 2002, the Cabinet Office-chaired Ad Hoc Group on Iraq (AHGI) co-ordinated all non-military cross-government work on post-conflict issues.

498. The AHGI was not tasked to consider in detail the operational requirements for humanitarian relief or wider reconstruction.

499. Nor was it required to examine systematically the different policy options for post-conflict Iraq, the UK's potential involvement in different scenarios or the associated risks.

500. The focus of the AHGI's work during autumn 2002 was a series of analytical papers by the FCO and other departments on the post-conflict administration and reconstruction of Iraq, and the possible consequences of conflict for the UK.

501. There was some visibility between military and civilian post-conflict analysis, but the two strands of work remained largely separate until the creation of the IPU in February 2003 (see Section 6.5). None of the analytical material produced by the AHGI in 2002 was put to Ministers for decision.

502. The AHGI was chaired by Mr Bowen and overseen by Sir David Manning. Its work was not shown routinely to Mr Blair.

503. The AHGI held its first meeting on 20 September.[276]

504. Mr Drummond wrote to Mr Bowen beforehand, suggesting topics for discussion and proposing departmental responsibilities for different subjects:

"In the absence of initiatives from the centre, a few departments have done their own work on the consequences of action in Iraq. We need to find out what has already been done and encourage departments to share it. So far I have only seen an FCO note on unintended consequences ... This identifies them but stops short

---

[274] House of Lords, *Official Report*, 24 September 2002, column 916.
[275] House of Lords, *Official Report*, 24 September 2002, column 1002.
[276] Minute Drummond to Manning, 23 September 2002, 'Ad Hoc Group on Iraq'.

of suggesting ways of mitigating and managing them. I suggest we focus on the following:

- The morning after in Iraq. What is the political process that secures a compliant, representative successor regime while Iraq retains its existing borders (FCO)? Reforming the security sector, civil service (MOD and DFID).
- Tactics for securing international support before and after the action. FCO need to write a paper …
- Impact on world growth and trade, and on the UK economy (HMT [the Treasury] to write a note if they haven't already).
- Securing oil supplies and effect of regime change on world oil markets (DTI).
- Consequences for air travel including viability of airlines (DfT).
- Environment. The after effects of CBW [chemical and biological weapons], oil fires, pollution in the Gulf etc … (DEFRA).
- Impact on the UK … (Home Office and Security Service should lead)."[277]

505. Mr Drummond suggested focusing on the main points needing discussion with the US, "probably the morning after and handling the region". He recommended that work on campaign objectives be kept in OD Sec and the Restricted COBR.

506. The AHGI remained the principal Whitehall co-ordination mechanism for non-military Iraq planning until the creation of the inter-departmental Iraq Planning Unit (IPU) in February 2003. Military planning continued to be restricted to a very narrow circle.

507. The record of the first meeting confirmed that:

"Most [departments] have begun considering implications of military action. These include Treasury on the macro economic impact, DTI on oil markets, DFID on humanitarian aspects, CCS [Cabinet Office Civil Contingencies Secretariat] on UK contingency planning, DfT on aviation security and the police and agencies on their range of issues …

"We should give priority to thinking through the morning after questions. The FCO have work in hand on this [in] preparation for talks with the US. They will share a draft with interested departments … They are already deeply engaged in discussions with the US about handling the regional players."[278]

---

[277] Minute Drummond to Bowen, 19 September 2002, 'Ad Hoc Group on Iraq (AHGI)'.
[278] Minute Drummond to Manning, 23 September 2002, 'Ad Hoc Group on Iraq'.

508. Mr Gray, the FCO attendee at the first meeting, commented to FCO colleagues:

"In practice this first meeting was largely an exercise in telling the FCO how to suck eggs. I'm sure future meetings will improve."[279]

FCO PAPER: 'IRAQ – CONSEQUENCES OF CONFLICT FOR THE REGION AND BEYOND'

509. The first FCO paper for the AHGI identified possible consequences of conflict for the Middle East and beyond. They included:

- **a refugee crisis;**
- **heightened anti-Western feeling;**
- **an easier environment for terrorists to operate in; and**
- **higher oil prices.**

510. The paper stated: "By preparing for the worst, we should be better placed to avoid it."

511. In Washington on 17 September, Mr Miller told Mr Ricketts that he had started a lot of work on post-conflict issues and expected to have the basics in place in two or three weeks.[280] Mr Ricketts suggested that UK and US experts should get together at that point and "stressed the importance of this work. We had to think through the unintended consequences of any action we might launch."

512. On 20 September, the FCO sent Sir David Manning a DSI paper on the regional and international impact of conflict in Iraq.[281] 'Iraq – Consequences of Conflict for the Region and Beyond' was the first of five FCO papers on post-conflict issues prepared over the following weeks and tabled at the AHGI on 11 October. The four others were:

- 'Scenarios for the Future of Iraq after Saddam';[282]
- 'Models for Administering a Post-Saddam Iraq';
- 'Vision for Iraq and the Iraqi People';
- 'What sort of relationship could the EU have with a rehabilitated Iraq?', shown to the AHGI in final form on 4 November.[283]

---

[279] Manuscript comment Gray on Minute Drummond to Manning, 23 September 2002, 'Ad Hoc Group on Iraq'.
[280] Telegram 1192 Washington to FCO London, 17 September 2002, 'Iraq: Ricketts' Visit to Washington, 17 September.
[281] Letter Sedwill to Manning, 20 September 2002, 'Iraq – Consequences of Conflict for the Region and Beyond' attaching Paper Directorate for Strategy and Innovation, undated, 'Iraq – Consequences of Conflict for the Region and Beyond'.
[282] A first version of this paper was also sent to Sir David Manning on 20 September. The Inquiry has seen no response. A revised version was sent on 26 September.
[283] Paper Middle East Department, 4 November 2002, 'What sort of relationship could the EU have with a rehabilitated Iraq?'

513. The introduction to the paper on international consequences stated:

"This paper identifies some of the possible impacts of war with Iraq on the immediate region and beyond over the short term. One of the aims is to identify the unintended consequences which could easily produce problems (cf the displacement of the Kurds in 1991). **The intention is not to predict catastrophe. But by preparing for the worst, we should be better placed to avoid it.**"

514. The FCO suggested that much would depend on the nature of the military campaign, but that it was possible to identify certain risks:

- "Humanitarian emergency in Iraq". This was possible unless the war ended quickly. The UK would be expected to play a major role in any international response. That response would need military support and to be co-ordinated with the military campaign. That would be difficult, with the US military unlikely to want humanitarian agencies on the ground complicating things.

- "Refugee Crisis". This might result from a prolonged or inconclusive conflict during which the Iraqi regime targeted parts of the population. Meeting refugees' needs would be a significant challenge and potentially destabilising for some of Iraq's neighbours. Senior Ba'athists would probably try to blend in with other refugees. There might need to be "some sort of screening process to identify those we would wish to interrogate and possibly bring criminal charges against".

- "Demonstrations, riots and political stability". Military action would heighten anti-Western feeling in the region. That could pose a threat to British nationals or interests and destabilise governments in the region. Much would depend on whether there was UN support and which countries joined the Coalition.

- "Terrorist attacks". With the US and others distracted, war in Iraq might create an easier environment for terrorists to operate in and would create a new incentive for them to act. UK Embassies and other interests might be attractive targets.

- "Environmental". Depending on Saddam Hussein's actions, a major environmental clean-up might be needed.

- "Non-related but potentially linked crises". With attention focused on Iraq, other crises "could easily flare up". Afghanistan and India/Pakistan were the main concerns. Russia might "increase suppression of the Chechens" or "turn the heat up on Georgia".

- "Economic". Oil prices would rise; stock markets would fall. Both should be short-term, but could be longer lasting. War would also be expensive. Germany, Saudi Arabia and Japan had been major players in 1991.[284] Would they be again? There were also potentially significant costs linked to reconstruction and Iraqi debt.

---

[284] Germany, Saudi Arabia, Japan and other countries made significant financial contributions to military operations in the 1991 Gulf Conflict.

- Two "problem multipliers" could make the situation worse: use of WMD by Iraq and an attack on Israel.

515. A month later, on 24 October, Sir David Manning asked Ms Anna Wechsberg, No.10 Private Secretary: "I have failed to do anything with this. Should I?"[285]

516. On 1 November, she replied that there was probably nothing in the paper that would be new to him and that the AHGI had taken it into account in their work.[286]

517. By then, a revised version, including comments from other departments, had been circulated to the AHGI. It is not clear whether it was seen by Sir David.

FCO PAPER: 'SCENARIOS FOR THE FUTURE OF IRAQ AFTER SADDAM'

518. **'Scenarios for the future of Iraq after Saddam', the second FCO paper for the AHGI, listed scenarios under which Saddam Hussein might lose power, the UK's four "overarching priorities" for Iraq, and how those priorities might be achieved.**

519. **The FCO recognised that the US would have the decisive voice in any externally-driven regime change, but concluded that the UK should be able to exert influence through its close relationship with the US, activity in the UN and its likely role in any military campaign.**

520. **The FCO concluded that the UK should:**

- **argue strongly for Iraq to remain a unitary state;**
- **avoid the root and branch dismantling of Iraq's governmental and security structures;**
- **argue for political reform, but not necessarily full democracy in the short term;**
- **aim for a political outcome to emerge from within Iraq;**
- **recognise the likely need for an interim administration and an international security force.**

521. On 12 September, Sir David Manning had commissioned a paper from the FCO on what a post-Saddam Hussein government might look like:

"If ... there is military action ... what sort of government structures should we try to construct? What should the relationship be between Baghdad and the regions ...? Who might make up this government?"[287]

---

[285] Manuscript comment Manning to Wechsberg, 24 October 2002, on Letter Sedwill to Manning, 20 September 2002, 'Iraq – Consequences of Conflict for the Region and Beyond'.
[286] Manuscript comment Wechsberg to Manning, 1 November 2002, on Letter Sedwill to Manning, 20 September 2002, 'Iraq – Consequences of Conflict for the Region and Beyond'.
[287] Letter Manning to McDonald, 12 September 2002, 'Iraq'.

522. The following day Mr Chaplin set out his views in a note to Mr Gray:

"In the aftermath of military action … we would have a particular responsibility to help hold the ring while a new government emerged … eg facilitating humanitarian relief, assuring minimum functioning of utilities and so on. But … unless the military campaign has been extremely destructive, civilian ministries should be able to resume work fairly quickly.

"… The job of the Coalition will then be to ensure stability, to allow a nation-building process of eg: a representative assembly; appointment of a provisional government; drawing up a new constitution; elections; formation of a new government.

"This process could take 6 to 9 months. Apart from providing security and humanitarian assistance, we may be in the business of providing technical help (eg reconstruction planning; constitution drafting). We will also have a role in preventing interference from neighbours, especially Iran."[288]

523. Mr Richard Stagg, FCO Director Public Diplomacy, raised with Mr Chaplin his "concern about the need to have greater clarity about our long-term vision for the Middle East post-Saddam, if we are to convince people that military conflict is the best available approach".[289]

524. Mr Stagg advised:

"We will make little or no headway with Arab opinion if our apparent goal is to install a pro-US puppet regime in Baghdad. We need an outcome which is not a victory for the US … but a victory for the region – by delivering benefits across the board in terms of stability and prosperity.

…

"I am not suggesting that we should be in a position now to say which individuals or parties will rule Iraq after Saddam, nor on what basis. But I think it would be helpful to have considerably greater clarity about:

(a) how we will go about establishing a future government in Iraq;

(b) how we will manage problems flowing from a more democratic system …;

(c) what sort of international presence we expect to remain in Iraq after a conflict (is there any chance of giving a major role to the UN?);

(d) what does this all mean for neighbouring countries …;

(e) who will control, and benefit from, Iraq's oil wealth;

---

[288] Minute Chaplin to Gray, 13 September 2002, 'Iraq: Post-Saddam Issues'.
[289] Minute Stagg to Chaplin, 13 September 2002, 'Iraq: Winning the War of Words'.

(f) what economic assistance will be available …;

(g) read-across to the MEPP."

525. The FCO paper 'Scenarios for the future of Iraq after Saddam' was sent to No.10 on 26 September.[290] It was circulated separately to the AHGI.

526. The covering letter explained that FCO officials had discussed some of the issues covered in the paper briefly with US officials earlier that day.

527. The paper, written by DSI and Research Analysts, addressed three themes:

- scenarios under which Saddam Hussein might lose power;
- the UK's four "overarching priorities" for Iraq; and
- how those priorities might be achieved.

528. The potential scenarios listed for Saddam Hussein's departure were: assassination by a member of his inner circle; resignation; military coup; popular insurgency; and externally-driven regime change.

529. The paper stated that popular uprisings were most likely "during or in the aftermath of any military campaign", when the situation would be most fluid and "after regular army units had been fragmented". Uprisings were unlikely to be successful "unless Saddam's military structures had collapsed and/or they received significant external assistance". If they did succeed, "the outcome would probably be chaos".

530. The FCO judged that Iraq's neighbours might find it difficult not to get sucked in and included an explicit reference to Iran as the neighbour most likely to become involved.

531. In the section on externally-driven regime change, the FCO reiterated that popular uprisings were one of the possible consequences of Coalition forces entering Baghdad and ejecting Saddam Hussein. If that happened and external rather than internal factors were the trigger, "the Coalition should have far more influence in shaping events. It would have large numbers of forces in many sensitive areas" and the local population would "probably be relatively passive".

532. The FCO stated that in each scenario, much would lie outside the UK's control:

"In most circumstances, the decisive voice would be that of the US. But we should be able to influence developments, through our close relationship with the US, our diplomatic activity in the UN and elsewhere and our likely role in any military campaign."

---

[290] Letter McDonald to Manning, 26 September 2002, 'Scenarios for the future of Iraq after Saddam' attaching Paper FCO, 'Scenarios for the future of Iraq after Saddam'.

533. The UK would need "the clearest possible sense of our objectives for Iraq". The UK's "fundamental interest in a stable region providing secure supplies of oil to world markets" suggested four overarching priorities:

- termination of Iraq's WMD programme and permanent removal of the threat it posed;
- more inclusive and effective Iraqi government;
- a viable Iraq which was not a threat to its neighbours; and
- an end to Iraqi support for international terrorism.

534. The FCO advised:

"We have stated that regime change is not one of our objectives. But once ground-war started it would rapidly become an almost inevitable outcome. The US would not settle again for a 1991-style solution. The question then arises of what constitutes the regime. It would certainly mean the removal of the whole of Saddam's family and inner circle.

"It is less clear how much of any remaining military and governmental structures we would want to see dismantled. This apparatus has facilitated much of what Saddam has done. His influence permeates the system. But removing it entirely would mean the removal of most of the structures of authority in Iraq. This could inhibit political and economic reconstruction."

535. The FCO stated that it was difficult to judge the extent to which government structures would survive Saddam Hussein's departure, but concluded:

- "The national Ba'ath superstructure would almost certainly collapse if Saddam fell as a result of military action, with the leadership seeking refuge. At lower levels, Ba'ath structures might continue ..."
- Local power lay with the Ba'ath Party leadership. The limited supporting bureaucracy was unlikely to be able to take on a more extensive role "without a radical overhaul".
- If Saddam Hussein fell, particularly after US-led military action, "tribal, regional and religious differences would probably come to the fore" in the army, causing splits within and between units. It was more likely that tribal leaders would seek to establish their own power bases than that the armed forces and security services would transfer their allegiance en masse to any new government.
- It was not clear whether there would be any enthusiasm for clerical rule or whether religion would be an effective rallying point for any post-Saddam Hussein administration.

536. On the scope of representative government, the paper stated:

"Some Americans have openly stated they want to see the establishment of democracy. We have avoided this position, because it is an unrealistic ambition in the short term."

537. Even if democracy were not a short-term option, presentationally it would be important for the international community to show that intervention was leading to better government. Difficult issues included:

- Iraq had no successful experience of representative or democratic government.
- A democratic Iraq would not necessarily be pro-Western.
- The Sunni minority would probably feel threatened by a more representative system.
- External opposition was weak and probably lacked sufficient legitimacy in Iraq to be credible.
- None of Iraq's neighbours would be keen to see a democratic Iraq.

538. The paper stated:

"To the extent possible, the Iraqis themselves should have the primary role in determining their future government and external intervention should appear to come from within the Arab world or the UN – perhaps through an international conference (but the Afghanistan model is not necessarily relevant)."

539. Because of the likely delay in putting in place longer term arrangements, the international community was likely to need to establish and provide staff for an interim administration:

"This would need to be set up quickly and on a large scale. It would maintain stability and provide basic services such as food rationing. It should probably have a UN mandate and would need strong support and participation from Arab countries. There are various models which could be adopted or drawn on, including the transitional administrations in Afghanistan, Cambodia, East Timor and Kosovo. We should start exploring what would be appropriate in the Iraqi context."

540. The FCO concluded that, in order to achieve its overarching priorities, the UK should:

- argue strongly for Iraq to remain a unitary state;
- "if possible avoid the root and branch dismantling of Iraq's governmental and security structures";
- accept that the political situation after Saddam Hussein's departure would "almost certainly be messy and unstable", that a new government "will possibly be military" and that "we should argue for political reform, but not necessarily full democracy in the short term";

- aim for a political outcome to emerge from within Iraq, but with the international community perhaps needing to host a conference to help reach a decision on Iraq's future government; and

- recognise the likely need for a plan for an interim administration and an international security force.

541. The AHGI concluded that the FCO paper on scenarios for Iraq after Saddam Hussein needed to be more ambitious.

542. Mr Jonathan Powell described it as "fairly useless". He advocated a UN administration in waiting followed by "some sort of democratic choice" and highlighted the importance of finding a way to stop the "terrible bloodletting of revenge".

543. Early indications from Washington suggested that the US favoured a post-conflict military governorate followed by a civilian administration before the transfer of authority to an Iraqi government.

544. There was no apparent role for the UN in the US approach.

545. Sir David Manning commissioned further advice from the FCO on possible models for a post-Saddam Hussein administration, including on where the UN would fit in.

546. When the AHGI discussed the FCO paper on scenarios for a post-Saddam Hussein Iraq on 27 September, it concluded that something more ambitious was required.[291] Six areas needed expanding:

- the duration of any international involvement in Iraq;
- the sustainability of UK forces there;
- the shape of Iraqi governance;
- SSR;
- economic recovery; and
- the humanitarian response.

547. The AHGI observed that US officials would not be available to discuss the paper until late October, but should be sent a copy well in advance.

548. Mr Powell commented to Sir David Manning:

"I think this is fairly useless. We need a UN Administration in waiting with some exiled Iraqi technocrats supported by an international military force. Then we need to come to some sort of democratic choice for the Iraqi people – a convention (or Loya Jirga!). The key things are to start identifying an Iraqi Karzai and to come up with a

---

[291] Minute Dodd to Manning, 30 September 2002, 'Ad Hoc Group on Iraq'.

way of stopping a terrible bloodletting of revenge after Saddam goes. Traditional in Iraq after conflict."[292]

549. On 28 September, the British Embassy Washington updated London on initial US thinking on the post-conflict administration of Iraq.[293] The latest NSC view was that an initial military governorate should be succeeded by a civilian administration, with the gradual draw down of the military presence ahead of the transfer of authority to an Iraqi government. The size of the military footprint, economic governance, oil and humanitarian and reconstruction needs were among issues yet to be properly addressed.

550. Sir David Manning drew on the comments from Mr Powell and the Washington Embassy in his response to the FCO paper on scenarios for the future of Iraq on 29 September.[294] He asked for more detailed advice on which were the most plausible of the possible models for a post-Saddam Hussein administration. With the US reported to be proposing a military governorate, the most immediate question was where the UN would fit in. In particular, what scope was there for preparing the blueprint for a UN administration-in-waiting drawing on currently exiled technocrats. Being very careful not to draw false analogies with Afghanistan, should a UN administration set out an early timetable promising democratic consultation on the Loya Jirga model, or would this risk chaos?

551. The MOD raised with the FCO the need to consider how assumptions about the UK's post-conflict role might inform decisions on the UK's military contribution to conflict.

552. Sir Christopher Meyer highlighted the need to keep sight of the UK's post-conflict commercial interests.

553. DFID commented on the importance of learning from DFID and inter-departmental experience elsewhere.

554. On 30 September, Mr Lee instructed Mr David Johnson, Head of the MOD Iraq Secretariat, to send the MOD's views to the FCO. He suggested that the FCO paper should include more detail on de-Ba'athification, how an international security force might be put together and how large it would need to be. Mr Lee also requested the inclusion of questions and assumptions that would make clear "the speculative nature of the current state of thinking". Those might include: whether the UN Security Council would supervise reconstruction if the US acted unilaterally; the role of neighbours, Russia, France and international bodies other than the UN; and whether it was possible to "determine criteria for UK military involvement".[295]

---

[292] Manuscript comment Powell to Manning on Letter McDonald to Manning, 26 September 2002, 'Scenarios for the future of Iraq after Saddam'.
[293] Telegram 1251 Washington to FCO London, 28 September 2002, 'US/Iraq'.
[294] Letter Manning to McDonald, 29 September 2002, 'Scenarios for the future of Iraq after Saddam'.
[295] Minute Lee to Head of Sec(Iraq), 30 September 2002, 'Scenarios for the Future of Iraq after Saddam'.

555. Mr Johnson set out the MOD's views in a letter to Mr Gray on 2 October.[296] He recommended that the FCO paper be clear about:

- The circumstances in which the UK might seek to establish democracy or set up "some kind of authoritarian regime" in Iraq. The UK's public position should "not raise expectations that we may subsequently disappoint".

- How much of Iraq's bureaucracy was "either redeemable or necessary". In the paper the FCO argued against root-and-branch dismantling of a system permeated by the Ba'ath Party, but also suggested that much of the Party would collapse anyway. "The key issue is surely the extent to which the existing bureaucratic structure will need to be retained (and no doubt re-educated) in order for the country to be governable in practice."

- The different options for an interim government. The paper needed to distinguish between the situation following military action explicitly authorised by the UN and that following what might be called "US unilateral action". In the latter case, was it still safe to assume the UN would take on the role of supervising reconstruction?

- The locus and role of other Permanent Members of the UN Security Council and neighbouring states.

- The potential role of multilateral institutions and states in reconstruction and security provision. For the UK, "a long-term commitment significantly over and above the forces currently in theatre, particularly following on from a war-fighting campaign, would have serious consequences for our ability to respond to other contingencies, or even perhaps our ability to sustain current tasks".

556. Mr Johnson commented that, although many of those questions might not be easy to answer at that stage, they needed to be raised, as did the issue of "whether and how an assumption about UK post-conflict involvement might feed back into our decision-making about our contribution to conflict (if it comes to that)".

557. Mr Johnson added that the DoD had expressed an interest in the subject. Mr Webb was planning to send a copy of the next version of the paper to Mr Feith.

558. Some of the MOD's suggestions were picked up in the next FCO paper, on models for administering Iraq, described later in this Section.[297]

559. Sir Christopher Meyer questioned whether the paper was right to classify the securing of UK reconstruction contracts as a second order objective.[298] Russia and France were, by all accounts, anxious about their economic interests in Iraq after Saddam Hussein's demise. UK interests were not something to press immediately, but

---

[296] Letter Johnson to Gray, 2 October 2002, 'Scenarios for the future of Iraq after Saddam'.
[297] Paper FCO, [undated, version received at AHGI, 11 October 2002], 'Models for Administering a Post-Saddam Iraq'.
[298] Telegram 1256 Washington to FCO London, 1 October 2002, 'Iraq: Dividing the Spoils'.

should be a "top priority" in post-Saddam Hussein contingency planning. Mr Blair would have to pursue the issue with President Bush if the UK was to have any impact.

560. Sir Christopher returned to the same theme during November, in the context of Iraqi oil contracts. The issue of oil contracts is addressed later in this Section.

561. DFID commented on the importance of learning from DFID and inter-departmental experience elsewhere.[299] Areas to consider included: SSR; civil-military co-ordination (CIMIC); DDR; economic recovery; UN co-ordination structures; donor financing; and the role of IFIs.

562. Some minor changes were made to the version of the FCO paper submitted to the AHGI on 11 October, including the addition of a reference to the need to plan on the basis that there would have to be "a major international effort, possibly for an extended period".[300]

STATE DEPARTMENT PAPER ON LESSONS OF THE PAST

563. On 26 September, Mr Richard Haass, State Department Director of Policy Planning, produced a 15-page policy paper on Iraq reconstruction for Secretary Powell.[301] Mr Haass described the paper, reproduced in full in *War of Necessity, War of Choice,* as "the largest single project we undertook during my tenure at Policy Planning". The paper was built on "an in-depth examination of the lessons of US experiences with nation building throughout the twentieth century" and concluded with:

"**Seven Lessons for Iraq**

- We must decide on the scale of our ambitions in Iraq, recognizing that goals that go beyond disarmament and regional stability and seek to build democracy, prosperity, and good governance will require a heavy commitment in resources, military involvement and diplomatic engagement. The strategic importance of Iraq points toward ambitious long-term goals …

- We must prevent a security vacuum from emerging in Iraq that could be exploited by internal spoilers, encourage external meddlers, and preclude reconstruction and humanitarian efforts …

- We should help formulate specific plans to transform the UN Oil-for-Food program into a mechanism that will simultaneously support the humanitarian needs of the Iraqi people, fund the broader reconstruction effort, and address outside claimants' justified interests … At the same time, the United States should avoid taking 'ownership' of the Iraqi oil industry.

---

299 Letter Conflict & Humanitarian Affairs Dept [junior official] to Gray, 4 October 2002, 'After Saddam'.
300 Paper FCO, [undated, version received at AHGI, 11 October 2002], 'Scenarios for the future of Iraq after Saddam'.
301 Haass RN. *War of Necessity, War of Choice: A Memoir of two Iraqi Wars.* Simon & Schuster, 2009.

- We should preclude only a small number of members of the old regime ... from participating in the post-Saddam political order. We will most likely need the assistance of many associated in some way with the old regime to maintain order and establish a new viable state ...

- We should avoid imposing a particular ruler or party on Iraq, but cannot allow Iraq to degenerate into chaos ... We should work with our partners to launch a political process that will allow the Iraqi people to move toward self-government ...

- We need to contain potential meddling by Iraq's neighbours, as well as by other international actors ... We need to maintain broad and effective bilateral dialogue with these countries, forge a six plus two-like forum[302] for co-ordination among Iraq's neighbours and most interested outside powers, and ... strive to develop new mechanisms to manage security concerns in the region as well as promote economic linkages ...

- ... We should assert forceful, public [US] leadership of the security operations, and then guide the other components of the reconstruction effort from behind the scenes as we are now doing in Afghanistan."

564. The Haass memorandum did not have an impact in Washington. Mr Haass recorded that Secretary Powell agreed most of it and sent copies to Secretary Rumsfeld, Dr Rice and Vice President Cheney:

"No one could argue that these perspectives had not been raised, although it was true that the lack of any meaningful inter-agency process or oversight of the aftermath made it too easy for the Defense Department (which was essentially left by the NSC to oversee itself) to ignore advice from the outside."

565. A copy of the memorandum was handed to UK officials by the State Department in late 2002.[303]

SPG PAPER, 30 SEPTEMBER 2002: 'UK MILITARY STRATEGIC THINKING ON IRAQ'

566. The "aftermath" section of the fourth edition of the SPG paper on UK strategic military thinking:

- **raised concerns about US post-conflict policy, including the US approach to de-Ba'athification, which could run counter to the need for basic governance and increase post-conflict reliance on the external authority;**

- **listed the principal post-conflict challenges in Iraq, including law and order and effective administration;**

---

[302] Afghanistan's six neighbours (Iran, Turkmenistan, Uzbekistan, Tajikistan, China and Pakistan), the US and Russia.
[303] Manuscript comment [unattributed] on Paper [unattributed and undated], 'Reconstruction in Iraq – Lessons of the Past'.

- **identified "key drivers" that would determine the extent and nature of post-conflict engagement, including levels of consent and damage to Iraq's infrastructure; and**
- **listed pre-invasion planning tasks, including establishing an FCO/DFID/MOD "framework plan".**

567. The 30 September edition of the SPG paper on UK strategic military thinking included an expanded section on what it called the "aftermath – resolution phase", the word "resolution" added in recognition of the possibility of a non-military, diplomatic resolution to the Iraq crisis.[304]

568. The paper summarised what was known about current conditions in Iraq:

"• Iraq though suffering from economic sanctions has great natural wealth, adequate water resources (with an antiquated urban distribution network) and an agricultural sector that is capable of producing food though in need of reform.

- Security structures are bound to the current leadership through ties of kinship and patronage at senior levels, and economic advantage and fear at the bottom.

- Iraq has a sophisticated though choking bureaucracy.

- Iraqi infrastructure is poorly maintained by the current regime with damage from the war of 1991 still not repaired, and water supplies becoming contaminated in major urban centres.

- Population has been ethnically mixed by current regime by internal displacement to weaken opposition; however though mixed ethnic, cultural, and religious divides persist with old scores remaining unsettled.

- Indebtedness to Russia. Other regional debts may also exist."

569. On US policy the paper stated:

"• US plans envisage a period of military authority exercised through a military governor. This would be followed by a gradual transition to civil authority and finally Iraqi self-rule.

- Allied to this is an extensive programme to dismantle and remove elements of the Iraqi regime closely related to Ba'athist rule.

- The UK will need to assess whether it can comfortably support the US intent to provide military stewardship rather than rapidly establishing an Iraqi transitional authority at the earliest opportunity.

- The US desire to remove the influence of the previous regime may also run counter to the need for basic administration and governance, further increasing the reliance on external authority. This may prove counter-productive."

---

[304] Paper [SPG], 30 September 2002, 'UK Military Strategic Thinking on Iraq'.

570. The principal challenges would be:

"• Law and order and effective administration.

• Ethnic/factional conflict.

• Humanitarian welfare.

• Regional agendas and interference.

• Remnant forces.

• Infrastructure shortfalls."

571. The paper also listed "key drivers" that would determine the extent and nature of post-conflict engagement:

"• Relationship with new leadership.

• Level of consent.

• Level of international support/perceived legitimacy.

• Speed of collapse/defeat.

• Extent of damage to infrastructure.

• Compliance/extent of defeat of Iraqi security forces.

• Requirement to remove elements of security apparatus to allow good governance."

572. Lists of post-conflict military tasks, dropped from the 4 September version of the paper, were reinstated with small amendments. Pre-invasion planning tasks were included for the first time:

"Pre-conflict:

- Establish FCO/DFID/MOD framework plan. Confirm in-country liaison arrangements.

- Explore US intent and acceptable scale of consequence management commitment.

- Develop agreed responsibilities for elements of consequence management.

- Account for post-conflict needs in targeting process.

- Identify Coalition sp [support] to Phase IV and any potential burden sharing.

- Identify regional attitudes to conflict and any possible reactions to outcomes."

573. The Chiefs of Staff agreed on 2 October that: "Phase IV considerations needed to be clearly understood, given that the inevitable UK involvement might result in an even greater burden than war-fighting per se."[305] The 25 September instruction to Lt Gen Pigott to "Explore options for potential UK involvement in Phase IV", remained on the list of "actions arising" attached to the minutes of the 2 October meeting, with an extended deadline of 16 October.

574. Lord Boyce told the Inquiry he doubted there had been very many Chiefs of Staff meetings where Phase IV had not been discussed:

"... half of most meetings was on Phase IV or half of the meetings about Iraq would be spent talking about Phase IV."[306]

575. More material on Phase IV was added to the 6 November edition of the SPG paper, described later in this Section.

576. The proposal for an FCO/DFID/MOD framework plan was not acted upon until late January 2003 (see Section 6.5).

JIC ASSESSMENT, 10 OCTOBER 2002: 'INTERNATIONAL TERRORISM: THE THREAT FROM IRAQ'

577. A JIC Assessment on 10 October judged that US-led military action against Iraq would motivate extremist groups and individuals to carry out terrorist attacks against Coalition targets.

578. On 10 October, at the FCO's request, the JIC assessed the terrorist threat from Iraq in the event of US-led military action or imminent military action.[307] The Assessment made no explicit reference to terrorist attacks against Coalition targets in Iraq, other than by Saddam Hussein during conflict, but stated:

"US-led military action against Iraq will motivate other [non-Iraqi] Islamic extremist groups and individuals to carry out terrorist attacks against Coalition targets. Al Qaida will use a Coalition attack on Iraq as further 'justification' for terrorist attacks against Western or Israeli interests ...

"A number of anti-West terrorist groups exploited the situation during the 1991 Gulf War ... Such attacks could be conducted again, by individuals and groups unconnected with Iraq. This may be exacerbated by weaker international support for Coalition action compared to 1991.

"**We judge that the greatest terrorist threat in the event of military action against Iraq will come from Al Qaida and other Islamic extremists**, but they will be pursuing their own agendas, not responding to direction from Iraq. In the longer term, a Coalition attack may radicalise increasing numbers of Muslims, especially Arabs, and boost support and recruitment for extremist groups."

[305] Minutes, 2 October 2002, Chiefs of Staff meeting.
[306] Public hearing, 27 January 2011, page 81.
[307] JIC Assessment, 10 October 2002, 'International Terrorism: The Threat from Iraq'.

579. The JIC addressed the wider terrorist threat in the event of military conflict on 10 February 2003 (see Section 6.5).

POSSIBLE MODELS FOR ADMINISTERING A POST-SADDAM HUSSEIN IRAQ

580. The FCO paper 'Models for Administering a Post-Saddam Iraq' identified a number of arguments against establishing a US military governorate, concluding that:

- **A UN mandate would be critical in any post-conflict scenario.**
- **The Coalition would need to retain responsibility for security for some time.**
- **The Coalition would also need to control and administer Iraq for an unknown period before the creation of an interim administration.**
- **A UN-led Transitional Authority would be most appropriate model for the interim administration.**

581. The FCO recommended that work should begin on examining a possible UN role in more detail.

582. It did not address the implications of the different models for the UK.

583. On 4 October, the FCO sent Sir David Manning a draft of the third paper in its series on post-conflict issues: 'Models for Administering a Post-Saddam Iraq'.[308]

584. A second version with a small number of revisions was handed to the AHGI on 11 October.[309]

585. The analysis in the paper rested on three assumptions:

"a. the US-led Coalition takes control of Iraq following a short campaign which does not cause a humanitarian crisis or extensive damage to infrastructure;

b. there has been no significant WMD usage; and

c. Saddam's regime has been removed almost entirely, no alternative regime had replaced him (eg a military junta) and there have been no uprisings by the Kurds or Shia."

586. The authors warned: "These assumptions are optimistic. The reality is likely to be more complicated, making the transition to a civilian administration harder." They also emphasised that much would depend on the legal basis of the campaign: in the absence

---

[308] Letter McDonald to Manning, 4 October 2002, 'Models for Administering a Post-Saddam Iraq' attaching Paper [draft] FCO, [undated], 'Models for Administering a Post-Saddam Iraq'.
[309] Paper FCO, [undated, version received at AHGI, 11 October 2002], 'Models for Administering a Post-Saddam Iraq'.

of a UN mandate it would be harder for the US-led Coalition to draw on the support of others in the "aftermath".

587. The body of the paper set out the immediate challenges and responsibilities the Coalition would face on arrival, and suggested models for managing the transfer of power to an Iraqi government. Immediate challenges included administering Iraq, providing security and preparing to hand over power:

- Administering Iraq would involve: "Provision of basic necessities ... Restoration of critical infrastructure ... Managing the economy ... Medical treatment ... Resettlement of refugees ... [and] Public information".

- A "strong security presence" would be needed to "Ensure the effective destruction of Iraq's WMD programme ... Provide internal and external security ... Protect any transitional administration ... Manage Prisoners of War ... [and] Initiate a disarmament, demobilisation and reintegration (DDR) programme."

- Preparing for the successful handover of power meant going into Iraq "with a clear idea of how [to] get out again". Iraqis should determine their own government, but it should be "representative of Iraq's diversity and ... deliver effective government". Three options were identified:
  - democracy (a government elected by a free vote and universal suffrage);
  - representative government (reflecting ethnic and regional interests); or
  - a unifying leader (although none was immediately identifiable).

588. The paper stated that, although it would be:

"... possible to explore ideas with Iraq exiles ... they have little credibility within Iraq. Any solution would almost certainly have to be sorted out once Saddam had gone ... We should avoid making promises (eg on the timing of any consultation process and possible government structures) which may later prove unworkable."

589. The section describing possible models for the transfer of power focused on the nature of the transitional authority to be established after the immediate post-conflict period:

"The US-led Coalition would almost certainly have to retain responsibility for the security function for some time after any conflict ...

"In the immediate aftermath of any war, the Coalition military forces would need to take control and administer Iraq at a basic level, including eg ensuring food and medical supplies. It is not clear how long this would last. Ideally, it would be a matter of weeks. But much would depend on the security situation. It is quite possible that it could become an extended period."

590. Once security had stabilised, "the Coalition would look to establish a clearer structure to carry out the full range of administrative functions ... the ideal would be to make as much use as possible of the existing Iraqi administrative apparatus".

591. One of the most difficult questions was the form that administration should take. Two options had been suggested: a US military governorate (with or without a UN mandate); and a UN or UN-supported transitional authority. The US preference was for a military governorate.

592. The authors cast doubt on any analogy with the rebuilding of Germany and Japan after the Second World War, but suggested that a military governorate could have advantages for the UK:

"It could guarantee US political and financial commitment to the reconstruction process. It would help ensure the civil administration and security elements of post-war government remained interconnected.

"But there are major disadvantages. It is questionable whether a military governorate would be able to carry out all the tasks outlined above effectively. Much would depend on who the US brought in to take on the key roles, including civilian personnel. It would be essential that full attention was paid to civilian reconstruction tasks …

"It is not clear what the legal basis for a governorate would be …

"Presentationally a US-led military governorate would be unattractive. Even with a UN mandate it would not be seen as impartial in the same way as a UN operation."

593. There were two possible models for a UN administration: a UN transitional authority as in Cambodia and East Timor, or a UN-supported transitional administration on the Afghanistan model. Ideally they would be endorsed by some sort of Iraqi political process. The paper explained:

"Under the Cambodia model, international personnel would take over the main governmental and military/security structures, replacing the senior officials and running the organisations themselves. More junior staff would remain in place …

"We consider the Cambodia model likely to be most appropriate for post-Saddam Iraq. Many senior figures in Iraq's bureaucracy and military are compromised by their connections with Saddam's regime, and also lower down. Rather than deciding immediately after any conflict who to retain and who to push out, it would be neater for the UN Transitional Authority to replace the top tier of leadership with international personnel immediately.

"Once this system was in place, the UN could then move towards the Afghanistan model, by gradually re-installing senior Iraqi officials as appropriate …"

594. The UN approach raised two further questions:

"a) Who would be the domestic figurehead? … There is no obvious candidate amongst the Iraqi exile/diaspora communities. It is doubtful whether they would have the credibility. But we should be open to suggestions. It is possible someone would emerge in the aftermath of conflict – Karzai did.

b) <u>Who would head the Transitional Authority</u>? It would be critical to identify a heavyweight figure to head the Transitional Authority. He or she would need to be acceptable to the Iraqis, within the region and wider Muslim world and to the US-led Coalition members …"

595. The authors concluded:

"– **Whatever we do, a UN mandate would be critical in any 'Day After' situation …**

– **The US and coalition partners would need to retain responsibility for Iraq's security for some time after any conflict, irrespective of the administrative arrangements** [removed from the 11 October version] …

– **The US-led military coalition would need to control and administer Iraq at a basic level for a period after the end of the conflict and before the creation of an interim administration. It is not clear how long this period would last** [replaced in the 11 October version with: "**The US-led military coalition would need to secure Iraq for a period after the conflict, including during the creation of an interim administration. It is not clear how long this period would last. We would want it to be as short as possible**"].

– **Our initial assessment is that a UN-led Transitional Authority would be most appropriate for the interim administration of Iraq …**

– **There are strong arguments against a US military governorate – practical, presentational and legal. We should not rule it out entirely, but need to understand better why the Americans favour this option and how it would work.**"

596. The paper stated that work should begin on examining a possible UN role in more detail, in particular:

- mapping key tasks and posts to be filled;
- identifying someone who could head a transitional authority;
- identifying Iraqis who could work in an international administration; and
- identifying "appropriate British personnel to take over key roles" [amended to "appropriate personnel (particularly Iraqis)" in the 11 October version].

597. The 11 October version of the paper contained an additional recommendation that:

"**Irrespective of the administrative arrangements, the US and Coalition partners would need to retain overall responsibility for Iraq's security for some time after the conflict. How the different security-related tasks (including security sector reform) should be carried out and by whom needs further consideration.**"

598. The FCO circulated follow-up papers on the possible shape of an international administration for Iraq and on SSR to the AHGI on 18 October. Both are described later in this Section.

599. Sir Peter Ricketts told the Inquiry:

"We started planning in the autumn of 2002, and at that point, of course, it wasn't clear exactly what scenario there would be in terms of a new regime in Iraq, but we assumed, I think, from that point onwards, that we would be dealing with an Iraq without Saddam Hussein and in the aftermath of a military intervention.

"Therefore, we based our planning on the assumption that the right vehicle for that would be the UN, which had had extensive experience of post-conflict stabilisation work in a number of different countries. But we looked at a range of scenarios and a range of possible outcomes from ones where it might be possible to work with large parts of the previous Iraqi administration to scenarios where it would not, and we had to look at a fairly wide range of scenarios."[310]

600. Iraq was discussed at a meeting Mr Ricketts attended with his US, French and German counterparts in Berlin on 14 October.[311] The record stated that there was an emerging consensus from the US Future of Iraq Project that "the Republican Guard and Ba'ath Party would have to go; but some feeling that medium and lower levels of government might remain, as might non-senior members of the military". Mr Ricketts indicated he thought it "likely the Ba'ath Party would implode post-Saddam".

601. In the US, the CIA considered the Ba'ath Party in two reports in October 2002.[312]

602. The first, 'Iraq: the Day After', dated 18 October, assessed that the Ba'ath Party would collapse along with Saddam Hussein's regime, but added:

"Despite the improbability that Ba'ath ideology will persist after Saddam, much of the infrastructure of the Party within civilian sectors, such as professional and civil associations, may sustain to facilitate a restoration of government services."

603. On the role of Iraqi military and security services, the paper stated that "many troops must be quickly disarmed and demobilized to remove a potential focal point for Sunni coup plotting", and that "certain units are so dominated by … pro-Saddam tribesmen or otherwise so intimately linked to the regime that their continued existence will be incompatible with democracy". The paper judged that officers who favoured a professional military ethos or saw themselves as guardians of Iraqi national values "may play a role in the post-Saddam military".

---

[310] Public hearing 9 December 2003, pages 62-63.
[311] Telegram 390 Berlin to FCO London, 14 October 2002, 'Iraq Restricted: Close Allies: 14 October: Iraq Post-Saddam'.
[312] US Senate Select Committee on Intelligence, *Report on Prewar Intelligence Assessments about Post-war Iraq*, 25 May 2007.

604. The second CIA report, 'The Iraqi Ba'ath Party: Inexorably Tied to Saddam', dated 31 October, assessed that many bureaucrats had joined the Ba'ath Party to attain their positions, were not "ardent supporters of Saddam" and "could probably remain … [after having been] investigated and vetted". The report stated, however, that the CIA did not know much about the loyalties, party affiliations, or potential criminal activities of most Iraqi military officers and government bureaucrats.

605. It is not clear whether either report was seen by officials in the UK.

606. FCO briefing on post-conflict issues for Mr Straw's visit to Washington on 14 and 15 October, prepared on 10 October, reflected the conclusions of the FCO papers for the AHGI.[313]

607. Suggested points for Mr Straw to raise included a list of reasons why it would not be easy to decide what new governmental structures should look like:

"– ethnic/religious/tribal mix;
– residual Ba'ath influence;
– uneven distribution of resources;
– lack of political infrastructure or unifying figure;
– scope for neighbours to meddle."

608. Officials suggested that Mr Straw seek agreement to "a few underlying principles:

– Iraq to remain a unitary state;
– no need for root and branch dismantling of government;
– Iraqis should determine their own government; and
– need for more representative government, but not necessarily full democracy in short term."

609. Other points covered in the briefing included the need for:

- "a credible legal base and UN framework";
- a clear exit strategy built on an understanding of what Iraq could look like and a process for getting there;
- a commitment to stay "as long as necessary"; and
- recognition that although it would be difficult to minimise the risk of Iraq's disintegration, it was important not to fall into the "opposite trap of exaggerating Iraq's fragility."

---

[313] Paper Middle East Department, 10 October 2002, 'Foreign Secretary's visit to Washington, 14-15 October, Iraq: forward thinking'.

610. On oil and gas, the briefing stated:

> "• … current speculation on post-Saddam arrangements in Iraqi oil sector are damaging public perceptions of our motives. See some risk of creating misimpression we are in this for the sake of spoils;
>
> • any new regime in Baghdad will need to be seen to honour legitimate existing commitments, and to maintain open bidding procedure for oil and gas investment (unlike Kuwait after 1991)."

611. Mr Straw and Secretary Powell discussed post-conflict issues on 14 and 15 October.[314]

FCO PAPER: 'VISION FOR IRAQ AND THE IRAQI PEOPLE'

612. The FCO's 'Vision for Iraq and the Iraqi People' was a statement of the UK's aspirations for Iraq.

613. It was intended to have a positive impact on UK and Iraqi Public opinion, but did not appear to reflect any assessment of the degree to which Iraqi citizens might share the UK's aspirations.

614. The 'Vision' was never used in its original form, but did inform the Government's statements on the future of Iraq in the run up to the invasion (see Section 6.5).

615. The fourth FCO paper on post-conflict Iraq, the 'Vision for Iraq and the Iraqi People', was put to the AHGI on 11 October. The record of the meeting stated that the paper was to "remain in reserve".[315]

616. The 'Vision for Iraq and the Iraqi People' was a one-page document by DSI containing echoes of the 2001 'Contract with the Iraqi People', described earlier in this Section.[316] It set out the UK's aspirations for the Iraqi people and how it would help achieve them. It stated that the UK had "no quarrel" with Iraqis and wanted to help them "restore Iraq to its proper dignity and place in the community of nations".

617. The UK's five aspirations were:

> "• <u>Freedom</u>: an Iraq which respects fundamental human rights, including freedom of thought, conscience and religion and the dignity of family life, and whose people live free from repression and the fear of torture or arbitrary arrest.
>
> • <u>Good Government</u>: an independent Iraq respecting the rule of law and ruled in accordance with democratic principles, whose government reflects the diversity of its population.

---

[314] Minute Straw to Prime Minister, 16 October 2002, 'Iraq: Conversation with Powell: No US Interlocutors'.
[315] Minute Dodd to Manning, 14 October 2002, 'Ad Hoc Group on Iraq'.
[316] Paper [draft] FCO, [undated], 'Vision for Iraq and the Iraqi People'.

- **International Respect**: an Iraq respected by its neighbours and the wider international community.

- **Peace**: a unified Iraq within its current borders living at peace with itself and with its neighbours.

- **Prosperity**: an Iraq sharing the wealth created by its economy with all Iraqis."

618. The UK would help by:

- working to bring an early end to sanctions;

- supporting Iraq's reintegration into the region;

- encouraging generous debt rescheduling;

- promoting increased aid from the international community;

- supporting an international reconstruction programme, "if one is needed";

- promoting investment in Iraq's oil industry;

- encouraging renewal of international education and cultural links;

- promoting institutional and administrative reform.

619. A revised 'Vision' was prepared in late February 2003 and is described in Section 6.5.

DFID PAPER: 'IRAQ: POTENTIAL HUMANITARIAN IMPLICATIONS'

620. During October, DFID produced two papers on Iraq: a paper on humanitarian contingency planning for the AHGI and a desktop analysis of central and southern Iraq for internal use in DFID.

621. The paper on humanitarian planning outlined possible humanitarian consequences of military action and the likely emergency requirements. It warned that DFID funds were likely to prove insufficient and that the international humanitarian system was becoming overstretched.

622. Before the 11 October meeting of the AHGI, Mr Alistair Fernie, Head of DFID Middle East and North Africa Department, circulated a draft paper on humanitarian planning not yet seen by Ms Short or other departments.[317] The paper outlined the provisions of OFF, considered the potential humanitarian consequences of military action and possible responses, and summarised NGO and multilateral agency contingency planning.[318]

623. The draft paper made two assumptions:

"a. That the UN is able to mount a coherent response to the developing situation in Iraq – before, during and after any conflict.

---

[317] Letter Fernie to Dodd, 11 October 2002, 'Iraq: Humanitarian Contingency Planning'.
[318] Paper DFID, 11 October 2002, 'Iraq: Potential Humanitarian Implications'.

b. That the UK role should be to develop and sustain a broad international coalition to deal with the humanitarian crisis in co-operation with the UN and other key international players."

It added:

"Assumption a) is credible if the UN has a mandate and active support from its members to do so. The situation might be different in the event of military action not backed by the UN. Assumption b) is in line with current UK humanitarian policy."

624. The draft listed possible humanitarian consequences of military action, including:

- large-scale civilian loss of life;
- internal and international population displacement;
- significant infrastructure and environmental damage;
- inter-factional clashes within Iraq; and
- use of chemical and biological weapons.

Likely emergency requirements included provision of basic needs and: "Early focus on recovery initiatives, particularly linking into infrastructure and environmental damage, and the impact on livelihoods."

625. The draft explained that DFID's Conflict and Humanitarian Affairs Department (CHAD) was undertaking a "short-term desktop study of the humanitarian situation" in central and southern Iraq. If restrictions on external contacts with humanitarian agencies were lifted, CHAD would obtain a fuller picture of contingency planning and agency capacities. The CHAD Operations Team (OT) was accelerating its post-Afghanistan refit and being brought up to its full authorised strength of 30.

626. The draft also stated that:

"Any large-scale UK humanitarian response would require additional funding from the Central Reserve. DFID's existing small (£6m) humanitarian programme in Iraq is fully committed; available humanitarian funds within CHAD are likely to be grossly insufficient and most of DFID's contingency reserve has already been allocated."

627. The draft paper did not consider whether there was a need for contingency plans should either of the underlying assumptions prove wrong.

628. The Inquiry has seen no indication that DFID addressed that possibility in any detail until February 2003.

DFID PAPER: 'CENTRAL/SOUTHERN IRAQ HUMANITARIAN SITUATION ANALYSIS'

629. The DFID desktop analysis of central and southern Iraq highlighted the extent of economic decline, the deterioration in public services and the vulnerability of the population.

630. The problems with Iraq's infrastructure and public services highlighted by the review were not addressed by DFID's planning for post-conflict Iraq over the coming months, which focused almost exclusively on the provision of humanitarian relief.

631. The DFID desktop analysis of central and southern Iraq, the second half of the Iraq review programme initiated in May, was completed on 17 October.[319]

632. Like the northern Iraq review in August, the 'Central/southern Iraq humanitarian situation analysis' was marked for DFID internal circulation only. The Inquiry has seen no evidence that it was distributed more widely.

633. Unlike the northern Iraq review, because of restrictions on external contacts by DFID officials, the analysis of central and southern Iraq was produced without consulting the UN, NGOs or bilateral partners, but did draw widely on external (including UN) publications.

634. Observations, some of which were repeated from DFID's report to Ms Short in May, included:

- "serial decline" or "collapse" in non-oil sectors of the economy;
- the negative impact on public services of the large number of public employees leaving their jobs;
- 50 percent of schools physically unsafe, unfit for teaching or learning and considered a public health hazard for children;
- 80 percent of primary schools in a "deteriorated" state;
- Umm Qasr port in a "dilapidated" state;
- only 50 percent of electricity demand being met;
- rising levels of waterborne diseases and salt intrusion in water systems in southern Iraq;
- transport infrastructure improving slowly "from a highly degraded base";
- the vulnerability of the population could be expected to increase as international pressure on the government grew; and
- in the event of military action, the scale and duration of a humanitarian crisis would be "dependent on efforts to stabilise the situation and address political, security, humanitarian and economic considerations coherently and rapidly".

635. Officials recommended that better data be sought as soon as contact with international agencies was authorised.

636. The two DFID reviews of northern and southern Iraq constituted a significant body of information on the scale of Iraq's social and economic decline.

---

[319] Email DFID [junior official] to Fernie, 17 October 2002, 'CSI analysis' attaching Paper Conflict & Humanitarian Affairs Department, October 2002, 'Central/southern Iraq humanitarian situation analysis'.

637. DFID should have shared that material with other participants in the AHGI to inform cross-government analysis of the state of Iraq and preparations for post-conflict reconstruction.

638. Sir Suma Chakrabarti, DFID Permanent Secretary from 2002 to 2008, told the Inquiry that DFID's knowledge of Iraq when it began contingency planning in 2002 was "pretty scanty" as DFID had not itself implemented humanitarian programmes in Iraq in the period leading up to the invasion, working instead through the UN agencies, NGOs and the International Committee of the Red Cross (ICRC).[320]

639. Sir Suma also stated that DFID focused on humanitarian issues "because we assumed that the UN would come in and show leadership on the post-conflict reconstruction and recovery phase" and there was "optimism about the UN being able to play that role".[321]

640. Mr Webb told the Inquiry that DFID was helpful on humanitarian issues and was ready "to bring in some of their expertise to help with some of the reconstruction".[322] He stated that: "the concentration on the humanitarian side, which we had expected might go on for a few months, had probably taken people's eye a bit off the reconstruction side …"

UK STRATEGIC POLICY OBJECTIVES FOR IRAQ

641. Mr Blair agreed draft UK strategic policy objectives for Iraq in early October.

642. Those objectives were published in January 2003.

643. There is no indication that Mr Blair sought Ministers' collective view on the strategic policy objectives between October 2002 and January 2003.

644. Nor did Mr Blair seek advice on whether the strategic policy objectives were achievable, and, if so, in what timeframe and at what cost.

645. The preparation of the objectives is described in detail in Section 3.5.

646. On 4 October, Mr Bowen submitted draft strategic policy objectives for Iraq, on which the Cabinet Office had been working with other departments, to Sir David Manning.[323] The "prime objective" was removal of the threat from Iraqi WMD. Other draft objectives included the end state approved by Mr Straw and Mr Hoon in May, to which a reference to "effective and representative government" had been added:

> "As rapidly as possible, we would like Iraq to become a stable, united and law-abiding state, within its present borders, co-operating with the international

---

[320] Public hearing, 8 December 2009, page 9.
[321] Public hearing, 8 December 2009, pages 61-62.
[322] Private hearing, 23 June 2010, page 59.
[323] Minute Bowen to Manning, 4 October 2002, 'Iraq: Strategic Policy Objectives'.

community, no longer posing a threat to its neighbours or to international security, abiding by all its international obligations and providing effective and representative government to its own people."

647. Mr Bowen commented that some had argued that the aspirations for the future of Iraq should be translated into the main objective. He had resisted "on the grounds that our purpose has been plainly stated by the Prime Minister as disarmament and because the effective implementation of that policy does not necessarily deliver our wider aspirations". The objectives would also need to "evolve with changing circumstances". If military action were authorised, the paper would need to be revised.

648. Mr Lee sent a copy of the draft to Mr Hoon's office, commenting that, while the text was "helpful in acknowledging the need to make military plans and preparations in case military action is required it does not, from our point of view, go far enough in providing direction for current military activity and an information strategy".[324] Mr Lee did not expect the draft to move forward until there was a clear UN position. He added that the Cabinet Office and No.10 accepted that the objectives would need to evolve. They were not for publication at that stage.

649. Draft military campaign objectives, building on the policy objectives, were prepared in late January 2003 and are addressed in Section 6.5.

650. On 22 October, Sir David Manning informed members of the Defence and Overseas Policy Committee (DOP) and the Home, Environment and Transport Secretaries that Mr Blair had approved the strategic policy objectives, which "should help guide work in departments for the current phase of activity".[325]

651. A version of the objectives was published as a Written Ministerial Statement by Mr Straw on 7 January 2003.

AHGI STOCKTAKE OF CONTINGENCY PLANNING

652. On 10 and 11 October, the House of Representatives and the Senate authorised US use of force in Iraq.[326]

653. Sir Christopher Meyer reported on 11 October that President Bush was "intensely suspicious of the UN", but had "bought the argument that it is worth trying to maximise international support by giving the Security Council one last chance".[327] That argument had "got stronger as the administration started to focus ... on 'day after' issues: it is one thing to go to war without ... UN cover, quite another to rule Iraq indefinitely without UN backing".

---

[324] Minute Lee to PS/Secretary of State [MOD], 7 October 2002, 'Iraq: Strategic Policy Objectives'.
[325] Letter Manning to McDonald, 22 October 2002, 'Iraq'.
[326] Almanac of Policy Issues, 15 October 2002, *Congressional Resolution Authorizing Force Against Iraq*.
[327] Telegram 1326 Washington to FCO London, 11 October 2002, 'US/Iraq: Will the President go to war'.

654. In a separate telegram on post-conflict issues sent the same day, Sir Christopher Meyer reported that the US media, briefed by an unnamed senior official, was saying that US views were coalescing around the idea of Iraq being governed by a US military commander in the initial period after Saddam Hussein's removal.[328] Sir Christopher explained that US Government views were yet to crystallise, but there was a strong inclination towards that approach, which was at odds with the UN-led solution in the recent FCO paper.

655. Sir Christopher concluded:

> "The bottom line is that the US will be firmly in the driving seat in organising any post-Saddam administration. We need to wake up to this reality and consider how best we can align ourselves to ensure not only a stable Iraq but also the maximum benefit for UK plc."

656. On 14 October, the Cabinet Office produced a grid of military and non-military contingency planning under way in Whitehall. Organised into "external" and "domestic" issues, work ranged from the FCO paper on administering post-Saddam Hussein Iraq to an ACPO review of counter-terrorism and counter-extremism policing.[329]

657. The grid listed 11 papers attributed to the FCO, including the five already circulated to the AHGI, and six others, "not yet ready for circulation", covering:

- consular contingencies in the region;
- reopening an Embassy in Baghdad (see Section 15.1);
- economic issues in Iraq and the region;
- SSR in Iraq;
- the vulnerabilities of UK diplomatic missions in the region; and
- contingency planning for a CBW attack on UK diplomatic missions.

658. The record of the meeting of the AHGI on 11 October stated that "sanitised" versions of the FCO paper on consequences of conflict had been shared with the US, and the scenarios for post-conflict Iraq with the US, France and Germany.[330]

659. The Cabinet Office grid listed three "external" MOD contingency planning activities:

- UK/US military liaison;
- discussion of Urgent Operational Requirements (UORs) with the Treasury and industry; and
- reorganisation of Operation FRESCO, the contingency plans to manage a prospective firefighters' strike (see Section 6.1).

---

[328] Telegram 1327 Washington to FCO London, 11 October 2002, 'Iraq: The Day After: US Views'.
[329] Minute Dodd to Manning, 14 October 2002, 'Ad Hoc Group on Iraq' attaching Paper Cabinet Office, 14 October 2002, 'Whitehall Iraq Contingency Planning'.
[330] Minute Dodd to Manning, 14 October 2002, 'Ad Hoc Group on Iraq'.

660. In addition, DFID was working on the paper on potential humanitarian implications of conflict in Iraq, and British Trade International (BTI) was identifying priority sectors in Iraq for British companies.

661. The grid also listed departments responsible for different aspects of domestic contingency planning, including community relations, refugee and asylum issues, the terrorist threat, and the economic consequences of conflict.

662. That work was later consolidated in a single paper produced by the CCS on 27 November, described later in this Section.

FCO PAPER: 'INTERNATIONAL ADMINISTRATION FOR IRAQ: WHAT, WHO AND HOW?'

663. The FCO paper 'International Administration for Iraq: what, who and how?' examined possible models for a UN role in the administration of Iraq.

664. The FCO concluded that a UN transitional administration working alongside an international security force would work, but planning needed to start as soon as possible.

665. Mr Gray sent the draft of a 12th FCO paper to the AHGI on 18 October.[331] 'International Administration for Iraq: what, who and how?' appears to have been produced in response to the recommendation in the FCO paper on models for administering a post-Saddam Hussein Iraq that work begin on examining a possible UN role in more detail. It drew on recent UN experience in Afghanistan, Cambodia, East Timor and Kosovo to distinguish between two approaches to international administration:

- a "light" approach, monitoring a local administration's decisions against principles set out in a mandate provided by the Security Council; and
- a more intrusive international administration implementing the mandate directly.

If the Iraqi regime fought to the end or the damage to Iraq was extensive, the international administration would need to assume control of key areas. If Saddam Hussein were overthrown quickly or "the bulk of Ba'ath apparatchiks switched sides", the lighter approach might be manageable.

666. In both cases, key elements of the Security Council mandate would include:

- reconstruction of war damage and delivery of humanitarian assistance;
- internal and external security;
- stopping Iraq's WMD programmes;
- ensuring respect for Iraq's territorial integrity;

---

[331] Letter Gray to Drummond, 18 October 2002, 'Papers for the AHGI' attaching Paper [unattributed], 17 October 2002, 'International Administration for Iraq: what, who and how?'

- a plan for a political process, which might emerge from the Iraqi opposition or within the country;
- ensuring full respect for human rights;
- administering OFF;
- reintegration of Iraq into the world economy; and
- a realistic exit strategy.

667. Security would remain the responsibility of the Coalition:

- internal security ("pacification of unrest"), which would fall to the military and be provided initially by the Coalition;
- external security, where Iraqi forces "would probably have to be replaced"; and
- "law and order issues", which "might be handled by local police forces but with strong international monitoring".

668. The FCO advised that tackling Iraq's administration and reconstruction called for a focus on key ministries, including defence, interior, justice, finance and oil, and the regional administration (18 governorates and Baghdad).

669. Some institutions (election machinery, parliament, a regional affairs ministry and Human Rights Commission) would need complete replacement or setting up from scratch. Some (the Revolutionary Command Council, intelligence and internal security services, the Ba'ath Party and the presidential apparatus) would need to be dismantled. Institutions in other areas (labour, planning, education, health and agriculture) could be left largely in Iraqi hands. That analysis applied whether the administration was headed by the US military or the UN.

670. The FCO suggested that the civilian administration be divided into "pillars" on the Kosovo model, with the Coalition taking on, as a minimum, defence and interior. Other pillars might include civil administration, reconstruction, economic reintegration, institution-building and justice and home affairs.

671. On the appointment of a UN "figurehead", the draft stated: "We would need a heavyweight Special Representative, ideally a Muslim, who would be prepared to spend time in Iraq leading the IA [interim administration], backed up by high-calibre senior staff."

672. There was no reference to any UK contribution.

673. The FCO advised that the number of Iraqis and non-Iraqis needed for civil administration would be large, but that the UN system was "unlikely to be able to produce all the people needed on time". The UK "should look at a range of other sources:

- Other international institutions, e.g. IMF and World Bank
- Coalition players

- Regional players and structures such as the EU and OIC [Organization of the Islamic Conference].[332] NATO?"

674. Previous interim administrations had cost up to US$500 million per year, with civil components of between 200 and 5,000 personnel, and military components between 40 and 15,000. Civilian police, where necessary, had numbered from 1,000 to 4,000. Iraq was comparable in size and population to Afghanistan, but much more developed:

"… the scale of intervention in its affairs will be much greater and more intrusive. Costs and numbers of personnel are likely therefore to be much greater than previous missions. Who paid would be a key question."

675. The FCO concluded:

"Administering Iraq and guiding it back to a sustainable place in the world community will be a major task. A UN transitional administration could do it, in parallel with an International Force to provide security and cover for the eradication of WMD. A model that could work would [be] an extensive Interim Authority, divided into pillars under the control of a variety of international players. The pace of eventual handover to Iraqi control could be different for each pillar … But to be successful, planning needs to start as soon as possible."

676. The Inquiry has not seen a final version of the FCO paper, but material from the 17 October draft was used in the 1 November Cabinet Office paper on models for Iraq after Saddam Hussein.

WAR CRIMES AND THE CREATION OF AN INTERNATIONAL CRIMINAL TRIBUNAL FOR IRAQ

677. In October, No.10 instructed the Attorney General's Office and the Cabinet Office to take account of the potential need to bring Saddam Hussein and his inner circle to justice as part of Whitehall work on the future of Iraq.

678. The creation of an international body to try senior members of Saddam Hussein's regime for war crimes was the founding purpose of INDICT, an NGO chaired by Ms Ann Clwyd, Vice-Chair of the Parliamentary Labour Party (PLP).

679. Ms Clwyd raised the possibility of using INDICT "as an alternative to war" at a meeting of the Parliamentary Committee (the executive body of the PLP) in July 2002.[333] Mr Blair is reported to have replied: "Why don't we do it?"

680. In his diaries, Mr Mullin recorded that Ms Clwyd told Mr Blair at the meeting of the PLP on 17 July: "We can indict the Iraqis now."[334] That had "seemed to come as news"

---

[332] Known since 2011 as the Organisation of Islamic Cooperation.
[333] Statement Clwyd, January 2010, 'The Work of INDICT', page 24.
[334] Mullin C. *A View from the Foothills: The Diaries of Chris Mullin*. Profile Books, 2009.

to Mr Blair even though Ms Clwyd "had been pressing the point for ages". Ms Clwyd offered to look into the issue for Mr Blair and get back to him.

681. At No.10's request, during September and October 2002, FCO officials started to consider the possibility of an international criminal tribunal for Iraq (ICTI).

682. In late September, the FCO advised Mr Blair that the UK would support international moves to prosecute leading members of Saddam Hussein's regime, but that there were a number of obstacles.[335] Those included the lack of International Criminal Court (ICC) jurisdiction over crimes committed before the ICC Statute entered into force on 1 July 2002 and limited support for the idea of establishing a UN tribunal for Iraq among members of the Security Council.

683. On 27 September, material was submitted to Lord Goldsmith, the Attorney General, on behalf of INDICT, arguing that the UK should assert jurisdiction over crimes committed against UK nationals by Saddam Hussein and Tariq Aziz (Iraqi Foreign Minister and Deputy Prime Minister) in 1990 and promote the formation of an ad hoc tribunal to deal with Saddam Hussein after he left office.[336]

684. Ms Clwyd sent the material to Mr Blair, who asked officials: "Can I have some proper work done on why this isn't a good idea, or could it have PR [public relations] value?"[337]

685. In their response on 15 October, FCO officials pointed out that, although President Bush had warned Saddam Hussein's generals in a speech on 7 October "that all war criminals will be pursued and punished", he had not identified the mechanism to be used.[338] They cautioned that "to pursue efforts to set up an ICTI now, when we are seeking to engage the UNSC on a range of substantive Iraq-related issues, would be a serious own goal".

686. Officials put forward four alternatives in the event of a change in the Iraqi administration:

- a special hybrid domestic tribunal, in connection with the UN and including international judges and prosecutors, similar to the tribunal established in Sierra Leone;
- special hybrid panels within the Iraqi criminal justice system along the lines of the panels established in East Timor and Kosovo;

---

[335] Letter Sedwill to Rycroft, 23 September 2002, 'Iraq: INDICT'.
[336] Note Montgomery, 27 September 2002, 'In the Matter of Iraqi Crimes Against Humanity'.
[337] Manuscript comment Blair on Note Montgomery, 27 September 2002, 'In the Matter of Iraqi Crimes Against Humanity'.
[338] Letter Sedwill to Rycroft, 15 October 2002, 'ICTY-Type Tribunal for Iraq'; Speech Bush, 7 October 2002, Cincinnati Museum Center.

- truth and reconciliation commissions for lower-level accused or where there was insufficient evidence for prosecution; and
- use of the existing criminal justice system in Iraq.

687. Mr Rycroft explained to Mr Blair that he expected Lord Goldsmith to reject the arguments put forward on behalf of INDICT relating to the 1990 hostage-taking cases on the grounds that there was almost no prospect of a successful prosecution. He also commented that the FCO advice on a tribunal "will … not enhance your view of government lawyers".[339]

688. Mr Rycroft advised Mr Blair that No.10 officials were "pushing back" on both issues. Mr Blair should tell Ms Clwyd he was interested in both proposals and that he had asked for "proper legal advice". On the tribunal, Mr Blair's line should be:

> "… it is essential that we take a strong line on human rights in Iraq (as we did in the dossier). We are considering whether we should propose the establishment of an International Criminal Tribunal for Iraq, or some other mechanism, to ensure that Saddam and others guilty of the most horrendous crimes can be brought to justice."

689. Mr Rycroft instructed the FCO, the Attorney General's Office and the Cabinet Office to take account of the potential need to bring Saddam Hussein and his inner circle to justice as part of Whitehall work on the future of Iraq.[340] He asked the FCO to do more work on options, including how best to let Saddam Hussein's inner circle know that their interests would be best served by breaking with him, and the Attorney General's Office to look again at the prosecution of the 1990 crimes: "On the face of it, there is much advantage in letting it be known that we are starting investigations against Saddam for these crimes."

690. The Attorney General's Office sent a holding reply on 17 October, explaining that Lord Goldsmith was still considering the material submitted on behalf of INDICT and had not yet responded to Ms Clwyd or INDICT.[341]

691. Lord Goldsmith sent a substantive reply to Ms Clwyd on 24 January 2003, which is addressed in the Box on INDICT in Section 3.6.[342]

692. Prosecution for war crimes was discussed at the first round of US/UK inter-agency talks on post-conflict Iraq in Washington on 6 November.

693. Updated FCO advice to No.10 followed in early December.

694. Both are addressed later in this Section.

---

[339] Minute Rycroft to Prime Minister, 16 October 2002, 'Iraq: Indicting Saddam'.
[340] Letter Rycroft to Sedwill, 23 October 2002, 'ICTY-type tribunal for Iraq'.
[341] Letter Adams to Rycroft, 17 October 2002, 'INDICT – Correspondence with Ann Clwyd MP'.
[342] Letter Goldsmith to Clwyd, 24 January 2003, 'Saddam Hussein, Tariq Aziz, Ali Hassan Al-Majid and Taha Ramadan'.

UK military options: war-fighting and reconstruction

695. Military planning for the deployment of UK land forces in northern Iraq as part of a US-led force gathered pace during October 2002.

696. On 31 October, Adm Boyce advised Mr Blair that a major contribution to the military campaign would reduce pressure on the UK to finance a share of the post-conflict reconstruction effort.

697. Mr Bowen informed Sir David Manning on 9 October that the Chiefs of Staff had concluded that a decision in principle in favour of Package 3 in the next few weeks would help the UK to influence US thinking to a greater extent than had been possible up to that point, "especially in relation to the aftermath of any military action".[343]

698. Section 6.1 sets out the detail of the discussion and the pressures driving the debate.

699. The need for a decision on the potential UK contribution to any US-led action against Iraq was set out in an urgent minute to Mr Hoon from Mr Johnson on 11 October.[344] Mr Johnson advised that US thinking on the "Day After" was "under-developed at present" and warned:

> "... there is likely to be a need for a substantial, potentially long-enduring commitment of forces. Assuming that military action had taken place under a UN umbrella, it is likely that the US would look to allies and the UK to play a major role in this, perhaps including providing a framework capability through the ARRC [Allied Rapid Reaction Corps]. We clearly have an interest in minimising the risk of a longstanding commitment ... in a part of the world that will not be retention-positive for our personnel: in terms of Defence Planning Assumptions, a rouled [rotating] medium scale PSO [peace support operation] in Iraq would only be manageable if our commitments elsewhere ... were capped at small scale. The more substantial our contribution to military action in the first place, the more plausibly we will be able to argue that we have done our bit."

700. After a meeting with senior advisers on 14 October, Mr Hoon wrote to Mr Blair on 15 October, seeking a decision that week on whether to tell the US they could assume a UK Land contribution in addition to the air, maritime and Special Forces package already offered for planning purposes.[345] Mr Hoon wrote:

> "There is likely to be a substantial and continuing post-conflict stabilisation task in Iraq. If we do not contribute Package 3, we may be more vulnerable to a US request to provide a substantial force for this potentially open-ended task."

---

[343] Minute Bowen to Manning, 9 October 2002, 'Iraq: Chiefs of Staff Meeting on 9 October'.
[344] Minute Johnson to PS/Secretary of State [MOD], 11 October 2002, 'Iraq: UK Contingency Planning'.
[345] Minute Hoon to Prime Minister, 15 October 2002, 'Iraq: UK Military Options'.

701. Sir David Manning advised Mr Blair:

"I am not much persuaded … that if we help with the war fighting, we shall be spared the post-conflict washing up. It didn't work like that in Afghanistan. Experience shows that once you are in, you're in deep, without queues of grateful countries waiting to take over when the shooting stops."[346]

702. Sir David suggested that Mr Blair explore a number of questions with Mr Hoon, including: "Can we afford Package 3?"

703. Mr Edward Oakden, Head of FCO Security Policy Department, advised Mr Straw to question whether the decision really had to be made that week.[347] Mr Oakden wrote that the MOD's suggestion that the UK could trade a more active role in fighting for "a smaller military role during reconstruction" seemed "optimistic": "On the contrary, if we have fought without international legal sanction, we could be left on our own with the US."

704. On 16 October, Mr Straw updated Mr Blair on his discussions with Secretary Powell on 14 and 15 October.[348] He and Secretary Powell had discussed the risks of acting without international backing and the problems of the "day after" which would be the "largest and most hazardous exercise in nation-building"; it would not be as straightforward as some thought.

705. Mr Blair, Mr Straw, Mr Hoon and Adm Boyce met on 17 October to discuss military options.[349] Mr Blair acknowledged the arguments in favour of Package 3, but:

"… remained concerned about costs. He concluded that he wanted to keep open the option of Package 3. But we must not commit to it at this stage."

706. Mr Campbell wrote in his diaries that at the meeting, Mr Blair said "it was not no, but it was not yet yes, and he wanted more work done analysing the cost".[350]

707. The minutes of the meeting of the Chiefs of Staff on 28 October stated that "it would be important to emphasise within forthcoming submissions that, although Package 3 might be considered expensive, the alternative of committing to ops [operations] during the aftermath would also require considerable resources".[351]

708. Mr Blair, Mr Straw, Mr Hoon and Adm Boyce discussed the MOD's wish to offer Package 3 to the US for planning purposes on 31 October.[352] Mr Blair asked about the additional costs of Package 3 and whether they had been discussed with the Treasury. Adm Boyce said that "he believed that if we made a major financial contribution to the

---

[346] Minute Manning to Blair, 16 October 2002, 'Iraq: UK Military Options'.
[347] Minute Oakden to Private Secretary [FCO], 16 October 2002, 'Iraq'.
[348] Minute Straw to Prime Minister, 16 October 2002, 'Iraq: Conversation with Powell: No US Interlocutors'.
[349] Letter Rycroft to Watkins, 17 October 2002, 'Iraq: UK Military Options'.
[350] Campbell A & Hagerty B. *The Alastair Campbell Diaries. Volume 4. The Burden of Power: Countdown to Iraq*. Hutchinson, 2012.
[351] Minutes, 28 October 2002, Chiefs of Staff meeting.
[352] Letter Wechsberg to Watkins, 31 October 2002, 'Iraq: Military Options'.

campaign through Package 3, we would be under less pressure to finance a share of the post-conflict reconstruction effort".

709. Mr Blair decided that the MOD should tell the US that the UK was prepared to "put Package 3 on the same basis as Package 2 for planning purposes, in order to keep the option open".

710. Asked why there might have been a reluctance in government during September and October to go beyond Package 2, Sir Kevin Tebbit told the Inquiry that one reason was:

> "… the lack of clarity of the overall plans still at that point. I think the Chiefs of Staff were very assiduous throughout this period of always asking whether, in the discussions with the United States … the US had 'a winning concept'.

> "… [U]nless and until the Chiefs of Staff were satisfied there was a winning concept – and remember, we were talking about aftermath or the day after as well as the actual operation itself - then obviously there was a reservation."[353]

711. The shift in UK military focus from northern to southern Iraq, and changes in the attitude of the Chiefs of Staff to the desirability of a significant UK military contribution to Phase IV early in 2003 are addressed in Section 6.2.

Growing concern about post-conflict planning

712. Between October and December 2002, UK officials expressed growing concern about the slow progress of post-conflict planning.

DFID CONTACT WITH THE US AND UN

713. By early October, restrictions on contacts with the US and UN were constraining DFID's ability to plan effectively.

714. After a visit to the US by Mr Chakrabarti in late September to discuss humanitarian planning, Ms Short stopped further contact between DFID and US officials, concerned about the potential political implications of DFID being seen to prepare for war.

715. DFID was also under instruction from the Cabinet Office not to discuss humanitarian issues with the UN system.

716. Those restrictions had been lifted by the beginning of November.

717. The DFID draft paper on humanitarian consequences of military action discussed by the AHGI on 11 October explained that planning was constrained by the shortage of

---

[353] Public hearing, 3 December 2009, pages 42-43.

information on Iraq's capacity to respond to the disruption of basic services.[354] Removal of "restrictions on initiating contact with relevant stakeholders" would allow DFID to fill the gap and develop a fuller picture of humanitarian agencies' contingency planning and regional capacity.

718. The Cabinet Office record of the meeting of the AHGI on 11 October observed that the DFID paper assumed there would be substantial UN involvement in post-conflict Iraq and added:

> "We have asked DFID not to discuss post-conflict Iraq humanitarian issues with [the] UN system yet, but they will need to do so to develop planning further."[355]

719. On 18 October, Mr Drummond informed Sir David Manning that departments' contingency planning was mostly confined to Whitehall.[356] Although there was no immediate pressure to extend existing external contacts, which included DTI contacts with the oil industry, the police with community leaders, and the FCO with the US, France and Germany, "some Departments such as DFID, who would like to link up with UN contingency planning, would find it helpful to be authorised to make contact soon, perhaps after the UNSCR is agreed".

720. On 30 September, Mr Chakrabarti had called on Mr Elliot Abrams, Head of the US inter-agency Humanitarian Working Group.[357] Mr Abrams outlined US thinking and suggested the UK and US keep in touch.

721. On 9 October, Mr Chakrabarti asked Mr Fernie to visit Washington in early November "for discussions with all the parts of the US Admin[istration] and with the World Bank".[358] He added that DFID needed to "thicken up our humanitarian/ development approach to Iraq".

722. On 15 October, Ms Anna Bewes, Ms Short's Principal Private Secretary, informed Ms Carolyn Miller, DFID Director Middle East and North Africa, that Ms Short had seen the record of Mr Chakrabarti's visit and agreed DFID should be planning for all humanitarian contingencies, including those not involving military action, but was "very wary" of attracting any publicity:

> "It could cause huge political difficulties if it emerged that … DFID is planning for war. For this reason the Secretary of State has asked me to make it clear that she does not authorise any discussion or document sharing with the US on our preparations for humanitarian crises in Iraq."[359]

---

[354] Paper DFID, 11 October 2002, 'Iraq: Potential Humanitarian Implications'.
[355] Minute Dodd to Manning, 14 October 2002, 'Ad Hoc Group on Iraq'.
[356] Minute Drummond to Manning, 18 October 2002, 'Iraq: Contingency Plans'.
[357] Minute [DFID junior official] to Chakrabarti, 9 October 2002, 'Call on Elliot Abrams, Special Assistant to the President & Senior Director for Democracy, Human Rights & International Operations, 30 September: Iraq'.
[358] Email Chakrabarti to Brewer/Fernie/Miller, 9 October 2002, 'Note on Call on Elliot Abrams'.
[359] Email Bewes to Miller, 15 October 2002, 'Iraq'.

723. Ms Short held a meeting on 21 October, attended by Mr Chakrabarti, to discuss contingency planning. At the meeting Ms Short agreed that DFID officials should "indicate an intention" to join the FCO-led delegation attending inter-agency talks in Washington on 6 November, with a final decision to follow later.[360]

724. Sir Suma Chakrabarti told the Inquiry that DFID received an email from the Cabinet Office on 23 October saying No.10 was happy for the department to talk discreetly to some NGOs if it was clear the aim was disarmament not war.[361]

725. Sir Suma stated that, although the email made no reference to contacting the UN, he and Ms Short had decided in early November that "we just had to do so".[362]

726. The Inquiry has not seen a copy of the Cabinet Office email.

727. Sir Suma Chakrabarti was asked by the Inquiry whether he had been instructed by his Secretary of State not to share information (with US officials).[363] He replied: "At no stage", and that he was "Absolutely sure" of that.

728. Sir Suma's evidence does not match the instruction sent out by Ms Short's office on 15 October.

729. Sir Jeremy Greenstock told the Inquiry that the first contact between UKMIS New York and the UN Secretariat to discuss post-conflict planning was in October 2002, "probably at their request".[364]

730. Sir Jeremy reported from New York on 30 October that UN post-conflict planning was "embryonic". There were indications of support for a "pillared" model for post-conflict administration somewhere between the approaches adopted for Kosovo and Afghanistan, but planning for a possible UN administration was happening at a very low level. That reflected an instruction from the Secretary-General that work on what was effectively planning for the UN to take over from the sovereign government of a member state should be very low key.[365]

731. On 31 October, the Cabinet Office reported to Sir David Manning that the wider instruction to departments not to engage external actors was, in practice, being overtaken.[366] There was particular pressure for consultation from the UK oil industry: a delegation from BP would be visiting the FCO on 6 November.

732. On 4 November, Ms Short agreed that a revised version of the DFID paper on the potential humanitarian implications of conflict in Iraq should be shared with the US

---

[360] Minute Bewes to Fernie, 22 October 2002, 'Iraq'.
[361] Public hearing, 8 December 2009, page 12.
[362] Public hearing, 8 December 2009, page 14.
[363] Public hearing, 8 December 2009, page 17.
[364] Public hearing, 15 December 2009, pages 4-5.
[365] Telegram 2073 UKMIS New York to FCO London, 30 October 2002, 'Iraq: Day After Planning: Possible UN Administration'.
[366] Minute Dodd to Manning, 31 October 2002, 'Iraq: After the UNSCR'.

as a work in progress, subject to the inclusion of an explicit reference to DFID's lack of financial resources to cover the humanitarian contingencies considered in the paper.[367]

733. The substance of the paper was little changed from October, but a new introduction made explicit reference to the need to consider the humanitarian consequences not just of military action, but also of regime change without major military action and of Iraqi compliance with UN resolutions.[368] The paper stated:

> "Most humanitarian planning is currently focused on the after-effects of conflict …
> But UK ministers are clear that humanitarian planning should also consider other
> contingencies and not assume conflict is the most likely, in line with current UK
> policy objectives for Iraq which focus on disarmament rather than conflict or regime
> change."

734. The paper also stated that DFID had begun informal contacts with UN agencies and that wider contacts might follow the passage of a resolution, a UN decision to start more active planning, or further UK Ministerial guidance.

735. Ms Short told the Inquiry that she had spoken to Mr Kofi Annan, the UN Secretary-General, and Ms Louise Fréchette, UN Deputy Secretary-General, a number of times, "sort of slightly breaching the No.10 ruling".[369] She believed that Mr Chakrabarti had also done so. It was "very fraught" for the UN because of divisions within the Security Council: "The UN prepared, but kept it quiet."

**736. There is no indication that temporary restrictions on DFID's contacts with
the UN and the US had a lasting impact on UK planning for post-conflict Iraq.
The Inquiry does not accept, however, that the political sensitivity of the UK
being seen to prepare for conflict while pursuing a negotiated solution to the Iraq
crisis should have interfered with discreet contingency planning for the possible
consequences of military action. It was necessary at all stages to consider and
prepare for the worst.**

737. At Ms Short's meeting with officials on 21 October, Mr Fernie reported that the FCO was not considering the possible humanitarian consequences of the use of WMD. Ms Short identified that as an area of legitimate focus for DFID and commissioned a paper for Mr Blair, to be produced, if possible, before 30 October.[370]

738. On 29 October, OD Sec wrote to Mr Robert Lowson, DEFRA Director for Environmental Protection Strategy, about oil-related environmental contingency planning. The letter also asked whether there was "any official UK capacity, beyond that of the MOD, to assist with CBW clear-up or in providing clean water in these

---

[367] Manuscript comment Short, 4 November 2002, on Minute Fernie to Private Secretary/Secretary of State [DFID], 4 November 2002, 'Iraq: Contingency Planning: Humanitarian Paper'.
[368] Paper UK Department for International Development, 5 November 2002, 'Iraq: Potential Humanitarian Implications'.
[369] Public hearing, 2 February 2010, page 52.
[370] Minute Bewes to Fernie, 22 October 2002, 'Iraq'.

circumstances".[371] The letter was copied to No.10, the FCO and the Cabinet Office, but not to DFID or the MOD.

739. Ms Short wrote to Mr Blair on 30 October, warning that the international community was not adequately prepared to cope with the potentially enormous human and financial costs if Iraq used chemical and biological weapons during any military conflict.[372] She concluded:

> "I accept of course that preparing for military options, among others, is necessary, but I am very concerned that in our work across Whitehall and with the USA, the examination of the humanitarian and possible political consequences of military action have not been properly explored. We should think through what it would mean to take responsibility for Iraq after a conflict involving WMD and also make contingency plans for other possible outcomes such as a fall of the regime without a war. I am concerned that Whitehall appears to be focusing on military action, not considering other scenarios, and not thinking through the consequences of the likely use of chemical weapons."

740. Mr Drummond informed Sir David Manning on 8 November that work so far on the effects of CBW had focused on military and consular dimensions.[373] Mr Drummond said that Ms Short was right that it should be extended to address wider humanitarian consequences. The DIS had been asked to follow this up, in consultation with DFID. Once the assessments were in, officials would need to consider how DFID would pursue them with humanitarian agencies. There were risks that information would be mishandled, but "there does need to be contingency planning".

741. Mr Watkins set out Mr Hoon's views to No.10 on 11 November.[374] Mr Hoon shared Ms Short's concerns about the potential use of WMD. The MOD was making sure UK military personnel were properly protected against the WMD threat, but it was:

> "… simply not possible (nor is it the MOD's role) to extend this protection to the civilian population of any country with whom we may be engaged in conflict. We can, however, offer the reassurance that we are working closely, through the Cabinet Office, with Departments across Whitehall, including DFID, on post-conflict strategy and are offering as much information as we can make available to assist planning."

742. There is no indication of any response from Mr Blair.

---

[371] Letter Dodd to Lowson, 29 October 2002, 'Iraq: Environmental Contingency Planning'.
[372] Letter Short to Blair, 30 October 2002, [untitled].
[373] Minute Drummond to Manning, 8 November 2002, 'Iraq: CBW'.
[374] Letter Watkins to Rycroft, 11 November 2002, 'Possible Iraqi Use of WMD'.

JIC ASSESSMENT, 23 OCTOBER 2002: 'IRAQ: THE KURDS AND SHIA'

743. On 23 October, at the FCO's request, the JIC assessed the likely reaction of the Kurdish and Shia population of Iraq to any US-led attack.[375] It evaluated how significant and unified the two groups were, their links to Iraq's neighbours and the external Iraqi opposition, and their aspirations and fears for a post-Saddam Hussein Iraq. The JIC assessed that "each population is a complex web of different groups and interests". UK knowledge of the Shia inside Iraq was "very limited". Senior religious leaders had "some influence over the Shia population", but the JIC could not gauge its extent.

744. The JIC assessed that Iraqi Shia contact with the outside world was "limited and ad hoc", and judged that:

> "... **currently neither Iran nor the external opposition has a significant influence over the Shia population as a whole**. On the contrary, we believe many Iraqi Shia fear Iran winning influence over the future of Iraq because of Tehran's supposed insistence on the centrality of Sharia in political life."

745. The JIC's conclusions included the assessment that:

> "... **spontaneous uprisings,** without any clear central leadership, are likely in both southern and northern Iraq ... should the regime's control collapse quickly. Army deserters (the Shia form the bulk of the Iraqi military's conscript force) could join these in large numbers. The pace of events in such a scenario **could overtake any planning by the KDP and PUK in the north, and in the south control could devolve by default to a patchwork collection of tribal leaders and religious figures** about whom we know little. In both areas there could be violent score settling ..."

746. The JIC assessment was not reflected in the Cabinet Office paper of 1 November on models for Iraq after Saddam Hussein.[376]

CABINET OFFICE PAPER: 'IRAQ: MODELS AND SOME QUESTIONS FOR POST-SADDAM GOVERNMENT'

747. At the beginning of November, the Cabinet Office sent No.10 a paper on models for Iraq after Saddam Hussein. It is not clear whether it was seen by Mr Blair.

748. The paper was to be the steering brief for the UK delegation to the first round of UK/US/Australia talks on post-conflict issues in Washington on 6 November.

---

[375] JIC Assessment, 23 October 2002, 'Iraq: The Kurds and Shia'.
[376] Minute Drummond to Manning, 1 November 2002, 'Iraq: Post-Saddam' attaching Paper 'Iraq: Models and some questions for post-Saddam government'.

749. It proposed that achieving the UK's preferred outcome of "a more representative and democratic Iraq" might involve three phases:

- **a transitional Coalition military government lasting up to six months;**
- **a UN administration lasting about three years; and**
- **a sovereign Iraqi government.**

750. The Cabinet Office sent a paper on models for Iraq after Saddam Hussein to Sir David Manning on 1 November.[377]

751. The Cabinet Office paper was the first attempted synthesis of some of the work undertaken by departments under the auspices of the AHGI. It was conceived as the steering brief for the FCO/MOD/DFID/Cabinet Office delegation to the forthcoming talks on post-conflict issues with the US in Washington and did not propose or allocate responsibility for next steps. Mr Drummond described it to Sir David Manning as a summary of latest thinking. The ideas in it would not be presented as UK policy.

752. The paper stated that there were many possible permutations of the "stable united and law abiding state … providing effective and representative government" sought by the UK, but focused on just two:

"a. an Iraq under a new, more amenable strongman;
b. a more representative and democratic Iraq."

753. In the event of Saddam Hussein being toppled by a new strongman from his inner circle before or during the early stages of a military campaign, the new regime could be recognised in return for agreement to certain conditions. But:

"Our leverage over the new regime would quickly dissipate as Coalition forces could not remain at invasion strength in the region for long. Any sanctions, once lifted, would be difficult to re-impose. This scenario for achieving our goal of Iraqi disarmament would be relatively simple and cheap, but there would be a high risk of the new strongman reverting to Saddam's policies …"

754. Assuming that Saddam Hussein's regime fell and Coalition forces reached Baghdad, the UK's preferred model for the future government of Iraq might fall into three phases:

- transitional Coalition military government;
- UN administration; and
- a "sovereign, representative and democratic government of Iraq".

755. Scenario 'b' assumed UN authorisation for military action and that the international community and UN system would be willing to assist with reconstruction.

---

[377] Minute Drummond to Manning, 1 November 2002, 'Iraq: Post-Saddam' attaching Paper 'Iraq: Models and some questions for post-Saddam government'.

756. The Coalition would make clear that it would transfer authority from a transitional military government to UN administration as soon as possible, but in practice that could take up to six months. The UN would then "rule" Iraq for about three years, during which time a new Iraqi constitution would be agreed, paving the way for the formation of a sovereign Iraqi government. The US would continue to have "overall responsibility" for security.

757. The Cabinet Office did not define "representative and democratic". The phrase contrasted with the more equivocal language in the FCO paper on scenarios for the future of Iraq, which proposed that the UK "should argue for political reform, but not necessarily full democracy in the short term", and with the reference to "effective and representative government" in the agreed definition of the desired end state, which was quoted elsewhere in the Cabinet Office paper.

758. The paper listed five priorities facing the transitional military government to be established by the Coalition after the collapse of the Iraqi regime.

759. The first, "establishing security", was to be achieved by disbanding the "inner rings" of Saddam Hussein's security apparatus. There would need to be screening of officers in the security forces. Some would be demobilised, some imprisoned and some tried.

760. The four other priorities were:

- Dismantling WMD.
- Addressing humanitarian needs. A UN presence would need to be established as soon as possible, accompanied by "a version of OFF". There would be a separate need for emergency work on infrastructure involving close co-ordination with civilian development agencies.
- Planning for a revival of the economy, which would require close co-operation with international financial institutions.
- Preparing for a UN administration. "A major task would be to decide as early as possible on the shape of a UN administration, and begin setting up as soon as the conflict ends. The Secretary-General, under guidance from the Security Council, would instruct the UN system to produce the necessary plan. Planning for SSR, economic recovery, and long-term reconstruction would also take place."

761. The paper's description of a possible UN administration drew heavily on the FCO paper on an international administration for Iraq described earlier in this Section. It went further than the FCO paper in proposing that a "UN Mission to Iraq (UNMI)" might be modelled on UNMIK, the UN Mission in Kosovo, where different roles had been sub-contracted by the UN to other multilateral bodies (the FCO paper listed the Kosovo model as one of a number of UN operations that could offer useful lessons). Organisations like the World Bank, OIC, UN and possibly the EU might lead on different strands. The paper proposed a parallel security structure under direct US military command, replicating NATO's parallel role in relation to UNMIK, "with as wide an inclusion of effective Coalition military partners as possible".

762. The level of intervention in individual ministries "would vary from total in the security field to … superficial in areas such as agriculture. The new senior cadres could be composed of UN staff, as far as possible from Muslim countries, émigré technocrats and non-tainted technocrats from within Iraq."

763. There would also need to be a political process managed by UNMI to prepare for a democratic government. The UN would:

"… engage in a process of political consultation which would lead to a convention of all Iraqi factions, both internal; and external … Under the UN administration, work could take place on reconstructing government, encouraging new political parties, facilitating free media and an active civil society. A new/revised/and possibly federal constitution will be drafted by Iraqi experts with international guidance. Municipal elections will take place."

764. The paper stated that UNMI would require:

"… at least in excess of one thousand international staff and several thousand foreign police. The security force would require tens of thousands of soldiers, although this figure would reduce over time. There are question[s] of how much this international effort would cost and how it would be funded. This could be done by national contributions or through the UN assessment system. An alternative would be to use oil revenue to pay administrative and military costs. This would require UN authorisation, and UNMI and security expenses would need to take account of debt repayment …"

765. There would also need to be a financial plan, involving detailed work by the IFIs, to reconcile payment of Iraq's "huge external debts" with reconstruction and development needs.

766. The SSR section of the Cabinet Office paper drew on an early draft of a longer FCO paper on the subject, the final version of which is described later in this Section. The Cabinet Office paper stated:

"Having dismantled Saddam's security apparatus, there will need to be a new one. This will need a comprehensive security sector plan agreed with and led by the US. The judiciary will need a total rebuild as well as the police. Decisions will need to be taken about the size and scope of the army and intelligence services."

767. The Cabinet Office paper concluded with a short section on establishing a "Sovereign Democratic Iraqi Government":

"To mark the end of UNMI there will be a progressive return of bureaucratic and political power to Iraqis. A new constitution will be promulgated. National elections will be held. International military forces will withdraw ... The new Iraq would be welcomed back to the international community. Under international guidance, the new government could be encouraged to sign a collective non-aggression pact with all states bordering the Gulf."

768. The paper did not address the UK's responsibilities and obligations during military occupation or the UK's wider post-conflict contribution.

769. Sir Peter Ricketts told the Inquiry:

"At the period we were developing our thinking about [the] UN lead in the summer of 2002, autumn of 2002, winter of 2002, it was not clear at all the timing on which military action might happen, indeed whether it would happen at all, and whether there would have been full UN authorisation in the second resolution for it.

"So at that period, we were talking in more general terms with the UN. By the time [in early 2003] it became clear, the timescale for military action, I think it was then also clear that the US would not be prepared to have UN administration. Therefore, by then we were on the track of working with ORHA [the DoD-led Office of Reconstruction and Humanitarian Assistance, see Section 6.5]. But I think it was a reasonable planning assumption in the autumn of 2002 that we could work for a UN transitional authority, and at that time the UN still had time to prepare for it."[378]

770. On 4 November, the AHGI took stock of all contingency planning papers nearing completion. The record of the meeting stated: "With the new UNSCR nearing adoption, it is time for those departments, which have not already done so, to conclude their initial contingency planning."[379] It listed papers close to completion on a range of subjects:

- the impact of conflict on the international and UK economies (Treasury);
- community relations in the UK (Home Office);
- humanitarian implications, including extra material on CBW use (DFID);
- Iraqi human rights abuses (FCO);
- environmental impact (DEFRA);
- impact on UK airlines and shipping (DfT);[380]
- consular planning (FCO);
- CBW dimensions of consular planning (FCO);

---

[378] Public hearing, 1 December 2009, page 81.
[379] Minute Dodd to Manning, 4 November 2002, 'Ad Hoc Group on Iraq'.
[380] Paper, Department for Transport, 12 November 2002, 'Possible Economic Impact on UK International Transport Operations of Action Against Iraq'.

- the Iraqi economy after Saddam Hussein (FCO);
- overview of post-Saddam Hussein scenarios (Cabinet Office, in preparation for inter-agency talks in Washington).

FCO PAPER: 'ECONOMIC ISSUES IN IRAQ AFTER POST-SADDAM REGIME CHANGE'

771. The FCO's second paper on rebuilding Iraq's economy identified the immediate tasks facing any new administration. Those included investing in infrastructure to build public support and taking control of public finances.

772. The paper stated that detailed analysis and planning needed to begin immediately.

773. A draft of the FCO paper on economic issues in Iraq, written at some point before 19 October,[381] was circulated to AHGI members on 4 November.[382] The paper described Iraq's economy as "distorted and very badly damaged", and consisting of a number of largely separate elements: the oil sector, which was efficiently run; the formal economy; the food distribution system; the informal economy ("an unrecorded, unregulated sprawl of trading and services"); the economy of northern Iraq; and the "partly secret regime/elite economy". The challenge would be to strip out the undesirable elements, retain the desirable and essential elements (the central bank and economic ministries "probably" still had competent staff below political appointees) and bring those together as a single economy.

774. Ensuring that there was "a smooth economic transition in the early months after regime change" would be the immediate task. Particularly high priority would have to be given to preserving food supplies and effective control of public finances, both of which were tied to the future of OFF.

775. The FCO paper stated that, in order to help build popular and regional support for the new administration, it might well be necessary to be able to show early gains:

"... the most obvious quick way of doing this would be to provide ... a significantly improved food ration, no doubt bolstered with a message about diverting resources from Saddam's extravagances ... Beyond the first 6-12 months the focus should turn more to targeting of reconstruction expenditure to achieve political quick wins.

"... Even if a new conflict produces little additional damage, the combination of neglect and war damage means that large investments in many areas and spread over many years, are needed if infrastructure and services are to recover even to their pre-1990 condition. Getting this process under way will be essential to economic revival, to the alleviation of humanitarian problems and to popular support for a new administration.

---

[381] Paper FCO, [undated], 'Economic issues in Iraq after post-Saddam regime change: internal policy and external engagement'.
[382] Minute Dodd to Manning, 4 November 2002, 'Ad Hoc Group on Iraq'.

"The two big constraints will be finance and implementation capacity. On the former the key will be a workable agreement between external stakeholders which guarantees a reasonable flow of resources to Iraq … On the latter there will be a need for detailed analysis and planning of the substance, some of which should be set in hand now … and also for the establishment of a competent central body within Iraq able to act as the focal point for reconstruction."

776. The FCO warned that Iraq's actual or potential financial obligations, including debt servicing and compensation payments, threatened to "swamp" the income available from oil. There would need to be co-ordination between external players on a package including new bilateral grants or loans and multilateral assistance.

777. The FCO advised that advance planning for the period immediately after regime change "falls to the US", but there was also a need for "good information and sound policy analysis" from the World Bank and IMF:

"… neither institution has done any substantive work for many years; if we leave it until regime change has happened to ask them to address the issues there is likely to be a considerable delay before they can produce anything useful. On economic grounds there is a good case for asking senior management in both institutions to put work in hand well in advance of military action … [S]ome useful preparatory assessments … would at least mean that an incoming regime, and its friends abroad, would not be flying completely blind on economic matters …"

778. The only comments on the draft seen by the Inquiry were from a junior official in DFID, who observed a need "to dovetail humanitarian relief efforts with a transition phase, reconstruction and longer-term reform".[383] The official recommended that "a revised version of OFF should incorporate **development planning** (sector development, economic planning and strategy), provide a clear structure of roles and responsibilities … and provide channels for supporting [Iraqi] government administrative and planning structures …"

TREASURY PAPER: 'ECONOMIC IMPACT OF A WAR IN IRAQ'

779. A Treasury paper on the impact of conflict on the global economy and the UK was circulated to the AHGI on 7 November.[384] The Treasury's assessment of the impact on the global economy remained unchanged from 6 September. The Treasury assessed that, in the UK, the conflict might lead to lower growth, higher unemployment and higher inflation, especially if it was protracted.

---

[383] Minute DFID [junior official] to Dodd, 31 October 2002, 'Economic issues in Iraq after post-Saddam regime change: internal policy and external engagement'.
[384] Letter Dodd to Ad Hoc Group on Iraq, 7 November 2002, 'Ad Hoc Group on Iraq' attaching Paper HMT, October 2002, 'Economic Impact of a War in Iraq'.

GOVERNMENT CONTACT WITH UK ACADEMICS

780. There is no indication that the Cabinet Office paper of 1 November or the individual papers on post-conflict Iraq prepared for the AHGI by other departments were shown to Mr Blair in the weeks before Christmas 2002, or that Mr Blair asked to see advice from officials on post-conflict issues.

781. Mr Blair did invite the views of academics working outside government.

782. In November, he and Mr Straw discussed Iraq with a number of academics.

783. During November a number of academics contributed to government discussion of post-conflict Iraq.

784. On 5 November, Mr Simon Fraser, FCO Director for Strategy and Innovation, reported to No.10 and a large number of FCO officials, including Sir Michael Jay, Mr Ricketts and Mr McDonald, a discussion on Iraq with Dr Charles Tripp of the School of Oriental and African Studies (SOAS).[385]

785. Mr Fraser highlighted a number of points raised by Dr Tripp, including his view that:

"Ordinary Iraqis were fairly passive towards the regime … Some among the Shia still considered Saddam to be the creature of America – 'without the Americans he would not be there now'. They would be cautious in welcoming any incoming army until they were convinced that Saddam really was on the way out …

"Analysts who tried to divide Iraq into three distinct ethnic/religious groups were being over simplistic …

"Federalism was not an option for Iraq … and could lead to polarisation between the north and south with a weak middle between …

"Establishing a representative government based on democratic principles would be costly both in political investment, money and military effort. There was no evidence that the US had either the stamina or the knowledge to carry this through. Many of those … who were talking about democracy in Iraq knew nothing about the country. A long-term international presence – whether US or UN-led – would be extremely vulnerable to Iraqi opposition movements, as well as to other elements such as Al Qaida who would want to see it fail … If this scenario were too daunting, then the best thing might [be] to go for a short-term fix involving one or more military strong men …

"Islamism was an underlying force in Iraq … If it came to a post-Saddam Iraq we would need to have thought through in advance how to respond …"

---

[385] Minute Fraser to Reynolds, 5 November 2002, 'Iraq Futures'.

786. Mr Fraser's note was included in No.10's briefing pack for Mr Blair before the No.10 seminar with six academics on 19 November.[386]

787. Mr Blair and Mr Straw held an off-the-record seminar on Iraq with six academics on 19 November. The participants were:

- Professor Lawrence Freedman, King's College London;
- Professor Michael Clarke, King's College London;
- Dr Toby Dodge, Chatham House;
- Professor George Joffe, Cambridge University;
- Mr Steven Simon (a former US diplomat), International Institute for Strategic Studies;
- Dr Tripp;
- Mr Jonathan Powell;
- Sir David Manning;
- Baroness Morgan;
- Mr Bowen;
- Mr Chaplin;
- Mr Rycroft.[387]

788. The seminar was proposed by Professor Freedman as a means to "raise some of the less obvious issues and perspectives that need to be discussed".[388]

789. Mr Rycroft advised Mr Blair to issue a disclaimer at the start of the seminar, which explained that:

"… this session is not about Iraq policy directly, the fact that we are having it does not mean anything about our policy, and any discussion of post-Saddam Iraq does not mean that our policy is regime change".[389]

790. No.10 issued a list of questions as an agenda for the seminar. Mr Rycroft explained to Mr Blair that the agenda was not designed to be adhered to religiously, but "to spark off an informal, free-flowing discussion":

"1. Can Iraq only be ruled by a strong authoritarian regime? Are other models possible? Why have they not worked in the past? Is regional devolution a starter?

2. Can the different communities work together? What are the aspirations of the Shia and the Kurds? What relations do the Iraqi Shia have with Iran?

---

[386] Manuscript comments Manning and Rycroft on Minute Fraser to Reynolds, 5 November 2002, 'Iraq Futures'.
[387] Letter Rycroft to Sinclair, 20 November 2002, 'Iraq: Prime Minister's seminar with academics, 19 November'.
[388] Email Freedman to Powell, 23 September 2002, 'Expert group'.
[389] Minute Rycroft to Prime Minister, 18 November 2002, 'Iraq: Seminar with Academics, Tuesday'.

3. What role does Islam play in Iraqi political life? How strong is Iraqi secularism? Would it survive the fall of the Ba'ath?

4. What links does Iraq have to terrorism these days?

5. Post-Saddam, how quickly would the Iraqi economy revive? Who would control the oil etc?

6. What is the future of Iraqi relations with Iran? Can they co-operate or are they condemned to remain rivals for power at the north of the Gulf?

7. Is there a prospect that Iraq can co-operate with the other Gulf Arab states, or will Baghdad, as the historical centre of power and the most populous Arab state in the region, always try to dominate? What are the possible models for security and stability in the Gulf region in the future? Can Iraq ever work with the GCC [Gulf Co-operation Council]?

8. Would change in Iraq destabilise other states like Syria (further undermining the credibility of the Ba'ath there) or Jordan? Is there really a prospect that change in Iraq could unlock movement on the MEPP?"

791. At the seminar, Mr Blair made clear that the discussion was off the record and "any discussion of post-Saddam Iraq did not imply that regime change was our policy or was inevitable".[390]

792. Not all the questions on the agenda were addressed at the seminar. The No.10 record stated that there were "no blinding insights". Points put forward by the academics included:

- Some members of the Iraqi regime were arguing that any change of regime would be worse for the Iraqi people: "Iraqis feared disorder; Saddam guaranteed stability".
- The most likely successor to Saddam Hussein was another General.
- Changing Iraq substantively would mean tackling:
    - the shadow state behind the publicly visible state;
    - the role of the armed forces; and
    - the political economy of oil, which led to a highly centralised bureaucracy and the power of patronage.
- There would be tricky decisions on the extent of co-operation with existing structures, including the Ba'ath Party, with differing views on whether it would survive Saddam Hussein's downfall.
- There was no existing process like the Afghan Loya Jirga that could be used to build future governance structures.

---

[390] Letter Rycroft to Sinclair, 20 November 2002, 'Iraq: Prime Minister's seminar with academics, 19 November'.

- Opposition groups outside Iraq had "zero credibility" in Iraq.
- The focus should be on building local councils (many Iraqis were localists at heart).
- A strong sense of Iraqi nationalism would hold the country together.
- There had been a shift of wealth from urban to rural and a rebirth of Iraqi agriculture.
- Reintegration into the global economy would throw up serious problems, including claims and debt.
- The Sunni majority [sic] would continue to dominate Iraq's government. There was scope for greater co-operation between Sunni, Shia and Kurds. An Iraqi Islamist movement could emerge and should perhaps be encouraged.
- Many Iraqis were relatively well disposed to the UK.

793. Dr Dodge told *The Independent on Sunday* in 2015: "We were heavily briefed … They said, 'Don't tell him [Mr Blair] not to do it. He has already made up his mind'."[391]

794. Professor Clarke, also speaking in 2015, explained that he was "agnostic" that day about what might happen after an invasion. He added: "Blair knew this was going to be serious … He was not blasé about it at all."

SPG PAPER, 6 NOVEMBER 2002: 'UK MILITARY STRATEGIC THINKING ON IRAQ'

795. **The last two editions of the SPG paper on UK military strategic thinking were emphatic about the strategic importance of the post-conflict phase of operations and the need for better co-ordination of planning and preparation across government.**

796. **On 6 November, the SPG advised:**

- **The post-conflict phase of operations had "the potential to prove the most protracted and costly phase of all".**
- **Planning needed to be flexible enough to accommodate a wide range of possible outcomes.**
- **Poor handling of post-conflict Iraq had the potential to fuel international tension and arm the forces of extremism.**
- **Planning for the post-conflict phase "must be complete before the start of offensive operations".**

797. **The paper highlighted the need for greater cross-Whitehall co-operation and deeper analysis of the nature of the Iraqi administration.**

798. **There is no indication of any response to the paper.**

---

[391] *The Independent on Sunday*, 25 January 2015, *What the six wise men told Tony Blair*.

799. The 6 November edition of the SPG paper on UK military strategic thinking included a rewritten section on the "Aftermath-Resolution Phase" that highlighted the strategic significance of the post-conflict phase of operations:

> "The lasting impression of Coalition legitimacy and success will not be set by military success in conflict – it will be determined by the nature of the Iraqi nation that emerges afterwards.

> "This phase has the potential to prove the most protracted and costly phase of all.

> "Planning must be flexible to accommodate a wide range of start states and possible outcomes ranging from fast and bloodless coup, a rapid and anarchic collapse, or a damaged and ungoverned state on the verge of disintegration.

> "Operations in Iraq may have a negative impact on the UK's policy objectives for international terrorism, as poor handling of a post-conflict Iraq has the potential to increase greatly anti-Western feeling in the region; fuelling the very international tensions we have sought to diffuse and arming the forces of extremism."[392]

800. The SPG paper listed four policy "pillars" needed to bring about the desired end state, "each composed of a range of lines of operation for different ministries, agencies and NGOs": judiciary and law; society and economy; governance; and security.

801. The SPG advised:

> "The Pillars only serve a purpose if they form the basis for interaction and co-operation between OGDs. The MOD can define some lines of operation in isolation, but early consultation is necessary for coherence.

> "Action is in hand by Cabinet Office to develop UK thinking.

> "From an MOD perspective, ideally OGDs should be invited to agree the policy pillars and outline their lines of operation within them, noting where they may seek assistance from, or interaction with, the military."

802. The SPG advised that, because of the US lead on military operations, much of the policy on post-conflict issues was likely to reflect US aims and principles. Early assessment of areas of potential difference was the key to avoiding UK principles being compromised. Governance and reform might be critical areas.

803. In the absence of an agreed US position on the post-conflict role of the UN, the SPG judged it "probable" the UK would accept: "an initial brief period of Coalition-run, largely military government; followed by an interim government run by either a UN international appointee or a UN approved Iraqi; leading to self-government".

---

[392] Paper [SPG], 6 November 2002, 'UK Military Strategic Thinking on Iraq'.

804. The SPG advised:

"A balance must be struck between the competing demands for reform and removal of Ba'athist influence and the need for effective administration. This dilemma shapes some clear information requirements …

- A detailed structural analysis of the current regime, its instruments of state power and its administration.

- An informed UK-US judgement on the degree to which reform will be required immediately, for effective operation, and eventually, to secure the end state.

- A rolling assessment of the effectiveness of state institutions as a result of Coalition action, linked to a mechanism for moderating or accelerating operations to set conditions for successful post-conflict efforts. **Throughout, military offensive action must be balanced against the longer-term objectives – the opportunity for counter-productive destruction is high.**"

805. The paper included a diagram showing the military activities ("lines of operation") supporting the four policy pillars and the expected duration of each activity across four phases:

- pre-conflict;
- immediate (six months);
- medium term (six months to two years);
- long term (2-10 years).

806. The military activities were focused on provision of security and SSR. Potential "supporting roles" included "administration, planning and co-ordination", emergency reconstruction, urgent humanitarian assistance, support to international courts and "info ops".

807. The SPG proposed a possible definition of the military end state:

"An accountable Iraqi security structure capable of assuming self-defence and internal security responsibilities in accordance with international law."

808. No firm date was given for achieving the military end state. The paper indicated that the UK might choose to set its own end state at as little as two years "to meet [the] aspiration for shorter engagement".

809. The diagram identified short-term military activities likely to last up to six months (emergency reconstruction; urgent humanitarian assistance; transitional law and order), medium-term activities of up to two years ("administration, planning and co-ordination"; WMD removal), and long-term activities lasting up to 10 years (force protection; control and reform of Iraqi armed forces and handover to those forces; maintenance of internal security and territorial integrity; infrastructure security).

810. In its summary of the implications of the post-conflict phase for military planning, the paper stated:

"• The impact of any enduring commitment on other operations would be significant. A recommendation on the size of force the UK is prepared to commit must be prepared, at least for the key six months following any operation. In parallel diplomatic efforts must seek partners to share, and eventually take, the burden.

…

• Planning for Resolution Phase operations must be complete before the start of offensive operations. Any UK land force HQ must have the capacity to conduct offensive and Resolution Phase operations concurrently.

• War-fighting forces must be able to contribute to Resolution Phase objectives until formal transition to resolution phase can be declared. Therefore clarity on post-Resolution Phase and likely UK contribution will be needed before operations commence."

811. The aftermath section of the SPG paper concluded with seven key judgements:

"• **Views on policy pillars and extent of support expected of military forces will be sought from OGD using current Cabinet Office machinery.**

• **The development of a jointly acceptable approach to Iraqi governance and reform in the Resolution Phase should be pursued with the US. Agreement on the role of the UN is essential.**

• **A structural analysis of the Iraqi system and the need for reform is required. Current FCO and DFID papers reveal key gaps in our knowledge (eg structure and efficiency of Iraqi police).**

• **A detailed analysis of the CoA [courses of action] of key actors is required. Military and non-military pre-emption capabilities and contingency plans must be prepared.**

• **The UK's intent to commit forces beyond offensive operations needs to be clarified to allow operational planning for the Resolution Phase, and to allow balancing of the wider commitments picture.**

• **Once principal Coalition partners have agreed on key issues, this will need to include agreement on Coalition management processes, early diplomatic activity to seek burden-sharing partners should be undertaken.**

• **Work to define force structure options must run concurrently with ongoing operational planning in order to ensure the UK is adequately prepared to conduct Resolution Phase operations."**

812. The SPG explained that a "full and detailed strategic estimate" for the post-conflict phase of operations was being prepared and would be presented in the next draft of the paper, which issued on 13 December and is described later in this Section.

First round of inter-agency talks, Washington, 6 November 2002

813. **US/UK differences on the potential role of the UN in post-conflict Iraq became increasingly apparent from November 2002.**

814. **In early November, the UK envisaged a six-month transitional Coalition military administration handing over to a UN administration for about three years. US planners foresaw a role for UN agencies (but not overall UN leadership) during a US-led transitional administration, with a gradual transfer of power to a representative Iraqi government.**

815. During talks in London on 13 September with Sir David Manning, Mr Haass proposed UK/US work on the political, economic, humanitarian and refugee issues that would result from Saddam Hussein's departure.[393] Sir David welcomed the proposal.

816. Before the talks took place, a "vigorous debate" about changes to US planning machinery led to a hiatus in US post-conflict planning lasting several weeks.[394]

817. In *War and Decision*, Mr Feith explained that, during October 2002, Secretary Rumsfeld reached the conclusion that one US official should be responsible for the political, economic and security aspects of reconstruction.[395]

818. Mr Feith explained the idea to the NSC on 15 October. He proposed that CENTCOM's post-invasion structure should consist of a military headquarters (the Combined Joint Task Force–Iraq (CJTF-I)) and a civil administration headed by a civilian "Iraq co-ordinator". Both would be under CENTCOM command. He also proposed that Secretary Rumsfeld should have overall responsibility for the post-war effort.

819. On 18 October, Secretary Rumsfeld told Mr Feith to set up a post-war planning office, only to reverse the decision soon afterwards. Mr Feith wrote that he only learned much later that this had been because President Bush was concerned that setting up such a unit would undercut his international diplomacy. As a result, each of the existing working groups for post-conflict issues carried on working independently. Planning for Phase IV of the military campaign, taking place at CENTCOM headquarters in Tampa, Florida, fell behind the other phases.

820. Mr Feith explained that the situation changed after Iraq's weapons declaration on 7 December. On 18 December President Bush had told the NSC that war was "inevitable". Mr Feith, who had never heard the President say that before, considered it a "momentous" comment. He also observed that the President's view was not shared by Secretary Powell.

---

[393] Letter Rycroft to Sedwill, 13 September 2002, 'Meetings with Richard Haass, 13 September'.
[394] Bowen SW Jr. *Hard Lessons: The Iraq Reconstruction Experience.* U.S. Government Printing Office, 2009.
[395] Feith DJ. *War and Decision.* Harper, 2008.

821. Mr Feith wrote that it now became possible to create a central post-war planning office:

> "The President knew that creating a new office … would be seen around the world as … a sign that war was likely and imminent. Now, however, the President was beyond that worry."

822. In late December, Secretary Rumsfeld asked Mr Feith to start drafting the charter for the new "central post-war planning office".[396]

823. Secretary Powell, quoted in *Hard Lessons*, explained:

> "[The] State [Department] does not have the personnel, the capacity, or the size to deal with an immediate post-war situation in a foreign country that's eight thousand miles away from here, so there was never a disagreement about this. It made sense."[397]

824. President Bush formalised the creation of the new office in January 2003 (see Section 6.5).

825. On 6 November, Mr Chaplin led an FCO/MOD/DFID/Cabinet Office delegation equipped with the Cabinet Office steering brief of 1 November to the first round of talks with a US inter-agency team and an Australian delegation in Washington.[398]

826. US participants included the NSC, the Office of the Vice President, the State Department, DoD and the military Joint Staff. USAID was not present at the inter-agency meeting, but did have separate discussions with DFID during the visit.

827. The British Embassy reported the outcome the following day:

> "Administration planning envisages a US-led international Coalition governing Iraq in the medium term, with a gradual transfer of power to a representative Iraqi government. Coalition control of WMD, and the preservation of internal and external security, are paramount objectives.

> "The US favour a role for UN agencies in the transitional phase, but not overall UN civil administration … We agree on the need to co-ordinate on humanitarian issues."

828. Mr Drummond, a member of the UK delegation, reported to Sir David Manning on 8 November that there were significant differences between the US and UK positions on some issues.[399] Where the UK assumed the Iraqi Government would need "radical

---

[396] Bowen SW Jr. *Hard Lessons: The Iraq Reconstruction Experience.* U.S. Government Printing Office, 2009.
[397] Bowen SW Jr. *Hard Lessons: The Iraq Reconstruction Experience.* U.S. Government Printing Office, 2009.
[398] Telegram 1456 Washington to FCO London, 7 November 2002, 'Iraq: UK/US Consultations on Day After Issues: 6 November 2002'.
[399] Minute Drummond to Manning, 8 November 2002, 'Iraq: Day After'.

reform", including removal of "the pervasive influence of the Ba'ath Party", the US believed "reasonably competent ministries" remained beneath permanent secretary level and that, because the Ba'ath Party operated as a parallel structure to government below that level, "less radical change is needed". Mr Drummond suggested that both the UK and US governments would need to develop and test their thinking more thoroughly.

829. On SSR, Mr Drummond reported agreement on the need for rapid and comprehensive reform of Iraqi security structures. He expected the US to "maintain a tight grip on this", but the UK had "urged them to think about the wider security sector including police and the need to arrive with a plan (ie not as in Afghanistan)".

830. The US seemed to be "well ahead with thinking about the humanitarian consequences of military action", though less so the impact of CBW use; was "focused on the need for urgent rehabilitation of infrastructure"; wanted to establish a trust fund for transparent administration of oil revenues; and agreed Iraqi debts would require rescheduling.

831. On war crimes, Mr Drummond said that the US was working to identify "the top 30 bad guys" with no future in a successor regime, but had not focused on how to deal with any who might survive the conflict: "Given the time and cost of international tribunals we offered to consider whether any Iraqi legal processes might be usable." Mr Drummond reported an absence of "serious thinking about Truth and Reconciliation", but suggested "that can be pursued later".

832. Mr Drummond concluded:

> "We expect a further meeting in London or Washington, before the end of the year. There is likely to be a separate session in December between DFID and NSC and USAID. But this was a useful start and revealed that the US had done some detailed work and inter-agency coordination is working."

833. Some of the differences between the UK and US positions described by Mr Drummond were addressed in a paper on possible interim administrations in Iraq produced by the FCO and shared with the US in mid-December. The FCO paper is described later in this Section.

834. Ms Miller, the DFID member of the UK delegation, provided her own assessment for Ms Short, reporting that the US was "reluctant to concede a meaningful role to the UN at any stage of the process", but that USAID took a slightly different position.[400] At her meeting with officials from USAID's Office for Foreign Disaster Assistance (OFDA), she had been told "we should assume a UN lead for planning purposes". Nevertheless, she was concerned that "USAID still see themselves and DFID as the two main Coalition leads".

---

[400] Minute Miller to P/S Secretary of State [DFID], 7 November 2002, 'Main Issues from Whitehall Visit to Washington: Iraq'.

835. Ms Miller added that, in the absence of USAID from the main inter-agency talks, Mr Abrams had led on humanitarian issues. He had said that the inter-agency Humanitarian Working Group was working closely with the US military, which he anticipated would take on most of the immediate post-conflict restoration of utilities.

836. At USAID, Ms Miller was told that OFDA was "preparing to take a major role in food delivery, health and water and sanitation". She reported that USAID was "extremely keen to hold more detailed conversations in a few weeks, possibly at an overly detailed level".

837. Mr Fernie visited Geneva on 7 November to discuss UN humanitarian contingency planning with UN agencies based there.[401] He reported that planning was being done discreetly and without political cover. He added that, although he had stressed throughout that the UK was thinking about a range of scenarios, including a deterioration of the humanitarian situation during further weapons inspections, no-one engaged on other options: "they are all planning for conflict".

838. Mr Fernie listed a number of next steps:

"We need to decide if/when we could support agency preparedness (we gave no commitment on this, citing policy and financial constraints) …

"… [W]e could consider promoting military-humanitarian co-operation on the implications of CBW use for civilian populations.

"We should consider with Whitehall colleagues how to co-ordinate our approaches with other donors – particularly the USA, in the light of what was learnt in Washington this week on US views of the UN's potential role."

839. UK officials drew encouragement from the adoption of resolution 1441 on 8 November.

840. At its meeting on 8 November, the AHGI was given an update on the imminent adoption of resolution 1441and the outcome of the Washington and Geneva visits.[402] Sir David Manning was informed that, at the AHGI, departments had been:

"… encouraged, where necessary, to engage those outside government in prudent contingency planning as long as such contact is discreet. This extends to DTI planning on the UK role in a post-Saddam economy, particularly in the oil sector."

841. The adoption of resolution 1441 on 8 November and Saddam Hussein's decision to re-admit UN weapons inspectors are addressed in detail in Section 3.5.

842. Mr Chaplin told the Inquiry there was "a surge of hope".[403] It seemed "there might, after all be a route to resolving this problem through the inspection route and without military action". He added:

---

[401] Minute Fernie to Miller, 8 November 2002, 'UN Humanitarian Contingency Planning'.
[402] Minute Dodd to Manning, 11 November 2002, 'Ad Hoc Group on Iraq'.
[403] Public hearing, 1 December 2009, page 26.

"… there was also a surge of hope, certainly on my part, that this would give us more time.

"Indeed, some exchanges I had with my opposite number in Washington suggested that, despite all the difficulties … it was not impossible to think that one could delay things until the autumn of 2003, and that would have been a very good thing, not least because we would then have extra time for the planning that was necessary."[404]

843. Mr Lee told the Inquiry that, by mid-November, there had been a lot of conceptual thinking and analytical work on day after planning in Whitehall and there was "a fairly clear idea of the sort of things that needed to be pursued".[405] His sense throughout the autumn was that, although the US "would agree with the propositions that we put to them", it had not made much progress "translating that into some sort of plan". During a visit to Washington on 11 and 12 November, he and Lt Gen Pigott had suggested post-conflict planning should be given the same level of attention and resource as conflict planning: "they recognised the point, and I think they had some sort of staff effort mobilised … towards post-conflict planning, but … nothing on the scale of the conflict planning".

844. The record of the 15 November meeting of the AHGI stated that UN planning for conflict and post-Saddam Hussein Iraq was deepening.[406] The UN was now in contact with the US. The US and UK agreed that the IMF and World Bank would have a leading role in helping economic recovery in Iraq. The AHGI agreed that the Treasury and DFID should instruct the UK Delegation to the IMF and the International Bank for Reconstruction and Development (IBRD) in Washington to find out what planning was in hand and encourage further work.

845. The record also stated that the Cabinet Office would consult departments on the best way to influence US thinking on whether the US or UN should lead an interim administration before the second round of US/UK discussions later in the year.

846. Two weeks later, at the 29 November meeting of the AHGI, it was reported that the FCO would start work on a further paper on the UN role in post-Saddam Hussein Iraq "to help bridge the gap with US thinking".[407] That paper and the FCO paper on SSR would need to be shared with the US before the next bilateral discussions.

847. Mr Fernie produced a separate summary of the main points discussed at the AHGI on 29 November, which recorded a difference of opinion between the Cabinet Office and the FCO on the timing of the next round of talks with the US, with the Cabinet Office preferring mid-December and the FCO early January.[408]

---

[404] Public hearing, 1 December 2009, page 40.
[405] Private hearing, 22 June 2010, pages 40-41.
[406] Minute Dodd to Manning, 18 November 2002, 'Ad Hoc Group on Iraq'.
[407] Minute Dodd to Manning, 3 December 2002, 'Ad Hoc Group on Iraq'.
[408] Minute Fernie to Brewer, 3 December 2002, 'Iraq: Contingency planning'.

848. Mr Chaplin discussed post-conflict issues with Mr William Burns, State Department Assistant Secretary Near East, on 22 November.[409] Mr Burns suggested that the US would want to follow the 6 November Washington talks with a visit to London in December or, if necessary, January. Mr Chaplin said the UK was working on a paper on the shape of a post-conflict administration of Iraq, the issue on which "the US and UK still seemed furthest apart".

849. The FCO paper on post-conflict administration was shared with the US on 12 December.[410]

Post-Saddam Hussein oil contracts

850. During October and November 2002, UK oil companies expressed concern to the Government about securing future oil contracts in Iraq.

851. Sir David Manning raised the issue with Dr Rice in early December.

852. An oil industry representative called on Mr Chaplin on 2 October, warning that "by sticking to the rules over Iraq and not going for post-sanctions contracts", major UK oil companies would lose out.[411] He was concerned that some other countries would sell their support for US policy for a guarantee that existing deals with the Iraqi regime would be honoured. Mr Chaplin explained that the FCO was "seized of the issue" and "determined to get a fair slice of the action for UK companies".

853. On 25 October, Mr Brenton reported a conversation with Vice President Cheney's office, in which he had been told that Mr Cheney was about to discuss Iraqi oil contracts with Mr Yevgeny Primakov, the former Russian Prime Minister. Mr Brenton was advised that Mr Primakov would be told the "bids of those countries which co-operated with the US over Iraq would be looked at more sympathetically than those which did not".[412]

854. UK companies' concerns persisted. Representatives of BP, Shell and British Gas discussed the issue with Baroness Symons on 31 October.[413] Baroness Symons reported to Mr Straw that she had said:

> "… we could not make any definitive undertakings, given our determination that any action in relation to Iraq is prompted by our concerns over WMD, and not a desire for commercial gains.

> "However, I undertook to draw this issue to your attention as a matter of urgency. They were genuinely convinced that deals were being struck and that British interests are being left to one side."[414]

---

[409] Telegram 622 FCO London to Washington, 25 November 2002, 'Iraq: US Views, 22 November 2002'.
[410] Minute Dodd to Manning, 19 December 2002, 'Ad Hoc Group on Iraq'.
[411] Email Chaplin to Gray, 2 October 2002, 'Iraq – Views of UK Business'.
[412] Letter Brenton to Chaplin, 25 October 2002, 'Iraq: Oil'.
[413] Minute Segar to PS/Baroness Symons, 31 October 2002, 'Iraq Oil'.
[414] Minute Symons to Straw, 1 November 2002, 'Iraqi Oil and Gas'.

855. BP raised its concerns with Mr Brenton in Washington the same day.[415]

856. On 6 November, the FCO hosted a presentation on Iraqi energy given by a team from BP.[416] The presentation spelt out Iraq's importance to oil companies: it had the second largest proven oil reserves in the world and "unique 'yet to find' potential", but the oil industry was "a mess" and had to run fast to stand still.

857. The record of the seminar was sent to Mr Powell and Sir David Manning as evidence of why Iraq was so important to BP.[417]

858. Mr Powell sent it to Mr Blair, who asked: "but what do we do about it?"[418]

859. BP called on Mr Brenton in Washington again on 11 November.[419] Sir Christopher Meyer told Sir David Manning that UK oil companies had been told by the Embassy that "US motivation as regards Iraq parallels our own: this is a matter of national security, not oil … Nevertheless, the rumours persist."

860. Sir Christopher continued:

> "We have seen a report from our team at CENTCOM which suggests that the Pentagon has already awarded a contract to Kellogg, Brown and Root, a subsidiary of Haliburton, to restore the Iraqi oil industry to production levels of 3m bpd [barrels per day]. (Haliburton is of course, the company of which Cheney was previously chairman). We have so far been unable to obtain collateral for this from the Administration, and it might well in any case amount to no more than prudent contingency planning to stabilise Iraqi oil facilities if Saddam attempts to damage them in a conflict.
>
> "Either way, there is clearly an issue here which we need to tackle. Raising it in an effective way with the Administration is a delicate matter. My view remains that the only realistic way in to this is via a PM intervention with Bush … The points to make would be:

> - Once Saddam has been disarmed … Iraq's oil industry will be central to … economic recovery.
> - We, as you, have energy majors who have skills and resources to help …
> - To give the lie to suggestions that this campaign is all about oil, it is vitally important that, once sanctions are lifted, there is seen to be a level playing field for all companies to work in Iraq."

---

[415] Telegram 1418 Washington to FCO London, 31 October 2002, 'BP & Iraqi Oil'.

[416] Minute Economic Policy Department [junior official] to Arthur, 13 November 2002, 'BP/Iraqi Energy'.

[417] Manuscript comment Rycroft, 18 November 2002, on Minute Economic Policy Department [junior official] to Arthur, 13 November 2002, 'BP/Iraqi Energy'.

[418] Manuscript comment Blair on Minute Economic Policy Department [junior official] to Arthur, 13 November 2002, 'BP/Iraqi Energy'.

[419] Letter Meyer to Manning, 15 November 2002, 'Iraqi Oil'.

861. Sir Christopher advised that this was the least the UK should do. He had been advised by Mr James A Baker III, the former US Secretary of State, to put down a marker with the Administration fast.

862. Sir David Manning raised oil and gas contracts with Dr Rice in Washington on 9 December.[420] He hoped UK energy companies "would be treated fairly and not overlooked if Saddam left the scene". Dr Rice commented that it would be particularly unjust if companies that had observed sanctions since 1991, a category which included UK companies, were not among the beneficiaries of post-Saddam Hussein Iraq.

863. UK and US policies on Iraqi oil and efforts to secure contracts for UK companies hoping to do business in Iraq are described in Section 6.5.

UK military options

864. **In November, the UK received a formal US request for UK military support in Iraq, including for post-conflict operations.**

865. **Lt Gen Reith submitted four proposals for the deployment of UK forces to the Chiefs of Staff, one for the North and three for the South.**

866. **The Inquiry has not seen any detailed analysis underpinning Lt Gen Reith's conclusion that the South of Iraq would be more manageable in the post-conflict period than the North.**

867. **Adm Boyce directed that the North should remain the focus of UK planners at that time.**

868. On 18 November, Mr Hoon's office informed No.10, the Cabinet Office, the FCO and Sir Christopher Meyer that Mr Hoon had received a formal US request for UK assistance with a military campaign in Iraq (see Section 6.1), including provision of "financial/material resources for a military campaign and for post-conflict efforts" and "constabulary forces and humanitarian assistance as part of post-conflict stability efforts".[421]

869. Lt Gen Reith submitted a paper to the Chiefs of Staff on 18 November setting out northern and southern options for a UK land contribution in Iraq (see Section 6.1).[422] He advised the Chiefs to think about "where we wish to be at the end of Phase III [combat operations], as this could impact directly on any UK involvement in Phase IV".

---

[420] Minute Manning to Prime Minister, 11 December 2002, 'Iraq'.
[421] Letter Williams to McDonald, 18 November 2002, 'Iraq – US request for UK support' attaching Paper [unattributed], 15 November 2002, 'Request for UK Support'.
[422] Minute Reith to DCDS(C), 18 November 2002, 'Options for the UK Land Contribution' attaching Paper CJO, 18 November 2002, 'Options for the UK Land Contribution'.

870. On the northern option, Lt Gen Reith advised:

"This could result in UK long-term leadership of the region during post-conflict operations: a position which the US would appear to favour. It would be a challenging area to control and develop, particularly in preserving regional stability between the Turks, Kurds and Sunnis. Whilst the UK has the necessary experience and capability, the challenges do need to be assessed in line with UK strategic guidance ..."

871. The post-conflict responsibilities in the South were presented as being more manageable:

"A post-conflict positioning of the UK division in the South could be attractive. The range of problems appears less complex and diverse, the long-term force structure requirements could be reduced and local conditions are likely to be more conducive to development and influence. The Northern Arabian Gulf (NAG) is also a traditional area of UK influence."

872. The MOD advised No.10 that post-conflict considerations needed to "guide thinking" on the conflict phase of operations and that the post-conflict phase would be "a challenge in its own right".

873. The MOD warned: "However successful the conflict phase, a badly-handled aftermath would make our intervention a net failure."

874. Mr Watkins wrote to Sir David Manning on 19 November, reporting the formal US request for UK support.[423] The letter was copied to Mr Straw's Private Office, Mr Brown's Private Office and Mr Bowen.

875. Mr Watkins highlighted the importance of the "aftermath":

"Our own work has increasingly convinced us that the aftermath of any military action will be a challenge in its own right. This needs to guide thinking on the conflict phase for all sorts of reasons:

- However successful the conflict phase, a badly-handled aftermath would make our intervention a net failure.

- Day 1 of conflict will also be Day 1 of the aftermath for some parts of Iraq.

- The nature of the conflict will influence the type of aftermath we find ourselves managing: in particular, Iraqi behaviour will have a big impact on the scale of the humanitarian and reconstruction tasks that might emerge.

- The forces we commit to conflict will also have to deal with the initial phase of the aftermath, simply by virtue of being there. And of course their location in the conflict phase will largely determine their post-conflict role ...

---

[423] Letter Watkins to Manning, 19 November 2002, 'Iraq: Military Planning after UNSCR 1441'.

- We also need to bear in mind that the aftermath could arise with little or no prior conflict, in the event that the regime collapses under pressure. Although the US tend to believe that the regime would indeed collapse very quickly, their thinking on the aftermath is, paradoxically, focused almost entirely on managing a post-conflict scenario."

876. Mr Watkins added that the US recognised the importance of aftermath planning, but their thinking remained:

"… somewhat immature, fitting the problem to their pre-conceived solution. In particular … they continue to have difficulty understanding why anybody might think that some kind of UN umbrella will be important in the aftermath stage. We need to keep trying to inject realism into their thinking."

877. Mr Watkins reported that Mr Hoon believed the UK should:

"Continue trying to influence US thinking on the aftermath, recognising that this is not something which can be neatly separated from any conflict phase (and indeed, might arise without conflict at all)."

878. Sir David Manning sent the letter to Mr Blair. He drew attention to separate advice on sensitivities associated with the call-out of UK military Reservists.[424]

879. The MOD was right to advise that a badly-handled aftermath would make intervention in Iraq "a net failure" and to conclude that thinking on the post-conflict phase should guide the UK's approach to the conflict.

880. The evidence seen by the Inquiry indicates that the MOD did start to consider post-conflict operations as an integral part of the overall military campaign, but against an assumption that the UK should seek to minimise the size and duration of its post-conflict deployment.

Parliamentary debates on resolution 1441, 25 November 2002

881. Post-conflict issues were raised by a small number of participants in the Parliamentary debates on resolution 1441.

882. The concerns raised included:

- **the need to start planning now;**
- **the importance of planning for the worst when preparing for the humanitarian consequences of conflict; and**
- **the need to consider unfinished business elsewhere in the world.**

---

[424] Minute Manning to Prime Minister, [undated and untitled], attaching Letter Watkins to Manning, 19 November 2002, 'Iraq: Military Planning after UNSCR 1441'.

883. Concerns about post-conflict preparations were raised during the House of Commons debate on resolution 1441 on 25 November, described in more detail in Section 3.6.

884. Mr Donald Anderson (Labour), Chair of the Foreign Affairs Committee, noted "that we need to plan for the post-conflict position now, rather than imagining that it will solve itself".[425]

885. Others focused on the importance of humanitarian contingency planning. The point was put most forcefully by Mr Peter Luff (Conservative):

"There is a strong view held with great sincerity by many UN Member States that to prepare for a humanitarian crisis is to acknowledge the inevitability of war. I do not accept that argument. To prepare for the worst is not to wish for the worst, and we should prepare for the worst. Indeed, that may have the incidental advantage of reinforcing in Saddam Hussein's mind the seriousness of the international community's purpose. Please let us do more to prepare for the humanitarian consequences of a war that none of us want."[426]

886. Dr Jenny Tonge (Liberal Democrat) asked Mr Straw to consider "unfinished business" elsewhere in the world:

"Do we have the capacity to cope? In Afghanistan, only $1bn has so far been committed out of the billions that were promised, and 70 percent of that has been spent on humanitarian aid. There is no security in Afghanistan outside Kabul, Afghanistan has asked for an extension of the international security assistance force, but where will the extra help come from? Will it come from the United States or from Britain? Where will it come from if we are facing war in Iraq and the Middle East? Very little progress has been made in Afghanistan despite the promises of the Prime Minister. It is unfinished business.

"Many members have rightly referred to the difficult situation in the Middle East ... more unfinished business.

"For many people, the Balkans are a distant memory, but it is still a very unstable region ... This year, only six percent of the aid promised in the famous Marshall Plan for the Balkans has been delivered. That is yet more unfinished business. We are very good at destroying, but not so good at rebuilding. I have not even mentioned Africa ..."[427]

887. Neither Mr Hoon nor Mr Straw addressed post-conflict issues during the debate.

---

[425] House of Commons, *Official Report*, 25 November 2002, column 89.
[426] House of Commons, *Official Report*, 25 November 2002, column 91.
[427] House of Commons, *Official Report*, 25 November 2002, column 115.

888. Mr Tony Colman (Labour), Chair of the All-Party Parliamentary Group on the UN, informed the House of Commons that he had been reassured by what he had been told about UN humanitarian planning during a recent visit to New York.[428]

889. In the House of Lords, Lord Moynihan (Conservative) warned that "the use of force against Iraq opens up the possibility of an on-going military and political entanglement" and asked for assurances that the UK would not enter into a conflict without a "clear, effective and well-planned exit strategy".[429]

890. Baroness Symons replied:

"The government of Iraq is a matter for the Iraqi people. We believe that the people of Iraq deserve a better government, one based on the rule of law, respect for human rights, economic freedom and prosperity. We welcome the external opposition's role in discussing the future of Iraq and in debating issues such as democracy, that cannot be discussed in Iraq … As at the end of the Gulf War, Britain would remain at the forefront of efforts to help the Iraqi people into the future."[430]

Domestic contingency planning

891. The first edition of a paper by the Civil Contingencies Secretariat (CCS) on the potential impact on the UK of operations against Iraq assessed that, the longer any dislocation lasted, the more likely it was that disruptive challenges would emerge. Those might include:

- **oil price rises;**
- **general uncertainty affecting the stock market;**
- **protests and counter-demonstrations;**
- **exploitation of the situation by Al Qaida and other Islamic extremist groups;**
- **military resources unavailable to cover industrial action other than the firefighters' dispute.**

892. On 27 November, Mr Drummond sent No.10 and the Private Offices of departments represented in the AHGI a CCS assessment of the potential impact on the UK of operations against Iraq.[431] The CCS assessed that:

"The most important factor within the UK will be public confidence and its extension, market and commercial confidence. The extent to which there is a public perception that everyday life and services have been altered and the terrorist threat increased will be a major factor. A short, successful campaign would have the minimum impact.

---

[428] House of Commons, *Official Report*, 25 November 2002, column 116.
[429] House of Lords, *Official Report*, 25 November 2002, columns 557-558.
[430] House of Lords, *Official Report*, 25 November 2002, column 558.
[431] Minute Drummond to Manning, 27 November 2002, 'Potential Impact on the UK of Operations Against Iraq' attaching Paper Civil Contingencies Secretariat, 21 November 2002, 'Potential Impact on UK of Operations Against Iraq'.

The longer dislocation lasts, particularly if there are major terrorist incidents, the greater the likelihood of real disruptive challenges emerging. The extent to which military operations have public support is also important. A strong patriotic factor will restrain disruption and increase tolerance of minor inconveniences."

893. The CCS formed a number of other "key judgements":

- Oil price rises would be the main economic factor. "General uncertainty" would affect the stock market and, possibly, domestic consumer spending. Tourism and air travel would be affected by dislocation of routes.

- The potential for further protests by anti-war groups and ethnic groups and counter-demonstrations would increase. There was "opportunity for violent confrontations between protest groups, ethnic groups, or targeted against ethnic groups, particularly in the aftermath of a major terrorist incident".

- The firefighters' dispute would probably go ahead.

- Heightened anxiety about terrorist attacks was likely to cause increased disruption from hoaxes and false alarms. The JIC assessed that the threat from Al Qaida and Islamic extremist groups remained "high". "Al Qaida and other Islamic extremists will seek to exploit the circumstances of a war situation".

- Military resources would be unavailable to cover industrial action contingencies other than the firefighters' dispute. A call up of medical Reservists would probably affect NHS provision.

894. The CCS stated that contingency planning by departments was in hand. In many cases, existing contingency plans were "adaptable to the circumstances arising from operations against Iraq".

895. The CCS paper continued to be updated until January 2003, when the AHGI established a Domestic Impact Sub-Group overseen by Mr Jonathan Stephens, Treasury Director Public Services, supported by the CCS (see Section 6.5).[432]

DFID engagement with Whitehall

896. In late November and early December 2002, DFID officials lobbied for a cross-government exercise to cost each of the military options being considered by the UK, and to include humanitarian costs.

897. During December, DFID officials also sought, with some success, to improve official-level co-ordination with the MOD and the rest of Whitehall on humanitarian issues.

898. In a meeting with DFID officials on 18 November, Ms Short expressed concern that not only was no money set aside for humanitarian actions, but that the issue was not

---

[432] Letter Stephens to Phillips, 20 January 2003, 'Iraq: Domestic Implications of Military Action' attaching Paper [draft] Civil Contingencies Secretariat, 17 January 2003, 'Potential Impact on UK of Operations Against Iraq'.

even being considered.[433] The meeting agreed that it would be important to cost each military option, including both military and "realistic humanitarian" costs.

899. Mr Fernie set out his understanding of Ms Short's position in an internal email the following week:

> "... HMT have been talking to MOD only about the military costs without taking into account the costs to the international community of any humanitarian response, post-Saddam transitional administration and/or reconstruction ..."[434]

900. Ms Short was reported to be "particularly keen" to make clear that DFID could not find substantial funds for such work from its existing budgets. Mr Fernie explained that DFID was trying to "cobble together some figures of possible costs – all a bit speculative ... but the point at this stage is to get others in Whitehall thinking about it."

901. On 3 December, Mr Fernie reported to Dr Nicola Brewer, DFID Director General Regional Programmes, that there had been no progress in interesting the Cabinet Office or the Treasury in costing "various scenarios".[435] Mr Drummond and the AHGI had both given a "clear negative response". The Cabinet Office position was that if DFID thought it would incur unaffordable extra costs, it should bid to the Treasury. DFID's Conflict and Humanitarian Affairs Department (CHAD) was working up preliminary costings, "but we currently have no consumer for the product". Mr Fernie asked how and when to report back to Ms Short.

902. Dr Brewer replied that she had spoken to Mr Ricketts who had been:

> "... slightly more willing to acknowledge that the likely costs ... should be factored into the decision-making process. But I got no sense at all that the FCO would either push for this or support us in doing so. Their sense is that the Prime Minister's mind will be made up by other factors."[436]

903. Dr Brewer suggested that the issue be raised with Sir David Manning or other Permanent Secretaries by Mr Chakrabarti, or at Cabinet by Ms Short.

904. DFID officials reported the lack of progress to Ms Short on 10 December.[437] Ms Short agreed that officials should raise US and DFID cost estimates at the next Cabinet Office meeting, and directed that DFID officials should increase discussions with the Treasury. It was also important to ensure that all costings included military and humanitarian factors.

905. At the same meeting, officials raised the need to consider training for DFID-funded personnel who might be deployed alongside the UK military. Ms Short pointed out that

---

[433] Minute Bewes to Miller, 19 November 2002, 'Iraq'.
[434] Email Fernie to Sparkhall, 26 November 2002, 'Iraq – expenditure implications across Whitehall'.
[435] Minute Fernie to Brewer, 3 December 2002, 'Iraq: Contingency planning'.
[436] Minute Brewer to Fernie, 5 December 2002, 'Iraq: contingency planning'.
[437] Minute Bewes to Fernie, 13 December 2002, 'Iraq'.

DFID would not usually deploy its own people, but would work through the UN or NGOs. She asked officials to revert to her before putting anyone through training.

906. On 3 December, Dr Brewer met Major General Tim Cross, Logistic Component Commander of the Joint Force being prepared for possible operations against Iraq, to discuss the potential for better MOD/DFID engagement in Iraq and elsewhere with.[438] Dr Brewer and Maj Gen Cross were joined later in the meeting by Mr Chakrabarti.

907. The record stated that Maj Gen Cross emphasised the non-official nature of his visit and requested that the meeting be conducted under Chatham House rules.[439] He was concerned that "the MOD was failing to engage at an early stage with other government departments particularly DFID and hence not paying sufficient heed in its planning to wider security and humanitarian issues". A number of action points were agreed to promote "immediate and sustainable" links between DFID and MOD, none specifically linked to Iraq.

908. Dr Brewer wrote to Mr Fernie on 5 December to express her concern about DFID's engagement with the rest of Whitehall:

> "I'm surprised that all of the Cabinet Office meetings so far seem to be at [relatively junior] Head of Department level: Peter Ricketts tells me that he is spending 50 percent of his time on Iraq ... are there Whitehall senior officials' meetings to which we are not being invited? We should be proactive about this ..."[440]

909. Sir Suma Chakrabarti explained to the Inquiry that Maj Gen Cross left the meeting on 3 December:

> "... agreeing a number of ways to try and resolve this. In fact, he even asked for Clare Short to write to the Defence Secretary, which I thought was interesting, to try and open up the military planning side.

> "On 12 December, Clare [Short] decided ... in the margins of Cabinet, to talk to the Prime Minister about this [military planning] and the Prime Minister suggested that she have a direct conversation with the Chief of Defence Staff, Lord Boyce, as he now is. And she did so, and Lord Boyce suggested that she or DFID officials talked to some other people in his office about this. She didn't seem to be making much progress. I took it up with the Cabinet Secretary. David Manning very kindly also rang the Chief of Defence Staff about it, and on 18 December MOD officials came across and we agreed a way forward whereby we could link up better the humanitarian assistance and the operational planning on the military side."[441]

---

[438] Minute DFID [junior official] to Brewer, 3 December 2002, 'Meeting with Major General Tim Cross – 3 December 2002'.
[439] The Chatham House Rule states that participants at a meeting in which it is invoked are "free to use the information received, but neither the identity nor the affiliation of the speaker(s) nor that of any other participant, may be revealed".
[440] Minute Brewer to Fernie, 5 December 2002, 'Iraq: Contingency Planning'.
[441] Public hearing, 8 December 2009, page 19.

910. Lord Turnbull told the Inquiry:

"There was one point in which – this is a sort of classic way in which the Cabinet Secretary intervenes, we get to December, I think, and the DFID come to me for – I think invoking my help, saying 'We are not satisfied that we are learning enough on what is going on in the military planning', and at the same time Clare Short raised it with Lord Boyce and the Prime Minister and it was very quickly sorted out."[442]

911. Although co-operation between DFID and the MOD improved, No.10 continued to block DFID participation in detailed discussions of military planning.

912. Ms Short was not briefed on UK military planning until 12 February.

913. At her request, Dr Brewer met Mr Stephen Pollard, Head of MOD Overseas Secretariat (Sec(O)), on 18 December, and Mr Lee and Mr Webb on 20 December.[443]

914. The DFID record of the meetings stated that the MOD appreciated the importance of DFID-MOD dialogue, especially on humanitarian issues, but that "the issue of Operational Security (Op Sec) is a hurdle to early and more consistent consultation". The issue was less the level of security clearance required than the "need to know", which was much more difficult to define.

915. Mr Webb was reported to be "clearly focused on aftermath planning". Dr Brewer set out Ms Short's interest in "post-conflict stabilisation strategies" and agreed that she (Dr Brewer) and he should discuss the issue on 10 January.

916. The record also stated that the meetings had confirmed that little thought was being given to humanitarian operations. Dr Brewer raised the issue of a stabilisation force and stated that: "Making a demonstrable (and rapid) difference to the civil population's lives was vital to the success of any political-military plan and to wider regional stability." Mr Lee "saw the advantage of HMG [Her Majesty's Government]-wide discussion".

917. Mr Lee commented afterwards to Lt Gen Pigott: "From a machinery of government and successful Iraq policy perspective all the arguments are surely in favour of including … DFID individuals in our discussions."[444] He explained that No.10 would not, however, accept this:

"At David Manning's meeting today … when asked by Peter Ricketts whether DFID could attend the COBR(R), David had immediately said 'no'. This was on the grounds that DFID officials would feel bound to report what they had heard to Clare Short … it was not acceptable to incorporate Ms Short herself into this level of debate."

---

[442] Public hearing, 13 January 2010, page 8.
[443] Minute [DFID junior official] to Brewer, 20 December 2002, 'Meetings with MOD officials'.
[444] Minute Lee to Policy Director, 20 December 2002, 'DFID Involvement in Iraq Planning and Preparations'.

918. Mr Lee also recorded that he had agreed with Dr Brewer that development of military campaign objectives needed to take account of humanitarian concerns.

919. The Inquiry considers that Ms Short's exclusion reflected No.10's position on her participation in the making of policy on Iraq. Ministerial decision-making is addressed in more detail in Section 2.

920. The discussion of DFID (and DTI) involvement in military planning by the Chiefs of Staff on 8 January 2003 is described later in this Section.

921. Dr Brewer told the Inquiry that the proportion of her time spent on Iraq changed significantly over that period:

"By about mid-December 2002 and then until early April 2003 it was taking up most of my time, displacing most of my other responsibilities as DG Regional Programmes. I handed over direct supervision of DFID's Iraq operations to Suma Chakrabarti a few weeks before Clare Short resigned in May 2003."[445]

922. Dr Brewer explained:

"From autumn 2002, Suma Chakrabarti and I kept under constant review staffing levels and responsibilities on Iraq, how work on Iraq was going, and the impact that our workload on Iraq was having on other DFID work in my areas of responsibility. In early April 2003, he and I agreed that he should take over from me direct supervision of DFID work on Iraq for the following reasons:

- co-ordination between DFID and OGDs, in particular MOD but also No.10, FCO and Cabinet Office, had significantly improved (which had been one of my key immediate tasks);

- the issue was reputationally critical for DFID, and therefore one on which the Permanent Secretary naturally needed to be engaged; and

- for me, as the relevant DG, as well as the Permanent Secretary also to continue to spend a considerable proportion of time on Iraq, risked both duplication of senior level supervision and significant neglect of the rest of my responsibilities."[446]

FCO preparation for handling an "all-out crisis"

923. In December 2002, the FCO introduced new machinery to manage its work on Iraq.

---

[445] Statement, 12 September 2010, page 1.
[446] Statement, 12 September 2010, page 14.

924. On 29 November, the FCO Board discussed priorities for the coming months, including reviewing Iraq policy and planning:

> "The Board agreed that the possibility of war in Iraq would remain the prime focus of attention over the next months. It discussed contingency plans being put in place. Work was in hand on staffing and establishing emergency units. Procedures were due to be tested in January … Board members stressed the need to keep the level of threat under review; and to keep examining and testing out the contingency plans."[447]

925. The Board also discussed whether further costs were likely to arise in the context of Iraq contingency planning. The MOD had already placed a claim on the Reserve and there was a strong case for an FCO claim "which would be strengthened if we could point to clear decisions being taken now to prioritise our spending".

926. FCO claims on the Reserve are addressed in Section 13.1.

927. A paper on FCO prioritisation was prepared for the Board in March 2003 and is described in Section 6.5.

928. On 2 December, Mr Ricketts sent Sir Michael Jay advice on "preparations for handling an all-out Iraq crisis".[448] In a brief description of how the FCO was "already geared up to deal with the increased intensity of work on Iraq", he included references to the procurement of items for the future Baghdad Embassy, contingency planning for CBW protection in the region, and consular contingency planning. Most of the advice addressed the role of the FCO Emergency Unit and choreography of departmental meetings.

929. Mr Ricketts explained that he held daily meetings at 9.00am to co-ordinate FCO activity, chaired in his absence by another FCO Board member or Mr Chaplin. He also described the Iraq-related responsibilities of FCO senior officials:

> "William Ehrman [Director General Defence and Intelligence] deals with JIC and MOD, Graham Fry [Director General Wider World] supervises work on consular planning …; Edward Chaplin and Charles Gray take the lead on policy advice, working with DSI for longer range thinking, with the UN and CFSP [Common Foreign and Security Policy] teams, with the Legal Advisers and others. I have deliberately involved a wide spread of senior managers, because we may well have to sustain an intense crisis for a significant period …
>
> "You will of course want to be closely involved in all the policy-making. One of the key tasks of the Emergency Unit is to prepare the Foreign Secretary and you for the [anticipated] No.10 meetings, to ensure the FCO is pro-active and thinking ahead. I propose to take responsibility under you as overall co-ordinator …

---

[447] Minutes, 29 November 2002, FCO Board.
[448] Minute Ricketts to PUS [FCO], 2 December 2002, 'Iraq: Handling the Crisis'.

"MED and Personnel Command discussed again this week the staff numbers required to produce this structure, and other essential augmentation (for example, for the Press Office and Consular Division) … But it will be vital that the Board meets early and decides which tasks can fall away …

"This all looks unwieldy, but I am confident that it will work … In managing this, the trick will be to have a clear co-ordinating and tasking arrangement, without vast meetings … We will need to keep [overseas] posts well briefed and targeted, while encouraging them to exercise maximum restraint in reporting …"

930. The Inquiry has seen no response to Mr Ricketts from Sir Michael Jay.

931. The first Iraq morning meeting for which the Inquiry has seen a record was on 24 December.[449] From 11 February 2003, Mr Ricketts chaired a second policy meeting most evenings.[450] The records of each morning and evening meeting were sent to Sir Michael Jay's office and copied widely in the FCO, to Dr Brewer in DFID, and, from 3 February 2003, to Dr Simon Cholerton, an official in Sec(O) in the MOD.

932. The records show that most meetings focused on negotiations at the UN. Post-conflict issues, including the preparation of briefing for No.10, key meetings with the US, and DFID's humanitarian preparations, were also discussed, but were often reported in less detail.

933. Mr Ricketts was right in December 2002 to try to ensure that the FCO was "thinking ahead" and to involve a wide range of senior managers responsible for areas of business affected by Iraq in the department's preparations for an "all-out Iraq crisis". But the new arrangements represented a missed opportunity to give greater prominence and coherence to the FCO's work on post-conflict issues.

FCO REPORT ON SADDAM HUSSEIN'S CRIMES AND HUMAN RIGHTS ABUSES

934. The FCO published a report on Saddam Hussein's crimes and human rights abuses in early December.

935. FCO officials advised Mr Straw that there continued to be differences between UK and US views on how to approach the prosecution of Saddam Hussein and his inner circle.

936. On 2 December the FCO published a report on Saddam Hussein's crimes and human rights abuses.[451]

---

[449] Minute Middle East Department [junior official] to PS/PUS, 24 December 2002, 'Iraq Morning Meeting: Key Points'.
[450] Minute Middle East Department [junior official] to PS/PUS, 11 February 2003, 'Iraq Evening Meeting: Key Points'.
[451] Foreign and Commonwealth Office London, *Saddam Hussein: crimes and human rights abuses*, November 2002.

937. The first draft of the FCO report had been produced in March 2002, in response to a request from Mr Blair for information on Saddam Hussein's record of human rights abuses, for publication alongside a paper on WMD.[452]

938. The development of a communications strategy on Iraq and the preparation of the Iraq dossier, which incorporated some material on human rights abuses, are addressed in Section 4.2.

939. The FCO report published on 2 December was "based on the testimony of Iraqi exiles, evidence gathered by UN rapporteurs and human rights organisations, and intelligence material".[453] It examined "Iraq's record on torture, the treatment of women, prison conditions, arbitrary and summary killings, the persecution of the Kurds and the Shia, the harassment of opposition figures outside Iraq and the occupation of Kuwait".

940. Mr Straw explained to the *BBC* that the report was being published "because it is important that people understand the comprehensive evil that is Saddam Hussein".[454]

941. The report was criticised by some as an attempt to influence public opinion in favour of war.[455]

942. On 11 December, in response to a request in October for more work on the criminal prosecution of Saddam Hussein and his inner circle, the FCO sent No.10 a paper on a possible international criminal tribunal for Iraq.[456]

943. The covering letter explained that, as requested, the question of a tribunal was being factored into Whitehall work on the future of Iraq. Officials had discussed the issue at the Washington talks on 6 November and consulted the State Department's War Crimes Office. The US did not appear to favour an international tribunal for Iraq along the lines of the International Criminal Tribunal for the former Yugoslavia (ICTY) and was giving close consideration to the Sierra Leone Special Court model.[457]

944. On the question of whether to circulate information about potential indictees in order to encourage them to break with Saddam Hussein, the FCO advised that there were various lists of possible targets in existence, including a list of 27 published by the Iraqi National Congress and a secret list produced by the US containing about 40 names, but that it would be inappropriate for a government to issue a list as it would pre-empt the role of the eventual prosecutor. It might also encourage those on the list to

---

[452] Minute McKane to Rycroft, 27 March 2002, 'Saddam's record of human rights abuses' attaching Paper, 'Iraqi Human Rights Abuses'.

[453] Foreign and Commonwealth Office London, *Saddam Hussein: crimes and human rights abuses*, November 2002.

[454] *BBC News*, 2 December 2002, *UK unveils 'torture' dossier*.

[455] *The Guardian*, 3 December 2002, *Anger over Straw's dossier on Iraqi human rights*.

[456] Letter McDonald to Rycroft, 11 December 2002, 'ICTY-Type Tribunal for Iraq' attaching Paper [unattributed and undated], 'Tribunal for Iraq'.

[457] The Sierra Leone Special Court (SLSC) is a special tribunal of domestic and international judges which exists outside the Sierra Leone criminal justice system. The SLSC prosecutes only those responsible for the most serious crimes.

resist to the end or to abscond. For those reasons, the US was cautious about the idea. The FCO intended to stay in touch with the State Department as thinking on transitional justice developed.

945. The FCO advised that prosecution of the range of allegations against Saddam Hussein's regime might require a combination of different judicial institutions. Issues to consider included:

- the capacity of the domestic criminal justice system, which was likely to need "substantial re-building and re-training to restore it as an independent and effective body";
- the difficulty of finding a legal basis for a number of the options if the UN was not involved in the administration of Iraq;
- the UK's wish not to be associated with the death penalty, which remained extant in Iraqi law; and
- categorisation of offenders, which might include:
    o political and military leaders;
    o others contributing to the commission of international crimes;
    o perpetrators of serious domestic crimes such as murder; and
    o those responsible for lesser offences.

946. Those issues were considered further by officials after the second round of inter-agency talks in Washington on 22 January 2003 (see Section 6.5).

947. **In a series of papers on post-conflict Iraq prepared in mid-December and shared with the US, the FCO identified:**

- **possible middle ground between UK and US positions on the post-conflict role of the UN;**
- **the need for more information on the capabilities of Iraq's civil service;**
- **the need to put SSR at the centre of post-conflict work;**
- **the risk of underplaying the importance of "Islamic forces in Iraq";**
- **the need to improve economic conditions as quickly as possible; and**
- **the importance of maintaining firm control of the internal security situation.**

948. **The British Embassy Amman also highlighted the tainted image of the UN in Iraq. It stated that a UN-led interim administration would be preferable to a US-led one, but would come in for much the same criticism from Iraqis.**

949. On 12 December, the FCO handed four papers to Ambassador Zalmay Khalilzad, US Ambassador at large for Free Iraqis, who was visiting London for the conference of the Iraqi Opposition from 14 to 17 December:

- 'Interim Administrations in Iraq: Why a UN-led Interim Administration would be in the US interest';
- 'Iraq: Security Sector Reform';
- 'Islamism in Iraq'; and
- a paper on war crimes.[458]

950. It is not clear from the documents seen by the Inquiry which paper on war crimes was handed to Ambassador Khalilzad. It seems most likely to have been the FCO paper published on 2 December, but could have been the paper on a tribunal for Iraq, which had been sent to No.10 on 11 December after a series of discussions on the subject between the FCO and the US Government.

951. The first three papers were tabled at the AHGI on 13 December.

952. The Cabinet Office undertook to circulate the paper on war crimes later.

FCO PAPER: 'INTERIM ADMINISTRATIONS IN IRAQ'

953. The FCO paper on interim administrations shared with US on 12 December was a response to the differences between the US and UK positions at the Washington talks on 6 November and was described as "work in progress".[459] The paper was tabled at the AHGI on 13 December. It is not clear who contributed to the draft.

954. The FCO paper set out the likely short- and medium-term functions of an interim administration, ranging from destruction of WMD stockpiles to reintegration of refugees. It cautioned:

"We cannot be sure of the scale of the problem before we encounter it (although we believe the US has done a lot of work in this area, particularly with the Iraqi exile community). Iraq has a reputation for being one of the better-run Arab countries with a well-educated civil service. But we have little first hand evidence of how things work nowadays. We need more information, and we are working with academics, the Iraqi exile community and our posts on this in order to tackle the following questions:

- To what extent are ministries infiltrated by Ba'athist elements? How central are the Ba'athists to the functioning of the ministries? Can the ministries work without them?
- How far do the Ba'athists have to be removed to ensure loyalty to an interim administration?

---

[458] Minute Dodd to Manning, 19 December 2002, 'Ad Hoc Group on Iraq'.
[459] Paper Middle East Department, 12 December 2002, 'Interim Administrations in Iraq: Why a UN-led Interim Administration would be in the US interest'.

- What has been the effect on good government of coping with sanctions? How much activity has moved to the 'black market'? How do we move black market activity back into the legitimate sector?

- To what extent have government practices become corrupted by non-transparent control over oil revenues?"

955. The FCO recognised that there were benefits and drawbacks with the US and UN models, and suggested a "third way":

"... a potential middle ground in which security requirements could be provided by Coalition Forces, answerable only to US leadership, and all other functions of administration provided through the UN. Or the tasks of an IA could be divided up so that US-led Coalition Forces retained the lead on some – eg defence, WMD, security sector reform – working alongside a UN-led civil interim administration.

"To achieve this sort of structure would require some innovative work in the UN Security Council ..."

956. The FCO concluded that international legitimacy was crucial to many aspects of the interim administration's mission and would be very difficult to achieve under US leadership. In the short term, the US-led model looked more likely to succeed, especially in the areas of SSR and WMD. Wider political and economic reforms were more likely to endure in the long term if the interim authority worked under UN auspices and maximised the contribution of Iraqis.

957. Comments on the paper from the British Embassy Amman were included in an annex:

"The crucial issue here is timing. If the US or UN were to control the initial period of post-conflict transition, their presence is likely to be accepted (if it brings peace and not a worse situation). This stage should not be long enough for the US or the UN to start expanding their duties beyond simply keeping the peace and avoiding major humanitarian problems."

958. The Embassy warned that the "fervour that could be whipped up" by any US attempt to run major Iraqi government departments "could be enough to endanger the international community's ability to affect the process of change at all". Equally:

"Whilst a UN-led authority would be undoubtedly better than a US-led one, the UN now has such a tainted image in Iraq that a UN-led IA would come in for much the same criticism. (The UN is felt to be under the control of the US anyway.)"

959. The Embassy concluded:

"There is a small group of Iraqis inside Iraq who could be trusted/used to bring about change in a transitional phase. They would need to be bolstered by Iraqi professionals willing to return from abroad.

"An interim authority would be best run by the Iraqis themselves with long-term technical and financial support from the international community. (The UK is in a particularly strong position to do this – we still maintain the image of being professional and knowledgeable!)"

FCO PAPER: 'IRAQ: SECURITY SECTOR REFORM'

960. During October and November, the FCO produced a number of drafts of a paper on SSR, one of which informed the 1 November Cabinet Office paper on models for post-Saddam Hussein Iraq.[460]

961. The last version seen by the Inquiry, dated 10 December, described SSR as a key task which, if carried out successfully, "should lead to Iraq giving up its attachment to WMD, dismantling its oppressive network of spies, informers and secret police, scaling down its huge armed forces and reforming its criminal justice system".[461] If SSR went well, Iraq would be "much less likely to pose the same threat to the region and its own people". The process would be shaped to a degree by post-conflict stabilisation and should be seen within the overall policy framework of promoting good government. There was a particularly clear overlap between SSR and those wider issues in areas of police and judicial reform, about which the UK knew little.

962. The paper listed the questions that any SSR plan for Iraq must answer:

- What security structures would be appropriate? That required an assessment of the internal and external threats to Iraq and knowledge of its future constitutional shape.

- Who should be in charge? SSR in Afghanistan had been hampered by the lack of international institutional architecture: "In Iraq's case, we should give a higher priority to organising SSR much earlier, ie ideally before military action … Good articulation between the body charged with overseeing SSR and the post S[addam] H[ussein] interim administration will be critical."

- Methodology. How far should the exclusion of members of the Tikriti clan be taken? The inner circle of security agencies around Saddam Hussein were ripe for abolition, but what about the civilian police and the judiciary?

- DDR. What mechanisms were need to bring perpetrators of crimes against humanity to justice?

- Qualitative and quantitative change. How to reform the security sector to operate on the basis of humanitarian values in support of a legitimate government?

- Accountability. How to establish the principle of civilian oversight?

---

[460] Letter Gray to Drummond, 18 October 2002, 'Papers for the AHGI' attaching Paper [unattributed], 17 October 2002, 'Iraq: Security Sector Reform'.
[461] Paper Middle East Department, 10 December 2002, 'Iraq: Security Sector Reform'.

963. The FCO described the paper as a "living document" and highlighted some emerging themes, including the need:

- to put SSR at the centre of post-conflict work, unlike in Afghanistan;
- to establish a UK working group to start the detailed assessment of "a number of complicated issues" that would allow the UK to engage with the US and UK academics on the issue;
- to involve the new Iraqi administration in the process as early as possible;
- to find out more about the judiciary and the civilian police; and
- for Ministers to decide the level of engagement "given our limited and stretched resources".

964. The record of the AHGI on 13 December stated that a Whitehall working group on SSR had been established and could undertake further work.[462]

965. The Government has been unable to supply evidence of activity by the SSR working group.

FCO PAPER: 'ISLAMISM IN IRAQ'

966. The FCO paper on Islamism in Iraq, written by DSI, described Iraq as "a relatively secular state", but warned:

"Many of the models for possible future governments, whether representative or even democratic, proposed by commentators, are broadly secular too. This may be the preferred outcome, but there is a risk we underplay the importance of Islamic forces in Iraq.

"In any period of post-Saddam political instability, it is likely groups will be looking for identities and ideologies on which to base movements. Ba'athism will have been largely discredited. Communism is no longer the force it once was in Iraq. Islamism, ethnicity and nationalism are obvious alternatives. This paper considers the possibility that Islamism emerges as one of the main organising principles for Iraqis."[463]

967. The paper stated that it was "almost certain that political Islam would become more prominent in post-Saddam Iraq" and drew four "tentative conclusions":

- Many popular groupings emerging after Saddam Hussein were likely to have religious agendas, some overtly anti-Western.
- The emergence of such groups was not inconsistent with moves towards more representative or democratic government.

---

[462] Minute Dodd to Manning, 19 December 2002, 'Ad Hoc Group on Iraq'.
[463] Paper DSI, [undated], 'Islamism in Iraq'.

- "We do not expect a massive surge in extremist sentiment". The Shia were unlikely to repeat the 1991 mistake of calling for a Khomeinist regime, a move which had alienated many Iraqis who might have joined them.

- A number of extremist groups were likely to use violence to pursue their political ends.

968. The FCO proposed a number of "practical steps" to provide stability.

969. In the short term, support for more extreme groups could be limited by:

- avoiding Shia shrines and important religious buildings during military action;
- improving economic conditions as quickly as possible;
- winning hearts and minds through public information and media campaigns;
- discouraging meddling by Iran and other regional players;
- maintaining Israel's neutrality during military action and making progress on Israel/Palestine; and
- "Maintaining firm control on the internal security situation and moving quickly to suppress any international terrorist groups in the country."

970. The FCO suggested that, in order to ensure longer-term stability and development, there would be an overriding interest in the rapid emergence of "a political class with whom we can do business". Focusing on pro-Western groups would be short-sighted. It could create:

"... a further breeding ground for resentment, extremism and ultimately terrorism directed both against any new regime and Western targets. It would be seen as another example of Western hostility to Islam and double standards. It would be a recipe for longer-term instability."

Instead, Islamist groups and religious leaders should be involved in the creation of the new Iraqi political system.

971. The FCO concluded:

- "We should plan on the basis that political Islam will be a significant force in many of the post-Saddam scenarios ...
- We should work to limit the support the extremist elements receive ...
- We should look to engage those moderate groups which are willing to work with us, even if they disagree strongly with some of our values. This means being prepared to accept the emergence of a religiously conservative and anti-Western regime if that is what Iraqis want.
- The approach the Americans adopt will be crucial. We should engage them on this issue."

972. On 30 December, Sir Michael Jay asked Mr Gray a number of questions about post-conflict issues, including how far FCO papers on post-conflict issues had been shared with the US and major EU partners.[464]

973. Dr Amanda Tanfield, Head of Iraq Section in MED, reported:

"Almost all the UK papers have been shared with the US. We have only withheld from them papers which have been overtaken by others that we have passed to them.

"We have been more selective with EU partners. Foreign ministry officials in France and Germany received the early planners [DSI] papers on 'Scenarios for the Future of Iraq after Saddam' and 'Consequences of Conflict for the Region'. We have given the French planners … the paper on 'Islamism in Iraq'.

"The difficulty with sharing a lot of thinking on day after with EU partners is that day after assumes regime change, which is difficult territory for many of them, particularly Germany. And some of the more recent papers have been drafted in the context of the ongoing UK-US official level day after talks, with the US readership very much in mind."[465]

974. In January 2003, Mr Chilcott commented that the UK had received little in return from the US (see Section 6.5).

975. Other issues raised by Sir Michael Jay on 30 December included:

- whether DFID's concerns about involvement in Iraq policy had been resolved; and
- whether the FCO had financial and other contingency plans if more close protection teams were needed for Embassy staff.[466]

976. Dr Tanfield confirmed that DFID was now "fully in the loop" and was represented at Mr Ricketts' daily Iraq meeting; and that contingency plans were in place for deploying close protection teams to Baghdad and five other Embassies in the region.[467]

Iraqi opposition conference, London

977. No senior UK official attended the conference of Iraqi opposition groups held in London from 14 to 17 December.

978. The conference cast further doubt on the credibility of many of those groups.

---

[464] Minute Jay to Gray, 30 December 2002, 'Iraq: The Day After Issues'.
[465] Minute Tanfield to PUS [FCO], 9 January 2003, 'Iraq: The Day After Issues'.
[466] Minute Jay to Gray, 30 December 2002, 'Iraq: The Day After Issues'.
[467] Minute Tanfield to PUS [FCO], 9 January 2003, 'Iraq: The Day After Issues'.

979. In late November, representatives of six Iraqi exile groups called on Mr Gray to seek "permission" to hold a conference of opposition groups in London after plans to hold it in Brussels had fallen through.[468]

980. Mr Gray informed Mr Straw's Private Office that he had made it clear to the group that he had no authority to authorise or prevent such a meeting and that they must make their own arrangements and abide by the law. He had also made it clear that attendance by Mr Blair or Mr Straw was "out of the question". Mr Gray recommended against attendance by a Minister or senior official, but advised that "it would be right to send a relatively junior observer perhaps from Research Analysts".

981. Mr Gray held to that view after the US informed the FCO that it would send "a large and senior delegation, probably led by Zalmay Khalilzad, Senior Director … at the National Security Council and Ambassador at large to the Iraqi Opposition".[469] Mr Gray advised Mr Straw's Private Office that the US had not urged the UK to raise the level of its attendance and there was no reason to do so. The event was "unlikely to be an edifying one, and I think we should be wary of association with it, even to please the Americans".

Iraqi opposition meetings in the UK

During 2002, representatives of the Iraqi opposition met in the UK a number of times, including under the auspices of the State Department's Future of Iraq Project. In each case, UK engagement was at junior official level, led by FCO Research Analysts. Significant events attended by FCO officials included:

- the US-hosted Democratic Principles Working Group of the Future of Iraq Project at Cobham, Surrey, on 4 and 5 September;[470]

- a follow-up meeting at Wilton Park on 10 and 11 October;[471]

- the first conference of the Iraqi National Movement at Kensington and Chelsea Town Hall on 28 and 29 September;[472] and

- the Iraqi opposition conference in London from 14 to 17 December.[473]

---

[468] Minute Gray to Private Secretary [FCO], 22 November 2002, 'Proposed Meeting of Iraqi Oppositionists, London, 10-15 December'.

[469] Minute Gray to Private Secretary [FCO], 5 December 2002, 'Iraq: Proposed Oppositionists' Conference. London, 13-15 December'.

[470] Teleletter Hetherington to Washington [junior official], 6 September 2002, 'Iraq: US-hosted 'Democratic Principles Working Group'.

[471] Telegram 104 FCO London to Amman, 20 November 2002, 'Iraqi Opposition Sitrep'; Report Democratic Principles Working Group, November 2002, 'Final Report on the Transition to Democracy in Iraq'.

[472] Teleletter Wilson to Amman [junior official], 30 September 2002, 'Iraq: Iraqi National Movement, First Conference, 28-29 Sept 2002'.

[473] Telegram 111 FCO London to Amman, 17 December 2002, 'Iraq: Opposition Conference 14-17 December'.

982. Early in December, the British Embassy Amman issued its November update on Iraq.[474] Unlike previous updates, which had only been sent to FCO addressees, the November report was copied to DFID and DIS.

983. The Embassy reported the recent release of all prisoners from Iraqi jails, noting that the policy had been criticised within and outside Iraq for causing a rise in crime. It also provided a general assessment of Iraqi public opinion:

"Iraqis do not want a war because they do not know what is next. (But they fully expect that a war will come) ...

"Iraqis do not want a 'US occupation' ...

"The biggest common denominator to emerge is that the Iraqi people do not know who to trust. They do not trust the US because they 'abandoned' them in 1991. They do not trust the regime or its religious men. They do not trust the opposition (who are corrupt or in the pockets of foreign governments). And they do not trust each other ... Any serious discussions tend to take place only within the very inner core of a family. All this makes an organised revolt seem improbable."

984. Over 300 representatives of a wide range of Iraqi opposition groups attended the conference in London from 14 to 17 December, which agreed a "Policy Statement of the Iraqi Opposition", a paper on the post-Saddam Hussein transition to democracy and appointed a 65 member co-ordinating committee.[475]

985. The FCO Research Analyst who attended the event reported "a palpable sense of relief" at those achievements, but predicted that:

"... given the intense differences displayed over the weekend and the chequered history of opposition conferences any show of unity is unlikely to last and there are enough people excluded who will already be briefing the press ... [T]he US will be unhappy at having such an unwieldy 65 to deal with."[476]

986. Those conclusions were echoed in the FCO Annual Review for Iraq, written in January 2003 by Research Analysts in the absence of an embassy in Baghdad.[477] The Review commented extensively on US involvement with Iraqi exiles. The US had encouraged the Iraqi opposition to convene and fund a conference to overcome emerging rivalries. After several postponements and changes of venue, the conference had been held in London and funded by the US. Competition between groups "cast doubt on whether a credible new front can emerge" and press reports suggested those groups had been "written out of the US's Iraq script". The Review also suggested that

---

[474] Teleletter Amman [junior official] to MED [junior official], 4 December 2002, 'Iraq: November sitrep'.
[475] *BBC News*, 16 December 2002, *Disputes mar Iraqi opposition talks*; Telegram 111 FCO London to Amman, 17 December 2002, 'Iraq: Opposition Conference 14-17 December'.
[476] Telegram 111 FCO London to Amman, 17 December 2002, 'Iraq: Opposition Conference 14-17 December'.
[477] Teleletter Wilson to Abu Dhabi, 16 January 2003, 'Iraq: Annual Review, 2002'.

the Future of Iraq Working Groups, originally to have been composed of technocrats, appeared to have been "hijacked" by opposition politicians.

987. On 19 December, Mr Masoud Barzani, leader of the Kurdistan Democratic Party (KDP), and Mr Jalal Talabani, leader of the Patriotic Union of Kurdistan (PUK), called on Mr Powell and Sir David Manning at No.10.[478] Mr Blair joined the meeting unannounced.

988. The briefing prepared for Mr Blair explained that the two party leaders did not know that he might drop in and that it was not essential that he did so.[479] If he did, he could ask about the opposition conference and the situation in "Kurdistan", and should state that the UK was committed to Iraq's territorial integrity.

989. The record of the meeting stated that Mr Blair agreed with the two leaders that all groups in Iraq should be involved in helping to reunite post-Saddam Hussein Iraq.[480]

990. Mr Blair wrote to Mr Barzani and Mr Talabani twice during March 2003 (see Section 6.5).

Military preparations gather pace

991. By December 2002, US military preparations were gathering pace.

992. The MOD informed No.10, the Cabinet Office, the FCO and the Treasury, but not DFID, that the US military was "gearing up" to be as ready as possible by 15 February.

993. Sir David Manning wrote to Mr Watkins on 27 November, requesting a note for Mr Blair on the progress of US planning (see Section 6.1).[481]

994. Mr Watkins advised Sir David Manning that it was "misleading to talk of firm plans", not just because of unresolved practical issues such as Turkish co-operation, but also because the US political strategy remained "unclear".[482] There had been "a significant shift in US military planning" as CENTCOM sought to "reduce the lead times between a political decision and military action". Secretary Rumsfeld had signed a number of deployment orders to take effect in early January, and the US was "increasingly moving beyond pure planning into at least some actual forward deployments".

995. Mr Webb visited Washington from 2 to 4 December for a US/European conference on post-conflict Iraq and two days of bilateral talks with US officials at the NSC, State Department and DoD.[483] In his report, copied to Mr Ehrman and Mr Chaplin in the FCO, Mr Webb observed that there was a good deal of activity on civil reconstruction under

---

[478] Letter Rycroft to Sinclair, 19 December 2002, 'Iraqi Kurds: Meeting with Prime Minister, 19 December'.
[479] Minute Rycroft to Prime Minister, 19 December 2002, 'Iraqi Opposition Leaders'.
[480] Letter Rycroft to Sinclair, 19 December 2002, 'Iraqi Kurds: Meeting with Prime Minister, 19 December'.
[481] Letter Manning to Watkins, 27 November 2002, 'Iraq: Military Planning'.
[482] Letter Watkins to Manning, 29 November 2002, 'Iraq: Military Planning'.
[483] Minute Webb to ACDS(Ops), 9 December 2002, 'Iraq Aftermath'.

way in the State Department involving expatriate Iraqis, but "no real connection to the military planning". He had explained to US officials, "somewhat repetitively", the need for an early start to post-conflict planning. Kosovo had shown that civil planning took longer and was more difficult than military planning. He reported that references to the UN's role had caused "an adverse reaction in many circles", and he had found it more productive to make the case for the UN as a source of legitimisation and co-ordination rather than as an executive instrument.

996. Mr Webb also reported a "big pitch by the Republican right for making democracy an objective" on the grounds that blood should not be spilt to replace Saddam Hussein with another strongman. "Weary Europeans said this was hopelessly unrealistic: modest ambitions for greater representation were more sensible."

997. In his next update on US military planning for No.10 on 5 December, Mr Watkins warned that it was increasingly difficult for the UK to plan without knowing where the UK land package would be based. In order to keep options open for significant UK military participation from mid-February onwards, the Armed Forces needed to "press ahead with further preparations".[484]

998. The US had "no formal position on the date by which they must be ready to act". It had a wide range of options, but assuming a political decision to take military action on 15 February (known as "P Day"), the MOD expected the air campaign and amphibious operations to start in early March.

999. Mr Watkins made no reference to post-conflict implications.

1000. In the US, CENTCOM's Phase IV planners held a post-conflict planning session with a 40-person inter-agency team on 11 December.[485] The event anticipated "rough going ahead". On the assumption that, initially, there would be no government in place, participants were "anticipating chaos".

1001. After a post-event briefing, Lieutenant General George Casey, Director of the Joint Staff, recognised the need to augment the Phase IV effort. A new Joint Task Force (JTF-4) was created in CENTCOM with an extra 58 staff.

SPG PAPER, 13 DECEMBER 2002: 'UK MILITARY STRATEGIC THINKING ON IRAQ'

1002. On 13 December, the SPG described the post-conflict phase of operations as "strategically decisive" and called for it to be "adequately addressed" in any winning concept.

1003. If the UK was not prepared to make a meaningful contribution to Iraq's physical and political rehabilitation, it should not be drawn into war-fighting.

---

[484] Letter Watkins to Manning, 5 December 2002, 'Iraq: Military Planning'.
[485] Bowen SW Jr. *Hard Lessons: The Iraq Reconstruction Experience.* U.S. Government Printing Office, 2009.

1004. The UK's strategy had to be flexible enough to respond to the situation on the ground, but there was a need for an urgent cross-government view on the area of Iraq for which the UK might want to accept responsibility "in order to make the task of scoping different scenarios possible".

1005. The Inquiry has seen no indication that the urgent, cross-government work recommended by the SPG took place.

1006. Development of the Government's thinking on the location and extent of the UK military Area of Responsibility (AOR) in Iraq is addressed in Sections 6.1 and 6.2.

1007. The introduction to the "aftermath" section of the final, 13 December, edition of the SPG paper on UK military strategic thinking pulled no punches:

> "The aftermath (AM) phase of operations is likely to be the strategically decisive phase of our engagement in Iraq. Only in this phase can our strategic objectives be met. It will also form the lasting impression of Coalition legitimacy and success.

> "The obvious deduction from this is that if we are not prepared to make a meaningful contribution to the physical and political rehabilitation of Iraq in the AM phase we should not be drawn into war-fighting. There is currently a risk that we view our engagement in reverse, considering post-conflict activity as a necessary but inconvenient adjunct to our war-fighting plans. The Winning Concept must address AM."[486]

1008. The material in the aftermath section was described as "key deductions distilled from a strategic estimate of the AM phase". The stated aim was to:

> "a. Set out a framework for the co-ordination of strategic planning between the MOD, OGDs, other nations and, where feasible, NGOs.

> b. Provide guidance for PJHQ on the development of operational plans."

1009. The paper listed nine "key judgements":

> "The AM phase will be the strategically decisive phase. We must be sure it is adequately addressed in our consideration of the Winning Concept.

> **"No overarching concept for the future of Iraq currently seems to exist. A framework for the development of a new Iraqi state must be agreed by any Coalition seeking to conduct military action that would result in the removal of the current regime.**

---

[486] Paper [SPG], 13 December 2002, 'UK Military Strategic Thinking on Iraq'.

"The development of a jointly acceptable approach to Iraqi governance and reform in the Resolution Phase should be pursued with the US. Agreement on the role of the UN is essential.

"A cross-government view on the area in Iraq for which the UK might want to accept responsibility is required urgently in order to shape or validate operational planning.

"Failure to ensure political agreement on the territorial integrity of Iraq could presage a break-up that would fix Coalition Forces in long-term stabilisation operations.

"We should encourage the US to begin work now on the future shape of the Iraqi armed forces in order to develop a sound SSR plan in advance of the start of operations. We should also undertake a review of the options for rapidly generating an Iraqi policing capability.

"Early engagement with OGDs and NGOs is required to scope the AM humanitarian situation and the degree to which it may fall to the military to ameliorate it. We should be prepared in advance for the real possibility thatwe may initially face a task beyond our means to rectify with little external support.

"An assessment of the options for rapidly meeting a surge requirement for additional forces at the start of the AM phase should be undertaken by PJHQ.

"The UK should be prepared to commit forces to Iraq at 'medium scale' for at least six months following the commencement of the AM phase, and possibly out to two years."

1010. The paper stated that a relatively small number of factors drove UK engagement. They were:

"a. Governance and reform – What is the UK vision for the future of Iraq? How realistic is the aim of retaining Iraqi territorial integrity? What replaces the Iraqi regime and what role will the UN play? How do we resolve UK/US differences on UN involvement?

b. Situation – Where will the UK operate and what situation will we face in that region? What is the intent of the various population groups and how badly damaged will the infrastructure be?

c. Iraqi armed forces – How do we manage the Iraqi armed forces in the short term and reform them in the long term?

d. Humanitarian situation – What humanitarian situation will be faced?

e. UK commitment – For how long, and to what extent, will the UK be a significant contributor to AM operations?"

1011. On governance and reform, the paper stated:

- Detailed military planning was proceeding with no clear view on the future of the Iraqi state. The UK had a valuable contribution to make to development of an overarching concept, "but the lead must rest firmly with the US as the only nation with sufficient resources to underwrite the task".

- There was considerable temptation for regional powers to develop bilateral relations with different ethnic groups, potentially leading to the "Balkanisation" of Iraq and a protracted role for Coalition forces.

- UK and US positions on the role of the UN were getting closer, but remained divided. For political and military reasons the UK must continue to stress the need to maximise UN and international involvement.

1012. The most significant factor in determining the scale and complexity of the post-conflict task, the situation in Iraq, was also the least predictable. It was not possible "to truly assess the state of Iraq and the intent of its principal actors in the AM phase until we are presented with them". The UK's strategy therefore needed to be flexible enough to respond to the situation on the ground. In order to make the task of scoping different scenarios possible, the UK needed to form an early view on where it wished to operate. The initial location might be driven by the UK's role in Phase III, "but we can shape this". To do that, three factors needed to be considered:

"a. Political – FCO:

What areas offer the UK an advantageous or influential role in the AM phase? Are oil fields a factor? Are there groups … whom we would rather not assume responsibility for? A reasoned policy view is required.

b. Military – MOD:

Where will our Phase III role place us and do we wish to shape it according to AM factors in any way? Are there areas where we judge there is a high risk of failure? Are there areas where UK strengths will be most effective, such as population centres? What size and nature of area can the UK force deployed realistically assume responsibility for?

c. Humanitarian – DFID:

What are the most significant areas of humanitarian risk? How will DFID engage and how can we effectively co-ordinate our efforts? How can we apply our limited military capacity to respond to best effect?

"This thought process must be undertaken urgently if we are to shape our Phase III role accordingly. Currently our involvement in the North or South is being driven by purely operational concerns. At the very least we must validate the current operational considerations strategically."

1013. The paper also set out the factors likely to determine the size of the UK military's post-conflict commitment:

"The scale of the UK commitment to AM will be determined by the size of force deployed for war-fighting in the first instance. Very rapidly, however, the demands of the AM phase are likely to drive the requirement for a different force structure. While the desire will evidently be to effect as rapid a drawdown as feasible, an initial increase in deployed strength may be required in order to stabilise the situation. A mass PW [prisoner of war] problem and/or a humanitarian crisis could both prompt this, requiring an increase in light forces and logistic effort. The options for meeting such a surge demand must be considered in advance in order to ensure a quick response.

"A final view on the extent of any long-term (post-12 months) UK commitment may not be required at this stage. It is necessary, however, to provide a baseline assumption for the level of commitment for the crucial 'first roulement' post-conflict in order to allow commitments to be balanced. It is suggested the assumption should be up to a medium-scale (Air and Land) commitment for up to six months of the AM phase. A requirement to commit at or around this level for up to two years might well be necessary to ensure any lasting progress towards the UK end state."

1014. The SPG paper was included in the Christmas reading pack prepared for Mr Blair by the MOD.[487]

1015. On 16 December Maj Gen Fry produced a paper on deployment of a UK stabilisation force in the event of the early collapse of the Iraqi regime or military leading to a "loss of control".[488]

1016. "Early collapse" was defined as the collapse of the Iraqi regime less than 60 days after "P Day"; "loss of control" as "the period between the collapse of the Iraqi regime and the establishment of an effective alternative providing law and order and security".

1017. Maj Gen Fry explained that:

"Rapid intervention by the Coalition may be required to stabilise the situation, including support to an interim government. Current Package 3 deployment timelines would limit the arrival of sufficient and appropriate UK military capability in time. Consequently there is a need to develop a contingency plan that would enable the UK to gain an early footprint on the ground, providing influence in theatre and achieving strategic impact."

---

[487] Letter Watkins to Manning, 20 December 2002, 'Iraq: Christmas Reading'.
[488] Paper DCJO(Ops), 16 December 2002, 'Provision of a UK Stabilisation Force'.

1018. Should the collapse occur after 60 days, the UK land component would be at full operating capability and would deal with the situation.

1019. In order to provide a quick response, the stabilisation force was "likely to be light" and its role limited to "wider peacekeeping and 'stabilisation' tasks", including controlling and denying access to WMD, security at key locations, disarmament and demobilisation. The proposal set out a number of options for different scenarios.

1020. The Chiefs of Staff discussed the paper on 18 December.[489] At the meeting, Lt Gen Reith commented that any stabilisation force would depend on timing and availability of resources, and that there was a synergy between the southern option and a stabilisation force.

1021. On 19 December, Mr Hoon's Private Office informed Sir David Manning and the FCO, Treasury and Cabinet Office that the US military was "gearing up" to be as ready as possible by 15 February, and advised: "we may well have to advance aspects of our own preparations if we are to remain in step".[490] The US now recognised that stabilisation and reconstruction of up to two thirds of Iraq would need to begin before the military campaign had concluded. This was "bringing home to the US military the need for more planning effort to be devoted to 'aftermath' issues now".

1022. The letter was not sent to DFID.

1023. The information on US planning in the letter from Mr Hoon's Private Office was repeated in a paper on US military thinking included in the Christmas reading pack sent to Mr Blair on 20 December.[491]

1024. Mr Watkins' covering letter to Sir David Manning highlighted "an increasingly pressing need to satisfy ourselves that the US has an overarching political strategy with which the Government is content" and "to address soon our campaign objectives", but made no reference to post-conflict planning.

Invasion plans take shape

UK objectives for post-conflict Iraq

1025. In January 2003, Mr Blair decided to publish the UK's strategic policy objectives for Iraq. They were closely based on those he had agreed in October 2002.

1026. Mr Straw issued a Written Ministerial Statement setting out the UK's objectives in Parliament on 7 January.

1027. Publication of the objectives is addressed in more detail in Section 3.6.

---

[489] Minutes, 18 December 2002, Chiefs of Staff meeting.
[490] Letter Williams to Manning, 19 December 2002, 'Iraq: Evolving US Military Thinking'.
[491] Letter Watkins to Manning, 20 December 2002, 'Iraq: Christmas Reading'.

1028. Mr Blair had been given clear warnings about the strategic significance of the post-conflict phase and the need to address inadequacies in US planning throughout the second half of 2002, including by:

- **Mr Hoon on 2 July;**
- **Mr Straw on 8 July;**
- **Mr Powell on 19 July;**
- **participants in Mr Blair's meeting of 23 July;**
- **Sir Christopher Meyer on 6 September;**
- **parliamentarians on 24 September and 25 November; and**
- **the MOD in Mr Watkins' letter of 19 November and in the SPG paper of 13 December.**

1029. Despite those warnings, there is no evidence that officials or Ministers addressed whether it was realistic to expect that the objectives could be achieved.

1030. Mr Campbell wrote to Mr Blair on 19 December, setting out the need to explain the UK's strategy.[492] He observed that: "Iraq is moving up a gear as an issue and as we enter the New Year we need to step up our communications efforts."

1031. Mr Campbell recommended that the objectives approved by Mr Blair in October should be published as soon as Parliament returned on 7 January, with a statement in the House of Commons from Mr Blair alongside publicity generated by the FCO Heads of Mission Conference. The statement would set out the strategic framework for the Government's overall approach and draw together the diplomatic, political and humanitarian strands of the strategy on Iraq as well as addressing issues of proliferation and terrorism.

1032. Mr Campbell argued that the communications strategy "should be rooted in where we think we will end up which currently looks like <u>a military conflict that ends in Saddam falling</u>". The major steps and key messages envisaged by Mr Campbell included: "Post-conflict: We're there to help for the long term."

1033. On 4 January, Mr Blair sent a long note to officials in No.10 (see Section 3.6).[493] On Iraq, he stated that there was "a big job of persuasion" to be done. That included showing "sensitivity to any humanitarian fall-out from war. Britain should take the lead on this, working with the UN."

1034. On 6 January, the Cabinet Office informed the FCO that Mr Blair had decided the policy objectives for Iraq should be placed in the public domain.[494]

---

[492] Minute Campbell to Prime Minister, 19 December 2002, 'Re: Iraq Communications'.
[493] Note Blair [to No.10 officials], 4 January 2003, [extract 'Iraq'].
[494] Letter Bowen to McDonald, 6 January 2003, 'Iraq' attaching Paper [unattributed], January 2003, 'Iraq: Policy Objectives'.

1035. In his diaries, Mr Campbell recorded the importance of publishing the objectives and his view that: "These strategy papers were as much about internal understanding as publicity."[495]

1036. Mr Straw issued a Written Ministerial Statement setting out the UK's objectives for post-conflict Iraq on 7 January.[496] The objectives were closely based on those approved by Mr Blair in October 2002.

1037. The UK's "prime objective" was "to rid Iraq of its weapons of mass destruction (WMD) and their associated programmes and means of delivery".

1038. Six "immediate priorities" were to:

- support the UN Monitoring, Verification and Inspection Commission (UNMOVIC) and International Atomic Energy Agency (IAEA) inspectors in Iraq;
- enable UNMOVIC and the IAEA to ensure long-term Iraqi compliance;
- maintain international solidarity behind the UN Security Council;
- preserve regional stability;
- continue to make military plans and preparations in case military action was needed; and
- continue to support humanitarian efforts to relieve suffering in Iraq.

1039. The undertaking to continue to support humanitarian efforts had been added since the first draft in October. Other changes included the addition of:

- a statement that the objectives were consistent with wider UK policy on the Middle East, WMD and terrorism; and
- an undertaking to act in conformity with international law to achieve the objectives.

1040. The definition of the post-conflict end state was unchanged, but with the aspiration to achieve it "as rapidly as possible" removed:

"We would like Iraq to become a stable, united and law abiding state, within its present borders, co-operating with the international community, no longer posing a threat to its neighbours or to international security, abiding by all its international obligations and providing effective and representative government to its own people."

1041. Questions about post-conflict planning continued to be raised in Parliament during January.

---

[495] Campbell A & Hagerty B. *The Alastair Campbell Diaries. Volume 4. The Burden of Power: Countdown to Iraq*. Hutchinson, 2012.
[496] House of Commons, *Official Report*, 7 January 2003, column 4WS.

1042. In the House of Commons on 7 January, Mr Hoon announced the first call out of Reservists for possible operations in Iraq and the deployment of the UK's Amphibious Task Group (ATG) to the Mediterranean.[497]

1043. In the debate that followed, Mr Tam Dalyell (Labour) asked what would happen when Coalition forces reached Baghdad.[498] Mr Hoon explained that Afghanistan provided "very recent experience on which to draw". He invited Mr Dalyell to "look carefully at the efforts that have been made by the United Kingdom, as part of the international community, to stabilise Afghanistan and provide it with very significant support as it grapples with the difficulties of rebuilding itself, its economy and ultimately, we hope, a democracy".

1044. During January, Written Parliamentary Questions on different aspects of post-conflict planning were addressed to Mr Straw, Ms Short and Mr Hoon:

- Dr Jenny Tonge (Liberal Democrat) asked Mr Straw what representations the UK had made to the US on post-war food, sanitation and water supplies. Mr Mike O'Brien, FCO Parliamentary Under Secretary of State, replied that no decision had been taken on military action and that the UK regularly discussed all aspects of Iraq policy with US colleagues.[499]

- Mr Hugo Swire (Conservative) asked Ms Short what assessment had been made of the potential humanitarian consequences of war. Ms Short replied that DFID was considering a wide range of contingencies which took into account the current humanitarian situation in Iraq.[500]

- Mr John Lyons (Labour) asked Mr Hoon what role British troops would play in post-war Iraq. Mr Adam Ingram, Minister of State for the Armed Forces, replied:

    "There is no inevitability about military action against Iraq; this question is therefore hypothetical at this stage. What I can say is that we take very seriously our current and potential responsibilities towards the Iraqi people. In the aftermath of any conflict, Britain would remain at the forefront of efforts to help the Iraqi people."[501]

UK military focus shifts to southern Iraq

1045. At the end of December 2002, the focus of the Chiefs of Staff and military planners switched from northern to southern Iraq, creating a contingent liability that the UK would be responsible for the post-conflict occupation and administration of a UK AOR in the region around Basra.

---

[497] House of Commons, *Official Report*, 7 January 2003, column 24.
[498] House of Commons, *Official Report*, 7 January 2003, column 30.
[499] House of Commons, *Official Report*, 20 January 2003, column 80W.
[500] House of Commons, *Official Report*, 22 January 2003, column 307W.
[501] House of Commons, *Official Report*, 27 January 2003, column 630W.

1046. PJHQ was given responsibility for Phase IV planning. PJHQ officials advised that:

- **If the UK were to take on the first Phase IV AOR in southern Iraq, it would effectively be "setting the standard" for the rest of Phase IV.**
- **PJHQ would need more support from other government departments if there was to be a joined-up approach to UK post-conflict planning.**

1047. Section 6.2 describes how, from the end of December 2002, the focus of UK military planning shifted from northern to southern Iraq.

1048. On 30 December 2002, Adm Boyce issued the 'CDS Planning and Preparation Directive for Operation TELIC',[502] authorising the military preparations needed for Coalition operations in Iraq.[503]

1049. The Directive, which included little material linked explicitly to the post-conflict phase of operations (Phase IV), stated:

"Delivering HMG's declared end state is likely to require UK engagement in follow-on operations but the possible scale and duration of 'aftermath operations' are uncertain and are in urgent need of clarification from US planners at all levels."

1050. Instructions to Lt Gen Reith included:

- to seek to influence US planning, as directed by MOD; and
- to prepare plans for humanitarian assistance in theatre, should it become necessary.

1051. Air Chief Marshal Sir Malcolm Pledger, Chief of Defence Logistics, was instructed to: "Be prepared to sustain follow-on forces at up to the medium scale of effort on land and air, and at small scale in the maritime environment for, initially, up to six months."

1052. The Planning and Preparation Directive was superseded by a first version of the Execute Directive on 4 March 2003 (see Section 6.5).

1053. On 5 January, Brigadier Albert Whitley, who had been deployed as Senior British Land Adviser (SBLA) to US Lieutenant General David McKiernan's Coalition Forces Land Component Command (CFLCC) HQ in Kuwait in early November 2002,[504] prepared a paper for PJHQ on "the imperatives for timely decision making for the commitment of UK Land Forces" to the US Operational Plan.[505] The paper is described in more detail in Section 6.2.

---

[502] Operation TELIC was the codename for the involvement of UK Armed Forces in the military campaign to remove the threat from Iraq's weapons of mass destruction.
[503] Paper CDS, 30 December 2002, 'CDS Planning and Preparation Directive for Operation TELIC'.
[504] Statement Whitley, 25 January 2011, page 3.
[505] Paper SBLA, 5 January 2003, 'Decision Imperatives'.

1054. Brigadier Whitley explained that, on 28 December, uncertainties about whether Turkey would allow transit of ground forces had led US and UK planners urgently to concentrate on developing robust operations from the south. Lt Gen McKiernan "would welcome the commitment of a UK division in the South from the start of the operation". The UK mission would be to "seize, secure and control" the rear area and right flank of the operation and provide a coherent transition to Phase IV operations in captured territory without loss of US combat forces. That would include securing infrastructure such as Umm Qasr and the Rumaylah oilfields, and fixing Iraqi forces in the Basra area. The Area of Operations (AO) was likely to be bounded by the Iraq/Kuwait border, the US V Corps/1 MEF (Marine Expeditionary Force) boundary, Jalibah airfield and the Euphrates, a similar land area to Kuwait.

1055. Brigadier Whitley strongly recommended acceptance, in principle, of "a UK Area of Operations and mission in an area of southern Iraq bounded in the north by the Euphrates".

1056. The Chiefs of Staff discussed the southern option on 6 January.[506] Lt Gen Reith described his latest paper on the land options, which was "based on a US offer for the UK to operate at division strength … in a discrete AOR in the South". That plan "appeared to offer strategic influence to the UK, especially in the move to Phase IV".

1057. Mr Paul Johnston, Head of FCO Security Policy Department, reported to Mr Straw's Private Office that, at the Chiefs of Staff Committee, Sir Kevin Tebbit and General Sir Michael Walker, Chief of the General Staff (CGS), both noted that the southern option for the UK was "part of an overall concept significantly different to that on which Ministers had so far been consulted".[507]

1058. In a paper on the southern option, dated 6 January and submitted after the discussion, Lt Gen Reith advised that the risks to a UK division were "minimal".[508] The "geographical area proposed would allow the UK to set the standard in the aftermath" and meant that it would be "strategically placed to exert maximum influence during Phase IV". Lt Gen Reith described the US plan as based on four assumptions, including: "The UK experience in wider peacekeeping, and subsequent ability to conduct early Phase IV – post conflict – operations."

1059. Lt Gen Reith recommended the deployment of a divisional headquarters and three brigades to the South; and that the armoured brigade should comprise four battlegroups.

---

[506] Minutes, 6 January 2003, Chiefs of Staff meeting.
[507] Minute Johnston to Private Secretary [FCO], 6 January 2003, 'Iraq: Chiefs of Staff Meeting, 6 January'.
[508] Minute Reith to COSSEC, 6 January 2003, 'Op TELIC – Southern Option' attaching Paper 'Op TELIC Southern Option – Revised'.

Definition and use of "Area of Operations (AO)" and "Area of Responsibility (AOR)"

"Area of Operations (AO)" refers to the UK military's area of combat operations during the invasion of Iraq (Phase III of operations). It is the term applied during conflict and is the area in which lethal force can be applied for a designated period of time.

"Area of Responsibility (AOR)" is a term usually applied during peace support operations. In Iraq, it refers to the area of southern Iraq for which the UK military was responsible during the post-conflict Occupation (Phase IV of operations).

The two terms were not used consistently and were sometimes applied interchangeably in the same document.

1060. On 7 January, Mr Paul Flaherty, MOD Civil Secretary at PJHQ, set out PJHQ's thoughts on preparations for Phase IV in a minute to Mr Lee.[509] In the absence of an agreed US inter-agency position on Phase IV planning, the CENTCOM commanders' conference in Tampa, Florida on 15 and 16 January was likely to have a significant impact on US policy-making. Phase IV planning was likely to be particularly important:

"... if, as now appears likely, the UK were to take on the first Phase IV AOR in southern Iraq. We would, in effect be setting the standard for the rest of Phase IV work. (And, of course, CJO [Lt Gen Reith] is, in any case charged in CDS' Directive with planning humanitarian assistance in theatre should it become necessary.)

"From our point of view ... we have to begin thinking very soon about the practical consequences on the ground of taking on the AOR. These include issues such as: food, water, displaced persons, oil (including accounting for its use), potential Iranian incursions, pollution as well as, in the slightly longer term, Security Sector Reform and reconstruction. Some, if not all of this will of course either determine, or more properly ought to be determined by, strategic considerations of post-conflict Iraqi structures."

1061. Mr Flaherty explained that PJHQ intended to establish a team charged with "developing planning for Phase IV implementation" as soon as possible, which would aim to take into account the lessons of the Balkans and Afghanistan. PJHQ was "in a reasonably good position to link up with US military thinking", but would need more support from other government departments to help produce "a fully joined up approach".

---

[509] Minute Flaherty to DG Op Pol, 7 January 2003, 'Op TELIC: Preparing for Phase IV'.

1062. Sir Kevin Tebbit told the Inquiry that during the shift from a northern to a southern option, he "felt that it was important to reappraise, to pause, to take stock as to what was going on".[510] He added:

> "The planning for post-conflict didn't seem to me to be very robust. As we could read it in the United States, a lot had been done, but it didn't seem to have bite and direction."[511]

1063. On 7 January, the SPG produced a paper analysing the advantages and disadvantages of a southern option.[512]

1064. The SPG advised the Chiefs of Staff that US combat power would deliver military success, but strategic victory would be "successful delivery of aftermath and limiting unintended consequences". The paper stated that adopting a southern option had the potential to:

> "Provide UK with leading role in key areas of Iraq (free of Kurdish political risks) in aftermath, and thus provide leverage in aftermath planning efforts, especially related to:
>
> – Humanitarian effort.
> – Reconstruction of key infrastructure.
> – Future control and distribution of Iraqi oil."

1065. The SPG concluded that adoption of the southern option would mean that the UK was likely to have a discrete AOR established early, with less demanding command and control than in the North. In addition:

> "UK will have made an early commitment to aftermath that will probably demand a commitment for a number of years. This would be hard to avoid in any event, and engagement in South offers significant advantages over possibly being fixed in North with Kurds."

1066. The SPG recommended that the Chiefs of Staff should agree Lt Gen Reith's recommendation for a force package to be deployed to the South.

1067. The analysis underpinning the SPG's conclusions did not appear to include any assessment of the conditions likely to be encountered or the tasks to be performed in either northern or southern Iraq during Phase IV.

1068. Lt Gen Reith introduced his 6 January paper on the southern option at the Chiefs of Staff meeting on 8 January.[513] He explained that:

---

[510] Public hearing, 3 February 2010, pages 24-25.
[511] Public hearing, 3 February 2010, pages 35-36.
[512] Paper SPG, 7 January 2003, 'Operation TELIC – Military Strategic Analysis of Pros/Cons of adopting a Southern Land Force Option'.
[513] Minutes, 8 January 2003, Chiefs of Staff meeting.

"Phase IV would need to begin at the same time as any offensive operations. There was a need for PJHQ to take ownership of Phase IV planning, which should include OGD input. The US were standing up JTF-4, which would be responsible for US Phase IV planning; UK staff were to be embedded."

1069. The Chiefs of Staff noted that there was still a need for the US formally to request any UK ground forces be switched to the South.

1070. Adm Boyce commented that:

"… it was inconceivable that the UK would not play a part in Phase IV operations, which could be enduring … There remained a need to test the plan as a winning concept, but against that caveat … the plan recommended in the paper represented a sensible military option with a valuable task, and … the option should be taken forward."

1071. Mr Bowen reported the discussion to Sir David Manning, emphasising the need for urgent preparatory work if the UK was to take on an AOR.[514]

1072. The military planning assumed a "decision date of 15 February and the start of hostilities in very early March". The UK was being offered an amphibious role at the start of hostilities. Thereafter, US forces would move north while the UK "took on stabilisation of a southern sector which would eventually include Basra".

1073. Mr Bowen concluded:

"While we are now getting more clarity about the shape of US military intentions in an attack on Iraq, and the potential UK role, precious little thought has gone into aftermath planning … [I]f the UK is to take on an Area of Responsibility for stabilisation operations, a lot of preparatory work is needed urgently. MOD have in mind to engage with FCO, DFID & DTI on this."

1074. By 14 January, PJHQ had established a team to examine post-conflict issues.[515]

1075. The PJHQ proposals for improved inter-departmental co-ordination began to take shape later in the month.[516]

1076. A letter from Mr Hoon's Private Office to Sir David Manning on 8 January reported the US offer of "an alternative role for a UK ground force in the South" and described potential roles for UK forces (see Section 6.2).[517]

---

[514] Minute Bowen to Manning, 8 January 2003, 'Iraq: Chiefs of Staff meeting on [8] January'.
[515] Minute Dodd to Manning, 15 January 2003, 'Iraq'.
[516] Minute PJHQ/Hd of J9 Pol/Ops to MA/DCJO(Ops), 20 January 2003, 'Op TELIC: Taking Forward Aftermath Planning'.
[517] Letter Williams to Manning, 8 January 2003, 'Iraq: UK land Contribution'.

1077. The letter proposed that the "final UK Divisional Area of Responsibility, including for aftermath operations, would be an area bounded by the Iraq/Kuwait border in the south, Jalibah airfield in the west, the Euphrates in the north, and the Shatt al Arab waterway in the east – a largely Shia area of some 1,600 sq km[518] [see Map 5 in Annex 4]".

1078. The letter suggested that the proposed UK role in the South "should enable US forces to reach further, faster, whilst providing a coherent transition to aftermath operations – an area of acknowledged UK expertise – in territory captured early in the campaign". Because the proposed UK role would be "crucial to the US plan in the South", it "would place us in a very awkward position if the US seemed likely to want to proceed in circumstances with which we were not content". Further MOD advice would follow "next week".

Cabinet, 9 January 2003

1079. Mr Blair told the Cabinet on 9 January that "the build up of military forces was necessary to sustain the pressure on Iraq".[519]

1080. Commenting on the preparations for the deployment of military forces to the Gulf, Mr Hoon told his colleagues that no decisions had been taken to launch military action. Nor had the US finalised its military planning.

1081. Mr Blair said that Cabinet the following week would "provide the opportunity for an in-depth discussion of Iraq".

1082. Discussion in Cabinet on 9 January is addressed in more detail in Section 3.6.

1083. Lord Turnbull, Cabinet Secretary from 2002 to 2005, told the Inquiry that, when Cabinet met on 9 January, Ministers were told:

> "... nothing was inevitable. We are pressing the UN option. No decisions on military action, whereas you can see that, at another level, the decisions on military action were hardening up quite substantially."[520]

1084. Lord Turnbull added:

> "I could see he [Mr Blair] did not want key discussions of ... who was going to bring what forces to bear where, and there is some sense in that. But the strategic choices that they implied ... didn't get discussed either. For example, the fact that if you have ground forces you become an occupying power."

---

[518] The figure of 1,600 sq km was used repeatedly in policy and briefing papers during January and February 2003. This was mistaken. It should have been approximately 16,000 sq km.
[519] Cabinet Conclusions, 9 January 2003.
[520] Public hearing, 25 January 2011, pages 15-16.

1085. The record of the AHGI on 10 January stated:

> "MOD is to begin work on the practicalities of a possible UK military role in administering immediate post-Saddam Iraq. It was agreed that this work needed to take place in the context of existing contingency planning and with the involvement of other interested departments. As a first step, the CO [Cabinet Office] would copy a complete set of post-Saddam Iraq papers to the MOD."[521]

DFID involvement in UK military planning

1086. One item not recorded in the minutes of the 8 January Chiefs of Staff meeting, but reported separately by Mr Ehrman, was a decision that DFID and DTI would be brought into MOD humanitarian and reconstruction planning, but "without being told US timelines".[522]

1087. Exactly how to engage DFID in military planning remained unresolved. On 8 January, Mr Webb wrote to Mr Lee:

> "The question is now before us of exactly who is going to organise CIMIC and the Civil Transition in any areas occupied by UK forces (let alone the wider problem with the US). It was agreed … today that we need to get DFID in on humanitarian and, with DTI, aftermath aspects of Iraq planning."[523]

Mr Webb added:

> "… I wonder whether we could use a 'wider group' approach in Whitehall that avoids military detail and dates (and I heard an interesting SPG idea for a proper planning conference to kick it off thoroughly) …

> "We might be able to go further subsequently with staff properly posted to PJHQ and the JFHQ [Joint Force Headquarters]. Experience has been generally good of DFID people deploying with JFHQs (especially to 'herd' NGOs) …"

1088. On 13 January Dr Brewer reported to Ms Short "some limited progress with MOD and FCO but not with No.10" in pursuing Ms Short's request "to persuade others in Whitehall that any UK military role in Iraq should focus on providing security for the Iraqi people (a 'stabilisation force')".[524]

1089. Dr Brewer asked Ms Short:

> "Are you content for us to work with MOD on a strategy for a later phase of stabilisation? I know your conception is of a UK military role limited to stabilisation.

---

[521] Minute Dodd to Manning, 13 January 2003, 'Ad Hoc Group on Iraq'.
[522] Minute Ehrman to Private Secretary [FCO], 8 January 2003, 'Iraq: military aspects'.
[523] Minute Webb to DG Op Pol, 8 January 2003, 'DFID Involvement in Iraq Planning and Preparations'.
[524] Minute Brewer to Secretary of State [DFID], 13 January 2003, 'Iraq: A Stabilisation Force'.

We can try to persuade David Manning ... that this should be our exclusive military focus. But it is the Prime Minister himself whose mind needs to be changed.

"You have talked to Suma [Chakrabarti] about the fact that we are still not getting access to all the military planning or intelligence on Iraq. We need to be in on David Manning's regular COBR meetings; I tried before Christmas and failed."

The decision to deploy UK forces

1090. The Chiefs of Staff discussed Phase IV on 15 January. Adm Boyce stated that the challenge would be to match the "top-down" work led by the FCO and the Cabinet Office with the "bottom-up" work in PJHQ.

1091. In view of the need for an urgent decision on military deployment, the Chiefs of Staff updated Mr Blair on the military plan on 15 January (see Section 6.2).[525] Mr Hoon, Mr Powell, Sir David Manning, Sir Kevin Tebbit and others were present. The FCO and DFID were not represented.

1092. The Chiefs of Staff discussed Iraq before meeting Mr Blair. The record of the discussion stated:

"CDS [Adm Boyce] underscored the potential dangers associated with 'catastrophic success' and the implicit need to develop thinking for aftermath management. In planning for Phase IV, the UK was adopting a twin track approach: the FCO and Cabinet Office were leading the top-down strand, and PJHQ was leading the bottom-up effort. The challenge which lay ahead was matching the two pieces of work ... The UK concept at the strategic level was to develop a model that could be offered to the US. It was assessed that the US was still working to an unrealistic assumption that their forces would be 'welcomed with open arms' by the Iraqi people during Phase IV operations, and there was an opportunity for the UK to lead the aftermath debate."[526]

1093. Lord Boyce told the Inquiry that:

"... in talking to senior people within the Pentagon ... there was this expectation that ... the Coalition would be seen as liberating the country and that they would be hugely welcomed ... It was impossible to persuade the people I spoke to, and this was so further down, to some of my subordinates as well, impossible to dissuade the Americans that this would not be the case."[527]

1094. Mr Johnson sent advice and a draft letter for No.10 to Mr Hoon's Private Office on 15 January.[528] He informed Mr Hoon that the Chiefs of Staff endorsed the proposed UK role in southern Iraq. Mr Hoon was advised that a number of issues needed to be resolved before it could be concluded that the US plan represented a winning concept,

---

[525] Minute MA/DCJO to MA/CJO, 15 January 2003, 'Briefing to Prime Minister'.
[526] Minutes, 15 January 2003, Chiefs of Staff meeting.
[527] Public hearing 27 January 2011, pages 76-77.
[528] Minute Johnson to PS/Secretary of State [MOD], 15 January 2003, 'Iraq: UK land contribution'.

including credibility of plans for the aftermath. Mr Johnson described the proposed UK AOR in the South as "a coherent one".

1095. Mr Hoon's letter to No.10 was sent on 16 January.

1096. The Inquiry has not seen any indication of the detailed analysis supporting the conclusion that the proposed AOR in the South was "a coherent one".

1097. Before the meeting with the Chiefs of Staff, Mr Rycroft provided Mr Blair with "some difficult questions" to raise, as suggested by Mr Powell, including on post-conflict issues:

> "–   What military involvement do you foresee in the aftermath?
>
> –   Will we be running Basra?
>
> –   Will the targeting in the campaign take account of the need to run (parts of) Iraq in the aftermath?"[529]

1098. Definitive answers to those questions required cross-departmental advice and collective consideration. There is no indication that other departments were consulted formally before or immediately after the meeting on 15 January.

1099. On 15 January, Mr Blair told the Chiefs of Staff "the 'Issue' was aftermath – the Coalition must prevent anarchy and internecine fighting breaking out".

1100. Mr Blair agreed that much greater clarity was needed on US intentions and asked the MOD to think through the unexpected, including on oil, use of WMD and internecine fighting.

1101. Several accounts of the 15 January meeting were produced by MOD participants, in addition to a No.10 record of the discussion (see Section 6.2).

1102. The "unofficial" PJHQ account of Mr Blair's meeting produced for Lt Gen Reith, who was in the Middle East at the CENTCOM Commanders' Conference, provided the fullest account of the discussion of post-conflict issues. Issues raised by Mr Blair included:

> "Worst Case. The PM wanted to know what CDS [Adm Boyce] thought was the worst case scenario. After much discussion about destroying the oil infrastructure, use of WMD and hunkering down in Baghdad and fighting it out, it was felt that the worst case was internecine fighting between Sunni and Shia, as well as the Kurds/ Turks/Iraqis.
>
> "Aftermath. This led on to a general discussion on aftermath, with the PM asking what the Iraqi view on it was. CDS stated that the thinking on this issue was 'woolly' at this stage, with work only just beginning. The PM stated that the 'Issue' was

---

[529] Minute Rycroft to Prime Minister, 14 January 2003, Iraq: Military Planning: Meeting with Chiefs of Staff'.

aftermath - the Coalition must prevent anarchy and internecine fighting breaking out."[530]

1103. Mr Blair asked the MOD to look at three issues:

> "• We need to be clear on what we are offering the Iraqi people and senior members of the regime (those below the top 100 on the list[531]) – removal of the senior hierarchy or minimising resistance or what?
>
> • Aftermath. We have to develop a feasible plan.
>
> • Look at the unexpected – think through the big 'what ifs'; oil, WMD, internecine fighting – and develop a strategy."

1104. The author of the record added some "personal observations", including:

> "The PM came across as someone with strong convictions that this should, and will, go ahead. He accepted the military advice being given to him, although he still sought reassurance that all aspects had been looked into and that plans are drawn up to deal with the unexpected or perceived worse cases. It is clear from the three areas that he asked further work to be done on that the Phase IV part of the plan is critical.

> …

> "Interestingly it was SofS [Secretary of State, Mr Hoon] who urged the PM to exercise a degree of restraint on POTUS [the President of the United States], whom he described as 'going for it'. SofS expressed concern about some of the US ideas and wanted to ensure that no irreversible damage was done to Iraq."

1105. After the briefing by the Chiefs of Staff, Mr Rycroft informed Mr Watkins that Mr Blair agreed that "much greater clarity about US intentions" on post-conflict issues was needed.[532] Mr Blair "would be keen to see the outcome of the Whitehall visit to Washington next week".[533]

1106. Mr Watkins instructed Mr Lee:

> "… we will clearly need to use all our regular contacts with the US, in both CENTCOM and the Pentagon. If appropriate, this [aftermath] is an issue that Mr Hoon could himself raise with Rumsfeld in their next regular phone call next week."[534]

---

[530] Minute MA/DCJO to MA/CJO, 15 January 2003, 'Briefing to Prime Minister'.
[531] The Inquiry has not seen any indication of what was meant by "the top 100 on the list". It is likely that it was a precursor to the list of 55 Iraqis featured on the "deck of cards" issued by the US military in April 2003.
[532] Letter Rycroft to Watkins, 15 January 2003, 'Iraq: Military Planning'.
[533] A reference to the second round of US/UK/Australia talks on post-conflict issues in Washington on 22 January.
[534] Minute Watkins to DG Op Pol, 16 January 2003, 'Iraq: Military Planning'.

1107. The first record seen by the Inquiry of a discussion of post-conflict issues between Mr Hoon and Secretary Rumsfeld was in Washington on 12 February (see Section 6.5).

1108. Lord Boyce told the Inquiry that his expression of concern to the Prime Minister at the briefing "was more about the immediate aftermath, immediately after the fighting phase, what would we need to do to provide security in the first instance, but also to provide what we saw as being the most immediate problem would be a humanitarian problem".[535]

1109. Lt Gen Reith attended the CENTCOM commanders' conference in Tampa, Florida on 15 and 16 January. The conference was described by Gen Franks as "likely to be the last chance for such a gathering to take place. It therefore had to be conclusive."[536]

1110. Maj Gen Wilson reported that "Phase IV responsibilities became a little clearer" at the commanders' conference: Gen Franks had demanded that JTF-4 deploy as soon as possible to Kuwait and had welcomed Lt Gen Reith's offer to embed four UK personnel in it. Gen Franks had also directed that "key Phase IV players should visit the Pentagon to ensure that planning was joined up".[537]

1111. In his record of the meeting with Gen Franks, Lt Gen Reith explained that UK staff embedded in JTF-4 would have "reach-back" to the Phase IV planning team in PJHQ, giving the UK "considerable influence over US planning".[538] He reported that Gen Franks had "agreed that we could plan on [the] UK having responsibility for the Basra region in Phase IV and would welcome our setting the standard for other nations. Clearly this will need Ministerial approval in due course." Lt Gen Reith also reported that the US had "a zillion dollar project to modernise and properly exploit the southern oilfields".

1112. Gen Reith told the Inquiry that, on 16 January, he told Gen Franks he was unhappy with the way planning was going:

> "... they were going into shock and awe, and we ... the British ... had been very much the custodians of 'Let's worry about Phase IV'. So we got on to Phase IV in our discussion and I made the point ... that the oilfields were absolutely essential for Phase IV, to provide revenue for Iraq for its reconstruction and therefore, we needed to secure the oilfields rather than have them destroyed. I also made the point to him that the more china that we broke, the more we would have to replace afterwards."[539]

---

[535] Public hearing, 27 January 2011, page 83.
[536] Minute Wilson to MA/CJO, 17 January 2003, 'CENTCOM Component Commanders' Conference: 15-16 Jan 03'.
[537] Minute Wilson to MA/CJO, 17 January 2003, 'CENTCOM Component Commanders' Conference: 15-16 Jan 03'.
[538] Minute Reith to PSO/CDS, 17 January 2003, 'Discussion with General Franks – 16 Jan 03'.
[539] Private hearing, 15 January 2010, pages 42-43.

1113. Maj Gen Wilson told the Inquiry:

"General Franks was very clear about the criticality of ... Phase IV [and] understood the need to have the resources available and the need for security and the relationship between reconstruction, humanitarian assistance, disposable funds and ... civil action."[540]

1114. In Cabinet on 16 January, Mr Blair listed priorities for the immediate future:

- **"preparatory work" on post-conflict planning and the role of the UN;**
- **the need to communicate to the Iraqi people a vision of a better life; and**
- **contingency work on the unexpected consequences of conflict.**

1115. The Cabinet discussed Iraq on 16 January. The discussion is also addressed in Sections 3.6 and 6.2.[541]

1116. Ms Short said that work on post-conflict issues needed to be taken forward urgently. She emphasised the need for extra resources, the potential effect of CBW on civilians and the importance of involving the UN.

1117. Summarising the discussion, Mr Blair said that the "priorities for the immediate future were:

- improved communications, which would set out the Government's strategy and be promoted by the whole Cabinet;
- preparatory work on planning the aftermath of any military action and the role of the United Nations in that, which should in turn be conveyed to the Iraqi people so that they had a vision of a better life in prospect; and
- contingency work on the unintended consequences which could arise from the Iraqi use of weapons of mass destruction, environmental catastrophe or internecine strife within Iraq."

1118. Despite Mr Blair's promise that military options would be discussed and the imminence of the formal decision to offer a significant land contribution, Cabinet was not briefed on the substance of the military options or the circumstances in which force would be used. It did not discuss the strategic implications of making a military contribution.

1119. On 17 January, Mr Blair approved the deployment of UK forces to support US military preparation in the region.

1120. He did so without clear advice on the wider strategic implications and contingent liabilities, including the potential UK responsibility for post-conflict administration and reconstruction in the event of military action.

---

[540] Public hearing, 4 December 2009, pages 39-40.
[541] Cabinet Conclusions, 16 January 2003.

1121. Mr Straw advised Mr Blair that much greater clarity was needed on US thinking on post-conflict issues.

1122. Mr Blair concluded that Mr Straw's concerns should not affect his decision to deploy forces.

1123. Mr Hoon wrote to Mr Blair on 16 January seeking agreement to the "key role in southern Iraq" proposed by the US for the UK.[542] The letter, described in more detail in Section 6.2, was copied to Mr Straw, Mr Brown and Sir Andrew Turnbull.

1124. Mr Hoon advised:

"Important questions remain to be resolved … But the role proposed for the UK is a sensible and significant one, and I recommend that with certain qualifications, we accept it. We need to decide quickly."

1125. Mr Hoon added that equipment and personnel would need to be moved early the following week and that, if Mr Blair agreed, he proposed:

"… to announce the composition and deployment of the force in an oral statement on Monday 20 January."

1126. Mr Hoon wrote that the proposed role for the UK was "essentially as described in my Office's letter of 8 January":

"The final UK Divisional Area of Responsibility, including for aftermath operations, would be an area bounded by the Iraq/Kuwait border in the south, Jalibah airfield in the west, the Euphrates in the north, and the Shatt al Arab waterway in the east – a largely Shia area of some 1,600 sq km [see Map 5 in Annex 4]."

1127. Mr Hoon advised that:

"… a number of issues still need finally to be resolved, before we can conclude that the overall US plan represents a winning concept. These include the legal basis for any operation as well as the credibility of plans for the aftermath, which the US accept will begin concurrently with combat operations.

…

"Assuming that outstanding issues can be resolved, I and the Chiefs of Staff are content that the role proposed for a UK ground force is both sensible and attractive. The plan will need further development to address a number of specific challenges (oilfields, displaced persons, handling Iran, etc) …

"The proposed final [UK] Area of Responsibility is a coherent one with largely natural geographical boundaries … and includes economic infrastructure critical to

---

[542] Letter Hoon to Blair, 16 January 2003, 'Iraq: UK Land Contribution'.

Iraq's future, including much of its oil reserves, critical communications nodes, a city (Basra) of 1.3m people and a port (Umm Qasr) about the size of Southampton. Although the establishment of UK control over this area will require careful presentation to rebut any allegations of selfish motives, we will be playing a vital role in shaping a better future for Iraq and its people."

1128. Mr Hoon stated that he had put work in hand to address the "three big issues" identified by Mr Blair at the meeting with the Chiefs of Staff:

- The "nature of the proposition" that was being put "to the Iraqi people including those in the governing apparatus who are not considered beyond the pale, and the way in which that would be conveyed to them without damaging operational security and losing the element of surprise".

- The need "Now that we have a proposed Area of Responsibility" to work on that "with greater clarity". The forthcoming visit of a Whitehall team to Washington was identified as "an opportunity to mould US thinking".

- Making sure the UK had the "best possible contingency plans for worst-case scenarios".

1129. On timing, Mr Hoon stated:

"CENTCOM assume that, unless Saddam changes his behaviour, a political decision to take military action may be made in mid-February. Air and ground operations could begin in early March, with the main effort by ground forces beginning in mid-March (although they still aspire to bring the main effort forward)."

1130. Mr Hoon recommended that the UK:

"… should inform the US that we agree that planning should assume the contribution of the proposed UK land force package to carry out the role the US has requested, subject to:

   i   the overall caveat that a further political decision would be required to commit UK forces to any specific operation;

   ii US assistance in facilitating the bed-down of UK forces, and provision of logistic support;

   iii further work to develop a satisfactory plan for the aftermath."

1131. Mr Hoon highlighted the significance of the post-conflict phase of operations in his advice to Mr Blair, but he did not:

- **identify the risks associated with deploying UK forces before decisions had been made on the scope or duration of their post-conflict role, or on the UK's wider post-conflict responsibilities;**

- **offer advice on what might constitute "a satisfactory plan for the aftermath" or the consequences of failure to reach agreement with the US on such a plan; or**
- **adequately consult the FCO or DFID before submitting his recommendation.**

1132. Mr Hoon should have questioned those omissions before advising Mr Blair on an issue of such significance.

1133. Sir Kevin Tebbit, as PUS, should have ensured that those issues were covered in more detail in the advice put to Mr Hoon.

1134. On Mr Ehrman's recommendation, Mr Straw sent a letter to Mr Blair on 17 January flagging up "three major issues" in Mr Hoon's proposal: targeting, Iraqi use of WMD and the "aftermath".[543] Mr Straw advised that:

> "… much greater clarity is required about US thinking and plans for the aftermath. How long would UK forces be expected to stay in the area of responsibility proposed for them? What would be their role in what form of administration, not least in Basra …? We need in particular far greater clarity on US thinking on management of the oilfields. As you know, we have sizeable differences of view from many in the US Administration who envisage Iraq being a US military governorate for an extended period of time. A UK team will be discussing this issue with the US next week. It will be putting hard questions, and highlighting our own view that there needs to be a move to UN administration, with Coalition forces remaining responsible for security, as soon as possible."

1135. Mr Straw's minute was not sent to Ms Short.

1136. Like Mr Hoon, Mr Straw did not give due consideration to what might constitute a satisfactory plan for the UK and whether UK participation in military action should be conditional on such a plan.

1137. Sir David Manning commented to Mr Blair: "Good questions. But I don't think they affect your decision in principle [to deploy forces]."[544]

1138. Mr Blair replied: "agreed".[545]

1139. Mr Hoon's recommendations were endorsed by Mr Blair on 17 January.[546]

---

[543] Minute Ehrman to Private Secretary [FCO], 16 January 2003, 'Iraq: UK Land Contribution';
Minute Straw to Prime Minister, 17 January 2003, 'Iraq: UK Land Contribution'.
[544] Manuscript comment Manning on Minute Straw to Prime Minister, 17 January 2003,
'Iraq: UK Land Contribution'.
[545] Manuscript comment Blair on Minute Straw to Prime Minister, 17 January 2003,
'Iraq: UK Land Contribution'.
[546] Letter Manning to Watkins, 17 January 2003, 'Iraq: UK Land Contribution'.

1140. The deployment of a UK land package was announced to Parliament on 20 January.[547]

1141. During the Parliamentary debate that followed, Mr Hoon responded to a question about post-conflict planning from Mr Bernard Jenkin (Conservative), by stating:

> "Certainly consideration is being given to aftermath issues and the question of humanitarian relief. Obviously, we will design force packages to ensure that we have soldiers in place who can deal with those issues as and when they arise."[548]

---

[547] House of Commons, *Official Report*, 20 January 2003, column 34.
[548] House of Commons, *Official Report*, 20 January 2003, column 37.

SECTION 6.5

PLANNING AND PREPARATION FOR A POST-SADDAM HUSSEIN IRAQ, JANUARY TO MARCH 2003

Contents

Introduction

1. Sections 6.4 and 6.5 consider the UK's planning and preparation for a post-Saddam Hussein Iraq between late 2001 and March 2003.

2. The two parts address:

- the development of UK post-conflict strategy and objectives;
- planning and preparation to implement those objectives;
- UK civilian and military planning machinery;
- UK influence on US planning and preparation and the impact of US planning on the UK; and
- Parliamentary interest in post-conflict planning and preparation.

3. The two parts do not consider:

- military plans for the invasion, which are addressed in Sections 6.1 and 6.2;
- intelligence on weapons of mass destruction (WMD) or preparations for the post-invasion search for WMD, addressed in Section 4;
- the financial and human resources available for post-conflict administration and reconstruction, addressed in Sections 13 and 15; and
- the outcome in post-conflict Iraq, which is addressed in Sections 9 and 10.

4. This Section covers the 10 weeks between the decision to deploy UK forces and the first post-invasion meeting between Mr Blair and President Bush at Camp David on 26 and 27 March 2003.

5. The preceding period, from mid-2001 to Mr Blair's decision on 17 January 2003 to deploy UK forces to support US military preparations, is addressed in Section 6.4.

6. Key findings for Sections 6.4 and 6.5 are listed at the start of Section 6.4.

7. The Inquiry's conclusions relating to both parts are at the end of this Section.

Second round of inter-agency talks, Washington, 22 January 2003

8. In the run-up to the second round of trilateral inter-agency talks on post-conflict issues in Washington on 22 January 2003, UK officials focused on how to influence US thinking on the post-conflict role of the UN.

9. Mr Peter Ricketts, FCO Political Director, predicted that discussion on the role of the UN would be "hard going". The US was wedded to a prolonged US occupation and opposed to any substantial role for the UN.

10. The first round of US/UK/Australia inter-agency talks on post-conflict issues took place in Washington on 6 November 2002 and is described in Section 6.4.

11. By the first week of January 2003, no date had been set for the second round.[1]

12. The FCO Iraq Morning Meeting on 7 January concluded that Sir David Manning, Mr Blair's Foreign Policy Adviser and Head of the Cabinet Office Overseas and Defence Secretariat (OD Sec), should ask Dr Condoleezza Rice, President Bush's National Security Advisor, to "unblock" the talks if US officials were unable to clear the way for a second round to take place in the week of 20 January.

13. Three days later, the FCO had arranged for the talks to take place on 22 January.[2]

14. Mr Ricketts visited Washington on 13 January. He reported to Mr Jack Straw, the Foreign Secretary, that the US had done good work on humanitarian issues, but was distrustful of the UN and "still clinging to … a wholly unrealistic expectation that they [the US] will be welcomed in as liberators".[3] Mr Ricketts suggested that the forthcoming UK/US/Australia post-conflict talks in Washington and visits by Mr Straw and Mr Blair later in the month were opportunities to influence official and Presidential thinking.

15. Mr Ricketts' report was copied to Sir David Manning.

16. Mr Ricketts' visit also exposed continuing differences between the UK and US on the post-conflict role of Iraqi exiles. During talks with National Security Council (NSC) officials about where to find suitable administrators for post-conflict Iraq, Mr Ricketts advised: "Iraqi exiles were unlikely to come into this category or carry much credibility in Iraq."[4]

17. At the first FCO Iraq Morning Meeting after his return from Washington, Mr Ricketts reported that:

> "… the US show no sign of accepting our arguments on transitional administrations. They are wedded to the idea of a prolonged US occupation, and opposed to any substantial role for the UN. We are likely to find the 22 January day after talks hard going in this respect."[5]

18. On 13 January, US officials briefed the British and Australian Embassies in Washington on US humanitarian planning. The British Embassy reported that the US had "what appeared to be a well researched and internally co-ordinated planning document", focused on the provision of emergency relief by the US military until the UN and non-governmental organisations (NGOs) could resume their activities. The US military would set up a Civil-Military Operations Centre (CMOC) HQ and regional branches. Each branch would incorporate a Disaster Assistance Response Team (DART) and a US Agency for International Development (USAID) presence to facilitate

[1] Minute Chilcott to PS/PUS [FCO], 7 January 2003, 'Iraq Morning Meeting: Key Points'.
[2] Minute Dodd to Manning, 13 January 2003, 'Ad Hoc Group on Iraq'.
[3] Minute Ricketts to Private Secretary [FCO], 14 January 2003, 'Iraq: The Mood in Washington'.
[4] Telegram 47 Washington to FCO London, 14 January 2003, 'Iraq: Day After Issues: Ricketts Visit to Washington. 13 January'.
[5] Minute Tanfield to PS/PUS, 15 January 2003, 'Iraq Morning Meeting: Key Points'.

co-operation with the military. CMOC and DART recruitment was under way. The US was co-ordinating closely with the UN and NGOs, had funded the UN High Commission for Refugees (UNHCR) to pre-position emergency assistance and expected the World Food Programme (WFP) to be a significant partner in the delivery of food.

19. The Embassy also reported that US officials had envisaged that the post-conflict talks in Washington on 22 January would focus on emergency relief and reconstruction, before accepting a UK and Australian suggestion that they also address future political structures for Iraq.[6]

20. The record of a restricted meeting of the cross-Whitehall Ad Hoc Group on Iraq (AHGI) on 14 January stated that the UK and Australia were being given full access to US aftermath planning.[7] The MOD had established a team at the Permanent Joint Headquarters (PJHQ) to examine aftermath issues. Relevant departments would be involved in the team's planning and the MOD would pass papers to the Cabinet Office for wider distribution. The record stated, however, that "without a higher level political and legal framework, MOD planning cannot advance very far".

21. On 14 January Mr Kofi Annan, the UN Secretary-General, announced publicly that the UN had begun humanitarian contingency planning for Iraq.

22. In response to a question at a press conference on 14 January about the humanitarian consequences of war, Mr Annan stated:

> "We have been doing some contingency planning on that and we are extremely worried about the fallout and consequences of any such military action. Obviously we do not want to be caught unprepared. So we have gone ahead and made contingency plans, and we are in touch with governments that can provide some financial assistance for us to move our preparations to the next level. But we are worried."[8]

23. On 22 January, Mr Straw approved the briefing prepared for the UK delegation to the US/UK/Australia inter-agency talks in Washington.

24. The briefing material focused on unresolved differences between the UK and US on the wider post-conflict role of the UN.

25. It envisaged the Coalition military handing over to an interim, civilian administration operating under UN auspices, "as soon as practically possible".

---

[6] Telegram 44 Washington to FCO London, 13 January 2003, 'US/IRAQ: Day After Humanitarian Planning'.
[7] Minute Dodd to Manning, 15 January 2003, 'Iraq'.
[8] UN News Centre, 14 January 2003, *Secretary-General's press conference*.

26. The briefing listed strategic decisions needed "very soon so that planning can proceed":

- **how to establish a secure environment;**
- **how to meet the basic needs of the Iraqi people;**
- **the level of ambition for political reform;**
- **the extent to which economic reform should be left to the International Monetary Fund (IMF) and the World Bank; and**
- **the environmental clean-up plan.**

27. The follow-up to the 6 November US/UK/Australia post-conflict talks in Washington took place on 22 January.

28. In his record of the 17 January meeting of the AHGI, Mr Jim Drummond, Assistant Head (Foreign Affairs) OD Sec, stated that preparations for the talks were on track and that the UK had supplied a number of papers on the main issues.[9] The US had not, so far, shared any papers with the UK.

29. Mr Drummond also stated that the MOD had started its own detailed aftermath planning, "just in case UK forces ended up controlling a part of Iraq". The questions raised would be used "to give a practical edge to the Washington discussions".

30. On 17 January, Mr Dominick Chilcott, FCO Middle East Department (MED), submitted an "Annotated agenda/overarching paper" to Mr Straw.[10]

31. In the covering minute, Mr Chilcott sought Mr Straw's agreement that UK officials should "argue for following a UN, rather than a unilateral, American-led, route on day-after issues" and "make clear that we need broad agreement soon on these issues, so that we can clarify the role which UK forces will play". Mr Chilcott reported that MOD officials were content with that approach.

32. Mr Chilcott explained that the UK had shared a number of papers on post-conflict issues with the US, but had received very little in return:

> "We had hoped that by now US thinking would be beginning to converge. But differences between departments remain as stark as before. At one end of the spectrum, the Pentagon, who regard the UN as irredeemably incompetent, advocate the US leading a day-after operation, co-opting willing allies for an extended period, until a new Iraqi government is ready to take over. At the other end sit the State Department who favour an internationalist approach with UN blessing. The NSC are somewhere in the middle. CENTCOM [Central Command] have set up a large military team to work up plans for taking over the government of Iraq. The risk is

---

[9] Minute Drummond to Manning, 21 January 2003, 'Ad Hoc Group on Iraq'.
[10] Minute Chilcott to Private Secretary [FCO], 17 January 2003, 'Iraq: Day-After Issues'.

that, in the absence of a consensus position on day-after, the CENTCOM plan will be followed *faute de mieux*.

"We believe any unilateral US day-after plan would be seriously flawed. It would lack international legitimacy, as the UN is unlikely to support it. We expect the Iraqis' euphoria at being liberated from Saddam to turn quickly into resentment and anger at being subject to a foreign army of occupation, a sentiment which is likely to be reflected more widely in the Arab world. In a hostile domestic and international environment, it will be more difficult to embed lasting political and economic reforms … All in all, a recipe for a mess, with Coalition forces obliged to stay on in Iraq for years.

"The arguments for following the UN route look compelling and … would be very much in US interests …

"As soon as practically possible, we envisage the Coalition military handing over to an interim, civilian administration operating under UN auspices. With international legitimacy, such an interim administration would be supported in the region and probably tolerated in Iraq. Reforms conducted under its supervision would be more likely to stick. And it would aim to oversee a sort of 'Bonn process'[11] for Iraq, under which the Iraqis themselves would create new political structures … Lasting reform in Iraq will take a long time and the UN is more likely than Washington to have the patience for the long haul.

"The Americans, not unreasonably, refuse to put their forces under UN control … The answer may be a Kosovo model, where parallel security and civilian presences co-exist, both blessed by the UN, with the security forces responsible for supporting and co-ordinating closely with the civil presence but not under UN control.

"We are unlikely to persuade all the agencies in Washington to see it our way on day-after in one session of talks on 22 January. But our aim remains to get an agreed Coalition approach. Without it the legal basis on which our own forces would act will be, at best, unclear and possibly unsafe. We also need broad agreement so that we can plan in detail how UK forces should conduct themselves in the aftermath of military action. The Secretary of State [Mr Straw] will arrive in Washington shortly after our talks conclude. We will … recommend how he might follow up in his talks with Colin Powell [US Secretary of State]. Day after issues should probably be on the agenda for the Prime Minister's meeting with President Bush on 31 January.

---

[11] A reference to the process initiated at the international conference on the future of Afghanistan convened by the UN in Bonn, Germany, in December 2001. At the Conference, Afghan leaders reached agreement on the creation of an Afghan Interim Authority.

"The Australians, as the other troop contributing nation, have been invited to join the day-after talks in Washington. We have spoken to their representatives here in London and understand that they share our strong views on the desirability of action through the UN."

33. Mr Chilcott concluded:

"We have no intention of surfacing this work. But if it leaks, we shall emphasise that it does not imply any change of the policy objectives and that it is simply prudent contingency planning."

34. The 'Annotated agenda/overarching paper' attached to Mr Chilcott's minute stated that "strategic decisions on the issues in this paper are needed very soon so that planning can proceed and a follow-up mechanism [be] agreed".[12] Issues were organised under five headings:

- Security

"An urgent task will be to **establish a secure environment** to facilitate humanitarian operations and to provide the foundation for normal society to flourish and self-sufficient development to begin … We shall need quickly to provide legitimate and transparent law and order and the necessary civil structures, backed by the Coalition military, to deliver it. Ideally, the ordinary Iraqi police should co-operate. But will they? And what is the basis of the law to be enforced – is it Iraqi law or something else?

"We shall also want to prevent internecine violence. Our handling of the defeated Iraqi forces will be critical. We shall need a DDR [demobilisation, demilitarisation and re-integration] plan for them, consistent with our vision for the future of Iraq's armed forces …"

- Relief and reconstruction

"The scale of the challenge will depend on the extent of damage and displacement following conflict and the extent of disruption to oil production … The main humanitarian issues are:

(a) **How will the basic needs of the Iraqi people – food, medicine, shelter, power, emergency reconstruction and protection/personal security – be met?** … Military action will disrupt the involvement of expats and NGOs in the distributions systems … We assume other UN agencies … and the ICRC [International Committee of the Red Cross] would be best placed to cope with refugees, although there may be a period when they cannot get access to them. How advanced is US thinking on civil/military co-operation?

---

[12] Paper Middle East Department, 15 January 2003, 'Second Round of US-UK talks, Washington: 22 January 2003'.

(b) Who will pay for humanitarian operations? What is the future of OFF [the UN-administered Oil-for-Food programme]? … Do the US think there is much potential for Iraq to borrow against future oil revenues to fund reconstruction?

(c) … What plans exist for dealing with zones contaminated by the use of CBW [chemical and biological weapons]?

(d) There will be a need to move quickly from **relief towards reconstruction** and generating local Iraqi economic activity … It will be particularly important to promote security and the rule of law at the local level to allow this to happen."

- Political

"We want S[addam] H[ussein]'s regime replaced with something much better. **How high should our level of ambition be in promoting political reform?** … Is a western-style democracy possible?

…

"We have no prescription for the **shape of a civilian administration (whether or not UN-led)**. But we shall want an arrangement that gives the Coalition military the freedom to operate alongside the UN interim administration, without putting their forces under UN command and control … What sort of courts should we have for bringing individuals in SH's regime to justice?

"A linked question is the extent to which we **replace Iraqis with international civilian** staff in the interim administration. We should probably dismantle the security agencies completely. But many ministries may be turned around with just a few changes at the top … To what extent shall we need to root out Ba'ath Party elements?

"The interim administration will need to set in hand **a process to allow new political structures to emerge**. We shall need visible Iraqi participation in such a process at an early stage. It should be for the Iraqi people themselves to produce the ideas … although the status within Iraq of many individuals in the exile community is low."

- Economic

"The interim administration will also have an important economic reconstruction and reform task. One of the keys to this will be ensuring that **Iraq's oil** revenues are maximised, consistent with the effect on the global oil market. We shall need to consider whether this is best achieved by returning control of Iraqi oil exports from an international civilian administration to Iraq rapidly or in slower time …

"To what extent do we leave the task of **promoting economic** reform … to the IMF/ World Bank? What is US thinking on rescheduling Iraq's US$100bn plus debt?"

- <u>Environmental</u>

"Do we have an **environmental clean-up plan**?"

35. The annotated agenda referred to a number of background papers[13] prepared over the preceding months:

- 'Scenarios for the future of Iraq post-Saddam' (FCO, 11 October 2002);
- 'Security Sector Reform' (FCO, 10 December 2002);
- 'International Administrations for Iraq, what, who and how?' (FCO, 17 October 2002);
- 'Interim Administrations in Iraq' (FCO, 12 December 2002);
- 'Bonn process' (FCO, January 2003);[14] and
- 'Economic issues in Iraq after post-Saddam regime change' (FCO, October 2002).

36. The annotated agenda made no reference to the UK's specific responsibilities in southern Iraq. Nor did it consider the possible contribution of different UK government departments to the UK post-conflict effort.

37. Mr Edward Chaplin, FCO Director Middle East and North Africa, commented to Mr Straw: "After 22 January we will need to raise the level of exchanges with the US, in order to reach agreement on these key issues."[15]

38. Mr Straw approved Mr Chilcott's recommendations and reported that Secretary Powell had told him the US working assumption was that the US and UK would be in Iraq for a long time after military action.[16]

39. The annotated agenda was shown in parallel to Mr Geoff Hoon, the Defence Secretary, and Ms Clare Short, the International Development Secretary.

40. Mr Stephen Pollard, Head of MOD Overseas Secretariat (Sec(O)), invited Mr Hoon to note the intended scope of the meeting.[17] Mr Pollard explained that, in the US:

"… much of the running is being made by CENTCOM, which has set up a large military team to work up plans for Phase IV[18] of the campaign. The MOD are well plugged in to this through our PJHQ representatives at Tampa. But other issues will need resolution at higher level, not least the legal authority for what will amount to an army of occupation following any hostilities, and the extent to which the UN will

---

[13] All but the paper on the Bonn process are described in Section 6.4.
[14] Paper Hetherington, January 2003, 'What would an Iraqi Bonn process look like?'.
[15] Manuscript comment Chaplin, 17 January 2003, on Minute Chilcott to Private Secretary [FCO], 17 January 2003, 'Iraq: Day-After Issues'.
[16] Minute Sinclair to Chilcott, 20 January 2003, 'Iraq: Day-After Issues'.
[17] Minute Pollard to APS/Secretary of State [MOD], 17 January 2003, 'Iraq: Phase 4'.
[18] The military term for the post-conflict phase of military operations in Iraq.

be involved, both in mandating any stabilisation and reconstruction activities and in overseeing them.

"… Unexpectedly, the FCO have just decided that they wish to seek the Foreign Secretary's approval for the general line they wish to take in discussion … that we should be pressing the US to follow a UN rather than a unilateral US-led route, in dealing with day-after issues. The FCO take the line that any unilateral US plan would lack international legitimacy, and that without an agreed Coalition approach the legal basis on which our own forces might operate would be at best unclear and possibly unsafe."

41. Mr Pollard stated that there was "some force" in the FCO argument and that Mr Ian Lee, MOD Director General Operational Policy (DG OpPol), was content to take part in the Washington talks on that basis.

42. Mr Pollard advised that the FCO was likely to brief Mr Straw to follow up the talks with Secretary Powell and was also expected to put post-conflict issues on the agenda for Mr Blair's meeting with President Bush on 31 January. The MOD would be closely associated with the drafting of that advice. Mr Lee would advise on his return from Washington whether Mr Hoon should raise the issue in his weekly telephone call to Mr Donald Rumsfeld, US Secretary of Defense.

43. Sir Kevin Tebbit, MOD Permanent Under Secretary (PUS),[19] commented separately to Mr Hoon:

"My main observation on what is a good paper is that this rather underplays the fissiparous tendencies within Iraq and the risk that groups are as likely to fight each other as Coalition forces. More detailed work is needed in my view on how to keep Kurds, Turkomans, Shia, Sunni and, perhaps Southern Marsh Shia together in one national entity – and indeed to handle those other three groups – people bent on revenge against S[addam] H[ussein]'s regime relics, and the outsiders/exiles who may find themselves less welcome than they expect. All points to the need for a very strong initial security presence, with a clear link to the political reform process. A still stronger case in my view for the US to want a wider Coalition, made possible under UN auspices."[20]

---

[19] In keeping with variations in use within departments, the Inquiry refers to the most senior civil servant in the FCO and the MOD as the Permanent Under Secretary (PUS), but in all other departments as the Permanent Secretary. The Permanent Under Secretaries and Permanent Secretaries are referred to collectively as Permanent Secretaries.

[20] Manuscript comment Tebbit on Minute Chilcott to Private Secretary [FCO], 17 January 2003, 'Iraq: Day-After Issues'.

44. Ms Carolyn Miller, DFID Director Middle East and North Africa and the DFID member of the UK delegation, informed Ms Short that the annotated agenda had been "put together rapidly", but DFID had been able to feed in a number of points, including:

"… the importance of establishing a secure environment for humanitarian aid; the need to factor in the risks of operating if CBW are used; the requirement for affordable financing arrangements for relief and reconstruction especially if OFF collapses; and the importance of moving from dependence on handouts to an Iraq-led economic recovery".[21]

45. Separate MOD briefing for the Washington talks listed questions to which "we must first have answers" before the UK assumed post-conflict responsibilities:

- **the future of the Iraq military, police and local and regional government;**
- **the legal basis for Coalition involvement in civil security;**
- **military sectors;**
- **the military's role in managing oil production; and**
- **when humanitarian agencies would take the lead in providing assistance.**

46. The briefing prepared for Mr Lee, the senior MOD member of the UK delegation for Washington, included "baseline assumptions" for UK force contributions in four post-conflict phases. The briefing stated that, in the absence of a US decision on timelines, the assumptions were only illustrative.[22]

47. The suggested UK land force contribution under each phase was:

- US military administration (0-6 months): war-fighting forces (large scale);[23]
- Coalition administration (6-12 months): large scale reducing to medium scale;[24]
- civil administration (12-24 months): medium scale reducing to small scale;[25] and
- full Iraqi governance (24 months plus): small scale reducing to advisory teams.

48. The briefing stated that the UK military would: "Take regional responsibility for AM [aftermath] operations in our current War-fighting JOA [Joint Operational Area], at least for the first six months." Military tasks would include setting the conditions for successful DDR/SSR (Security Sector Reform) programmes. The military would also support a civil/NGO lead in:

- humanitarian operations, including distribution of food and water, provision of shelter and control of internally displaced persons;

---

[21] Minute Miller to PS/Secretary of State [DFID], 18 January 2003, 'UK/US/Australia talks in Washington: 22 January'.
[22] Minute Sec(O)4 to DG Op Pol, 21 January 2003, 'Visit to Washington – Iraq Aftermath'.
[23] Defined in the 1998 *Strategic Defence Review* (SDR) as deployments of division size or equivalent.
[24] Defined in the 1998 SDR as "deployments of brigade size or equivalent" for war-fighting or other operations.
[25] Defined in the 1998 SDR as "a deployment of battalion size or equivalent".

- support to local government and administration; and
- emergency reconstruction.

49. The briefing included questions to which "we <u>must first</u> have answers" if the UK was to contribute along those lines:

- What should be the future of the Iraqi military, police and local and regional government, and at what level should the Coalition do business with them, "as we will have to do"?
- What would be the legal basis for Coalition forces' involvement in civil security?
- Did the US envisage "sectorisation" as in Bosnia or "central locations and force projection" as in Afghanistan as the model for Phase IV Coalition Force structure? If sectorisation, would the US provide additional forces in the UK sector to perform humanitarian tasks for which UK capacity was limited?
- What role would the military have in managing oil production?
- When did the US assume humanitarian agencies would take the lead in providing humanitarian assistance?

50. On 20 January, Mr William Ehrman, FCO Director General Defence and Intelligence, advised Mr Straw that clarity on US thinking would follow the talks in Washington on 22 January.[26] In the meantime, on a personal basis, he suggested: "we should start to think internally about elements relating to aftermath that might need to go into a future Security Council resolution … Such elements include: aftermath UN administration; oil management; and the future of IAEA [International Atomic Energy Agency]/UNMOVIC [UN Monitoring, Verification and Inspection Commission]."

51. On 20 January, two days before the second round of post-conflict talks in Washington, President Bush confirmed publicly his decision that all US post-conflict activity was to be placed under the leadership of Secretary Rumsfeld.

52. On 18 December 2002, President Bush decided in principle to place the Department of Defense (DoD) in charge of all post-conflict activity (see Section 6.4).

53. That decision was confirmed publicly on 20 January, when President Bush issued National Security Presidential Directive 24 (NSPD 24), consolidating all post-conflict activity in the new DoD-owned Office of Reconstruction and Humanitarian Assistance (ORHA).[27]

---

[26] Minute Ehrman to Private Secretary [FCO], 20 January 2003, 'Iraq: military aspects and aftermath'.
[27] Bowen SW Jr. *Hard Lessons: The Iraq Reconstruction Experience.* U.S. Government Printing Office, 2009.

54. The consolidation of post-conflict planning in ORHA led to a "turbulent" period of adjustment.[28]

55. Mr Frank Miller, NSC Senior Director for Defense Policy and Arms Control, who in summer 2002 had been appointed to head the NSC Executive Steering Group on Iraq in order to "jump-start" US post-war planning (see Section 6.4), recalled DoD officials saying "you guys stay out, we don't need your help".[29]

56. Mr James Kunder, acting Deputy Administrator of USAID, described USAID as "stunned" by the sudden disappearance of the NSC Humanitarian Working Group led by Mr Elliot Abrams, NSC Senior Director for Democracy, Human Rights and International Organizations.

57. *Hard Lessons*, Mr Stuart Bowen's account, as US Inspector General for Iraq Reconstruction, of the US experience of reconstruction between 2002 and 2008, explained that Lieutenant General (retired) Jay Garner, Head of ORHA, faced a range of challenges.[30] They included:

- the practical tasks of staffing, housing and equipping the new organisation;
- lack of access to material produced by the earlier inter-agency planning process;
- ambiguity in the division of responsibilities between ORHA and Joint TaskForce 4 (JTF-4), the separate post-conflict planning unit embedded in CENTCOM; and
- disagreement with General Tommy Franks, Commander-in-Chief CENTCOM, over ORHA's operational independence from CENTCOM.

58. Against that difficult background, Lt Gen Garner succeeded in organising ORHA into three "pillars": humanitarian assistance, civil administration and reconstruction. The humanitarian pillar took on the food programme and disaster relief from the NSC Humanitarian Working Group. The reconstruction pillar started using contracts negotiated by USAID to engage technical experts. The civil administration pillar faced the difficulty of finding credible information about public services and ministry functions in Iraq and was the least well developed of the three.

59. Ms Short described the decision to make the Pentagon responsible for all post-conflict planning as "stunning".[31] She told the Inquiry:

"… if you then wanted the world to come together and support the reconstruction of Iraq, you needed … the military to do their bit, and then you needed to bring

[28] Bowen SW Jr. *Hard Lessons: The Iraq Reconstruction Experience*. U.S. Government Printing Office, 2009.
[29] Bowen SW Jr. *Hard Lessons: The Iraq Reconstruction Experience*. U.S. Government Printing Office, 2009.
[30] Bowen SW Jr. *Hard Lessons: The Iraq Reconstruction Experience*. U.S. Government Printing Office, 2009.
[31] Public hearing, 2 February 2010, page 58.

everybody in, and that's what we were trying to achieve. So to hand it all over to the military is a bit foolish, because your chances then of getting co-operation from the rest of the international system may be diminished."[32]

60. Ms Short also said that:

"... all this enormous State Department planning, which included the danger of chaos and sectarian fighting and so on, was thrown away. ORHA and the Pentagon took over. They believed there wasn't going to be any trouble and people would be waving flowers at them, and off they went. They believed their own propaganda, and the British Government's capacity to think better ... was just subverted and thrown away, to our deep, eternal shame."[33]

61. Sir Kevin Tebbit described some of the consequences of the changes:

"I had numerous ... meetings with very senior people in the Pentagon ... where we were trying to stress the importance of actually getting the right sort of planning in to Phase IV for the aftermath ... where ... they had discarded the State Department's advice, and indeed people ... and I could not get across to them the fact that ... the Coalition would not be seen as a liberation force where flowers would be stuck at the end of rifles ... [T]his was absolutely not accepted, and I think, as far as the Pentagon was concerned ... they just thought that Iraq would be fine on the day ... and everybody would be happy."[34]

62. Sir Peter Ricketts told the Inquiry:

"I think the crucial problems [with post-conflict planning] arose from the late decisions in the US to put a department and an organisation in charge which had not been prepared for this role. I do think, if the careful State Department work had been allowed to feed through into operational planning for the post-conflict phase, that would have been more successful. I think it would have been easier for us to dock with it, and the overall effect on the ground would ... have been a stronger operation from earlier on."[35]

63. Mr Alastair Campbell, Mr Blair's Director of Communications and Strategy from 2000 to 2003, told the Inquiry: "Assumptions were made about the State Department planning." He asserted that: "once we had realised ... that the Pentagon appeared to be taking the lead on almost every level ... the Prime Minister was ... rattling a lot of cages within the British system and asking for an awful lot of things to be done".[36]

---

[32] Public hearing, 2 February 2010, page 61.
[33] Public hearing, 2 February 2010, page 85.
[34] Public hearing, 3 December 2009, page 62.
[35] Public hearing, 1 December 2009, page 92.
[36] Public hearing, 12 January 2010 (afternoon session), pages 69-70.

64. **In his evidence to the House of Commons Liaison Committee on 21 January, Mr Blair emphasised the importance of the post-conflict phase:**

"You do not engage in military conflict that may produce regime change unless you are prepared to follow through and work in the aftermath of that regime change to ensure the country is stable and the people are properly looked after."

65. In his evidence to the House of Commons Liaison Committee on 21 January, Mr Blair stated:

"It is a terrible responsibility ever to commit troops to action, but I believe we were right to do it in both Kosovo and Afghanistan. When I say is it right and is it do-able, is it do-able militarily but also is the aftermath something that you can handle as well, because I think that is important too."[37]

66. Asked about the risks of military action for stability in Iraq and the region, Mr Blair stated:

"That is precisely why part of any preparations is to make clear, firstly that the territorial integrity of Iraq is sacrosanct … and … why we must make sure that we try and do everything we can to follow through. That is why I say military conflict, if it comes to that, is not the end of the issue; there are humanitarian questions, there are questions of what type of government, and all these things have got to be looked at very carefully. We are obviously in detailed discussion with people about them."[38]

67. Asked about the role of opposition groups in a reconstructed Iraq, Mr Blair said:

"I think it is important that we try to make sure that any potential successor government has the requisite stability but, also, has as broad a representation as possible … One of the things I am wary about at this point in time is saying 'Look, this is exactly what we believe should happen' in circumstances where we have not actually got to the point of saying we should have a conflict."[39]

68. Sir George Young (Conservative) asked Mr Blair:

"Is it not the case that actually the more difficult stage is stage two [nation-building], and that is the stage at which we might get more involved. To what extent are you confident that the whole strategy will not be undermined because stage two does not follow through the success of stage one [military action]?"[40]

---

[37] Liaison Committee, Session 2002-2003, *Minutes of Evidence Taken Before the Liaison Committee Tuesday 21 January 2003*, Q 67.
[38] Liaison Committee, Session 2002-2003, *Minutes of Evidence Taken Before the Liaison Committee Tuesday 21 January 2003*, Q 110.
[39] Liaison Committee, Session 2002-2003, *Minutes of Evidence Taken Before the Liaison Committee Tuesday 21 January 2003*, Q 112.
[40] Liaison Committee, Session 2002-2003, *Minutes of Evidence Taken Before the Liaison Committee Tuesday 21 January 2003*, Q 117.

69. Mr Blair replied:

"You do not engage in military conflict that may produce regime change unless you are prepared to follow through and work in the aftermath of that regime change to ensure the country is stable and the people are properly looked after.

…

"I think that if stage one is successful, then you will find that the international community wants to come behind that and make sure the Iraqi people are given the chance to develop free from the repression of Saddam. I expect that there will be considerable international support for that, and it is important that we do it … I think it is extremely important that we do not take our eye off Afghanistan … Getting rid of the Taliban was not the end, for me. The end is Afghanistan reconstituted as a country that has got its own internal system working properly and does not threaten the outside world. In exactly the same way in Iraq, if we come to changing the regime … then I think it is extremely important that we make the most detailed preparations and work within the international community as to what happens afterwards."

70. In his memoir, Lord Mandelson, who had resigned from the Government in January 2001, recalled that, in January 2003, he asked Mr Blair:

"'What happens after you've won? … You can go in there, you can take out Saddam but what do you do with Iraq? You're going to have a country on your hands. I don't know what your plan is. I don't know how you are going to do it. Who is going to run the place?' Tony replied: 'That's the Americans' responsibility. It's down to the Americans.'"[41]

71. Asked by the Inquiry whether the assumption had been that the US would do most of the post-conflict planning, Mr Blair stated that:

"… the Americans, of course, would have the primary responsibility, but let me be absolutely clear I was most certainly not thinking it was to be left to the Americans. The reason why we had done a lot of planning ourselves was precisely because we knew we were going to be part of the aftermath …"[42]

72. The second round of official-level talks between the US, the UK and Australia took place in Washington on 22 January.

73. The talks made little progress.

74. US officials advised that US/UK differences on the role of the UN would need to be resolved between Mr Blair and President Bush.

---

[41] Mandelson P. *The Third Man: Life at the Heart of New Labour*. Harper Press, 2010.
[42] Public hearing, 21 January 2011, page 124.

75. UK participants commented on the small amount of time left to prepare post-conflict plans.

76. On 22 January, Mr Chaplin led an FCO/MOD/DFID delegation to Washington for talks on post-conflict planning with the NSC, State Department, DoD, USAID and an Australian delegation.

77. The British Embassy summarised the outcome:

"Some progress in persuading the Administration of the merits of a UN role – but NSC advise that this will need Prime Minister/Bush discussions to resolve.

"Overall, US Day After planning is still lagging far behind military planning. But they have agreed to two working groups: on the UN dimension; and on economic reconstruction issues. Experts will stay in touch on humanitarian co-ordination, bringing war criminals to justice, and the legality of any international presence in Iraq."[43]

78. The Embassy also reported "confusion" over how the decision to establish ORHA, operating out of DoD alongside JTF-4, would work in practice.

79. On de-Ba'athification, the Embassy reported that Ambassador Zalmay Khalilzad, NSC Senior Director and Ambassador at large to the Iraqi Opposition, had stated that, after Saddam Hussein's departure, top officials in Iraqi ministries should be replaced by "internationals", who would rely as much as possible on remaining Iraqi personnel not tainted by the former regime.

80. Sir Christopher Meyer, British Ambassador to the US from 1997 to 2003, told the Inquiry that, in January 2003, a contact in the NSC informed him:

"… we are going to have to get rid of the top people, Saddam's henchmen, but we can't de-Ba'athify completely, otherwise there will be no administration in Iraq and no school teachers and no nothing and we are going to need some of these people".[44]

81. Mr Chaplin, Mr Lee and Ms Miller produced supplementary reports for their respective Secretaries of State.

82. Mr Chaplin informed Mr Straw that the talks had gone "better than expected", but had revealed that, "as we expected, apart from on humanitarian relief and immediate post-conflict reconstruction, the US have not yet made much progress on a lot of the day-after agenda. Most of the issues have not yet gone to principals."[45] The US "seemed very confident that Coalition forces would have the right in international law to occupy and administer Iraq after a conflict", which was not the view of FCO lawyers.

---

[43] Telegram 89 Washington to FCO London, 23 January 2003, 'Iraq: US/UK/Australia Consultations on Day After Issues: 22 January 2003'.
[44] Public hearing, 26 November 2009, page 98.
[45] Minute Chaplin to Secretary of State [FCO], 22 January 2003, 'Iraq: "day-after" issues'.

83. Mr Chaplin reported that since "military action could start within a few weeks", it had been agreed to have the first meetings of the new working groups the following week, if possible.

84. Mr Lee reported to Mr Hoon that the US was beginning to take the aftermath seriously and was willing to work with the UK and Australia in the various working groups, but there was little time left.[46] During his visit Mr Lee had arranged a call on Lt Gen Garner at which he had said the UK was "keen to be involved" as ORHA took shape. Lt Gen Garner had been grateful and suggested that the UK feed in ideas rather than wait for him to make requests.

85. Mr Lee recommended that Mr Hoon raise post-conflict planning in his next phone conversation with Secretary Rumsfeld in terms that it was a vital issue that needed "to be sorted now because it affects both the UK decision to commit to hostilities … and also international support", and that there was a need for clarity on "who is responsible to whom for what on day after planning and then execution".

86. Ms Miller informed Ms Short that the talks had provided a useful opportunity to deepen understanding between DFID and the MOD. Unlike the US participants, members of the UK delegation had been in agreement on the main lines of policy.[47] She added that support from Australia on the role of the UN and humanitarian concerns had been particularly helpful.

87. Mr Chaplin told the Inquiry:

> "By January 2003, though, as it turned out, that was rather late in the day, though we hoped we would have more time, the Americans were at least listening … So we bombarded the Americans with lots of good advice, we hoped, on the handling of the aftermath and said it needed to be considered, which actually matched pretty well with what the State Department had done."[48]

88. Mr Straw told Secretary Powell on 23 January that the UK expected its troops to be in Iraq for "quite a long time".

89. Mr Straw saw Secretary Powell in Washington the day after the inter-agency talks.[49] The Embassy reported that, in addition to emphasising the need to involve the UN in

---

[46] Minute Lee to PS/Secretary of State [MOD], 23 January 2003, 'Aftermath: Visit to Washington'.
[47] Minute Miller to PS/Secretary of State [DFID], 23 January 2003, 'UK/US/Australia talks, Washington: 22 January 2003'.
[48] Public hearing, 1 December 2009, page 37.
[49] Telegram 91 Washington to FCO London, 23 January 2003, 'Iraq: Foreign Secretary's Lunch With US Secretary of State, 23 January'.

post-conflict administration, Mr Straw responded to a question about how long UK troops would stay, saying:

> "... our assumption was that they would be around for quite a long time. We had gone for the biggest of the three options we had considered ... partly in order to help with the occupation."

90. Before he had seen the record of the Washington talks, Mr Mike O'Brien, FCO Parliamentary Under Secretary of State, set out his views on the creation of a democratic federal Iraq in a note to Mr Straw.[50] Mr O'Brien argued that US plans for a post-conflict "military regime" would "go down badly in the Muslim world". Instead, the period between a second resolution and the start of military action should be used to set out a programme for bringing about a democratic federal Iraq run by Iraqis. He recommended "a major exercise" to bring together opposition groups to negotiate a constitution, with Western assistance, as soon as possible. Mr O'Brien added that a transitional authority "would need to rely on the recruitment of Iraqis from within the Saddam Hussein administration as well as some of the diaspora opposition".

91. Mr Chaplin commented:

> "I have no problem in setting democracy as a goal for Iraq ... But we have to be careful how we present this. To most Arabs 'democracy' means imposing Western style institutions on the Arab world, for our own benefit. It is wiser ... to talk about the application of universal principles such as democratic <u>values</u>, good governance, the rule of law and so on ...

> "My only point of disagreement in Mike O'Brien's analysis is that 'we' ie the Coalition should negotiate a new constitution for Iraq with Iraqi opposition groups. Firstly ... a new constitution must be seen to be developed by the Iraqis themselves. What we will be doing is holding the ring to allow that process to take place. Secondly Iraqi opposition groups are a very disparate bunch. A few of them ... represent a constituency on the ground in Iraq. Most of them represent only themselves."[51]

Follow-up to the inter-agency talks

92. Immediately after the 22 January Washington talks, the Cabinet Office told departments that follow-up work was urgent. Officials were instructed to take the initiative with the US.

93. The AHGI co-ordinated follow-up to the Washington talks.[52]

---

[50] Minute O'Brien to Straw, 22 January 2003, 'Post Saddam Iraq'.
[51] Minute Chaplin to PS/Mr O'Brien, 28 January 2003, 'Iraq: Day After'.
[52] Letter Drummond to Chaplin, 23 January 2003, 'Iraq: Working Groups'.

94. On 23 January, Mr Drummond allocated responsibility for following up the five issues on which the participants in the Washington talks had agreed the need for further co-ordination:

- The role of the UN. The NSC would lead for the US; Mr Stephen Pattison, Head of FCO United Nations Department (UND), for the UK.

- Economic issues. State Department to lead for the US; FCO Economic Advisers for the UK.

- Humanitarian issues. DFID was already working with the NSC and USAID and would continue to co-ordinate with the FCO, MOD and others.

- War crimes. The US appeared to favour a two-tier approach, with the Iraqi legal system trying those suspected of war crimes against the Iraqi people and a different system for war crimes against Coalition Forces, though this was not agreed policy. US and UK lawyers and policy-makers on both sides would discuss, with the FCO in the lead for the UK.

- Rights of the Occupying Power. FCO and MOD legal advisers would pursue with US legal advisers.

95. Mr Drummond added that Brigadier William Rollo, MOD Director of Military Operations, would take forward post-conflict military planning through the British Embassy Washington and links into CENTCOM.

96. Mr Drummond emphasised that the work was urgent. The UK "should take the initiative in arranging the work of the groups" and individual leads should report progress to the Cabinet Office by 7 February.

97. The first meeting of UK members of the UN group was held on 31 January and the first meeting of the economic group on 3 February.[53]

98. UK members of both groups travelled to Washington in the week of 3 to 7 February for inter-agency discussions.

The UK Common Document

99. UK military planners were encouraged by the level of detail in US Phase IV plans presented at the CENTCOM planning conference on 23 and 24 January, but expressed concern about:

- **whether the level of ambition in US planning would be matched by political will and resources;**

- **the underlying assumption that the plan could be implemented without international support or interference;**

---

[53] Minute Dodd to Manning, 3 February 2003, 'Ad Hoc Group on Iraq'.

- **the assumption that the UK military would remain welcome in Iraq; and**
- **lack of clarity on medium- and long-term objectives.**

100. PJHQ proposed a "Common Document" that would be endorsed by the FCO and DFID, to ensure the UK delivered the consistent message needed to influence US post-conflict planning.

101. On 20 January, a PJHQ official provided Major General Rob Fry, Deputy Chief of Joint Operations (Operations), with "a proposed way forward on Phase IV work".[54] The official advised:

"The first issue that we have faced in doing this work is that many (senior) people have been generating ideas to contribute to the Phase IV planning, but to date without a conceptual framework … The result has been a sense of increasing concern that the issue is not being adequately gripped (which in turn has prompted further high level input). To address this and using a slightly modified version of CENTCOM's framework, we have formulated just such a framework and called it 'the Common Document' … The aspiration is that … we will be able to produce a cross-Government agreed UK 'manifesto', from which we would be able to guide subsequent engagement with the US. It also provides a mechanism for systematically identifying issues that need to be resolved.

"… We also need to integrate any SPG [Strategic Planning Group] work that has been done on this subject and cross-check it against UK peacekeeping doctrine … [I]t is in the first instance intended as a planning tool, a mechanism for pooling UK thinking on aftermath. We should not be in the business of doing the thinking, just collecting it and making it coherent.

"… The Common Document has yet to be briefed outside the department, but will need FCO and DFID input to be any use …

…

"Unfortunately time is not on our side, however, and we have an increasing concern about our ability to populate the framework in the time available … We recommend, therefore, that we should hold a week long cross-government planning seminar to help complete the document. Effectively this would be a single 'big-push' to pull together all government thinking on aftermath …

"Overcoming the institutional resistance to such a proposal would also be a challenge … To make it work, we would need <u>active</u> support (not just acquiescence) from the top of MOD, the FCO and DFID (and probably the Cabinet Office). This might take some effort …

---

[54] Minute PJHQ/Hd of J9 Pol/Ops to MA/DCJO(Ops), 20 January 2003, 'Op TELIC: Taking Forward Aftermath Planning'.

"Nevertheless, I think the arguments for pursuing the idea are persuasive. First and foremost is the fact that Iraq seems to be the Prime Minister's Main Effort, and aftermath his chief concern. So far we seem to have little to reassure him. Second, time is not on our side … Third, because of the way this war is being planned in the US, we risk missing a major trick if we do not give the UK components the policy guidance they need to inform the US planning."

102. A joint MOD/PJHQ delegation attended a Phase IV planning conference convened by the US Joint Staff at CENTCOM in Tampa on 23 and 24 January.[55] Participants addressed Phase IV planning in more detail than at the Washington talks on 22 January.

103. The PJHQ record stated that the conference "substantially enhances confidence in US planning", but that:

"Significant strategic issues [are] not yet resolved, including whether the level of ambition evident in US planning will be matched by US political will, and therefore by resources.

"… The strength of the US approach to Phase IV … is that their plan has been prepared in isolation, on the basis that the US needed to be ready to go it 'alone, unafraid and unilateral'. As a result it is clear that they have a detailed operational model that broadly covers all the bases and makes sense. Conversely, the weakness of the US approach is that the plan has been developed on the assumption that it can be implemented without the acceptance of, or interference from, the international community."[56]

104. The MOD participants endorsed the PJHQ assessment.[57] They stated that, although the UK delegation had left Tampa "enormously heartened" by the level of detail in US planning:

"… US military (and other) planners have made a number of very big assumptions (eg that they will remain welcome) in developing plans for delivering success in the aftermath. The lack of clarity on how the medium- to long-term objectives will be delivered, and how these will be conditioned by the short term, was our greatest area of concern."

105. The Chiefs of Staff approved the creation of the Common Document as a means to establish a framework for UK policy that would guide those trying to influence US thinking.

---

[55] Minute DOMA AD(ME) and Sec(0)4 to MA/DCDS(C), 27 January 2003, 'US Iraq Reconstruction Conference – Tampa 23-24 Jan 03'.
[56] Minute Op TELIC CPT Ldr to MA/DCJO(Ops), 24 January 2003, 'Reconstruction Planning Integration Conference held at US Central Command: 23/24 Jan 03'.
[57] Minute DOMA AD(ME) and Sec(0)4 to MA/DCDS(C), 27 January 2003, 'US Iraq Reconstruction Conference – Tampa 23-24 Jan 03'.

106. Lieutenant General John Reith, Chief of Joint Operations (CJO), proposed the creation of a Common Document to "capture the UK's position across the range of Phase IV issues" in a paper for the Chiefs of Staff on 27 January.[58]

107. Lt Gen Reith stated that US planning had developed rapidly. It was based on a single unified plan for Iraq with which Coalition partners would be expected to comply. The US distinction between humanitarian assistance and post-conflict reconstruction remained. USAID/CENTCOM plans for the former were "relatively well advanced", with the "Humanitarian Assistance Plan" already endorsed by President Bush. Reconstruction options were "well-formed on paper", but waiting on key strategic decisions.

108. Lt Gen Reith argued that the UK needed immediate engagement, at the right levels, with a consistent message, if it was to influence US plans. He proposed a document, with DFID and FCO buy-in, that would mirror the terminology used in US planning and set out UK aspirations and potential involvement against each of the current US planning objectives. Without it, it would be "difficult to deliver to our embedded liaison staffs the necessary guidance that they require to shape early US thinking, or to ensure that UK policy guidance is met". That was needed as soon as possible.

109. Lt Gen Reith proposed a two day planning seminar the following week. It would need to be more than a "talking shop". Its aim should be to deliver "an authoritative account of 'UK policy'", to be validated by senior staff from across government before being put to Ministers.

110. The Chiefs of Staff discussed the proposal at their meeting on 29 January. They concluded that "the Phase IV Common Document … would establish a framework UK policy, which would … provide guidance to the embedded UK staffs charged with influencing US thinking".[59]

111. The PJHQ Phase IV planning seminar took place on 5 February and is described later in this Section.

Post-conflict discussions with the French

112. Meetings in late 2002 and early 2003 revealed a strong convergence between senior UK and French officials' views on post-conflict issues.

113. French officials warned that the UK should not let optimistic scenarios blind it to potential problems, including political disintegration.

114. France would want to play a role in post-conflict Iraq, but would not want to "dive into a quagmire".

---

[58] Minute Reith to COSSEC, 27 January 2003, 'Op Telic: UK Approach to Phase IV Planning'.
[59] Minutes, 29 January 2003, Chiefs of Staff meeting.

115. Mr Chilcott visited Paris on 29 January to update the French Government on UK thinking on post-conflict issues. His visit was the latest in a series of contacts between FCO officials and their French counterparts at which post-conflict issues had been discussed.

116. Mr Giles Paxman, Deputy Head of Mission at the British Embassy Paris, had discussed UK thinking on post-Saddam Hussein Iraq with two senior French officials on 16 October 2002.[60] One official was reported to have commented that he:

> "... feared that the removal of Saddam would lead to general anarchy in Iraq with attacks on Ba'ath Party symbols, settling of accounts and widespread violence as in Albania. It might need a relatively authoritarian regime to re-establish order. We should not rule out the possibility that this might be done by the Ba'ath Party organisation."

117. In December, Mr Simon Fraser, FCO Director for Strategy and Innovation, reported that a French interlocutor had:

> "... argued that we needed to think carefully about the potential for political disintegration in Iraq after a war. There could be many unforeseen consequences including political instability motivated by revenge. We should not let the optimistic scenarios blind us to the potential problems. The same went for the wider regional implications."[61]

118. The purpose of Mr Chilcott's visit on 29 January was to be "as transparent as possible" to "prepare the ground in case we had to move quickly on the day after, not least so that the EU should be engaged at that point".[62] Mr Chilcott reported that he was struck by how far UK and French views converged. The officials he had seen were confident France would want to play "a proactive role" in any aftermath, even if they did not participate in the military operation, but they would not want to "dive into a quagmire".

UK military campaign objectives

119. Draft UK military campaign objectives were circulated to the FCO, MOD and DFID in late January.

120. Mr Desmond Bowen, Deputy Head of OD Sec, reported to Sir David Manning that Ministers were "generally content" with the draft, but that there needed to be a lot of work on the objectives covering the period between the end of hostilities and the establishment of a new Iraqi government.

---

[60] Letter Paxman to Fraser, 18 October 2002, 'Scenarios for the future of Iraq after Saddam'.
[61] Minute Fraser to Ricketts, 23 December 2002, 'Planning talks: Paris: 20 December'.
[62] Minute Chilcott to Chaplin, 30 January 2003, 'Day After Talks with the French'.

121. On 22 January, Mr Bowen consulted Mr Lee, Mr Chaplin and Dr Nicola Brewer, DFID Director General Regional Programmes, on draft military campaign objectives.[63]

122. Dr Brewer copied the draft objectives to Ms Short, explaining that the MOD had consulted DFID on three other papers that day: two on the impact of CBW on civilians and a more general paper by the MOD Defence Intelligence Staff (DIS).[64] Dr Brewer observed "signs … that MOD and the military are beginning to take more seriously the humanitarian implications for military planning and of any conflict".

123. Sir Suma Chakrabarti, DFID Permanent Secretary from 2002 to 2008, told the Inquiry that, from January 2002, there were much better links between military and DFID planners: "until that point we didn't have much of an idea of what military planning consisted of and how humanitarian assistance should link into that".[65]

124. Mr Bowen requested written comments on a revised draft of the military campaign objectives on 28 January.[66]

125. Dr Brewer informed DFID colleagues that the revised objectives incorporated the main points she had made at a meeting chaired by Mr Bowen to discuss the draft. Those were:

- the need to highlight humanitarian consequences of military action earlier in the draft;
- the need to factor in "stabilisation" objectives from the start, not just during the "aftermath"; and
- the need for references to essential infrastructure to cover utilities, "especially electricity", transport and key buildings, as well as oil.[67]

126. Mr Bowen sent a revised draft to Sir David Manning on 29 January.[68]

127. The draft incorporated a number of additional written comments proposed by DFID and agreed by Ms Short.[69]

128. Mr Bowen explained to Sir David Manning that the objectives "flow from our policy objectives published on 7 January". They had not been agreed by departments, although Ministers had seen them and were "generally content".

---

[63] Letter Bowen to Lee, 22 January 2003, 'Iraq: Military Campaign Objectives'.
[64] Manuscript comment Nicola [Brewer] to PS/SOS [DFID] on Fax Bowen to Lee, 23 January 2003, 'Iraq: Military Objectives'.
[65] Public hearing, 8 December 2009, page 19.
[66] Letter Bowen to Lee, 28 January 2003, 'Iraq: Military Campaign Objectives'.
[67] Manuscript comment Brewer to Fernie on Fax Bowen to Lee, 28 January 2003, 'Iraq: Military Campaign Objectives'.
[68] Minute Bowen to Manning, 29 January 2003, 'Iraq: Military Campaign Objectives' attaching Paper [unattributed and undated], 'Iraq: Military Campaign Objectives'.
[69] Manuscript comment Short on Minute Bolton to PS/Secretary of State [DFID], 28 January 2003, 'Iraq: Military Campaign Objectives'.

129. Mr Bowen emphasised that those objectives covering the period between the end of hostilities and the establishment of a new Iraqi government needed a lot of work:

"... these would need to go a lot wider in terms of civil administration (involving the UN) and a process for arriving at representative government. Much of this latter area is nowhere near agreed between the US and the UK ...

"It will be important before the Coalition embarks on military action to ensure that we share the same military objectives with the US, otherwise the strategic direction of the campaign risks falling apart ..."[70]

130. Mr Bowen sent a further revision of the military campaign objectives, incorporating comments from Mr Straw and Whitehall departments, to Sir David Manning on 11 February.

Mr Blair's talks with President Bush, 31 January 2003

131. In late January, Mr Blair suggested to President Bush that delaying military action by one month would provide additional time to work up more coherent post-conflict plans.

132. Mr Blair sent President Bush a Note on 24 January, in which he wrote that the biggest risk they faced was internecine fighting in Iraq when a military strike destabilised the regime.[71]

133. Mr Blair also listed a number of potential advantages in delaying military action by one month to late March/early April, including the additional time that would allow for working up more coherent post-conflict plans.

134. Sir David Manning told the Inquiry that delay would have opened "all sorts of possibilities", including an awareness of the risks being run by setting up ORHA very late.[72]

135. Ms Short commented that, given the lack of preparedness, she expected the date to be put back: "I wouldn't have believed we would go that quickly, given how unready everything was."[73]

136. FCO briefing for Mr Blair's meeting with President Bush on 31 January advised Mr Blair to make two points: that "the US needs to pay much more attention, quickly, to planning on 'day after' issues; and that the UN needs to be central to it".

---

[70] Minute Bowen to Manning, 29 January 2003, 'Iraq: Military Campaign Objectives' attaching Paper [unattributed and undated], 'Iraq: Military Campaign Objectives'.
[71] Letter Manning to Rice, 24 January 2003, [untitled] attaching Note Blair.
[72] Public hearing, 30 November 2009, page 85.
[73] Public hearing, 2 February 2010, page 64.

137. Officials explained that operational planning was constrained by the continuing absence of an overall framework for post-conflict Iraq.

138. Section 3.6 describes the range of advice prepared for Mr Blair's meeting with President Bush on 31 January.

139. Advice on post-conflict issues was included in a number of documents prepared separately by the FCO, the MOD, the Cabinet Office and DFID.

140. Briefing prepared by the FCO included in its list of objectives: "To convince President Bush … the US needs to pay much more attention, quickly, to planning on 'day after' issues; and that the UN needs to be central to it."[74] Key messages included:

"– Our officials … need agreement from us [Mr Blair and President Bush] on overall framework to carry out operational planning.

– Coalition needs an overall 'winning concept'. Should embrace both military action and 'day-after' administration in Iraq. Would be pointless and damaging to win war and lose peace.

– Would be irresponsible to abandon Iraq quickly after toppling Saddam. Risk of civil war would be real. And Iraq's neighbours would get dragged in, creating instability in the whole region.

– We must leave Iraq and region better off after our intervention. As well as disposing of Iraq's WMD and its oppressive security forces that means presiding over wide political and economic reforms. Will take time to introduce and take root, and will go beyond a military occupation. So international community is in for long haul.

– All the evidence from the region suggests that Coalition forces will not be seen as liberators for long, if at all. Our motives are regarded with huge suspicion. The Iraqis, including those in exile, (and the Arabs more generally) want us gone quickly. Our occupation and administration of Iraq will become more unpopular and its lawfulness more debatable, the longer it continues.

– Blunt fact is that in those circumstances any reforms are unlikely to stick. Iraqis will need legitimate international presence holding the ring while they themselves set up new, Iraqi, structures. Can't foist these on them. Iraqi opposition groups can be involved but should not be parachuted into power.

– So we should plan to keep period of government by military Coalition as short as possible, and introduce quickly an international administration with UN blessing.

---

[74] Paper Middle East Department, 30 January 2003, 'Prime Minister's visit to Camp David, 31 January: Iraq'.

- Our joint irritation at some aspects of the UN should not blind us to the significant advantages it can bring in Iraq after the conflict.

  - Iraqis more likely to accept a UN-mandated transitional administration than a Coalition or US one. Same goes for Arab world …

  - By reducing hostility to the Coalition UN route reduces risk that our actions serve as a recruiting sergeant for Islamist terrorist organisations.

  - Makes sense for UN to be in charge of oil revenues to avoid accusations that aim of military action was to get control of oil.

  - UN provides best forum for managing humanitarian agencies …

  - UN will make it easier for other countries to support practically and politically, reforms we want.

  - By making burden sharing easier, UN provides the best prospect of a clean exit strategy.

  - UN has the stamina to stay in Iraq for a long time, which will be needed for our ambitious reforms to stick.

- UN's record on transitional administrations is not perfect. But getting better with experience …

- Understand US concern to keep control of military and security issues. Agree UN should not take this on – at least, not at first …

- … Can get best of both worlds: UN legitimisation and freedom of action with a UNSC [UN Security Council] mandate …

- UNSG [UN Secretary-General] must appoint right Special Representative …

- Restoring oil production will be an immediate challenge. Oil sector will need some technology and a lot of capital. We must encourage an open investment regime and a level playing field for foreign companies.

- Our media and Parliament have not yet focused on day-after questions. But it would be very difficult to sustain a UK contribution to day-after if our occupation of Iraq were opposed, in Iraq and in region. Don't want a repeat of the 1920s."

141. The background note stated that US hostility to the UN:

"… should not be allowed to prejudice the Coalition against the crucial advantages it brings. Putting the UN in the centre of reforming Iraq, after the Coalition topples Saddam is as important as following the UN route to disarm Iraq.

"The way to present the case is to focus on the practical advantages of involving the UN. But there is also the question of international legitimacy. We shall need UNSC authorisation for practical purposes eg any change to the sanctions regime and to the Oil-for-Food arrangements, as well as for the far-reaching reforms we plan to introduce to Iraq. The lawfulness of an occupation, post-conflict, will also be related to the lawfulness of the military action itself."

142. The note stated that the US was "putting a huge effort into humanitarian relief and immediate post-conflict reconstruction, which the military expect to control", but US thinking on the transition between Coalition military administration and the transfer of power to a new Iraqi government was "bogged down in inter-agency disputes".

143. On Iraqi exiles, the background note stated that they "can join the debate on Iraq's future but will have to test their credibility with the Iraqi people, not be parachuted in by the US/UK".

144. The background note concluded that Mr Blair's visit was well timed to influence US planning:

"Without agreement, which can only come from President Bush and the Prime Minister, on the overall framework for day-after, operational planning will continue to be handicapped."

145. The briefing provided by the MOD included a section on "aftermath".[75] Suggested lines for Mr Blair to use with President Bush included:

- There was no doubt the Coalition could win the war, but it was "equally certain that we face a risk of 'losing the peace'".
- Any post-conflict honeymoon would be brief, if it occurred at all.
- Strategic questions about future governance were not academic and needed answering quickly.
- Choices made early in the campaign "can shape – often irrevocably – our options months, even years later".

146. The short Cabinet Office paper from Mr Drummond offered a "few OD Sec points, just in case they slip through the briefing".[76] Those included:

- the importance of offering a clear public vision for the future of Iraq;
- the need to press for agreement on the post-conflict role of the UN;
- the importance of integrated Coalition planning on post-conflict issues;
- the need for "top political impetus" on post-conflict issues;

---

[75] Letter Williams to Rycroft, 29 January 2003, 'Prime Minister's briefing – Iraq' attaching Paper [unattributed and undated], 'Iraq – Aftermath'.
[76] Minute Drummond to Rycroft, 28 January 2003, 'Iraq: US Visit'.

- the importance of transparent use of oil revenues; and
- the need to argue for a level playing field for UK companies on new oil exploration contracts.

147. In response to a request from Mr Blair, Mr Chaplin provided additional briefing on:

- The humanitarian situation – described as "the one area where US Day After planning is reasonably advanced". Mr Chaplin attached a short note from DFID listing three key issues from a humanitarian and developmental perspective:
  - ○ refining the military options to minimise civilian suffering, damage to essential services and disruption to existing humanitarian systems;
  - ○ a leading UN role in relief and reconstruction as soon as possible;
  - ○ agreement on affordable financing mechanisms for relief and reconstruction.[77]
- Options for a second resolution (see Section 3.6). Mr Chaplin attached a note from UND suggesting additional material for a second resolution, which would affirm the Security Council's willingness to take on the post-conflict administration of Iraq.[78] The proposed material was close to that in resolution 1244 (1999) establishing a UN administration in Kosovo.
- UN involvement in the aftermath, where the UK delegation had made "some impact" in the talks on 22 January, but which was "only likely to make progress if the US side gets a signal from the President to take it seriously".[79]

148. Mr Chaplin advised that, even if the US remained unwilling to endorse a UN administration specifically in a second resolution, it might be possible to agree compromise language, "including reaffirmation of commitment to Iraq's sovereignty and territorial integrity, the UN's readiness to help facilitate a political process to encourage the development of new institutions, readiness to mobilise resources for the reconstruction of key infrastructure, protection of human rights, the safe return of refugees and so on".

149. In his diaries, Mr Campbell described preparations for the meeting between Mr Blair and President Bush, including the preparation of a further Note on the strategy (see Section 3.6).[80]

150. A four-page document entitled 'Countdown' appears in the No.10 files for 30 January 2003.[81]

---

[77] Paper DFID, 30 January 2003, 'Briefing for Prime Minister's Meeting with President Bush'.
[78] Paper UND, 30 January 2003, 'Iraq: Second Resolution – Additional Elements'.
[79] Letter Sinclair to Rycroft, 30 January 2003, 'Iraq: Prime Minister's visit to Camp David, 31 January: Additional Briefing' attaching Paper Chaplin, 30 January 2003, 'Prime Minister's visit to Camp David, 31 January: Iraq'.
[80] Campbell A & Stott R. *The Blair Years: Extracts from the Alastair Campbell Diaries*. Hutchinson, 2007.
[81] Note [Blair to Bush], [undated], 'Countdown'.

151. The Cabinet Office could not confirm the origin of the document but it appears to be the Note referred to by Mr Campbell and has manuscript additions in Mr Blair's hand.

152. The document comprised a series of headings with very short bullet points, including "Aftermath Questions":

- What would happen immediately, "a new Iraqi government or US run?"
- What type of Iraqi government would be the aim in the medium term?

153. Mr Blair raised aftermath planning issues with President Bush and Dr Rice in Washington on 31 January.[82]

154. Mr Blair was told that detailed planning on humanitarian issues was progressing well, but a dilemma remained over how to handle the transition to civil administration and what sort of Iraqi government should emerge. Mr Blair suggested that a UN badge was needed for what the US and UK wanted to do, and would help with the humanitarian problems.

155. The minutes of the 3 February FCO Iraq Morning Meeting stated that the talks between Mr Blair and President Bush had not focused on day after issues and that the MOD had "flagged up the urgent need for progress on the key questions".[83]

156. Mr Blair's comments to President Bush did not convey the full extent of UK concerns about the state of post-conflict planning.

157. Section 6.4 explains that Mr Hoon had advised Mr Blair on 16 January that:

- **"a satisfactory plan for the aftermath" was needed before any decision to use UK forces deployed to the region; and**
- **a US political decision on military action could be taken in mid-February, with operations beginning in mid-March.[84]**

158. By 31 January, time was running out to ensure that, before the conflict began, there was an agreed US/UK plan for the post-conflict administration and reconstruction of Iraq.

159. Mr Blair's conversation with President Bush represented a missed opportunity to exert pressure on the US to add necessary impetus to that task.

---

[82] Letter Manning to McDonald, 31 January 2003, 'Iraq: Prime Minister's Conversation with President Bush on 31 January'.
[83] Minute Tanfield to PS/PUS [FCO], 3 February 2003, 'Iraq Morning Meeting: Key Points'.
[84] Letter Hoon to Blair, 16 January 2003, 'Iraq: UK Land Contribution'.

160. Nor did Mr Blair take prompt action after his conversation with President Bush. His next interventions on post-conflict planning were:

- **to tell Cabinet on 6 February that post-conflict planning "needed greater emphasis"; and**
- **to convene a first Ministerial meeting on humanitarian issues on 13 February, a meeting that did not address wider post-conflict concerns.**

161. Mr Blair did not raise post-conflict issues again with President Bush until his Note of 19 February and did not discuss the subject with him until 5 March.

162. During the talks in Washington Dr Rice handed Sir David Manning two documents:

- 'Iraq Relief and Reconstruction Planning', a document dated 7 January prepared by Mr Abrams' inter-agency Humanitarian Working Group; and
- 'Immediate Post-War Concerns', a document dated 31 January incorporating an updated version of the US strategy document 'Iraq: Goals, Objectives, Strategy' (see Section 6.4).[85]

163. Sir David Manning asked the FCO, the MOD, the Joint Intelligence Committee (JIC) and the Cabinet Office for comments on the two documents. DFID was not consulted.

164. Mr Drummond proposed using a special meeting on "aftermath" scheduled to replace the AHGI on 7 February to co-ordinate a response.[86] He suggested that the agenda also cover:

- "State of preparedness" on a range of issues including the political process, oil, humanitarian issues and SSR;
- "Timetable for completion of work"; and
- "Gaps".

165. The meeting on 7 February appears to have focused on preparing key messages on post-conflict issues for Mr Hoon and Sir David Manning to put to Secretary Rumsfeld and Dr Rice in Washington on 12 February.[87] The Inquiry has seen no evidence that it addressed the other agenda items.

---

[85] Letter Manning to McDonald, 2 February 2003, 'Iraq: Post-War Reconstruction Planning' attaching Paper [unattributed], 7 January 2002 [sic], 'Iraq Relief and Reconstruction Planning' and Paper [unattributed], 31 January 2003, 'Immediate Post-War Concerns'.
[86] Letter Drummond to Chaplin, 4 February 2003, 'Iraq: Aftermath'.
[87] Letter Drummond to Chilcott, 10 February 2003, 'Iraq: Key Messages'.

Official-level discussions with the US

166. On 29 January the US asked whether the UK would be prepared to take the lead on restoring Iraq's judicial system and police force in the two months after regime change.

167. The US also requested that the UK help it "get to grips" with war crimes.

168. Mr Straw instructed officials to help on judicial and police issues "as much as possible", but "on the basis of what is practical".

169. On 29 January, Mr Peter Gooderham, Political Counsellor at the British Embassy Washington, reported that the NSC had asked whether the UK, as one of the Occupying Powers, would be willing to take lead responsibility for getting the Iraqi judicial system and police "up and running within 60 days" of regime change, and whether someone from the UK could spend a week in Washington to help "get to grips" with war crimes.[88] The US would want the Coalition to deal with war crimes committed by Iraqis during hostilities, but questions remained about prosecution of crimes from previous conflicts. The NSC had been given two weeks to come up with answers.

170. FCO officials advised Mr Straw that two junior officials planned to visit Washington the following week to develop a joint policy on war crimes with the US, but that taking lead responsibility for the judicial system and the police would be:

> "… a massive undertaking, with implications for the UK's role as an 'Occupying Power', that should more properly be an international effort, mandated by the UN. So we shall avoid getting drawn on this request."[89]

171. The FCO advice was copied to the Cabinet Office, but not to any other department.

172. On 3 February, Mr Straw instructed that the UK "should help the US on police and judicial matters as much as possible", but accepted that "this help has to be on the basis of what is practical".[90] He requested further advice after the next round of US/UK talks on post-conflict issues.

173. UK support for SSR and judicial issues is addressed in Section 12.

174. At the trilateral UK/US/Australia UN working group on 5 February, the US rejected UK compromise proposals for a hybrid governance structure in Iraq that might satisfy US and UK views on the role of the UN.

---

[88] Letter Gooderham to Chaplin, 29 January 2003, 'Iraq: Day After: US Requests for Assistance on Judicial Issues'.
[89] Minute UND [junior official] to Private Secretary [FCO], 31 January 2003, 'Iraq the Day after – US Requests for Assistance on Judicial Issues'.
[90] Minute [FCO junior official] to UND [junior official], 3 February 2003, 'Iraq the Day after – US Request for Assistance on Judicial Issues'.

175. Dr Rice was firm: there could be no high-level UN administrator or UN involvement in running even technical Iraqi ministries.

176. At the meeting of the trilateral UN working group in Washington on 5 February, the UK delegation, headed by Mr Pattison, shared preliminary UK thinking on the potential scope and structure of UN involvement in a transitional civil administration with a US inter-agency team led by Mr Abrams.[91]

177. Mr Pattison reiterated that the UK believed that UN involvement in post-conflict administration would produce political and practical benefits including:

- local support for an international reforming presence;
- the potential for burden sharing and "capturing expertise"; and
- better prospects for an exit strategy.

178. The UK understood that the US would seek to maintain freedom of operations on security, SSR and the pursuit of WMD and war criminals, but the UK believed that it was possible to devise a "hybrid" structure that would meet UK and US concerns and achieve a prosperous, stable and representative Iraq. Mr Pattison added that "UN involvement in an international presence was a top priority for the UK as the Prime Minister had told Bush".

179. The UK presented elements of a draft Security Council resolution, emphasising that these did not represent an agreed UK position. Key elements included:

- a Coalition security presence with a broad security mandate, headed by a US general;
- a civilian transitional administration with a defined reformist mandate and monitoring function, headed by a UN executive administrator;
- a separate political process involving a Special Representative of the Secretary-General along the lines of the Bonn (Afghanistan) or Dayton (Bosnia Herzegovina) models;
- a consultative mechanism to involve the Iraqi people; and
- a Joint Implementation Board (JIB) consisting of representatives of the international security presence and international civilian presence.

180. Mr Abrams commented that the UK seemed to envisage a much larger role for the UN than the US had been considering. The US continued to be cautious about embracing a more extensive role for the UN and was sceptical about the UN's ability to deliver.

---

[91] Telegram 167 Washington to FCO London, 5 February 2003, 'Iraq: US/UK/Australia talks on "Day After" Issues'.

181. After the talks, Mr Tony Brenton, Deputy Head of Mission at the British Embassy Washington, explained to Mr Abrams that the UK "very much hoped" to be consulted before the US took decisions on areas in which the UK had "a crucial interest", including the post-conflict role of the UN and governance of the Iraqi oil sector. Mr Abrams suggested that Sir David Manning should ask Dr Rice to share emerging US thinking.

182. The British Embassy reported the next day that Mr Abrams had discussed the UN role with Dr Rice.[92] Her view was firm: the US agreed that some kind of UN mandate should be sought as the basis for post-conflict Coalition activity, but there was no question of any high-profile UN role in administering the country. UN agencies' contribution to humanitarian relief and reconstruction would be crucial, but there could be no high-level UN administrator or UN involvement in running even technical Iraqi ministries.

183. After the first meeting of the trilateral economic working group, UK officials reported that DoD had prepared detailed contingency plans for Iraq's oil industry, but that there was "a conspicuous disconnect" between those plans and civilian planning for economic development and management.

184. The UK delegation to the meeting of the trilateral economic working group in Washington on 5 February included representatives of the FCO, DFID, the Treasury, the British Embassy and the UK Delegation to the IMF/IBRD (International Bank of Reconstruction and Development).[93] The US delegation included a team from the State Department and representatives of DoD, USAID, the NSC and the US Treasury.

185. The British Embassy reported that the working group had agreed to co-operate on defining practical economic steps to be taken in the first three to six months of military occupation. The UK would contribute its ideas by 14 February.

186. US thinking on short-term reconstruction was reported to be at an early stage. Little thought had been given to the financing gap that might arise if Iraqi oil output were severely constrained.

187. The Embassy reported that DoD had detailed contingency plans to protect and restore the oil sector and was well aware of the importance of that sector for reconstruction. In the best case (minimal damage, current levels of output restored after two to three months) it estimated that the sector could make a net contribution of US$12bn in the first year after any conflict; in the worst case it could be a net cost of US$8bn.

---

[92] Telegram 172 Washington to FCO London, 6 February 2003, 'Iraq: Day After'.
[93] Telegram 169 Washington to FCO London, 6 February 2003, 'Iraq: Meeting of Trilateral Working Group on "Day After" Economic Issues: Short Term Reconstruction'.

188. The Embassy also reported that US planning on longer-term external financing had made little progress.[94] The US recognised the difficult external financial challenges that were facing Iraq in the longer term and agreed to the early informal involvement of international financial institutions (IFIs). It favoured rescheduling rather than forgiveness of Iraq's Paris Club debt and inclined towards extending rather than cancelling compensation payments for damage caused by the 1991 invasion of Kuwait.

189. The UK delegation stressed that early progress was important. Donors needed some certainty about Iraqi liabilities before they would be prepared to commit substantial new resources.

190. The FCO member of the UK delegation, the Economic Adviser for the Middle East and North Africa, reported separately to Mr Drummond that the UK participants had stressed that a substantial UN role in the transitional post-conflict administration was "not only politically important but crucial to hopes of effective financial burden-sharing and key to the early attraction of investment in the oil sector".[95] He added:

> "DoD are ploughing ahead with detailed contingency planning for the oil sector in the initial military administration phase. But – apart from USAID preparations on the humanitarian side – there was a conspicuous disconnect between this and civilian planning for economic management and policy development within Iraq ..."

191. The FCO delegate reported that it had also been agreed that the UK and US would approach the IMF and IBRD separately to make clear there was a major role for both organisations and to encourage them to step up their analysis and contingency planning.

DFID humanitarian contingency planning

192. The House of Commons debated humanitarian contingency planning on 30 January.

193. Ms Short explained that:

- **The international community needed to agree that the UN should lead on post-conflict reconstruction.**
- **Preparations by UN humanitarian agencies were as good as could be expected, but the international humanitarian system was "under considerable strain".**
- **DFID would play its part in the humanitarian system, but its own resources were limited.**

---

[94] Telegram 170 Washington to FCO London, 6 February 2003, 'Iraq: Meeting of Trilateral Working Group on "Day After" Economic Issues: External Finance Issues'.
[95] Teleletter FCO [junior official] to Drummond, 6 February 2003, 'Iraq: Meeting of US/UK/Australian Working Group on "Day After" Economic Issues: Assessment and Follow Up'.

194. On 30 January, Mrs Caroline Spelman, Opposition spokesperson for International Development, introduced an Opposition Day debate in the House of Commons on humanitarian contingency planning. She contrasted the Government's "worrying silence" on humanitarian aspects of war in Iraq with the numerous statements from Mr Hoon and Mr Straw on the military build-up and diplomatic activity, and sought reassurances from Ms Short that there were "comprehensive humanitarian contingency plans" in place.[96]

195. In response, Ms Short stated:

"It is necessary to prepare to minimise harm if military action is taken and to make arrangements for the reconstruction of the country as rapidly as possible. To achieve that, we need to ensure that the UN takes the lead in the reconstruction, as it did in Kosovo, East Timor and Afghanistan. That needs to be agreed across the international community."

196. Ms Short explained that:

"All parties have recently been more willing to prepare for all contingencies, including the military in the United States of America, but it has not been easy to get discussions and analysis going across the international system to prepare for all those. Anyone who pauses to reflect intelligently on the strains and tensions across the international system because of the crisis would realise why that has been difficult … but my department has been working for a considerable time on all contingencies. That work is developing and we are getting more co-operation from some of our international partners which was difficult to get before."

197. Ms Short reported that Iraq's infrastructure was:

"… in chronic disrepair. Hospitals, clinics, sanitation facilities and water treatment plants suffer from a terrible lack of maintenance. The result is that the Iraqi people's lives are perilously fragile. Their coping strategies have been worn away by years of misrule. The public facilities to help them cope are run down, often to the point of uselessness."[97]

198. Preparations by UN humanitarian organisations and the UN Office for the Co-ordination of Humanitarian Affairs (OCHA) were "as good as they can be", but given the number of risks and uncertainties, it was very difficult to prepare.

199. Ms Short set out five humanitarian risks of military action:

- the "very serious risk" of "large-scale ethnic fighting";
- damage to water and sanitation facilities as a result of attacks on electricity supplies to Iraqi anti-aircraft facilities;

---

[96] House of Commons, *Official Report*, 30 January 2003, columns 1042-1043.
[97] House of Commons, *Official Report*, 30 January 2003, columns 1053-1054.

- environmental damage and delays to reconstruction because of booby-trapped oil installations;
- disruption to OFF; and
- use of CBW.

200. Ms Short added that collaboration between military and humanitarian planners needed to keep improving.[98] She warned that the international humanitarian system was "under considerable strain" with:

> "… enormously complicated problems with drought and food shortages in southern Africa, the horn of Africa and Angola. Every day five million people in Afghanistan need food aid, and the humanitarian situation on the west bank and Gaza is very serious and getting worse. My department's resources and those of the international humanitarian system are therefore strained."

201. In response to a question from Mr Crispin Blunt (Conservative) about the resources available to DFID, Ms Short explained that the UK contribution to any international humanitarian crisis, as determined by the Organisation for Economic Co-operation and Development (OECD), was just over 5 percent of the total. She cautioned that, faced with demands elsewhere, the international humanitarian system and DFID's own budget were strained: "We will play our part in the international system, but the Department is not flush with resources – I must frankly warn the House that they are short."[99]

202. At the end of January, officials advised Ms Short that the UK might be expected to make a contribution to humanitarian relief and reconstruction in Iraq that was much larger than DFID's contingency reserve.

203. On 21 January, at Ms Short's request, Mr Alistair Fernie, Head of DFID Middle East and North Africa Department, advised "how to maximise the chances of securing additional funding from the Treasury to cover the costs of [a] DFID humanitarian response".[100]

204. Mr Fernie recommended that Ms Short should speak, rather than write, to Mr Gordon Brown, the Chancellor of the Exchequer. A letter would invite a formal response, and Treasury officials were likely to caution Mr Brown against providing any broad assurance on funding and might recommend that DFID "unpick" its 2003/04 spending plan, to be agreed shortly, in order to provide more funding for Iraq.

---

[98] House of Commons, *Official Report*, 30 January 2003, columns 1055-1056.
[99] House of Commons, *Official Report*, 30 January 2003, columns 1057-1058.
[100] Minute Fernie to PS/Secretary of State [DFID], 21 January 2003, 'Iraq contingency planning: financial provision'.

205. Mr Fernie continued:

"Mr [Mark] Lowcock's [DFID Director Finance and Corporate Performance] advice is that the best time to extract maximum funds from the central Reserve is when the political pressure is at its height. We might guess that such a time will come in a month or so – by which time budgets for our existing programmes would be more secure, with our 2003/04 framework finalised and on its way to publication."

206. Ms Short commented: "No – I don't want to ring Ch X [the Chancellor of the Exchequer] … I wanted to put humanitarian considerations into Gov[ernment] mind not just to squeeze some money."[101] Rather than write or speak to Mr Brown, she would write to Mr Blair. That letter was sent on 5 February.[102]

207. On 31 January, in response to a further request from Ms Short, a DFID official provided advice on how much the UK might be expected to contribute to "humanitarian relief/reconstruction" in Iraq.[103] Assuming the UK provided 5.6 percent of the total humanitarian/reconstruction costs (in line with the UK's share of OECD Gross National Income), the UK's contribution could reach US$640m (£400m) a year for the next three years.

208. The official added:

"It is important to consider that DFID 'traditionally' (Balkans/Afghanistan) contributes between 8-10 percent for total relief/reconstruction costs … This would mean that under a high case military scenario, with low oil revenues and where reparation/debt claims are not reduced, **annual costs to HMG** [Her Majesty's Government] **could be in excess of US$1bn**."

209. The minutes of the 3 February FCO Iraq Morning Meeting recorded that DFID was coming under pressure to step up its humanitarian planning after the House of Commons debate on 30 January.[104] Dr Brewer had explained to the meeting that there were serious domestic and international financial constraints.

210. DFID's financial resources are addressed in more detail in Section 13.1.

211. FCO lawyers advised UK participants in the post-Washington talks on the rights of the Occupying Power that, under international law, aspects of the post-conflict reconstruction of institutions and infrastructure could fall outside the competencies of an Occupying Power.

---

[101] Manuscript comment Short, 22 January 2003, on Minute Fernie to PS/Secretary of State [DFID], 21 January 2003, 'Iraq contingency planning: financial provision'.
[102] Email DFID [junior official] to Fernie, 22 January 2003, 'Iraq: submission of 21 January'.
[103] Minute DFID [junior official] to PS/Secretary of State [DFID], 31 January 2003, 'Iraq: cost of humanitarian relief/reconstruction and potential UK contribution' attaching Paper [draft], 'Iraq: Relief and reconstruction: implications for UK Government'.
[104] Minute Tanfield to PS/PUS [FCO], 3 February 2003, 'Iraq Morning Meeting: Key Points'.

212. On 31 January Mr John Grainger, a Legal Counsellor in the FCO, sent Mr Pattison a "basic principles" paper on rights under international law to occupy and administer post-conflict Iraq. The paper was for use by Mr Pattison during talks in Washington the following week and was copied to Mr Ricketts, Mr Ehrman and other FCO officials.[105] The paper was also copied to Mr Martin Hemming, the MOD Legal Adviser, but it is not clear whether it had been discussed with the MOD in draft.

213. Mr Grainger explained that he had discussed occupation rights with the State Department Legal Advisors, who acknowledged they had not done any systematic thinking on the issue, but that he had not yet discussed the issue with DoD.

214. Mr Grainger's paper stated:

"The rights of Coalition forces to occupy Iraq following a conflict would be closely related to their rights under international law to use force. It is likely that those rights will be based on the express or implicit authorisation of the United Nations Security Council ... to be interpreted within the overall objective of Iraqi compliance with disarmament obligations imposed by the Security Council and the requirement for restoring international peace and security in any area ... As regards Occupation post-conflict, the authorisation will again only justify such steps as are necessary to achieve the above objectives.

"To the extent that Iraq came under Coalition control during the course of any conflict the rights and obligations of the Coalition would be those of an Occupying Power, as set out in detail in Articles 42 to 56 of the Regulations annexed to Hague Convention IV of 1907, and in Geneva Convention IV ... of 1949 ... In general, the Occupying Power must take all measures in its power to restore and ensure public safety by respecting, unless absolutely prevented, the law in the occupied State ... Detailed provisions include limited rights to take possession of and use state property ...; to remove officials and judges ...; and to amend the penal laws of the occupying territory ... The Geneva Convention also provides a comprehensive code on the protection of the civilian population and internees.

"In these and other areas it is likely that aspects of reconstruction of institutions and infrastructure post-conflict could fall outside the competencies of an Occupying Power under international law. For these reasons it is important that a further Security Council resolution be adopted under Chapter VII as soon as possible to confer upon the Coalition and/or other States and international organisations as appropriate the necessary powers ... A United Nations administration would not be an occupying power and would not be constrained by the provisions of international humanitarian law though it should apply general international law ... Equally a

---

[105] Minute Grainger to Pattison, 31 January 2003, 'Rights Under International Law to Occupy and Administer Iraq after a Conflict' attaching Paper [unattributed and undated], 'Rights Under International Law to Occupy and Administer Iraq after a Conflict'.

military presence in Iraq post-conflict mandated by the UN would no longer be an occupying power regulated by the Hague and Geneva Conventions."

215. Mr Michael Wood, the FCO Legal Adviser, sent a copy of Mr Grainger's paper to Mr Straw on 28 February.

Parliamentary discussion of post-conflict issues, 3 February 2003

216. In Parliament on 3 February, Mr Blair offered "absolute assurances" that the UK would deal with any humanitarian consequences of conflict and undertook to "try to ensure that we move in to help get Iraq back on its feet".

217. Mr Mandelson asked Mr Blair about preparations for recovery and reconstruction in the House of Commons on 3 February:

"In addition to the need for political transition, the humanitarian and refugee demands could be immense. Will he outline to the House what preparation is being made for that at the United Nations and by key members of the international community? What structure for reconstruction is being put in place? In terms of donor funding, will Britain join America – and, I think Switzerland and Canada – in making an early offer of resources for those purposes?"[106]

218. Mr Blair replied:

"… we must deal with those vital points. We are in discussion with allies and the United Nations about reconstruction. The Foreign Secretary and I have spoken to the Secretary-General of the United Nations about that. If there is a conflict and Saddam's regime is removed, it is important to give absolute assurances and undertakings to the people of Iraq that we shall deal with any humanitarian consequences. In such circumstances, we must also try to ensure that we move in to help get Iraq back on its feet as quickly as possible. This country is willing to play its part in that with others."

219. In answer to a question from Mr Tony Baldry (Conservative) about the extent of discussions taking place with UN agencies, Mr Blair replied that detailed discussions were under way and that: "We are well aware that we must have a humanitarian plan that is every bit as viable and well worked out as a military plan."[107]

220. Sir Christopher Meyer told the Inquiry:

"… the worry at the time, was that there would be some kind of humanitarian disaster … What just disappeared from the calculations was the understanding that, after Saddam was toppled, you were going to have to maintain law and order and

---

[106] House of Commons, *Official Report*, 3 February 2003, column 28.
[107] House of Commons, *Official Report*, 3 February 2003, column 36.

guarantee the continuity of the central services; otherwise you would lose the Iraqi population very rapidly, and that was discussed."[108]

221. In early February, Mr Ricketts advised Mr Straw that the 22 January Washington talks had made little progress on the principle of UN involvement in post-conflict administration, and that the US envisaged the UK being responsible for administering one-fifth of Iraq. The UK risked being drawn into a "huge" and "complex" commitment in Iraq for an uncertain period.

222. Mr Ricketts recommended using a series of forthcoming Ministerial contacts at Cabinet level, which he described as a moment of "maximum leverage" on the US, to press the case for UN involvement.

223. In his minute to Mr Straw on 7 February, copied to Mr O'Brien, Sir Michael Jay (FCO PUS), and other FCO senior officials, Mr Ricketts stated:

> "As we approach the critical phase on Iraq, I thought it would be useful to look ahead to the decisions that will be needed on issues where the FCO is leading and set out the work coming forward to the Foreign Secretary."[109]

224. Mr Ricketts reported on the follow-up to the 22 January post-conflict talks in Washington. He stated that Mr Pattison had led a team "to have another go at getting into the US bloodstream the advantages of UN authorisation and involvement of the UN and its agencies in the civil administration of Iraq. He made a bit of headway. But this is water on a stone." Meanwhile, the Pentagon was accelerating planning for a Pentagon-run "aftermath organisation" under a US civil administrator alongside the continuing US military presence. With the US envisaging the UK being responsible for administering one-fifth of Iraq, "we risk being drawn into a huge commitment of UK resources for a highly complex task of administration and law and order for an uncertain period".

225. Mr Ricketts continued:

> "So we have a pressing interest in convincing the Americans to accept the benefits of a model giving the UN the lead on civil administration. Coalition military forces would then be responsible for carrying out security tasks, including dealing with WMD, while a civilian transitional administration would be set up headed by a UN executive administrator and drawing on the resources of the UN, IFIs and a broad range of countries, as well as involving Iraqis themselves in the administration as quickly as possible. This would not only be more realistic and sustainable, but also be much more acceptable to Arab opinion than US/UK military-led occupation. (It is also a further argument for getting a second resolution in advance of conflict, which may be one reason for the allergic reaction in parts of the US system to a UN-led administration.)

---

[108] Public hearing, 26 November 2009, page 93.
[109] Minute Ricketts to Private Secretary [FCO], 7 February 2003, 'Iraq Strategy'.

"Since most of the US work is going on in the Pentagon, a key opportunity to influence the Americans will be the Defence Secretary's talks with Rumsfeld in Washington on 12 February. A brief setting out the best points in favour of the UK's model is being co-ordinated in the Cabinet Office, and will be served up to Mr Hoon, and also to the Foreign Secretary and David Manning, for use later in the week with Powell and Rice.

"This is a key issue with huge resource implications. Now is our moment of maximum leverage on the Americans, and I think it should be a high priority for discussions with them over the next fortnight. It may be an issue to be taken up by the PM with Bush before US thinking sets in concrete."

226. Mr Ricketts also informed Mr Straw that there was inter-departmental agreement that "the FCO should lead policy work on planning for post-conflict Iraq". The first task of the new Iraq Planning Unit (IPU) would be "to start assembling answers to the many questions thrown up by PJHQ as they begin to plan for coping with the situation military forces will find in Iraq as soon as conflict finishes".[110]

227. Mr Straw commented: "Good note … I need to talk to [Secretary] Powell re this."[111]

Creation of the Iraq Planning Unit

228. The inter-departmental (FCO/MOD/DFID) Iraq Planning Unit (IPU), based in the FCO, was established on 10 February to improve Whitehall co-ordination on post-conflict issues.

229. Although the IPU was an inter-departmental unit, its head was a senior member of the Diplomatic Service and it was integrated into the FCO management structure.

230. The draft Terms of Reference for the IPU stated that:

- **The IPU would report to Mr Chaplin in the FCO. The Terms of Reference did not define the relationship between the IPU and senior officials in DFID and the MOD.**
- **The IPU would work "within broad policy guidelines set by the Cabinet Office".**
- **The main purpose of the IPU would be to provide "policy guidance on the practical questions" that UK civilian officials and military commanders would face in Iraq.**
- **The IPU was intended "to bring influence to bear on US plans".**

---

[110] Minute Ricketts to Private Secretary [FCO], 7 February 2003, 'Iraq Strategy'.
[111] Manuscript comment Straw on Minute Ricketts to Private Secretary [FCO], 7 February 2003, 'Iraq Strategy'.

231. Tasks assigned to the IPU by the AHGI included consideration of:

- **the shape of the Iraqi political process needed to underpin the transition to Iraqi rule;**
- **management of Iraq's oil; and**
- **whether and where the UK should run its own sector before the restoration of Iraqi sovereignty.**

232. After the creation of the IPU, the AHGI remained responsible for co-ordination of all post-conflict planning and preparation across government, including consular planning and civil contingencies.

233. At the FCO Iraq Morning Meeting on 3 February, Mr Alan Charlton, FCO Personnel Director, asked about military timing.[112] Mr Ricketts advised that "the newspapers weren't a bad guide: 'we need to have our preparations in place by end Feb[ruary]'".

234. The same day, Mr Ehrman reported to Mr Ricketts that the Pigott Group, an MOD-led, inter-departmental group of senior officials (see Section 6.4), had decided that there was a need for a senior FCO official to co-ordinate full-time with the MOD, DFID and others the rapidly increasing volume of work on aftermath planning.[113]

235. Mr Ehrman suggested that "in addition to work on overall legality ... we will need sub-groups on WMD, OFF, SSR, humanitarian, reconstruction, judicial, possibly terrorism. All this to feed into and influence the various aftermath groups in Washington."

236. Mr Ricketts informed Mr Chaplin on 4 February that he had agreed with Sir Michael Jay and Mr Ehrman that:

> "... the FCO should consolidate the lead we have already taken in this area [post-conflict issues] with the work that Dominick Chilcott has been doing under your supervision.

> "I am sure that this work will now grow fast, particularly with the prospect of the UK inheriting responsibility for a good slice of southern Iraq following a military conflict."[114]

237. Mr Bowen chaired a meeting in the Cabinet Office on 4 February, attended by officials from the FCO, the MOD and DFID, at which it was decided to set up an inter-departmental (FCO, MOD and DFID) unit.[115] The unit would be headed by an FCO official, Mr Chilcott, to "prepare for the aftermath in practical operational terms". Wider strategy would continue to be co-ordinated through the AHGI.

---

[112] Manuscript comment Brewer, 3 February 2003, on Minute Tanfield to PS/PUS, 31 January 2003, 'Iraq Morning Meeting: Key Points'.
[113] Minute Ehrman to Ricketts, 3 February 2003, 'Pigott Group, 3 February'.
[114] Minute Ricketts to Chaplin, 4 February 2003, 'Iraq: Day After Planning'.
[115] Letter Bowen to Ehrman, 5 February 2003, 'Iraq: Operational Policy Unit'.

238. Mr Bowen explained to participants at the meeting that there was "a good deal of uncertainty about American intentions in administering Iraq in the event of (and after) hostilities to remove Saddam Hussein's regime". Meetings in Washington that week should bring greater clarity but were unlikely to produce decisions.

239. Mr Bowen reported that participants at the meeting had recognised that:

"… even if some of the big strategic issues remained unresolved, a lot of detailed management issues were likely to arise. Much was likely to emanate from CENTCOM, which had the prospectively imminent task of administering a country whose leadership had been removed. With this in mind we agreed that we should set up an Iraq Operational Policy Unit with contributions from the FCO, DFID and MOD … My view was that we needed an integrated unit with high calibre representation to work through the sort of issues that would confront the Coalition on the 'day after'. **Their initial remit would be to develop policy guidance to enable the administration of Iraq pending the appointment of a transitional civil administration, consistent as far as possible with the longer term vision for the future of Iraq.** They would need to work their way, with the US, through issues as diverse as humanitarian relief, policing, administration of justice, local government and provision of utilities, environmental recovery and priorities for the return to normality. The view we all reached was that this unit ought to be up and running from Monday 10 February … It will need staff who think strategically and operationally and have some background in state reconstruction from other cases (in order to feed in the lessons of eg Kosovo and Afghanistan)."

240. Mr Bowen explained that the new unit would work alongside the FCO consular and emergency units (described in more detail in the Box 'The FCO Emergency Unit' later in this Section), and with the Defence Crisis Management Centre (DCMC) in MOD and the Conflict and Humanitarian Affairs Department (CHAD) in DFID.

241. The UK's expectation was that:

"… General Franks of CENTCOM will be in overall charge of Iraq, with the military chain of command operating, which would involve [Major] General [Robin] Brims [General Officer Commanding 1st (UK) Armoured Division (GOC 1 (UK) Div)], being in charge of a sector of Iraq. Brims would need civilian support in theatre (beyond an MOD Polad [policy adviser]), but it was too early to judge at what level; it was clear that there would need to be FCO and DFID input. The extent to which the US were planning on providing civil support to a British sector was as yet unclear."

242. Mr Bowen reported that participants at the meeting had identified other possible requirements, including "a British office in the UK sector, a special envoy and an Ambassador". The new unit was only the first step.

243. Mr Bowen suggested "Iraq Operational Policy Unit" as a name for the new body. He asked Mr Ehrman, Ms Miller, Mr Pollard and Brig Rollo to take action to set up the unit and reported that Sir David Manning supported the thrust of the proposed approach.

244. The Chiefs of Staff meeting on 5 February was informed that: "Output from the FCO unit would feed US planning through the newly appointed Major General Tim Cross, the senior UK secondee to ORHA, working for Lt Gen Garner."[116] The unit would be informed by the PJHQ seminar on post-conflict issues.

245. Mr Ricketts explained to Mr Straw that the new unit would be headed by Mr Chilcott, located in the FCO's Middle East and North Africa (MENA) Directorate and include participants from the MOD and DFID. It would be closely linked to the Cabinet Office co-ordinating machinery.[117]

246. The IPU, headed by Mr Chilcott, was established on 10 February.[118]

247. On 11 February, Mr O'Brien chaired an internal FCO briefing on post-conflict issues, at which he commissioned work from the IPU and "stressed the need to consider how our work fitted into a managed exit strategy".[119] Mr O'Brien suggested that other Arab states' contribution to the modernisation of Iraq "would assist in [the] process of exiting and handover".

248. The record of the FCO Iraq Evening Meeting on 27 February stated that Mr Straw had asked Mr O'Brien to focus on post-conflict issues.[120]

249. The Inquiry has seen no other evidence of that decision or explanation of the role Mr O'Brien was expected to play.

250. Mr O'Brien was actively engaged on post-conflict issues after the creation of the IPU, including a visit to New York and Washington to discuss Phase IV with the US and UN in March.[121]

251. On 17 February, Sir Michael Jay sent draft terms of reference for the IPU to Sir Andrew Turnbull, the Cabinet Secretary, copied to Whitehall Permanent Secretaries. The draft, which had already been discussed with DFID, the MOD and the Cabinet Office, stated:

> "The unit will operate within broad policy guidelines set by the Cabinet Office. In the FCO, it will report to the Director Middle East and North Africa Command [Mr Chaplin]. Its main customers will be British military planners in PJHQ, MOD and,

---

[116] Minutes, 5 February 2003, Chiefs of Staff meeting.
[117] Minute Ricketts to Private Secretary [FCO], 7 February 2003, 'Iraq Strategy'.
[118] Minute Chilcott to Private Secretary [FCO], 20 February 2003, 'Iraq: Day-After (Phase IV)'.
[119] Minute APS/Mr O'Brien to Chilcott, 11 February 2003, 'Iraq: Day After Issues'.
[120] Minute Tanfield to PS/PUS [FCO], 27 February 2003, 'Iraq Evening Meeting: Key Points'.
[121] Minute Chilcott to Private Secretary [FCO], 3 March 2003, 'Iraq: Phase IV (Day After)'.

mainly through them, British officers and officials seconded to the Pentagon and CENTCOM.

"The main purpose of the unit will be to provide policy guidance on the practical questions that British civilian officials and military commanders will face, in the event of a conflict in Iraq. The advice will be designed to help them to minimise the suffering of the Iraqi people and to deal with the civil administration of any sector of Iraq under the control of British forces, particularly during the period before a transitional civilian administration is established. It will aim to ensure that British operational military planning for the post-conflict phase in Iraq is consistent with and promotes the UK's policy objectives on the future of Iraq. In doing so it will take particular account of the key role of the UN.

"The unit will aim to bring influence to bear on US plans by providing similar guidance, through PJHQ and MOD, to seconded British personnel working within the US military planning machinery and through the Embassy to the NSC and other parts of the US Administration.

"The unit will also provide a focus in Whitehall for developing policy advice and recommendations, as required, on strategic questions concerning a post Saddam Iraq.

"The role of the unit will be reviewed in three months."[122]

252. The record of the 17 February meeting of the AHGI stated that the US and UK military build-up continued and the US "impetus to war" had not slowed.[123] The IPU had been formed initially "to meet a UK military planning need for detailed policy guidance on occupation issues". In the event of UK participation in the occupation of Iraq it was likely to expand considerably.

253. The record continued:

"We need to agree with the US on the role of the UN in any civilian transitional administration. We see advantage in a major UN role for reasons of legitimacy, expertise in certain areas and burden-sharing. However, in exchange for sanctioning a transitional administration, the UN Security Council may require a larger UN role than the US currently envisage.

"Our original planning envisaged a period of up to three months of military rule. Latest reports from CENTCOM suggest the US envisage moving to civilian rule more quickly …

---

[122] Letter Jay to Turnbull, 17 February 2003, 'Iraq Planning Unit' attaching Paper [unattributed and undated], 'Proposed Terms of Reference for the tract [sic] Planning Unit'.
[123] Minute Dodd to Manning, 17 February 2003, 'Ad Hoc Group on Iraq'.

"The Planning Unit [IPU] will also focus on the shape of the Iraqi political process needed to underpin a handover to Iraqi rule, which the US see as occurring 18 months to two years after invasion. Other issues include the management of Iraq's oil and whether and where the UK should run its own sector until Iraqi sovereignty is restored."

254. The record of the next meeting, on 21 February, described the co-ordinating role of the AHGI:

"... the Ad Hoc Group draws together work related to Iraq as follows:

- Work on post-Saddam issues led by the Iraq Planning Unit. This includes the HMT [HM Treasury]-led sub-group on economic and financial issues;
- Consular planning; and
- HMT/CCS [Civil Contingencies Secretariat]-led domestic contingency planning (the Stephens Group).

"AHGI receives updates on military and intelligence issues, but these issues are handled elsewhere. AHGI provides a forum for deciding how to cover any new Iraq-related issues. There is some read across from pre-existing DTI [Department of Trade and Industry] and HMT Whitehall groups looking at oil."[124]

255. **The evidence in this Section indicates that, after the creation of the IPU, neither Sir Michael Jay, nor Mr Ricketts as the senior FCO official tasked by Sir Michael to direct all aspects of FCO Iraq work, instructed the IPU or other parts of the FCO contributing to the IPU to:**

- **provide thorough analysis of a range of possible post-conflict scenarios, not just the best case;**
- **identify the need for contingency plans and preparations to address each of those scenarios; or**
- **provide a realistic assessment of the UK's civilian capabilities and resources in the light of its likely obligations in Iraq.**

Domestic contingency planning: the Stephens Group

256. After expressions of concern by Permanent Secretaries about the possible impact on the UK of war in Iraq, Sir Andrew Turnbull had agreed in January 2003 that the AHGI should conduct further work on domestic contingencies.[125]

---

[124] Minute Dodd to Manning, 25 February 2003, 'Ad Hoc Group on Iraq'.
[125] Minute Dodd to Manning, 13 January 2003, 'Ad Hoc Group on Iraq'.

257. On 10 January, the AHGI had agreed that:

- The Treasury should review its November 2002 paper on the impact of conflict on the UK economy (see Section 6.4).

- The DTI would revisit its October 2002 paper on the oil market (see Section 10.3) and look at the potential impact of conflict on UK industry.

- The Department for Transport (DfT) would review its November 2002 transport paper (see Section 6.4).

- The Cabinet Office would circulate the latest version of the CCS paper on the potential impact on the UK of operations against Iraq (see Section 6.4) for comments from departments.

- The CCS would draft an Action Plan to be circulated to the AHGI for comment, setting out actions the Government would need to take should conflict be imminent.

258. Mr Jonathan Stephens, Treasury Director Public Services, circulated a revised draft of the CCS paper to Permanent Secretaries on 20 January.[126] He invited each department to identify key actions that needed to be taken to manage and mitigate risks.

259. Mr Stephens also announced the creation of a Domestic Implications Sub-Group of the AHGI (subsequently known as the Stephens Group), which would meet for the first time on 24 January.

260. The Stephens Group continued to work on the domestic implications of military action during February and March.[127]

261. On 19 March, the Private Office of Mr Gus O'Donnell, Treasury Permanent Secretary, sent a paper by Mr Stephens on the domestic implications of military action to Permanent Secretaries.[128] The paper stated that initial work on the issue had identified priority risks requiring further work. Those had been grouped into three cross-cutting areas:

- public behaviour and community cohesion;
- health and public service implications of military requirements; and
- fuel disruption, tourism and unemployment.

---

[126] Letter Stephens to Phillips, 20 January 2003, 'Iraq: Domestic Implications of Military Action' attaching Paper [unattributed and undated], 'Domestic Impact of an Iraq Operation – Risk to PSA Targets', and Paper Civil Contingencies Secretariat Assessments Team, 17 January 2003, 'Potential Impact on UK of Operations Against Iraq'.
[127] Minute Dodd to Manning, 17 March 2003, 'Ad Hoc Group on Iraq'.
[128] Email Martin to Permsecs, 19 March 2003, 'Domestic Implications of Military Action' attaching Paper Stephens, 'Domestic Implications of Military Action with Iraq – Next Steps'.

262. Mr Stephens summarised the key issues:

- <u>Demands on police resources</u> arising from the possibility of simultaneous challenges, including "heightened security environment, support to military preparations, public order and the possible renewal of the firefighters' dispute". Mr Stephens stated that the Cabinet Office and Home Office had work in hand on the issue, in conjunction with the police and the MOD.

- <u>Policy on bringing Iraqi prisoners of war or civilian casualties to the UK for treatment</u>. The IPU and CCS were co-ordinating work on the issue.

- <u>Fuel disruption</u>. DTI and CCS had identified short-term mitigation measures and longer-term resilience options.

- <u>Military Aid to the Civil Authorities (MACA)</u>. Departments had confirmed that there were no major concerns. The Cabinet Office was working separately on provision of military resources for civil contingencies.

- <u>Impact on departments of fuel price rises</u>. Departments had confirmed they did not expect major problems.

263. Mr Stephens listed additional action points for departments on specific issues related to public order, community cohesion, asylum and the NHS.

PJHQ planning seminar

264. The PJHQ planning seminar to discuss the UK Common Document took place on 5 February.

265. Participants were told by PJHQ that US planning was moving fast and that within a week or so it would be very difficult to reverse what the US had decided.

266. The PJHQ Phase IV planning seminar on 5 February was attended by junior officials from the Cabinet Office (Mr Tom Dodd, OD Sec), DFID (Mr Fernie) and the FCO.[129] Discussion centred on the PJHQ Common Document (given the title 'Iraq – Phase IV Subjects'), which set out UK and US positions on post-conflict security, reconstruction, civil administration and humanitarian assistance, and issues needing resolution.

267. The FCO record of the seminar was addressed to Mr Chilcott and summarised the key messages from PJHQ planners:

- US planning was "going ahead fast, whether we like it or not". Once Secretary Rumsfeld had signed it off "in about a week's time" it would be "very difficult to reverse what has been decided".

---

[129] Minute MED [junior official] to Chilcott, 6 February 2003, 'Iraq: PJHQ Meeting on "Aftermath"' attaching Paper [unattributed], 5 February 2003, 'Iraq – Phase IV Subjects'.

- Steers were needed for Maj Gen Brims and two UK officers in "key planning positions": Brigadier Albert Whitley (Senior British Land Adviser (SBLA) at the Coalition Forces Land Component Command (CFLCC) in Kuwait) and Maj Gen Cross,[130] working to Lt Gen Garner in ORHA.

268. The record of the FCO Iraq Morning Meeting on 6 February stated that: "PJHQ have a large number of practical questions, on which they need urgent policy guidance."[131]

269. Maj Gen Whitley told the Inquiry that US Lieutenant General David McKiernan, Coalition Forces Land Component Commander, had initially asked him to lead on planning for "post hostilities" and to be his "eyes and ears" on the subject with other headquarters.[132] With the creation of ORHA and the augmentation of CFLCC by Combined Joint Task Force 7 (CJTF-7, the post-invasion military command), Lt Gen McKiernan, who already had deputies for Operations and Support, had felt it essential that the then Brigadier Whitley be given more authority. In mid-February 2003, with the agreement of Lt Gen Reith, Lt Gen McKiernan appointed Brigadier Whitley Deputy Commanding General (Post Hostilities), with the rank of (acting) Major General.

270. Maj Gen Whitley told the Inquiry he was instructed to: "Do what you can, with what we have and when we can. Produce a plan for CFLCC for Phase IV." That plan came to be known as Eclipse II and is described in the Box 'Eclipse II – the CFLCC plan for Phase IV' later in this Section.

271. MOD officials briefed Mr Hoon on the IPU and the Common Document on 12 February:

> "In the UK officials have set about establishing a bespoke structure that will provide policy guidance on aftermath issues – initially, principally to the UK military, but also more widely …

> "Central to this effort is the Iraq Policy Unit [sic] … Advising this in an expert capacity is the Iraq Aftermath Strategic Planning Group in the MOD. The main effort of the IPU is to populate a document ('The Iraq Stage IV Subjects Document') that is essentially a structured list of questions with answers that will allow departments to give policy guidance, and will form a 'core script' that will permit our various personnel embedded in US structures to give a unified message on the UK vision for post-conflict Iraq. Many of these are issues of detail, but they have real practical import (for example – whether the US plans to dollarize the Iraqi economy will affect the currency that is issued to 1 Div, who will need to pay contractors in their AO [Area of Operations])."[133]

---

[130] The author of the record was unsure of the name of the individual working to Lt Gen Garner, but must have meant Maj Gen Cross.
[131] Minute Tanfield to PS/PUS [FCO], 6 February 2003, 'Iraq Morning Meeting: Key Points'.
[132] Statement, 25 January 2011, page 3.
[133] Minute Sec(O) [junior official] to PS/Secretary of State [MOD], 12 February 2003, 'Iraq: Aftermath – Briefing for Meeting with OGD Ministers'.

272. A briefing note prepared for staff in the UK National Contingent Headquarters (NCHQ) in Qatar referred to a revised version of the Common Document dated 11 February that has not been seen by the Inquiry.[134]

273. The Inquiry has seen no evidence that the IPU updated the Common Document during preparations for the US inter-agency Rock Drill on post-conflict issues on 21 and 22 February.

274. The Rock Drill is addressed in detail later in this Section.

275. On 20 February, Mr Chilcott updated Mr Straw on the first nine days of the IPU. It had "a core staff (from FCO, MOD and DFID), a large room, and IT". The Unit was working well with other departments and UK military planners and had "successfully contracted out a lot of work".[135]

276. Mr Chilcott told Mr Straw that ORHA was emerging as the IPU's key counterpart in the US and that Maj Gen Cross and the IPU were "two sides of the same coin and [would] work increasingly hand in glove".

277. Mr Chilcott told the Inquiry that, although numbers were small ("maybe only six, eight, ten, for the first couple of weeks"), the IPU drew on expertise elsewhere in Whitehall that allowed it to pull together a strategic view.[136] While military planners and PJHQ were planning what would be needed as troops occupied territory and became "responsible … for the administration of where they were", the IPU was "thinking about the political process and the big issues about the development fund for Iraq or oil policy or what to do about war criminals or the importance of legitimacy and legal questions".

278. Asked how influential the IPU had been, Mr Chilcott stated:

"… I don't think our main issue was having to convince other parts of the government machinery that they should be doing things that they didn't want to do.

"I think we were really synthesising the views and expertise across government.

"Where we needed to have clout … was in influencing the United States, and I think, there, we … had no more clout than a sort of body of middle to senior ranking British officials would have had with their American counterparts."[137]

279. On the relationship with ORHA, Mr Chilcott said that: "ORHA in some ways weren't really our counterparts because they were the sort of operational implementers … as well as the drawers up of the plan, whereas we … were writing policy papers and briefing and lines to take."[138]

---

[134] Paper SO2 [NCHQ], 13 February 2003, 'Introductory Note to Folder on Phase IV Planning'.
[135] Minute Chilcott to Private Secretary [FCO], 20 February 2003, 'Iraq: Day-After (Phase IV)'.
[136] Public hearing, 8 December 2009, pages 7-8.
[137] Public hearing, 8 December 2009, pages 8-9.
[138] Public hearing, 8 December 2009, page 20.

280. Mr Bowen told the Inquiry that one reason for establishing the IPU was to set up a counterpart to ORHA: "as soon as we … understood where the centre of gravity was in America … we set up … a centre of gravity that could interact with it". At this early stage in the relationship, before misgivings about ORHA had begun to emerge in Whitehall, that seemed still to be the intention.

Preparing for the UK's "exemplary" role in the South

281. On 3 February, Maj Gen Brims told UK military commanders that, in the event of an invasion, UK forces could "set the pace" for Phase IV operations.

282. Maj Gen Brims issued the first GOC Directive for UK military commanders involved in Operation (Op) TELIC[139] on 3 February.[140] It stated: "We only win on successful implementation of Phase IV", and continued:

> "The Phase IV requirements have yet to emerge. I am confident that our people have the physical and mental agility to attend to it quickly, thoughtfully and effectively … But two important points:
>
> a. There must be no triumphalism … we must restore, foster, Iraqi dignity in our AO and work together as far as possible to achieve Phase IV for their benefit.
>
> b. We shall probably be the first Coalition forces to implement Phase IV. We can set the pace. The world media will be reporting our activities."

283. Also on 3 February, DFID officials recommended to Ms Short that DFID second six Civil/Military Humanitarian Advisers to the UK military and ORHA, in order "to take further forward our objective of refining the military planning options to ensure the humanitarian consequences of any conflict in Iraq are fully addressed".[141]

284. The Inquiry has not seen Ms Short's response, but DFID did second a number of staff over the following weeks.[142]

285. Later in February, DFID officials sought policy guidance from Ms Short on the scope of DFID co-operation with military forces in "complex emergencies".

---

[139] Operation TELIC was the codename for the involvement of UK Armed Forces in the military campaign to remove the threat from Iraq's weapons of mass destruction.
[140] Minute Brims to various, 3 February 2003, 'Op Telic – GOC's Directive One'.
[141] Minute Conflict & Humanitarian Affairs Department [junior official] to PS/Secretary of State [DFID], 3 February 2003, 'Iraq: Refining the Military Options'.
[142] Letter Warren to Rycroft, 7 March 2003, [untitled] attaching Paper DFID, [undated], 'DFID Planning on Iraq'.

286. Ms Short informed Mr Blair on 5 February that, "after a slow start", DFID was "getting real co-operation" from the MOD, FCO and Cabinet Office.[143] It was involved in drafting military campaign objectives and was experiencing more co-operation from UN agencies and the US. Ms Short reported that she had approved a limited number of DFID secondments to UK and US military planning units.

287. Ms Short stated that the main outstanding issue was the scale of the UK contribution to the humanitarian and reconstruction effort in Iraq. A "fair share" would be about 5.6 percent of the total, equivalent to the UK share of OECD gross national income, and would amount to approximately £440m a year for three years. It was for Mr Blair to decide whether he thought the UK should make a "modest" contribution along those lines, or "aim higher". If so, it would need to be an effort on behalf of the whole government, not just DFID.

288. Ms Short concluded:

> "I think the way in which you could best help is to make clear across the system that you want humanitarian considerations to be given more weight. In addition it would help if we could settle the financial questions."

289. The same day, Mr Lee sent Mr Hoon a request from Ms Short to be briefed by MOD officials on the planned military campaign. The request was for Ms Short to be briefed "on similar lines" to Mr Straw and Lord Goldsmith, the Attorney General.[144] Mr Lee debated whether the briefing should focus on post-conflict issues, but concluded: "As full and frank a briefing within the constraints of operational security will be a key element in achieving a joined up approach and help build on the good relationships we have set up over the last few weeks." He also advised that No.10 had asked to be consulted on the terms of any briefing for Ms Short.

290. Mr Martyn Williams, Mr Hoon's Private Secretary, asked: "Doctrinally pure advice on involving DFID SofS [Secretary of State]. Are you happy for me to consult No.10?"[145]

291. Mr Hoon agreed to the proposal.[146]

292. The Inquiry has seen no record of No.10 approving the briefing for Ms Short, which took place on 12 February.

293. Mr Annan told the press on 5 February that there was no agreement on the post-conflict role of the UN.

---

[143] Letter Short to Blair, 5 February 2003, 'Iraq: Humanitarian Planning'.
[144] Minute Lee to PS/Secretary of State [MOD], 5 February 2003, 'Iraq: Briefing the international development secretary'.
[145] Manuscript comment to SofS [MOD] on Minute Lee to PS/Secretary of State [MOD], 5 February 2003, 'Iraq: Briefing the international development secretary'.
[146] Manuscript comment Hoon, 6 February 2003, on Minute Lee to PS/Secretary of State [MOD], 5 February 2003, 'Iraq: Briefing the international development secretary'.

294. At a press conference after the meeting of the Security Council on 5 February (addressed in Section 3.7), Mr Annan stated that, after any conflict, "the UN always had a role to play".[147] He added that the post-conflict role of the UN in Iraq:

> "… has not been discussed. As you know, we are doing some contingency planning on the humanitarian side. This is also something that we have given some preliminary thought to, but we are not there at all."

295. Mr Blair told Cabinet on 6 February that planning for the aftermath and humanitarian relief needed "greater emphasis".

296. The same day, he commissioned a paper on "aftermath and humanitarian issues", to be co-ordinated by the FCO.

297. Mr Blair told Cabinet on 6 February that "planning for the aftermath of military action and humanitarian relief needed greater emphasis".[148]

298. Mr Straw said that the aftermath was "being discussed intensively" with Ms Short and Mr Hoon.

299. Points made in discussion included:

- The word "aftermath" was "ill-chosen: it incorrectly implied that Iraq would be utterly destroyed by military conflict whereas we should gear our thinking around the future of the people of Iraq and their interests".

- The reconstruction and development of Iraq would "provide opportunities for British companies to be involved".

- The focus after hostilities "had to be on civil society which had suffered 35 years of tyranny that had reduced the country to the point where 60 percent of the population relied on United Nations food programmes".

- It was "essential" that the UN should be involved in Iraq's redevelopment after any military action "to avoid the military occupation being viewed as an army of occupation".

300. On 6 February, Mr Blair held a meeting with Mr Straw, Mr Hoon and senior officials from the MOD, the Secret Intelligence Service (SIS), No.10 and the Cabinet Office to discuss how to minimise civilian casualties during an air campaign. The meeting is described in more detail in Section 6.2.

301. At the meeting, Mr Blair commissioned a paper on "aftermath and humanitarian issues" for 14 February.[149] No.10 instructed the FCO to co-ordinate with the MOD, DFID and the Cabinet Office.

---

[147] UN News Centre, 5 February 2003, *Secretary-General's press encounter following Security Council meeting and Luncheon on Iraq (unofficial transcript).*
[148] Cabinet Conclusions, 6 February 2003.
[149] Letter Rycroft to Watkins, 6 February 2003, 'Iraq: Prime Minister's Meeting, 6 February'.

302. The request appears to have been overtaken by a further Ministerial meeting on humanitarian issues on 13 February at which DFID, the FCO and the MOD were asked by Mr Blair to co-ordinate advice for him to use with President Bush.[150]

303. In separate letters to Mr Blair on 10 February, Mr Straw and Mr Hoon endorsed Ms Short's views on improved co-operation between departments.

304. Mr Straw told Mr Blair that DFID, the MOD and the Cabinet Office had been co-operating closely on humanitarian issues.[151] Work on humanitarian and other long-term planning issues would be strengthened by the creation of the IPU.

305. Mr Straw commented that humanitarian planning was the area of "long-term work" where the UK probably had fewest differences with the US. It was an area, unlike some others, where the US seemed to agree on the need for close UN involvement. The US and UK Missions in New York were working on the fine-tuning of OFF arrangements to make them better suited to the circumstances of post-conflict Iraq. In addition, the US military was:

> "… developing detailed plans for relief and reconstruction teams to follow in the wake of advancing military forces in Iraq to begin immediately the urgent tasks of restoring water and electricity supplies and repairing public buildings. The US are clearly aware of the importance of delivering quick wins to show the Iraqi people and the world the benefits of Coalition action."

306. Mr Straw explained that much work remained to be done on economic reconstruction. An inter-departmental visit to Washington that week had revealed that, although there were, "as always", clear differences between US government agencies, there did still seem to be an opportunity to influence their thinking.

307. Mr Hoon responded to Ms Short's question about the scale of the UK humanitarian contribution.[152] He accepted that, in the "very short term", the UK military would play "a very significant role", but early thought would also need to be given to the timing of transition to purely civil structures. The key issue was to resolve differences with the US over the role of the UN.

308. A JIC Assessment on 10 February warned of the possibility of terrorist attacks against Coalition Forces in Iraq, during and after conflict.

309. On 10 February, at the request of the MOD and the FCO, the JIC produced its second Assessment on the potential terrorist threat in the event of conflict in Iraq.[153]

310. The earlier Assessment, produced on 10 October 2002, is described in Section 6.4.

---

[150] Letter Cannon to Bewes, 13 February 2003, 'Iraq: Humanitarian Issues'.
[151] Minute Straw to Prime Minister, 10 February 2003, 'Iraq: Humanitarian Planning'.
[152] Letter Hoon to Blair, 10 February 2003, 'Iraq: Humanitarian Planning'.
[153] JIC Assessment, 10 February 2003, 'International Terrorism: War with Iraq'.

311. The "Key Judgements" in the February Assessment included:

> "I. The threat from Al Qaida will increase at the onset of any military action against Iraq. They will target Coalition forces and other Western interests in the Middle East. Attacks against Western interests elsewhere are also likely, especially in the US and UK for maximum impact. The worldwide threat from other Islamist terrorist groups and individuals will increase significantly.
>
> …
>
> III. Al Qaida associated terrorists in Iraq and in the Kurdish Autonomous Zone in Northern Iraq could conduct attacks against Coalition forces and interests during, or in the aftermath of, war with Iraq."

312. An updated Assessment, produced on 12 March, judged that: "Senior Al Qaida associated terrorists may have established sleeper cells in Iraq, to be activated during a Coalition occupation."[154]

313. Treasury briefing for Mr Brown on 11 February warned of the possibility of substantial pressure on the UK to make a disproportionate contribution to post-conflict Iraq.

314. On 11 February, Treasury officials invited Mr Brown's views on their "preliminary thinking" on the Treasury's interests in a post-Saddam Hussein Iraq.[155] The paper drew on earlier Treasury work in September 2002 on the implications of war in Iraq for the global, regional and Iraqi economies.[156] Officials advised that the Treasury's main interest was to ensure Iraq's prosperity and stability while sharing fairly the cost of achieving that outcome. The cost was difficult to predict but "potentially massive". It comprised:

- peacekeeping costs; the peacekeeping force in Yugoslavia had numbered 40,000 at its peak, with the cost to the UK of the Kosovo Force (KFOR) reaching £325m in 1999/2000. Iraq would probably need more troops, given its ethnic and religious tensions, the likelihood of score-settling and its sheer size;
- humanitarian expenditure;
- environmental costs arising, for example, from the use of WMD or oil fires;
- "general reconstruction", which could cost between US$1.5bn and US$8bn a year (including humanitarian costs); and
- economic stabilisation, through an IMF programme.

---

[154] JIC Assessment, 12 March 2003, 'International Terrorism: War with Iraq: Update'.
[155] Minute Treasury [junior official] to Chancellor, 11 February 2003, 'HMT policy on post-Saddam Iraq' attaching Paper CEP/HMT, [undated], 'What should HMT policy be on post-war Iraq?'
[156] Email [Treasury junior official] to Bowman, 6 September 2002, 'What would be the economic impact of a war in Iraq?' attaching Paper HMT, September 2002, 'What would be the economic impact of war in Iraq?'

315. The paper warned that there could be substantial pressure on the UK to make a "disproportionate" contribution, and suggested that an "emerging policy position" would be to:

- maximise Iraqi contributions;
- push for debt rescheduling;
- maximise contributions from the multilateral development banks, and secure IMF and World Bank engagement;
- push for bilateral contributions to the reconstruction effort to take into account military contributions (with countries that would make no military contribution paying a higher share of reconstruction costs); and
- ensure a finance ministry/IFI lead on financing issues, with no money committed until a proper needs assessment had been done.

316. The Treasury informed the Inquiry that Mr Brown did not comment on the paper.[157]

317. Treasury officials sent Mr Brown further updates on the likely total cost of war, including humanitarian and reconstruction costs, later in February.

318. The Treasury's response to departments' requests for additional funding to cover the anticipated costs of post-conflict Iraq is covered in detail in Section 13.1.

319. **The FCO sent guidance on post-conflict issues to overseas posts on 7 February. The guidance stated that:**

- **The UK was planning on a contingency basis for what the international community should do if Saddam Hussein were removed.**
- **The UK wanted to hand back power to the Iraqi people as quickly as possible, but with Iraq "radically reformed for the better".**
- **Timing of the three stage transition was uncertain.**
- **Iraq's public administration could be expected to work "adequately" once senior regime officials had been removed.**
- **The role of the UN was still a matter of active debate.**

320. On 7 February, the FCO sent guidance on "day after" issues to all overseas posts.[158] The guidance stated that the UK's goal was disarmament of Iraq's WMD, not regime change, but that, since military action could not be ruled out, it was "sensible to plan on a contingency basis, for what the international community should do in Iraq" if Saddam Hussein's regime were removed from power.

---

[157] Email Treasury to Iraq Inquiry, 26 February 2010, [untitled].
[158] Telegram 67 FCO to Abidjan, 7 February 2003, 'Iraq: "Day After" Questions'.

321. In the background material for posts, not to be used with external contacts, the FCO explained that Coalition Forces would become the de facto government of Iraq as soon as Saddam Hussein fell. The UK would aim to hand back power to the Iraqi people as quickly as possible, but would want to see Iraq "radically reformed for the better" before doing so.

322. The FCO explained that the timing of the three stage transition was uncertain. Coalition military rule was likely to last as long as it took to establish a civilian transitional administration, "perhaps weeks, rather than many months". The transitional administration would last "rather longer", as it would take time to agree political structures to introduce reforms.

323. The FCO stated that Iraq had "a relatively sophisticated public administration" and expected that:

> "… it will work adequately once the most senior old regime officials have been removed. Iraq should not be like Kosovo, where ministries and public services had to be created from scratch."

324. The FCO explained that the role of the UN was "still a matter of active debate" in the US and between the US and UK. It concluded:

> "We are in contact with a number of international players, including in particular the US, about these sensitive matters. We are not making the content of these contingency talks public. Nor should you."

Maintaining pressure on the US

325. **The Chiefs of Staff were briefed on the three-phase US Phase IV Plan on 10 February. They were told:**

- **US planning was evolving slowly because of disputes in Washington about the primacy of the different bodies involved.**
- **Without a common approach to the underlying issues in the UK, it would not be possible to exert influence on the US process.**

326. **The Chiefs of Staff commented that there would be a significant requirement for other countries to share the post-conflict burden. The FCO undertook to explore the issue.**

327. Maj Gen Fry updated the Chiefs of Staff on US Phase IV planning on 10 February.[159] The US had divided Phase IV into three stages: IVa – Stabilisation; IVb – Recovery; and IVc – Transition to Security.

---

[159] Minute Fry to COSSEC, 10 February 2003, 'Aftermath Planning' attaching Paper DCJO(Ops), 10 February 2003, 'Aftermath Planning'.

328. Maj Gen Fry invited the Chiefs to note that:

- The US intended the immediate post-conflict stabilisation period to last between three and six months: "By necessity and tactical imperative there is implicit UK acceptance of this direction."

- US thinking on the recovery phase, expected to last up to two years, was evolving and could be shaped by the UK: "The UK has a comprehensive network of embedded staff who need clear direction if they are to meet UK intent."

- It was not clear where the Combined Joint Task Force (CJTF) responsible for security sector issues from the start of the recovery period would be found: "A UK view on the potential role of HQ ARRC [Allied Rapid Reaction Corps] is required."

- Boundaries within Iraq would change with the transition from stabilisation to recovery: "If the UK wish to retain Sector South East a clear message needs to be sent to CFC [Coalition Forces Commander, Gen Franks]."

- The US assumed continued UK two-star leadership and "prolonged commitment" of a brigade. The duration of the UK's commitment needed clarification.

- The US needed to take critical decisions about UN involvement soon.

329. Maj Gen Fry explained that US planning was evolving slowly because of disagreement between DoD and the State Department over governance and the primacy of CFLCC, JTF-4 and the "Iraq Office of Post-war Planning [ORHA]". The UK had a colonel and small team in CFLCC "with the lead on the stabilisation stage" and a colonel with a small team in JTF-4 "with a focus on the recovery stage". Maj Gen Cross would deploy to ORHA with a small team shortly. To exert influence, there needed to be a common UK approach to the issues, which was "currently lacking". The IPU had been tasked to take that work forward.

330. Under existing US plans, once "post-hostility conditions" were achieved, CJTF would take over from CFLCC as the military headquarters responsible for Phase IV, but a decision was still needed on CJTF's "parentage". One option was to deploy the ARRC to take over as CJTF Iraq, incorporating JTF-4.

331. The paper described key tasks for the stabilisation phase, but offered no assessment of troop numbers needed to perform them.

332. The first detailed estimate of the type (but not the size) of force required to deliver different tasks was in Lt Gen Reith's draft Concept of Operations for Phase IV on 25 March.

333. The Chiefs of Staff discussed Maj Gen Fry's paper on 12 February.[160] They observed that there would be a substantial requirement for other countries to share the burden. The FCO undertook to explore the issue.

334. General Sir Mike Jackson, Chief of the General Staff, questioned whether the potential role for the ARRC was for the UK AO or all of Iraq, and whether it was to be used in its NATO or national role.

335. The potential deployment of the ARRC is addressed in Section 6.2.

336. MOD officials briefed Ms Short on the military campaign on 12 February.

337. On 12 February, MOD officials explained to Ms Short the general shape of the campaign, the policy on targeting and the approach to post-conflict operations.[161] The record stated she was: "reassured that MOD was 'catching up with the reality' … that humanitarian operations need to be an integral part of … campaign planning", but "reiterated in the strongest possible terms" her belief that the practical benefits of a second resolution were worth a delay until the autumn. Ms Short's main interest was mitigation of the impact of conflict on the Iraqi people, including in the event of CBW use. Working with the military in any UK Area of Responsibility (AOR), she wanted the UK to set "a benchmark standard for recovery and reconstruction".

338. Briefing for Mr Hoon's discussion of post-conflict issues with Dr Rice on 12 February listed eight "Key Gaps/US-UK policy differences", including the role of the UN, de-Ba'athification, SSR and economic policy.

339. Mr Hoon discussed post-conflict issues with Dr Rice and Secretary Rumsfeld in Washington on 12 February.

340. Briefing prepared by the MOD Iraq Secretariat stated that US aftermath planning was "impressive on details", but "riddled with holes at the political and strategic levels".[162] With the US divided on the merits of involving the UN, the key issue was the legal basis for any continuing occupation of Iraq. The UK assessment was that a specific mandate was needed. Without that the Coalition would "face both obligations and constraints which will face us with a choice between illegality and ineffectiveness".

341. The briefing listed eight "Key Gaps/US-UK policy differences" on post-conflict planning:

- UN mandate.
- Transitional administration. The UK wanted to see transition to a UN-led civilian administration as soon as possible.

[160] Minutes, 12 February 2003, Chiefs of Staff meeting.
[161] Minute Lee to PS/Secretary of State [MOD], 13 February 2003, 'Briefing for International Development Secretary'.
[162] Minute Johnson to PS/Secretary of State [MOD], 10 February 2003, 'Secretary of State's Visit to Washington: Iraq'.

- <u>Vetting policy</u>. "Is it the US aim to de-Saddam, or de-Ba'ath Iraq? If the latter, how much of the party structure do we wish to remove? In the short term, and in the long term? What level of compromise/co-operation with Iraqi officialdom will be necessary and/or acceptable in the early stages of Phase IV? Depending on the US intention, can they provide UK forces with means of identifying particular officials for removal from office or detention? How will the Coalition process those removed from office? … How will government functions be maintained if key officials are removed?"

- <u>Oil</u>. The UK would press for transparency of oil management, greater UN involvement than was envisaged and early setting of the date for handing control of oilfields back to Iraq.

- <u>National governance</u>. A decision on the final shape of an Iraq administration (the end state) was of "critical importance" to the earliest phases of the military effort.

- <u>Economic policy</u>. What were the plans for preventing macroeconomic collapse?

- <u>SSR</u>. What would the new security apparatus look like? At a tactical level, UK forces needed guidance on how to treat different parts of the Iraqi security infrastructure as they encountered them.

- <u>Humanitarian</u>. The source of the extra resources needed by the UK military to deliver humanitarian assistance in the absence of a significant NGO or UN presence was not known and there was no plan for the worst case scenario.

342. It is not clear whether the FCO or Cabinet Office saw the MOD briefing.

343. Separately, Mr Drummond sent Mr Lee "key messages" on post-conflict Iraq for Mr Hoon to use with Secretary Rumsfeld and for Sir David Manning to use with Dr Rice later in the week.[163] The messages, agreed by officials in other departments and No.10, included material on the importance of securing a UN mandate to legitimise international rule, establishing a substantial UN role in post-Saddam Hussein Iraq, engaging IFIs to plan economic reconstruction, avoiding the perception of a UK/US "oil grab" and securing "a level-playing field for UK business in oil and other areas".

344. The proposed message on dismantling the Iraqi regime was:

"Must detain senior leadership and leading members of Saddam's security forces and put them through proper legal process. But we will need Iraqi technocrats, who may have gone along with Saddam's regime, to run the country. Our officials are talking about handling war criminals etc. Must have an agreed policy this month."

345. It is unclear whether the reference to "an agreed policy" referred to war criminals, technocrats, or both.

---

[163] Letter Drummond to Lee, 11 February 2003, 'Iraq Post Conflict: Key Messages' attaching Paper Cabinet Office, 11 February 2003, 'Iraq Post Conflict: Key Messages'.

346. The British Embassy Washington reported that on 12 February Mr Hoon raised the issue of financing reconstruction from oil sales with Secretary Rumsfeld, who agreed that oil proceeds were key and should not be misinterpreted as a reason for the conflict.[164] DoD would make it clear that oil proceeds should go to Iraq's people. OFF was a good basis on which to work.

347. The Embassy also reported agreement during Mr Hoon's talks with Secretary Rumsfeld and Dr Rice that "broad UN cover for day after management in Iraq would bring political, financial and legal benefits. But this cover should not come with inefficient micro-management by UN agencies."[165] The Embassy commented that, although ORHA remained "disputed turf" and Mr Hoon had heard conflicting accounts of its role while in Washington, it would be the "key body in ruling and reconstructing a defeated Iraq". The UK was "slightly ahead of the game" in already having Maj Gen Cross there, but the US would welcome more UK secondees.

348. Neither the Embassy's report of Mr Hoon's meeting with Secretary Rumsfeld nor the record written by Mr Peter Watkins, Mr Hoon's Principal Private Secretary, referred to any discussion of de-Ba'athification.[166]

349. Mr Hoon told the Inquiry that, at the meeting, he handed Secretary Rumsfeld a paper which, while not using the word "de-Ba'athification", had:

> "… emphasised … that there would be people who had joined the Ba'ath Party … not because they necessarily were enthusiastic supporters of Saddam Hussein, and we felt that there ought to be a distinction between those who were enthusiastic supporters and those who simply joined the party in order to gain position … and I think a similar argument arises in relation to the army".[167]

350. The Inquiry has been unable to identify the paper handed over by Mr Hoon.

351. During Mr Hoon's meeting with Dr Rice she expressed concern that the existing military campaign plan for the South of Iraq assumed local administrators would remain in place. Her assessment was that those individuals, who were mainly Sunni in an otherwise Shia area, would flee after the collapse of Saddam Hussein's regime.[168] Mr Hoon's response was to point to the value of achieving UN cover for Coalition operations in Iraq.

---

[164] Telegram 203 Washington to FCO London, 13 February 2003, 'Iraq: Defence Secretary's Visit to Washington'.

[165] Telegram 204 Washington to FCO London, 13 February 2003, 'Iraq: Defence Secretary's Visit to Washington: Day After Management'.

[166] Minute Watkins to Policy Director, 13 February 2003, 'Meeting with Donald Rumsfeld: 12 February 2003'.

[167] Public hearing, 19 January 2010, page 160.

[168] Letter Watkins to Manning, 13 February 2003, 'Defence Secretary's call on Condi Rice: 12 February 2003'.

352. Mr Hoon told the Inquiry:

"… we were concerned that the planning for the aftermath was not as detailed and as comprehensive as we would have liked. Indeed, in a visit to the Pentagon in … February, I took with me a list of the things that we hoped that the United States would take account of."[169]

353. Mr Hoon added:

"… they welcomed the suggestions that we were making, but … I accept that not all of those items on my list were followed up and followed up in the timescale that we expected".

354. Sir Kevin Tebbit discussed post-conflict planning with Mr Frank Miller, NSC Senior Director for Defense Policy and Arms Control, on 12 February. Sir Kevin was told that ORHA was responsible for implementation only; policy remained with the NSC-led inter-agency group. Sir Kevin stressed the importance of UK involvement in both strands but was informed that the UK knew all there was to know: US planning was thin, but was all the system could cope with at that point.[170]

355. US officials' evidence to the Senate Foreign Relations Committee on 11 February revealed "enormous uncertainties" around US post-conflict plans.

356. The Committee's response was one of "incredulity".

357. Sir David Manning emphasised to officials in No.10 and the Cabinet Office the need to keep pressing the US for the work to be done.

358. On 11 February, Mr Marc Grossman, US Under Secretary of State for Political Affairs, and Mr Douglas Feith, US Under Secretary of Defense for Policy, gave evidence on US post-conflict plans to the Senate Foreign Relations Committee.[171]

359. The British Embassy Washington reported that the message to the Foreign Relations Committee was "liberation not occupation", with an assurance that the US did not want to control Iraq's economic resources.

360. The Embassy highlighted the degree of uncertainty surrounding US plans:

"In the ensuing discussion, Feith said that military occupation could last two years. Both admitted to 'enormous uncertainties'. They said that they did not know how the Iraqi oil industry would be managed, who would cover the costs of oil installation reconstruction, or how the detailed transition to a democratic Iraq would operate.

---

[169] Public hearing, 19 January 2010, pages 82-83.
[170] Minute Tebbit, 13 February 2003, 'Note for File: Phone Call with Frank Miller – 12 February'.
[171] Telegram 196 Washington to FCO London, 12 February 2003, 'Iraq "Day After": US Makes Initial Planning Public'.

The Committee's response was one of incredulity, with encouragement to plan for the worst, as well as the best, case."

361. Sir David Manning commented to Mr Bowen, Mr Matthew Rycroft (Mr Blair's Private Secretary for Foreign Affairs) and Mr Nicholas Cannon (Mr Blair's Assistant Private Secretary for Foreign Affairs):

"Last para[graph] shows scale of problem post-Saddam. We <u>must</u> keep pushing for this work to be done."[172]

Revised UK military campaign objectives

362. The UK shared its draft military campaign objectives with the US in mid-February.

363. Those objectives relating to the post-conflict phase of operations emphasised the role of the UN and the international community, and the UK's wish to withdraw from Iraq as soon as possible.

364. The objectives made no reference to the UK's obligations and responsibilities as an Occupying Power.

365. There is no indication that the objectives were linked to any assessment of feasibility or the resources needed for implementation.

366. Ministers had expressed themselves "generally content" with the draft objectives in January, but did not have an opportunity collectively to discuss the issues raised until Mr Blair's meeting on post-conflict issues on 6 March.

367. Sir David Manning described the objectives to Dr Rice as compatible with but not identical to US objectives.

368. Lord Goldsmith's approval of the objectives before publication is addressed in Section 6.2.

369. On 11 February, Mr Bowen sent Sir David Manning a revised draft of the UK's military campaign objectives, incorporating comments from Mr Straw and Whitehall departments.[173] Only DFID offered comments on post-conflict issues.

370. FCO concerns centred on how to present any reference to regime change.

---

[172] Manuscript comment Manning on Telegram 196 Washington to FCO London, 12 February 2003, 'Iraq "Day After": US Makes Initial Planning Public'.
[173] Minute Bowen to Manning, 11 February 2003, 'Iraq: Military Campaign Objectives' attaching Paper Cabinet Office, February 2003, 'Iraq: Military Campaign Objectives'.

371. In his advice to Mr Straw, Mr Chaplin had argued against avoiding all mention of regime change:

> "It seems to me unrealistic to expect that the Americans will sign up to a common set of campaign objectives which does <u>not</u> include explicit mention of regime change (put in the context of disarmament), especially once military action has begun. At that point it would be very difficult to claim publicly that, although we were taking part in military action, we did not intend or expect the regime to fall."[174]

372. Mr O'Brien had proposed specific wording to Mr Straw that "should satisfy the Americans but stop short of making regime change an explicit element of UK objectives" by establishing more clearly that regime change was needed to secure long-term disarmament:

> "The UK's overall objective for the military campaign is to create the conditions in which Iraq disarms in accordance with its obligations under UNSCRs [UN Security Council resolutions] <u>and creates the circumstances in which Iraq remains disarmed in the long-term</u>."[175]

373. Mr Straw included that proposal in a letter to Mr Blair on 11 February, in which he expressed "serious concerns" about the presentation of military campaign objectives:

> "It is particularly important to explain carefully any reference to regime change. We must underline that this is only necessary because Iraq has consistently refused to comply with UN Security Council resolutions. Otherwise people here and in the region will assume that we had been intent on regime change all along."[176]

374. The MOD comments on the draft objectives had focused on whether they provided "enough top cover to derive appropriate CDS and targeting directives to enable us to work in coalition with the US".[177]

375. DFID had proposed the addition of references to:

- addressing, rather than minimising, any adverse humanitarian consequences of the military campaign;
- demonstrating to the Iraqi people, rather than reassuring them, that their security and well-being was the UK's concern; and
- ensuring that sanctions were lifted and that the OFF programme and resources were available to meet the needs of the Iraqi people.[178]

---

[174] Minute Chaplin to PS [FCO], 4 February 2003, 'Iraq: Military Campaign Objectives'.
[175] Minute [FCO junior official] to Private Secretary [FCO], 7 February 2003, 'Iraq: Military Campaign Objectives'.
[176] Letter Straw to Prime Minister, 10 February 2003, 'Iraq: Military Campaign Objectives' attaching Paper [unattributed], 'Iraq: Military Campaign Objectives'.
[177] Letter Lee to Bowen, 4 February 2003, 'Iraq: Military Campaign Objectives'.
[178] Letter Brewer to Bowen, 4 February 2003, 'Iraq: Military Campaign Objectives'.

376. The draft circulated by Mr Bowen on 11 February stated:

> **"The UK's overall objective for the military campaign is to create the conditions in which Iraq disarms in accordance with its obligations under UNSCRs and remains so disarmed in the long term."**[179]

377. The Coalition's main tasks in support of that objective were to:

"a.　overcome the resistance of the Iraqi security forces;

b.　deny the Iraqi regime the use of weapons of mass destruction now and in the future;

c.　remove the Iraqi regime, given its clear and unyielding refusal to comply with the UN Security Council's demands;

d.　identify and secure the sites where weapons of mass destruction and their means of delivery are located;

e.　secure essential economic infrastructure, including for utilities and transport, from sabotage and wilful destruction by Iraqis; and

f.　deter wider conflict both inside Iraq and the region."

378. The UK's wider political objectives in support of the military campaign were to:

"a.　demonstrate to the Iraqi people that our quarrel is not with them and that their security and well-being is our concern;

b.　work with the United Nations to lift sanctions affecting the supply of humanitarian and reconstruction goods, and to enable Iraq's own resources, including oil, to be available to meet the needs of the Iraqi people;

c.　sustain the widest possible international and regional coalition in support of military action;

d.　preserve wider regional security, including by maintaining the territorial integrity of Iraq and mitigating the humanitarian and other consequences of conflict for Iraq's neighbours;

e.　help create conditions for a future, stable and law-abiding government of Iraqis;

f.　further our policy of eliminating terrorism as a force in international affairs."

---

[179] Minute Bowen to Manning, 11 February 2003, 'Iraq: Military Campaign Objectives' attaching Paper Cabinet Office, February 2003, 'Iraq: Military Campaign Objectives'.

379. The paper listed seven immediate military priorities in the aftermath of hostilities:

"a.   provide for the security of friendly forces;

b.   contribute to the creation of a secure environment so that normal life can be restored;

c.   work in support of humanitarian organisations to mitigate the consequences of hostilities and, in the absence of such civilian humanitarian capacity, provide relief where it is needed;

d.   work with UNMOVIC/IAEA to rid Iraq of its weapons of mass destruction and their means of delivery;

e.   facilitate remedial action where environmental damage has occurred;

f.   enable the reconstruction and recommissioning of essential infrastructure for the political and economic development of Iraq, and the immediate benefit of the Iraqi people; and

g.   lay plans for the reform of Iraq's security forces."

380. The paper stated that:

- Those tasks would, "wherever possible", be carried out in co-operation with the UN.
- UK military forces would withdraw as soon as possible.
- The UK hoped to see early establishment of a transitional civilian administration.
- The UK would work with the international community to build the widest possible international and regional support for reconstruction and the move to representative government.

381. The paper concluded with the 7 January description of the desired end state for a post-Saddam Hussein Iraq (see Section 6.4).

382. On 12 February, the Chiefs of Staff noted that work on the UK objectives paper had been concluded, but not finally endorsed. The paper would be "ready for release at the start of any offensive campaign".[180]

383. Mr Hoon discussed the objectives with Secretary Rumsfeld in Washington on 12 February.[181]

---

[180] Minutes, 12 February 2003, Chiefs of Staff meeting.
[181] Letter Manning to Rice, 14 February 2003, 'Iraq: Military Campaign Objectives'.

384. Sir David Manning sent a copy to Dr Rice on 14 February.[182] He explained that the UK military campaign objectives were "compatible but not identical" to 'Iraq: Goals, Objectives, Strategy' (the US document handed to Sir David by Dr Rice on 31 January).

385. Sir David explained that the UK and US were committed to ridding Iraq of WMD and recognised the need to remove the current Iraqi regime if military action proved necessary, but the UK document avoided references to "liberation". No firm decision had been taken, but the likelihood was that the UK would publish its objectives if and when military action was decided.

386. A final version of the military campaign objectives, with changes to the introductory paragraphs (reflecting the outcome of negotiations in the UN Security Council) but not to the objectives themselves, was placed in the Library of the House of Commons by Mr Hoon on 20 March.

387. In a speech on 11 February, Mr Straw explained that the UK's first objective in Iraq was disarmament. The next priority was to work with the UN to help the Iraqi people recover.

388. In a speech at the International Institute for Strategic Studies on 11 February, Mr Straw stated that if military action did prove necessary, "huge efforts" would be made "to ensure that the suffering of the Iraqi people" was "as limited as is possible".[183] They deserved "the chance to live fulfilling lives free from the oppression and terror of Saddam"; and to "choose their own destiny and government, and to pursue a prosperous life within a safe environment". The UK's first objective was disarmament, but the "next priority would be to work with the United Nations to help the Iraqi people recover … and allow their country to move towards one that is ruled by law, respects international obligations and provides effective and representative government".

Mr Blair's meeting on humanitarian issues, 13 February 2003

389. Mr Blair convened two Ministerial meetings on post-conflict issues in February and March 2003. The first, on 13 February, covered the specific question of humanitarian assistance. The second, on 6 March, addressed wider post-conflict issues and is addressed later in this Section.

390. At the meeting on 13 February, Mr Blair listed three UK post-conflict priorities:

- **that the UN "must play a key role", which he did not define;**
- **a UK lead on humanitarian issues in southern Iraq; and**
- **mobilisation of other contributors.**

---

[182] Letter Manning to Rice, 14 February 2003, 'Iraq: Military Campaign Objectives'.
[183] *The Guardian*, 11 February 2003, *The Foreign Secretary's address to the International Institute for Strategic Studies*.

391. The lack of precision in the instructions to departments from No.10 after the meeting was indicative of the Government's persistent failure to define the component parts of the post-conflict task and how different departments would be responsible for addressing them.

392. In particular, the relationship between humanitarian relief and wider reconstruction, and between short-, medium- and long-term post-conflict tasks, tended to be overlooked or left unclear.

393. Throughout the planning process Mr Blair continued to request, and receive, separate advice on post-conflict issues from Mr Straw, Mr Hoon and Ms Short.

394. Mr Blair convened a meeting on humanitarian issues with Mr Straw, Mr Hoon, Ms Short, Admiral Sir Michael Boyce (CDS) and No.10 officials in the margins of Cabinet on 13 February.[184] Sir Michael Jay, Sir Kevin Tebbit and Mr Chakrabarti were not present.

395. The IPU briefing for Mr Straw set out three objectives for the meeting, including:

"• encourage Ms Short to engage fully in planning;

• persuade Ms Short that she should allow DFID money to finance small scale [reconstruction] projects in the area administered by a UK commander."

396. On the assumption that discussion might stray beyond humanitarian issues, the briefing included "a background note on other key 'Day After' issues", including:

"**For how long do we want to run a geographical sector of Iraq?**

"... it seems very likely that UK forces (under US command) will find themselves occupying an area of south-east Iraq ...

...

"In practical terms, administration of a geographical sector will be very labour intensive. It will be dangerous and difficult ...

"There is likely to be a hybrid model of both geographical sectors under different interim administrations, and lead countries responsible for some issue nation-wide. So, for example, the US want to lead on military issues throughout Iraq. But the detail of a hybrid model remains unclear."[185]

---

[184] Letter Cannon to Bewes, 13 February 2003, 'Iraq: Humanitarian Issues'.
[185] Minute Iraq Planning Unit [junior official] to Private Secretary [FCO], 12 February 2003, 'Meeting on Iraq Day After Issues Before Cabinet 13 February'.

397. The other issues listed were:

- whether the UK wanted to lead on justice;
- the role of the UN; and
- UK commercial involvement.

398. Before the meeting, Mr Bowen advised Sir David Manning that:

"The Prime Minister will … want to seek Clare [Short]'s engagement in the potential humanitarian relief operation and reconstruction – which will need funding and the commitment of human resources as a priority."[186]

399. The No.10 briefing note for Mr Blair stated that the purpose of the meeting was to discuss "humanitarian aspects of developments in Iraq", but that there also needed to be "quick agreement on a US/UK policy for a post-conflict Iraq, so that plans can be made".[187]

400. Those wider issues were not addressed.

401. At the meeting, Mr Hoon reported on his Washington visit.[188]

402. Ms Short commented on the scale of the potential humanitarian crisis, stressed that military assets should not be used for humanitarian operations and suggested that NGOs would want to see a UN role.

403. In response to a question from Mr Blair about whether the UK should "take the lead on humanitarian action in the southern zone", Ms Short said that she was in favour. The UK could do an "exemplary job" in the zone on both military and humanitarian fronts.

404. The No.10 record of the meeting stated that Mr Blair concluded:

- "The UN must play a key role, both to reassure the NGOs and also for political reasons, to avoid the impression of a US takeover of Iraq. He asked DFID, FCO and MOD to co-ordinate advice so that he could discuss with President Bush.
- We should seek to take the lead on humanitarian issues in the southern zone of Iraq.
- We must work up a strategy for mobilising other contributors on the humanitarian side: France and Germany could play a role, as could Japan."

405. No further instructions were sent to departments by No.10.

---

[186] Minute Bowen to Manning, 13 February 2003, 'Meeting on Iraq: Humanitarian Follow-up'.
[187] Minute Cannon to Prime Minister, 13 February 2003, 'Iraq: Humanitarian Planning'.
[188] Letter Cannon to Bewes, 13 February 2003, 'Iraq: Humanitarian Issues'.

406. Mr Hoon instructed MOD officials to take forward work with the FCO and DFID.[189] Mr Watkins explained to Mr Simon Webb, MOD Policy Director:

"As he has discussed with CDS, PUS and you, the Secretary of State is clear that the MOD should act as the conduit for UK views to the US Post War Planning Office [ORHA] which has been established in the Pentagon. If the UK is to influence the Office's approach, it must present it with a consistent joined-up line: we cannot allow individual Whitehall departments to transmit possibly disparate messages to their secondees in the Office.

"The underlying theme of yesterday's meeting was that all relevant government departments need to contribute to what will be a major undertaking. The role of pulling together the Whitehall line on this side of the Atlantic belongs naturally to the FCO. Mr Hoon presumes that the FCO will now move quickly to pull together the views of the relevant departments … Mr Hoon's clear recollection is that all three Secretaries of State concerned were asked to provide the Prime Minister with co-ordinated advice on how the UK should structure its approach to post-conflict planning and what level of contribution it should be prepared to make (not just the narrow UN point …). I have spoken to No.10 and the Foreign Secretary's Office accordingly.

"Mr Hoon would be grateful if you would speak to your counterparts in the FCO and DFID to ensure this work is being taken forward in the right lines."

407. In his statement of 14 January 2011, Mr Blair explained to the Inquiry that:

"… we broke down planning into three parts: humanitarian – the priority for DFID; Military – with the MOD; and political with the FCO …

"Though the Iraq Planning Unit was formally established in February 2003, some planning was already under way and co-ordinated by the ad hoc officials group [AHGI] from October 2002 … but above all planning was under way within departments …

"… [I]ndividual Secretaries of State were responsible for each separate stream. The Cabinet was debating the issue and there was a constant process of exchange at official level passed up to me and the Ministers. As we came to recognise … it would have been better to have had more integrated planning at an earlier time; and certainly there is a lesson there."[190]

---

[189] Minute Watkins to Policy Director, 14 February 2003, 'Iraq: Humanitarian Issues'.
[190] Statement, 14 January 2011, pages 13-14.

408. On 14 February, Ms Short advised Mr Blair of constraints on the UK's ability to perform an "exemplary" humanitarian role in Iraq.

409. In response, Mr Blair restated the need to "get the US to accept the UN role".

410. Ms Short sent Mr Blair a letter on 14 February setting out "key humanitarian issues and some thoughts on the UN's role which we need to pursue with the US".[191] Ms Short advised:

> "The vulnerability of the Iraqi people to humanitarian catastrophe should not be underestimated … Iraq should be an upper middle or high income country. Instead its average earnings have plummeted in the last two decades, its population is largely dependent on food handouts, its agricultural sector operating well below capacity. Iraqi people's lives are perilously fragile – their private coping strategies worn away by years of misrule … The situation in the centre and south of Iraq is much worse than in the north …"

411. Ms Short also expanded on her comments on the UK's ability to do an "exemplary" job, made at Mr Blair's meeting on 13 February. She told Mr Blair there was a "great opportunity" for the UK to play "an exemplary humanitarian role" in a sector under UK control, within an agreed international framework set out in a second resolution. Such a resolution "should address the UN's lead role after conflict and underline the prioritisation of humanitarian considerations".

412. Ms Short also highlighted budgetary constraints. She could not:

> "… take resources from other poor and needy people to assist post-conflict Iraq. Without some understanding on finance, I cannot responsibly commit DFID to the exemplary partnership with MOD which we discussed."

413. In her evidence to the Inquiry, Ms Short focused on the resolution's importance to reconstruction, rather than humanitarian efforts:

> "… we knew that if we didn't get another UN resolution, we were in big trouble. We could do humanitarian, but you can't reconstruct the country, and that became an absolute obsession of Whitehall."[192]

414. Mr Blair wrote on his copy of the letter: "We must get the US to accept the UN role."[193]

---

[191] Letter Short to Blair, 14 February 2003, 'Iraq: Humanitarian Planning and the Role of the UN'.
[192] Public hearing, 2 February 2010, page 68.
[193] Manuscript comment Blair on Letter Short to Blair, 14 February 2003, 'Iraq: Humanitarian Planning and the Role of the UN'.

UN preparations

415. Mr Annan briefed members of the UN Security Council on humanitarian contingency planning on 13 February.

416. Mr Annan and Ms Louise Fréchette, UN Deputy Secretary-General, briefed members of the Security Council on the UN Secretariat's humanitarian contingency planning and financial requirements on 13 February.[194]

417. Mr Annan reported that Ms Fréchette had led a steering group of the relevant UN departments, funds and programmes since November 2002 to prepare contingency plans in case of conflict. The task would be complex because of the large number of Iraqis already dependent on international aid through OFF.

418. Ms Fréchette explained that the UN agencies had developed an integrated humanitarian plan for Iraq, working with the six neighbouring countries, the ICRC and NGOs. US$30.6m had already been pledged and the UN was preparing a request for a further US$88.8m. Much more would be needed in the event of a "medium-case scenario" of two to three months' acute conflict, which would trigger a "flash appeal".

419. The US$2.22bn UN Flash Appeal for Iraq was launched on 28 March (see Section 10.1).

420. Mr Straw raised the Security Council briefing with Mr Annan on 14 February.[195] Mr Annan's concerns were understandable, but "the US was doing a huge amount on this, and the UK was contributing and planning also. DFID were active, and keen on UN cover for an operation." Mr Annan stated that all the humanitarian agencies also wanted UN cover, including for the reconstruction effort.

421. Mr Straw "pointed out that there was in this area an inverse relationship between loudness of rhetoric and willingness to contribute hard cash".

422. Sir Jeremy Greenstock, UK Permanent Representative to the UN from 1998 to 2003, told the Inquiry that the UK Permanent Mission to the UN in New York (UKMIS New York) discussed post-conflict Iraq with the UN Secretariat in February 2003.[196] There were very clear indications the UN did not want the administration of Iraq to become its responsibility. It was more focused on the things it was very good at:

> "... food supply, some policing perhaps, help for the political process and other aspects of services to a population or territory in trouble but not to take full responsibility."

---

[194] Telegram 257 UKMIS New York to FCO London, 14 February 2003, 'Iraq: UN Humanitarian Contingency Planning'.
[195] Telegram 268 UKMIS New York to FCO London, 15 February 2003, 'Iraq: Foreign Secretary's Meeting with the UN Secretary-General: 14 February'.
[196] Public hearing, 15 December 2009, page 5.

The absence of a "winning concept"

423. In mid-February, officials expressed concern about two significant risks:

- the potential "nightmare scenario" of no second resolution and, at best, only a weak legal basis for military action; and
- the continuing absence of a coherent plan for the administration of Iraq.

424. Over the previous year, Ministers, the military and officials had identified effective preparation for the post-conflict phase as a requirement for strategic success.

425. Mr Hoon had reminded Mr Blair as recently as 16 January that a satisfactory post-conflict plan was needed before a decision was taken to deploy UK forces (see Section 6.4).

426. As the extent of US opposition to a UN lead on civil administration became clearer and the likely start date for military action approached, the Government needed to reassess policy and prepare for the possibility that the US could not be persuaded of the UK view.

427. No reassessment of UK policy took place.

428. Section 3.7 describes Mr Chaplin's analysis of the prospects for a Ministerial-level meeting of the Security Council on 14 February. On 13 February, he advised Mr Ricketts that it was:

"… probably the last opportunity to reflect on whether we can extract … a better outcome … than at present looks likely.

"… No SCR and a feeble, at best, legal basis for military action is a nightmare scenario … A quick collapse of the Iraqi regime (quite likely); subsequent clear proof, because we find the stuff, that we were right all along about the Iraqi WMD threat (*questionable – what convinces the experts may not convince public opinion unless it is pretty spectacular); and a smooth transfer to a democratic and stable government (improbable, especially without UN cover) would reduce the damage. But this is a high risk route."[197]

429. On 14 February, officials advised No.10 of the critical importance of a satisfactory post-conflict plan as part of an overall "winning concept" for Iraq.

430. A Cabinet Office paper on "winning the peace" gave a clear description of the potential scale of the post-conflict task and the long list of issues still to be resolved with the US.

---

[197] Minute Chaplin to Ricketts, 13 February 2003, 'Iraq: The Endgame'.

431. The paper warned that there was "no coherent plan of how Iraq will be governed beyond the first 3 to 6 months".

432. On 14 February, in response to a request for a note on key messages for use with the US, Mr Drummond sent Sir David Manning a paper on "winning the peace", cleared with the IPU.[198]

433. Mr Drummond stated: "A satisfactory plan for post-conflict is critical to whether we have a 'winning concept'."

434. "Victorious Coalition forces" could expect to find an Iraq with certain "broad characteristics":

- the remains of a command state with "some sound technical institutions, which should recover with Saddam's influence removed";
- a "brutal security apparatus with the layers closest to Saddam requiring disbandment and the rest substantial reform";
- a "dysfunctional judicial system";
- large numbers of displaced people;
- the majority of the population hungry should the OFF programme collapse;
- health, education and other public services that had declined rapidly over the last 20 years;
- damage to key infrastructure, "perhaps less than other conflicts if the campaign is quick";
- an oil-dependent country with potential and the skills available to recover quickly if well managed;
- a secular Islamic state "with potential for much greater fundamentalism";
- tribal, sectarian and, especially, ethnic divisions;
- neighbouring states "keen to press their interests" and a region "deeply nervous, if not hostile, to a continuing US military presence in Iraq".

435. It was expected that any Iraqi welcome for the removal of Saddam Hussein would be short lived:

"… liberation will quickly become occupation … So the Coalition must have a clear public plan for restoring Iraqi representative government, for the use of oil revenues for the benefit of all Iraqis, and the means to bring early benefits of change to the Iraqi people. This will also help with the region and those members of the international community who did not support military action.

"We must not underestimate the task. In recent years, we have had to remove governments in Kosovo and East Timor and replace them with international

---

[198] Minute Drummond to Manning, 14 February 2003, 'Iraq: Winning the Peace' attaching Paper OD Secretariat, 11 February 2003, 'Iraq: Post Conflict: Key Messages'.

administrations, but they are much smaller both in size (Wales not France) and population (2.5m in Kosovo, 25m in Iraq). In Afghanistan we have worked with a local political process and administration. In Iraq we face having to replace a government and remove a political party which has dominated Iraqi politics and institutions for over 40 years. So some similarities to post-war Germany."

436. On post-conflict planning, the paper stated:

"The US has assumed for planning purposes that it will lead the government of Iraq following military victory. It has consulted extensively with the Iraqi exile population, many of whom are well informed about the situation in Iraq, but have their own agenda. There has been extensive CENTCOM and DoD planning for the military campaign and the first 60 to 90 days. PJHQ are plugged into this well, and have helped to shape some aspects of it. There is also good progress in planning to follow up the military advance with immediate humanitarian support for the Iraqi population. But there is no serious US assessment of the consequence of CBW use on the civilian population.

"PJHQ started their own detailed planning exercise as soon as it became clear that UK forces might have control over the Basra area of southern Iraq (city population 1.5m alone) from the very early stages of the campaign … Whitehall inter-departmental teams have visited [the US] several times since last autumn to discuss the issues. Some decisions cannot of course be made until the Coalition can assess the situation post-conflict. But there is no coherent plan of how Iraq will be governed beyond the first 3 to 6 months. This risks the continuation of a military government becoming increasingly unpopular. This would be even more likely if the US proceeded with a plan of dividing Iraq into three sectors for military government.

"The US envisages that there will be three phases post-conflict:

- A military government led by a US general for the first 3 to 6 months to re-establish security and deal with the humanitarian crisis.
- Then a civilian-led international government charged with rebuilding democracy from the bottom up, restoring key services and increasing oil production. The US hope this would last 12 to 18 months but accept it might take longer.
- Handover to an Iraqi representative government at which point Coalition forces would withdraw.

"Our key concerns are to manage the task, by ensuring that we have legal cover, as much support as possible within Iraq and internationally, and as much help in both money and skills from the international community."

437. The paper stated that decisions needed to be reached with the US on:

- Legitimacy. The US had been told that the UK required the UN to legitimise the post-conflict government of Iraq and to resolve legal problems around sanctions and OFF. "This would require a further resolution. It should be achievable if the Security Council is satisfied with the extent of UN involvement in the transition … Even Rumsfeld is beginning to accept the need for it. On current plans it would not be presented until the end of the conflict."

- UN administration. This would make sense for "international acceptability and for the skills, which the UN could bring … But the US is set against, because they believe the UN has performed poorly elsewhere. We are therefore proposing that the UN's expertise should be used in technical areas such as education and health. A UN Special Representative … will be required to pull the UN machinery together locally … We have given the US proposals for UN involvement. Mr Hoon pursued with Rumsfeld, and you will want to follow up with Condi Rice."

- The political process. "We need urgently to pin down a process so that it can be announced as soon as a decision is taken to remove Saddam by force … Again we have given the US outline proposals, but should firm them up."

- Humanitarian issues. "Although the US has good plans to bring in humanitarian relief behind the military it has not thought through how to encourage NGOs and UN specialised agencies to engage. The international community also needs a contingency financing plan …"

- The economy. A joint working group with the US was working on a plan for transparent management of Iraq's oil revenues, which needed "a political push in the US".

- Reconstruction contracts. The US needed to be encouraged to create "a level playing field".

- Security. The Pentagon wanted to withdraw units from Iraq as quickly as possible. "We must prevent the UK bearing a disproportionate share of the security burden at a time when military overstretch is causing problems with meeting our other priorities. If we are not to replicate the problems seen in Afghanistan, we will also need the US to agree early on to [a] single holistic plan for Security Sector Reform. We have offered outline proposals for the security sector. We should offer a plan."

- Justice. The US had asked the UK to lead on the revival of the Iraqi justice system.

- Sectorisation. The UK needed "urgently to understand the recent US suggestion that Iraq be divided into three geographical sectors and that we should run one of them (a much bigger area than the Basra Area of Operations) with enormous personnel and financial implications".

- The timeframe. "US plans are very ambitious. The reforms planned are unlikely to be achieved within a two year period. We are likely to need longer engagement in Iraq if we are to leave a durable legacy, but we should deliver the latter stages under an Iraqi administration. The US will need to be persuaded of this fact."

438. The paper did not address the scale of the potential UK contribution.

439. Mr Drummond explained that the IPU would take forward detailed planning, aiming for a paper that Sir David Manning could send to Dr Rice for Mr Blair to discuss with President Bush the following week.

440. It is not clear whether Mr Blair saw the paper.

441. Sir David Manning instructed Mr Cannon to "have [a] first look + mark up", but there is no evidence of further action.[199]

442. The Inquiry has seen no comment on the paper from No.10.

443. There is no indication that Mr Drummond's paper was discussed further or that the IPU prepared a second paper before Mr Blair's conversation with President Bush on 19 February.

444. On 14 February, Secretary Rumsfeld identified lessons for Iraq from the experience of nation-building in Afghanistan. The goal in Iraq was not to impose a US template, but to create conditions for Iraqis to form their own government.

445. Secretary Rumsfeld stated that a US-led Coalition in Iraq would stay as long as necessary and leave as soon as possible.

446. In a speech in New York on 14 February, Secretary Rumsfeld drew lessons for Iraq from the US experience of nation-building in Afghanistan:

> "Afghanistan belongs to the Afghans. The objective is not to engage in what some call nation-building. Rather it is to help the Afghans so they can build their own nation. This is an important distinction. In some nation-building exercises well-intentioned foreigners … can create a dependency."[200]

447. Secretary Rumsfeld stated that a US-led Coalition in Iraq would be guided by two commitments, to "[s]tay as long as necessary and to leave as soon as possible":

> "We would work with our partners as we are doing in Afghanistan to help the Iraqi people establish a new government …
>
> "The goal would not be to impose an American-style template on Iraq, but rather to create conditions where Iraqis can form a government in their own unique way, just as the Afghans did with the Loya Jirga which produced a representative government that is uniquely Afghan.

---

[199] Manuscript comment Manning to Cannon, 18 February 2003, on Minute Drummond to Manning, 14 February 2003, 'Iraq: Winning the Peace' attaching Paper OD Secretariat, 11 February 2003, 'Iraq: Post Conflict: Key Messages'.
[200] US Department of Defense, 14 February 2003, *Speech: Beyond Nation Building*.

"This is not to underestimate the challenge that the Coalition would face. Iraq has several advantages over Afghanistan. One is time. The effort in Afghanistan had to be planned and executed in a matter of weeks after September 11th. With Iraq, by contrast, there has been time to prepare. We have set up a Post War Planning Office to think through problems and co-ordinate the efforts of Coalition countries and US Government agencies. General Franks in an inter-agency process has been working on this for many months.

"A second advantage is resources. Afghanistan is a poor country that has been brutalized by continuous war – civil war and occupation. Iraq has a solid infrastructure with working networks of roads and [resources] and it has oil to help give free Iraq the means to get on its feet."

448. In his speech to the Labour Party Spring Conference, Mr Blair stated that the UK should be as committed to rebuilding Iraq as to removing Saddam Hussein.

449. He offered no detail on what form that assistance might take.

450. Before his speech to the Labour Party Spring Conference in Glasgow on 15 February, Mr Blair asked officials for information on a number of issues, including some raised by Ms Short in her letter of 14 February:

"(a) How many Iraqi children under the age of five die each month? (We have seen the figure of 150 deaths per 1000. Is this accurate, and what does it mean in actual numbers?)

(b) How many political prisoners are there in prison in Iraq at any time?

(c) Is Northern Iraq better administered than the rest of Iraq? If so, what concrete examples can we give?

…

(f) How were the Shia and Kurd uprisings after the Gulf War put down?

(g) What was Iraq's standard of living in the 1960s compared with eg Portugal, Taiwan, and others? And today?"[201]

451. The FCO response emphasised the unreliability of the available data, in particular for infant mortality and the number of political prisoners.[202] The FCO also advised that the comparative figures on GDP per capita came from different sources and should only be used as indicators, although the comparison between Iraq and Portugal was "particularly illuminating".

---

[201] Minute Rycroft to Owen, 14 February 2003, 'Iraq: Prime Minister's Speech'.
[202] Letter Owen to Rycroft, 14 February 2003, 'Iraq: Prime Minister's Speech'.

452. At Mr Rycroft's request, the FCO later provided additional comparators for GDP growth and new figures on infant mortality agreed with DFID.[203]

453. Mr Rycroft drew on the FCO response to recommend text for inclusion in Mr Blair's speech.[204] Mr Rycroft made no reference to the reliability of the data.

454. Some of the material provided by the FCO and Mr Rycroft was incorporated into the speech, in which Mr Blair described Iraq as:

"A country that in 1978, the year before he [Saddam Hussein] seized power, was richer than Malaysia or Portugal. A country where today, 135 out of every 1,000 Iraqi children die before the age of five[205] – 70 percent of these deaths are from diarrhoea and respiratory infections that are easily preventable. Where almost a third of children born in the centre and south of Iraq have chronic malnutrition.

"Where 60 percent of the people depend on food aid.

"Where half the population of rural areas have no safe water.

"Where every year and now, as we speak, tens of thousands of political prisoners languish in appalling conditions in Saddam's jails and are routinely executed.

"Where in the past 15 years over 150,000 Shia Muslims in southern Iraq and Muslim Kurds in northern Iraq have been butchered, with up to four million Iraqis in exile round the world, including 350,000 now in Britain."[206]

455. Mr Blair concluded:

"If the international community does not take note of the Iraqi people's plight but continues to address it casually this will breed terrorism and extremism within the Iraqi people. This cannot be allowed to happen.

"Remember Kosovo where we were told war would destabilise the whole of the Balkans and that region now has the best chance of peace in over 100 years.

"Remember Afghanistan, where now, despite all the huge problems, there are three million children in school, including for the first time in over two decades one and a half million girls, and where two million Afghan exiles from the Taliban have now returned …

---

[203] Fax Owen to Rycroft, 14 February 2003, 'PM's Speech Question'; Fax Owen to Rycroft, [undated], 'Iraq: Prime Minister's Speech'.
[204] Minute Rycroft to Prime Minister, 14 February 2003, 'Iraq: Scotland Speech'; Minute Rycroft to Prime Minister, 14 February 2003, 'Iraq: Scotland Speech – additional points'.
[205] The figure of 135 per 1,000 appears to have been taken from Ms Short's letter of 14 February to Mr Blair and not the material supplied by the FCO. Ms Short's letter made clear that the figure referred only to central and southern Iraq and quoted a figure of 72 per 1,000 for the north.
[206] *Scoop Independent News*, 17 February 2003, *Prime Minister Tony Blair's Glasgow Party Speech*.

"Ridding the world of Saddam would be an act of humanity. It is leaving him there that is in truth inhumane.

"And if it does come to this, let us be clear: we should be as committed to the humanitarian task of rebuilding Iraq for the Iraqi people as we have been to removing Saddam."

DFID contingency planning

456. In mid-February, DFID officials sought Ms Short's views on how DFID should deploy its limited resources and what balance to strike between planning for an "exemplary role" in southern Iraq and supporting the UN and the wider international effort throughout the country.

457. Officials recommended certain actions to ensure that DFID was adequately prepared for a range of roles.

458. Ms Short rejected a number of her officials' recommendations on the grounds that they might imply that military action was a certainty or presupposed a significant role for DFID to which it could not yet commit.

459. Ms Short did so despite accepting that, as a consequence, DFID would not be prepared for an immediate response in the event of military action or a humanitarian crisis on the ground.

460. Ms Short withdrew her objections by early March.

461. On 17 February, DFID officials advised Ms Short on the implications of the decisions taken at Mr Blair's meeting on 13 February.[207] DFID needed to balance the decision that the UK should take the lead on humanitarian issues in southern Iraq with its commitment to support the international system, in particular the UN, in humanitarian work across Iraq and the region. DFID needed to prioritise its "scarce human and financial resources" between those activities.

462. DFID officials had discussed the idea of an "exemplary role" briefly with senior UK military officers and the MOD, who were ready to contribute "in circumstances where the military may be the only people able to deliver humanitarian assistance, or they are needed to facilitate access by others". The Chiefs of Staff would discuss the humanitarian role of the UK military on 19 February. Officials recommended to Ms Short that, at that meeting, DFID would need to give a clearer steer on the role it expected to play and what it thought the military should do.

---

[207] Minute Conflict & Humanitarian Affairs Department to PS/Secretary of State [DFID], 17 February 2003, 'Iraq – Contingency Planning: Deployment Plan'.

463. Officials recommended that:

"... we plan at this stage to do all four of these activities:

a) Support humanitarian needs nationally and in the region, primarily through the UN and Red Cross/Red Crescent movement

b) Work alongside and influence humanitarian action by US DART teams

c) Work alongside the UK military

d) Undertake DFID bilateral humanitarian action.

"These activities are complementary and doing them all could maximise our impact – working in an exemplary way in a part of the country under UK military control (though activities b), c) and d) will have greater influence if we are co-operating closely with the UN and US delivery of assistance elsewhere in the country (through activities a) and b))."

464. Officials also recommended a number of "pre-deployment steps which we need to initiate now to be adequately prepared to play these roles effectively":

- establishing a forward base in Kuwait to allow DFID to build its capacity for deployment into Iraq, potentially including a field presence in a UK military AOR and/or Baghdad;
- deployment of a Humanitarian Adviser to Amman to liaise and work with humanitarian partners;
- regional assessment missions, including to Cyprus, Egypt, Turkey and Iran;
- deployment of a Civil-Military Humanitarian Adviser to 1 (UK) Div in Kuwait and regular visits to CENTCOM in Qatar; and
- secondments to support humanitarian co-ordination, initially to the UN Humanitarian Information Centre (HIC) in Cyprus.

465. Officials warned Ms Short:

"If we do not have people and assets in place and ready in time, we will not be able to respond quickly and as may be needed. Once conflict has begun logistical constraints will make it extremely difficult to respond unless we have put the preparations in place."

466. Officials advised that the US was planning to carry out humanitarian work across Iraq, including in the South. If the UK did not agree with that approach, it would need to convince the US at "very senior level" that it should change its plans and that the UK was adequately resourced to play an exemplary role, which was not currently the case. It might be more realistic to supplement and influence US efforts in a UK sector. Officials recommended working alongside the US DART field office in Kuwait, "to protect and supplement the proposed exemplary role for UK humanitarian action".

467. On working alongside the UK military, the advice stated that:

- The military was considering how to revise plans to allocate resources to a potentially significant humanitarian role, but that, given the military's resource constraints, it could be "highly advantageous" if Coalition military units could supplement the UK effort with medical teams and NBC units, where it was weakest.

- DFID needed to retain flexibility to deal with the possibility that, initially, the UN and other humanitarian organisations might not be able to operate in Iraq. In those circumstances, "we would need to rely on military forces supported by embedded DFID civil/military humanitarian advisers and/or a DFID operational team".

- Significant planning and preparation had been carried out, but some sectors were poorly covered, including "fuel supply (supporting electricity generation and distribution systems), water and sanitation and the power sectors". The security environment and the ability of humanitarian agencies to engage was a "principal concern". Past experience showed that "direct DFID/UK military humanitarian action can save lives [and] alleviate suffering, and assists the process towards recovery and stabilisation".

468. On DFID-led interventions, officials advised that the military might provide security and logistics to support DFID "assessments" and:

"… depending on priority needs potentially including the maintenance and management of key infrastructure including water and sanitation, transport infrastructure and electricity generation and transmission infrastructure in an AOR. Under these circumstances DFID would assist with technical programme support directly or via specialist contractors retained internationally. However, it has to be noted that our human resource capacity is limited (CHAD-OT [Operations Team] can provide around 25 specialists, including recruiting additional experts) and the scale of need could be immense and we may face … the threat of CBW. Therefore we should concentrate on those tasks where our experience and expertise would add most value. Working alongside Coalition military where necessary and with US DART capacity where it would enhance humanitarian response."

469. The advice concluded with a section on resource constraints. Until DFID received an indication from the Treasury or No.10 that further funds would be forthcoming, it was planning on the basis that "a substantial share of DFID's Contingency Reserve" would supplement CHAD's emergency funds and MENAD's Iraq programme budget. If a total of £60m were available from those sources in 2003/04, DFID would plan initially to commit £35m for immediate relief. Exactly how to allocate that amount would depend on the nature of the conflict and other factors, but an indicative allocation might be:

- £20m to support the work of UN agencies, the Red Cross and NGOs across Iraq;

- £5m to fund UK military Quick Impact Projects (QIPs) to help generate stability within communities; and

- £10m for DFID's own rapid response capacity.

470. The advice stated:

"Under many scenarios, £35m is unlikely to be perceived as an adequate UK contribution to any immediate relief effort, particularly if OFF collapses. Leaving £25m for further humanitarian need, medium-term rehabilitation and reconstruction could also look very sparse. Action in response to the Secretary of State's previous two letters [Ms Short's letters of 5 and 14 February] to the Prime Minister on this rests with No.10.

"If the military is involved in the direct delivery of humanitarian assistance, there will be an issue about who pays. MOD claim to be financially stretched and are keen for DFID to pay ..."

471. Ms Short held a meeting to discuss those recommendations on 18 February, attended by Dr Brewer, Ms Miller, Mr Fernie and other DFID officials.[208] Mr Chakrabarti was not present, but was sent a copy of the record.

472. Ms Short stated that she was unwilling, without a clear financial package, to plan to do more than "support the UN, key international agencies, and perhaps provide some financial assistance to the UK military for Quick Impact Projects". She had repeatedly made it clear in various forums (to Mr Blair in person and in writing, and in the House of Commons) that DFID did not have the financial resources to play a major role.

473. Within those constraints, Ms Short was content for officials:

- to start discussions about possible support to NGOs not yet involved in Iraq that had specific technical expertise in areas such as water and sanitation;

- to work closely with the US on a humanitarian response, but only if there was an overarching UN mandate and financial cover; and

- "in principle", to make money available to the UK military for QIPs, to be re-examined if there was no UN mandate and the UK military was "working under a US lead".

474. Ms Short did not agree to a forward base in Kuwait on the grounds that it would imply that military action was a certainty. DFID could make scoping visits to the region and arrange for vehicles to be ready for transportation, but the equipment should not be pre-positioned in the region. Ms Short "accepted that this would mean that DFID would not be prepared for an immediate response in the event of military action or a humanitarian crisis on the ground". She suggested that DFID consider providing more

---

[208] Minute Bewes to Conflict and Humanitarian Affairs Department, 19 February 2003, 'Iraq Contingency Planning: Update'.

funds to the ICRC, which was undertaking similar preparations to those recommended by DFID officials.

475. Ms Short also rejected the proposed deployments to Amman and the HIC in Cyprus, on the grounds that it pre-supposed a significant role for DFID, which it was as yet unable to promise.

476. The meeting considered DFID's response to three possible scenarios:

"a. US/UK bilateral action; no second Security Council resolution (SCR); US military governor without UN mandate:

–   DFID would work through whichever international agencies were willing to engage: the UN, Red Cross, and others.

b. Second SCR but overall US lead:

–   DFID would provide funding to UK military for QIPs; and work through the UN, Red Cross and others.

c. Second SCR with UN mandate:

–   DFID would wish to be positively engaged – exactly how would depend on financial package available."

DFID would need to consider each scenario, and variations on them, in the light of the amount of finance made available.

477. Ms Short also asked officials to reconsider wording used in draft replies to Parliamentary Questions that suggested DFID had "well-established systems for responding to humanitarian crises". Iraq was a very different case.

478. Dr Brewer briefed the Chiefs of Staff on DFID's approach to humanitarian planning on 19 February.

479. Ms Short's meeting was a key exchange that defined DFID's approach to the immediate pre-conflict period:

- **DFID would prioritise "humanitarian considerations" over wider reconstruction.**
- **In the absence of further resources for humanitarian assistance and to avoid suggesting that military action was a certainty, DFID:**
    - o **would prioritise support for the UN and the wider international effort throughout Iraq and the region;**
    - o **would not prepare for contingencies that exceeded its current resources; and**
    - o **would not deploy its full humanitarian response capability to support the immediate humanitarian effort in Iraq.**

480. Although Mr Chakrabarti did not attend the meeting on 18 February, by then he should have been aware:

- of the possibility that the UN would not lead the post-invasion reconstruction effort;
- that the US might fail to produce a satisfactory post-conflict plan; and
- that the UK military required effective DFID support if the UK was to meet its likely obligations in Iraq.

481. In those circumstances, as Permanent Secretary, Mr Chakrabarti should have:

- ensured that DFID officials had:
  - analysed the risks associated with DFID's plans for a limited contribution to the UK's humanitarian and reconstruction effort in post-conflict Iraq;
  - assessed the need for contingency preparations for a much broader role in humanitarian relief and reconstruction; and
- shared the findings with Ms Short.

482. There is no indication that Mr Chakrabarti engaged on the issue with Ms Short, DFID officials or the military, either before the meeting on 18 February or in the weeks remaining before the invasion.

"Sectorisation"

483. During February, UK officials became increasingly concerned about the risk that the UK might agree to take responsibility for a geographical sector of Iraq before the implications of doing so had been examined.

484. A draft IPU paper on "sectorisation", not yet agreed with the MOD, recommended that the UK should make clear to the US that it was unwilling to take responsibility for a sector for more than 60 days unless its presence was authorised by the UN and there was to be an early move to a UN transitional administration.

485. IPU guidance for UK officials attending the US inter-agency Rock Drill on post-conflict issues on 21and 22 February stated that, in the very short term, the UK would have to administer a small area, most likely around Basra, where its troops were present at the end of hostilities.

486. The UK would not make a commitment to administer a division-sized area in the medium to long term.

487. On 14 February, Mr Ehrman reported to Mr Ricketts that at a "[Sir David] Manning meeting" on post-conflict issues, Sir David had "expressed strong concern that junior

CENTCOM planners seemed to be dreaming up an ever larger area of Iraq for the UK to administer".[209] The Chiefs of Staff had advised Mr Blair that it would be easier for the UK to play a smaller post-conflict role if it was part of a Coalition fighting force; the opposite now seemed to be the case. Sir David had said that:

> "[Mr Richard] Armitage [US Deputy Secretary of State] was talking of military administration for two years. The Pentagon seemed to be more sensible, talking of six months. Did we [the UK] not need to reduce our 40,000 troops to around 5,000 by the end of six months? And who would pay for all this? Some on the US side seemed to be saying: you pay for what you administer."

488. Mr Ehrman had suggested to Sir David that if the UK were to take on a sector it should be getting as many like-minded allies as possible to join it:

> "We should use the Anglo-Italian and Anglo-Spanish summits for this. Simon Webb wondered whether Spain and Italy would be able to contribute. They were almost fully committed in Kosovo, and we were trying to line up Spain as the next ISAF [International Security Assistance Force in Afghanistan] lead. David Manning however favoured using the summits for the purpose I suggested. He also said we should look to involve Arab countries: Egypt, Jordan, UAE, and maybe also Malaysia and Pakistan."

489. Mr Ehrman informed Mr Ricketts that Sir David Manning had asked the MOD:

> "... to get the best information they could, at a senior level, on what size of sector was really being proposed for the UK; and FCO, with MOD, then to let No.10 have views on the issues which would be involved in its administration, and how we would seek to deal with these".

490. Mr Ehrman said that the FCO would be setting up a meeting with the MOD at official level the following week.

491. On 17 February, the IPU sent Mr Ehrman a paper on sectorisation as part of his briefing for a meeting on post-conflict issues chaired by Lieutenant General Anthony Pigott, Deputy Chief of the Defence Staff (Commitments) (DCDS(C)).[210]

492. In the covering minute, the IPU proposed objectives for the meeting, including agreement on the need for "express international authorisation of any Coalition occupation of Iraq (ie a 'third' Security Council resolution)", and for:

> "... an early move from a Coalition military occupation to a UN interim administration: we need to make clear to the US that we shall not be prepared to stay at all long (60 days?) under a US/Coalition administration. If there is an early move to a

---

[209] Minute Ehrman to Ricketts, 14 February 2003, 'Iraq: Day After'.
[210] Minute Iraq Planning Unit [junior official] to Ehrman, 17 February 2003, 'Iraq: General Pigott's Meeting: Sectorisation and UN Involvement' attaching Paper [undated and unattributed], 'A UK Geographical Sector of Iraq?'.

UN interim administration, we should be prepared to be 'lead nation' for a sector. It would be useful to discuss what this might mean in practice. A lead on security and willingness to take a lead role in UN discussions?"

493. The IPU explained that there was "a slight difference" between MOD and FCO advice being prepared for No.10. The FCO proposed that the UK should take the lead on security in a sector "only if there is a <u>UN interim administration</u>". The MOD "appear willing to contemplate taking on a rather greater burden in a sector so long as there is a <u>UN-authorised Coalition/US administration</u>".

494. The two positions were reconciled in the joint briefing on post-conflict UN involvement prepared by the IPU for Mr Blair's conversation with President Bush on 19 February.

495. In the paper on sectorisation, prepared with input from UND and FCO Legal Advisers, the IPU assumed that under any military plan UK forces would secure a "UK sector" in southern Iraq. Four questions then arose:

"•   how long should UK forces remain?

•   should other UK civilians/administrators be in Iraq?

•   what should be their task?

•   which area should they be in?"

496. Options ranged:

"•   <u>from</u> occupying as small an area as possible (initial plans were for around 1,600 sq km[211] around Basra and Umm Qasr) for as short a time as possible (until we can hand over to someone else, or simply withdraw without leaving a bloodbath)

•   <u>to</u> occupying a large area of south-eastern Iraq and administering it as an occupying power for perhaps 2-3 years, until an Iraqi administration takes over."

497. The paper listed four constraints on the UK approach to sectorisation:

•   growing debate about the legality of occupation the longer Coalition Forces remained in Iraq without a UN mandate;

•   UK and US interpretations of their responsibilities under international law might differ;

•   reduction in UK force numbers "must begin by July/August, to achieve reduction to medium scale by October/November";

•   financing: military costs alone would be £2.5bn. The paper asked: "MOD: is this known to Treasury?"

---

[211] The figure of 1,600 sq km was used repeatedly in policy and briefing papers during January and February 2003. This was mistaken. It should have been approximately 16,000 sq km.

498. The IPU listed pros and cons of sectorisation:

"<u>Pros</u>

International Profile (though this could be negative).

Ability to make a real difference: exemplary administration of a sector, setting the standard for others operating elsewhere.

Control: less dependent on others (US in particular).

<u>Cons</u>

Exposure: the former colonial power again administering Iraq. Possible resentment, even resistance. Much would depend on the international environment.

Expense. Long-term commitment / military overstretch / drain on other human resources (NHS staff, armed policemen).

We want a united (albeit federal) Iraq. Lengthy occupation of sectors by [a] different power would mean different systems of administration, and make a united Iraq more difficult to achieve. (? Bosnia)"

499. The IPU offered a tentative conclusion, in which it square bracketed all references to the possible duration of the UK's responsibility for a sector. The IPU stated that "in any foreseeable circumstances, the UK has the capacity to secure and occupy for [six] months" the 1,600 sq km initially envisaged, "though we think it is in fact rather larger than that", and to "take on a wide range of tasks". The larger the sector, the shorter the time the UK could administer it for. On that basis, the IPU recommended:

"We need to make clear to the US that **we are unwilling to take responsibility for a sector for more than [60 days] unless our presence is clearly and expressly authorised by the UN, and there is to be an early move to a UN transitional administration**. So we can operate as 'lead nation' (ensuring security) within a UN transitional administration, but are not willing to take on a medium-term (two year) administration on our own, under a US occupation of Iraq which lacks UN authorisation. We should tell the US that, were we to find ourselves in that position, we would want to hand over to them [at the end of 60 days]. And they would find it extremely difficult to find anyone to share the burden."

500. The record of Mr Ricketts' Iraq Evening Meeting on 18 February stated that "a possible UK sector" had been one of the subjects discussed at post-conflict talks with the MOD attended by Mr Ehrman and Mr Chilcott.[212]

---

[212] Minute Tanfield to PS/PUS [FCO], 18 February 2003, 'Iraq Evening Meeting: Key Points'.

501. The IPU paper's broad assumption in favour of administration of a small sector for a short period was reflected in the guidance for UK officials attending the US inter-agency Rock Drill on post-conflict issues on 21 and 22 February.[213]

502. The guidance, agreed by Mr Ehrman and Lt Gen Pigott, was submitted to Ministers on 20 February.[214]

503. In the second half of February, Treasury officials expressed concern about the resource implications of the UK taking on responsibility for a geographical sector of Iraq.

504. They advised that the "emerging politics" of post-conflict Iraq pointed to a much longer and larger commitment than initial MOD estimates suggested.

505. Papers by No.10 and the Treasury on the financing of post-conflict reconstruction also emphasised the risk of a significantly higher cost to the UK in the absence of a UN mandate.

506. On 19 February, Treasury officials updated Mr Brown on post-conflict issues for meetings with Mr John Snow, the US Secretary of the Treasury, and other G7 Finance Ministers:

> "Iraqi reconstruction may come up at this meeting. Even if Mr Snow does not raise it, you may wish to. Our sense is that momentum on the issue is developing very fast, and there is a risk that the financing agenda could be set by policy decisions taken in Foreign and Defence Ministries. Sharing ideas with Mr Snow may be a useful way to begin to redress this balance. An additional approach would be to write round Whitehall colleagues sharing your concerns (for instance, about the economic and financing implications of foreign and defence policy decisions)."[215]

507. Officials attached a paper identifying three "pitfalls" on the path to achieving Treasury objectives in Iraq (establishing prosperity and stability while sharing the cost fairly):

- UN cover. Without this, the UK would have to contribute more to the reconstruction effort, IFIs would find it hard to engage, and the international community would be unable to resolve crucial financing issues such as debt rescheduling.

- Being realistic about the decisions a transitional Iraqi government could take. It could be illegitimate and destabilising for the transitional government to take decisions on Iraqi economic policy.

---

[213] Minute Chilcott to Private Secretary [FCO], 20 February 2003, 'Iraq: Day-After (Phase IV)' attaching Paper [unattributed], 'Iraq Day After: Guidance for Officials at US ROCK Drill'.
[214] Minute Pollard to PS/Secretary of State [MOD], 20 February 2003, 'Iraq: Day After'.
[215] Minute [Treasury junior official] to Chancellor, 19 February 2003, 'Update on Iraq' attaching Paper Country Economics and Policy Team, 19 February 2003, 'Iraqi reconstruction: pitfalls and process'.

- The implications of establishing administrative sectors in Iraq: "If the UK takes on one, the cost – in terms of money and administrative burden – could rocket, and our stay lengthen."

508. The paper stated:

"… we should learn and apply some generic post-conflict lessons including: ensuring UN involvement does not stretch to running economic policy or co-ordinating reconstruction; not committing resources until a needs assessment has been done; and trying to prevent foreign ministries taking financing decisions (even by default).

"The momentum of this issue makes it difficult for us to influence decisions, as does the concentration of decision-making in the US White House/NSC and Department of Defense. But the UK is feeding into this at official level via a new Iraq Planning Unit – we are leading an economic sub-group within this."

509. Mr John Dodds, Head of the Treasury Defence, Diplomacy and Intelligence Team, sent comments to Mr Brown the same day, focusing on sectorisation:

"… a key decision that will need to be taken very soon is whether … the country should be split into sectors for administrative and peacekeeping purposes and whether the UK should take responsibility for one of the sectors.

"This is a decision that will have substantial public expenditure implications. If there were a UK sector we would find ourselves locked into the management of the aftermath for a substantial period (perhaps as long as five years) rather than allowing other countries – who will not have borne any costs of the conflict itself – to make their contribution."[216]

510. Mr Dodds added that the net additional cost to the UK "would certainly be hundreds of millions of pounds a year", more if there were no UN authorisation. The US appeared to favour a sectoral approach, but the need to bring in expertise from the widest possible range of sources and to avoid the perception that the UK was occupying "part of the Arab world" argued for a more internationalist approach. Mr Dodds explained that Treasury officials were taking every opportunity to stress to FCO and MOD colleagues that Mr Brown would want to have an input to any decision on sectorisation, but recommended that he underline the point himself with Mr Blair, Mr Straw and Mr Hoon.

511. The following day, a Treasury official provided further advice to Mr Brown and Mr Paul Boateng, Chief Secretary to the Treasury.[217] He reported that the Treasury now had the MOD's first estimates of the likely total cost of conflict in Iraq "if a decision is

---

[216] Minute Dodds to Chancellor, 19 February 2003, 'Iraq – "Aftermath" – UK Role' attaching Paper Dodds/ [Treasury junior official], 19 February 2003, 'Iraq conflict – public expenditure impact'.
[217] Minute [Treasury junior official] to Chancellor, 20 February 2002, 'Iraq: update on potential cost and how should we present them?'

made to stay … and provide a medium-term stabilisation/peace keeping force". The upper limit, based on what was feasible in military terms, was a two-year commitment at a total cost of £1.6bn. The advice continued:

> "The extent to which any of this is optional is unclear. We think that, because of our Geneva convention obligations, it will be impossible to resist keeping a substantial force in theatre for at least six months post the end of fighting … In practice the emerging politics of a post-conflict Iraq point to a much more substantial commitment both in terms of size and length of stay."

512. The official raised the need to take into account the cost of humanitarian and reconstruction assistance. He did not expect that the Treasury's insistence that departments (mainly DFID) should meet those costs through budget reprioritisation would hold. As a "worst case", he anticipated £250m for humanitarian costs and £250m for reconstruction costs in the UK financial year 2003/04 (with figures for future years to be determined later).

513. On 24 February, Mr Jeremy Heywood, Principal Private Secretary to Mr Blair, sent Mr Mark Bowman, Mr Brown's Principal Private Secretary, a paper on financing Iraqi reconstruction prepared by the No.10 Policy Directorate. Mr Blair wanted to share the paper with the US as soon as possible.[218] The paper was also sent to the FCO, DFID, DTI and the Cabinet Office.

514. The No.10 paper stated that the cost of "reconstruction and nation-building" in Iraq would be between US$30bn and US$105bn, excluding the direct cost of conflict and post-conflict peacekeeping. Only an administration enjoying the legitimacy provided by the UN would be free to engage with the financial markets to secure funding for Iraq's long-term future.

515. Mr Bowman replied on 25 February, explaining that the Treasury "fully supports the main message of the paper, that, in the absence of a UN mandate, the financing costs of reconstructing Iraq will be significantly higher".[219] Mr Bowman offered detailed comments on the text and pointed out that the Treasury was already involved in complementary work alongside the IPU and in liaison with the US and Australia.

516. Mr Straw's Private Office reinforced the message that work was already under way elsewhere, adding that "interdepartmental discussion is needed to get the complex issues touched on right".[220] It added that, while it was welcome that No.10 wanted to share UK concerns and explore options with the US at a high level, the paper needed improvement. If shared with the US in its current form it would undermine efforts to build up a constructive bilateral dialogue on post-conflict economic issues.

---

[218] Letter Heywood to Bowman, 24 February 2003, 'Iraq: Reconstruction' attaching Paper [unattributed and undated], 'Financing the Reconstruction of Iraq'.
[219] Letter Bowman to Heywood, 25 February 2003, [untitled].
[220] Letter Owen to Heywood, 25 February 2003, 'Iraq: Reconstruction'.

517. A revised draft was prepared, but not shared with the US.[221]

518. UK/US discussion of the post-conflict financing of Iraqi reconstruction is described in Sections 10.1 and 10.2.

The post-conflict Rock Drill

519. The stated aim of the UK delegation to the US inter-agency Rock Drill on 21 and 22 February was to encourage the US to draw the conclusion that the job of administering Iraq was too large for the US, that a large Coalition was the key to success, and that this could only be achieved by securing UN authorisation for Phase IV.

520. Instead, the Rock Drill only confirmed the scale of the shortcomings in US post-conflict planning, including the deficiencies of ORHA, and the continuing gap between UK and US positions on the role of the UN.

521. Sectorisation remained unresolved after the Rock Drill.

522. On 19 February, the Chiefs of Staff discussed post-conflict planning in the context of the forthcoming US Rock Drill, an inter-agency rehearsal for post-conflict administration convened by Lt Gen Garner and scheduled for 21 and 22 February.[222] The FCO (Mr Ehrman), the Cabinet Office (Mr Bowen), SIS, Maj Gen Cross and, for the first time, DFID (Dr Brewer) and the IPU (Mr Chilcott) were present.

523. Lt Gen Reith reported that Mr Blair wanted:

"... an exemplary aftermath but [was] not committed to any particular size of UK AOR pending further advice on objectives, capability and capacity to sustain. It was ... unclear who the US anticipated placing as sector leaders given that few other nations would be able to support the task within three months. Therefore, there may be an unsupportable expectation that the UK would control a relatively large area. Pragmatically, however, aftermath operations would commence locally whenever and wherever hostilities ceased, not necessarily coincident with any plan.

"The FCO view was that other nations should be involved as soon as possible and that early commitment to any nascent US sector plan should be avoided ...

"The UK line to take at the Rock Drill would be the commitment in principle to the immediate involvement in aftermath ops but not yet to any long-term plan, noting the PM's wish to exert maximum influence in aftermath planning. Clarity was needed on the proposed command chain in Phase IV and whose political and legal authority would prevail."

---

[221] Manuscript comments Manning and Drummond on Email Heywood to Banerji, Manning, Powell and Adonis, 3 March 2003, 'Financing the Reconstruction of Iraq' attaching Paper [unattributed], 'Financing the Reconstruction of Iraq'.
[222] Minutes, 19 February 2003, Chiefs of Staff meeting.

524. Dr Brewer set out DFID's approach to humanitarian planning. The UK was "well placed to play an exemplary role in humanitarian support in the UK AOR but saw UN authorisation as essential to effective involvement". DFID had identified four potentially complementary routes for delivering support (through UN agencies, the US military, UK military and DFID bilaterally), subject to five possible scenarios ranging from no UNSCR to an "all embracing UN mandate". At the two extremes, it would only be "politically possible" to provide a small amount of assistance without a second resolution, while a "full UN mandate" would require funding of £300m-£400m per year. Training for a small number of DFID staff had begun, but their deployment would depend on progress at the UN. Ms Short, while working for full commitment through the UN, would not be seeking additional resources beyond DFID's £100m contingency reserve.

525. Dr Brewer restated DFID's position in a letter to Mr Bowen on 24 February, which was copied to the MOD, FCO and Treasury.

526. The Chiefs of Staff agreed that humanitarian operations formed an essential part of the overall campaign, not least as a force protection measure, and should therefore attract Treasury contingency funding. Adm Boyce directed that humanitarian assistance be covered in the joint FCO/MOD position paper on post-conflict issues for the Rock Drill, which should make clear the potential for conflict and post-conflict phases to run in parallel from an early stage.

527. Adm Boyce summarised the key points of the discussion on post-conflict preparations, including that:

- the Rock Drill should be used "to secure maximum [UK] influence without early commitment to detail";
- a "UN-approved international civilian administrator" would be required;
- UK Phase IV activity should centre on the region around Basra; and
- the UK military commitment should be "scaled down from large to medium in the autumn".[223]

528. On 20 February, Mr Chilcott sent Mr Straw an IPU guidance note for officials taking part in the Rock Drill.[224] It had been agreed with Mr Ehrman, the MOD and the Cabinet Office, but not DFID.

529. Mr Chilcott's covering minute to Mr Straw stated:

"There is barely any mention of the UN in the CENTCOM plans we have seen for Phase IV (post-conflict) to date. But there are gaps in the plan, which is still fluid and which we have the opportunity to influence. We shall encourage the US players at

---

[223] The only reference to reducing troop numbers "in the autumn" seen by the Inquiry. All subsequent references are to a reduction "by the autumn".
[224] Minute Chilcott to Private Secretary [FCO], 20 February 2003, 'Iraq: Day-After (Phase IV)' attaching Paper [unattributed], 'Iraq Day After: Guidance for Officials at US ROCK Drill'.

the Rock Drill to draw the conclusion that the job of administering Iraq is too large even for the US to undertake, that putting together a large Coalition – drawing on Arab countries – is the key to success, and that this can only be achieved by getting UN authorisation for Phase IV."

530. The attached guidance note focused on the arguments participants should deploy in support of "at least UN authorisation of the transitional administration, and ideally … a UN transitional administration" and offered them "strategic" guidance on the UK contribution.

531. The guidance note stated that the UK and US agreed that "there must be a phased approach to the 'day after'". For the UK, that meant "(a) military administration, (b) a UN transitional administration and (c) handover of power to a new Iraqi government". The US referred to "stabilisation", "recovery" and "transition to security".

532. On sectorisation, the guidance stated:

"• UK will have, in the very short term, to administer the area where its forces are at the end of hostilities. No commitment to administer divisional size area in the medium to longer term. More likely a small area around Basra.

• No commitment to administering any part of Baghdad.

• Where we are involved in administration, will want to be so in an exemplary fashion."

533. On the UN, it stated:

"We need at least UN authorisation of the transitional administration, and ideally want a UN transitional administration. UN authorisation means a non-US figurehead. We need to explore further the right mix of US, UN and other elements to achieve a transitional administration which:

–   is acceptable to the Iraqis;

–   gains UN Security Council support;

–   looks competent enough for the US.

"We should argue for:

• A UN executive administrator overseeing the international civilian transitional administration. Possibly a central European, with a high preponderance of Americans beneath him.

• The UN supervising/mentoring the majority of Iraq's technical ministries, eg health, agriculture, finance, energy.

• A separate UN figure, supported by the international community and acting in close liaison with the US, overseeing the political process leading to a new constitution, a referendum and elections.

- The US-led Coalition providing security, mandated by the UNSC but not answerable to the UN.
- The World Bank and IMF overseeing economic reconstruction, both the policy framework and the award of contracts above a certain threshold, under UN authority."

534. The guidance stated that the UK force would reduce from large scale (three brigades plus) to medium scale (one brigade plus) "if possible by the autumn".

535. The UK would make no commitment on any "vertical" (functional) sector, but, in keeping with Mr Straw's instruction of 3 February, the paper stated that the UK would consider, but not commit to, providing support for UN-led justice sector reform "provided we had the right cover".

536. Mr Straw commented that he was "very glad" to see how much the paper highlighted the UN's role and that he was "ready to weigh in at any time with [Secretary] Powell".[225]

537. Mr Pollard showed the IPU paper to Mr Hoon the same day.[226] He explained that a more detailed cross-government paper, setting out potential UK involvement in Iraq in the short, medium and long term, would be prepared after the Rock Drill.

538. The first paper matching that description was the 'UK Vision for Phase IV', sent to No.10 on 26 February and described later in this Section.

539. The Rock Drill on 21 and 22 February was the first time representatives of all US military and civilian agencies involved in post-conflict administration had met in one place.[227]

540. The UK team was led by Mr Chilcott, accompanied by a military secondee to the IPU, a DFID representative, Maj Gen Cross and (acting) Maj Gen Whitley.[228]

541. The British Embassy Washington reported that:

"The inter-agency rehearsal for Phase IV … exposes the enormous scale of the task … Acknowledgment that this is beyond US capabilities. Private realisation by some that it will require a UN umbrella, but planning does not take account of this …

"Overall, planning is at a very rudimentary stage, with the humanitarian sector more advanced than reconstruction and civil administration."[229]

---

[225] Minute Owen to Chilcott, 21 February 2003, 'Iraq: Day-After (Phase IV)'.
[226] Minute Pollard to PS/Secretary of State [MOD], 20 February 2003, 'Iraq: Day After'.
[227] Bowen SW Jr. *Hard Lessons: The Iraq Reconstruction Experience.* U.S. Government Printing Office, 2009.
[228] Telegram 235 Washington to FCO London, 24 February 2003, 'Iraq: Day After: Rehearsal of Office of Reconstruction and Humanitarian Assistance'.
[229] Telegram 235 Washington to FCO London, 24 February 2003, 'Iraq: Day After: Rehearsal of Office of Reconstruction and Humanitarian Assistance'.

542. The record of the FCO Iraq Morning Meeting on 24 February stated that the Rock Drill:

"... revealed a large gap between the US's ambitious plans and their ability to deliver. Our message, that they need the Coalition and, therefore, UN authorisation, appeared to hit home."[230]

543. On 25 February, Lt Gen Garner discussed the Rock Drill with Maj Gen Cross. According to Maj Gen Cross, Lt Gen Garner was irritated at US colleagues' lack of understanding of the scale of the task ahead, but did not seem to have tackled the issue with Secretary Rumsfeld. Maj Gen Cross added that Lt Gen Garner was being "run pretty ragged briefing people" and had little time to lead ORHA.[231]

544. Maj Gen Cross told the Inquiry that:

"... [the IPU] was very small and at that stage I sensed that we had no thoughts of our own post-war.

"So when Dominick [Chilcott] and the team came out to the Rock Drill ... all that happened was that people listened to this debate rather than saying, 'This is what we think we should be doing.'"[232]

545. Mr Chilcott told the Inquiry:

"We saw ORHA for the first time in action at a Rock Drill in the United States on 21 and 22 February, and there, I think, we realised quite how undercooked ORHA was as an operation ...

"... [T]hey hadn't been in place very long, and although Jay Garner ... was a thoughtful, reasonable man who had experience of Iraq ... most of the people who he had asked to join him were at that stage, you know, like him, former retired military officers and one didn't get a sense that this was drawing on the best information and best knowledge that was available to the US administration ...

"... And I remember at the Rock Drill thinking that the scale of the challenge that they are taking on is absolutely enormous, and the time they have got to do it is very short and the number of people they have got to do it who really know about how to run these things is actually very small.

"... [I]t wasn't an organisation or an event, the Rock Drill, that inspired, I think, any of us with a great deal of confidence that this was going to go smoothly.

...

---

[230] Minute Tanfield to PS/PUS [FCO], 24 February 2003, 'Iraq Morning Meeting: Key Points'.
[231] Minute Cross to DCDS(C), 25 February 2003, 'Bullet Points from Cross Since VTC with DCDS(C)'.
[232] Public hearing, 7 December 2009, page 20.

"So we had misgivings about whether we should be too closely associated with what ORHA was doing. We also had other reasons to hesitate about the day after, which was to do with the legality of ORHA's ambition. ORHA had quite a high degree of ambition in the amount of reform and reconstruction it was proposing, and we felt without specific Security Council authorisation this would go beyond what we were allowed to do as Occupying Powers on the basis of the Geneva Convention and the Hague Regulations. So we had a legal issue and we had a kind of policy issue about whether this should be a DoD beast, that made us hesitant. We certainly reported our views on the shortcomings of ORHA when we went back."[233]

546. Asked what the reaction had been in London, Mr Chilcott explained:

"We doubled our efforts in our bilaterals with the Americans to try and swing them back into a sort of concept of operations that we felt was more likely to bring success.

"So the ORHA Rock Drill was on 21 and 22 February, the Prime Minister chaired a Ministerial meeting on day after issues on 6 March, which … raised the high level of Ministerial engagement on these issues, and Mike O'Brien … led discussions on day after issues on 13 March, which I attended as well, and then there was the 16 March Azores Summit.

"So there were a series of high level events where we were making our points to the Americans."

547. Mr Chilcott added:

"I can't remember the lack of sense of preparation on the American side for a clear post-war plan ever being brought up as a reason for the UK not to be involved in whatever operation might be coming, because at the same time we had much bigger things to worry about.

…

"And this may seem difficult to believe, but even until quite late in the day, we were not sure ourselves in the Foreign Office … whether the UK would be involved … we were only absolutely sure a relatively few number of days before things kicked off that we were going to be involved.

"And there was even that wobble … when Rumsfeld said on television that if the UK wants to come with us that's fine, but if they don't, we understand and we will go it alone [see Section 3.8]. And that, I think, reflected at the time genuine doubt, certainly within the IPU and, I think, more widely in Whitehall, as to whether we were really going to be engaged or not."[234]

---

[233] Public hearing, 8 December 2009, pages 21-23.
[234] Public hearing, 8 December 2009, pages 25-26.

548. In his written evidence to the Inquiry, Maj Gen Whitley explained:

"A 'Rock Drill' is US parlance for a complete mission rehearsal which assumes there is a plan – there was not. Instead this conference ranged across US departments describing how they were going to rewrite children's history books, form an Iraqi Fanny Mae,[235] what training for personnel was needed for ORHA, what weapons they would have and so on …

"I have no idea if there were any UK objectives for the aftermath at all. The only US articulation of an end state was 'A country within current borders with a democratically elected government'. The only direction I am aware of from the Prime Minister was that 'the behaviour of British Forces is to be exemplary'. Both inadequate …

"The appointment of Garner and the creation of ORHA provided very clear indications that DoD would take control of the aftermath. This became very clear during the Rock Drill during which the State Department was publicly sidelined … I … repeated my misgivings but without any great belief there was anything [the] UK could do even if it was prepared to get engaged …"[236]

549. After the Rock Drill, Mr Chilcott reported that the US military envisaged seven sectors in post-conflict Iraq, while ORHA would organise into three.

550. Mr Chilcott advised against accepting a likely US offer for the UK to head an ORHA sector.

551. Sectorisation remained unresolved after the Rock Drill. Mr Chilcott set out his understanding of the latest position on 24 February:

"Sectors mean different things at different times in Phase IV. And the military and ORHA have different sized sectors in mind …"[237]

552. Mr Chilcott explained that it was not yet possible to know how large the UK Division's AOR would be in Phase IVa, the stabilisation phase. In Phase IVb, the recovery phase, CENTCOM planners envisaged Iraq being divided into seven sectors, each headed by a two-star general. Whether a two-star general would have a division under his command would depend on the availability of forces and the degree of difficulty in maintaining stability:

"If there is organised resistance to the Coalition's presence, the number of boots needed on the ground could considerably outstrip the Coalition's ability to provide them. In Belfast, a city of 750,000, during the troubles, some 250 terrorists kept

---

[235] The US Federal National Mortgage Association.
[236] Statement, 25 January 2011, page 9.
[237] Paper Iraq Planning Unit, 24 February 2003, 'Iraq: Phase IV: Sectorisation'.

16 battalions busy. Basra province (the most likely UK AOR) has a population of about two million."

553. Mr Chilcott reported that (acting) Maj Gen Whitley needed guidance from London on the size of the UK commitment to Phase IV. He added that, at the Chiefs of Staff Committee on 19 February, Adm Boyce:

"… thought we should aim to reduce to a medium size (ie one brigade) within six months and then stay at that level for as long as necessary.[238] Provided we can attract suitable partners to join us (and that would almost certainly depend on having UNSCR authorisation for Phase IV), having a UK two-star in charge of one of the sectors would be a reasonable outcome."

554. Mr Chilcott explained that ORHA would organise into three sectors – north, central and south, aligned with military sectors containing "very large numbers of people". For as long as ORHA had no UN mandate, its work would be politically controversial and was "likely to be very messy". Mr Chilcott advised against accepting an expected offer from Lt Gen Garner for Maj Gen Cross to lead one of the three sectors.

555. It is not clear who saw Mr Chilcott's paper, but some of the issues raised were discussed at a meeting chaired by Mr Blair on 6 March.

556. Lord Boyce told the Inquiry:

"… the initial expectation was that we would be there for a while, without defining exactly what it was. But we certainly weren't expecting, the day after achieving success, to start drawing down our numbers; we were expecting to be there for a considerable period of time."[239]

557. Lord Boyce explained: "I thought we would be there for three or four years at least, and said so at the time." He added:

"The theoretical planning against the defence planning assumptions is you don't do this sort of operation for an extended period longer than about six months. But it never seemed to me very likely that we would be out [of] there in six months."

Seeking US agreement on the post-conflict role of the UN

558. Mr Blair's Note to President Bush on the second resolution, sent on 19 February, said little about post-conflict issues.

559. There is no indication that, when Mr Blair discussed Iraq with President Bush on 19 February, he raised either post-conflict planning or the post-conflict role of the UN.

---

[238] The minutes of the Chiefs of Staff meeting, quoted earlier in this Section, recorded Adm Boyce as saying only that the UK military commitment should be "scaled down from large to medium in the autumn".
[239] Public hearing, 3 December 2009, page 101.

560. On 18 February, in response to a request for advice for Mr Blair's discussion with President Bush the next day (see Section 3.7), Sir David Manning wrote that there would be a much better chance of gaining support for the second resolution:

- if it was clear that the UN would have a "key role" after any military action and that a "massive humanitarian aid programme" would be instituted; and
- by publishing and implementing the Road Map on Israel/Palestine before any military action.

Sir David advised Mr Blair that both points would be a "tough sell" with President Bush, but "both are very important in helping us to win the argument".[240]

561. Mr Blair sent President Bush a six page Note on 19 February, reflecting the seriousness of the UK's concerns about the second resolution.[241] The Note is addressed in detail in Section 3.7.

562. At the end of the Note, Mr Blair offered "two further thoughts":

- Publishing the Middle East Peace Process (MEPP) Road Map would have "a massive impact".
- There was a "need to start firming up the humanitarian work for the aftermath of the conflict … and show how we will protect and improve the lives of Iraqi people".

563. Mr Blair and President Bush spoke by telephone on 19 February.[242]

564. Before the call, the FCO submitted the advice on key messages for use with President Bush commissioned at Mr Blair's meeting on 13 February.[243] The briefing paper was prepared by the IPU in collaboration with the MOD, the Treasury, DFID and the Cabinet Office, and listed reasons for moving quickly to a UN interim administration operating alongside a "robust Coalition military presence to ensure security".

565. The FCO concluded:

"The greater the degree of UN involvement, the greater our ability to take part in aftermath. Without UN involvement, ongoing UK participation will be very difficult – real legal and legitimacy problems."

566. The conversation between Mr Blair and President Bush is described in Section 3.7.

---

[240] Minute Manning to Prime Minister, 18 February 2003, 'Iraq: Points for Bush'.
[241] Note [Blair to Bush], [undated], 'Note'.
[242] Letter Rycroft to McDonald, 19 February 2003, 'Iraq and MEPP: Prime Minister's Telephone Conversation with Bush, 19 February'.
[243] Letter Owen to Rycroft, 19 February 2003, 'Iraq Day after: UN involvement' attaching Paper FCO, [undated], 'Iraq Day After: UN Involvement'.

567. There is no indication in the record that Mr Blair raised either post-conflict planning or the post-conflict role of the UN during his conversation with President Bush.[244]

568. Mr Mandelson raised UK military concerns about post-conflict planning with Mr Blair on 23 February.

569. On 23 February, after visits to Japan, Korea, Bahrain and Qatar, Mr Mandelson emailed Mr Blair and Mr Jonathan Powell, Mr Blair's Chief of Staff, about Iraq, commenting that "people are more worried about what follows a war than winning it".[245] Mr Mandelson stated that:

> "American occupation and rule will be highly de-stabilising and will, in my view, radicalise opinion far more than the military action itself … At the moment, the Arab League is well balanced … If post-Saddam Iraq goes wrong we can expect mounting trouble. I should add here that Air Marshal Brian Burridge [UK National Contingent Commander (NCC)] and [Major] General Peter Wall [Deputy Chief of Operations] whom I saw at the US/British HQ outside Doha are also worried about post-Saddam planning. I am not sure exactly what is worrying them so much but they fear an FCO reluctance to 'post plan' too much, that we are not developing our own independent views but following in the American train and that we will not have sufficient strength on the ground to enforce our own judgements and will over the best arrangements for Iraqi governance after the hostilities.
>
> …
>
> "They wonder whether the perceived lack of British pre-planning over the humanitarian follow up is because Clare [Short] won't accept the likelihood of war. They emphasise the clear up – in different scenarios – will be huge. Are we all really ready for it, they wonder."

The potential for violence in the South

570. The potential scale and complexity of the post-conflict task facing the UK in southern Iraq was made clear in a February JIC Assessment.

571. The JIC warned that failure to meet popular expectations over humanitarian aid and reconstruction and rapidly to restore law and order could undermine support for any post-Saddam Hussein administration.

---

[244] Letter Rycroft to McDonald, 19 February 2003, 'Iraq and MEPP: Prime Minister's Telephone Conversation with Bush, 19 February'.
[245] Email Mandelson to Powell, 23 February 2003, 'Back from travels'.

572. On 19 February, at the request of the Cabinet Office, the JIC produced the Assessment 'Southern Iraq: What's in Store?'.[246] Key Judgements included:

- "Coalition forces will face large refugee flows, possibly compounded by contamination and panic caused by CBW use. They may also face millions of Iraqis needing food and clean water without an effective UN presence and environmental disaster from burning oil wells."

- "Iran does not have an agreed policy on Iraq beyond active neutrality. Nevertheless Iran may support small-scale cross-border interventions by armed groups to attack the Mujahideen e Khalq (MEK). The Islamic Revolutionary Guards Corps (IRGC) will continue to meddle in southern Iraq. Iranian reactions to a Coalition presence in southern Iraq remain unclear but are unlikely to be aggressive."

- "Post-Saddam the security situation in the South will be unpredictable. There is a high risk of revenge killings of former regime officials. Law and order may be further undermined by settling of scores between armed tribal groups."

- "Popular support for any post-Saddam administration in the South will depend on adequately involving the Shia in the government of Iraq as a whole as well as engaging the remains of the state bureaucracy in the South, local tribal leaders and Shia clerics in local government."

573. The JIC emphasised that intelligence on southern Iraq was limited.

574. In addition to assessments of Iraqi military dispositions and the immediate Iraqi and Shia responses to an attack, the JIC looked at Iranian policy and the post-Saddam Hussein political and security landscape.

575. The Assessment stated that Iran's aims in response to a Coalition presence in Iraq included:

- preventing refugee flows into Iran;
- ensuring a leading role for its allies among the Iraqi Shia (the Supreme Council for an Islamic Revolution in Iraq (SCIRI) and its armed wing the Badr Corps);
- minimising the size and duration of a US presence; and
- destroying the MEK.

576. Iran had interests throughout Iraq, but might consider that it had the greatest influence to pursue them in the South, through armed Shia groups such as the Badr Corps. The Badr Corps was estimated to be 3,000 to 5,000 strong, but "with the addition of reservists this may increase up to 20,000".

---

[246] JIC Assessment, 19 February 2003, 'Southern Iraq: What's in Store?'

577. The JIC assessed that:

"If the Coalition does not deal with the MEK, Iran may make limited cross-border rocket attacks on them … [T]he Iranian Revolutionary Guard Corps (IRGC) might act to undermine any post-Saddam peace that did not take Iran's concerns into account … We judge that both Iranian conservatives and reformers are anxious to avoid provoking a US-led attack on Iran. We therefore assess that **Iranian-inspired terrorist attacks on Coalition forces are unlikely, unless the Iranians thought the US had decided to attack them after an Iraq campaign.**"

578. The JIC assessed that the Iranian regime was preoccupied with domestic concerns and was not in a strong position to project its power into Iraq.

579. Shia politics in post-Saddam Hussein Iraq were described as "highly unpredictable":

"Saddam's regime has centralised power and stifled opposition. The only networks of influence in the South that exist outside of the Ba'ath Party are the tribes and the followers of some of the senior Shia clerics. Once the regime has collapsed, Coalition forces will find the remains of the state's bureaucratic structures, local tribal sheiks and religious leaders. There will also be a number of fractious armed groups, some strengthened by arms seized during the collapse of the regime. The external opposition will attempt to assert authority, but only those with armed forces on the ground or support from senior Shia clerics, such as SCIRI or Da'wa, another Shia Islamist group, are likely to succeed to any extent …

"Given that the Shia in southern Iraq have borne the brunt of regime oppression since 1991, there is a high probability of revenge killing of Ba'ath officials, both Sunni and Shia. This could be particularly widespread and bloody … Beyond that the extent of any further breakdown of law and order is difficult to predict. But there will be large numbers of armed groups and some potential for tribal score-settling … Overall there is a risk of a wider breakdown as the regime's authority crumbles. There are no indications, however, of Shia preparations for an all-out civil war against Sunni Iraqis … Iraqis may not welcome Coalition military forces, despite welcoming the overthrow of Saddam. **The establishment of popular support for any post-Saddam administration cannot be taken for granted.** It could be undermined by:

- damage to holy sites;
- major civilian casualties;
- lack of a UNSCR authorising a new administration;
- heavy-handed peace enforcement;
- failure to meet popular expectations over humanitarian aid and reconstruction;
- failure rapidly to restore law and order;

- failure to involve the Shia adequately in a post-Saddam administration; and
- failure to be seen to run the oil industry in the interests of the Iraqi people."

Two factors might work in the UK's favour:

"•   surviving networks of influence with whom we could work, including remains of state bureaucracy and food-distribution networks, tribal leaders and religious figures; and

-    receptivity of the population to information from external media and leaflet drops."

580. Mr Blair asked officials for advice on the implications of the JIC Assessment.[247]

581. Mr Cannon explained that the Cabinet Office and the IPU were "co-ordinating policy work in Whitehall on a range of issues likely to face our forces in southern Iraq regardless of whether there is a formal UK zone of control".[248] The Rock Drill had provided an opportunity to put across the UK's views on UN involvement and showed "the extent of US determination, at the highest level, to go it alone with minimal UN cover".

582. Mr Cannon's advice did not refer to the comment on the "rudimentary" state of US planning included in the report on the Rock Drill from the British Embassy Washington, which was not received in Whitehall until late on 24 February.

583. Mr Cannon provided Mr Blair with a list of IPU activities, drawn from Mr Chilcott's note of 20 February, as an indication of the extent of the work in hand. Mr Cannon drew particular attention to a paper in preparation "outlining our principles and 'red lines' for a post-Saddam Iraq … for use initially by David Manning with Condi Rice and … possibly by you with President Bush".

584. A set of IPU papers addressing those issues was sent to No.10 on 26 February.

585. In his statement to the Inquiry, Mr Blair wrote:

"… what we anticipated, was not what we found … for example, the JIC report of 19 February 2003, specifically on the South of Iraq, says the risks were refugees, environmental damage and the impact of CBW strikes."[249]

586. Mr Blair subsequently told the Inquiry:

"The benefit of the South was that it was Shia absolutely predominantly. So I felt we were going to be in an Area of Operation where it was frankly going to be easier for us …

---

[247] Minute Cannon to Prime Minister, 24 February 2003, 'Southern Iraq: Aftermath Issues'.
[248] Minute Cannon to Prime Minister, 24 February 2003, 'Southern Iraq: Aftermath Issues'.
[249] Statement, 14 January 2011, page 14.

"... [W]hat they [the JIC] were warning of was obviously right and important, but we felt that we had a better chance of managing this.

"I would just draw attention also to what they say about Iran too, because ... their basic view is that it is unlikely that Iran would be aggressive."[250]

587. Mr Blair's views on pre-invasion analysis of post-conflict Iraq are addressed later in this Section.

588. **Several contributions to a paper published by the International Institute for Strategic Studies (IISS) in January 2003, read by Mr Blair in February, described the potential for violence in a post-Saddam Hussein Iraq.**

589. **The paper prompted Mr Blair to ask a number of questions about plans for post-conflict.**

590. In mid-February Mr Blair read the Adelphi[251] Paper *Iraq at the Crossroads: State and Society in the Shadow of Regime Change*, published by the IISS.[252]

591. Several contributors to the Adelphi Paper warned of the potential for violent disorder in post-conflict Iraq.[253]

592. Dr Isam al Khafaji (International School of Humanities and Social Sciences, University of Amsterdam) cautioned that "the horrendous task of overthrowing Saddam's regime may prove to be less painful than that of dealing with the interest groups that have taken firm root in Iraqi society and owe varying forms and degrees of allegiance to the power structure that has been in place since 1968".[254] He considered that violence was likely in the immediate aftermath of US military action but did not anticipate a civil war along sectarian (Sunni versus Shia) lines. He also considered that a period of foreign occupation was likely to be resented by the Iraqi population and become a cause for violence.

593. Looking at southern Iraq, Dr Faleh Jabar (Birkbeck College, London) cautioned against assumptions that the Shia community was homogenous and likely to be quiescent in the transition to a post-Saddam Hussein Iraq.[255] He warned that, while the Shia south might welcome an end to Ba'athist rule, the internal dynamics of the

---

[250] Public hearing, 21 January 2011, pages 120-121.

[251] The IISS website describes the Adelphi series as "the principal contribution of the IISS to policy-relevant original research on strategic studies and international political concerns".

[252] Letter Rycroft to McDonald, 20 February 2003, 'Iraq: Political and Military Questions'.

[253] Dodge T & Simon S (eds). *Iraq at the Crossroads: State and Society in the Shadow of Regime Change.* IISS Adelphi Paper 354. Oxford University Press, January 2003.

[254] Al Khafaji I. *A Few Days After: State and Society in a Post-Saddam Iraq.* In: Dodge T & Simon S (eds). *Iraq at the Crossroads: State and Society in the Shadow of Regime Change.* IISS Adelphi Paper 354. Oxford University Press, January 2003.

[255] Jabar FA. *Clerics, Tribes, Idealogues and Urban Dwellers in the South of Iraq: the Potential for Rebellion.* In: Dodge T & Simon S (eds). *Iraq at the Crossroads: State and Society in the Shadow of Regime Change.* IISS Adelphi Paper 354. Oxford University Press, January 2003.

community (tribal loyalties and divisions, and increased Islamic fundamentalism) "could also bring forth unfettered chaos".

594. Mr David Ochmanek (RAND Institute) concluded that, even if any invasion were successful in defeating the Iraqi military and deposing Saddam Hussein's regime:

"Success in the endgame – providing a secure environment for the remaking of the political system and culture of Iraq – cannot simply be assumed. The emergence of tribally-based or ethnically-based insurgent or terrorist groups unreconciled to the post-Saddam order cannot be ruled out, particularly if the regime in Iran chose to sponsor and harbour such groups …"[256]

595. The Adelphi Paper prompted Mr Blair to ask the FCO, the MOD and DFID a number of questions about the military campaign (addressed in Section 6.2) and post-conflict issues on 20 February.[257] The three departments were asked to provide answers by 24 February.

596. On post-conflict issues, Mr Blair asked:

"How do we prevent the Shias rising up to take over from the Sunnis?

"What is our plan for the successor Government in Iraq? Is it a military ruler? Or a military ruler first then a path to more democratic rule mapped out?

"What is the UN role in the new Government?

"What are the precise humanitarian issues we need to address and what are our plans for them?"

597. The FCO and DFID answered Mr Blair's questions on post-conflict issues.

598. FCO officials advised that:

- **The Shia response to the removal of Saddam Hussein would depend to a great extent on the length of the Coalition occupation.**
- **The US plan to put a US general in charge of the transitional civilian administration was flawed.**
- **The duration of the transitional administration was "anyone's guess".**
- **The very high level of US ambition was not matched by resources.**
- **There was no reason the Iraqi civil service should not continue to function.**
- **UN involvement was needed to provide the legal mandate to reform and restructure Iraq.**

---

[256] Ochmanek D. *A Possible US-led Campaign Against Iraq: Key Factors and an Assessment*. In: Dodge T & Simon S (eds). *Iraq at the Crossroads: State and Society in the Shadow of Regime Change*. IISS Adelphi Paper 354. Oxford University Press, January 2003.
[257] Minute Rycroft to McDonald, 20 February 2003, 'Iraq: Political and Military Questions'.

599. DFID explained that its humanitarian plan involved working primarily through the UN. If additional resources were made available, it would consider a more active bilateral role in any UK-controlled zone. The department also expressed severe doubts about the adequacy of US humanitarian preparations.

600. The FCO answered three of Mr Blair's questions of 20 February about post-conflict issues.[258] On preventing a Shia uprising, it advised the key would be:

"… to assure the varied Shia communities that they will be fairly represented in future Iraq … A majority would probably hope to see a secular government … Much will also depend on the length of a Coalition 'occupation'. If they see Western control becoming quasi-permanent, this too may arouse opposition, probably encouraged by neighbours like Iran."

601. Mr Blair told the Inquiry that, from autumn 2002:

"… we focused very much on what we would find and how we would deal with it. Also … I raised this issue myself several times, you know, how would the Sunni/Shia relationship work out?

…

"There was very much discussion of the Sunni/Shia issue, and we were well aware of that … people did not believe that you would have Al Qaida coming in from outside and … that you would end up in a situation where Iran … would then try deliberately to destabilise the country."[259]

602. On plans for a successor government, the FCO stated:

"We and the US envisage a three-stage process following the conflict.

"Immediately after military action, the effective ruler of Iraq will be General McKiernan, the Coalition Land Forces Commander, reporting to General Franks in the US.

"Once the country has been stabilised, the US intend to establish a civilian administration in Iraq. To do this they have created … ORHA … We think this part of the US plan is flawed. We have argued for a UN-led or UN-authorised civil administration, and we do not think having a US General in charge is sensible.

"How long the [civilian] Transitional Administration would operate is anyone's guess. The US argue it will be 18 months – 2 years … Their level of ambition is very high and not matched by their resources … They aim to help the Iraqis rewrite their constitution and establish pluralist politics, to hold elections and to create a free market economy.

---

[258] Letter Sinclair to Rycroft, 25 February 2003, 'Iraq: Political and Military Questions'.
[259] Public hearing, 29 January 2010, pages 192-194.

"The first elections would be local. The goal of the Transitional Administration will be to create an environment in which national elections are possible. After elections, the Transitional Administration will be able to hand over to an elected national government.

"We believe that, contrary to the assumptions sometimes made, the Transitional Administration will be able to draw on a relatively competent Iraqi civil service. The Iraqi civil service has continued to function through several regime changes,[260] and we see no reason why it should not do so again, with changes at the highest level only."

603. Mr Blair told the Inquiry that, if there had been "even more focus" on planning, the UK "would still have been focusing essentially on the humanitarian side, with an assumption that we would inherit a functioning civil service infrastructure, and it was that assumption that proved to be wrong".[261] The UK "didn't plan for … the absence of this properly functioning civil service infrastructure".

604. In response to Mr Blair's question about the role of the UN in the new government, the FCO stated that any Transitional Administration would require UN Security Council authorisation.

605. The FCO advised that UN involvement would also be needed to:

- provide the legal mandate to reform and restructure Iraq;
- secure international and regional support;
- bring in the IMF and World Bank;
- adapt the OFF and sanctions regimes; and
- verify WMD finds and destruction.

606. The FCO added that the Coalition would still need to lead on security, and that Security Council authorisation would be required for both civilian and security functions.

607. DFID answered the fourth of Mr Blair's questions, on humanitarian issues and the UK plan to address them.[262] The department advised that the scale of the humanitarian crisis would depend on the nature of the conflict. A key priority was therefore to minimise risks to civilians, infrastructure and, in order to protect Iraqi revenues, oil production. DFID emphasised that:

"There is more scope to **refine the Coalition military options and minimise these risks**. If this is not done, the consequences … are potentially too great for the international humanitarian system to plan on current resources."

---

[260] It is not clear what this referred to. The Ba'athist regime had been in place since 1968.
[261] Private hearing, 29 January 2010, pages 180-181.
[262] Minute Rycroft to Prime Minister, 26 February 2003, 'Political and Military Questions on Iraq' attaching Paper DFID, 24 February 2003, 'DFID Input to Prime Minister's questions of 20 February'.

608. DFID also stated that the military would need adequate plans to deal with the civilian impact of CBW use before the UN and NGOs arrived. More generally, the role of UN agencies and NGOs would be determined by the extent of UN cover. There were also "severe doubts about the adequacy of US humanitarian preparations".

609. Mr Blair's question about the plan for addressing humanitarian issues was answered in one sentence:

> "DFID is planning to work primarily through UN agencies, unless extra financial resources are available, in which case a more active bilateral role in any UK-controlled zone could be considered."

A UN "badge" for post-conflict Iraq

610. Mr Blair raised the importance of a UN "badge" with Gen Franks on 25 February.

611. He told Parliament later the same day that the UN must have a "key role" in post-conflict Iraq and that discussions were under way on exactly what that role would be.

612. Sir David Manning explained to Dr Rice that Mr Blair attached importance to the UN's role, but was clear that UN involvement must not be at the expense of efficient administration and effective reconstruction.

613. On 25 February, Mr Blair told Gen Franks that he "still hoped that the UN could be brought on board" and that: "In any post-Saddam administration, the UN 'badge' would help pull the international community, including the Arabs and European public opinion back on board."[263]

614. Mr Blair and Gen Franks also discussed the possibility that "an occupation could work in several ways on a continuum from a US occupation of Japan model downwards" and that "it was important to work on the details, to avoid any perception of a US occupation".

615. Mr Watkins informed Mr Hoon (who was due to meet Gen Franks in Qatar on 26 February) that, during a meeting earlier in the day, Gen Franks had told Adm Boyce that Iraq would need to be under Coalition control for some time, during which there would need to be discussion with the UN on establishing a UN mandate.[264] Gen Franks had added that, contrary to press speculation, the US was not seriously considering anything along the lines of post-Second World War Germany or Japan. He had also agreed with a comment from Mr Webb that, in order to convince regional opinion of its intent, the US needed to start talking to the UN, but the US did not want to do anything

---

[263] Letter Cannon to Owen, 25 February 2003, 'Iraq: Prime Minister's meeting with General Franks'.
[264] Minute Watkins to Secretary of State [MOD], 25 February 2003, 'Meeting with General Franks: 26 February'.

that looked like pre-emption while the second resolution was still under discussion. Mr Watkins recommended that Mr Hoon use that opening to pursue with Gen Franks the UK's preference for "a 'transitional civilian administration' under UN auspices".

616. Mr Hoon and AM Burridge met Gen Franks in Qatar on 26 February. The MOD record makes no reference to discussion of the duration of a transitional administration or a UN mandate.[265] During an exchange on the build-up of Coalition Forces in the region, Mr Hoon told Gen Franks that "politicians had a natural tendency to put off decisions. It was important that the military robustly told the politicians when they had to go."

617. Mr Blair made no reference to post-conflict planning in his statement on Iraq to the House of Commons on 25 February.[266]

618. In response to questions from Mr Iain Duncan Smith, Leader of the Opposition, about UN humanitarian contingency planning and "what contingencies the Government have planned for a representative government in Iraq", Mr Blair stated:

> "In relation to humanitarian considerations and what type of government might succeed the government of Saddam … that is something we are discussing closely with allies and the UN. I should like to emphasise that in my view if it comes to conflict the UN's role in the resulting humanitarian situation and in finding the right way through for Iraq will be immensely important …"[267]

619. Mr Charles Kennedy, Leader of the Liberal Democrats, asked Mr Blair:

> "… what post-war scenario do the Government envisage? Would they prefer a United States-administered post-conflict Iraq or some form of UN protectorate? What will our contribution be in such circumstances?"[268]

620. Mr Blair stated that, if it came to conflict, he had:

> "… made it clear that the UN must have a key role; exactly what that role will be is another thing that we are discussing with the UN and with allies now."[269]

He did not answer Mr Kennedy's question about the UK contribution.

---

[265] Minute Williams to DG Op Pol, 27 February 2003, 'Secretary of State's call on General Franks (CENTCOM) – 26 February 2003'.
[266] House of Commons, *Official Report*, 25 February 2003, column 126.
[267] House of Commons, *Official Report*, 25 February 2003, column 128.
[268] House of Commons, *Official Report*, 25 February 2003, column 129.
[269] House of Commons, *Official Report*, 25 February 2003, column 129.

621. In response to a question from Mr Tony Worthington (Labour) about whether he had been party to plans, reported in the US press, for a US general to administer Iraq, Mr Blair replied:

"… no decisions have yet been taken on the nature of how Iraq should be administered in the event of Saddam's regime being displaced by force. I said earlier that I thought that the role of the UN had to be well protected in such a situation. The discussions that we are having on that matter are proceeding well. When we have reached conclusions and decisions, we can announce them so that people can discuss them."[270]

622. Parliamentary debate on Iraq on 25 and 26 February is addressed in more detail in Section 3.7.[271]

623. Sir David Manning and Dr Rice discussed post-conflict issues on 25 February.[272] Both agreed the need to think soon about the "aftermath" and to keep discussing the role of the UN.

624. Sir David told Dr Rice that it would be important to show that the UN was fully involved in running post-Saddam Hussein Iraq:

"If we had gone the UN route to disarm him, it would be entirely consistent to maintain the UN route to rebuild the country once his regime had gone. There were also important questions of expertise and financing to consider. The UN was a critical source of both. This was an important issue for the Prime Minister, although he was clear that UN involvement must not be at the expense of efficient administration and effective reconstruction."

625. Sir David offered to send Dr Rice a paper setting out the UK's ideas.

The DIS Red Team

626. In late February, the MOD established a small "Red Team" within the Defence Intelligence Staff (DIS) to give key planners in Whitehall an independent view of intelligence assumptions and key judgements.

627. Key judgements in the first report produced by the DIS Red Team included:

- the need for Coalition Forces to prevent the emergence of a security vacuum;

---

[270] House of Commons, *Official Report*, 25 February 2003, column 137.
[271] House of Commons, *Official Report*, 25 February 2003, column 123.
[272] Letter Manning to McDonald, 25 February 2003, 'Iraq: Conversation with Condi Rice'.

- **the danger that Iraqi support would erode rapidly in the absence of an acceptable interim administration and a clear road map to an Iraqi-led administration; and**

- **the risk of creating fertile ground for Al Qaida.**

628. In late February, the MOD established a small "Red Team" within the DIS to give key planners in Whitehall an independent view of intelligence assumptions and key judgements, to challenge if appropriate and to identify areas where more work was needed.[273]

629. Papers were copied to the Chiefs of Staff, PJHQ, the MOD, the FCO, the IPU and the JIC. There is no evidence that they were seen in No.10.

The DIS Red Team

Between February and April 2003 the DIS Red Team produced five reports on post-conflict issues:

- 'Regional Responses to Conflict in Iraq and the Aftermath';
- 'Obtaining and Retaining the Support of the Iraqi People in the Aftermath of Conflict';
- 'What Will Happen in Baghdad?';
- 'The Future Governance of Iraq';
- 'The Strands of the Rope' (an assessment of the steps needed to achieve an effective Iraqi Interim Administration and hand over to a representative government of Iraq).

The first two reports are addressed in this Section. The other three were issued in April, after the start of the invasion, and are described in Section 10.1.

Four of the five reports were described as drawing on "a variety of sources inside the Allied intelligence community and ... a panel of regional experts assembled ... by Kings College, London".[274] Professor Sir Lawrence Freedman was listed as one of the contributors to the first paper.

The fifth report, on Baghdad, "sought the perspectives of academic sources and members of the Iraqi exile community in UK (military and civilian) to gain fresh insights, and to a certain extent reflects their views".[275]

All five reports were copied widely within the MOD, to PJHQ (Lt Gen Reith), the JIC (Mr Scarlett) and to the FCO/IPU (Mr Ehrman and Mr Chilcott). The last three were also addressed to the MOD/DIS US Liaison Officer. It is not clear how they were used.

---

[273] Minute PS/CDI to APS2/SofS [MOD], 25 February 2003, 'Iraq: Red Teaming in the DIS'.
[274] Minute PS/CDI to APS2/SofS [MOD], 28 February 2003, 'Iraq Red Team – Regional responses to conflict in Iraq and the Aftermath' attaching Paper, DIS Red Team, 'Regional Responses to Conflict in Iraq and the Aftermath'.
[275] Minute PS/CDI to various, 7 April 2003, 'Iraq Red Team – What Will Happen in Baghdad?'

630. The first Red Team report ('Regional Responses to Conflict in Iraq and the Aftermath') was issued on 28 February.[276] It described Iraq as "a very complex society" and cautioned that "any attempt to analyse it in neat categories based on religion, ethnicity or tribe will almost certainly be over simplistic". The report advised that, by comparison with the previous British mandate in Iraq, which had relied on advisers like Gertrude Bell with an intimate knowledge of the country and its people, "our understanding of Iraqi society today can be shallow".

631. The Red Team's key judgements drew heavily on earlier JIC Assessments and included:

- the need for Coalition Forces to assume immediate responsibility for law and order to avoid other forces stepping into an internal security vacuum;

- that most Iraqis would initially view the Coalition as a liberating force, but support was likely to erode rapidly if the interim administration was not acceptable to the population and it could not see a road map towards a pluralist, representative Iraqi-led administration;

- the risk of creating fertile ground for Al Qaida, which could deliberately cause civilian casualties to undermine the establishment of a representative Iraqi-led administration.

632. The report stated that Al Qaida:

"… seeks removal of Western presence/influence from the Gulf and wants to see the US/UK operation go badly. AQ [Al Qaida] are currently in some disarray but will wish to take the opportunity presented by the US/UK operation to re-establish credibility and encourage widespread anti-Western activity in the region. However:

- Initially AQ shares a common goal with the Coalition: regime change. Once completed, goals will diverge rapidly and UK/US forces will present a rich target for terrorist attack.

- AQ fears the establishment of a pluralist, representative Iraqi government as it undermines their argument that Muslims can only achieve self-determination in a unitary Islamic theocracy. They could deliberately cause civilian casualties to undermine the Coalition's position."

Obstacles to an "exemplary" UK effort

633. Dr Brewer set out Ms Short's views on the scale of DFID's post-conflict contribution in a letter to departments on 24 February.

---

[276] Minute PS/CDI to APS2/SofS [MOD], 28 February 2003, 'Iraq Red Team – Regional responses to conflict in Iraq and the Aftermath' attaching Paper, DIS Red Team, 'Regional Responses to Conflict in Iraq and the Aftermath'.

634. **Ms Short was keen for DFID to support an exemplary humanitarian effort in any UK-controlled sector, but DFID's role would be constrained by:**

- **the extent of the UN mandate; and**
- **the financial resources available (under most scenarios DFID would want to allocate significant funding to UN agencies working throughout Iraq).**

635. **DFID was doing scoping work on the role it might play if there were a UN mandate, but the department did not have Ms Short's authority to deploy operationally or to make substantive plans to deploy "in an exemplary role".**

636. **Ms Short stated her position in Cabinet on 27 February.**

637. Ms Short held a meeting on Iraq with DFID officials, including Dr Brewer and Mr Fernie, on 24 February.[277] The record was copied to Mr Chakrabarti's Private Office.

638. The record stated that there was "increased recognition across Whitehall of the likely scale of post-conflict activity, and the essential nature of UN involvement and authority if this was to be effectively addressed". Ms Short emphasised the importance of a "substantive" second resolution that clearly justified any action taken under it. She asked officials "to keep closely abreast of the debate on the legality of occupation of Iraq without any UN mandate".

639. Officials reported that ORHA's state of preparedness was "extremely worrying":

- Humanitarian plans were the most advanced, but ORHA did not yet have sufficient funds, staff or capacity to deliver them.
- Reconstruction plans were "not nearly as well advanced as they should have been at this point".
- Civil administration plans were the least advanced, and ORHA "would not be ready by the six week deadline they had been set".
- Logistical support planning had only just begun. ORHA had "not even started on such vital areas as telecommunications".

640. The record of the meeting stated that Ms Short would write to Mr Blair after Dr Brewer's forthcoming visit to New York, setting out the dangers this situation would pose in the event of early military action that was not authorised by the UN and did not enjoy wide international support.

641. The meeting also considered financial issues. Although the MOD and FCO "appeared to be more aware of the financial constraints, and the need for the widest possible burden sharing within the international community, we [DFID] had as yet no clear response to the issue of the limitation of DFID's engagement imposed on it by our

---

[277] Minute Bewes to Miller, 25 February 2003, 'Iraq contingency planning: update'.

financial situation". Ms Short reported that Mr Brown "had indicated to her, in a private conversation, that he 'would do what he could to help'".

642. The same day, Dr Brewer sent Mr Bowen and senior officials in the MOD, FCO and Treasury a letter setting out Ms Short's position on what DFID could do following any conflict.[278] The letter reflected the conclusions of Ms Short's meeting with DFID officials on 18 February and Dr Brewer's presentation to the Chiefs of Staff on 19 February.[279]

643. Dr Brewer stated:

> "Although she [Ms Short] would be keen for DFID to support an exemplary humanitarian effort in any UK-controlled sector, our [DFID's] role will be constrained by the extent of the UN mandate and the financial resources available to us. We have a strong commitment to the UN agencies, and would want to allocate significant funding to them under most scenarios. Drawing heavily on our contingency reserve and existing humanitarian aid and Iraq budget lines is unlikely to release more than £60-70m for humanitarian assistance to Iraq in 2003/04. Given our predictions of the humanitarian needs, with this level of funding we would not be able to play the exemplary role [in the South] the Prime Minister has asked for, and it would be irresponsible of us to plan to do so."

644. On the UN mandate, Dr Brewer stated:

> "The role which DFID can play in funding our usual humanitarian partners may be further constrained by perceptions of the legality of any conflict and what happens afterwards, and also by humanitarian principles of impartiality and independence. UN mandates justifying not only military force but also a continuing international presence afterwards are critical to ensuring the international community can engage fully with the predicted enormous needs."

645. Dr Brewer described DFID's potential role under four scenarios closely based on those discussed at the DFID meeting on 18 February:

- "No second UNSCR, no mandated UN humanitarian role." DFID would fund those international agencies willing to accept UK money and best placed to respond.

- "Second UNSCR but no mandated UN humanitarian role (overall US lead)." DFID would additionally fund UK military QIPs, although without additional resources, the total was unlikely to exceed £5m. "We have doubts about how much the UN would be able to do beyond immediate relief with only a thin second SCR if a US-led Coalition assumed medium-term control of the country."

---

[278] Letter Brewer to Bowen, 24 February 2003, [untitled].
[279] Minute Fernie to Private Secretary/Secretary of State [DFID], 21 February 2003, 'Iraq: Deployment Options'.

- "Second UNSCR and clear humanitarian mandate." DFID would want to be "positively engaged" with the UK military, US humanitarian effort and the UN. It would also "consider bilateral operations in any UK sector", but commitments to UN agencies across Iraq and the region would "severely financially constrain what we could do in a UK-controlled sector with the UK military and other partners".

- "Second UNSCR, clear humanitarian mandate and additional resources." With adequate finances, DFID "would be able to play the exemplary role suggested by the Prime Minister". Without, DFID could discuss with the MOD what the exemplary role might entail, but could not plan for it "without more comfort on resources".

646. Dr Brewer stated that DFID staff were committed to advising the MOD and Armed Forces in all circumstances and that MOD-DFID links were now strong. DFID was also doing "scoping work" on the role it might play if there were a UN mandate:

"But we do not currently have political authority to deploy operationally, or to make substantive plans to deploy in an exemplary role (eg commissioning or pre-positioning material). Our Secretary of State has made our financial position clear in two letters to the Prime Minister."

647. **Dr Brewer's letter illustrated the absence of an agreed UK approach to the provision of humanitarian relief, highlighting the gap between DFID's focus on supporting the UN, Red Cross and NGOs across Iraq and the UK military's focus on the humanitarian situation in its Area of Operations (AO) in the South.**

648. **MOD officials expressed growing concern about UK preparations for the delivery of humanitarian assistance and longer-term reconstruction in the South.**

649. On 26 February, Mr David Johnson, Head of the MOD Iraq Secretariat, expressed concern to Mr Hoon's Private Office about humanitarian assistance during the early stages of military conflict.[280] The MOD and DFID believed US plans for humanitarian assistance were inadequate, in particular because they relied on delivery by NGOs, which would not be there in numbers early on. The UK military would therefore need:

"... immediate access to sufficient expertise and resources to ... make good the deficiencies in the US plans. In particular ... DFID experts deployed in theatre, who can advise what is actually required ... (as opposed to soldiers making it up as they go along) ... There are lead-times associated with this ... Waiting till after a second SCR is leaving it too late. We know DFID haven't got any money. That is why they need to ask for some, now."

---

[280] Email sec(O)-Iraq to sofs-ps [MOD], 26 February 2003, 'Humanitarian Assistance'.

650. Mr Webb commented on Dr Brewer's letter on 27 February.[281] He suggested to Mr Lee that there were "wider consequences for the overall success of the campaign from the effectiveness of the CIMIC [civil-military] component, to which we should draw Ministers' attention collectively".

651. Sir Kevin Tebbit, who saw Dr Brewer's letter a few days later, commented on 7 March:

"The problem here is that DFID have a wrong view of what the Armed Forces can or should do to administer humanitarian relief, as distinct from civil, UN and NGO agencies – including DFID themselves."[282]

652. Mr Blair told Cabinet on 27 February that humanitarian and reconstruction planning needed to take "centre stage" and that he would raise the issue with President Bush.

653. In Cabinet on 27 February, Mr Hoon reported on his meeting with General Franks in Qatar the previous day (see Section 3.7).[283] Mr Hoon had discussed concerns with General Franks that:

"Not enough planning had been done on the post-conflict phase of operations, including humanitarian relief. British forces could find themselves in charge of a portion of Iraq quite quickly if resistance to Coalition military action collapsed. It would be helpful if experts from the Department for International Development could work with military planners in the region and consider pre-positioning humanitarian supplies so that there was no hiatus in the event that military action took place."

654. Ms Short told Cabinet that experts had been involved in talks in the Pentagon. Preparations were "just beginning and needed to be expedited". A UN legal mandate was "essential" for the humanitarian and reconstruction tasks that lay ahead. Without that, "proper preparation was impossible". That matter "needed to become a priority for the Coalition". It would be "difficult" to accommodate action in Iraq within her department's contingency reserve: "Greater resources were likely to be needed."

655. The Inquiry considers that Ms Short's reluctance to prepare for a wider UK post-conflict role, though not critical to the outcome, and consistent with DFID's statutory role, contributed to the Government's failure to ensure that the UK was adequately prepared and resourced to carry out its likely obligations in Iraq.

656. Mr Blair said that he would continue to push for a further Security Council resolution.[284] President Bush's commitments the previous day on the MEPP

---

[281] Manuscript comment Webb to DG Op Pol, 27 February 2003, on Letter Brewer to Bowen, 24 February 2003, [untitled].
[282] Manuscript comment Tebbit, 7 March 2003, on Letter Brewer to Bowen, 24 February 2003, [untitled].
[283] Cabinet Conclusions, 27 February 2003.
[284] Cabinet Conclusions, 27 February 2003.

(see Section 3.7) were "helpful". Looking beyond the current divisions in the international community, it would be "important to seek unity of purpose through the humanitarian and reconstruction work which would follow any military action". Planning in this field "needed to take centre stage". He would pursue that with President Bush "in the coming days". The "transitional civil administration in Iraq should have a United Nations mandate, although the scale of United Nations involvement should balance the administrative effectiveness with the necessity for proper authority".

657. In his diaries, Mr Campbell wrote:

> "At Cabinet, things were pretty much rock solid … I could sense a few of them only fully realising … the enormity of the decisions, the enormity of the responsibility involved … Clare [Short] was doing her usual … and for her was relatively onside. She wanted to do a big number on aftermath preparations but TB was there ahead of her. He was very calm, matter of fact, just went through where we were on all the main aspects of this."[285]

658. Mr Straw sought advice from Mr Wood on the legal authority for post-conflict reconstruction.

659. Mr Wood set out the legal constraints on an Occupying Power. He stated that the longer an occupation lasted and the further the tasks undertaken departed from the objective of the military intervention, the more difficult it would become to justify an occupation in legal terms.

660. On 10 March, Mr Wood told the Attorney General's Office that the UK view of the legal framework for occupation appeared to be getting through to the US.

661. Mr Straw's Private Office requested advice from Mr Wood on Ms Short's observation in Cabinet that there appeared to be no legal authority for post-conflict reconstruction:

> "Is this true? The Foreign Secretary thinks that it is. If so, it underlines the importance of having effective UN authority in place very quickly (the so-called third resolution). The Foreign Secretary knows that officials are already in touch with DFID about this but would like this work to be given even higher priority."[286]

---

[285] Campbell A & Hagerty B. *The Alastair Campbell Diaries. Volume 4. The Burden of Power: Countdown to Iraq*. Hutchinson, 2012.
[286] Minute McDonald to Wood, 27 February 2003, 'Iraq Post-Conflict'.

662. On 28 February, Mr Wood advised:

"The legal basis for the occupation of Iraq by Coalition forces in a post-conflict phase would depend initially on the legal basis for the use of force. That legal basis is likely to be Security Council authorisation for military action to enforce Iraq's WMD obligations under SCRs. But the longer an occupation went on, and the further the tasks undertaken departed from this objective, the more difficult it would become to justify an occupation in legal terms.

"Without a Security Council mandate for the post-conflict phase, the status of the occupying forces would be that of belligerent occupants, who would have the rights and responsibilities laid down by international humanitarian law as set out in particular in the Hague Regulations of 1907 and the Geneva Conventions of 1949. The rights of belligerent occupants are quite limited …

"FCO Legal Advisers are closely involved in the establishment of our policy on the post-conflict phase. This stresses the need for rapid UN involvement, and in particular for UN authorisation of, if possible, the presence of and the activities to be undertaken by the Coalition. The Foreign Secretary will know of the efforts we are making to persuade the US of the merits of our position. We understand that they are almost ready to share with us a draft of the so-called third resolution."[287]

663. Mr Wood attached copies of:

- Mr Grainger's advice of 31 January on the general position in international law;
- FCO legal advice to the IPU on occupation rights relating to oil; and
- FCO legal advice to the IPU on occupation rights and the administration of justice.

664. Mr Grainger had sent advice on occupation rights relating to oil to the IPU on 14 February.[288] In it, he advised that, under the 1907 Hague Convention:

"… the Occupying Power acquires a temporary right of administration, but not sovereignty. He does not acquire the right to dispose of property in that territory except according to the strict rules laid down in those regulations. So occupation is by no means a licence for unregulated economic exploitation."

665. Mr Grainger also advised that, in the event of there being no government in active control of Iraq, there would need to be changes to existing arrangements for OFF, which assumed a degree of Iraqi Government involvement in the programme's operation.

---

[287] Minute Wood to McDonald, 28 February 2003, 'Iraq Post-Conflict'.
[288] Minute Grainger to Iraq Planning Unit [junior official], 14 February 2003, 'Occupation Rights: Iraqi Oil'.

666. FCO Legal Advisers had sent the IPU an overview of the legal framework for the post-conflict administration of justice on 16 February.[289] The paper, which was copied to the MOD, explained that:

- With certain exceptions, the penal laws of the occupied territory would remain in force (Geneva Convention IV, Article 64).

- Again with certain exceptions, the administration of justice should remain in the hands of the incumbent administration and courts (Geneva Convention IV, article 64; Hague Regulations, Article 43).

- Where possible, existing personnel involved in the administration of justice should remain in their positions (Geneva Convention IV, Article 54).

667. The paper also listed some of the issues "it may be useful to consider ... in advance of a conflict":

- identification of laws to be applied, amended, repealed or enacted by an occupying force;

- a scoping study of the current state of the criminal justice system;

- identification of systems for seizure and preservation of evidence and maintenance of known crime sites; and

- development of a public information and awareness campaign.

The legal framework for Occupation

As Occupying Powers, the UK and US were bound by international law on belligerent occupation. Its rules are set out in the 1907 Hague Regulations (Articles 42 to 56), the Fourth Geneva Convention on the Protection of Civilian Persons in Time of War of 1949 (Articles 27 to 34 and 47 to 78) and the 1977 First Protocol to the Geneva Conventions of 1949 Relating to the Protection of Victims of International Armed Conflicts.[290]

Article 42 of the Hague Regulations defines an Occupation as follows:

"Territory is considered occupied when it is actually placed under the authority of the hostile army. The occupation extends only to the territory where such authority has been established and can be exercised."

Article 43 of the Hague Regulations provides that the Occupying Power "shall take all the measures in his power to restore, and ensure, as far as possible, public order and safety while respecting, unless absolutely prevented, the laws in force in the country".

---

[289] Minute Hood to UND [junior official], 16 February 2003, 'Occupation Rights: the Administration of Justice'.
[290] International Committee of the Red Cross, 29 October 2010, *The ICRC's mandate and mission*; International Committee of the Red Cross, 29 October 2010, *War and international humanitarian law*.

> Sir Michael Wood, the FCO Legal Adviser from 1999 to 2006, explained in his second witness statement:
>
> "While some changes to the legislative and administrative structure may be permissible if they are necessary for public order and safety, more wide-reaching reforms of governmental and administrative structures are not lawful. That includes the imposition of major economic reforms."[291]

668. Mr Straw commented on Mr Wood's advice on 1 March:

"This is good advice: having UN authority for post-conflict Occupation makes sense politically as well as legally. I'd be happy to receive further advice from Michael Wood, or talk to him, about whether I should lobby C Powell on progress."[292]

669. Mr Simon McDonald, Mr Straw's Principal Private Secretary, sent those comments to Mr Wood on 4 March, after Mr Straw had spoken to Secretary Powell.[293]

670. Mr Straw told the Inquiry:

"I was clear that under international law … we would be bound by the 1907 Hague Regulations as well as the Fourth Geneva Convention of 1949. We would therefore be considered an Occupying Power with responsibility for providing 'public order and safety, while respecting, unless absolutely prevented, the laws in force in the country'. We would need specific UNSCR authorisation for powers and duties beyond these instruments."[294]

671. Ms Cathy Adams, Legal Counsellor in the Legal Secretariat to the Law Officers, told Mr Wood on 28 February that the Attorney General had received a letter from Mr William Haynes, General Counsel at DoD, which, among other issues, dealt with post-conflict questions.[295] Ms Adams advised:

"We have not seen here any papers relating to post-conflict planning. I expect the Attorney [General] would be interested to know how matters are progressing on this issue particularly as regards outstanding legal concerns."

672. Mr Wood replied on 10 March, the same day as Sir David Manning sent Dr Rice a UK draft of a possible third resolution. Sir Michael explained that a good deal of thought had been given to the issue in the FCO and MOD.[296] The UK view had been urged on

---

[291] Statement, 15 January 2010, pages 2 and 3.
[292] Manuscript comment Straw, 1 March 2003, on Minute Wood to McDonald, 28 February 2003, 'Iraq Post-Conflict'.
[293] Minute McDonald to Wood, 4 March 2003, 'Iraq Post-Conflict'.
[294] Statement, 19 January 2011, page 18.
[295] Letter Adams to Wood, 28 February 2003, 'Letter from General Counsel of the US Department of Defence [sic]'.
[296] Letter Wood to Adams, 10 March 2003, 'Letter from General Counsel of the US Department of Defence [sic]'.

the US "and appears gradually to be getting through". He suggested that in any reply to Mr Haynes's letter, the Attorney General "might refer briefly to this matter, and to our wish to remain in close contact on legal issues".

673. On 27 February, DFID officials had sought Ms Short's guidance on "the scope of DFID co-operation with UK (and potentially other) military forces in support of UK government objectives in a complex humanitarian emergency".[297] Officials explained that the approach adopted in Kosovo and developed in Afghanistan, but not universally accepted as good practice in DFID, provided for:

- UK and/or allied military forces to assist vulnerable populations directly when there was insufficient humanitarian capacity to meet their needs;
- funding of military QIPs "which contribute to the security and stability of the environment thus facilitating humanitarian, recovery and development programmes and enabling legitimate political developments to take root";
- secondment of humanitarian specialists to UK military forces; and
- "the flexibility to decide … the degree of co-operation with combatant military forces whose operation may, or may not, be endorsed by the UN".

674. Ms Short replied: "Thanks – I am minded to maintain our position. We must check if [there are] any legal implications."[298]

675. On 28 February, a junior DFID official advised:

"I cannot see any International Development Act problems here. Section 3 of the Act … says: 'The SofS [Secretary of State] may provide any person or body with assistance for the purpose of alleviating the effects of a natural or man-made disaster or other emergency on the population of one or more countries outside the UK'.

"… [W]hich pretty much allows you to do what you like, so long as it is for the purpose of alleviating the effects of a disaster or emergency on the population of a country outside the UK.

"This is understood as applying pretty much to the immediate effects of an emergency, and not to long term rehabilitation or development … Once you move into development assistance you must be motivated by poverty reduction. But you can still use soldiers to provide assistance if that is the best way of reducing poverty."[299]

---

[297] Minute DFID [junior official] to PS/Secretary of State [DFID], 27 February 2003, 'Civil Military Relations in Complex Emergencies – DFID Position'.
[298] Manuscript comment Short, 27 February 2003, on Minute DFID [junior official] to PS/Secretary of State [DFID], 27 February 2003, 'Civil Military Relations in Complex Emergencies – DFID Position'.
[299] Email [DFID junior official] to Mosselmans, 28 February 2003, 'Civil Military Relations in Complex Emergencies – DFID Position'.

676. It is not clear whether that advice was seen by Ms Short.

677. On 28 February, the MOD warned No.10 that the UK was "currently at risk of taking on a very substantial commitment that we will have great difficulty in sustaining beyond the immediate conclusion of conflict". Specific concerns included:

- **the extent of practical US support for UK humanitarian assistance;**
- **the absence of an ORHA plan for administering Iraq;**
- **the US expectation that the UK would take on an unsustainable commitment in the South-East;**
- **US decision-making moving so fast that, even though the UK was trying to influence US thinking, "UK policy will have largely to be about managing the consequences of US decisions that are taken for us";**
- **the risk that the UK, as an Occupying Power, might be expected to make up a significant part of any funding shortfall for reconstruction.**

678. Lt Gen Garner was reported to be attracted to the idea of abandoning the plan to have three ORHA sectors in Iraq in favour of mirroring the seven proposed military sectors.

679. On 28 February, Mr Hoon's Private Office sent Sir David Manning an update on military planning.[300] The paper was also sent to the Private Offices of Mr Straw and Mr Brown, and to Mr Bowen, but not to DFID.

680. Much of the section on post-conflict planning was devoted to US preparations. The paper stated:

> "For the immediate aftermath, most of the planning is now considered to be complete, but there remains significant effort required to agree how those plans should be implemented. There are significant outstanding policy issues which require resolution before the beginning of operations. For the later stages of the aftermath, planning is also gathering speed (meaning that important policy decisions are being made now by the US that will dictate the course of the aftermath)."

681. The paper stated that CFLCC and ORHA were taking forward planning, but that there were "important issues of dispute between them". The UK was "very heavily engaged in military (CFLCC) planning at a senior level", with (acting) Maj Gen Whitley as Deputy Commanding General (Post Hostilities), and had "good visibility" of ORHA thinking thanks to the embedded UK staff.

682. The paper stated that orders for the initial aftermath would issue shortly, setting out the responsibilities of an Occupying Power. There was also a "superficially impressive"

---

[300] Letter Williams to Manning, 28 February 2003, 'Iraq: Military Planning and Preparation' attaching Paper [unattributed], 28 February 2003, 'Iraq: Military Planning Update – 28 February 2003'.

plan to manage early provision of humanitarian assistance, but "a distinct lack of planning by the US" on local and national civil administration:

"An initial plan to divide the country in two (largely arbitrary) parts, with Baghdad as a third entity, may not last the test of time … Garner has now seen the CFLCC '7 sectors' map and appears attracted to mirroring those for civil administration – but there is still no concept of how to interact with either current Iraqi civil governance structures … or the military divisions. This might be an area where [the] UK can provide some useful guidance."

683. The paper listed several UK concerns:

- "Humanitarian Assistance/Stability Provision." The UK plan was "to make most use of the US humanitarian provision", but DFID and the UK military had concerns about the level of practical US support that would be available and the likely initial absence of NGOs and international organisations. Because of the block on the deployment of DFID advisers to Kuwait, UK military planning to cover the gap was going ahead without guidance. The absence of funding was even more pressing.

- "Roll-out of regional administration." ORHA had still not thought through the detail of how it would administer Iraq. There was a risk of giving the impression of a military occupation.

- "Military lay-down." It was "absolutely clear" that, of the seven military sectors, the US expected the UK to take leadership of the South-East. Without Coalition partners that would be beyond UK capabilities in the "medium term". The UK was "**currently at risk of taking on a very substantial commitment that we will have great difficulty in sustaining beyond the immediate conclusion of conflict**".

- "Policy lacunae." There were still many unresolved details in US planning. The UK was seeking to influence US thinking, but US decision-making was moving so fast that "UK policy will have largely to be about managing the consequences of US decisions that are taken for us".

- "Funding." This remained "a great unknown". US planning assumed the rest of the world would pick up 75 percent of the bill for reconstruction. That was "possibly hopelessly optimistic". As an Occupying Power, the UK would be at the front of the queue of countries the US would approach to make up any deficit.

684. Mr Cannon commented: "Prime Minister and Jonathan Powell should see."[301]

685. Some of the issues raised in Mr Hoon's letter were discussed at Mr Blair's meeting on post-conflict issues on 6 March.

---

[301] Manuscript comment Cannon, 28 February 2003, on Letter Williams to Manning, 28 February 2003, 'Iraq: Military Planning and Preparation' attaching Paper [unattributed], 28 February 2003, 'Iraq: Military Planning Update – 28 February 2003'.

686. In a Written Parliamentary Question on 28 February, Dr Tonge asked what financial provision had been made to fund the reconstruction of Iraq in the aftermath of war.[302] Mr Boateng replied: "The Government believe that the role of the United Nations and other multilateral institutions will be vital in addressing the reconstruction of Iraq in the aftermath of any war and are liaising closely with allies on this issue."

The 'UK Vision for Phase IV'

687. The 'UK Vision for Phase IV' equated the scale of change envisaged for Iraq to post-Communist reforms in central Europe. Success would require "huge efforts", "a large coalition" and "a lot of time".

688. On 26 February, the FCO sent No.10 a set of papers commissioned by Sir David Manning:

- key talking points for Mr Blair to draw on with President Bush;
- a 'UK Vision for Phase IV';
- an outline structure for the interim civil administration, already sent to Lt Gen Garner;
- a draft letter from Sir David Manning to Dr Rice setting out arguments for a UN-authorised transitional administration; and
- a list of "11 good reasons" for a third resolution.[303]

689. The papers were copied to the Private Offices of Mr Brown, Mr Hoon and Ms Short, but it is not clear from the correspondence how extensively they had been discussed with Treasury, MOD and DFID officials beforehand.

690. It is not clear whether any of the papers were seen by Mr Blair.

691. The covering letter from Mr Straw's Private Office to Mr Rycroft explained:

"You will see that the key point to make to the Americans remains the need to have UN Security Council authorisation for the civil transitional administration. There are signs that General Franks and Jay Garner … understand this. But convincing Mr Rumsfeld will be much more difficult."

692. The proposed messages for Mr Blair to deliver to President Bush were:

"– Winning the peace is important, but more difficult, than winning the war. We need to leave Iraq radically changed for the better.

– We are committing just under a third of our Armed Forces to the fighting. We shall also be staying on for the 'aftermath' – Phase IV. But we shall have to

---

[302] House of Commons, *Official Report*, 28 February 2003, column 760W.
[303] Letter Owen to Rycroft, 26 February 2002, 'Iraq: Phase IV'.

reduce by a third within six months. You can continue to count on us to do our bit.

— The Phase IV task is huge, comparable to the transformation of central European countries after the fall of the Berlin Wall – beyond what even the US can manage by itself. We shall need to build a broad coalition. We shall need more countries to provide peacekeeping forces. We must involve the UN agencies, other countries and international organisations in reconstructing the country. We need their expertise and finance.

— … I would like to begin lobbying potential contributors now. Can we agree to this?

— … [I]n order to ease the passage of the second UN Security Council resolution … there could be advantage in explaining our intention to go for a third resolution for Phase IV.

— It will take some weeks and months, after securing UN authorisation, to get a provisional civil administration ready to move to Iraq. So for the initial post-conflict period, our Coalition forces, supported by Jay Garner's Office of Reconstruction and Humanitarian Assistance, will be in charge of Iraq. The choices we make in those first weeks and months will significantly shape the future development of Iraq. Then we can hand over the task to the wider international effort, mandated by the UN.

— We should be absolutely clear that Coalition military forces will remain under General Frank's command.

— I am not starry-eyed about the UN's management record. I do not propose that the UN should take over the running of Iraq. But the Security Council's authorisation is crucial to building support internationally for our efforts.

— We need to identify a senior international figure (but not a Brit, American or Australian) who could serve as the Head of Civil Administration.

— Our officials have excellent links on the detailed planning for Phase IV. They should continue to work closely together on the key issues. These include … how to deal with those closest to Saddam's regime … and rebutting the accusation that this is a war about oil …

— One last important thing – it will be very helpful to get the weapons inspectors back into Iraq quickly to verify findings of Iraqi WMD."

693. The 'UK Vision for Phase IV', written by the IPU, opened with the statement:

"A successful mission means winning the peace as well as the war. We should aim to leave Iraq radically changed for the better. That means an Iraq which:

- Has given up its attachment to WMD
- No longer supports terrorism
- Has appropriately sized, reformed armed forces and intelligence/security agencies
- Does not threaten its neighbours
- Complies with its international obligations
- Enjoys a broad-based, representative government, which respects human rights
- Has a fair justice sector
- Has been weaned off its dependency on the Oil-for-Food programme and is determinedly travelling along the path towards becoming a free market economy
- Trades normally and is set to normalise its relations with international financial and trading organisations.[304]

"That is a lot to achieve – similar in scale to the post-communist reforms of central European countries. Success will require huge efforts from the Iraqis themselves and from the wider international community. The support of countries in the region will also be critical. We shall need to pull together a large coalition to provide the resources for the task. And it will take a lot of time – perhaps many years – to achieve success."

694. The paper set out the UK's expectations for the three stages of Phase IV:

- <u>Phase IV Alpha</u>. Military administration by CFLCC, then, when conditions permit, ORHA, under CENTCOM command. Key issues would be:
  - constraints placed on the military's powers to administer Iraq by international humanitarian law;
  - the urgent need to provide clean water, sanitation, food, shelter and medicines; most of that task would fall to UN agencies and NGOs, with the Coalition providing the secure environment in which assistance could be delivered;
  - early resurrection of OFF;
  - maximising Iraqi involvement from the outset through a consultative council to advise the military and ORHA; and

---

[304] Paper Iraq Planning Unit, 25 February 2003, 'UK Vision for Phase IV'.

- ○ working with existing Iraqi structures as far as was consistent with the security of Coalition Forces and the objectives of military action.
- Phase IV Bravo. In the UK's view, this would begin as soon as there was a UN mandated international civil transitional administration (CTA) in place, supported by UN-mandated Coalition military:
  - ○ With a UN mandate it would be possible to increase the number of countries contributing forces in what could still be an uncertain environment.
  - ○ The aim of Phase IV Bravo would be to transform Iraq "along the lines of the vision".
  - ○ The UK was still working with the US on possible elements for the CTA's composition: "The trick will be to make it sufficiently international and UN friendly to win the support of the UNSC but not to put the UN in charge of areas where it has a poor management track record".
  - ○ The duration of Phase IV Bravo would be determined by the time taken to draw up a new constitution and to elect a new government.
- Phase IV Charlie. Coalition Forces and the CTA would withdraw, but Iraq would continue to need help restructuring its economy and possibly with public administration more generally.

695. The FCO letter to No.10 also enclosed an outline structure for the interim civil administration during Phase IV Bravo, which had already been sent to Lt Gen Garner.[305] The outline stated:

"Once Iraq is stabilised and it becomes possible to move to Phase IVb (recovery), it would be desirable to transition the Interim Civil Administrative structure to a more broadly-based structure, authorised by a UN Security Council resolution. That would enable wide international support, and could make the most of international experience without hindering effective leadership.

"The structure would be headed by a 'High Representative' ... ideally a Muslim figure ... Beneath him would be several co-ordinators heading up vertical pillars covering humanitarian assistance, reconstruction, civil administration and 'democratisation'. To assist him in his task, and until such time as the 'democratisation' pillar delivered appropriate constitutional reform and a broadly based, representative system, there would be an Iraqi Consultative Council. Working alongside him would be a security co-ordinator who would be responsible for security sector reform and liaison with the Coalition military commander."

---

[305] Paper [unattributed and undated], 'Phase 4b Organization'.

696. The thinking behind the vision was expressed most clearly in the draft letter from Sir David Manning to Dr Rice, which stated that it would be helpful to be able to say soon how the US and UK saw the government of Iraq after Saddam Hussein:

"Our starting point is that the humanitarian, reconstruction and civil administration tasks are too complex and too resource intensive for the US and UK to undertake alone … Most potential contributors … will only feel comfortable participating … if there is a UN authorising mandate. They will not arrogate to themselves the right to redesign Iraq, however desirable the end state. And nor would we. We shall need Security Council authorisation for legal reasons too."[306]

697. The draft letter concluded:

"Handing Iraq's reconstruction over to a UN-authorised CTA will allow us to reduce our presence in Iraq and leave the country with honour. Indeed, unless we do so, I am far from convinced that we can succeed in Phase IV."

698. The FCO explained that the draft letter did not refer to the outline for Phase IVb that had been shared with Lt Gen Garner, "in case David Manning thought it was a bridge too far, at this stage, to put to Condi Rice".[307]

699. The letter appears never to have been sent. When Sir David next wrote to Dr Rice, on 10 March, it was in the context of work on a draft Security Council resolution.

700. The FCO sent a separate draft 'Vision for Iraq and the Iraqi People' to No.10 on 28 February.

701. President Bush described the US post-conflict commitment to Iraq in a speech on 26 February. He stated that rebuilding Iraq would take "a sustained commitment from many nations, including our own: we will remain in Iraq as long as necessary, and not a day more".

702. In a speech at the American Enterprise Institute on 26 February, described in more detail in Section 3.7, President Bush stated:

"If we must use force, the United States and our Coalition stand ready to help the citizens of a liberated Iraq …

"We will provide security against those who try to spread chaos … We will seek to protect Iraq's natural resources from sabotage by a dying regime, and ensure those resources are used for the benefit of the owners – the Iraqi people.

"The United States has no intention of determining the precise form of Iraq's new government … All Iraqis must have a voice in the new government, and all citizens must have their rights protected.

---

[306] Letter [draft] Manning to Rice, 24 February 2003, 'Iraq: Phase IV'.
[307] Letter Owen to Rycroft, 26 February 2002, 'Iraq: Phase IV'.

"Rebuilding Iraq will require a sustained commitment from many nations, including our own: we will remain in Iraq as long as necessary, and not a day more. America has made and kept this kind of commitment before – in the peace that followed a world war …

"There was a time when many said that the cultures of Japan and Germany were incapable of sustaining democratic values … Some say the same of Iraq today. They are mistaken. The nation of Iraq – with its proud heritage, abundant resources and skilled and educated people – is fully capable of moving toward democracy and living in freedom."[308]

UK commercial interests

703. UK oil firms had begun to express concern about access to post-Saddam Hussein oil contracts in the second half of 2002 (see Section 6.4).

704. By 27 February, officials were concerned that UK reticence in contacts with the US was disadvantaging UK firms across a range of business sectors.

705. In early 2003, UK companies in other sectors approached Trade Partners UK (TPUK), the division of British Trade International (BTI) responsible for promoting UK exports, for advice on business opportunities in post-conflict Iraq.[309] A number of companies expressed concern about a repeat of the situation in 1991, when UK firms lost out heavily to US companies on reconstruction contracts in Kuwait.

706. On 12 February Mr Bill Henderson, TPUK Director International Group 1, explained to Baroness Symons, joint FCO/DTI Minister of State for International Trade and Investment, that, until early February 2003, UK Government discussion of commercial opportunities in Iraq had largely been restricted to officials in order "to avoid giving undue prominence to the commercial aspects of HMG's handling of the crisis".[310]

707. Mr Henderson reported that, on 12 February, he had chaired a meeting with the FCO, the Export Credit Guarantee Department (ECGD) and, for the first time, a representative of the British Consultants and Contractors Bureau (BCCB) to discuss how best to provide assistance to UK companies outside the oil and gas sector. Mr Henderson expressed concern that "the overall Whitehall agenda appears to attach little importance to the commercial aspects and the interest of UK companies".

708. The need to secure "a level-playing field for UK business in oil and other areas" was one of the key messages for the US on post-conflict Iraq, agreed on 11 February.

709. On 27 February, Mr Henderson remained concerned that UK reticence was disadvantaging UK companies: "the US (and probably France who have a Trade Office

---

[308] *The Guardian*, 27 February, *Full text: George Bush's speech to the American Enterprise Institute*.
[309] Minute Henderson to Symons, 12 February 2003, 'Iraq: post-conflict commercial issues'.
[310] Minute Henderson to Symons, 12 February 2003, 'Iraq: post-conflict commercial issues'.

in Baghdad) are ahead of us on this, and are taking a much more open stance".[311] He recommended to Baroness Symons that she agree a "more open, pro-active approach" to dealing with UK companies.

710. Baroness Symons sent that advice to Mr Straw and Ms Patricia Hewitt, Secretary of State for Trade and Industry, stating that:

"... the pressure from businesses is building and I fear that some of our business community fear we are not engaged. Some think that the US and France are ahead of the game already ..."[312]

711. Government lobbying on behalf of UK firms is addressed in more detail in Section 10.3.

The UK 'Vision for Iraq and the Iraqi People'

712. **The UK 'Vision for Iraq and the Iraqi People', written by the FCO in October 2002, was revised at the end of February 2003.**

713. **Mr Straw saw its principal value as a means to reassure domestic and Iraqi public opinion of the UK's intentions in Iraq.**

714. **The 'Vision' was a statement of aspirations that assumed a level of agreement with the US that did not yet exist on plans for post-conflict Iraq.**

715. **The 'Vision for Iraq and the Iraqi People' was a separate document to the 'UK Vision for Phase IV', which is addressed earlier in this Section.**

716. On 27 February, Mr Straw discussed the draft 'Vision for Iraq and the Iraqi People', originally prepared by FCO officials in October 2002 (see Section 6.4), with Mr Campbell.[313] The draft had been shown to the AHGI on 11 October 2002, when it had been decided that the paper should "remain in reserve".[314]

717. Mr Straw believed that "public commitment on the lines of the draft could have a powerful impact in Iraq and the region as well as on the British domestic debate". The 'Vision' should not be launched or trailed until the UN had voted on the second resolution because of the risk that it would be presented as "discounting" the role of the Security Council. Care would also be needed to avoid confusing the message that the justification for military action rested firmly on disarmament of WMD.

718. Mr Straw thought it essential that the UK, US and "other Coalition members" spoke to a common script. That underlined the importance of making progress with the US on

---

[311] Minute Henderson to Symons, 27 February 2003, 'Iraq contingency planning: commercial aspects'.
[312] Minute Symons to Straw and Hewitt, undated, 'Iraq: Commercial Aspects'.
[313] Letter Owen to Rycroft, 28 February 2003, 'A Vision for Iraq and the Iraqi People' attaching Paper [unattributed and undated], 'A Vision for Iraq and the Iraqi People'.
[314] Minute Dodd to Manning, 14 October 2002, 'Ad Hoc Group on Iraq'; Paper [draft] FCO, [undated], 'Vision for Iraq and the Iraqi People'.

day after planning. Although there was nothing in the UK draft that "could not be squared with US policy" as set out in President Bush's speech, "elements ... go further than the US has so far done in public or, on some issues including UN involvement, in private".

719. The FCO sent No.10 the latest draft of the 'Vision', which had been seen by officials in the MOD, Cabinet Office, Treasury and DFID, explaining that work was in hand to ensure coherence with military campaign objectives already agreed by Ministers.[315]

720. The new version expanded the criticism of Saddam Hussein, added a reference to the military consequences should he refuse to co-operate with the UN and inserted two references to "democratic government" in place of the previous version's single reference to "democratic principles".

721. The new description of overall aims explained that:

"Our aim is to disarm Saddam of his weapons of mass destruction, which threaten his neighbours and his people. Our presence in Iraq if military action is required to secure compliance with UN resolutions will be temporary. But our commitment to support the people of Iraq will be for the long term. The Iraqi people deserve to be lifted from tyranny and allowed to determine the future of their country for themselves. We pledge to work with the international community to help the Iraqi people restore their country to its proper dignity and place in the community of nations, abiding by its international obligations and free from UN sanctions."

722. The five principal aims remained unchanged from the October paper:

- "Freedom";
- "Good Government";
- "International Respect";
- "Peace";
- "Prosperity".

723. The list of ways in which the UK/Coalition would help was also largely unchanged, offering support with:

- an early end to sanctions;
- Iraq's reintegration into the region;
- generous debt rescheduling;
- increased aid from the international community;
- an international reconstruction programme;
- investment in Iraq's oil industry;

---

[315] Letter Owen to Rycroft, 28 February 2003, 'A Vision for Iraq and the Iraqi People' attaching Paper [unattributed and undated], 'A Vision for Iraq and the Iraqi People'.

- renewal of international education and cultural links; and
- institutional and administrative reform.

There were three additions to the October 2002 list:

- ensuring the military campaign was as swift and carefully targeted as possible;
- working with the UN and the international community to meet emergency humanitarian needs; and
- enabling Iraqis "to establish their own democratic government as quickly as possible" and encouraging UN involvement in the process.

724. Mr Bowen commented on the draft on 4 March.[316] He suggested that, in addition to drawing on wording in the military campaign objectives, the draft could:

"... reflect more closely how we would wish post-Saddam Iraq to be governed ... We are also concerned about the extent to which the document implies responsibility for Iraq's future being largely the UK's rather than that of the international community."

725. Specific recommendations included:

- replacing the reference to an "independent and democratic Iraq" with "an Iraq with effective and representative government"; and
- extensive redrafting of the section on UK/Coalition support in order to distinguish between the Coalition contribution "in the immediate wake of conflict" and what "we" and the international community, working with the Iraqi people, would do within months of the conflict.

726. Mr Hoon endorsed Mr Bowen's proposed redraft, commenting that "it would be useful in terms of credibility to be able to set out our vision in the more specific text ... recognising that this may add to the challenge of reaching agreement with the US".[317]

727. Both sets of comments were copied to No.10.

728. A revised version of the 'Vision for Iraq and the Iraqi People' was sent to No.10 on 15 March, the day before the Azores Summit. It incorporated Mr Bowen's proposal to replace "democratic" with "effective and representative government", but did not reflect his broader recommendation for extensive redrafting.

729. On 27 February, the British Embassy Washington reported that the US was showing "growing acceptance" of the idea of a civilian administrator backed by a UN mandate.

---

[316] Letter Bowen to Owen, 4 March 2003, 'Vision for Iraq and the Iraqi People'.
[317] Letter Williams to Owen, 5 March 2003, 'A Vision for Iraq and the Iraqi People'.

730. The British Embassy Washington reported the outcome of a call on ORHA and the NSC by Dr Brewer on 27 February. Thinking on the UN was evolving. The US accepted it would need technical help with humanitarian and reconstruction work and was showing growing acceptance of an international civilian administrator backed by a UN mandate, but remained opposed to a direct reporting line to the UN.[318]

731. Separately, the Embassy suggested giving more support to ORHA. It would be vital to the long-term success of UK action in Iraq and any assistance would be "gratefully received and effectively used". So far three staff had been provided, including Maj Gen Cross. That was "a drop in the bucket". The Embassy suggested staff already earmarked for posting to Baghdad might be one source.[319]

732. The secondment of UK officials to ORHA is addressed in Section 15.

733. Mr Straw spoke to Secretary Powell on 3 March (see Section 3.7). He reported to No.10 that, in the context of a discussion about the lack of serious planning for post-conflict, he had told Secretary Powell that, "whilst the US Administration had to be the best judge of its long term interests", he "thought it would reap a whirlwind if it failed to secure legitimacy for what it was doing in respect of Iraq. We were not there yet."[320]

734. By 4 March, senior members of the US Administration were said to have accepted the need for a Security Council mandate, a role for the UN after the initial military occupation and the need for a UN Special Co-ordinator.

735. Mr Tony Brenton, Chargé d'Affaires at the British Embassy Washington, reported overnight on 3/4 March that senior members of the US Administration had accepted the need for a Security Council mandate, a role for the UN after the initial military occupation and the need for a UN Special Co-ordinator, although there were differing views over how the UN figure would relate to an Iraqi Interim Council.[321] The US hoped to organise a "Bonn Conference" on the Afghan model, four to six weeks after the invasion, involving external opposition figures and tribal leaders from inside Iraq. The conference would produce an administrative council, which would gradually take on authority over a period of months as it moved Iraq towards elections or a constituent assembly. Mr Brenton reported that he had underlined to the US the UK's wish to see a structure which brought international legitimacy and buy-in, and had expressed "polite scepticism" about the qualities of those members of the external opposition best known to the UK.

---

[318] Telegram 256 Washington to FCO London, 27 February 2003, 'Iraq Day After: US Views on UN Role'.
[319] Telegram 257 Washington to FCO London, 27 February 2003, 'Iraq Day After: UK Role in Post-Conflict Iraq'.
[320] Letter Straw to Manning, 4 March 2003, 'Iraq: Conversation with Colin Powell, 3 March'.
[321] Telegram 284 Washington to FCO London, 4 March 2003, 'Iraq: Day After'.

736. At the FCO Iraq Morning Meeting on 4 March, Mr Chilcott described Mr Brenton's report on the evolving views of US Principals as:

"... a further good example of even the most senior levels of the US Administration showing themselves open to good arguments firmly put at the right time. We needed to go on making these arguments."[322]

Growing pressure for Ministerial decisions

737. Mr Blair produced a manuscript Note on 3 March setting out a list of potential actions to help secure Security Council support for the second resolution. Potential actions included agreeing:

- a UN role in post-conflict Iraq;
- a broad-based government;
- the humanitarian effort.[323]

738. Mr Blair's Note is addressed in more detail in Section 3.7.

739. On 4 March, Mr Ricketts told Mr Straw that he and Sir David Manning had discussed advice from Sir Jeremy Greenstock on the second resolution and believed that the "best package" might include for the US to make clear that it "accepted a significant UN role in post-conflict Iraq".[324]

740. On 3 March, the AHGI advised Sir David Manning that Ministers needed to give their urgent attention to the possibility that the UK could be running an area of Iraq within weeks.

741. The record of the 28 February meeting of the AHGI was sent to Sir David Manning on 3 March.[325] On the question of the UK assuming responsibility for a sector of Iraq it stated:

"Although military action is not certain, we may be confronted with the realities of running a part of Iraq within weeks.

"The question of geographical sectors, whether for security or to provide civilian government as well, whether we should offer to lead one and how much it would cost, is of increasing concern. The US military plan, which has been adopted, has the UK running a sector covering a significant part of Iraq. In the event of war, UK forces will end in occupying part of Iraq, but a sector covering four provinces, as the US propose, is probably beyond our national capacity. There are concerns in home departments about implications for their resources of any commitment to provide

---

[322] Minute Tanfield to PS/PUS [FCO], 4 March 2003, 'Iraq Morning Meeting: Key Points'.
[323] Note [Blair], 3 March 2003, [untitled].
[324] Minute Ricketts to PS/Straw, 4 March 2003, 'Iraq: UN Tactics'.
[325] Minute Dodd to Manning, 3 March 2003, 'Ad Hoc Group on Iraq'.

civil government in a UK sector. We [the AHGI] agreed that Ministers needed to give this question their urgent attention."

742. On 4 March, Adm Boyce issued the first draft of the Execute Directive for Op TELIC, for planning and guidance purposes only.

743. He instructed Lt Gen Reith to work closely with US commanders on preparations of Phase IV.

744. Adm Boyce issued the first version of the Execute Directive for Op TELIC on 4 March.[326] In his covering minute to Lt Gen Reith, he explained that the Directive was being issued in draft form for planning and guidance purposes only. It was to be read on the clear understanding that no political decision had yet been taken on combat operations, but "events could move very fast". Lt Gen Reith's focus would be to work closely with US commanders "on all aspects of potential operations in support of Phases III and IV".

745. The Directive itself was addressed to the Commander Joint Operations (Lt Gen Reith) and listed three objectives "in Support of the UK's Higher Political Intent:

(1) Support efforts of humanitarian organisations to mitigate the consequences of hostilities.

(2) Facilitate international efforts for the rehabilitation and reconstruction of Iraq.

(3) Contribute to the preservation of the territorial integrity of Iraq and the wider regional security …"[327]

746. A number of specific tasks were linked to those objectives, including:

- "Protect, and be prepared to secure, essential Iraqi political, administrative and economic infrastructure from unnecessary destruction in order to reassure the Iraqi people and facilitate rapid regeneration."
- "Deter opportunistic inter-ethnic and inter-communal conflict."
- "Within available resources, be prepared to support humanitarian efforts to mitigate the consequences of conflict."
- "As quickly as possible, establish a safe and secure environment within which humanitarian aid agencies are able to operate."
- "If directed, be prepared to contribute to the reform of Iraq's security forces."

747. A final version of the Directive, authorising military action in Iraq and with the points listed above unchanged, was issued on 18 March.

---

[326] Minute CDS to CJO, 4 March 2003, 'Chief of Defence Staff Execute Directive to the Joint Commander Operation TELIC'.
[327] Paper MOD, 28 February 2003, 'Chief of Defence Staff Execute Directive to the Joint Commander Operation TELIC'.

748. Lt Gen Reith presented two papers to the Chiefs of Staff on 4 March advocating an expanded combat role for UK forces. He advised that the implications for Phase IV should be a consideration.

749. Mr Hoon and the Chiefs of Staff agreed that the UK should not actively seek a wider role, but should be ready to consider any unsolicited US requests on their merits. Implications for Phase IV operations would be one of a number of considerations.

750. On 4 March, Lt Gen Reith sent the Chiefs of Staff two papers setting out proposals for employing UK land forces on combat missions with or without "a dedicated 'UK box'" based on "the agreed 1 (UK) Div AO". The papers are described in more detail in Section 6.2.[328]

751. Lt Gen Reith explained that a UK box would "allow UK forces to move first in a ground offensive and thereby set the conditions for the 'exemplary performance' in Phase IV", but US resistance to the creation of a UK box would "probably only be overcome by high level intervention".

752. In the first of the two papers, Lt Gen Reith addressed the advantages and disadvantages of "UK ownership of its full AO from the start". Under the existing Base Plan, the UK AO would expand into space vacated by US forces as they moved north and UK forces would not be able to shape their own Phase IV AOR. Lt Gen Reith explained that one of the contingency plans already worked up by the Land Component Command (LCC) assumed full UK ownership of its AO from the start. There could be "no doubt at all that this represents a far better option for UK forces than the Base Plan".

753. In the second paper, Lt Gen Reith explained that his forthcoming meetings with Lt Gen McKiernan and others would "almost certainly be the last chance that the operational commanders will have to discuss the plan face to face before ground operations commence". US commanders were likely to press him on UK land contributions beyond the provisions in the Base Plan.

754. Lt Gen Reith put forward two options:

- "National focus with limited operational exposure." The Base Plan, involving "operations within the AO as presently defined, concentrating on making the early transition from Phase III to Phase IV, with an end state defined as 'exemplary performance' in Phase IV within Basra region".

- "Coalition focus with unconstrained operational exposure." Among the disadvantages of this approach was a reduction in the number of troops

---

[328] Minute Reith to COSSEC, 4 March 2003, 'Op Telic employment of UK forces' attaching Paper CJO, 3 March 2003, 'Op TELIC Land Options for 1(UK) Armoured Division – update' and Paper CJO, 4 March 2003, 'Op TELIC Land Options for 1(UK) Armoured Divisions – Alternative Options'.

available for Phase IV operations in the UK AO, which "may impact on our ability to produce exemplary early effect during Phase IV".

755. Lt Gen Reith concluded:

"US commanders are likely to press on branch planning and UK land contributions beyond the provisions of the Base Plan.

"The situation is changing: the potential for a UK box remains my aspiration but is in practical terms receding …

"In discussing the campaign, and subject to their [the Chiefs of Staff] agreement, CJO will balance the desire to husband our land forces for Phase IV in our own AO, against the possible Coalition requirement to take a greater part of the Phase III effort, with the risks this implies in terms of the ease with which we transition to Phase IV."

756. The Chiefs of Staff discussed the papers on 5 March.[329] They rejected the proposal for a UK box.

757. In Lt Gen Reith's absence, Maj Gen Fry sought guidance from the Chiefs of Staff on offering "UK 'niche' contributions beyond the provisions of the Base Plan" in the context of the requirement to deliver an exemplary Phase IV.

758. The Chiefs of Staff noted that delivering an exemplary Phase IV required "the concomitant resources and OGD [other government department] commitment". Adm Boyce stressed that Phase IV could not be delivered by military activity alone.

759. Adm Boyce directed Lt Gen Reith to "push for a 'niche' role for the UK … and make it clear that the UK was ready to be asked to contribute further in order to exploit any operational opportunities that arose during the campaign", subject to US logistics support and assurances that UK forces would be "relieved-in-place" as soon as possible for Phase IV activities in the South.

760. Mr Watkins informed Sir David Manning on 6 March that Mr Hoon and the Chiefs of Staff judged that "it would not be wise at this late stage to seek a major revision to the US plan", but that the plan could make better use of some of the niche capabilities in 1 (UK) Division.[330] Mr Hoon had agreed that the UK should encourage US commanders to identify a niche role. The US was looking at a number of variations to its plan, including involving 7 Armoured Brigade in "decisive manoeuvre operations beyond south-eastern Iraq" and "possibly in a decisive phase around Baghdad". That would raise a number of issues, including for post-conflict operations.

---

[329] Minutes, 5 March 2003, Chiefs of Staff meeting.
[330] Letter Watkins to Manning, 6 March 2003, 'Iraq: Options for Employment of UK Land Forces'.

761. Mr Watkins explained that Mr Hoon and the Chiefs of Staff had therefore agreed that the UK "should not actively seek this sort of wider role, but that we should be prepared to consider any unsolicited US requests on their merits".

762. President Bush and Mr Blair discussed Iraq on 5 March.

763. Mr Blair told Cabinet the following day that President Bush had agreed that the UN should be "heavily involved" in post-conflict Iraq.

764. There was no clarification of what was meant by "heavily involved".

765. Mr Blair and President Bush discussed Iraq on 5 March.

766. Mr Rycroft advised Mr Blair that the key points he should make to President Bush included that it was: "Crucial to have [a] UN role post-conflict."[331]

767. Mr Blair spoke to President Bush proposing further amendments to the draft resolution. Mr Blair and President Bush also briefly discussed the military plan.[332] Mr Rycroft informed the FCO that Mr Blair considered it important that there was a "UN badge" for post-conflict work.

768. Mr Blair told Cabinet on 6 March that he had agreed with President Bush on the need for the UN to be "heavily involved" in "the post-conflict situation, in the event that military action was necessary".[333]

769. Points made in discussion included that the reconstruction of Iraq would require a UN mandate, not just UN involvement; otherwise the right of Coalition Forces to engage in reconstruction work would be limited by their status as an occupation force.

Mr Blair's meeting on post-conflict issues, 6 March 2003

770. Before Mr Blair's meeting on humanitarian and other post-conflict issues on 6 March, the UK remained without an agreed approach to humanitarian relief.

771. On 5 March, PJHQ warned the MOD that DFID had indicated that it would focus its humanitarian effort on areas of Iraq with the greatest need and not necessarily the UK's AO.

772. On 5 March, PJHQ alerted the MOD to its concerns about provision of humanitarian assistance in a UK AO in the immediate aftermath of conflict.[334] PJHQ advised that it had planned to "piggy-back" on US arrangements, but it was now apparent that the US plan depended heavily on the provision of funding to international organisations (IOs) and NGOs. Those organisations were unlikely to be present in the

---

[331] Minute Rycroft to Prime Minister, 5 March 2003, 'Bush Call'.
[332] Letter Rycroft to McDonald, 5 March 2003, 'Iraq: Prime Minister's Conversation with Bush, 5 March'.
[333] Cabinet Conclusions, 6 March 2003.
[334] Minute PJHQ [junior official] to MOD Sec(O) 4, 5 March 2003, 'Op TELIC: resourcing of humanitarian assistance'.

first weeks after any conflict. PJHQ had also assumed that DFID would be responsible for providing humanitarian assistance. Dr Brewer's letter of 24 February to Mr Bowen suggested that DFID believed that the most effective way to distribute humanitarian assistance was through IOs and NGOs, and that they would focus their resources on areas of greatest need (rather than necessarily on the UK's AO). PJHQ estimated that between £30m and £50m a month for two months would be required to cover the provision of humanitarian assistance in the UK AO in the immediate aftermath of any conflict.

773. Ms Short informed Mr Blair that, without resources greater than her department's entire contingency reserve, "it would be impossible for DFID to take a leading role in humanitarian delivery in the South-East" of Iraq.

774. Ms Short held a meeting with DFID officials to discuss Iraq, and in particular the legality of "reconstruction work" without a covering UN mandate, on 5 March.[335] Ms Short concluded that without a clear mandate for reconstruction, DFID could only legally fund or undertake humanitarian work. The meeting agreed that:

"... under circumstances where DFID would be involved in humanitarian work only, DFID's contingency reserve could be drawn upon. This might provide around £60-65m. In the event that a wider DFID role was possible, should we be asked by No.10 or others how much funding DFID would need, we should mention an initial sum of £100m."

775. Ms Short also agreed the need to:

"... move away from any expectation that DFID would undertake an 'exemplary' role, or ... focus exclusively on any one area. This decision was taken on the basis that there would be substantial need elsewhere in Iraq other than simply in the South East; that the extent of our involvement would not be clear for some time, as the different variables affecting it fell into place; and that we needed to avoid being so closely associated with one area that we were seen as the 'donor of last resort', for all unfunded needs. However, we should make clear that, given the right UN mandate and authority, we would aim to work alongside the UK military, as well as elsewhere, with others, as appropriate."

776. Ms Short said that she would use Mr Blair's meeting on 6 March to press him to:

- examine carefully the legality of different post-conflict options for the UK;
- press the US on the need for "sufficient preparation" before any conflict began; and
- consider options for extending the deadline before the vote on a Security Council resolution or putting forward a revised text.

---

[335] Minute Bewes to Fernie, 6 March 2003, 'Iraq update: 5 March'.

777. Ms Short set out her views in a letter to Mr Blair before the meeting:

"… the reconstruction of Iraq without an explicit UN mandate would breach international law. Without the UN mandate the Coalition would be an occupying army with humanitarian duties under the Geneva Convention, but – like the Israelis in the Occupied Territories – without any rights to change institutional arrangements. The UN is clear that without the right mandate they could only respond to immediate humanitarian needs. My understanding is that the US has not yet accepted all our arguments on the UN role. Unless they do, DFID could do no more than support UN humanitarian efforts, and few others would be willing to engage.

…

"You should be aware that the US and the international humanitarian community are not properly prepared to deal with the immediate humanitarian issues. Visits to Washington suggest that the newly created US Office for Reconstruction and Humanitarian Assistance is well led but under-staffed, under-resourced and under-prepared for the scale of the challenge …

"But the US is improving its humanitarian preparedness daily. A little more time would make the US much better able to deal with some of the humanitarian consequences of conflict. My department is doing what we can to advise the UK military on preparations for delivering humanitarian assistance including in the initial absence of the UN and most international NGOs. We too could also be better prepared given more time.

"You must also be aware that without resources larger than my whole contingency reserve – just under £100m – it would be impossible for DFID to take a leading role in humanitarian delivery in the South-East …"[336]

778. Ms Short's letter was also sent to Mr Brown, Mr Straw and Mr Hoon.

779. On 6 March, Mr Blair chaired the first Ministerial meeting convened solely to address humanitarian and other post-conflict issues.

780. Officials recommended that the UK should not seek responsibility for general administration of a geographical area of Iraq in the medium term and pressed Ministers to take an urgent decision on the issue.

781. No decision was taken.

782. Officials asked Ministers to agree a new set of objectives and guiding principles for the post-conflict occupation of Iraq.

783. The objectives and guiding principles were not discussed at the meeting.

---

[336] Letter Short to Blair, 5 March 2003, 'Post Conflict Iraq: UN and US Roles'.

784. Although there was no guarantee at that stage that a UN mandate along the lines sought by the UK would be forthcoming, Mr Blair stated that planning for "medium-term post-conflict action" should continue on the assumption that there would be a UN mandate.

785. For the first time, Mr Blair requested a consolidated UK plan for post-conflict Iraq, including the key decisions for Ministers to take.

786. DFID and the MOD remained unable to agree a joint approach to UK humanitarian operations in the area likely to be occupied by UK forces.

787. After Cabinet on 6 March, Mr Blair chaired a meeting on post-conflict issues with Mr Brown, Mr Hoon, Ms Short, Baroness Symons, Sir Michael Jay and "other officials".[337]

788. The IPU prepared an annotated agenda in consultation with other departments.[338]

789. With the invasion possibly only weeks away, the IPU explained that US and UK planning assumed that, in the "medium term after the conflict", Coalition Forces would be "re-deployed into six or seven geographical sectors in order to provide a secure environment for the civil transitional administration to conduct humanitarian assistance and reconstruction work". The US expected the UK Division in Iraq to be responsible for a geographical sector (see Section 6.2), which would be very expensive and carry wider resource implications. The UK Division would probably be based in or near Basra, with the size of its AOR depending on a number of factors, including the permissiveness of the environment and the size of the Division in relation to the rest of the Coalition.

790. The annotated agenda stated: "Ministers need urgently to take a view on this before the military planning assumptions become a fait accompli." Ministers were asked:

- <u>Whether they agreed that the UK did not have the resources to make an "exemplary" effort in providing for basic humanitarian needs in the area controlled by a UK Division</u>. The potential cost of making a "significant difference" in a UK AO likely to contain 20 percent of Iraq's population was estimated at between US$400m and US$2.4bn for the first year, depending on disruption to OFF and the extent of the damage caused by conflict. That was "well beyond" the financial and implementing capacity of DFID and the MOD, and could become a significant medium-term commitment if the local population became dependent on UK assistance. The alternative to an "exemplary effort" was to "give our assistance to UN agencies and NGOs", supplemented by support for QIPs in the UK's area.

- <u>To choose between options for a medium-term post-conflict military presence</u>. The Chiefs of Staff believed it would be necessary to reduce the UK's military

---

[337] Letter Cannon to Owen, 7 March 2003, 'Iraq: Post-Conflict Issues'.
[338] Paper IPU, 5 March 2003, 'Planning for the UK's role in Iraq after Saddam'.

contribution from about 45,000 to 15,000 in the "medium term (by the autumn)" to "avoid long term damage to the Armed Forces". At the same time, the US expected the UK to contribute forces "for the security of a geographic area … over the medium term". The IPU considered it "reasonable to assume that a brigade should be able to manage a single, well-populated province" the size of Basra, but there were four options available:

- a brigade responsible for security in a single province;
- a UK divisional headquarters could take responsibility for security, under Coalition command, in a wider area of Iraq (US planners envisaged Basra, Maysan, Dhi Qar and Wasit being a single sector), supported by Coalition partners, which, the paper recognised, could be difficult to find;
- deployment of the ARRC in addition or as an alternative to a brigade;
- withdrawal of all forces in the medium term, though the paper warned that would be politically difficult.

- <u>Whether to follow the US plan to administer Iraq as a whole and not seek general UK responsibility for the administration of any geographic area in the medium term</u>. The US plan was to administer Iraq as a whole from Baghdad, "which must be right". In any area where the UK took responsibility for security, it could, with a UN mandate, also take on wider responsibility for reconstruction (including humanitarian assistance and aspects of civil administration), but that would "very likely be beyond the resources of the UK alone and have implications for domestic departments".

- <u>Whether any UK involvement in the medium term should be conditional on a UN mandate</u>.

- <u>To agree a set of objectives for post-conflict occupation of Iraq</u>. The UK's objectives would be achieved when Iraq had been "radically changed for the better". The US ambition was reform leading to "a liberal market economy and multi-party democracy", and was consistent with UK objectives as set out by Mr Straw in Parliament on 7 January. From a UK perspective, the IPU envisaged an Iraq that:

- had "a broad-based, effective and representative government";
- had "given up its attachment to WMD";
- had armed forces and intelligence services of "an appropriate size … well on the way to being reformed";
- complied with its international obligations;
- respected human rights and made "significant progress towards a fair and effective justice sector";
- was not dependent on OFF and was "well on the way to becoming a free market economy";

- ○ was not subject to sanctions and had "begun to regularise its relations with international financial and trading organisations, with a view to it not being economically hamstrung by debt and reparations".

- <u>To agree a set of principles that would be useful from a planning perspective and guide UK involvement in the short term</u>. Those principles were that the UK would:

  - ○ meet its international legal obligations;

  - ○ minimise the suffering of the Iraqi people;

  - ○ be limited in what it could do to change Iraq until there was a new UN Security Council mandate;

  - ○ help Iraqis to help themselves by using their own institutions to run the country;

  - ○ stress that its presence in Iraq was temporary, but the commitment to support the people of Iraq was for the long term;

  - ○ stress that Iraq's natural resources were for the people of Iraq;

  - ○ as far as possible, ensure that short-term involvement did not exceed resources currently committed and "keep options open for the medium term";

  - ○ expect evidence of WMD to be verified by UN inspectors;

  - ○ seek to internationalise its presence in Iraq "as soon as possible". Ministers were asked whether they were content for officials to approach potential contributors.

791. The IPU checklists of objectives and guiding principles made no reference to operational preparations for the UK's post-conflict role in Iraq.

792. MOD advice to Mr Hoon was explicit about the inadequacy of those preparations:

- **UK involvement in post-conflict administration would require a significant civilian component: none had been identified.**

- **Under existing US plans, the UK would need substantial military support from other nations: there were no formal arrangements to gather such support.**

- **US planners assumed a UK contribution to Phase IV that was potentially greater than could be sustained: if Ministers wanted to set limits, they should do so now.**

- **There was a need to consider the worst case: an enduring large scale military commitment with commensurate civilian support.**

793. The MOD advice to Mr Hoon stated:

"… any UK involvement in the administration of post-conflict Iraq will necessarily require a significant civilian administrative and specialist component; this component has not yet been identified or resourced by OGDs. **This is the key issue. The success of civil administration will be essential to Iraq's long term future. The UK military cannot do this on their own.**

"… [T]he current defence planning assumption is that UK forces can only sustain large scale operations for a period of six months without doing long term damage to capability. This implies that UK forces reduce to a Medium Scale (i.e. roughly one brigade) post-conflict TELIC commitment.

"… US planning is currently tending to assume UK involvement in Phase IV at a level that is the maximum, if not higher than, that we can sustain. **If Ministers wish to set limits on the UK's Phase IV contribution they should be set <u>now</u> so that US planning can be adjusted** …

"… [A]s US planning stands, the UK will need substantial support from other nations. There are no arrangements yet in place formally to gather such support. Such support will be largely contingent on a suitable second/third UNSCR and a UN mandate for the occupation of Iraq. The FCO need to build on their recent 'market survey' to identify candidates and persuade them to shorten the time it will take them to deploy."[339]

794. Possible levels of UK commitment to Phase IV were set out in an annex:

"i.   **Maximum payoff (and maximum cost):** Tackle a problem area (eg Basra) with a UK two-star lead (subsequently becoming a multinational HQ). A UK Brigade in the SE sector. HQ ARRC taking on the CJTF(I) role early for six months. UK involvement (but <u>not military</u>) in a reconstruction pillar. <u>This would be contingent on US burden sharing on HQ ARRC CIS</u> [communications and information systems].

ii.   **Regional (+):** The SE Sector with a UK two-star lead (subsequently becoming a multinational HQ). A UK Brigade in the SE sector. No HQ ARRC but UK involvement (including military) in a reconstruction pillar and a significant staff contribution to CJTF-I.

iii.   **Regional:** The SE Sector with a UK two-star lead (subsequently becoming a multinational HQ). A UK Brigade in the SE sector.

---

[339] Minute Sec(O)4 to PS/Secretary of State [MOD], 6 March 2003, 'Iraq: Aftermath – Medium to Long Term UK Military Commitment'.

iv. **Regional (-):** A UK Brigade in the SE sector – not UK led. UK involvement (including military) in a reconstruction pillar.

v. **Regional (- -):** A UK Brigade in the SE sector – not UK led."

795. Mirroring the urgency expressed in the IPU annotated agenda, the MOD warned that, in the absence of settled UK policy on the scale or duration of the UK contribution to post-conflict Iraq, that contribution risked being determined "by decisions being taken by CENTCOM now".

796. The MOD identified a number of specific concerns, including:

- US plans envisaged the UK having responsibility for security in one of seven sectors. The UK had neither agreed formally nor challenged the US assumption. Nor had other departments scoped what non-military UK contributions could be sustained. The UK was "**currently at risk of taking on an unsustainable task if there is no further Coalition contribution to the occupation of Iraq**".

- If the UK did lead a military sector, there was a risk of the UK military being "intimately involved" in the civil administration, "not a role they would seek". There was "**a pressing need to identify civil capacity across the international civil admin effort, including to support civil administration in a UK military sector**".

- The UK was "**carrying some risk of early humanitarian assistance failures in the UK AO**".

797. The policy considerations included:

- the degree to which the UK wanted to stand "shoulder to shoulder" with the US, "a fundamental political judgement … where are the UK's red lines?"; and

- the UK's attitude to the future of Iraq. "Does the UK wish to become intimately involved in reconstruction and civil administration? This is not a military task … but it will both affect and be affected by the level of military engagement. It will also have significant resource implications, across government."

798. The briefing concluded with a section on the worst case:

"Much of the above is predicated on best-case assumptions for the progress of a conflict (swift, short and successful), the condition of Iraq post-conflict (infrastructure not greatly damaged by fighting, limited internecine conflict) and the degree of international buy-in with civil and military resources, including cash (considerable and UN endorsed). The Secretary of State may wish to take the opportunity of this meeting to remind his colleagues that there is at least a credible possibility that none of these conditions will obtain.

> "Even if there is a second (and possibly third) UNSCR this is no guarantee of broad-based international buy-in into Phase IV ... [T]here is a real possibility of the UK (along with the US and a few forward leaning smaller military nations) being committed to Phase IV engagement without international burden sharing and without an immediate exit strategy. At its worst this could expose the UK to an <u>enduring Large Scale military commitment (20-30,000 in theatre) – *and* the commensurate civil support required to contribute to the rebuilding of Iraq</u> ... The potential consequences are severe ... This is not the most likely risk, but it is one that increases the further the outcome post-conflict is from a UN-mandated solution."

799. In a speaking note for Mr Hoon, officials highlighted concerns about the tendency of discussion of the post-conflict phase, and the IPU annotated agenda, to focus on the military contribution:

> "A military presence will be a necessary but not a sufficient condition for success in Iraq. **A large, organised and properly funded humanitarian assistance plan (supported by DFID) is needed from the outset.**

> "... The UK should identify now what <u>civil</u> contribution it will make to rebuilding in Iraq and consider the cross-Government resource consequences.

> "We must not shy away from the fact that there remains a very credible worst case scenario that we shall want to proceed without either a second UNSCR or wider international <u>practical</u> support. The possible implications of this for the UK, across the board, are severe ...

> "We should put in hand detailed work to consider these implications and ways of mitigating possible effects."

800. The record of the meeting on 6 March shows that Mr Hoon raised the question of DFID/MOD co-ordination. There is no indication that Ministers discussed the wider issues raised by MOD officials.

801. Mr Cannon told Mr Blair that Ministers needed to make progress on three interlinked issues: the humanitarian response; the UN mandate; and whether the UK should "take over control of" a geographical sector in Iraq.[340] Mr Cannon explained:

- Ms Short's demands for additional UN cover and funding had left the military concerned that the job of securing Basra might be compromised by lack of DFID advance planning.

- Reports from Washington indicated the US had "moved a long way" on the UN mandate.

- Basra was "the obvious choice" if the UK decided to take on one of seven geographical sectors in Iraq.

---

[340] Minute Cannon to Prime Minister, 5 March 2002, 'Iraq: Post-Conflict Issues'.

802. At the meeting on 6 March, Ms Short repeated her concerns about the need for a UN mandate.[341] She also stated that DFID humanitarian advisers had been deployed in support of UK forces and that the DFID contingency fund would prioritise Iraq. The funding available to DFID would not, however, provide for an exercise on the scale of Kosovo.

803. Mr Brown commented that the military operation would be very costly. Estimates for a major humanitarian operation were running at US$1.9bn to US$4bn. The burden of reconstructing Iraq should not be borne by just the US and the UK; other countries and the EU should contribute. In the long term, Iraq's oil should fund the country's reconstruction. Mr Brown was particularly concerned that UK funds should not be used to repay Iraq's debts to Germany, France and Russia.

804. Mr Hoon warned that a humanitarian crisis "could cause operational problems for the military and expose us to public criticism", underlining the need for joint DFID/MOD planning.

805. The record stated:

"The <u>Prime Minister</u> concluded that:

(a) DFID and MOD should draw up a plan for immediate humanitarian action in the Area of Operations of British forces.

(b) Planning for medium-term post-conflict action should continue on the assumption that a UN mandate (the 'third/fourth resolutions') would be forthcoming. The FCO should draft the necessary resolutions, which we should share with the US. The FCO should prepare a Phase IV plan with other departments, including the key decisions for Ministers to take.

(c) The Chancellor should draw up a funding plan, including securing funding from wider international sources …

(d) The Prime Minister was prepared to pursue with President Bush our need for a UN mandate for a post-conflict administration."

806. Mr Blair also stated that sectorisation would need to be addressed and should be covered in the Phase IV plan.

807. Ministers "did not have time to address" the IPU's draft objectives for post-conflict Iraq or the principles to guide UK involvement in the short term.[342] Both were re-submitted to Mr Blair on 12 March.

---

[341] Letter Cannon to Owen, 7 March 2003, 'Iraq: Post-Conflict Issues'.
[342] Minute Cannon to Prime Minister, 12 March 2003, 'Iraq: post-conflict planning: objectives and principles'.

The UK plan for Phase IV

808. The FCO described the 'UK overall plan for Phase IV', prepared by the IPU and shown to Mr Blair on 7 March, as "work in progress".

809. The plan stated that the US was leading on Phase IV planning and that UK personnel were well placed to influence that work.

810. It listed three sets of decisions that Ministers needed to take either immediately, before the conflict began or very soon after the start of hostilities.

811. The plan contained little detail on post-conflict tasks and no new material on sectorisation, but warned:

"… we need to be clear that if we take on leadership of a military sector, previous deployments of this type suggest that we are likely to inherit wider responsibilities than purely security."

812. Officials recommended postponing decisions on the extent of the UK's post-conflict commitment until after the start of hostilities.

813. The 'UK overall plan for Phase IV' was shown to Mr Blair on 7 March.[343] Much of the plan, prepared by the IPU, was drawn from the annotated agenda prepared for the meeting on 6 March.

814. A letter from Mr Straw's Private Office stated that the plan was:

"… work in progress. A full plan could say quite a lot more about the shape of civilian government, the treatment of war criminals and other matters, most of which we are working on."[344]

815. The IPU described Phase IV as "the military term for the part of the plan that takes place after the fighting has finished" and stated: "In practice Phase IV starts the moment Coalition forces enter Iraq."[345]

816. The plan stated:

"The US is leading on post-conflict or Phase IV planning. The military part in this is being led by CENTCOM's Land Component Headquarters, and the civil piece by its Office of Reconstruction and Humanitarian Assistance (ORHA). We have military officers and officials seconded to both. They are well placed to influence planning. The UN is also carrying out contingency planning. We are tracking that as well. There are decisions for Ministers to take about the level of UK engagement in Phase IV and key points on which to influence US planning."

---

[343] Minute Rycroft to Prime Minister, 7 March 2003, 'Iraq: Weekend Papers'.
[344] Letter Owen to Rycroft, 7 March 2003, 'Iraq: Phase IV'.
[345] Paper Iraq Planning Unit, 7 March 2003, 'The UK overall plan for Phase IV'.

817. The IPU listed actions needed that week:

- "UK forces will be ready to fight soon. By then **we need to have promulgated some principles**[346] **to guide the campaign** for the first few days of Phase IV. And UK forces are likely to be the first to confront this."

- "Of equal urgency is the need **to ensure our humanitarian relief effort is in place**. The scale of the UK effort for humanitarian operations depends on assessed need and the expected contributions of others. **Ministers will need to agree this**." Issues of concern included:
  - the absence of detailed US plans for humanitarian operations;
  - the impact on UK planning of uncertainty about the legitimacy of military conflict and the status of the Occupation;
  - the dependence of some DFID plans on further financing decisions; and
  - UK forces' lack of funding and capacity to fulfil their humanitarian obligations in the absence of other providers.

  The UK military needed resources for humanitarian assistance to reduce the risk of humanitarian disaster. Ms Short and Mr Hoon needed "**to agree on the modalities**".

818. Before the conflict began, there needed to be agreement with the US on:

- A Security Council resolution allowing OFF to continue.

- An "**authorising UNSCR for Phase IV**". The agreement should be announced "to encourage/galvanise the international community to advance their own preparations". US policy was "moving in our direction but still has some way to go". The UK needed to:
  - work with the US to identify and define the role of the head of the interim civilian administration; and
  - "push US thinking" on an Iraqi consultative council towards arrangements visibly inclusive of all segments of the population. Getting the right political framework was "crucial" given that the initial period of Phase IV would be perceived as a military occupation and that "the work done during the first weeks and months will shape the mould for what follows".

- Objectives for the day power was handed back to Iraq (as set out in the annotated agenda of 5 March).

819. Very soon after the start of hostilities the UK needed "**to agree what our medium-term contribution to Iraq should be (say from the autumn onwards). For this will shape our conduct in the short term**." Sectorisation would be a key determinant of UK policy.

---

[346] The principles were broadly as set out in the annotated agenda of 5 March.

820. The IPU repeated the advice in the annotated agenda of 5 March that the UK should follow the US plan to administer Iraq as a whole and not seek "general UK responsibility for the administration of any geographic area of Iraq in the medium term". The IPU added:

> **"However, we need to be clear that if we take on leadership of a military sector, previous deployments of this type suggest that we are likely to inherit wider responsibilities than purely security."**

821. The Inquiry has seen no response to the Phase IV plan.

822. Mr Rycroft put five other FCO papers to Mr Blair, most of which had been prepared before Mr Blair's request of 6 March:

- elements of a resolution "authorising our post-conflict requirements";
- issues UK forces might confront in the first 48 hours of hostilities;
- the role of UN weapons inspectors (see Section 4.4);
- 'Iraq Day After – Oil'; and
- 'Preliminary UK Views on Economic Actions in First 30/60 Days'.[347]

823. The IPU prepared the paper on oil. It is not clear which, if any, of the others was written by the IPU.

824. The FCO advised No.10 that the paper setting out elements for a possible resolution was "broadly in line with emerging US thinking". The suggested elements included the proposal that a UN Special Co-ordinator (UNSC) would be appointed, and would in turn appoint or supervise the creation of an Iraqi Interim Council.[348]

825. Other core elements of the draft resolution were:

- authorisation for Member States acting under unified command to provide an international security presence in Iraq;
- continuation of OFF, overseen by the Security Council, to ensure the transparent and fair use of Iraqi oil revenues;
- creation of a UN Assistance Mission for Iraq (UNAMI) to co-ordinate the work of NGOs and UN agencies.

826. UK efforts to secure a UN mandate for a post-conflict administration, culminating in the adoption of resolution 1483 on 22 May, are described in detail in Section 9.1.

---

[347] Minute Rycroft to Prime Minister, 7 March 2003, 'Iraq: Weekend papers'.
[348] Paper [unattributed and undated], 'Iraq: Phase IV Elements for a possible resolution'.

827. The paper on issues for the first 48 hours listed 16 questions that would need answering, but offered no answers.[349] It is not clear whether the MOD or DFID had been consulted before the document was sent to No.10.

828. The list of questions included:

- Which economic assets would need securing?
- What message should be delivered to the Iraqi people?
- What would be the most effective UK contribution to humanitarian relief?
- "With Whom Should UK Forces Work?
  - Who should be indicted ('black list'), or detained until the situation is secure ('grey list')?
  - Who can we identify in advance as Iraqis we might work with? ('White list')?
  - How are these people to be identified on the ground?
  - What should be the immediate handling of members of Iraqi security organisations? Presumably key players on the National Security Council, the leadership of the Special Security Organisation and the Special Republican Guard would be on a black list?
  - What about the police and regular Army?"
- How far should UK forces respond to civil unrest in urban areas?
- What assurances could be given to Russia or France about the security of their assets?

829. The IPU paper on oil policy had been shown to Mr Straw on 28 February.[350] Mr Chilcott described it as "preliminary, official-level thinking", incorporating comments from a range of departments. He explained to Mr Straw that the IPU intended to share the paper with the US "in due course".

830. In the paper, the IPU judged that it would take "enormous investment over a number of years" to overcome decades of underinvestment in Iraq's oil infrastructure. That work should be a major focus for the international administration, but much of the initial work would fall to the interim administration. It would be important to ensure any such moves by the interim administration were "clearly in the interests of the Iraqi economy and people" and carried out transparently, and that production was "not pushed beyond OPEC-type depletion rates, even though this could be in the interests of the Iraqi people".

---

[349] Paper [unattributed and undated], 'The first 48 hours'.
[350] Minute Chilcott to Private Secretary [FCO], 28 February 2003, 'Iraq Day After – Oil Policy' attaching Paper IPU, 27 February 2003, 'Iraq Day After – Oil'.

831. The IPU saw no reason for a radical overhaul of an industry which was "relatively well run given the circumstances". The US had identified individuals in Iraq and the diaspora who could take on key roles. The UK should do the same. "Winning hearts and minds" among oil workers and making sure they were paid would be vital. The UK would want to be seen to help get oil pumping while putting out "robust messages" that it had no selfish interest in doing so.

832. Four types of oil contract needed to be considered: OFF oil purchase contracts, which should continue with minimal disruption; and new contracts for tackling fires, investment in new fields and rehabilitation of infrastructure, all of which would need to be transparent and open to UK firms. It was important to make sure the US kept the UK Government in the picture.

833. As next steps, the IPU recommended the UK should:

- convene a meeting with UK oil companies to make use of their expertise;
- obtain the US data on the Iraqi oil sector, including personnel;
- carry out detailed research on key oil infrastructure in the UK sector;
- hold preliminary discussions with UK firms to ensure they were well placed to pick up contracts;
- develop an oil sector information campaign;
- calculate the cost of paying Iraqi oil workers;
- factor rapid assistance for oil field installations into UK military planning;
- start work on appropriate UN resolutions, including for the continuation of the OFF programme; and
- research existing oil investment agreements with Iraq.

834. On 2 March, Mr Straw had commented: "V[ery] good paper."[351]

835. UK policy on the management of Iraq's oil reserves is addressed in Section 10.3.

836. The last paper in the set shown to Mr Blair, on economic actions in the first 30 to 60 days, had been written in mid-February as the UK contribution to the trilateral working group on economic issues.[352]

837. The paper did not allocate responsibility for individual post-conflict tasks or identify the likely resources needed, but is the most detailed piece of non-military planning for post-conflict Iraq seen by the Inquiry.[353]

---

[351] Manuscript comment Straw, 2 March 2003, on Minute Chilcott to Private Secretary [FCO], 28 February 2003, 'Iraq Day After – Oil Policy'.
[352] Minute Dodd to Manning, 3 March 2003, 'Ad Hoc Group on Iraq'.
[353] Paper [unattributed], 14 February 2003, 'Iraq Day After: Preliminary UK Views on Economic Actions in First 30/60 Days'.

838. The paper set out strategic and operational objectives against six different issues: humanitarian relief; public finances; oil; Ba'ath Party and former elite economic issues; reconstruction and economic strategy; and effective economic administration. The operational objectives were divided into action needed before the fall of the existing Iraqi regime, "immediate" actions for the first 30 days afterwards and "pressing" actions for between 30 and 60 days.

839. The section on public finances included as one of its key strategic objectives: "Avoiding disintegration of civil service and public services." The "specific operational objective" before regime change was to reassure employees that salaries would be paid. Objectives for the 30 days after regime change included ensuring salaries continued to be paid and "decisions about pay policy towards security services and military".

840. The paper was unchanged from a version shared with the US State Department on 14 February, when it had been described to US officials as "very much work in progress, not completely co-ordinated here [in London]".[354]

841. The Inquiry has seen no evidence of further work on the document.

TREASURY DISCUSSIONS WITH THE IMF

842. Mr Jon Cunliffe, Treasury Managing Director for Macroeconomic Policy and International Finance, called on the IMF internal task force on Iraq in Washington on 6 March.[355]

843. The UK Delegation to the IMF reported that the task force had made "some significant progress", but that staff emphasised the sheer scale of the debt problem facing Iraq, well in excess of the capacity to pay. Without taking account of the need to front-load reconstruction costs, IMF staff estimated it could take 20 years to pay off less than a third of Iraq's potential debt burden of US$300bn (incorporating external debt of US$90bn and compensation payments to Iran and Kuwait). IMF staff were pulling together background information on the economy, the state of institutions and priorities in case the IMF became involved in either policy advice or technical assistance. Potential areas of involvement included currency reform, fiscal policy, the oil sector and external debt. Planning was "highly tentative". Experience of other post-conflict situations had taught the IMF that "the situation on the ground can turn out to be extremely different from prior expectations and that this then impacts on the policy advice".

---

[354] Letter Economic Policy Department [junior official] to US State Department official, 14 February 2003, 'Iraq Day After: Trilateral Economic Discussions – Follow-up'.
[355] Telegram 21 UKDel IBRD Washington to FCO London, 7 March 2003, 'Iraq and IMF'.

DFID update on humanitarian assistance

844. **A DFID update on humanitarian planning for No.10 on 7 March stated that:**

- **In the event of conflict, DFID would assess the scale of the humanitarian need, identify the UN agency best placed to respond and provide immediate funding.**

- **DFID would also be advising the military, to whom immediate responsibility for assistance would fall.**

- **Reconstruction plans were less well advanced. DFID's focus had been on ensuring the international community and the US recognised the scale of the task and the need for a UN mandate.**

845. **DFID urged Mr Blair to press the case with the US immediately for a resolution authorising reconstruction. UK participation in military action should be made conditional on such a resolution.**

846. **Sir David Manning advised Mr Blair to engage President Bush on the issue the following week, but to focus first on the second resolution.**

847. Mr Blair received a DFID update on humanitarian assistance and reconstruction planning on 7 March.[356] The paper stated that the principle underlying DFID's humanitarian assistance was "to provide rapid support to whoever is best placed to meet the immediate needs of the people". There was now a DFID staff presence in ORHA and 1 (UK) Div in Kuwait, with further deployments to the region and UN agencies imminent. £10m had been earmarked for UN and NGO contingency planning and supplies were in place to provide shelter for up to 25,000 people. DFID would:

> "… respond to the humanitarian needs of the Iraqi people through supporting the international humanitarian system, principally the UN, Red Cross/Crescent and key NGOs to save lives and alleviate suffering. We would be able to allocate up to £65m from our contingency reserve."

848. In the event of conflict, DFID would assess the scale of the humanitarian need, identify the UN agency best placed to respond and provide immediate funding for it to do so, although immediate responsibility for assistance would fall to the military, to whom DFID would be giving advice.

849. The paper stated that reconstruction plans were less well advanced. The focus of DFID's work, in collaboration with other government departments, had been "to ensure the international community, especially the US, realises the enormous scale of the task and the necessity of a UN mandate". Uncertainty over that issue was holding up planning, but DFID had held discussions with the World Bank and other partners. One of

---

[356] Letter Warren to Rycroft, 7 March 2003 attaching Paper DFID, [undated], 'DFID Planning on Iraq'.

the first tasks would be to put Iraq's debt on an agreed international footing. DFID would aim, with the Treasury, "to play a lead role in the IFIs in gaining such an agreement".

850. Dr Brewer sent Sir David Manning supplementary material for Mr Blair to use with President Bush, which explained the need for a resolution to authorise reconstruction activity and the financial advantage of having one.[357] Dr Brewer explained that the draft speaking note had been seen by Ms Short, Mr Chakrabarti, Mr Chilcott (in Mr Ricketts' absence) and Mr Bowen. She concluded:

> "We judge that the time to press our case with the Americans is now: they need to know how much this matters for us and for the prospects of others engaging in the reconstruction effort."

851. The suggested points for Mr Blair to put to President Bush included:

- the constraints on occupying forces in the absence of a resolution expressly authorising a continued international presence in Iraq; and
- the negative impact the absence of a resolution was having on planning by large parts of the international system.

852. The DFID draft included the suggestion that Mr Blair conclude with the statement: "That apart, I need this UN mandate before I can give the go-ahead."

853. Sir David Manning forwarded Dr Brewer's letter to Mr Blair on 8 March, with the comment:

> "You will need to engage Bush on this soon – but my view is that we should concentrate on 2nd Resolution this w/e [the weekend of 8 and 9 March] and start on the UN heavy lifting on Monday/Tuesday [10 and 11 March]."[358]

854. Mr Blair discussed the need for a further resolution on post-conflict Iraq with President Bush on 12 March.

DIS Red Team report on retaining the support of the Iraqi people

855. The second report by the DIS Red Team stated that internal Iraqi support was likely to be the single most important factor in achieving success in Iraq.

856. The Red Team recommended that, if there was any doubt about the Coalition's ability to meet Iraqi expectations in an exemplary fashion, steps should be taken as soon as possible to lower those expectations.

---

[357] Letter Brewer to Manning, 7 March 2003, 'Iraq/Post Conflict: Legal and Financial Imperatives' attaching Paper [unattributed], 7 March 2003, 'Iraq/Post Conflict: Legal and Financial Imperatives: Points for the Prime Minister to use with President Bush'.
[358] Manuscript comment Manning to Prime Minister, 8 March 2003, on Letter Brewer to Manning, 7 March 2003, 'Iraq/Post Conflict: Legal and Financial Imperatives'.

857. The aim of the second report from the DIS Red Team ('Obtaining and Retaining the Support of the Iraqi People in the Aftermath of Conflict'), issued on 7 March, was: "To identify the optimum structure of the Immediate and Interim Administrations in Iraq and other measures most likely to obtain and retain the support of the Iraqi people."[359]

858. The Red Team listed six key judgements and three key considerations:

"Key judgements:

- Internal Iraqi support is likely to be the single most important factor to the success of the whole operation. After a 'honeymoon period', Iraqi support is likely to become fragile and will depend on the way the early phases of the military campaign were conducted and the effectiveness of the immediate post-conflict administration.

- The Immediate Administration will be established as a 'belligerent occupation', which will require Coalition forces to provide a wide range of administrative support, as well as maintaining law and order.

- The form of the Interim Administration is not yet clear, but in descending order of acceptability is likely to be:
  - UN Assistance Mission with strong US/UK civilian and military contributions.
  - US-led civilian administration.
  - 'Full blown' UN administration – on the lines of UNMIK [UN Mission in Kosovo] or UNTAET [UN Transitional Administration in East Timor].

- The critical success factor from the outset will be the engagement of local representatives in advisory bodies at national, regional and local level. Iraqi representation must not be restricted to Iraqi exile bodies.

- Opportunities must be taken to hand over administrative responsibility to local authorities as they become competent and are approved by advisory bodies.

- Law and order, including the judicial process, will require special handling and the retention of executive authority by the Interim Administration.

...

"Key Considerations.

- **Fragility of Popular Support** ... There is likely to be widespread support for Coalition forces in the immediate aftermath, but it will be extremely fragile. Retaining support will depend on:
  - The conduct of the early phases of the campaign ...
  - Providing food, water, medical assistance and shelter ...
  - Prompt action to mark and clear unexploded ordnance ...

---

[359] Minute PS/CDI to APS2 SofS [MOD], 7 March 2003, 'Iraq Red Team – Obtaining and Retaining the Support of the Iraqi People in the Aftermath of Conflict' attaching Paper DIS Red Team, 7 March 2003, 'Obtaining and retaining the support of the Iraqi people in the aftermath of conflict'.

- Preventing interference in internal Iraqi affairs by outside states (principally Turkey and Iran).
- Providing a credible promise of increasing Iraqi involvement in administration with a road-map to Iraqi-led government, whilst ensuring no particular group feels unduly disadvantaged.

"If any of these conditions are not met, we must expect support rapidly to evaporate in all or part of the country.

- **Clarity of the Information Campaign message …**
- **Legal Position:** in the post-war period, irrespective of the status of UNSCRs, the US/UK forces in Iraq will be in 'belligerent occupation'. This obliges them to:
  - Restore and maintain public order and safety by *respecting the laws in force … in the occupied state*'.
  - Assume responsibility for administering the occupied area.
  - Take responsibility for the medical care of inhabitants.
  - Supply the civil population with food, medical supplies, clothing, bedding and shelter.
  - Facilitate relief schemes, if required.
  - Facilitate the operation of postal facilities, religious observance and schools.
  - Issue a proclamation making the existence, extent and special regulations of the occupied territory clear to the inhabitants.
- UK forces are also obliged to apply the standards of the European Convention on Human Rights, whereas US forces are not. This could present complications with respect to the removal of detainees from Iraq, for example.
- These responsibilities remain in force until the Occupation ceases.
- Expectations that the Coalition forces will be able to deliver these responsibilities are high; so if there is doubt over our ability to meet them in an 'exemplary' fashion we should take steps to lower expectations as early as possible."

859. The section of the report on "Post-War Structures" stated that Iraq was "not a 'failed state'", nor was it recovering from a bloody civil war. The people were "proud" and would "respond badly to condescension or perceived insults".

860. On law and order and the judicial system, the Red Team judged that:

- "[O]nce an assessment has been made of the effectiveness of local police forces it should be increasingly possible to include them in military-led law and order operations".
- The Iraqi judicial system was "largely dysfunctional" and an "interim judicial system may be necessary".
- The prison system was likely to need "a complete overhaul and supervisory regime", although the infrastructure might be "useable".

861. The Red Team concluded that:

"• Iraqis look forward to improved circumstances post-conflict and their expectations that they will be engaged by the Coalition in achieving this need to be accommodated.

• The way the military campaign is run, and the early stages of post-war operations, will determine the degree of support the Coalition receives from the Iraqi people; if it is not well handled, we risk compromising overall success."

862. There is no indication of any response to either of the Red Team's pre-conflict reports, including the warning of the terrorist threat from Al Qaida against civilians and Coalition Forces in Iraq.

UK military and humanitarian co-ordination in the South

863. In early March, Lt Gen Reith discussed the expansion of the UK combat role with US commanders. He continued to advise the Chiefs of Staff to extend the UK AO.

864. Lt Gen Reith visited the Middle East from 5 to 7 March, where he discussed optimising the use of 1 (UK) Div combat power "in some detail" with General John Abizaid, Gen Franks' Deputy Commander (Forward), and then with Lt Gen McKiernan.[360] The record of the visit stated that Lt Gen Reith "offered" two options for UK forces to play a role in later operations: providing additional combat power to the US advance on Baghdad, or deploying forward by air to the Baghdad area to "assist in developing stability in case of sudden regime collapse".

865. A manuscript note on Maj Gen Fry's copy of the record stated:

"CDS was most unhappy … COS [Chiefs of Staff] & SofS [Secretary of State] riding instructions were to not offer anything outside the UK AO but be receptive to requests ('request mode rather than push mode'). CDS wanted to talk to CJO [Lt Gen Reith] immediately – but will close the loop on Saturday [8 March]. In the meantime this note is being kept away from Ministers' offices."[361]

866. Gen Jackson visited UK forces in Kuwait between 6 and 8 March and was involved in Lt Gen Reith's discussion with Lt Gen McKiernan (see Section 6.2).[362] He reported to Adm Boyce that:

"Hampered by lack of domestic and international consensus on Phase III, planning for Phase IV remains the most immature aspect of the operation. The key to success in Phase IV will be legitimisation through multi-nationality, if possible underpinned by a further UNSCR … Early multi-nationalisation of the occupying force should provide

---

[360] Minute Dutton to PSO/CDS, 7 March 2003, 'CJO visit to Middle East 5-7 Mar 03'.
[361] Minute MA/CJO to PSO/CDS, 7 March 2003, 'CJO visit to Middle East 5-7 Mar 03'.
[362] Minute CGS to CDS, 10 March 2003, 'CGS Visit to Op TELIC'.

the perception of legitimacy that the current narrow Coalition lacks. But realistically, current ill-feeling may run deep enough to prevent a thaw …

"… Lt Gen Abizaid would like to avoid an occupation model based on sectors as used in the Balkans … I observed that a territorial solution may be difficult to avoid as nations would wish to influence a given sector and military commanders would want clear boundaries for operations and interaction with civil authorities …

"… I judge that, realistically, it will be some time before Coalition partners join US and British forces in any real strength, if at all. I draw two conclusions from this: first, that as much as possible of Iraq's administrative and military structure should be preserved; and second, that we should beware rapid US drawdown on the American assumption that UK (perhaps through the ARRC) will form the focus for an international force that in the event fails to materialise.

"… GOC 1 Div [Maj Gen Brims] made it clear to me that in clarifying his role in Phase IV, he needed simply to know what his title was, to whom he would be responsible, and how quickly a civil administrator would be appointed. While he judges that Basra has adequate short-term food stocks, it will urgently need water, electricity and medical supplies … Only the ICRC has humanitarian stocks in position … there was little confidence within 1 Div that DFID has a coherent plan in place. I support GOC 1 Div's intent to manage Phase IV with as light a touch as possible, but it will be important to establish the rule of law quickly – the question, as in Kosovo, will be whose law? …"

867. Gen Jackson concluded:

"We are ready not just to demonstrate solidarity with our Coalition partner, but to contribute considerable and potentially decisive combat power to achieve rapid success in Phase III. Rapid success will set the conditions for Phase IV, which in turn will determine the overall success of the enterprise."

868. A "Critical Decision Checklist" prepared for Mr Hoon on 7 March listed actions that had to be taken before UK forces were committed to action, including provision of resources for immediate humanitarian assistance.

869. DFID and the MOD remained unable to agree a joint approach to UK humanitarian operations in the area occupied by UK forces.

870. On 7 March, Mr Lee prepared a "Critical Decision Checklist" for Mr Hoon, listing actions that "have to be taken before forces could be committed to action".[363] Three were linked to post-conflict planning:

- "Provision of resources for immediate humanitarian assistance (in hand)";

---

[363] Minute Lee to PS/Secretary of State [MOD], 7 March 2003, 'Critical Decision Checklist'.

- "Agreement with US on Phase IV assumptions (IPU in hand)"; and
- "Finalisation of military campaign objectives (Cabinet Office, in hand)".

871. Separate MOD advice to Mr Hoon stated that DFID expected to distribute humanitarian relief through IOs and NGOs that would not be present until the environment was benign.[364] UK forces could find themselves in control of part of Iraq, including Basra, before IOs and NGOs were willing to enter the country. Ms Short's agreement that DFID should take part in planning to manage the consequences of war was welcome, but DFID's likely plan was to distribute relief wherever there was a need, not just in the UK AO. There was a danger that, even with DFID engagement, UK troops would lack the resources to deal with the humanitarian difficulties they faced. Officials recommended that the only way to be sure UK forces had access to the humanitarian supplies they might need was for DFID to channel its funding directly through the military.

872. Section 13.1 describes the subsequent exchange between the MOD, DFID and the Treasury on how to fund delivery of humanitarian assistance in the UK's AO.

873. On 9 March, Ms Short threatened to resign from the Government if the UK took military action against Iraq without UN authorisation.

874. In an interview for *BBC Radio 4* on 9 March, Ms Short said she would resign from the Government if the UK took military action against Iraq without UN authority.[365] Asked whether she thought Mr Blair had acted "recklessly", Ms Short described the situation as "extraordinarily reckless". She continued:

> "… what worries me is that we've got the old spin back and we have detailed discussions either personally or in the Cabinet and then the spin the next day is: 'we're ready for war' …

> "If it takes another month or so, that is fine … And I think you could get a world where we see the UN in authority … proper care for the people of Iraq, because at the moment the preparations to care for the humanitarian aftermath of any military conflict are not properly in place.

> "And there's another major legal point – if there isn't a UN mandate for the reconstruction of Iraq … [i]t will in international law be an occupying army and won't have the authority to make changes in the administrative arrangements in Iraq."

875. In her memoir, Ms Short wrote that when she arrived in DFID on 11 March, Mr Chakrabarti and senior officials had obviously been asked by No.10 to find out what

---

[364] Minute MOD D/Sec to PS/Secretary of State [MOD], 7 March 2003, 'OP Telic: DFID involvement and the funding of immediate humanitarian assistance'.
[365] *BBC News*, 10 March 2003, *Clare Short Interview*.

it would take to make her stay on as International Development Secretary.[366] After discussion, they agreed that the conditions were:

"1. Publish Road Map [for the Middle East]

2. Absolute requirement UN mandate for reconstruction

3. UN mandate for military action."

876. Mr Chakrabarti wrote to Sir Andrew Turnbull later on 11 March to explain Ms Short's position and to recommend "more frequent and systematic discussion of these issues between senior Ministers" and between Mr Blair and Ms Short, who needed reassurance that her concerns would be taken fully into account. Mr Chakrabarti understood that Mr Blair might ask senior Ministers to meet more regularly if conflict started, but advised starting these meetings sooner, "given the scale and significance of the decisions being taken".[367]

877. Sir Andrew Turnbull informed officials in No.10 and the Cabinet Office of revised arrangements for Ministerial meetings on 18 March.

878. On 10 March, the House of Commons International Development Committee published its Report *Preparing for the Humanitarian Consequences of Possible Military Action Against Iraq*. The Committee stated: "We are not yet convinced that there is, to use the Prime Minister's words, 'a humanitarian plan that is every bit as viable and well worked out as a military plan'."[368] The Committee advised: "it is essential that in planning for the possible humanitarian consequences of military action the worst case scenario, involving ethnic conflict, is considered".[369] The Committee recommended that DFID issue a statement immediately outlining its humanitarian contingency plans.

879. Ms Short's statement on 13 March is described later in this Section.

MR STRAW'S STATEMENT TO THE HOUSE OF COMMONS, 10 MARCH 2003

880. Mr Straw made a statement on Iraq to the House of Commons on 10 March, described in more detail in Section 3.8, in which he addressed the potential consequences of military action. Mr Straw stated that the international community would have "a duty to build a secure, prosperous future for the Iraqi people". In his meeting with Mr Annan on 6 March, he had proposed "that the UN should take the lead role in co-ordinating international efforts to rebuild Iraq, and that they should be underpinned by a clear UN mandate".[370]

---

[366] Short C. *An Honourable Deception: New Labour, Iraq and the Misuse of Power*. The Free Press, 2004.
[367] Letter Chakrabarti to Turnbull, 11 March 2003, 'Iraq'.
[368] Fourth Report from the International Development Committee, Session 2002-2003, *Preparing for the Humanitarian Consequences of Possible Military Action Against Iraq*, HC 444-I, page 5.
[369] Fourth Report from the International Development Committee, Session 2002-2003, *Preparing for the Humanitarian Consequences of Possible Military Action Against Iraq*, HC 444-I, page 17.
[370] House of Commons, *Official Report*, 10 March 2003, column 23.

DIS REPORT: 'BASRA: POST SADDAM GOVERNANCE'

881. On 11 March, the DIS reported anecdotal evidence that Iraqi citizens were arming themselves as protection against an anticipated breakdown in law and order after the removal of Saddam Hussein.

882. The same report identified the Ba'ath Party as Basra's most important administrative institution.

883. On 11 March, the DIS produced the paper 'Basra: Post Saddam Governance'.[371] It was the first of a series of DIS reports on southern Iraq and came with the caveat that much of the content was "necessarily speculative".

884. It is not clear who saw the DIS report, but it seems likely that it would have been sent to all those, including senior officials in the MOD and the FCO, but not DFID, who received copies of the Red Team reports.

885. The report listed a range of possible local responses to military action, ranging from reprisals against Ba'ath Party and Security Force personnel to the collapse of law and order.

886. The DIS described the Ba'ath Party as "Basra's most important administrative institution". The local organisation mirrored that of the rest of the country:

> "Most party members will have joined for reasons of professional and social advancement. It can be assumed most prominent members of Basra's professional classes (eg senior port officials, heads of local government departments, University Heads etc.) will be party members. They may however have little role in directing the party or ensuring regime control."

887. The DIS stated that the "upper echelons … (Director level)" of most Basra governorate departments, which covered the full range of local administrative functions, would be members of the Ba'ath Party.

888. The DIS advised that there was "very limited reporting on the organisation of Iraq's Civil Police. And we have no information specific to Basra." It added that there was anecdotal evidence from elsewhere in Iraq suggesting civilians were fearful of a general breakdown in law and order and were arming themselves. Disarming them "might be interpreted as running contrary to cultural norms and could be resisted by the civil populace".

889. Those conclusions were broadly consistent with views expressed in US intelligence briefings produced in January and March.

---

[371] Report DIS, 11 March 2003, 'Basra: Post Saddam Governance'.

890. In January 2003, a US National Intelligence Community Assessment had judged that a post-Saddam Hussein authority in Iraq would face "a deeply divided society with a significant chance that domestic groups would engage in violent conflict with each other unless an occupying force prevented them from doing so".[372] The Assessment identified three divisions:

- The "principal division" between Sunni Arabs, the Shia and the Kurds. Based on ethnicity and religion, it also had a geographical aspect, with the groups concentrated in the central, southern and northern regions of Iraq respectively.

- Divisions between "tribal identities". Although 75 per cent of Iraqis identified with a tribe, many of those would be urban residents who probably felt little allegiance to their tribal leaders. Many Iraqi tribes were associated with Saddam Hussein, although for most this was based on self-interest and they could be expected to seek accommodation with any successor regime.

- Divisions between those associated with Saddam Hussein's regime and its victims.

891. A March 2003 CIA report on the Iraqi police and judiciary provided a general description of both, but highlighted the lack of information held by the US on local level officials, including their identities, loyalties and involvement in human rights abuses under Saddam Hussein's regime.[373] The issue had been a lower intelligence collection priority than Iraqi WMD, conventional military capabilities and leadership dynamics.

DFID'S HUMANITARIAN STRATEGY AND IMMEDIATE ASSISTANCE PLAN

892. DFID produced an outline 'Humanitarian Strategy and Immediate Assistance Plan' for Iraq on 12 March.

893. The paper, prepared for Ms Short, was a statement of DFID's, rather than the UK's, priorities. It sought to retain "maximum operational flexibility" for DFID in the face of continuing uncertainty and limited resources.

894. On 12 March, DFID officials sent Ms Short DFID's outline 'Humanitarian Strategy and Immediate Assistance Plan' for Iraq.[374] The covering minute explained that the strategy aimed to address DFID's key objectives of "saving lives and relieving the suffering of the Iraqi people whilst adhering to our principles of impartial humanitarian response. In view of the uncertainties and our limited resources, we are planning to retain the maximum operational flexibility."

---

[372] US Senate Select Committee on Intelligence, *Report on prewar intelligence assessments about post-war Iraq*, 25 May 2007.

[373] US Senate Select Committee on Intelligence, *Report on prewar intelligence assessments about post-war Iraq*, 25 May 2007.

[374] Minute Conflict and Humanitarian Affairs Department [junior official], 12 March 2003, 'Iraq: Humanitarian Strategy and Immediate Assistance Plan: Information Note'.

895. Officials highlighted three issues:

- The UK military had an obligation under international law to provide humanitarian assistance. DFID was helping the MOD to plan and prepare for those responsibilities in the UK AOR, "making it clear that DFID and international agencies will be focused on the Iraq-wide humanitarian needs".

- Until there was a permissive security environment, CHAD-OT remained ready to deploy, but not immediately to establish a forward base, which might affect DFID's ability to respond on the ground in Iraq.

- Planning was based on the assumption that £65m was available for "immediate response needs". Given the scale of potential need in Iraq, those funds would be committed quickly and certainly within the first three months.

896. The attached paper stated that the humanitarian strategy was "based on DFID's humanitarian principles, which includes seeking the best possible assessment of needs and giving priority to the most urgent cases of distress". It listed four aims:

- to save lives and relieve suffering;
- to respond to immediate humanitarian needs in Iraq and neighbouring countries;
- to protect and restore livelihoods; and
- to support rapid transition from relief to recovery.[375]

897. The paper explained that policy development and operational planning were constrained by six factors:

- the uncertain military outcome;
- the wide range of humanitarian scenarios;
- limited DFID human resources;
- uncertainty over financial resources;
- the need to differentiate between support to Coalition Forces and support to "traditional humanitarian partners"; and
- the need for a clear DFID security policy in response to the NBC threat.

898. The humanitarian strategy would focus on:

- ensuring co-ordination of the international effort;
- working with the UN to maintain OFF;
- providing assistance through the UN, Red Cross and NGOs;
- supporting the UK military's stabilisation and relief effort; and
- designing humanitarian interventions that take account of longer-term recovery and reconstruction issues.

---

[375] Paper Conflict and Humanitarian Affairs Department, 12 March 2003, 'Iraq Humanitarian Strategy and Immediate Assistance Plan'.

899. On the single page describing the "Operational Plan", officials explained that: "In view of DFID's limited resources, we will retain **maximum flexibility to respond to changing scenarios and needs**." It listed seven actions that were planned or under way:

- "Information Management": CHAD-OT staff in Kuwait and Jordan were to collate, analyse and disseminate field information. DFID was evaluating the need to send staff to Turkey, Iran and Cyprus, and would retain a limited capacity to deploy assessment teams to localised crisis points.

- "Humanitarian Advice/Funding": CHAD advice in the field and in London to inform policy and funding decisions.

- "Direct Support to the UN": secondment of specialists to support the co-ordination and information activities of the UN's Humanitarian Assistance Centre (HIC) and Joint Logistic Centre (UNJLC).

- "Advice to the Military/Coalition": two secondees advising 1 (UK) Div and one official in ORHA, all contributing to DFID's "information gathering system", and a further secondment to the National Component HQ in Qatar under consideration.

- "Material Support": DFID's stockpile of non-food items, vehicles and equipment brought to immediate readiness, with some elements positioned in Kuwait and elsewhere in the region.

- "Direct Implementation": officials ready to assess and undertake limited relief and immediate rehabilitation operations through supervised QIPs "implemented by our traditional partners and possibly the UK military. This could include building or repairing critical infrastructure required for the humanitarian effort."

- "Oil-for-Food Programme": maintaining and protecting OFF or a variant mandated by the UN.

900. Ms Short responded: "Thanks."[376]

901. On 12 March, Mr Hoon's Private Office informed No.10 that MOD and DFID advisers had been working together for some time, but that it was only "very recently", with the decision to deploy a DFID adviser to HQ 1 (UK) Div, that it had been possible to engage in detailed planning for humanitarian operations within the UK AO.[377] "As a consequence our planning is far less mature than we would ideally like." The absence of funding for 1 (UK) Div to undertake humanitarian assistance was of "crucial concern".

902. In a letter to Mr Blair on 12 March, Ms Short appeared to distance herself and her department from collective responsibility for the UK's humanitarian and reconstruction effort in Iraq.

---

[376] Manuscript comment Short on Minute Conflict and Humanitarian Affairs Department [junior official], 12 March 2003, 'Iraq: Humanitarian Strategy and Immediate Assistance Plan: Information Note'.
[377] Letter Williams to Cannon, 12 March 2003, 'Iraq Post-Conflict Issues'.

903. The letter stated that DFID humanitarian preparations were well in hand; those of the UN humanitarian agencies and the US and UK military were not.

904. On 12 March, Ms Short set out her misgivings about the state of humanitarian planning in a letter to Mr Blair.[378] DFID preparations were well in hand; those of the UN humanitarian agencies and the US and UK military were not. Ms Short argued that "UK Armed Forces are not configured or supplied to provide substantial humanitarian relief" and that the US military were even less prepared:

> "Their focus is on recovery and reconstruction, whereas the most critical period for their involvement will be during the immediate relief phase, during which the implementing partners on whom their plans rely will almost certainly be unable to deliver."

905. Ms Short listed three critical steps, in addition to a UN mandate, needed to improve the situation:

- giving the lead co-ordinating role to the UN;
- clarity over the resources available to DFID to support the provision of humanitarian and reconstruction assistance; and
- more time.

906. Ms Short also confirmed that DFID had "earmarked £65m for Iraq … the majority of my entire contingency reserve for next year [2003/04]".

907. The letter was also sent to Mr Hoon, Mr Straw, Mr Brown and Sir Andrew Turnbull.

908. Mr Hoon responded on 14 March.[379] He endorsed Ms Short's conclusion that international preparedness was insufficient, but insisted the UK and US military were doing all they could with available resources, and argued that she understated the priority the US attached to humanitarian issues.

909. Ms Short outlined DFID's humanitarian preparations to Parliament on 13 March.

910. In her statement, Ms Short announced that DFID was also considering longer-term reconstruction and reform issues.

911. In response to the request from the International Development Committee on 10 March for DFID to issue a statement outlining its humanitarian contingency plans, Ms Short issued a Written Ministerial Statement to Parliament on 13 March.[380] She described how planning had progressed over the previous month: "My assessment of the overall level of preparedness of the international community to cope with the

---

[378] Letter Short to Blair, 12 March 2003, [untitled].
[379] Letter Hoon to Blair, 14 March 2003, 'Iraq: post conflict issues'.
[380] House of Commons, *Official Report*, 13 March 2003, column 21WS.

humanitarian challenges which may lie ahead in Iraq is that it is limited, and this involves serious risk."

912. Ms Short stated that DFID would have two roles in the event of conflict:

- to help advise UK Armed Forces on their obligations under the Hague and Geneva Conventions; and
- to use the funds, expertise and influence available to it to support delivery of humanitarian assistance by the international community.

913. She added that DFID was deploying staff to key locations in the region, had brought DFID's stockpile of non-food items, vehicles and equipment "to immediate readiness", was procuring additional supplies and was positioning some of those stocks in Kuwait and elsewhere in the region.

914. Ms Short explained that she had decided to supplement the extra £3.5m announced on 10 February[381] to support UN humanitarian contingency planning with a further £6.5m, part of which would support a small number of NGOs in their contingency preparations. That was in addition to DFID's ongoing humanitarian programme for Iraq, expected to amount to £8m in 2002/03, and its regular funding to the UN and other humanitarian agencies, which included provision for emergency preparedness worldwide.

915. Ms Short announced:

"My Department is also considering the longer term reconstruction and reform issues. It is clear that a UN mandate will be required to provide legal authority for the reconstruction effort, and to make possible the engagement of the international financial institutions and the wider international community."

916. DFID provided further information in its detailed response to the Committee's report on 21 March.[382]

917. **The Inquiry has seen no evidence that a cross-government humanitarian plan for Iraq was ever produced.**

918. **One week before the invasion, with no reference to potential timescales, costs or measurable outcomes, the DFID paper did no more than restate DFID's position on an issue where there was no cross-government consensus.**

919. **The 'Humanitarian Strategy and Immediate Assistance Plan' was the last DFID plan prepared before the invasion of Iraq.**

---

[381] House of Commons, *Official Report*, 10 February 2003, column 526W.
[382] House of Commons International Development Committee Second Special Report of Session 2002-03, *Preparing for the Humanitarian Consequences of Possible Military Action Against Iraq: Government Response to the Committee's Fourth Report of Session 2002-03*, HC 561.

920. DFID did not produce any proposals for longer-term reconstruction until 27 March.

Extending the Oil-for-Food programme

921. Dr Rice gave Sir David Manning an account of White House thinking on the handling of Iraqi oil on 13 March. The OFF programme should be left in place, but sanctions lifted to allow Iraq to use the proceeds as it chose. OFF should be phased out when there was an Iraqi entity ready to take over revenues. The US also wanted to make clear that military operations would not be paid for out of Iraqi oil money. In response, No.10 asked the FCO to prepare a note on UK plans for Iraqi oil revenues for Mr Blair to use in public.[383]

922. On 14 March, the FCO instructed the UK Mission to the UN in New York to start discussions with the US delegation on a possible resolution to modify the OFF programme and sanctions regime should military action lead to the absence of an effective Iraqi government.[384]

923. The UK position was summarised in the FCO background papers for the Azores Summit, sent to No.10 on 15 March:

> "If the Iraqi regime falls, new arrangements will need to be put in place to enable the OFF to keep functioning. Our current plan is to table a resolution soon after conflict starts … We are seeking to amend some of the procedures to speed up the process for humanitarian goods …

> "We would hope that the Secretary-General would be able to transfer full control over oil revenues to a properly representative Iraqi Government as soon as possible (not as the US have suggested, an Iraqi 'entity', which could, particularly if US appointed, fuel suggestions that the Coalition was seeking to control Iraqi oil)."[385]

924. Resolution 1472, adopted unanimously on 28 March, transferred authority for administering the OFF programme to the UN Secretary-General for a period of 45 days, with the possibility of further renewal by the Security Council.

Plans and preparations on the eve of the invasion

925. In early March, the structure of ORHA and of the post-conflict Iraqi Interim Authority (IIA) remained uncertain.

926. On 6 March, a UK official working for ORHA in Washington reported to Mr Chilcott that ORHA would welcome "UK ideas on how to handle [the] Iraqi Foreign Ministry" and

---

[383] Minute Cannon to Owen, 14 March 2003, 'Iraq: Iraqi Oil Post-Conflict'.
[384] Telegram 149 FCO London to UKMIS New York, 14 March 2003, 'Iraq – Military Action – Sanctions and Oil for Food – Strategy Paper'.
[385] Letter Owen to Rycroft, 15 March 2003, 'Azores Summit' attaching Paper FCO, 'Iraq – Oil for Food Programme (OFF) and Sanctions'.

"UK information on Iraqi ministries – structure, numbers, who are good Iraqis to work with".[386] The official stated that Principals had still not agreed ORHA's structure in Iraq, ORHA's relationship to the UN or to the IIA, or the role of different Iraqi groups in the IIA. The official also commented that: "ORHA has an overwhelmingly military feel, despite Gen Garner's best efforts to be called 'Mr'."

927. An IPU official sent Mr Chaplin and Mr Chilcott a set of possible principles to guide the composition of the IIA on 10 March.[387] Those included:

- sensitivity to ethnic and sectarian balance, the secular/religious mix and the role of tribes, without reinforcing or reinventing divisions in Iraqi society;
- ensuring that diaspora returnees included technocrats and "religious charitable organisations";
- remembering that many of the diaspora were in Arab countries; and
- that members of the external opposition "must have hands-on skills and/or real support within Iraq".

928. Mr Chaplin agreed with all but the last. He argued that:

"… external oppositionists of any stripe should be free to try their luck back in Iraq. The Coalition can perhaps judge their skills, but not their political credibility. Only Iraqis can do that."[388]

929. On 10 March, Mr Fraser sent Sir Michael Jay and Mr Ricketts advice on the implications of military action for the international system.[389] Mr Fraser attached a paper prepared by the Directorate of Strategy and Innovation (DSI) listing "the risks and opportunities of quick, successful, UN-sanctioned military action leading to the installation in Iraq of an international administration (ie a best case scenario)", to "help us to focus on some of the issues we may confront quite early on the morning after".[390]

930. The risks covered Iraq, the region and more general issues. Under "Iraq internal", the paper listed:

"–   Internal rebellion; major unrest

–   External military intervention (eg by Turkey; Iran)

–   Power vacuum (providing ideal conditions for criminal elements; drugs; people-trafficking)

–   Iraqi oil fields rendered unusable."

---

[386] Email [British Embassy Washington junior official] to Chilcott, 6 March 2003, 'ORHA: reporting'.
[387] Email [IPU junior official] to Chilcott, 10 March 2003, 'ORHA: reporting'.
[388] Email Chaplin to Chilcott, 10 March 2003, 'ORHA: reporting'.
[389] Minute Fraser to Jay, 10 March 2003, 'Iraq: Implications for the International System'.
[390] Paper DSI, [undated], 'Iraq – Risks and Opportunities'.

931. The paper warned that seeking but failing to secure a second resolution would increase many of the risks listed, including by "reducing the effectiveness of any Day After work (so eg increased chance of a power vacuum forming in parts of Iraq or external intervention)".

932. On 10 March, the British Embassy Washington reported that the US had agreed a broad outline for the transitional administration of Iraq:

- **a Civilian Administrator responsible for key ministries and reporting to Coalition Forces;**
- **a UN Special Co-ordinator responsible for UN agencies and reporting to the Security Council; and**
- **an IIA under Coalition oversight, administering the less sensitive ministries.**

933. UK officials commented that the US seemed to be "moving in the right direction". No.10 would be asked to inject the UK's advice on Phase IV.

934. Mr Brenton reported on 10 March that the US had agreed the "broad outlines of the structure of transitional arrangements" in Iraq in the period between military rule and Iraqi government.[391] The three components of the transitional arrangements were:

- a Civilian Administrator reporting to Coalition Forces and responsible for key ministries;
- a UN Special Co-ordinator responsible for UN agencies and reporting to the Security Council; and
- an IIA to administer the less sensitive ministries and agencies, under Coalition oversight.

935. There was agreement in Washington that those arrangements "would need to be blessed via a UNSCR". The State Department had been commissioned to start work on a draft. But the Coalition would remain in overall control until it felt comfortable enough to hand authority to the Iraqis: the US would "not allow sovereignty to be passed to the UN".

936. On 10 March, Sir David Manning wrote to Dr Rice, enclosing a draft resolution on post-conflict Iraq.[392] He described the purpose of the resolution as:

- to provide legal and political "cover" for the UK and other nations to contribute to reconstruction;
- to build support in Iraq and the Arab world for reform;

---

[391] Telegram 321 Washington to London, 10 March 2003, 'Iraq: Day After Planning'.
[392] Letter Manning to Rice, 10 March 2003, 'Iraq: Post-conflict administration'.

- to "provide an exit strategy"; and
- to re-unite the international community.

937. The record of the 11 March FCO Iraq Morning Meeting stated that: "US Principals still seem to be moving in the right direction on 'Day After' thinking. No.10 will be asked to hurry along the injection of our Phase IV advice."[393]

938. On 12 March, Mr Chaplin updated heads of key FCO posts abroad on progress "as we enter the endgame".[394] He reported that the post-conflict phase "should offer opportunities to rebuild a degree of international consensus after the blood spilled over the second SCR". Guidance would issue separately (the Phase IV Core Script), but heads of post could already stress to interlocutors the principles guiding the UK approach, including a major role for the UN and giving clear responsibility to the Iraqi people (not just exiles) to decide the constitution and institutions they wanted.

939. On 13 March, Sir Michael Jay informed FCO staff in London and at posts abroad that the FCO Emergency Unit would be open from 0900 on 14 March and the Consular Crisis Centre from 17 March.[395]

The FCO Emergency Unit

The FCO Emergency Unit, responsible for co-ordination of all aspects of FCO Iraq policy during the military campaign, opened on 14 March.

The FCO Consular Crisis Centre opened on 17 March.

Both operated 24 hours a day throughout the military campaign.

Sir Michael Jay informed FCO staff on 13 March that the FCO Emergency Unit would be open from 0900 on 14 March and the Consular Crisis Centre from 17 March.[396] Sir Michael explained:

"This does not imply that military action is inevitable, or that a date has already been set for its start should it become unavoidable. We continue to work flat out to secure a further UN resolution that will lead to Iraq's disarmament. But we must be prepared for all contingencies, and events are moving fast.

"Peter Ricketts ... together with William Ehrman ... is co-ordinating the FCO's overall response to the crisis. Edward Chaplin ... is Deputy Crisis Co-ordinator. They will continue to work from their current offices. Charles Gray ... has been appointed Crisis Manager.

"As well as political and briefing sections ... the EU [Emergency Unit] will also include a Pol Mil [politico-military] Section ... which will be responsible for liaison with the MOD. There will also be a member of Consular Division embedded in the Unit, who will liaise with the Consular Crisis Centre. The Emergency Unit will work in close

---

[393] Minute Tanfield to PS/PUS [FCO], 11 March 2003, 'Iraq Morning Meeting: Key Points'.
[394] Telegram 33 FCO London to Riyadh, 12 March 2003, 'Iraq: The Endgame'.
[395] Telegram 130 FCO London to Abidjan, 13 March 2003, 'Opening of FCO Emergency Unit'.
[396] Telegram 130 FCO London to Abidjan, 13 March 2003, 'Opening of FCO Emergency Unit'.

co-operation with the various other [FCO] geographical and functional departments engaged in crisis related work … and Press Office. It will also work closely with the Iraq Planning Unit which, for the moment, continues to lead on the less immediate, longer-term, post-conflict planning issues."

Mr Ricketts had been chairing regular FCO morning and evening meetings on Iraq since late 2002 (see Section 6.4). The last of those meetings took place on the morning of 14 March.[397]

After the closure of the Emergency Unit on 2 May, Mr Ricketts resumed daily Iraq policy meetings in his office from 6 May.[398]

On 20 March, Sir Michael Jay informed Mr Straw that almost 5 percent of FCO staff in London had been redeployed to work on Iraq, including 170 volunteers to temporary positions in the two emergency units.[399]

That number far exceeded the combined total of appointments to the IPU, to the new Embassy in Baghdad and to ORHA (see Section 15.1).

940. On 13 March, Mr Blair told Cabinet that President Bush had promised a UN mandate for reconstruction.

941. Mr Blair spoke to President Bush on the afternoon of 12 March (see Section 3.8).[400] Among the issues discussed was a US statement on the need for a further UN resolution on post-conflict Iraq.

942. Mr Blair told Cabinet on 13 March that work continued in the UN to obtain a second resolution (see Section 3.8).[401] He also stated that "the reconstruction of Iraq after a conflict would need a United Nations Security Council resolution". The US had "now agreed" to that.

943. In the discussion, points made included that UN authority for the reconstruction of Iraq was "essential so that all countries and international institutions could contribute".

944. In her memoir, Ms Short wrote that, after Cabinet on 13 March, Mr Blair told her that President Bush had "promised [a] UN mandate for reconstruction".[402]

---

[397] Minute Kernahan to PS/PUS, 14 March 2003, 'Iraq Morning Meeting'.
[398] Minutes, 1 May 2003, FCO Emergency Unit Iraq Meeting.
[399] Minute Jay to Secretary of State [FCO], 20 March 2003, 'Iraq Contingency Planning and Prioritisation'.
[400] Letter Rycroft to McDonald, 12 March 2003, 'Iraq: Prime Minister's Telephone Conversation with President Bush, 12 March'.
[401] Cabinet Conclusions, 13 March 2003.
[402] Short C. *An Honourable Deception: New Labour, Iraq and the Misuse of Power*. The Free Press, 2004.

Presidential approval of US post-conflict plans

Between 10 and 12 March, President Bush approved important elements of the US post-conflict plan:

- a policy of "light" de-Ba'athification that would preserve Iraq's administrative capacity;
- use of the Iraqi Army as a labour force for reconstruction, but not its demobilisation;
- the transfer of governance authority to an Iraq Interim Authority (IIA) with Iraqi exiles and Kurdish groups at its core, and the Coalition determining the pace at which power was transferred.

On 10 March, Lieutenant General (retired) Jay Garner, Head of the Office of Reconstruction and Humanitarian Assistance (ORHA), briefed President Bush on ORHA's post-conflict plan, warning that: "a tremendous amount of work was still necessary to make the inter-agency post-war plans operational".[403] He identified three priorities: funding for Iraq's public service, police and army; the rapid deployment of "international stability forces" after the fall of Saddam Hussein; and the need to use the Iraqi Army for reconstruction. The President authorised Lt Gen Garner's proposal to use the Iraqi Army "to populate a large labor force for reconstruction efforts".

The same day, Mr Frank Miller, NSC Senior Director for Defense Policy and Arms Control, secured President Bush's agreement to a policy of "light" de-Ba'athification in order to preserve Iraq's administrative capacity.

Two days later, on 12 March, Mr Douglas Feith, US Under Secretary of Defense for Policy, briefed President Bush that the Iraqi Army would not be demobilised. He also proposed the transfer of power "shortly after Saddam's fall" to an IIA. Iraqi exiles and Kurdish groups would become the core of the IIA, working in partnership with the Coalition's transitional authority so that Iraqi citizens would have some political control from the outset, with the Coalition determining the pace at which power was transferred.

President Bush endorsed the plan. *Hard Lessons* observed that the plan assumed Iraqi governmental institutions would emerge from the war reasonably intact and that the plan's implementation was therefore dependent on the course of the war.

The post-conflict demobilisation of the Iraqi Army is addressed in Section 12.1.

945. **After talks in Washington on 13 and 14 March, UK officials suggested that UK/US thinking on the role of the UN was "80 percent congruent".**

946. **Sir David Manning was informed that the principal point of difference was US resistance to a UN representative exercising control over the transitional administration.**

---

[403] Bowen SW Jr. *Hard Lessons: The Iraq Reconstruction Experience.* U.S. Government Printing Office, 2009.

947. Mr O'Brien and Mr Chilcott discussed post-conflict issues in Washington on 13 March.[404] The British Embassy reported that US interlocutors accepted the need for a "UN badge" for Phase IV and that there was "general agreement that the [UK] draft [resolution] was 80 percent congruent with the [US] Administration's position", but the US wanted to retain as light a UN touch as possible, with Coalition control over a Transitional Civilian Administration (TCA) and the IIA. Finding the right UN Special Co-ordinator would be key.

948. The Embassy reported that Mr O'Brien's US interlocutors had confirmed that the administration of Iraq would be "uniform". ORHA would not treat areas controlled by UK forces differently and there was "no question of food distribution or public sector salaries stopping at the borders of any British sector". Although the Ba'ath Party would be disestablished, "the vast majority of members would need to be left in place".

949. Mr Chilcott stayed in Washington for a second day of talks on 14 March.[405] The Embassy reported that US participants had stated that control over the TCA, and in particular the IIA, could not be given to a UN Special Co-ordinator and that most of the tasks the UK assigned to a UN Assistance Mission for Iraq (UNAMI) would be carried out by the Coalition-led TCA.

950. The AHGI discussed the UK/US consultations on the role of the UN on 14 March, before officials in London had seen the report of Mr Chilcott's second day of talks in Washington.[406]

951. On 17 March, Mr Dodd reported the AHGI discussion to Sir David Manning:

"There is '80 percent agreement' with the US on the role of the UN. For example, the US agrees that food distribution and civil service salaries should be organised nationally. The remaining significant point of difference is whether the transitional administration should be subordinate to a UN representative. The FCO believe it unlikely that the UN Security Council will mandate the administration unless it is."

952. Mr Dodd also reported that the IPU was considering how best to approach other donors for support on Phase IV.

953. Concerns remained about UK companies' access to reconstruction contracts in Iraq.

954. Mr O'Brien used his visit to Washington on 13 March to lobby on behalf of UK firms.

---

[404] Telegram 341 Washington to FCO London, 13 March 2003, 'Iraq day after: Mr O'Brien's visit'.
[405] Telegram 346 Washington to FCO London, 14 March 2003, 'Iraq day after: US proposals for post-conflict administration'.
[406] Minute Dodd to Manning, 17 March 2013, 'Ad Hoc Group on Iraq'.

955. On 10 March, Mr Brenton had reported that "a commercial contact" had passed the British Embassy Washington a version of a USAID invitation to select US companies to bid for a US$600m contract for infrastructure reconstruction.[407] USAID had confirmed that the invitation had been issued on 12 February with a closing date of 27 February. Mr Brenton had pressed for more transparency.

956. Mr Brenton also reported that it was not clear how that USAID contract related to a separate contract "allegedly being let by the US Army Corps of Engineers" and reported in the UK press on 9 March.

957. That contract, the US$7bn contract for "repair work on Iraq's oil sector" awarded to US engineering firm KBR, a subsidiary of Halliburton, by the US Army Corps of Engineers on 8 March, later emerged as the single largest reconstruction contract in Iraq.[408]

958. On 13 March, during his visit to Washington, Mr O'Brien lobbied Mr Andrew Natsios, USAID Administrator, for UK companies to be awarded reconstruction contracts.[409] Mr Natsios advised that, for security reasons, USAID had invited only a few US companies with the necessary clearances to bid for the 17 primary reconstruction contracts. There were no such constraints on subcontracts, and he hoped that UK companies and NGOs with the right expertise would be successful in securing those contracts. In response to a question from Mr O'Brien, Mr Natsios said that it would be possible for UK companies to acquire the necessary security clearances to bid for primary contracts.

959. Mr O'Brien also lobbied the European Directorate of the NSC on oil contracts.[410] He accepted that it was reasonable for US companies to be the recipients of DoD money for emergency contracts to repair damage to oil infrastructure, but the field should be opened up "once Iraqi money came on stream". The NSC official agreed.

960. On 14 March, Mr Straw commented on Baroness Symons's minute, described earlier in this Section, in which she drew attention to concerns in the UK business community about the level of the Government's engagement with the US on commercial issues. Mr Straw stated: "This is really important."[411] His office instructed Mr Chilcott to factor Baroness Symons's concerns into the IPU's follow-up to Mr O'Brien's discussions in Washington.[412]

---

[407] Telegram 320 Washington to FCO London, 10 March 2003, 'Iraq Day After: Infrastructure Reconstruction Contracts'.
[408] Bowen SW Jr. *Hard Lessons: The Iraq Reconstruction Experience.* U.S. Government Printing Office, 2009.
[409] Telegram 341 Washington to FCO London, 13 March 2003, 'Iraq Day After: Mr O'Brien's Visit'.
[410] Letter Gooderham to Chilcott, 13 March 2003, Iraq: Day After: The Oil Sector'.
[411] Manuscript comment Straw, 14 March 2003, on Minute Symons to Straw and Hewitt, [undated], 'Iraq: Commercial Aspects'.
[412] Minute McDonald to Chilcott, 14 March 2003, 'Iraq: Commercial Aspects'.

961. No.10 officials updated Mr Blair at his request on 15 March, following press and Parliamentary interest in UK access to reconstruction contracts and the involvement of Halliburton.[413] Mr Blair was informed that UK companies would be eligible for subcontracted work under the US$600m USAID contract and that Mr O'Brien had agreed to send USAID a list of "trustworthy UK companies", including those with experience of contracting for the MOD, which might acquire security clearance to bid for primary contracts. The briefing note made no mention of the US$7bn oil repair contract.

962. Government lobbying on behalf of UK companies and the involvement of UK firms in post-conflict reconstruction is addressed in Section 10.3.

The UK military plan

963. **On 14 March, Mr Blair approved a proposal to extend the UK's AO northwards during Phase III if commanders on the ground judged it sensible.**

964. Lt Gen Reith sent the Chiefs of Staff an update on military planning options on 10 March (see Section 6.2).[414] The update reflected the Chiefs' comments on Lt Gen Reith's two papers of 4 March and his discussions with senior US commanders between 5 and 7 March.

965. Lt Gen Reith recommended that the Joint Command be authorised to operate north of the current planned UK AO, no further than al-Amara, "on the understanding that the Division will only exploit forward as far as security and transition to Phase IV within the current AO allows".

966. Lt Gen Reith outlined the plan to extend the UK AO to the north at the Chiefs of Staff meeting on 10 March.[415] He stated that the "current UK AO could potentially result in enemy forces around Basra interfering with Phase IV operations". There was "a clear military task to ensure that enemy forces in the areas outside the current UK AO were unable to interfere with the UK Main Effort".

967. The Chiefs of Staff were "concerned that extending the AO would overstretch Phase III and Phase IV resources and potentially detract from the Main Effort in the UK AO".

968. Adm Boyce directed Lt Gen Reith "to proceed with the main effort, of an exemplary Phase IV, in the original AO (Southern AO) with operations in the Northern AO as required to achieve a speedy and successful Phase III and to shape Phase IV".

---

[413] Minute Cannon to Prime Minister, 15 March 2003, 'Iraq: Reconstruction Contracts'.
[414] Minute Reith to COSSEC, 10 March 2003, 'Iraq – Military Planning Options Update' attaching Paper CJO, 10 March 2003, 'Iraq military planning options – an update'.
[415] Minutes, 10 March 2003, Chiefs of Staff meeting.

969. AM Burridge wrote in his Hauldown Report in early May:

"Our overriding consideration was for the GOC [Maj Gen Brims] to condition his own AO, in preparation for stability operations (Phase IV), rather than inherit circumstances [created by others] ..."[416]

970. Mr Blair held a meeting with Mr John Prescott (the Deputy Prime Minister), Mr Hoon, Lord Goldsmith, Adm Boyce, Sir Andrew Turnbull and No.10 staff on 11 March to discuss legal and military issues.[417] Mr Straw attended part of the meeting.

971. The meeting is addressed in more detail in Sections 3.8 and 6.2.

972. The briefing note for Mr Blair stated that the "main purpose of the meeting" was confirmation of the viability of the overall military plan.[418] Questions for Mr Blair to raise included whether the US had a "winning concept" and what conditions UK forces should expect in Basra.

973. Adm Boyce told the meeting he was "confident that the battle plan would work".[419]

974. Asked about that statement and whether it included the aftermath, Lord Boyce told the Inquiry: "No, not in that statement."[420]

975. After the meeting, Mr Watkins sent Sir David Manning an outline of the military plan for Iraq and advice on decisions needed on the development of the UK's role (see Section 6.2).[421]

976. On the question of the expansion of the UK AO northwards, Mr Watkins explained:

"The US Land Component Commander has ... developed a plan that would expand the UK Area of Operations by up to 150km up to and beyond al-Amara [in Maysan province] (but short of al-Kut [in Wasit province]) ...

"The case for pushing a UK formation northwards will ultimately have to be judged at the time. Clearly it will depend to some extent on what is happening in the Basra area. It is also the case that an exemplary Phase IV operation depends on a satisfactory conclusion to the conflict phase. The Defence Secretary therefore judges that the senior UK operational commander (the Chief of Joint Operations) should be authorised to expand the Phase III Area of Operations northwards if that is required to achieve a satisfactory outcome to Phase III. The focus for the UK in Phase IV should, however, remain the South-Eastern Area of Operations as currently understood."

---

[416] Report Burridge to CJO, 8 May 2003, 'NCC Operation Telic Hauldown Report: 07 Feb 03 – 08 May 03'.
[417] Letter Rycroft to McDonald, 11 March 2003, 'Iraq: Legal and Military Aspects'.
[418] Minute Rycroft to Prime Minister, 11 March 2003, 'Iraq Military: 1300 Meeting'.
[419] Letter Rycroft to McDonald, 11 March 2003, 'Iraq: Legal and Military Aspects'.
[420] Public hearing, 27 January 2011, page 85.
[421] Letter Watkins to Manning, 11 March 2003, 'Iraq: the Military Plan'.

977. Mr Watkins reported that Mr Hoon judged that the UK should be "forward-leaning" on the idea of extending the UK AO north during the conflict phase, "provided that UK commanders judge this sensible in the circumstances at the time".

978. Mr Watkins sent the letter to the Private Offices of Mr Straw and Mr Brown, and to Mr Bowen, but not to DFID.

979. Mr Blair approved the plan on 14 March.[422]

980. The advice on which Mr Blair based his decision was incomplete.

981. Mr Hoon stated in January 2003 that credible plans for the aftermath were needed before it could be concluded that the overall US plan represented a "winning concept", and that further work was needed on a satisfactory plan for the aftermath before the UK committed forces to military action, but he failed to press the point further with Mr Blair.

982. Mr Hoon's advice to Mr Blair on military options in October 2002, on the shift to the South and the deployment of UK forces in January 2003, and on the expansion of the UK's AO and AOR in March 2003, while recognising the significance of the post-conflict phase, offered little analysis of wider, non-military implications.

983. It was Sir Kevin Tebbit's responsibility, as PUS, to ensure that military advice from Adm Boyce to Mr Hoon was placed firmly in that wider context and reflected broader analysis of the UK's overall obligations, capabilities and strategic objectives.

984. Lt Gen Reith was emphatic about the strategic significance of Phase IV in a paper on the UK response to the "legal, security and humanitarian assistance demands of Phase IVa" sent to the Chiefs of Staff on 11 March.[423]

985. In his covering minute, Lt Gen Reith informed the Chiefs of Staff that "legal obligations placed on the UK as an Occupying Power will be extensive". He advised:

> "Phase IVa is likely to be the decisive phase of this campaign. This is recognised by the US and considerable inter-agency planning effort has gone into creating structures and providing resources to deal with anticipated security and H[umanitarian] A[ssistance] issues; we can have confidence in these plans. However, Phase IVa will not be the initial main effort; some political expectation management may be required."

---

[422] Letter Manning to Watkins, 14 March 2003, 'Iraq: The Military Plan'.
[423] Minute Reith to COSSEC, 11 March 2003, 'Phase IVa – A UK Response' attaching Paper Reith, 11 March 2003, 'Phase IVa – A UK Response'.

986. The paper on the UK response to Phase IVa described Phase IV as "strategically decisive" and highlighted a number of significant gaps in post-conflict planning:

- the absence of a detailed UK/US policy on the role of the military in maintaining law and order and detaining civilians;

- a risk that UK forces would face a humanitarian situation for which they were not resourced unless there was early agreement that DFID would fund humanitarian assistance through military channels;

- the military was still waiting for the Treasury's agreement to an initiative for £10m to be made available to UK forces for QIPs; and

- the absence of a decision on how or whether the UK would pay Iraqi public sector salaries.

987. The paper included, in full, US definitions of the end state for Phases IVa, b and c:

- Phase IVa: "a stable environment in which the territorial integrity of Iraq is intact; civil order is maintained; repairs to damaged civil infrastructure are under way; humanitarian assistance is provided by the civilian sector; and an interim administration is in place".

- Phase IVb: "responsibility for stability and security passing from Coalition military to responsible Iraqi institutions; rule of law is fully established; necessary civil infrastructure is functioning and economic development is under way; lessening dependence on humanitarian assistance; and a transitional civil administration is in place with increasing Iraqi participation".

- Phase IVc: "a durable, secure and stable Iraq sustained by Iraqis, in which the rule of law is well established and civil order is maintained by Iraqi authorities; civil infrastructure is functioning and economic development continuing; lessened dependence on humanitarian assistance; authority had been transferred to an Iraqi national government".

988. In the paper, Lt Gen Reith explained that CFLCC had instructed all commanders to:

"… liaise with and monitor local administrations within their area of responsibility … but … only to directly intervene in the administrative process when necessary to maintain public order and safety, or to prevent human suffering. Existing Iraqi government organisations should be allowed and encouraged to function as normal and no attempt should be made to reorganise or replace existing structures."

Eclipse II – the CFLCC plan for Phase IV

The CFLCC plan for Phase IV, known as Eclipse II, was the product of the post-conflict planning effort led by (acting) Major General Albert Whitley, CFLCC Deputy Commanding General (Post Hostilities). Eclipse II had close links to CFLCC's combat operations planning, but not to broader Washington policy debates.[424]

After Saddam, the 2008 RAND report for the US Army on US post-conflict planning, stated that Eclipse II had been through 15 revisions by the middle of March 2003, with the final draft released on 12 April.[425]

The RAND report concluded that CFLCC "was gaining a realistic appraisal of the potential security challenges that would confront Coalition forces", but failed to challenge military planning assumptions, including the degree to which the remnants of the Iraqi Government would provide essential services and security.

In his written statement to the Inquiry, Maj Gen Whitley explained that Eclipse II was named after the 1945 US plan for post-war Germany.[426] It was "an attempt to produce some coherence for the military aspects of Post Hostilities and give subordinate commands, responsibilities, direction and tasks". The "tiny" planning team in ORHA produced the civil mirror image.

Maj Gen Whitley judged that the plan had "some local practical effect", but was "inadequate".

---

989. On 11 March, at the height of the UK's effort to secure Security Council backing for a second resolution (see Section 3.8), Mr Straw advised Mr Blair of the need for a "Plan B" for the military in the event that the Government failed to secure a majority in the Parliamentary Labour Party for military action.

990. Mr Straw's Plan B envisaged the UK "taking responsibility for a sector and for humanitarian and reconstruction work" in order to make "a major UK contribution to the overall campaign" without being directly involved in the invasion.

991. At that stage, officials were still pressing, without success, for Ministers to agree draft objectives for post-conflict Iraq and principles to guide short-term UK involvement that could be shared with the US.

992. It is not clear whether Mr Straw had discussed the feasibility of his idea with others.

993. On 11 March, Mr Straw advised Mr Blair that he should not go to Parliament seeking approval for military action unless he could be sure of a majority in the

---

[424] Dale C. *Operation Iraqi Freedom: Strategies, Approaches, Results and Issues for Congress.* Congressional Research Service, 15 December 2008.
[425] Bensahel N, Oliker O, Crane K, Brennan RR Jr, Gregg HS, Sullivan T & Rathmell A. *After Saddam: Prewar Planning and the Occupation of Iraq.* RAND Corporation, 2008.
[426] Statement, 25 January 2011, page 12.

Parliamentary Labour Party and the House of Commons. He advised of the need to "start working up a Plan B for our Armed Forces if we cannot be sure of the [House of] Commons' approval for their inclusion in the initial invasion of Iraq".[427]

994. Mr Straw advised:

> "… it need not be a disaster for you, the Government, and even more important for our troops, if we cannot take an active part in the initial invasion, provided we get on the front foot with our strategy.

> "I am aware of all the difficulties … But I understand that the US could if necessary adjust their plan rapidly to cope without us. In these circumstances we could nevertheless offer them a major UK contribution to the overall campaign. In addition to staunch political support, this would include … as soon as combat operations are over, full UK participation in the military and civilian tasks, including taking responsibility for a sector and for humanitarian and reconstruction work. We could also take the lead in the UN on securing the … resolution to authorise the reconstruction effort and the UN role in it which the US now agree is necessary."

995. Efforts to secure Parliamentary approval for military action in Iraq are addressed in Section 3.8.

UK objectives for post-conflict Iraq

996. The draft objectives and guiding principles for post-conflict Iraq were resubmitted to Mr Blair for approval on 12 March.

997. No decision was taken and there is no indication that Mr Blair discussed the objectives and principles with Ministers.

998. In the absence of a decision from Mr Blair, post-conflict planners remained without clear Ministerial guidance on the nature and extent of the UK's post-conflict commitment.

999. On 12 March, one week before the start of the invasion, Mr Cannon re-submitted to Mr Blair the IPU's draft objectives for post-conflict Iraq and principles to guide short-term UK involvement.[428]

1000. One item had been added to the objectives prepared for Mr Blair's meeting on 6 March: that the new Iraqi government should maintain Iraq's territorial integrity.

1001. Mr Cannon stated that the IPU proposals were "not contentious in UK terms", but "clear policy approval now would assist our planning for post-conflict operations". He explained that the objectives had not been drafted for publication: the UK's aims would

---

[427] Minute Straw to Prime Minister, 11 March 2003, 'Iraq: What if We Cannot Win the Second Resolution?'
[428] Minute Cannon to Prime Minister, 12 March 2003, 'Iraq: post-conflict planning: objectives and principles'.

be set out in the "vision for Iraq and other public messages (likely to be held back until we are … actually at war: until then we would not wish to be seen to be actively pursuing regime change …)".

1002. On the principles, Mr Cannon stated:

"The **principles** are those which should guide our occupation, if only short-term, of Iraqi territory. They are pretty uncontroversial. But our military commanders would find this sort of guidance, endorsed by Ministers, very useful."

1003. Mr Cannon concluded:

"If you approve these objectives and principles, the next step would be for Iraq Planning Unit to share them with the Americans. There is no reason to think that they cut across American views in any way."

1004. The evidence seen by the Inquiry indicates that Mr Blair saw Mr Cannon's minute, but not whether he approved the draft objectives and principles.[429]

1005. There is no indication that Mr Blair discussed the objectives and principles with Ministers.

1006. Mr Bowen sent a revised draft set of 'British Post-Conflict Objectives' to senior officials in the FCO, the MOD and DFID on 25 March, six days after the start of the invasion.

1007. The first Treasury paper on financing post-conflict reconstruction to be shared with No.10 recommended spreading the burden as widely as possible.

1008. If the UN was not involved, the resources available would be substantially smaller and the IMF and World Bank would be unlikely to engage.

1009. On 14 March, Mr Bowman sent No.10 the paper on financing Iraqi reconstruction requested by Mr Blair on 6 March.[430]

1010. The paper was the first Treasury paper on post-conflict financing to be shared with No.10.

1011. The Treasury estimated the total cost at up to US$45bn for the first three years, in addition to military costs, and warned that, without UN authorisation of arrangements for a transitional administration, Iraqi oil might only pay for a fraction of the total.

1012. The best way to pay for reconstruction would be to spread the burden as widely as possible, drawing in contributions from non-combatants, IFIs and Iraq itself, and

---

[429] Manuscript note [tick] on Minute Cannon to Prime Minister, 12 March 2003, 'Iraq: post-conflict planning: objectives and principles'.
[430] Letter Bowman to Cannon, 14 March 2003, [untitled] attaching Paper HM Treasury, March 2003, 'Financing Iraqi Reconstruction'.

ensuring Iraqi revenues were not diverted into debt or compensation payments. By far the most significant factor in making that happen would be political legitimacy conferred by the UN.

1013. The Treasury stated that OFF provided "an obvious way to pay for immediate humanitarian needs", by using the approximately US$4bn unspent in the UN OFF account and restarting oil exports. That depended on oil production facilities surviving the conflict relatively intact. In the most benign circumstances, with rapidly increasing production and high oil prices, oil revenues "could make a very significant contribution" to ongoing relief and reconstruction. Future oil revenues were another possible source of funds, but, officials warned, Iraq had already accumulated "massive and probably unsustainable debts" that way.

1014. The Treasury concluded that, given fiscal constraints in the UK and US, total resources for reconstruction would be "substantially smaller if the UN were not involved". That, combined with the likelihood that the IMF and World Bank would be unable to engage in such circumstances, "could make it harder to put Iraq on a path to peace, stability and democracy".

The Azores Summit, 16 March 2003

1015. Mr Blair discussed preparations for the Azores Summit with President Bush on 14 March.[431] Mr Blair said that "at some point we needed to set out our views on post-conflict, including humanitarian issues".

1016. The UK's revised 'Vision for Iraq and the Iraqi People', sent to No.10 before the Azores Summit, was intended to reassure the Iraqi people and wider audiences of the Coalition's intentions for Iraq after Saddam Hussein's departure.

1017. The wording of the UK draft and the later text agreed with the US and Spain at the Summit made no specific or measurable commitments for which the Coalition could be held directly to account.

1018. The FCO background papers sent to No.10 before the Azores Summit included a revised version of the UK's 'Vision for Iraq and the Iraqi People'.

1019. The IPU explained to Mr Straw's Private Office that the intention was for the Vision to be:

"... launched in a manner that provides maximum impact, both with the Iraqi people and with wider public opinion. The Vision and the messages accompanying its launch will be critical to reassuring Iraqis and the Arab world about our post-conflict objectives ...

---

[431] Letter Rycroft to McDonald, 14 March 2003, 'Iraq: Prime Minister's Conversation with Bush, 14 March'.

"The text is now being shared with US contacts. The purpose of this is to ensure that there are no surprises and that our Vision is consistent with any similar exercise that the US plans to conduct. We do not though plan to produce a joint document or simply to reflect US views in our own."[432]

1020. Changes to the earlier text circulated on 28 February included:

- removal of the reference to freedom from the fear of torture;
- under the heading "Good Government", removal of the words "and democratic" from the phrase "an independent and democratic Iraq";
- removal of the commitment to work "to ensure a military campaign is as swift and carefully targeted as possible";
- the addition of a commitment to "prioritise resources to feed and care for the people of Iraq";
- a reference to enabling the Iraqi people to establish their own "effective representative government" to replace the earlier reference to establishing "democratic government";
- "Seeking a fair and sustainable solution to Iraq's debt problems" in place of "Negotiating generous debt rescheduling";
- the addition of a commitment to help "the transition to a more prosperous and dynamic economy"; and
- the addition of a reference to Iraq's oil industry being managed "fairly and transparently".[433]

1021. Mr Straw's Private Office explained to No.10 that "Washington is negotiating with the NSC on the Vision for Iraq. We hope to ensure that the final version has the presentational impact of the UK's … draft."[434]

1022. The FCO also suggested that Mr Blair talk to Mr Annan from the Azores. Key messages might include: "look forward to the United Nations having a significant role after any conflict in helping Iraq move quickly towards new prosperity and stability".

---

[432] Minute Bristow to Private Secretary [FCO], 14 March 2003, 'A Vision for Iraq and the Iraqi People'.
[433] Letter Owen to Rycroft, 15 March 2003, 'Azores Summit' attaching Paper FCO, 'A Vision for Iraq and the Iraqi people'.
[434] Letter Owen to Rycroft, 15 March 2003, 'Azores Summit'.

1023. Sir David Manning had already consulted Sir Jeremy Greenstock on whether Mr Blair should speak to Mr Annan.[435] Sir David informed Mr Blair that Sir Jeremy felt that "on balance" Mr Blair should speak to Mr Annan "to keep him in play". Sir Jeremy suggested explaining that, if the second resolution failed and conflict occurred:

"… we shall want to involve the UN as rapidly, and fully, as possible, once military action is over. We are pressing for a real role for a UN Special Co-ordinator. One of our principal concerns has been, and will remain, to try to safeguard the UN system."

1024. Sir David commented to Mr Blair:

"Incidentally, this would play well with Clare [Short] who has sent me a message saying how important she thinks it is that you are in close consultation with Kofi [Annan] over Iraq."

1025. Mr Blair spoke to Mr Annan on 16 March, before the start of the Azores Summit (see Section 3.8).[436] They discussed the importance of a strong UN role in post-conflict Iraq, the need for a relationship between the UN and "whoever was occupying Iraq", and a resolution establishing the relationship between the occupying force and occupied Iraq.

1026. At the Azores Summit, Mr Blair emphasised the presentational benefits of UN involvement in post-conflict Iraq. He told President Bush and Mr José María Aznar, the Prime Minister of Spain:

- **it was necessary to give the impression that the administration of Iraq was under UN authority, and the clearer the UN role the better; and**
- **the UN should be seen to give overall authorisation, but could certainly not run everything.**

1027. At the Azores Summit, Mr Blair, President Bush and Prime Minister Aznar discussed the likelihood that the invasion would be welcomed, but the risk that there would be communal violence. They also discussed the role the UN should play, including that it would not be able to deal with communal violence.[437] That would need to be "handled rapidly by the military".

1028. Mr Blair stated that the role of the UN in post-conflict Iraq must be defined very carefully:

"We must give the impression that the administration was under UN authority. The clearer the UN role, the better. It was vital that UK public opinion understood that we were not taking possession of Iraq's oil."

---

[435] Minute Manning to Prime Minister, 14 March 2003', 'Iraq: Contact with Kofi Annan'.
[436] Letter Campbell to Owen, 16 March 2003, 'Iraq: Kofi Annan, 16 March'.
[437] Letter Manning to McDonald, 16 March 2003, 'Iraq: Summit Meeting in the Azores: 16 March'.

1029. Mr Blair also stated that the UN should be seen to give overall authorisation, but it could certainly not run everything. He wanted the UN Security Council to remain seized of the Iraqi issue.

1030. The record of the discussion was to be shown only to Mr Straw and Mr Hoon and their Principal Private Secretaries.

1031. The Azores 'Vision for Iraq and the Iraqi People' incorporated many elements of earlier UK drafts, but the wording on democracy, terrorism and the nature of the Iraqi threat to the world reflected US priorities.

1032. The 'Vision for Iraq and the Iraqi People' issued by Mr Blair, President Bush and Prime Minister Aznar at the Summit on 16 March is described in more detail in Section 3.8. It adopted a more oratorical tone than the UK text, but shared much of the substance.[438] Key differences included:

- the omission of any explicit reference to oil;
- insertion of a reference to terrorism ("We will fight terrorism in all its forms. Iraq must never again be a haven for terrorists of any kind");
- insertion of a reference to democracy ("We will support the Iraqi people's aspirations for representative government that upholds human rights and the rule of law as cornerstones of democracy"); and
- insertion of named references to Iraq's constituent peoples (Iraq's "rich mix of Sunni and Shiite Arabs, Kurds, Turkomen, Assyrians, Chaldeans, and all others").

1033. On post-conflict reconstruction, the three leaders declared:

"We will work to prevent and repair damage by Saddam Hussein's regime to the natural resources of Iraq and pledge to protect them as a national asset of and for the Iraqi people. All Iraqis should share the wealth generated by their national economy …

"In achieving this vision, we plan to work in close partnership with international institutions, including the United Nations … If conflict occurs, we plan to seek the adoption, on an urgent basis, of new United Nations Security Council resolutions that would affirm Iraq's territorial integrity, ensure rapid delivery of humanitarian relief, and endorse an appropriate post-conflict administration for Iraq. We will also propose that the Secretary-General be given authority, on an interim basis, to ensure that the humanitarian needs of the Iraqi people continue to be met through the Oil-for-Food program.

---

[438] Statement of the Atlantic Summit, 16 March 2003, 'A Vision for Iraq and the Iraqi People'.

"Any military presence, should it be necessary, will be temporary and intended to promote security and elimination of weapons of mass destruction; the delivery of humanitarian aid; and the conditions for the reconstruction of Iraq. Our commitment to support the people of Iraq will be for the long term."

1034. Mr Blair commented further at the concluding press conference:

"… should it come to conflict, we make a pledge to the people of Iraq … who are the primary victims of Saddam …

"… [W]e will help Iraq rebuild – and not rebuild because of the problems of conflict, where if it comes to that we will do everything we can to minimise the suffering of the Iraqi people, but rebuild Iraq because of the appalling legacy that the rule of Saddam has left …"[439]

1035. On 16 March, in a television interview with Sir David Frost, Mr Brown said the UK "would be committed, if there were to be military action, to the reconstruction of Iraq".[440] He explained that reconstruction "should take place under the auspices of the United Nations".

1036. Mr Straw set out the UK's approach to reconstruction in more detail in a speech to the Newspaper Society Annual Conference on 1 April (see Section 13.1).

Post-Azores concerns

1037. UK concerns about shortcomings in post-conflict planning and preparation, and uncertainty about the nature and scope of the UK's role in post-conflict Iraq, persisted after the Azores Summit.

1038. FCO legal advice on 17 March about the compatibility of post-conflict tasks with the rules and obligations of military occupation stated that Security Council authorisation:

- **was not needed for humanitarian assistance or "rehabilitation" in the sense of essential repair work closely connected with humanitarian assistance; but**
- **would be required for any reconstruction or institutional reform beyond what was necessary for the relief effort.**

---

[439] *The Guardian*, 17 March 2003, *Full text: Azores press conference.*
[440] *BBC News*, 16 March 2003, *BBC Breakfast with Frost Interview: Gordon Brown, MP, Chancellor of the Exchequer March 16th 2003.*

1039. Mr Huw Llewellyn, an FCO Legal Counsellor, wrote to the IPU on 13 March to emphasise the need for concrete information about ORHA's plans now that there were UK secondees in the organisation. He stated:

> "This is important because if UK forces are in control of the Basra area, the UK will be the Occupying Power in that area and it will be the UK's international obligations which are engaged."[441]

1040. Mr Llewellyn wrote to the IPU again on 17 March to explain that he had intended to comment in detail on an ORHA plan for "post-liberation" Iraq but that, after meeting Maj Gen Cross, it had become clear that "ORHA plans in reality are much more limited".[442] ORHA now appeared to intend to "do the minimum necessary to allow Iraqi ministries to function" before handing over to a "UN Security Council authorised administration after about ninety days". Given Maj Gen Cross's planned role, Mr Llewellyn suggested that developments should be monitored and views fed in as necessary through him.

1041. The same day, Mr Llewellyn also advised the IPU on the compatibility of various post-conflict activities with the rules of military occupation.[443]

1042. Mr Llewellyn explained that Security Council authorisation was not required for humanitarian assistance. The position was more complicated for "rehabilitation" and "reconstruction":

> "Rehabilitation
>
> "As I understand it, this means essential repair work, (for example to schools, hospitals, government buildings, roads). It is closely connected with basic humanitarian assistance.
>
> "… Article 55 of the Hague Regulations requires the Occupying Power to 'safeguard' the capital of public buildings etc. Repair work would be consistent with that obligation …
>
> "Reconstruction
>
> "You list under this heading matters such as reform of the judiciary, security sector and police reform, demobilisation, reform of government and its institutions, the education system, and the banking system … it might also include the building of new roads and other structures to assist the regeneration of Iraq.

---

[441] Minute Llewellyn to Bristow, 13 March 2003, 'ORHA Plans'.
[442] Minute Llewellyn to Bristow, 17 March 2003, 'ORHA Plans for the Administration of Iraq: Military Occupation'.
[443] Minute Llewellyn to IPU [junior official], 17 March 2003, 'Potential Humanitarian and Reconstruction Activities in Iraq'.

"Construction of entirely new roads and buildings may in some circumstances be permissible – where this is necessary for the relief effort or, for example for maintaining security or public order. As you know, the scope for action on the other issues … is limited. Any action going beyond these limits would require Security Council authorisation."

1043. Mr Llewellyn offered further observations on 18 March, in which he emphasised that "sweeping" institutional and personnel changes would not be permitted.[444]

1044. The FCO informed No.10 that the UK continued to make progress reconciling UK and US positions on the post-conflict role of the UN, but significant differences remained.

1045. The US accepted the need to internationalise Phase IV activity but wanted to keep the "whip hand", an approach that was "almost certainly not negotiable in the UN Security Council".

1046. The FCO advised that the US must be held to the commitments made at the Azores Summit. No Security Council authorisation would mean no wide international effort and the likelihood of a much less consensual environment in which to operate.

1047. As "best friends" of the US, the UK should continue to offer advice on what would and would not work.

1048. On 17 March, the FCO informed Sir David Manning that the UK continued "to make some good progress" in bringing together UK and US positions on the UN.[445] The US now accepted that:

- "The Phase IV reform and reconstruction task is much too big for the US/UK to go it alone. All the traditional nation-builders will be required – the IFIs, the UN, NGOs, and the big bilateral donors (eg the EU and Japan). We need wide international support to allow us an exit strategy."

- Security Council authorisation would make it easier to secure international support.

- The international community would need a new Security Council mandate to have a legal basis for a reform programme which would go beyond what was allowed by the laws of armed conflict.

---

[444] Minute Llewellyn to IPU [junior official], 18 March 2003, 'Potential Humanitarian and Reconstruction Activities in Iraq'.
[445] Letter Owen to Manning, 17 March 2003, 'Iraq: Phase IV (Day-After): US/UK Discussions on an Authorising UNSCR'.

1049. At the same time, some important differences remained. In particular, the US wanted:

- the resolution authorising Phase IV to identify the US-led civil transitional authority as the main body leading reform and reconstruction;
- the UN Special Co-ordinator to be subordinate to the Coalition military commander;
- the US to oversee the process leading to the creation of the IIA;
- the IIA to be managed closely by the Coalition rather than lightly supervised by the UN Special Co-ordinator; and
- the Coalition to continue to exercise control over IIA decisions in areas for which the IIA had been given responsibility.

1050. The FCO concluded:

"... the US want the UN Security Council to authorise them to take charge of the reform and reconstruction of Iraq. Although they accept the need to internationalise activity in Phase IV, they want to keep the whip hand.

"The US approach is almost certainly not negotiable in the UN Security Council. And the last thing we need is another prolonged and acrimonious wrangle in the Council over the details of the day after arrangements ...

"We made clear to the US last week, (and many times before that) our view on the shortcomings of their Phase IV concept. President Bush's public statement at the Azores Summit and the US/UK/Spanish vision for Iraq provide good foundations on which to build. We must keep the US to these commitments. The alternative would be grim – no Security Council authorisation would mean no wide international effort, and the likelihood of a much less consensual environment in which to operate: in short, far from a recipe for mission success.

"The next procedural step is for the US to send us their version of the draft UNSCR for Phase IV ... Meanwhile, we should continue to offer our advice, as their best friends, on what is and is not likely to work.

"The key to reconciling US and UK differences may lie in the personality of the figure identified as the UN Special Co-ordinator."

1051. The FCO did not address the implications for the UK of a failure to reconcile those differences.

1052. Ms Short advised Mr Blair of continuing shortcomings in humanitarian preparations.

1053. On 17 March, at Ms Short's request, DFID officials prepared a paper on shortcomings in humanitarian preparations and steps needed to address the situation.[446]

1054. Ms Short sent the paper to Mr Blair with the comment: "This summarises what needs to be done to improve humanitarian preparedness. Perhaps we could really focus on this next week."[447]

1055. A No.10 official advised Mr Blair that the main problems identified by DFID were:

- underfunding of humanitarian agencies;
- agencies not ready to respond effectively and lacking experience outside northern Iraq;
- the need for Coalition forces to provide humanitarian assistance until there was a permissive security environment; and
- the risk that OFF might break down.

1056. The official informed Mr Blair that DFID's proposed solutions included:

- increased funding for DFID and the MOD;
- rapid securing of a permissive security environment; and
- a resolution transferring management of OFF to the UN Secretary-General.[448]

1057. The official assessed that the DFID analysis was "probably about right". The MOD had been pressing DFID to help for some weeks, so it was useful that DFID now recognised the need to help. DFID was seconding two people to work with the US and the Cabinet Office was working to broker a deal on additional funding with the Treasury (see Section 13.1).

1058. The official recommended a meeting with Mr Brown, Mr Hoon, Mr Straw and Ms Short to discuss humanitarian issues later in the week.

1059. Mr Annan told the press on 17 March that the UN would need a Security Council mandate for some of the post-conflict activities it would have to undertake in Iraq.

1060. Mr Annan spoke to the press after a meeting of the Security Council on 17 March:

> "… if there is military action, the [Security] Council of course will have to meet to discuss what happens after all that. I think I have made it clear that regardless

---

[446] Minute Conflict and Humanitarian Affairs Department [junior official] to Private Secretary/Secretary of State [DFID], 17 March 2003, 'Iraq: Humanitarian Assistance' attaching Paper [unattributed and undated], 'Iraq: What is lacking in terms of being prepared for an effective humanitarian response and what would it take to address that?'
[447] Manuscript comment Short on Minute Conflict and Humanitarian Affairs Department [junior official] to Private Secretary/Secretary of State [DFID], 17 March 2003, 'Iraq: Humanitarian Assistance'.
[448] Minute [No.10 junior official] to Prime Minister, 17 March 2003, 'Iraq: Humanitarian Assistance: DFID Views'.

of how this current issue is resolved, the Security Council is going to have a role to play. And I think that was also implied in the communiqué that came out of the Azores. That the UN has an important role to play in the post-conflict Iraq and the Council will have to discuss that. The Council will have to give me a mandate for some of the activities that we will need to undertake."[449]

1061. Sir David Manning spoke to Dr Rice on 18 March and explained that the UK hoped to see the US draft of a post-conflict resolution.[450] He welcomed the news that Dr Rice planned to see Mr Annan in New York the following week. Sir David considered it "extremely important to emphasise our commitment to the UN's post-conflict role, as we had done at the Azores Summit".

1062. Mr Blair told Cabinet on 17 March that the US had confirmed that it would seek a mandate for post-conflict reconstruction.

1063. A specially convened Cabinet attended by Lord Goldsmith, the last before the invasion, was held at 1600 on 17 March (see Section 3.8).[451]

1064. Mr Blair told Cabinet that the US had confirmed that it "would seek a UN mandate for the post-conflict reconstruction of Iraq". Oil revenues would be administered under the UN's authority.

1065. Late on 17 March, Ms Anna Bewes, Ms Short's Principal Private Secretary, informed Mr Heywood that, subject to her deciding she could remain in government, Ms Short would like to take up Mr Blair's suggestion that she visit New York and Washington to follow up his conversations with Mr Annan and "to take forward discussions on humanitarian and reconstruction assistance with the UN, IFIs and US".[452] Ms Short would report back to Cabinet on 20 March.

1066. On 17 March, Mr Blair met Dr Barham Salih, the Patriotic Union of Kurdistan (PUK) "Prime Minister" of northern Iraq, at No.10.

1067. Section 6.4 describes Mr Blair's meeting with Mr Masoud Barzani, leader of the Kurdistan Democratic Party (KDP), and Mr Jalal Talabani, leader of the PUK, at No.10 on 19 December 2002.[453]

---

[449] *UN News Centre*, 17 March 2003, *Press Encounter with the Secretary-General at the Security Council stakeout (unofficial transcript)*.
[450] Letter Manning to McDonald, 18 March 2003, 'Iraq: Conversation with Condi Rice'.
[451] Cabinet Conclusions, 17 March 2003.
[452] Letter Bewes to Heywood, 17 March 2003, [untitled].
[453] Letter Rycroft to Sinclair, 19 December 2002, 'Iraqi Kurds: Meeting with Prime Minister, 19 December'.

1068. Mr Blair wrote to Mr Barzani and Mr Talabani on 12 March 2003 and again on 17 March in response to concerns they had raised about regional security in northern Iraq.[454] In the letter of 17 March, Mr Blair stated that he knew from the meeting in December 2002 that Mr Barzani and Mr Talabani shared the UK's "vision of an Iraq which has a genuinely representative government and where there are greater human rights for all Iraqi people, greater liberties and greater democracy".

1069. During a meeting with Mr Blair at No.10 on 17 March, Dr Salih said that it would be important to hand over quickly to the Iraqi people as much of the running of Iraq as possible, but that he did not want the UK and US military to leave early.[455]

1070. Concerns about ORHA continued to grow as ORHA staff deployed from Washington to Kuwait in the days immediately before the invasion.

1071. FCO officials expressed concern about the small number of civilians working for an organisation that was expected to be responsible for the initial post-conflict civil administration of Iraq.

1072. On his way to Kuwait, Maj Gen Cross gave Mr Blair a clear picture of the inadequate state of post-conflict plans.

1073. ORHA staff left Washington for Kuwait on 16 March.[456] The inter-agency tensions that had hampered post-conflict planning in the US were soon compounded by new logistical obstacles. Although Gen Franks had placed ORHA under the operational command of Gen McKiernan's CFLCC, when Lt Gen Garner's advance party arrived at CFLCC headquarters, there was no space available for them. Post-conflict planners in ORHA, JTF-4 and CENTCOM were soon scattered across five locations in Kuwait, the US and Qatar.

1074. Maj Gen Cross deployed to Kuwait on 18 March, travelling via London.[457]

1075. In his written statement to the Inquiry, Maj Gen Cross said that while in London he briefed Mr Blair:

> "I was as honest about the position as I could be, essentially briefing that I did not believe post-war planning was anywhere near ready. I told him that there was no clarity on what was going to be needed after the military phase of the operation, nor who would provide it. Although I was confident that we would secure a military victory I offered my view that we should not begin that campaign until we had a much more coherent post-war plan."[458]

---

[454] Letter Blair to Barzani and Talabani, 12 March 2003, [untitled]; Letter Blair to Barzani and Talabani, 17 March 2003, [untitled].
[455] Letter Rycroft to Owen, 17 March 2003, 'Northern Iraq: Prime Minister's Meeting with Salih, 17 March'.
[456] Bowen SW Jr. *Hard Lessons: The Iraq Reconstruction Experience.* U.S. Government Printing Office, 2009.
[457] Statement Cross, 2009, page 15.
[458] Statement, 2009, page 15.

1076. Maj Gen Cross told the Inquiry:

"He [Mr Blair] was engaged … So we had a very sensible conversation, and at the end of it I do remember saying, in so many words, I have no doubt at all we will win this military campaign. I do not believe that we are ready for post-war Iraq …

"He nodded and didn't say anything particularly. But I'm sure he understood what I was saying."[459]

1077. In his written statement, Maj Gen Cross explained that:

"… after all of the many briefings and conversations I had in the UK at that time, my sense was that:

- Not everyone believed that there would actually be a war; if there was to be one, then there was certainly no consensus that we (the UK) should be involved;
- There was no coherent UK, pan-Whitehall, view of what post-war Iraq should look like;
- There was serious reluctance to take on the US over their views;
- If events did unfurl differently to 'the plan' – such as it was – there was an underlying belief that the US would quickly be able to bring whatever was necessary to bear;
- There was, therefore, some seriously wishful and woolly, and un-joined up, thinking going on!"[460]

1078. Maj Gen Cross told the Inquiry he had found no single cross-Whitehall perspective on events and that it took some time to get agreement that he should go to Kuwait:

"At this stage it is very, very late in the day to be deciding whether or not we are going to be engaged in these post-war operations. So I felt very isolated is the truth."[461]

1079. Mr Straw discussed the "military feel" of ORHA with Secretary Powell on 19 March.

1080. On 14 March, Mr Ehrman had raised the need to "civilianise" ORHA with Mr Straw. There were three FCO personnel there, but only one representative of the State Department.[462] ORHA would provide the initial civilian government of Iraq and it was strongly in the UK's interests to increase the size of the civilian contingent within it. He hoped that Mr Straw would raise the issue with Secretary Powell when they next spoke.

---

[459] Public hearing, 7 December 2009, page 34.
[460] Statement, 2009, page 16.
[461] Public hearing, 7 December 2009, page 31.
[462] Minute Ehrman to Private Secretary [FCO], 14 March 2003, 'Iraq: Military Aspects and Day After'.

1081. Mr Straw raised the issue on 19 March.[463] Secretary Powell agreed with Mr Straw's view that "ORHA had a fairly military feel".

1082. The development of UK policy towards ORHA is described in Sections 9.1 and 10.1.

1083. In response to advice from officials on the global diplomatic agenda that would follow a short and successful military campaign, Mr Straw asked what would happen if there were "a long and unsuccessful war".

1084. Mr Straw's question was not put to officials and there is no indication that it was considered further.

1085. On 18 March Mr Fraser sent Mr Straw a paper on "the diplomatic agenda in the aftermath of a short and successful war in Iraq", covering the US, the EU, NATO, the wider Middle East, the UN and the global economy.[464] The paper stated that:

> "Much will depend on how the military campaign goes, the success of the post-war settlement and whether we are able to provide useable evidence to the international community that Saddam presented a real threat. **For the purposes of this paper, we assume a positive outcome on all three.**"

1086. The section on relations with the US recommended focusing on "a relatively small number of deliverables" on Iraq, the MEPP, WMD proliferation, the World Trade Organization (WTO) and climate change. On Iraq, the paper recommended:

> "We should continue to argue strongly for US agreement to a genuine UN role in the administration and reconstruction of Iraq, including an effective EU contribution … We should also seek to ensure that UK companies get a fair crack of the whip in post-conflict Iraq."

1087. On 21 March, Mr Straw asked: "What about if it is a long and unsuccessful war?"[465]

1088. Mr Straw's question was not included in the formal response to Mr Fraser's paper sent from Mr Straw's Private Office on 1 April.[466] There is no indication that it was considered further.

---

[463] Letter McDonald to Manning, 19 March 2003, 'Iraq: Foreign Secretary's Conversation with US Secretary of State, 19 March'.
[464] Minute Fraser to PS [FCO], 18 March 2003, 'Iraq: Implications for the International System' attaching Paper DSI, [undated], 'Iraq – Implications for the International System'.
[465] Manuscript comment Straw, 21 March 2003, on Minute Fraser to PS [FCO], 18 March 2003, 'Iraq: Implications for the International System'.
[466] Minute McDonald to Fraser, 1 April 2003, 'Iraq: Implications for the International System'.

1089. Asked why, given US opposition to a leading role for the UN in post-conflict Iraq, the UK did not have a plan B, Mr Straw told the Inquiry:

> "... the only plan B ... in the absence of a central role for the UN, was a central role for the Occupiers, which were the US and the UK. Those were the two alternatives. There was lots and lots of discussion with the United States system ...

> "... [I]t wasn't for the want of trying that we ended up in the position we did, but this was one of those absolute classics where the American decision making process was opaque ... you put all these things in and it just sort of flows around and one day there is a decision."[467]

1090. Mr Straw had been aware since January, when Mr Ricketts had likened the process of changing US views to "water on a stone", that it would be extremely difficult to secure US support for the UK's preferred option.

1091. It was Mr Straw's responsibility as Foreign Secretary to give due consideration to the range of options available to the UK should that effort fail. Those included making UK participation in military action conditional on a satisfactory post-conflict plan.

1092. Section 6.4 states that Mr Straw did not do so in January 2003.

1093. Nor did he address that gap between January and March.

1094. FCO guidance on Phase IV sent to all UK diplomatic posts on 19 March stated: "Providing the conditions for success exist – a legal basis for action from the UNSC and a secure environment in which to act – we would expect all the traditional nation-builders to take part."

1095. On 19 March, the FCO sent a "Core Script" on Iraq for all diplomatic posts to use at their discretion with key contacts.[468]

1096. The same text was circulated to No.10 and key departments the next day.[469] The covering letter to No.10 stated:

> "Until now we have been reluctant to discuss openly how we see Phase IV unfolding. As military action begins, we shall wish to ensure that our ideas for Phase IV – the means by which we shall deliver our 'Vision for Iraq and the Iraqi People' – are given greater prominence."

1097. The paper carried the caveat that it represented current UK thinking, not necessarily agreed Coalition policy, and would evolve as Phase III unfolded. If military

---

[467] Public hearing, 2 February 2011, pages 118-119.
[468] Telegram 150 FCO London to Abidjan (parts 1 and 2), 19 March 2003, 'Iraq: Core Script – Phase IV'.
[469] Letter Owen to Rycroft, 20 March 2003, 'Iraq: Phase IV: Core Script' attaching Paper Iraq Planning Unit, 19 March 2003, 'Iraq: Core Script – Phase IV (Post-Conflict)'.

action led to the collapse of Saddam Hussein's regime, the UK's goal would be "to transform Iraq along the lines set out in the UK's 'Vision for Iraq and the Iraqi people', launched at the Azores Summit".

1098. Once most of Iraq had been stabilised, ORHA would take on supervision of the civil administration, calling itself the International Transitional Civil Authority (ITCA): "We hope that the vast majority of the Iraqi public sector will remain in place and be able to carry on its work, albeit under ITCA's overall direction." In the first weeks, the Coalition's task would be to provide a secure environment for the delivery of humanitarian relief by UN agencies and NGOs.

1099. After "some weeks", the UN should appoint a Special Co-ordinator for Iraq and set out a mandate for the international community's presence in the country, leading to the establishment of an IIA under the "light supervision" of the Special Co-ordinator. The IIA would establish a constituent assembly along the lines of the Bonn Conference on Afghanistan to agree a constitution. The constitution would be put to a referendum and lead to the election of a "broad-based, representative government".

1100. On reconstruction:

"Providing the conditions for success exist – a legal basis for action from the UNSC and a secure environment in which to act – we would expect all the traditional nation-builders to take part. The aim will be to introduce widespread economic and political reforms, as well as improvements in the functioning of the public administration."

1101. The core script concluded:

"An important objective for HMG is to ensure a level playing field for UK companies to compete for commercial opportunities that arise in the reconstruction of Iraq."

1102. The core script made no reference to the role of the Iraqi opposition or Iraqi exiles in post-conflict arrangements.

Parliamentary debate on Iraq, 18 March 2003

1103. In his speech to the House of Commons on 18 March, Mr Blair restated the importance of bringing sustainable development, democracy, human rights and good governance to Iraq.

1104. Mr Blair did not explain how, other than by seeking a UN resolution, the UK would contribute.

1105. The motion tabled by the Government on 18 March stated that:

"... this House ... in the event of military operations requires that, on an urgent basis, the United Kingdom should seek a new Security Council resolution that would affirm Iraq's territorial integrity, ensure rapid delivery of humanitarian relief, allow for the earliest possible lifting of UN sanctions, an international reconstruction programme, and the use of all oil revenues for the benefit of the Iraqi people and endorse an appropriate post-conflict administration for Iraq, leading to a representative government which upholds human rights and the rule of law for all Iraqis ..."[470]

1106. In his speech in the House of Commons on 18 March, addressed in more detail in Section 3.8, Mr Blair called for a "larger global agenda: on poverty and sustainable development; on democracy and human rights; and on good governance of nations".[471] He added:

"That is why what happens after any conflict in Iraq is of such critical significance. Here again there is a chance to unify around the United Nations. There should be a new United Nations resolution following any conflict providing not only for humanitarian help, but for the administration and governance of Iraq. That must be done under proper UN authorisation.

...

"The UN resolution that should provide for the proper governance of Iraq should also protect totally the territorial integrity of Iraq. And this is also important: that the oil revenues, which people falsely claim that we want to seize, should be put in a trust fund for the Iraqi people administered through the UN.

...

"Let the future Government of Iraq be given the chance to begin the process of uniting the nation's disparate groups, on a democratic basis ...

...

"The process must begin on a democratic basis, respecting human rights, as, indeed, the fledgling democracy in northern Iraq – protected from Saddam for 12 years by British and American pilots in the No-Fly Zone – has done remarkably. The moment that a new Government are in place, committed to disarming Iraq of weapons of mass destruction, is the point in time when sanctions should be lifted, in their entirety for the people of Iraq."

1107. Mr Blair stated:

"I have never put the justification for action as regime change. We have to act within the terms set out in resolution 1441 – that is our legal base. But it is the reason why I say frankly that if we do act we should do so with a clear conscience and a strong heart ... Iraq is a potentially wealthy country which in 1979, the year before Saddam came to power, was richer than Portugal or Malaysia. Today it is impoverished,

---

[470] House of Commons, *Official Report*, 18 March 2003, column 760.
[471] House of Commons, *Official Report*, 18 March 2003, columns 771-772.

with 60 percent of its population dependent on food aid. Thousands of children die needlessly every year from lack of food and medicine. Four million people out of a population of just over 20 million are living in exile.

"The brutality of the repression – the death and torture camps, the barbaric prisons for political opponents … is well documented … We take our freedom for granted. But imagine what it must be like not to be able to speak or discuss or debate or even question the society you live in. To see friends and family taken away and never daring to complain. To suffer the humility [sic] of failing courage in face of pitiless terror. That is how the Iraqi people live. Leave Saddam in place, and the blunt truth is that that is how they will continue to be forced to live.

"We must face the consequences of the actions that we advocate. For those … who are opposed to this course, it means … that for the Iraqi people, whose only true hope lies in the removal of Saddam, the darkness will simply close back over."[472]

1108. In his memoir, Mr Blair stated that the "moral case for action – never absent from my psyche – provided the final part of my speech and its peroration, echoing perhaps subconsciously the Chicago speech of 1999" (see Section 1.1).[473]

1109. A small number of MPs raised post-conflict issues in the debate that followed Mr Blair's speech.

1110. In the debate that followed Mr Blair's speech, Mr Duncan Smith stated that it would be wrong not to acknowledge the consequences of military action:

"That is why the Opposition have constantly urged the Government to set out their plans for humanitarian assistance. Our view of the lack of preparedness was endorsed by the Select Committee on International Development …

"We welcome the written statement made last week by the Secretary of State for International Development, but it did not explain what is being done to improve co-ordination between the Ministry of Defence and DFID. It did not establish whether DFID would set up a mechanism to co-ordinate the UK humanitarian response. It did not set out what will replace the Oil-for-Food programme … It did not spell out DFID's plan in the event of Saddam Hussein unleashing any of his arsenal of chemical and biological weapons on his own people. Nor did it give details of how to cope with the flight of refugees … The questions need to be answered."[474]

---

[472] House of Commons, *Official Report*, 18 March 2003, columns 772-773.
[473] Blair T. *A Journey*. Hutchinson, 2010.
[474] House of Commons, *Official Report*, 18 March 2003, column 777.

1111. In response to an intervention from Mr Elfyn Llwyd (Plaid Cymru) as to why he was "so keen on going to war" if those preparations were so ill-advanced, Mr Duncan Smith stated:

"The hon. Gentleman betrays a certain ignorance. The reality is that we need to deal with Saddam Hussein regardless of those arrangements."

1112. Later in the debate, Mr Alex Salmond (Scottish National Party) asked: "Will the nation-building work? The record of the United States on nation-building has not been impressive."[475]

1113. Mr Tony Worthington (Labour) raised concerns about the scale of the challenge in Iraq:

"What bothers my constituents – it is one of the reasons why the Prime Minister fails to persuade them of the rightness of his approach – is that little or no attention is being paid to the consequences of the action that we are about to take.

…

"We are going to invade a country of Balkanesque complexity where occupying forces will be unable easily to withdraw. We are rapidly in danger of becoming piggy in the middle for every discontented ethnic or religious group in the area. There seems little doubt of speedy, initial victory, but it is worth remembering that the six-day war in the Middle East is still going strong after 35 years. This war has similar potential.

…

"We have to consider the scale of the humanitarian problem. Iraq is a huge country, the size of France. We have to think about feeding 26 million people instantly. That has to be done by the UN, not by the Office of Reconstruction and Humanitarian Assistance … I hope that the Minister will be absolutely clear in his winding-up speech whether the UN or American generals will be in control …"[476]

1114. Mr John Baron (Conservative) stated that insufficient thought had been given to the consequences of military action:

"Who and what will replace Saddam Hussein? What plans exist for humanitarian relief? We know little about that. What effect will the action have on the stability of neighbouring states?"[477]

---

[475] House of Commons, *Official Report*, 18 March 2003, column 821.
[476] House of Commons, *Official Report*, 18 March 2003, columns 832-834.
[477] House of Commons, *Official Report*, 18 March 2003, column 835.

1115. Mr Michael Ancram, Shadow Foreign Secretary, while expressing support for military action, asked Mr Straw to explain what provision had been made for humanitarian relief:

"We are told that all is in hand, but we have not yet heard what is in hand or how it will be delivered ... [I]n Yugoslavia we started but we did not finish. This time we must finish.

"We must also ensure that what replaces Saddam Hussein's brutal regime is a truly representative government, accepted by the Iraqi people and, as Kofi Annan said and the Azores meeting agreed, under the auspices of the United Nations ... If the administration are not representative – if they are not balanced – they will fail ... Above all we must preserve the territorial integrity of Iraq ..."[478]

1116. In his concluding remarks, Mr Straw stated:

"As the Prime Minister, President Bush and Prime Minister Aznar agreed in the Azores on Sunday ... a new resolution will be put before the Security Council. I hope very much that it will attract the fullest possible support ... and that the United Nations will be fully and actively involved in the reconstruction effort."

1117. In response to a question from Mr Salmond about the cost of reconstruction, Mr Straw stated:

"... Iraq is an astonishingly wealthy country. The oil is important to this extent: it has the second largest oil reserves in the Middle East. One of the other agreements clearly reached in the Azores, which must also be endorsed by a United Nations Security Council resolution, which we shall propose, is that every single cent and penny of those oil revenues are not plundered by Saddam Hussein and his friends, but used for the benefit of the Iraqi people. I am quite clear that, when that happens, the costs of reconstruction to the rest of the world will be remarkably insignificant. I can also tell the hon. Gentleman that we have already provided funds for contingency work to ensure the smooth passage of the reconstruction work."[479]

1118. In the House of Lords, concerns were raised about the potential for ethnic and political violence after Saddam Hussein's departure.

1119. In the House of Lords debate on Iraq, Lord Redesdale (Liberal Democrat) warned:

"Even with regime change, there will be no simple solution. We will not be able to install a democratic government in the short term. Looking back to the previous Gulf War, there was enormous letting of blood, settling of scores and political upheaval. That will increase ...

---

[478] House of Commons, *Official Report*, 18 March 2003, column 894.
[479] House of Commons, *Official Report*, 18 March 2003, column 899.

"We must consider the situation in the context of what has just happened in the United Nations. It could be ourselves and the Americans who have to pick up the pieces in Iraq in the short to medium term."[480]

1120. Lord Elton (Conservative) described the 'Vision for Iraq and the Iraqi People' issued at the Azores Summit as "aspirational rather than inspirational".[481] He asked how the Vision would be achieved:

"… what is to be the cost, and under what government. It took the Americans 12 years to get out of Japan after the last world war, and it took us 50 years to unite Germany. It troubles me that so little has been thought and said on this matter until so late in the programme …

"… [W]e have to remember with compassion the people of Iraq who suffered horrors under tyranny. We must ensure that they do not suffer horrors after a war due to munitions left behind or through internecine strife …"

Revised arrangements for Ministerial discussion of Iraq

1121. **Daily meetings of the "War Cabinet" began on 19 March.**

1122. **Proposals for the creation of a wider Ministerial group covering post-conflict issues were kept under review.**

1123. The first Ad Hoc Meeting on Iraq, also known as the "War Cabinet", took place at 8.30am on 19 March.[482]

1124. The Ad Hoc Meeting took place daily from 19 March to 12 April, with the exception of Sundays 30 March and 6 April, and was chaired by Mr Blair. Attendees included Mr Straw, Mr Hoon and Ms Short.

1125. The remit of the Ad Hoc Meeting was to "cover … military and other updates and the day's events", and "to focus on longer term policy decisions", although the time for that would be limited and would need to be "rationed carefully".[483]

1126. When Sir Andrew Turnbull explained the new arrangements to Mr Heywood, he proposed that:

"There might also be a case for having a weekly meeting of DOP [the Defence and Overseas Policy Committee] … perhaps convening just before Cabinet. This would provide an opportunity for wider Ministerial involvement, including on day after issues. I suggest that this is something that David Manning keeps under review."[484]

---

[480] House of Lords, *Official Report*, 18 March 2003, column 157.
[481] House of Lords, *Official Report*, 18 March 2003, columns 207-208.
[482] Minutes, 19 March 2003, Ad Hoc Meeting on Iraq.
[483] Minute Drummond to Rycroft, 19 March 2003, 'Iraq Ministerial Meeting'.
[484] Minute Turnbull to Heywood, 18 March 2003, 'Iraq'.

1127. The first meeting of the Cabinet Committee set up to oversee all aspects of the reconstruction of Iraq, the Ad Hoc Ministerial Group on Iraq Rehabilitation (AHMGIR), took place on 10 April.

1128. The creation of the AHMGIR and its role in setting the direction of UK post-conflict policy are addressed in Section 10.1.

1129. Mr Rycroft's briefing for Mr Blair before the first Ad Hoc Meeting on 19 March explained that there would be a standard agenda each day, including "Humanitarian and reconstruction".[485]

1130. Mr Blair told the meeting on 19 March that it was a priority to get a Security Council resolution for the post-conflict phase that would "bring in those who had been opposed to military action".[486] He requested a meeting with Ms Short on 21 March, on her return from discussions with Mr Annan and the US on preparations for humanitarian relief and reconstruction.

1131. At their meeting on 19 March, the Chiefs of Staff observed that the US appeared to be shifting its focus to Phase IV and that there had been "much greater US physical preparation for Phase IV than in any previous operation".[487] Adm Boyce instructed Lt Gen Reith "to report the detail of the preparations in-theatre, particularly the nature and tonnage of humanitarian aid stocks".

Mr Blair's conversation with President Bush, 19 March 2003

1132. Mr Blair and President Bush spoke at 1240 on 19 March (see Section 3.8).[488] They discussed the military plans and timetable. Mr Blair said that he had "reviewed the military plans and was confident that they would work". Post-conflict issues would be the focus of conversation when they met. A full day meeting was envisaged to cover the ground. Mr Blair suggested that the discussions might include bringing in allies who had opposed military action and co-ordinating a communications strategy.

1133. Mr Blair and President Bush discussed post-conflict issues at Camp David on 26 and 27 March, a week after the start of the invasion.

Prime Minister's Questions, 19 March 2003

1134. Asked in Parliament on 19 March about the UK's plans for post-conflict Iraq, Mr Blair explained that discussions were under way and referred to the principles set out in the Azores 'Vision for Iraq and the Iraqi People'.

---

[485] Minute Rycroft to Prime Minister, 19 March 2003, 'Iraq: 0830 Ministerial Meeting'.
[486] Minutes, 19 March 2003, Ad Hoc Meeting on Iraq.
[487] Minutes, 19 March 2003, Chiefs of Staff meeting.
[488] Letter Cannon to McDonald, 19 March 2003, 'Iraq: Prime Minister's Conversation with Bush, 19 March'.

1135. At Prime Minister's Questions on 19 March, Mr David Rendel (Liberal Democrat) asked for assurances that sufficient funds for post-conflict reconstruction would be made available quickly.[489]

1136. Mr Blair replied that the purpose of the reconstruction programme in Iraq was not, primarily, to do with the consequences of conflict, "but is actually to do with reconstructing the country after the years of Saddam Hussein and his rule". Funds had already been earmarked for the purpose and Ministers were doing all they could "to make sure that we co-ordinate with American allies and also with other UN partners to ensure that the funds are available and also that the programme is available, so that in the post-conflict situation in Iraq the people of Iraq are given the future that they need".

1137. Mr Duncan Smith observed that, when he had asked in the past about the plans for post-conflict Iraq, Mr Blair had been "quite legitimately and understandably, reluctant to give full answers because he would not have wanted to give the impression that war was inevitable".[490] Would Mr Blair now explain what plans there were "to put in place a civilian representative government in Iraq"?

1138. Mr Blair replied:

"We are in discussion now with not just the United States, but other allies and the United Nations. We want to ensure that any post-conflict authority in Iraq is endorsed and authorised by a new United Nations resolution, and I think that will be an important part of bringing the international community back together again."[491]

1139. Mr Blair referred Mr Duncan Smith to the 'Vision for Iraq and the Iraqi People'. He suggested that the principles of peace, prosperity, freedom and good government included in the Vision "will go some way toward showing that if there is a conflict and Saddam Hussein is removed, the future for the Iraqi people will be better as a result".

Security Council debate on Iraq, 19 March 2003

1140. Mr Annan told the Security Council on 19 March that, in any area under military occupation, responsibility for the welfare of the population fell to the Occupying Power.

1141. The UN would do whatever it could to help, without assuming or diminishing the responsibility of the Occupying Power.

1142. The Security Council held an open debate on Iraq on 19 March. The debate is addressed in more detail in Section 3.8.[492]

---

[489] House of Commons, *Official Report*, 19 March 2003, column 930.
[490] House of Commons, *Official Report*, 19 March 2003, column 931.
[491] House of Commons, *Official Report*, 19 March 2003, columns 931-932.
[492] UN Security Council, '4721st Meeting Wednesday 19 March 2003' (S/PV.4721).

1143. During the debate, Sir Jeremy Greenstock stated that: "Whatever the present divisions and resentments, we the Security Council, we the United Nations, have a central role to play on Iraq and on the wider issues associated with it." That included rapid delivery of humanitarian relief and the earliest possible lifting of sanctions. Sir Jeremy hoped that, "with the active contribution of the Secretary-General", rapid progress could be made "on this crucial area". Ms Short was in New York to discuss humanitarian issues and the UK had already set aside "about US$110m for immediate humanitarian provision if there is a conflict" and was likely to announce further funding.

1144. Mr Annan said that the "plight of the Iraqi people" was now his "most immediate concern". In the short term, a conflict could "make things worse – perhaps much worse". The members of the Security Council should agree to "do everything we can to mitigate this imminent disaster".

1145. Mr Annan stated that:

> "Under international law, the responsibility for protecting civilians in conflict falls on the 'belligerents'. In any area under military occupation, responsibility for the welfare of the population falls on the Occupying Power.

> "Without in any way assuming or diminishing that ultimate responsibility, we in the United Nations will do whatever we can to help."

1146. Mr Annan explained that there would be an appeal for additional funds to finance relief operations and that decisions by the Council would be needed to adjust the Oil-for-Food programme.

1147. Mr Annan concluded by expressing the hope that:

> "... the effort to relieve the sufferings of the Iraqi people and to rehabilitate their society after so much destruction may yet be the task around which the unity of the Council can be rebuilt."

1148. Mr Straw told the Inquiry that, on 19 March, Mr Annan was reported to have said he did not think there was a role for the UN in the circumstances of internationally controversial military action.[493] Mr Straw said that Mr Annan's remarks "made an extensive role for the UN doubly difficult". There had been "no prospect at that stage ... of a central role [for the UN]".

Straw/Hoon joint minute to Mr Blair

1149. Most of the issues raised at Mr Blair's meeting on 6 March, including the role of the UN, sectorisation and the nature of the UK's post-conflict contribution in Iraq, remained unresolved as the invasion began.

---

[493] Public hearing, 2 February 2011, page 117.

1150. **On 19 March, Mr Straw and Mr Hoon informed Mr Blair that:**

- **the UK would not be expected to contribute resources to anything other than security during the first phase of the US post-conflict plan (a transitional administration headed by ORHA);**
- **it would be premature to take a view on the merits of sectors for the following phase; but**
- **it would help the US and military planners to agree on the UK's medium-term contribution.**

1151. **The minute concluded with a warning that Coalition partners were thin on the ground. If the campaign did not go well, there would not be many who would be prepared or able to take part.**

1152. **Mr Straw and Mr Hoon considered only the UK's military presence in Iraq. They made no reference to the civilian contribution.**

1153. **Sir Kevin Tebbit expressed concern about the transition from a primarily military effort to longer-term civilian-led reconstruction. It would be necessary to work hard to avoid dependence on the Armed Forces to carry out civilian tasks.**

1154. Mr Straw and Mr Hoon sent Mr Blair a joint minute on the UK military contribution to post-conflict Iraq on 19 March.[494]

1155. The draft was subject to "intensive consultations" at official level in the MOD and the FCO.[495]

1156. In the FCO, Mr Ricketts sent the draft to Mr Straw's Private Office with the comment:

"This is a clear note on a crucial issue. If the Secretary of State [Mr Straw] could OK it (I showed him a slightly earlier draft this morning) it can go to No.10 tonight, for discussion at the PM's meeting at 0830 on 20 March."[496]

1157. In the MOD, the draft was cleared by Adm Boyce and Sir Kevin Tebbit.

1158. Sir Kevin commented:

"In terms of our military capacity, with an eye to the aftermath, it would clearly be preferable to confine ourselves to SE Iraq and not bite off more than we can chew. I accept, however, that we should be prepared, initially, for our forces to be fairly

---

[494] Minute Straw and Hoon to Prime Minister, 19 March 2003, 'Iraq: UK Military Contribution to post-conflict Iraq'.
[495] Minute Chilcott to Private Secretary [FCO], [undated], 'Iraq: The UK's Military Contribution to Post-Conflict Iraq'.
[496] Manuscript comment Ricketts to Private Secretary [FCO], [undated], on Minute Chilcott to Private Secretary [FCO], [undated], 'Iraq: The UK's Military Contribution to Post-Conflict Iraq'.

widely dispersed across Iraq, depending on how Phase III goes, because without successful Phase III, Phase IV becomes harder, if not academic. The trick will be to be able to regroup in a smaller area of SE Iraq once hostilities are ended.

"I also agree that we should be clear about our medium/long-term scale of military commitment. While we are putting all we can into the war effort, we should plan ahead to stay broadly within … [*Strategic Defence Review* guidelines].[497]

"What concerns me most is the process of transiting from a primarily military effort to the civil-led longer-term humanitarian and reconstruction phase. Recent history does not offer too much encouragement and we shall have to work hard to avoid 'dependence culture' on the armed forces to do things which should be for civil departments – initially through aid, subsequently through Iraqi own efforts. The politics of the issue do, I believe, point in the same direction. To meet the PM's wish for us to play an exemplary role, we shall need to remember that memories of the UK in the region from the 1920s are not all positive, and we should make clear our desire to hand over and withdraw on the <u>right</u> basis as early as we can."[498]

1159. In their joint minute, Mr Straw and Mr Hoon warned that some issues "could confront us as early as next week" and invited agreement to five propositions:

"(a) The maximum size of task that UK forces would contribute to in the early days should not exceed our overall military capability. A focus in the South-East of Iraq would be reasonable.

(b) The UK contribution to such a task in advance of a Security Council resolution would be limited to the facilitation of humanitarian assistance and a secure environment and the elimination of WMD.

(c) We therefore need to agree urgently with the US a realistic authorising Security Council resolution for post-conflict Iraq.

(d) We should agree urgently a plan with the US to help us find military partners to enable us to draw down and, in due course, design an exit strategy.

(e) In broad terms the MOD will need to draw down its scale of effort to nearer a third of its commitment by the autumn."[499]

---

[497] It is not clear whether Sir Kevin Tebbit referred to the *Strategic Defence Review* or the Defence Planning Assumptions. The MOD has been unable to provide a version of Sir Kevin Tebbit's manuscript note including the missing words.
[498] Manuscript comment Tebbit on Email DCMC CRISIS 04-S to CDS/PSO-S, 19 March 2003, 'Joint Defence and Foreign Secretaries Minute to PM on "Sectors"'.
[499] Minute Straw and Hoon to Prime Minister, 19 March 2003, 'Iraq: UK Military Contribution to post-conflict Iraq'.

1160. Mr Straw and Mr Hoon gave little detail of what UK forces would be required to do immediately after the invasion:

"Much will depend on how the campaign develops, but in the first few weeks we should expect Coalition forces to be spread across Iraq. The expectation is that UK forces will end up in southern Iraq, loosely centred on Basra. However, we should be prepared for elements of our forces to be dispersed fairly widely across Iraq …

"US military planning continues to be fluid. But it envisages Coalition forces re-deploying into a more tailored security framework as soon as the situation permits. The military task will be to facilitate a secure environment (including law and order, deterring adventurism and a variety of military-technical tasks) to enable immediate humanitarian relief to be conducted. To help UK forces win hearts and minds, HMT have allocated them £30m for humanitarian purposes in the first month as well as £10m for quick win projects. (Clare [Short] has allocated £20m for UN agencies' preparations and earmarked another £60m from DFID's contingency reserve for humanitarian operations. But this is a drop in the ocean; in the worse case, if the Oil-for-Food programme ground to a halt, Iraq could need as much as a billion dollars a month for humanitarian aid.)

"The expectation is that UK forces would be responsible for a task focused on Basra and other key military objectives in the South-East of Iraq, which could include 20 percent of the Iraqi population. This task is broadly proportionate to the size of the UK's contribution to overall Coalition land forces …

"In parallel, and under the overall military command, the US plan to bring in a transitional administration[500] to co-ordinate immediate civil relief and humanitarian assistance. The transitional administration is making plans for allocating its limited resources, including provision of public sector salaries, on a nation wide, Coalition basis. There is no expectation that the UK would be asked to contribute any resources to anything other than security. So there is no suggestion that the UK would be left to foot the bill for the civil administration or the costs of humanitarian relief and reconstruction in any area."

1161. Mr Straw and Mr Hoon reported that US planning remained "sensibly flexible" once the initial phase was over and "a major part of Iraq has been stabilised". It advised that US planning:

"… recognises that parts of Iraq will be more permissive than others and that security could well be provided through something other than sectors. It would be premature now to take a view on the merits of sectors for this stage. We are well placed to influence US thinking with a number of military officers and officials embedded within their military headquarters and in ITCA. **It would be helpful for**

---

[500] A footnote explained: "The Office of Reconstruction and Humanitarian Assistance (ORHA) becomes the transitional administration once it is established inside Iraq."

them, and for military planners generally, to agree what our scale of effort should be in our medium-term contribution to Iraq."

1162. Mr Straw and Mr Hoon advised that it would be necessary to reduce the UK military contribution "to nearer a third by no later than the autumn in order to avoid long-term damage to the Armed Forces" and to remain within current defence planning assumptions: "If Ministers wanted us to, we would need decisions now so that we would be able to recommend what would have to give elsewhere." Scaling down to nearer a third would limit the UK contribution thereafter to "a maximum of around one brigade, a two-star headquarters and possibly a contribution to higher level command and control". They recommended telling the US now, for planning purposes, that this was the upper limit of the UK contribution.

1163. Mr Straw and Mr Hoon also recorded that the ARRC featured in current CENTCOM planning as a multinational headquarters that could play a role in post-conflict Iraq, but would be the subject of a separate paper (see Section 9.1).

1164. Mr Straw and Mr Hoon ended with a section on "**Setting the conditions for success**". The conditions in which UK forces operated needed to be conducive to success. There needed to be a resolution authorising international activity in the post-conflict period and: "We should also let the US know the key importance of internationalising the security arrangements now so that we can reduce our commitment as set out above. And we would expect US support in building a wider Coalition to operate alongside our forces, allow us to draw down and eventually to provide us with an exit strategy."

1165. Mr Straw and Mr Hoon concluded:

"We should be realistic about the limited prospects of our finding any genuine military capability to help us take this task on. New … Coalition partners are thin on the ground and, if the post-conflict phase does not go well, there will not be many nations who will be prepared or able to take part.

"And finally, we shall need to return to this issue once we are clear how the campaign is developing and look at our wider contribution in the round."

1166. **The Cabinet Office took a different position on whether it would be "premature" to take a view on the merits of sectors.**

1167. Before the joint minute from Mr Straw and Mr Hoon reached No.10, Mr Drummond advised Mr Rycroft that "we need Ministers to decide on sectors". The joint minute and the question of sectors should be on the agenda for the Ad Hoc Meeting on Iraq (the "War Cabinet") on 20 March, with Ms Short given the chance to comment on the minute on her return from the US on 21 March.[501]

---

[501] Minute Drummond to Rycroft, 19 March 2003, 'Iraq Ministerial Meeting'.

1168. Mr Drummond suggested that Ministers would want to agree the proposals in the joint minute:

"… provided they are satisfied that:

- UK Forces will be capable of providing security for an area around Basra including about 20 percent of Iraq's population.

- How long will we have this responsibility, and what is the exit strategy (benign security environment created, UK forces replaced by others). Will we be able to limit 'our area' to say Basra by the autumn, when we want to withdraw two-thirds of our troops?

- That the assertion that the transitional administration will handle civil administration including humanitarian reconstruction issues is correct: This is clearly the plan, but it must be doubtful that ORHA will have the capacity, and therefore the troops on the ground may be called on to help. The UK certainly doesn't have civilian capacity to help govern 20 percent of Iraq."

1169. The joint minute was not discussed at the Ad Hoc Meeting on Iraq at 10am on 20 March, where Mr Blair stated that decisions on the minute were needed at the next meeting on 21 March.[502]

1170. Mr Rycroft showed the Straw/Hoon joint minute on the UK military contribution to post-conflict Iraq to Mr Blair on 20 March. Mr Rycroft commented:

"For discussion at 1500 on Friday [21 March]. Do you agree? Key points to fix are: size of our sector, length of time of commitment, exit strategy, proper UN authorisation."[503]

1171. On the eve of the invasion, there remained considerable uncertainty about the three phase model for post-conflict Iraq.

1172. In the absence of UN authorisation for post-conflict activity or agreement on a UN role, the model, as understood by the UK, remained as much aspiration as plan.

1173. Asked by the Inquiry whether, on the eve of the invasion, there had been a reasonably clear understanding of the UK's military, political and diplomatic objectives for Phase IV, Mr Chilcott replied:

"Yes, I think the UK view of it was well understood within the UK Government, and I have no reason to think it wasn't well understood in the UK military as well, which was that we were working on broadly this three-phase model in our minds that we would have a period of occupation, where we would be governed by, as

[502] Minutes, 20 March 2003, Ad Hoc Meeting on Iraq.
[503] Manuscript comment Rycroft to Prime Minister, 20 March 2003, on Minute Straw and Hoon to Prime Minister, 19 March 2003, 'Iraq: UK Military Contribution to post-conflict Iraq'.

I said, the Geneva Conventions and the Hague Regulations, where we would be responsible for the welfare of the people. And our main concern at that stage would be establishing a secure environment and ensuring that humanitarian relief was able to get through to those that needed it.

"But we wanted that period to be as short as possible, after which we would move to some interim administration authorised by the UN Security Council.

"It was clear, I think, on the eve of the invasion that we weren't going to have a UN-run interim administration, but an interim administration authorised by the Security Council was going to be good enough for us. And that would begin the process of reform and reconstruction in Iraq and, at the same time, we would have the UN involved in a political process in parallel that would lead to some kind of convention or conference that would enable a new constitution to emerge and elections on the basis of the new constitution, whereupon with a new Iraqi Government, we could hand over power completely to the new Iraqi Government. And that coalition security forces would be needed for as long as the new Iraqi Government wanted them."[504]

The invasion

1174. The transition from conflict (Phase III) to post-conflict (Phase IV) military operations began immediately Coalition troops started to occupy Iraqi territory.

1175. When that transition began the Government had not taken firm decisions on the nature or duration of the UK's military commitment in post-conflict Iraq or on the extent of the UK AOR. There had been no systematic analysis of the UK's military or civilian capacity to fulfil its likely obligations in the South in a range of circumstances, including:

- **in the prolonged absence of an authorising resolution;**
- **in the absence of additional Coalition partners;**
- **in a hostile security environment with low levels of Iraqi consent; and**
- **over different timescales, in particular the medium and long term.**

1176. Each of those issues had been identified as a potential risk to UK strategic objectives in Iraq, but no detailed contingency plans or preparations were in place to mitigate those risks.

1177. Ministers, officials and the military continued to assume that:

- **there would be early agreement on a post-conflict resolution;**
- **levels of consent would rise steadily across most of Iraq; and**

---

[504] Public hearing, 8 December 2009, pages 33-35.

- **despite the scale of the undertaking, the international community would succeed in realising the Azores vision for the social, political and economic transformation of Iraq.**

1178. Above all, it was assumed that the US, even without a convincing post-conflict plan, could act as guarantor of the UK's objectives in Iraq.

1179. Those assumptions shaped continuing discussions about the nature, duration and extent of the UK's post-conflict military and civilian deployment.

1180. Two days after the start of the invasion Mr Blair sought further advice from officials on the size of any UK sector, the duration of the UK commitment and the exit strategy.

1181. The invasion of Iraq began overnight on 19/20 March 2003. Military operations during the invasion are described in Section 8.

1182. Adm Boyce issued the Execute Directive, the order to Lt Gen Reith to implement Op TELIC, on 18 March.[505]

1183. Lt Gen Reith was directed to "assume the UK Phase IV AO will be centred on Basra". In line with the military plan approved by Mr Blair on 14 March, the Directive set clear limits on the expansion of the UK AO during the conflict phase of military occupations. It stated that, to "assist the Coalition in a timely and successful Phase III and to help in shaping Phase IV conditions in the UK AO", Lt Gen Reith should exploit no further north than an east-west line running 90km south of al-Kut, ending at a point 50km north-east of al-Amara.

1184. The Directive also stated that it was Adm Boyce's "current intent ... that the UK should aim to draw down its deployed force to medium scale within four months of commencing offensive operations".

1185. Mr Hoon placed a document setting out the UK's Military Campaign Objectives, approved by Lord Goldsmith, in the Library of the House of Commons on 20 March (see Section 8).[506]

1186. The Execute Directive did not refer explicitly to the Military Campaign Objectives, but was consistent with them.

---

[505] Minute CDS to CJO, 18 March 2003, 'Op TELIC: Authorisation for Military Operations in Iraq' attaching Paper CDS, 'Chief of Defence Staff Execute Directive to the Joint Commander for Operation TELIC (Phases 3 and 4)'.
[506] House of Commons, *Official Report*, 20 March 2003, column 1087.

1187. The Military Campaign Objectives defined the overall objective for the military campaign as:

> "… to create the conditions in which Iraq disarms in accordance with its obligations under UNSCRs and remains so disarmed in the long term".[507]

1188. In aiming to achieve the objective as swiftly as possible, the military was required to make "every effort … to minimise civilian casualties and damage to essential economic infrastructure, and to minimise and address adverse humanitarian consequences".

1189. On post-conflict issues, the objectives stated that the UK would "work with the United Nations to lift sanctions affecting the supply of humanitarian and reconstruction goods, and to enable Iraq's own resources, including oil, to be available to meet the needs of the Iraqi people", and "help create conditions for a future, stable and law-abiding government of Iraq".

1190. The document stated that the "immediate military priorities" for the Coalition in the wake of hostilities were to:

> "a. provide for the security of friendly forces;
>
> b. contribute to the creation of a secure environment so that normal life can be restored;
>
> c. work in support of humanitarian organisations to mitigate the consequences of hostilities and, in the absence of such civilian humanitarian capacity, provide relief where it is needed;
>
> d. work with UNMOVIC/IAEA to rid Iraq of its weapons of mass destruction and their means of delivery;
>
> e. facilitate remedial action where environmental damage has occurred;
>
> f. enable the reconstruction and recommissioning of essential infrastructure for the political and economic development of Iraq, and the immediate benefit of the Iraqi people; and
>
> g. lay plans for the reform of Iraq's security forces."

1191. The end state for Iraq remained as defined in Mr Straw's Written Ministerial Statement of 7 January (see Section 6.4).

1192. In his Address to the Nation on 20 March (see Section 3.8), Mr Blair stated:

> "Removing Saddam will be a blessing to the Iraqi people. Four million Iraqis are in exile. 60 percent of the population dependent on food aid. Thousands of children die every year through malnutrition and disease. Hundreds of thousands have been driven from their homes or murdered.

---

[507] Iraq: Military Campaign Objectives, 18 March 2003.

"I hope the Iraqi people hear this message. We are with you. Our enemy is not you, but your barbarous rulers.

"Our commitment to the post-Saddam humanitarian effort will be total. We shall help Iraq move towards democracy. And put the money from Iraqi oil in a UN trust fund so that it benefits Iraq and no-one else."[508]

The role of the UN

1193. Ms Short set out to Mr Annan the need for a central UN role in humanitarian and reconstruction work.

1194. Mr Annan emphasised the need to have clarity on US thinking for UN planning to proceed.

1195. Ms Short visited New York and Washington on 19 and 20 March for talks with the UN, US, World Bank and IMF.

1196. In New York, Ms Short underlined to Mr Annan and senior UN officials "the political, legal and practical necessity for a central UN role in humanitarian and reconstruction work, and the strong contribution the UK would make to this".[509] Mr Annan agreed and emphasised the need for clarity on US thinking so planning could proceed.

1197. In Washington, Ms Short emphasised to senior officials in USAID, the NSC and the State Department the need for early agreement on a resolution to extend OFF.[510] She also raised the issue of an "omnibus" resolution on post-conflict administration. It was "practically and politically" important to the UK that the UN play a central role in the administration of post-Saddam Hussein Iraq.

1198. At the IMF and World Bank, Ms Short was informed that both institutions were well advanced with preparatory work and ready to engage in Iraq as soon as conditions allowed.[511] Ms Short explained that a resolution on OFF would be followed by a resolution to establish an interim authority with the necessary legitimacy to open the door to IMF and World Bank engagement and allow the comprehensive restructuring of Iraq's economy to begin.

1199. How the overall cost of reconstruction would be met remained unclear.

1200. Ms Short informed the Treasury that reconstruction costs would need to be considered in the longer term, after the completion of an IFI-led needs assessment in Iraq.

---

[508] The National Archives, 20 March 2003, *Prime Minister's Address to the Nation*.

[509] Telegram 501 UKMIS New York to FCO London, 21 March 2003, 'Iraq Humanitarian/Reconstruction: Clare Short's Visit to New York'.

[510] Telegram 370 Washington to FCO London, 21 March 2003, 'US: Iraq: Ms Short's Visit'.

[511] Telegram 25 UKDel IMF/IBRD Washington to FCO London, 24 March 2003, 'IMF/World Bank: Iraq: Visit of Secretary of State for International Development'.

1201. On 21 March, Ms Short explained to Mr Boateng that reconstruction costs would need to be considered in the longer term, "once the post-conflict situation is clearer and we have an IFI-led needs assessment".[512] The aim should be "to have most of the bill paid from the proceeds of sales of Iraqi oil and support from the IFIs".

1202. The time taken to complete the UN/World Bank Joint Needs Assessment (JNA) for Iraq and the implications for UK planning and Iraq's post-conflict reconstruction are addressed in Section 10.1.

1203. On 21 March, Mr Cannon sent Mr Blair a background note for the Ministerial meeting on post-conflict issues scheduled for that afternoon.[513] Mr Cannon summarised the Straw/Hoon position on the scale of the UK's medium-term military effort:

- that the US be told now that drawdown of the UK military effort to around one-third by the autumn represented the upper limit of the UK contribution;
- that the UK would seek partners for Phase IV, but the MOD and FCO were not optimistic about the prospects for success; and
- that the US planned an Iraq-wide transitional administration and "the possibility of our taking over civil administration in a 'British sector' has fallen away".

1204. Mr Cannon attached an FCO paper on areas of agreement and disagreement with the US on a post-conflict resolution. He explained that:

"The Americans want the Coalition to set the IIA up: we think it would have more legitimacy with the UN playing a lead role. The Americans have just shown us a draft SCR enshrining their ideas: we doubt that it will run in the Security Council. The attached FCO paper sets out where we agree and disagree with the Americans: to close the gap it recommends initially that the Foreign Secretary write to Colin Powell … and if necessary you talk through the basic principles with President Bush."

1205. Mr Cannon also reported that problems with DFID/MOD co-operation on humanitarian operations "appear to be falling away".

1206. Post-conflict co-operation between DFID and the MOD, including reports of friction between military and DFID personnel in the UK AO, is addressed in Section 10.1.

1207. After the Ministerial meeting on post-conflict issues on 21 March, Mr Rycroft informed the FCO and the MOD that Mr Blair agreed to the Straw/Hoon recommendations, subject to further urgent advice on the size of any UK sector, the duration of the UK commitment and the exit strategy.[514] Mr Rycroft's letter was copied to the Treasury, DFID, the Cabinet Office, SIS and Sir Andrew Turnbull.

---

[512] Letter Short to Boateng, 21 March 2003, 'Iraq Humanitarian Funding: Reserve Claim'.
[513] Minute Cannon to Prime Minister, 21 March 2003 [wrongly dated 20 March 2003], 'Iraq: Post-Conflict Issues'.
[514] Minute Rycroft to McDonald and Watkins, 21 March 2003, 'Iraq: UK Military Contribution to Post-Conflict Iraq'.

1208. Joint FCO/MOD advice followed on 25 March.

1209. At the Ad Hoc Meeting on Iraq on 22 March, Mr Blair requested advice from Mr Straw on the UK's approach to reconstruction "and associated conferences".[515]

1210. Mr Blair discussed the need for a UN "badge" for post-conflict activity with President Bush on 22 March. He suggested that there should be two separate resolutions: one on OFF, which should proceed quickly; and a second on post-conflict administration to follow.

1211. In a telephone call on 22 March, Mr Blair raised the UN's role with President Bush.[516] Mr Blair said that it was essential to get a UN "badge" for post-conflict efforts and that, while the Coalition did not want to hand over the results of its efforts to the UN, a Security Council resolution on post-conflict administration would help the Coalition get access to UN funding, including from the IFIs.

1212. Mr Blair proposed that different parts of the draft resolution should proceed on different timescales; a resolution on OFF should move quickly, with one covering administration after the conflict to follow.

1213. On 23 March, Mr Blair reassured Ministers that UK and US positions on the role of the UN were not far apart. He believed the US was misreading the implications of UN authorisation.

1214. On 23 March, Mr Blair told the Ad Hoc Meeting on Iraq that, on the draft resolution, "British and American positions were not so far apart".[517] He believed that the US was misreading the implications of what UN authorisation meant and added: "It was more a matter of timing than substance."

1215. At the UN, Mr Annan told Sir Jeremy Greenstock that he would not want to see an arrangement "subjugating UN activity to Coalition activity".

1216. Mr Annan also made it clear, in public, that during any occupation it was the Occupying Power that was responsible for the welfare of the people. Without detracting from those responsibilities, the UN would do whatever it could to help the Iraqi population.

1217. Sir Jeremy Greenstock discussed post-conflict Iraq with Mr Annan on 24 March, in advance of a meeting between Mr Annan and Dr Rice later in the day.[518] Sir Jeremy told Mr Annan that he "assumed that the UN would not want to run Iraq nor its security sector". Mr Annan told him that "Coalition respect for Iraqi sovereignty, territorial integrity

---

[515] Minutes, 19 March 2003, Ad Hoc Meeting on Iraq.
[516] Letter Cannon to McDonald, 22 March 2003, 'Iraq: Prime Minister's Conversation with Bush, 22 March: Post-Conflict Issues'.
[517] Minutes, 23 March 2003, Ad Hoc Meeting on Iraq.
[518] Telegram 526 UKMIS New York to FCO London, 25 March 2003, 'Iraq Phase IV: UN Dynamics'.

and political independence would be a precondition for a UN role" and that he "would not wish to see any arrangement subjugating UN activity to Coalition activity".

1218. After meeting Mr Annan, Sir Jeremy spoke to Mr John Negroponte, US Ambassador to the UN, who observed that the focus within the Security Council on "no legitimisation of Coalition military action" might make it impossible to secure its authorisation.[519] Sir Jeremy reminded him that without a resolution there would be no IFI or other international funding for reconstruction and it would be "hard to drum up troop contributors to permit an exit strategy for US/UK forces".

1219. Mr Annan told the press:

> "… the proposal before the [Security] Council is we would want to resume our work as soon as possible. And whichever authority is seen in charge at the end of the hostilities, we will work with them. We don't know what – if it is Iraqis, if it's somebody else – we will need to find a way of working, but we will be working for the Security Council, in accordance with Security Council resolutions covering the Oil-for-Food …

> "… I have made it clear in my discussion with the Council and publicly, that in times of war, it is the belligerents who are responsible for the welfare and safety of the people. I've also indicated that, in any situation under occupation, it is the Occupying Power that has responsibility for the welfare of the people. Without detracting from those responsibilities, the UN will do whatever it can to help the Iraqi population."[520]

1220. Sir Jeremy Greenstock told the Inquiry that Mr Annan managed the tension within the UN between a Secretariat "full of resentment" that the UN had been "bypassed" in the decision to go to war, and Mr Annan's own view and that of some others, that the UN should not be "absent from its responsibilities" in post-conflict Iraq.[521] Sir Jeremy commented that the Secretariat was "in quite an angry mode", but "got down to the planning work in quite a responsible way".[522]

MOD update on Phase IV planning

1221. Lt Gen Reith warned the Chiefs of Staff on 21 March that there were already signs that pre-conflict assumptions about the nature and duration of the conflict had been wrong, with implications for Phase IV planning.

1222. Lt Gen Reith advised that the Coalition "must be prepared" for high, medium and low levels of consent.

---

[519] Telegram 526 UKMIS New York to FCO London, 25 March 2003, 'Iraq Phase IV: UN Dynamics'.
[520] UN News Centre, 24 March 2003, *Remarks by the Secretary-General upon arrival at Headquarters (unofficial transcript)*.
[521] Public hearing, 15 December 2009, pages 8-9.
[522] Public hearing, 15 December 2009, page 21.

1223. Lt Gen Reith produced an update on Phase IV planning for the Chiefs of Staff on 21 March.[523] He warned that Phase IV delivery remained subject to "uncertain US dynamics at the pol/mil [politico-military] level". US planning continued, but was "primarily bottom-up", and CFLCC was still seeking guidance on key issues including governance, payment of salaries and "regeneration" of the military.

1224. Lt Gen Reith advised that there were already signs that previous assumptions about the nature and duration of the conflict might have been wrong. Phase IV(a) now looked likely to be far shorter than previously expected, while the arrival of other Coalition partners and NGOs looked like taking longer. All this added pressure. The paper listed a number of issues needing resolution, pointing out that some were already well known. They included: the system of governance under Phase IV(b); how to approach SSR; provision of salaries to Iraqis; and how to engage with the Iraqi military and judiciary.

1225. On "military realities", Lt Gen Reith stated that: "The Coalition must be prepared for high/medium/low consent and variations thereof in time and space, including asymmetric attack and intra-factional violence." "How to deal with non-compliance" was listed as one of the "key issues requiring resolution".

1226. In a second paper, Lt Gen Reith updated the Chiefs of Staff on humanitarian assistance.[524] USAID had led the development of the CMOC/DART structure to provide immediate relief as Coalition forces advanced. UK forces would draw primarily on the US DART, but had developed national contingency plans in case demand outstripped supply, including funding for QIPs and DFID-funded medical supplies.

1227. On 24 March, Treasury officials advised Mr Brown that:

- **The Chiefs of Staff considered a medium scale deployment of 10,000-15,000 to be the most the UK could sustain in the medium term without lasting damage to the UK's forces.**

- **It was unlikely, except in the most benign post-conflict scenario, that the maximum envisaged UK force would be able to deal with all the challenges on its own.**

- **No significant Coalition partners were likely to come forward without an appropriate UN resolution.**

- **Treasury and MOD views differed on the wisdom of taking on a two-star command without "the necessary guarantees".**

---

[523] Minute Reith to COSSEC, 21 March 2003, 'Phase IV Planning – Taking Stock'.
[524] Minute Reith to PSO/CDS, 21 March 2003, 'Humanitarian Assistance for Iraq'.

1228. Mr Dodds sent advice on the Straw/Hoon joint minute to Mr Brown on
24 March.[525]

1229. Mr Dodds reported that the picture looked "rather different to that presented in
the correspondence":

> "The Defence Chiefs say that a 'medium size' deployment (ie 10,000-15,000) is the
> most we could sustain in the medium term without lasting damage to our forces.
> MOD officials tell us they had intended the submission [the joint minute] to pose the
> question 'do you want us to do as much as we can (ie this medium size deployment)
> or as little as we can get away with (ie less)?' The question is not posed in that form
> and hence is not answered. **The choice is essentially political, but it is essential
> to note that the cost of a deployment on this medium scale is about £1bn
> a year.**"

1230. Mr Dodds reported that the concept of sectors in US military planning had
moved on:

> "The plan now appears to have four 'two-star commands (ie divisions)' outside of
> Baghdad, focusing more flexibly on the tasks that need to be done, rather than being
> tied down to specific narrow locations.

> "The MOD ambition is to have a UK-led 'two-star command'. However:

> - the scale of military effort needed will depend on the permissiveness of the
>   environment … and the relationship between the military and civil powers;
> - it is unlikely, except in the most benign scenario, that the maximum
>   envisaged size of UK force would be able to deal with all the challenges …
>   on its own;
> - without an appropriate UN resolution to legitimise the aftermath, MOD
>   believe it unlikely that any significant Coalition partners will come forward to
>   share our burden …"

1231. Mr Dodds commented that, in that context, Mr Blair's questions of 21 March about
the size of the UK sector, the duration of the UK commitment and the exit strategy were
"excellent questions", but could not be answered easily. More relevant was:

> "… how to ensure a permissive environment as quickly as possible, and how to
> maximise the number of militarily-capable Coalition partners to share our burden.

> "And given past experience, while going all out for a suitable resolution, it would be
> wise to ask what our Plan B would be if we couldn't get one. MOD currently don't
> have an answer to that!"

---

[525] Minute Dodds to Chancellor, 24 March 2003, 'Iraq: UK Military Contribution to Post-Conflict Iraq'.

1232. Mr Dodds recommended that the UK:

- should continue to emphasise to the US that a further UN resolution was vital;
- should stress to the US that UK military capability was stretched to the limit; and
- should not be too ready to take on a two-star command in the aftermath without "the necessary guarantees". It carried the risk of costs "we cannot afford both militarily and financially". This was an issue on which the Treasury disagreed with the MOD. Mr Brown's input "could be invaluable".

1233. Mr Dodds advised that Mr Brown might have a view on "whether to press for a smaller commitment than the £1bn 'medium' scale deployment that MOD/FCO have offered".

1234. Mr Dodds explained that the Treasury was feeding those thoughts into FCO papers for Mr Blair's meeting with President Bush at Camp David on 26 and 27 March. He concluded that it would be useful if Mr Brown could "make an input" at Cabinet (see Section 10.1).

Draft UK post-conflict objectives

1235. The FCO response to Mr Blair's request of 21 March for further advice on the narrow question of the UK military contribution to post-conflict Iraq continued the pre-invasion pattern of analysis and advice that separated military from civilian concerns.

1236. The FCO advice, which reflected Treasury concerns and had been agreed with the MOD, warned of the substantial risk that, without a resolution, the UK "would become trapped" into a higher level of commitment than planned.

1237. The FCO advised that it would not be possible to decide on the size of a UK military sector before establishing the nature of the task and the scale of the Coalition resources available.

1238. The FCO did not address the relationship between the size of a military sector and the wider contingent liabilities, including the impact on potential UK civilian responsibility for administration and reconstruction.

1239. On 25 March, the FCO sent its response to Mr Blair's request for further advice on the size of any UK sector, the duration of the UK commitment and the exit strategy.[526]

1240. The FCO advice, agreed with the MOD and copied to DFID and the Treasury, emphasised the risk of "serious long term damage to the Armed Forces" if the UK commitment was not reduced to a third of existing levels by the autumn, but stated that it

---

[526] Letter Owen to Rycroft, 25 March 2003, 'Iraq: UK Military Contribution to Post-Conflict Iraq'.

was not possible to answer Mr Blair's questions definitively. Reducing troop numbers by the autumn and devising an exit strategy depended on a number of factors:

- the outcome of the military campaign;
- the attitudes of the US and the Iraqi people;
- negotiation of an authorising resolution;
- the ability to build a broader Coalition; and
- success in achieving Coalition objectives for Iraq.

1241. The FCO warned:

"There is therefore a substantial risk that if we fail to obtain a UNSCR, we will not be able to build the Coalition under overall US leadership. We would become trapped into maintaining a higher level of commitment for longer, with all that this would mean in terms of cost and for the long-term health of the Armed Forces."

1242. On the size of the UK sector, the FCO expanded on the advice in the Straw/Hoon joint minute:

"… we need to determine in the first instance the nature of the military task, and make an assessment of the UK and other Coalition resources likely to be available. Only then can we answer the question about geographical coverage. If the task is to promote a secure environment, the size of the area will depend on the number of troops that are available and the attitude of the Iraqis. The expectation is that Basra, and the area around it, linked to existing administrative boundaries, should be the focus. Plans need to remain flexible until we are able to define the task and confirm the attitude of the population. US thinking appears to have moved away from too early definition of 'sectors' for exactly the reasons explained above."

1243. The Inquiry has seen no response from No.10.

1244. The Cabinet Office sent draft UK post-conflict objectives to senior officials in the FCO, the MOD and DFID on 25 March.

1245. The draft objectives were to be shown to Ministers before being submitted for formal approval.

1246. The objectives restated a familiar list of broad UK aspirations for the future of Iraq that had been under discussion since late 2002.

1247. There is no indication whether the objectives were ever adopted formally.

1248. Mr Bowen sent draft 'British Post-Conflict Objectives' to senior officials in the FCO, the MOD and DFID on 25 March.[527] The draft incorporated earlier comments from some departments.

1249. The draft stated that it remained the UK's wish to see Iraq:

"… become a stable, united and law abiding state, within its present borders, co-operating with the international community, no longer posing a threat to its neighbours or to international security, abiding by all its international obligations and providing effective and representative government to its own people."

It added:

"Our objective is to create conditions for a future Iraqi government which will act to make this aspiration a reality. We will work with the Iraqi people, the UN and other international organisations, and the wider international community to this end."

1250. The draft also stated:

"British forces will continue to contribute, for no longer than is necessary at a sustainable level, to the US-led Coalition military presence in the interests of promoting a secure environment in Iraq …

"We have made plans with our international partners to assist the Iraqi people in the process of transition. With others, we will assist in the return to full Iraqi sovereignty …

"With others, we will help revive the Iraqi economy and assist reform by:

a. working with the UN to manage Iraq's oil revenues in order to achieve the maximum benefit for the Iraqi people in an accountable and transparent manner;

b. supporting an international programme for the reconstruction and repair of Iraq's infrastructure …;

c. fostering economic reform …;

d. agreeing a comprehensive financial framework of transitional support for Iraq …;

e. helping reform Iraq's public administration …;

f. supporting the observance of human rights, and legal and judicial reform …;

g. helping Iraq generate reformed and accountable security forces acting in accordance with international human rights standards."

---

[527] Letter Bowen to Chaplin, 25 March 2003, 'Iraq: Post Conflict Objectives' attaching Paper [draft], 25 March 2003, 'Iraq: British Post-Conflict Objectives'.

1251. Mr Bowen suggested that officials should show the draft paper to their Ministers, if they had not already done so: "We will then see the outcome of the Prime Ministerial visit to Camp David and consider formal submission early next week."

1252. There is no indication whether the objectives were ever adopted formally.

1253. Officials expressed concern about the absence of an Iraqi perspective in UK and Coalition planning.

1254. Mr Lee expressed concern to MOD colleagues about the apparent absence of any Iraqi perspective in the objective-setting process:

> "I get no sense in anything we're doing of an Iraqi input. (State Dept in Washington have had a large 'Future of Iraq' project going for some time addressing exactly this point – but it seems to have dropped off the table)."[528]

1255. Dr Robert Wilson, an FCO Research Analyst, commented on the failure to engage with Iraqis as the invasion began in a minute to Mr Chilcott on 27 March:

> "A point that is being made with increasing force by members of the Iraqi community is that the Coalition is failing to engage them in the process of their liberation …

> "Several people have made the point to me that we need to get Iraqis visibly involved on the side of the Coalition, and in whatever way is possible establish a sense of partnership between the Coalition and the Iraqi population. If we do not do so, we may find that we are dealing not with a jubilant population but one that says, 'OK, you've got rid of Saddam. Now what?' …

> "The sense of a lack of partnership is unfortunately strengthened by our own focus on the humanitarian side – handing out food, bringing in 'aid'. Iraqis are proud and don't feel they need aid or handouts …"[529]

1256. The Inquiry has seen no response either to Mr Lee or to Dr Wilson.

1257. The first detailed military planning papers for Phase IV were presented to the Chiefs of Staff on 25 March.

1258. On 25 March, Mr Watkins reported to No.10 that: "Southern Iraq is effectively under Coalition control although significant resistance remains in Basra."[530]

1259. The same day, Lt Gen Reith presented the Chiefs of Staff with a draft Operational Concept and draft planning guidance for Phase IV.

---

[528] Minute Lee to Policy Director, 24 March 2003, 'Iraq: Camp David Meeting'.
[529] Minute Wilson to Chilcott, 27 March 2003, 'Failure to Engage with the Iraqis'.
[530] Letter Watkins to Rycroft, 25 March 2003, 'Prime Minister's visit to Washington. Iraq: Review of the Military Situation'.

1260. Discussion of the two documents and the emergence of the UK AOR in southern Iraq are addressed in Section 8.

Mr Blair's meeting with President Bush, Camp David, 26 and 27 March 2003

1261. In advance of the meeting between Mr Blair and President Bush at Camp David on 26 and 27 March, Mr Straw's Private Office sent Mr Rycroft a negotiating brief for what was to become resolution 1483, the resolution defining the roles of the UN and the Coalition in post-conflict Iraq.[531]

1262. The negotiating brief, prepared by the IPU, described what was known about the "first few weeks" after the combat phases of the military campaign:

"Immediately after the conflict, the Coalition will be in control of Iraq.

"As soon as it is safe to do so, Jay Garner and his Office of Reconstruction and Humanitarian Assistance (ORHA) will arrive behind the military and become a transitional administration. Their aim will be to work with the existing Iraqi public administration, so far as possible. Garner will then take forward the reconstruction process. His people will be inserted into the top of the Iraqi ministries, with senior US officials being assigned to each ministry as 'shadow ministers' …

"ORHA is understaffed and began preparing for its task only a few weeks ago. There are now some ten or so UK secondees embedded in it. Garner would like to be out of Iraq within 90-120 days. Whether ORHA will be able to get any reform programme started in that time is moot. This period is likely to be dominated by humanitarian and security concerns."

1263. The IPU advised that ORHA and the Coalition might enjoy a "brief honeymoon", but not if the Coalition seemed set on administering Iraq for more than a brief period. It was therefore necessary to put in place interim arrangements for post-conflict administration that would be accepted by the Iraqi people and the Arab and Islamic world.

1264. A resolution was required to authorise those interim arrangements, and to provide a legal basis for "reconstruction and reform":

"Without a UNSCR, other countries, international organisations, the IFIs, UN agencies and NGOs will be comparatively limited in what they can do … That would leave US/UK with no viable exit strategy from Iraq and a huge bill."

---

[531] Letter Owen to Rycroft, 25 March 2003, 'Prime Minister's visit to Washington: Iraq: UN Security Council Resolution on Phase IV' attaching Paper Iraq Planning Unit, 25 March 2003, 'Iraq: Phase IV: Authorising UNSCR'.

1265. The IPU stated that the task for Camp David was to build on five areas where there was already agreement between the UK and US:

- The Coalition, through ORHA, would be responsible for the administration of Iraq for the first few weeks.
- The UN should not be asked to run Iraq.
- The objective should be Security Council authorisation or endorsement for an international presence that would include the UN.
- Coalition, not UN, troops would provide security on the ground.
- As soon as possible, Iraq should govern itself.

1266. The differences between the UK and US positions remained significant. The IPU explained that the US approach amounted to:

"… asking the UNSC to endorse Coalition military control over Iraq's transitional administration, its representative institutions and its revenues until such time as a fully-fledged Iraqi government is ready to take over. It would marginalise the role of a UN Special Co-ordinator. These ideas are a non-starter for the Security Council, would be denounced by the Iraqis and the wider Arab/Islamic world, and would not provide the stability needed to develop the new Iraq."

1267. The brief stated that there was "still some distance to go if we are to agree a way forward to avoid an inchoate start to Phase IV".

1268. The IPU set out a number of "propositions" which it hoped Mr Blair and President Bush could agree. Those propositions and the progress of the negotiations on resolution 1483 are addressed in Section 9.1.

1269. Mr Straw sent Mr Blair an FCO paper on Phase IV issues in advance of Camp David.[532] Mr Straw said that he hoped Mr Blair would counter any tendency by President Bush to conclude that the UN had failed over Iraq:

"… the US will need to go on working through the UN, both to authorise the post-conflict work in Iraq so that a wide range of countries can join the peacekeeping and reconstruction effort, and to provide an exit strategy for the US/UK and because the UN itself and its agencies have important expertise to offer".

1270. The FCO paper on Phase IV issues stated that, in addition to US agreement on a UN resolution, the UK needed US agreement on a number of other important political, humanitarian and economic issues, including:

- A Baghdad conference. The US was still thinking of a Coalition conference with the UN in a supporting role. That was the wrong way round for international acceptability.

---

[532] Minute Straw to Blair, 25 March 2003, 'Camp David: Post-Iraq Policies'.

- <u>The role of the IIA</u>. An early statement of intent to hand over power to an IIA while helping the Iraqi people to build a democratic future "should go down well". The UN Special Co-ordinator should have veto power over the IIA's decisions.

- <u>Humanitarian issues</u>. UK and US efforts were substantial: "we should play them up in the media".

- <u>Economic issues</u>. After several wars and 12 years of sanctions, Iraq's oil revenues alone would not meet the "very heavy" cost of reconstruction, particularly in the short term. "We need to share the burden with other developed countries … But contacts with them tell us they will make **their contribution conditional on there being an authorising UNSC resolution for Phase IV**." The World Bank would need to prepare a rigorous needs assessment, but that too would probably need UN cover.[533]

1271. On the UK's bilateral effort, the paper stated that Ms Short was considering where the UK might help with the longer-term contribution to "reform and reconstruction". SSR and reform of the public administration were two areas where the UK had a comparative advantage. UK public finances were "tight". If the UK was to keep armed forces in Iraq, "the scope for a major effort on reform and reconstruction will be limited".

1272. The paper stated that the UK's Armed Forces were fully stretched and would need to scale down to about a third of current levels by the autumn. President Bush would have similar concerns:

> "So **we both need an exit strategy**. The key to that will be to get new Coalition partners, **which needs an authorising UNSCR**. US/UK officials are working up a lobbying strategy. But we must be realistic. The number of countries who have real capability to offer is small."

1273. Efforts to secure additional Coalition partners are addressed in Sections 8 and 10.1.

1274. **Mr Blair discussed post-conflict issues with President Bush at Camp David on 26 and 27 March.**

1275. **Mr Blair recommended postponing the debate about what sort of post-conflict resolution was required until victory was secured and the UK and US were in a position of strength.**

1276. Mr Blair and President Bush met at Camp David on 26 and 27 March. The meeting is addressed in more detail in Section 9.1.

1277. At dinner on the first evening, Mr Blair told President Bush that he did not want his visit to Camp David to focus primarily on a UN resolution to deal with post-conflict

---

[533] Paper FCO, 25 March 2003, 'Iraq: Phase IV Issues'.

Iraq. The question about what sort of resolution was needed for the administration and reconstruction of Iraq should be parked. Mr Blair said that:

> "The time to debate this would come when we had secured victory, and were in a position of strength."[534]

1278. Mr Blair raised Phase IV issues with President Bush the next day. They discussed the need to push for a quick agreement on the resolution to continue the OFF programme, and for a separate resolution that would free up financial and troop contributions from other nations, secure World Bank and IMF involvement and put reconstruction on the right footing.[535]

1279. Mr Rycroft recorded that Mr Blair had identified the main issue as whether the UN formed the future Iraqi government or whether the Coalition did so with UN endorsement, but had said that "it was not helpful to expose this distinction yet".

1280. After returning to the UK, Mr Blair told the Ad Hoc Meeting on Iraq that in relation to the post-conflict administration of Iraq, "quiet and effective diplomacy" was the tactic to achieve a new resolution.[536]

1281. The process leading to the adoption of resolution 1483 in May 2003 is addressed in Section 9.1.

1282. Ms Short told DFID officials on 26 March that Mr Blair had given her responsibility for reconstruction in Iraq.

1283. Ms Short held a meeting with key DFID officials on 26 March at which she stated: "The important thing was for the world to know that a resolution for a UN mandate was coming."[537]

1284. At the meeting, officials reported a sense in Whitehall that a resolution on reconstruction might not be achieved. Ms Short made clear that "significant engagement" on reconstruction would need a UN resolution. The Attorney General had been clear at Mr Blair's meeting that morning that, under the Geneva and Hague Conventions, no changes could be made to the administration by the Occupying Powers, except to keep systems working for civilians. Ms Short asked her office to request that the Attorney General's advice be committed to paper.

1285. Ms Short reported that "the Prime Minister had given her responsibility for reconstruction in Iraq". She stated that her role should be underpinned by a Cabinet Office Committee chaired by Mr Chakrabarti, adding: "This area was our lead in

---

[534] Letter Manning to McDonald, 28 March 2003, 'Prime Minister's Meeting with President Bush at Camp David: Dinner on 26 March'.
[535] Letter Rycroft to McDonald, 27 March 2003, 'Prime Minister's Meeting with President Bush at Camp David: Iraq Phase IV'.
[536] Minutes, 28 March 2003, Ad Hoc Meeting on Iraq.
[537] Minute Warren to Fernie, 26 March 2003, 'Iraq: Meeting with Secretary of State'.

Whitehall and we needed to ensure that this was recognised." Mr Chakrabarti reported that he had already spoken to Sir Andrew Turnbull and Mr O'Donnell about the issue.

1286. Ministerial responsibility for post-conflict reconstruction is addressed in Section 10.1.

1287. DFID produced its first substantive paper on post-conflict reconstruction at the end of March.

1288. DFID described the paper to the Cabinet Office as a "work-in-progress" that set out some "preliminary ideas on reconstruction planning".

1289. DFID officials told Ms Short that it would be useful to show No.10 and the Cabinet Office that DFID was not only the natural lead on the UK's overall approach to rebuilding Iraq, but also had the human resources and experience to dedicate to it.

1290. On 27 March, Mr Fernie sent a draft paper on reconstruction planning to Ms Short.[538] She had seen an earlier draft on 20 March. Officials were:

"… now thinking how to take this forward as part of a more comprehensive DFID-led process across Whitehall, looking at the whole range of international activities needed to help Iraq recover from conflict, sanctions and years of misrule".

1291. Mr Fernie explained that the draft had been revised to take account of comments from Ms Short on:

"… getting the multilateral system working to support Iraqi institutions, the importance of sustainable debt and reparations strategy, and focusing on using and developing Iraqi talent rather than bringing in too many international consultants".

1292. Comments had also been received from the FCO, The Treasury and the Cabinet Office. Those centred on:

- "What we would do if there were no UNSCR authorising reconstruction." Mr Fernie advised that, with the Attorney General's advice now in writing, "we should stick to our position that without an SCR the UK can only support humanitarian relief and basic civil administration reform to ensure public security".
- "Setting reconstruction planning within a wider post-conflict context." Mr Fernie advised that a broader, more strategic paper would be needed.

---

[538] Minute Fernie to Private Secretary/Secretary of State [DFID], 27 March 2003, 'Iraq: Iraq Reconstruction Planning' attaching Paper DFID, 27 March 2003, 'Iraq – Reconstruction Planning: Objectives and Approach'.

1293. Mr Fernie explained that the paper would be tabled at a Cabinet Office meeting the next day. He added:

> "We will discuss the process for the more comprehensive paper tomorrow afternoon – it will be useful to show to No.10 and the Cabinet Office that DFID is not only the natural lead on this approach but also has the human resources and experience to dedicate to it."

1294. On 28 March, Mr Fernie sent the draft to the Cabinet Office as a "work-in-progress" setting out some "preliminary ideas on reconstruction planning".[539] Mr Fernie explained that the paper benefited from comments offered by FCO, MOD and Cabinet Office officials at a meeting chaired by DFID, which had raised wider issues about how reconstruction fitted with the UK's overall approach to rebuilding Iraq and securing international consensus behind that approach. DFID's view was that the UK needed to "start working now on a broader strategy which binds together the many bits of work going on across Whitehall".

1295. The development of DFID's approach to post-conflict reconstruction is addressed in Section 10.1.

1296. The extent of the work still to be done on planning and preparing for the range of post-conflict tasks was apparent from a list of issues prepared by the Cabinet Office on 28 March for consideration by the new Ad Hoc Ministerial Group on Iraq Rehabilitation (AHMGIR).

1297. On 28 March, Mr Drummond sent Mr Bowen a list of issues for consideration by the AHMGIR, including, for some items, an assessment of current plans:

- humanitarian assistance;
- role of ORHA: "competence and UK links with and involvement in";
- wider UN role on reconstruction;
- political process/fate of the Ba'ath Party: "Outline plan exists, not agreed with US";
- economy: "Good contacts with US";
- reconstruction of infrastructure: "Depends on damage. Beginning now. Disagreements with US on role of Iraqis";
- SSR: "Ideas offered to US, but no plan";
- public administration reform and service delivery: "No plan yet?";
- commercial opportunities: "Needs wider policy agreement with US";
- legal issues: "Some contact with US. No firm agreement. No plan";

---

[539] Letter Fernie to Drummond, 28 March 2003, 'Iraq Reconstruction Planning' attaching Paper DFID, 27 March 2003, 'Iraq – Reconstruction Planning: Objectives and Approach'.

- disarmament: "No agreement with US on extent of involvement of UN inspectors"; and

- re-integrating Iraq into the international community.[540]

Witness comments

1298. A number of witnesses to the Inquiry commented on the efficacy of the UK's post-conflict planning and preparation. They identified a range of factors shaping the UK approach, including:

- **the unpredictability of the situation on the ground;**

- **the breakdown in US inter-agency co-ordination;**

- **limits to UK influence on the US;**

- **optimism bias, including the hope that conflict could be averted and that any problems that arose after the conflict could be resolved;**

- **separate departmental priorities;**

- **the absence of a senior figure responsible for post-conflict planning and preparation;**

- **inadequate planning machinery;**

- **insufficient analysis of risk; and**

- **a focus on preparations for humanitarian relief at the expense of wider post-conflict issues.**

1299. The extent to which those factors, and others, shaped UK planning and preparation is addressed in the conclusion to this Section.

1300. Witnesses told the Inquiry that it would not have been possible to predict the exact circumstances on the ground after an invasion, and that advice prepared in government did not predict the circumstances that did arise.

1301. In his memoir, Mr Blair wrote:

"... the aftermath was more bloody, more awful, more terrifying than anyone could have imagined. The perils we anticipated did not materialise. The peril we didn't materialised with a ferocity and evil that even now shocks the senses."[541]

1302. Mr Blair added:

"There has never been, there never will be, a campaign of any nature that does not turn out differently from what is anticipated.

---

[540] Minute Drummond to Bowen, 28 March 2003, 'Iraq: Reconstruction Agenda'.
[541] Blair T. *A Journey*. Hutchinson, 2010.

"… We were told there would be a functioning Iraqi civil service. There wasn't. We were told there would be a humanitarian disaster. It was averted. We were warned that Saddam might fight to the bitter end. He collapsed.

"We were told that Shia/Sunni sectarian violence would be a factor. Actually, to begin with it was much less than feared …"

1303. Mr Blair told the Inquiry "there was nothing that was putting us on notice about the problem we ended up with".[542] Planning took place, but:

"The trouble was we were planning (a) on an assumption that Iraq had a functioning bureaucracy and civil service, which in the end it didn't, and (b) our focus really was on humanitarian, environmental and the possibility of use of chemical/biological weapons and so on. I mean, I would say there was a significant amount of planning that went on, unfortunately directed at the wrong things."[543]

1304. Mr Straw told the Inquiry:

"… the consequences of war are unpredictable … it's an inherently chaotic process. So the possibilities of aftermath of military action are greater than they are for many other human actions … What was extremely difficult to predict was the exact circumstances on the ground … [I]f you look at the detailed planning documents we produced and the State Department produced in early 2003 both we and the Americans were predicting all the things that then happened. What we weren't able to predict was the exact mix of these things. I mean … yes, there was a prediction about the possibility of terrorism. We didn't predict its extent …"[544]

1305. Lt Gen Reith, who had extensive experience of working with humanitarian agencies and NGOs during the 1999 Kosovo campaign,[545] told the Inquiry that, on arrival in Iraq, he had been surprised by the state of the country's infrastructure:

"All of our intelligence assets were looking at the Iraqi forces. What they weren't looking at was the infrastructure, and … when we arrived in there, I was amazed … that it was completely broken …"[546]

1306. Sir John Sawers, British Ambassador to Egypt before becoming the Prime Minister's Special Representative on Iraq in mid-2003, told the Inquiry:

"Very few observers actually highlighted the scale of the violence that we could face. I think about the only person in my recollection who got it right was President

---

[542] Public hearing, 21 January 2011, page 27.
[543] Public hearing, 21 January 2011, pages 122-123.
[544] Public hearing, 2 February 2011, pages 121-122.
[545] Fourteenth Report from the Defence Committee, Session 1999-2000, *Lessons of Kosovo*, HC 347-I, paragraph 222.
[546] Public hearing, 15 January 2010, page 45.

Mubarak[547] who warned of unleashing 100 Bin Ladens. The combination of an undefeated Ba'athist regime melting away and coming back as a gradually more potent insurgency combined with the attractiveness of Iraq as a means for international terrorists under the umbrella of Al Qaida to have a go at the Americans, combined with Shia extremists supported from Iran, this combination creating the level of violence, the onslaught of violence that I have mentioned, this was not thought through by any observer.

"I think had we known the scale of violence, it might well have led to second thoughts about the entire project. And we could certainly have mitigated some aspects of it had we had a clearer appreciation of it in advance …

"But I don't think it is reasonable to assume that we should have predicted all this violence in advance, because very few people did actually do that. That wasn't the anticipated scenario that we were stepping into and it was an unprecedented scenario that we found ourselves in."[548]

1307. Lord Boyce told the Inquiry that a number of assumptions had been made about the state of Iraq after the invasion, which, with the benefit of hindsight, were "probably optimistic, to say the least".[549] There had been:

"… an expectation that we would find more of a structure which was ready to step into place than actually turned out to be the case in May [2003], even before the de-Ba'athification and the disbandment of the Iraqi army …"

1308. Mr Lee told the Inquiry that the Government had identified many of the problems that emerged later, but failed to analyse the risk they represented.

1309. Mr Lee commented on the UK's failure to build on its own analytical platform:

"I think there is a valid criticism that on the one hand we had identified an awful lot of these problems, and had identified quite explicitly, as I recall, the question of the aftermath as a crucial element of the campaign overall, and the whole concept of a successful campaign and winning including a successful outcome to that …

"But we didn't actually carry that through … into an analysis at the time of what the post-conflict plans actually were on the level of uncertainty that remained, and therefore the level of risk that remained, in the plan on those issues …"[550]

---

[547] Mr Hosni Mubarak, President of Egypt from 1981 to 2011.
[548] Public hearing, 16 December 2009, pages 81-82.
[549] Public hearing, 27 January 2011, page 68.
[550] Private hearing, 22 June 2010, pages 46-47.

1310. Mr Lee told the Inquiry that the question of whether the post-conflict period carried too much uncertainty to risk embarking on the conflict had never been asked in those terms:

"… however much you intellectually or analytically describe the wider campaign, psychologically the focus is on the conflict itself. A certain amount of … optimism, hope, creeps in in respect of the aftermath. That will be sorted out, and there are too many things unknown there to do too much more planning. Therefore you go ahead and hope that you've got enough of a structure which can then be supplemented by ad hoc arrangements afterwards, and therefore it will all be sorted out.

"I think, as we know, in practice it turned out to be a lot more difficult than we thought at the time."

1311. Several witnesses highlighted the breakdown in US inter-agency co-ordination as a significant obstacle to effective planning.

1312. Mr Straw described it as "the fundamental problem".

1313. In his statement, Mr Blair wrote:

"There was interaction at every level between the UK and the US system. Some of that, as evidence to the Inquiry makes clear, was unsatisfactory, due mainly to inter-agency issues in the US. It is correct also that the shift from the State Department to the Department of Defense in January 2003 made a difference. The shortcomings of the US planning have been well documented and accepted. Our own planning was complicated both by the difficulties of being fully inserted into the US system and the fact that the planning was taking place against the backdrop of fast-changing political and military plans."[551]

1314. Mr Straw went further in directly attributing difficulties with UK planning to the situation in the US. He told the Inquiry that "a significant number of the problems we faced … could have been avoided by better planning and co-ordination, above all in Washington".[552] The UK "got caught up in internal administration politics", but that "didn't become completely clear until after the invasion".[553]

1315. Mr Straw concluded:

"… the fundamental problem … was not a lack of planning in London … [but] the breakdown in co-ordination in Washington between the Department of Defense and the State Department".[554]

---

[551] Statement, 14 January 2011, page 14.
[552] Public hearing, 21 January 2010, page 15.
[553] Public hearing, 8 February 2010, page 104.
[554] Public hearing, 8 February 2010, page 107.

1316. Sir Peter Ricketts told the Inquiry that the state of US planning had been "one of a number of concerns as the peace process ended and the conflict loomed".[555] He added:

"I do think, if the careful State Department work had been allowed to feed through into operational planning for the post-conflict phase, that would have been more successful. I think it would have been easier for us to dock with it, and the overall effect on the ground would … have been a stronger operation from earlier on."[556]

1317. A number of witnesses to the Inquiry commented on the difficulty the UK faced in trying to influence the US.

1318. Sir David Manning told the Inquiry that Mr Blair:

"… was insistent throughout that a lot of thought needed to be given to what happened on what has been called 'the morning after'. He raised that with the President. This was raised by, I think, most British interlocutors with their American interlocutors.

"I don't think I could say to you that that was a condition in the end when the UN route failed for military action, but it was certainly something that was important to him."[557]

1319. Sir David also told the Inquiry:

"The Prime Minister throughout is very clear that there has to be a clever plan afterwards, the UN have to be involved, and you can't do this simply as a military operation.

"The second thing he is absolutely insistent … [on] is the Middle East peace process.

"So I think he is very clear that it isn't just a military operation, but getting the American machine to respond to this proves to be enormously difficult."[558]

1320. Sir David added:

"I don't know whether the Prime Minister discussed a blueprint for Iraq – I don't think he did, I don't recall it – with the President. He might have done in his private conversations. But insisting that they had to think about what came next, insisting on the importance of having the UN in there, he was very clear about that. And I suppose the fact that the Americans were doing a lot of planning for Iraq was a reassurance to him."[559]

---

[555] Public hearing, 1 December 2009, pages 59-60.
[556] Public hearing, 1 December 2009, page 92.
[557] Public hearing, 30 November 2009, page 41.
[558] Private hearing, 24 June 2010, pages 42-43.
[559] Private hearing, 24 June 2010, page 58.

1321. Asked at what stage the UK would have needed to exert its influence in Washington for post-conflict planning to have been more effective, Sir Christopher Meyer told the Inquiry: "if the Americans had their act together in September/October [2002], and we did likewise, then you could have done it".[560]

1322. Mr Chaplin stated that Ministers "constantly stressed to their American opposite numbers the need for proper aftermath planning", but the US was "obviously going to be the greater partner of this enterprise and we were going to be the junior partner".[561]

1323. Mr Chaplin added:

"The message … we constantly got from the American side, particularly those that were frustrated with the lack of planning, as they saw it, was, 'Please, could we make this clearer at a higher level in the US administration?' Colin Powell didn't need to be convinced, but President Bush and Donald Rumsfeld did."

1324. Mr Chaplin explained that the UK response had been "to keep feeding in the ideas of what we thought was the sensible way ahead on the issues" and to provide "people to sit alongside the US opposite numbers, in particular, General Tim Cross".

1325. In his statement to the Inquiry, Maj Gen Cross suggested that UK efforts to exert influence on US thinking achieved little: "I got no sense of UK pressure on the US; no 'demands' for clarity over the intended 'End State' or the planning to achieve it."[562]

1326. Maj Gen Cross provided an example of his own difficulties in influencing US thinking during his time in Washington in February and March 2003.[563] At a lunch with Secretary Rumsfeld and others, he had challenged the assumption that the overthrow of Saddam Hussein would be greeted with such relief in Iraq that the US would be able to move on quickly:

"I argued that this was, perhaps, fine as a Plan 'A' – but what was desperately needed was a Plan 'B' and a Plan 'C', and a recognition that what would probably emerge would be an amalgam of the last two. It was made clear that my views were not welcomed."

1327. Mr Chilcott told the Inquiry: "we could have any number of variations of our own plan, but what mattered was influencing the American plan, and that was where our main effort was concentrated".[564]

1328. FCO witnesses spoke of the difficulty of working for a negotiated settlement while preparing for conflict.

---

[560] Public hearing, 26 November 2009, page 96.
[561] Public hearing, 1 December 2009, pages 58-59.
[562] Statement, 2009, page 10.
[563] Statement, 2009, page 14.
[564] Public hearing, 8 December 2009, page 19.

1329. Asked by the Inquiry whether the FCO had been slow to recognise the inevitability of conflict and whether, as a result, it had been too late to make full preparations for what was going to happen, Lord Jay responded:

"I think there are two points there … There is, was it our judgment that, whatever happened, the Americans were likely to go to war in Iraq and, secondly, if they did, was it inevitable that we should join them?

"On the first point … I would not put it as inevitable. I think I would say it was … certainly towards the end of 2002 quite difficult to see the scenario in which the Americans would conclude that they would not try to seek Saddam Hussein by force. I don't think it was inevitable. It was always possible that Saddam Hussein could go … That would clearly have been preferable.

"I would never say that conflict was inevitable. I would say that, from the end of 2002 onwards, it was probable. There was a separate question as to whether Britain would take part in that. When one looks back on it now, with all that has been said since then, the inevitability of Britain taking part seems much greater than it did at the time. It did not seem clear at the end of 2002 and the beginning of 2003 … it did not seem clear to us in the Foreign Office, that a British participation in the conflict was inevitable. There was an option not to take part in it."[565]

1330. Lord Jay suggested that it was "an extremely difficult thing to do in the minds of the same people, to try to prevent something happening and to prepare for that failure and I don't think we had the structures available to us to do that".

1331. Sir Peter Ricketts told the Inquiry:

"All along, right through to the eve of the second resolution, I thought it was possible, perhaps not likely, but possible, that Saddam Hussein would choose, rather than face overwhelming military force, to co-operate and comply. So it was never for sure that the UK would be part of military operations or even really that military operations were inevitable. I always thought there was another option."[566]

1332. On the role of the UN, Sir Peter stated:

"In Kosovo, we had had a UN-led transitional administration, building on existing structures there. In Afghanistan, we had had a very strong UN presence led by Mr Brahimi,[567] supporting a Loya Jirga, and then a domestic process, and so we approached it in the same frame of mind, that the UN had real experience in dealing

---

[565] Public hearing, 30 June 2010, pages 69-71.
[566] Public hearing, 1 December 2009, page 25.
[567] Mr Lakhdar Brahimi, Special Representative of the UN Secretary-General for Afghanistan from 2001 to 2004 and Chairman of the Bonn Conference.

with post-conflict situations, a unique legitimacy in doing so and that was our preferred route."[568]

1333. Sir Peter added that the FCO was:

"… very doubtful indeed about the neo-con assumption that international forces would be welcomed as liberators and … that somehow very quickly Iraqi political life would resume and the occupying forces would not carry these responsibilities … We warned Ministers that this would be a long period of post-conflict work for the international community, which is why we then said that we thought it was important that, if possible, the UN should take on the lead."[569]

1334. Mr Chilcott commented that, in the IPU:

"… because it was contingency planning, because right up until the last moment we didn't know for sure that we were going to be involved in the military action, that maybe psychologically had an effect on us …"[570]

1335. Witnesses commented on the responsibilities and priorities of different departments.

1336. Ms Short stated that DFID "got down to planning against all eventualities within the difficult atmosphere we had in Whitehall about communications".[571] The principal planning failure had been the UK and US military's failure to plan for "catastrophic success".[572] Rapid military success followed by ethnic conflict had been foreseen as a risk, but the military "didn't prepare for their Geneva Convention obligations" of keeping order and providing basic humanitarian relief.[573]

1337. Sir Suma Chakrabarti saw the FCO as the natural lead department for post-conflict issues.[574] He commented that the FCO was "more focused on the second resolution than planning for the day after … There was a vision for Iraq that I think the Foreign Office put together … So there was thinking going on, but, yes, second resolution was the main issue in their minds, no doubt."

1338. Lord Jay told the Inquiry that "the FCO and DFID were not on the same page in the lead-up to the war … because … there were differences between our Ministers on the desirability and the likelihood of war … What we were faced with … was not something which DFID had been geared up to do or Clare Short found comfortable."[575]

---

[568] Public hearing, 1 December 2009, page 30.
[569] Public hearing, 1 December 2009, page 65.
[570] Public hearing, 8 December 2009, pages 47-48.
[571] Public hearing, 2 February 2010, page 48.
[572] Public hearing, 2 February 2010, page 46.
[573] Public hearing, 2 February 2010, page 47.
[574] Public hearing, 8 December 2009, page 55.
[575] Public hearing, 30 June 2010, page 72.

1339. Sir Kevin Tebbit told the Inquiry that "the so-called comprehensive concept did exist in Whitehall, the idea that we needed to have integrated planning to bring all the instruments of government to bear on the issue … and we certainly had transparency", but argued that this was very difficult to achieve quickly across different departmental cultures.[576]

1340. Sir Kevin added: "I always felt that we could not quite get other departments to share the urgency that we felt in the Ministry of Defence in terms of their own planning with us."

1341. Lord Boyce told the Inquiry that the MOD did not consider that it was its role to take the lead on post-conflict issues: "It was something that possibly should have been done by the Foreign Office or even DFID."[577]

1342. Witnesses offered differing views on whether the Government's performance would have been improved by the appointment of a senior individual responsible for directing post-conflict planning or the earlier introduction of better planning machinery.

1343. Asked by the Inquiry whether UK planning could have been better, Mr Blair stated:

> "I do accept that, yes … If we were sitting down today, now, if we were in a situation of nation-building again, I think there are changes in our approach that certainly should be done …
>
> "I think … the real issue is what you focus on less than the structure; in other words, you could say that we should have had one Minister focusing on the pre-planning, but I would debate that actually, but you may conclude that … The core of the problem was the focus of what that planning was."[578]

1344. Lord Turnbull shared Mr Blair's view that the absence of Ministerial oversight was not necessarily the "real issue".[579] Asked about the absence of an individual or body with overall responsibility for planning, he argued that, although there was no "single controlling mind" and co-ordination should have been better, this was "not material to the outcome".

1345. Sir Suma Chakrabarti took a different view. He told the Inquiry:

> "… it would have been better to have had the IPU earlier, firstly, and, secondly, probably a Minister, preferably of Cabinet rank … who was … the overlord Minister for this, either in the Cabinet Office or in the Foreign Office … because this was a

---

[576] Public hearing, 3 December 2009, pages 116-117.
[577] Public hearing, 27 January 2008, page 68.
[578] Public hearing, 21 January 2011, pages 130-131.
[579] Public hearing, 25 January 2011, pages 55-56.

top priority for the British Government and various trade-offs had to be made and someone had to make them on a day-to-day basis for the Prime Minister."[580]

1346. Mr Chilcott warned against being "dazzled" by the IPU's late creation: "a lot of the work that the IPU was able to bring together in a more intense atmosphere had been going on for some time".[581] But he did accept that the IPU could have been set up sooner:

"... one of the lessons is obviously you can't begin this sort of thinking too early, and although we did begin serious thinking about the day after in the preceding October ... we could have created the IPU earlier. We could have had a greater sense of the reality of what we were doing."[582]

1347. A number of witnesses commented on the Government's focus on humanitarian preparations at the expense of other post-conflict issues.

1348. In his statement to the Inquiry, Mr Blair wrote:

"The over-riding concern was the humanitarian fall-out from conflict, together with the potential damage, from firing oil wells to the environment and WMD attacks."[583]

1349. Mr Straw told the Inquiry:

"... we had anticipated the problem of a humanitarian crisis sufficiently well that, on the whole, we were able to avoid that, which was good. What we had not anticipated was the extent of the inefficacy of ORHA ..."[584]

1350. Lord Turnbull told the Inquiry that, although the UK prepared for the worst case on the humanitarian front, it failed to anticipate the collapse of civil order: "The real problem was security and we probably spent too much time on humanitarian ... if we didn't establish security, nothing else counted for anything."[585]

1351. Similarly, Lord Boyce stated:

"First of all, we recognised there could very well be a humanitarian problem ... and a lot of our focus was I think at the humanitarian level rather than the governance of the country, in other words, picking up the point about law and order and so forth ...

"I think that we probably took too narrow a view about what might be required in the aftermath in terms of the governance aspects of life."[586]

---

[580] Public hearing, 8 December 2009, page 56.
[581] Public hearing, 8 December 2009, pages 17-18.
[582] Public hearing, 8 December 2009, pages 47-48.
[583] Statement, 14 January 2011, page 13.
[584] Public hearing, 8 February 2010, page 111.
[585] Public hearing, 13 January 2010, page 39.
[586] Public hearing, 27 January 2011, pages 67-68.

1352. Witnesses identified a number of lessons, including the need to:

- **assume the worst;**
- **understand the underlying nature of the society;**
- **seek maximum legitimacy and maximum support; and**
- **identify the resources needed.**

1353. In his additional statement to the Inquiry on planning lessons learned, Mr Blair wrote:

"Where military action is to remove the regime of a corrupted and brutal state, assume the worst about its capacity, its governing infrastructure and the integrity of its Government systems. There will be nation-building and governance capacity required to be established over a significant time period …

"… the challenge confronting any nation when a powerful, all encompassing grip is taken away, is formidable. There are powerful, interacting religious and tribal elements and influences. These are hard to manage. Everything we take for granted in our countries in government, public services, institutions and even private sector has to be built or at a minimum, substantially reformed. We simply do not have the international capacity to do this. It needs to be grown …

"The planning for any aftermath should go deep into an analysis not only of government and governing structures and the readily available information and data, but into the underlying nature of the society, the impact particularly of the regime's brutality and corruption on the social and business capital of the country and any cross currents to do with religious, tribal or other affiliation, as they have been affected by the regime …

"The number and nature of forces required for the aftermath of regime change may be radically different from those required for the removal of the regime, in scale, in type of training, in force posture and deployment. These really are genuinely separate missions and should be treated as such …"[587]

1354. Asked whether more effort should have been put into planning for different post-conflict scenarios, Sir Peter Ricketts told the Inquiry:

"It is always possible to say that one could do more. I think we needed a plan that was sufficiently flexible to respond to any scenario that arose after the conflict."[588]

1355. Mr Chaplin told the Inquiry:

"… the main lesson learned was you have to have a strategy and have a proper plan. You do a lot more preparatory work than was done in this case … and crucial

---

[587] Statement, [undated], 'The Planning Lessons Learned', pages 1-6.
[588] Public hearing, 1 December 2009, page 95.

to that is ... contriving circumstances in which you have maximum legitimacy and therefore maximum support ...

"When you have done all that ... you need to identify the resources that are necessary to carry that out."[589]

Conclusions

1356. Clear warnings were given before the invasion of Iraq about the potential for post-conflict political disintegration and extremist violence, the inadequacy of US post-conflict planning and the risk that, in the absence of UN authorisation, additional international support would not be forthcoming.

1357. Despite those warnings, the Government failed to ensure that the UK was adequately prepared for the range of circumstances it might encounter in southern Iraq in the short, medium and long term.

1358. The Inquiry does not conclude that better planning and preparation would necessarily have prevented the events that unfolded in Iraq between 2003 and 2009, described in Sections 9 and 10, nor that it would have been possible to prepare for every eventuality. Better plans and preparation, however, could have mitigated some of the risks to which the UK and Iraq were exposed, and increased the likelihood of achieving the outcomes desired by the UK and the Iraqi people.

1359. The lessons identified by the Inquiry in relation to both the planning and preparation for post-conflict operations and to post-conflict operations themselves are set out in Section 10.4.

What was known on the eve of the invasion

1360. The evidence described earlier in this Section shows that, although there were large gaps in the information on Saddam Hussein's Iraq available to the UK Government before the invasion, much was known about the state of the country and the possible impact of military action.

1361. The degraded state of Iraq's infrastructure was recognised by UK analysts in January 2002 and was known to Mr Blair by the end of July 2002.

1362. The most comprehensive pre-invasion report on the state of Iraq's infrastructure was the DIS paper of mid-January 2002, seen by Mr Blair at the end of July 2002.[590] With the exception of road and rail transport, the situation described in the paper was comprehensively bleak. The DIS assessed that Iraq's theoretical power generation capacity was about 10,000 megawatts (MW), but that the "practical limit" was about 5,000 MW, well below "even the most basic demand".

---

[589] Public hearing, 1 December 2009, page 93.
[590] Paper DIS, 18 January 2002, 'Infrastructure Briefing Memorandum: Iraq'.

1363. The potential consequences of Iraq's poor infrastructure for post-conflict operations were identified in the 4 September edition of the SPG paper on military strategic thinking, which stated:

> "Given fractious nature of Iraqi politics, broad regional concern on nature of new Iraqi government, and poor state of Iraqi infrastructure, delivery of stated post-conflict objectives will require lengthy engagement."[591]

1364. The 30 September edition of the SPG paper stated that Iraqi infrastructure was "poorly maintained by the current regime with damage from the war of 1991 still not repaired".[592]

1365. The FCO paper 'Models for Administering a Post-Saddam Iraq', presented to the AHGI on 11 October, stated that administering Iraq would involve restoration of critical infrastructure.[593]

1366. The Cabinet Office paper on models for Iraq after Saddam Hussein, sent to Sir David Manning on 1 November, listed priorities facing the transitional military government to be established by the Coalition after the collapse of the Iraqi regime.[594] Those included emergency work on infrastructure involving close co-ordination with civilian development agencies.

1367. The implications of the fragile state of Iraq's infrastructure for the Iraqi people and for achieving post-conflict objectives were clearly stated in an FCO paper for the AHGI in November 2002 and by Ms Short in Parliament on 30 January 2003.

1368. The FCO paper on economic issues in Iraq, sent to AHGI members on 4 November 2002, described Iraq's economy as "distorted and very badly damaged".[595] The FCO stated:

> "Even if a new conflict produces little additional damage, the combination of neglect and war damage means that large investments in many areas and spread over many years, are needed if infrastructure and services are to recover even to their pre-1990 condition. Getting this process under way will be essential to economic revival, to the alleviation of humanitarian problems and to popular support for a new administration."

---

[591] Paper [SPG], 4 September 2002, 'UK Military Strategic Thinking on Iraq'.
[592] Paper [SPG], 30 September 2002, 'UK Military Strategic Thinking on Iraq'.
[593] Paper FCO, [undated, version received at AHGI, 11 October 2002], 'Models for Administering a Post-Saddam Iraq'.
[594] Minute Drummond to Manning, 1 November 2002, 'Iraq: Post-Saddam' attaching Paper 'Iraq: Models and some questions for post-Saddam government'.
[595] Paper FCO, [undated], 'Economic issues in Iraq after post-Saddam regime change: internal policy and external engagement'.

1369. Ms Short told the House of Commons on 30 January 2003 that Iraq's infrastructure was:

> "… in chronic disrepair. Hospitals, clinics, sanitation facilities and water treatment plants suffer from a terrible lack of maintenance. The result is that the Iraqi people's lives are perilously fragile. Their coping strategies have worn away by years of misrule. The public facilities to help them cope are run down, often to the point of uselessness."[596]

1370. Papers written in the weeks before the invasion and concerned with the military objective of minimising further damage during conflict did not address the risk to Coalition objectives represented by the underlying fragility of Iraq's infrastructure.

1371. Mr Drummond's paper on "winning the peace", sent to Sir David Manning on 14 February 2003, stated that Coalition Forces could expect to find an Iraq with certain "broad characteristics", including damage to key infrastructure, but "perhaps less than other conflicts if the campaign is quick".[597]

1372. The Military Campaign Objectives published on 20 March, stated that, in aiming to achieve the objective as swiftly as possible, the military was required to make "every effort … to minimise civilian casualties and damage to essential economic infrastructure".[598]

1373. The seven immediate military priorities in the aftermath of hostilities listed in the Military Campaign Objectives included: "enable the reconstruction and recommissioning of essential infrastructure for the political and economic development of Iraq, and the immediate benefit of the Iraqi people".[599]

1374. Section 6.2 addresses military planners' efforts to minimise damage to Iraq's infrastructure during conflict.

1375. UK planners had little information on which to build an assessment of the capabilities of Iraq's civil bureaucracy.

1376. The FCO and the SPG recommended further work to address gaps in the UK's knowledge.

1377. There is no indication that those gaps were filled.

---

[596] House of Commons, *Official Report*, 30 January 2003, columns 1053-1054.
[597] Minute Drummond to Manning, 14 February 2003, 'Iraq: Winning the Peace' attaching Paper OD Secretariat, 11 February 2003, 'Iraq: Post Conflict: Key Messages'.
[598] Iraq: Military Campaign Objectives, 18 March 2003.
[599] Minute Bowen to Manning, 11 February 2003, 'Iraq: Military Campaign Objectives' attaching Paper Cabinet Office, February 2003, 'Iraq: Military Campaign Objectives'.

1378. Because the Ba'ath Party was closely intertwined with Iraq's bureaucracy, the failure of the US and UK to agree an approach to de-Ba'athification compounded uncertainty about how the bureaucracy might perform after Saddam Hussein's departure.

1379. In January 2002, the DIS stated that the Ba'ath Party, the Iraqi civil bureaucracy and the armed forces were intertwined: "any 'regime insider' succeeding Saddam would find the functional roles of the Party indispensable in administering the state and controlling the populace".[600]

1380. The DIS paper was included in Mr Blair's summer reading pack at the end of July.

1381. The DFID 'Northern Iraq Desktop Review', circulated within DFID on 8 August, stated that many civil servants had resorted to alternative sources of income or left the country in order to secure a stable income.[601]

1382. The FCO paper 'Scenarios for the future of Iraq after Saddam', sent to No.10 on 26 September, stated that it was difficult to judge the extent to which government structures would survive Saddam Hussein's departure:

- "The national Ba'ath superstructure would almost certainly collapse if Saddam fell as a result of military action, with the leadership seeking refuge. At lower levels, Ba'ath structures might continue".

- Local power lay with the Ba'ath Party leadership. The limited supporting bureaucracy was unlikely to be able to take on a more extensive role "without a radical overhaul".

- If Saddam Hussein fell, particularly after US-led military action, "tribal, regional and religious differences would probably come to the fore".[602]

1383. The "aftermath" section of the 30 September edition of the SPG paper on UK military strategic thinking raised concerns about the US approach to de-Ba'athification, which could run counter to the need for basic governance and increase post-conflict reliance on the external authority.[603]

1384. The FCO paper 'International Administration for Iraq: what, who and how?', sent to the AHGI on 18 October, assessed that, if Saddam Hussein were overthrown quickly or "the bulk of Ba'ath apparatchiks switched sides", a "light" approach to international administration might be possible, monitoring a local administration's decisions against

---

[600] Paper DIS, 1 February 2002, 'The Iraqi Ba'ath Party – its history, ideology and role in regime security'.
[601] Minute CHAD Operations Team [junior official] to [DFID junior official], 8 August 2002, 'Northern Iraq Desktop Review and Background Briefing Document' attaching Paper, Conflict and Humanitarian Affairs Department, July 2002, 'Northern Iraq Desktop Review and Background Briefing Document'.
[602] Letter McDonald to Manning, 26 September 2002, 'Scenarios for the future of Iraq after Saddam' attaching Paper FCO, 'Scenarios for the future of Iraq after Saddam'.
[603] Paper [SPG], 30 September 2002, 'UK Military Strategic Thinking on Iraq'.

principles set out in a mandate provided by the Security Council.[604] If the Iraqi regime fought to the end or the damage to Iraq was extensive, the international administration would need to assume control of key areas.

1385. The importance of a "structural analysis of the Iraqi system and the need for reform" was one of seven key judgements in the 6 November edition of the SPG paper on strategic military thinking, which stated that current FCO and DFID papers had revealed "key gaps in our knowledge".[605]

1386. The SPG stated that a "balance must be struck between the competing demands for reform and removal of Ba'athist influence and the need for effective administration". There needed to be a "detailed structural analysis of the current regime, its instruments of state power and its administration".

1387. Mr Drummond, a member of the UK delegation to the talks on post-conflict issues in Washington on 6 November, made a similar point to Sir David Manning.[606] He reported that, where the UK assumed the Iraqi Government would need "radical reform", including removal of "the pervasive influence of the Ba'ath Party", the US believed "reasonably competent ministries" remained beneath permanent secretary level and that, because the Ba'ath Party operated as a parallel structure to government below that level, "less radical change is needed". Mr Drummond suggested that both the UK and US Governments would need to develop and test their thinking more thoroughly.

1388. At Mr Blair's seminar with academics on 19 November, points made in discussion included that there would be difficult decisions on the extent of co-operation with existing structures, including the Ba'ath Party. Views differed on whether the Ba'ath Party would survive Saddam Hussein's downfall.[607]

1389. The FCO paper on interim administrations, shared with the US on 12 December, stated:

"... Iraq has a reputation for being one of the better-run Arab countries with a well-educated civil service. But we have little first hand evidence of how things work nowadays. We need more information ..."[608]

1390. Officials were reported to be working with academics, the Iraqi exile community and diplomatic posts to tackle a number of questions, including: "To what extent are ministries infiltrated by Ba'athist elements? How central are the Ba'athists to the functioning of the ministries? Can the ministries work without them?"

---

[604] Letter Gray to Drummond, 18 October 2002, 'Papers for the AHGI' attaching Paper [unattributed], 17 October 2002, 'International Administration for Iraq: what, who and how?'
[605] Paper [SPG], 6 November 2002, 'UK Military Strategic Thinking on Iraq'.
[606] Minute Drummond to Manning, 8 November 2002, 'Iraq: Day After'.
[607] Letter Rycroft to Sinclair, 20 November 2002, 'Iraq: Prime Minister's seminar with academics, 19 November'.
[608] Paper Middle East Department, 12 December 2002, 'Interim Administrations in Iraq: Why a UN-led Interim Administration would be in the US interest'.

1391. The annotated agenda for the second round of talks on post-conflict issues in Washington on 22 January 2003 asked to what extent Iraqis should be replaced with international civilian staff in an interim administration.[609] Many ministries might be turned around with "a few changes at the top".

1392. Briefing for Mr Hoon's discussion of post-conflict issues with Dr Rice and Secretary Rumsfeld on 12 February listed eight "Key Gaps/US-UK policy differences" on post-conflict planning, including on de-Ba'athification:

> "Is it the US aim to de-Saddam, or de-Ba'ath Iraq? If the latter, how much of the party structure do we wish to remove? In the short term, and in the long term? What level of compromise/co-operation with Iraqi officialdom will be necessary and/or acceptable in the early stages of Phase IV? Depending on the US intention, can they provide UK forces with means of identifying particular officials for removal from office or detention? How will the Coalition process those removed from office? … How will government functions be maintained if key officials are removed?"[610]

1393. The 19 February JIC Assessment 'Southern Iraq: What's in Store?' stated that the only networks of influence in the South outside the Ba'ath Party were the tribes and the followers of some senior Shia clerics.[611] The external opposition would try to assert authority, but only those with armed forces on the ground or support from senior Shia clerics were likely to succeed to any extent.

1394. Advice to Mr Blair on 25 February 2003 stated that "a relatively competent Iraqi civil service" should continue to function "with changes at the highest level only".

1395. In advice to Mr Blair on 25 February, the FCO stated:

> "We believe that, contrary to the assumptions sometimes made, the Transitional Administration will be able to draw on a relatively competent Iraqi civil service. The Iraqi civil service has continued to function through several regime changes, and we see no reason why it should not do so again, with changes at the highest level only."[612]

1396. The FCO made no reference to the absence of agreement with the US on the extent of de-Ba'athification.

1397. The DIS paper on "the 'post-Saddam' political and security environment" in Basra, produced on 11 March, described the Ba'ath Party as "Basra's most important administrative institution".[613]

---

[609] Minute Chilcott to Private Secretary [FCO], 17 January 2003, 'Iraq: Day-After Issues'.
[610] Minute Johnson to PS/Secretary of State [MOD], 10 February 2003, 'Secretary of State's Visit to Washington: Iraq.'
[611] JIC Assessment, 19 February 2003, 'Southern Iraq: What's in Store?'
[612] Letter Sinclair to Rycroft, 25 February 2003, 'Iraq: Political and Military Questions'.
[613] Report DIS, 11 March 2003, 'Basra: Post Saddam Governance'.

1398. Despite concerns about the implications of de-Ba'athification, by 28 March there was no agreement with the US on the issue.[614]

1399. During 2002 and early 2003, UK analysts described Iraq as:

- **"potentially fundamentally unstable"; and**
- **facing "a risk of a wider breakdown as the regime's authority crumbles".**

1400. Mr Blair insisted that the Coalition must prevent anarchy and internecine fighting breaking out.

1401. He told President Bush that Iraq would be at risk of internecine fighting when a military strike destabilised the regime.

1402. On 13 June 2002, the SPG described Iraq as "potentially fundamentally unstable".[615] Iraq was held together by a strong security apparatus. It would require considerable force to break the security structure, but when that happened the regime would "shatter". Among the military tasks for the first six months would be the provision of external and internal security, and law and order, "to prevent any potential for inter-ethnic violence".

1403. On 15 January 2003, Mr Blair told the Chiefs of Staff "the 'Issue' was aftermath – the Coalition must prevent anarchy and internecine fighting breaking out".[616] He asked the MOD to look at the big "what ifs", including internecine fighting, and to develop a strategy.

1404. The annotated agenda for the second round of talks on post-conflict issues on 22 January stated that establishing a secure environment would be an urgent task and: "We shall also want to prevent internecine violence. Our handling of the defeated Iraqi forces will be critical."

1405. Mr Blair's Note to President Bush on 24 January stated that the biggest risk they faced was internecine fighting in Iraq when a military strike destabilised the regime.[617]

1406. The JIC Assessment of 19 February stated that there were "large numbers of armed groups and some potential for tribal score-settling" and "a risk of a wider breakdown as the regime's authority crumbles".[618] But there were "no indications ... of Shia preparations for an all-out civil war against Sunni Iraqis".

1407. MOD advice for Mr Hoon before Mr Blair's 6 March meeting on post-conflict issues stated that much of the UK preparation for post-conflict Iraq was based on

---

[614] Minute Drummond to Bowen, 28 March 2003, 'Iraq: Reconstruction Agenda'.
[615] Minute Driver to PSO/CDS, 13 June 2002, 'Supporting Paper for COS Strategic Think Tank on Iraq – 18 June' attaching Paper [unattributed], 12 June 2002, [untitled].
[616] Minute MA/DCJO to MA/CJO, 15 January 2003, 'Briefing to Prime Minister'.
[617] Letter Manning to Rice, 24 January 2003, [untitled] attaching 'Note'.
[618] JIC Assessment, 19 February 2003, 'Southern Iraq: What's in Store?'

"best-case assumptions" on the progress of the conflict, including limited internecine conflict.[619] Officials suggested that Mr Hoon remind Ministerial colleagues that there was "at least a credible possibility that none of these conditions will obtain".

1408. At the Azores Summit, Mr Blair, President Bush and Mr Aznar discussed the risk of communal violence and the need for it to be "handled rapidly by the military".[620]

1409. From September 2002, the FCO warned that war in Iraq might create an easier environment for terrorists.

1410. "Maintaining firm control on the internal security situation" was among the "practical steps" to provide stability proposed by the FCO.

1411. In late February 2003, the DIS Red Team warned of the risk of Coalition military action creating fertile ground for Al Qaida, which could deliberately cause civilian casualties to undermine the establishment of a representative Iraqi-led administration.

1412. The first FCO paper for the AHGI, written in September 2002, stated that war in Iraq might create an easier environment for terrorists to operate in and would create a new incentive for them to act. UK Embassies and other interests might be attractive targets.[621]

1413. Three JIC Assessments, on 10 October 2002, 10 February 2003 and 12 March 2003, judged that the greatest terrorist threat in the event of military action against Iraq would come from Al Qaida and other Islamic extremists.[622]

1414. The 6 November 2002 edition of the SPG paper on UK military strategic thinking on Iraq stated:

> "Operations in Iraq may have a negative impact on the UK's policy objectives for international terrorism, as poor handling of a post-conflict Iraq has the potential to increase greatly anti-Western feeling in the region; fuelling the very international tensions we have sought to diffuse and arming the forces of extremism."[623]

1415. The FCO paper on Islamism in Iraq, shared with the US in December 2002, warned that it was likely groups would be looking for "identities and ideologies on which

---

[619] Minute Sec(O)4 to PS/Secretary of State [MOD], 6 March 2003, 'Iraq: Aftermath – Medium to Long Term UK Military Commitment'.

[620] Letter Manning to McDonald, 16 March 2003, 'Iraq: Summit Meeting in the Azores: 16 March'.

[621] Letter Sedwill to Manning, 20 September 2002, 'Iraq – Consequences of Conflict for the Region and Beyond' attaching Paper Directorate for Strategy and Innovation, [undated], 'Iraq – Consequences of Conflict for the Region and Beyond'.

[622] JIC Assessment, 10 October 2002, 'International Terrorism: The Threat from Iraq'; JIC Assessment, 10 February 2003, 'International Terrorism: War with Iraq'; JIC Assessment, 12 March 2003, 'International Terrorism: War with Iraq: Update'.

[623] Paper [SPG], 6 November 2002, 'UK Military Strategic Thinking on Iraq'.

to base movements".[624] It was "almost certain that political Islam would become more prominent in post-Saddam Iraq". The FCO did not expect "a massive surge in extremist sentiment", but did anticipate that a number of extremist groups were likely to use violence to pursue political ends.

1416. The paper proposed a number of "practical steps" to provide stability, including: "Maintaining firm control on the internal security situation and moving quickly to suppress any international terrorist groups in the country."

1417. Briefing prepared by the FCO for Mr Blair's meeting with President Bush on 31 January 2003 included in its list of objectives: "To convince President Bush … the US needs to pay much more attention, quickly, to planning on 'day after' issues; and that the UN needs to be central to it."[625] One of the advantages of the UN route was that, by reducing hostility to the Coalition, it "reduces risk that our actions serve as a recruiting sergeant for Islamist terrorist organisations".

1418. Mr Ochmanek, one of the contributors to the Adelphi Paper read by Mr Blair in mid-February, concluded that, even if an invasion were successful in defeating the Iraqi military and deposing Saddam Hussein's regime:

> "Success in the endgame – providing a secure environment for the remaking of the political system and culture of Iraq – cannot simply be assumed. The emergence of tribally-based or ethnically-based insurgent or terrorist groups unreconciled to the post-Saddam order cannot be ruled out, particularly if the regime in Iran chose to sponsor and harbour such groups …"[626]

1419. The first DIS Red Team report, issued on 28 February, warned of the risk of creating fertile ground for Al Qaida, which could deliberately cause civilian casualties to undermine the establishment of a representative Iraqi-led administration.[627]

1420. Potential Iranian interference in post-conflict Iraq was a theme of UK analysis from February 2002.

1421. In February 2003, the JIC assessed that Iranian reactions to a Coalition presence in southern Iraq were unclear, but "unlikely to be aggressive". Iran's aims included ensuring a leading role for its allies among the Iraqi Shia.

---

[624] Paper DSI, [undated], 'Islamism in Iraq'.
[625] Paper Middle East Department, 30 January 2003, 'Prime Minister's visit to Camp David, 31 January: Iraq'.
[626] Ochmanek D. *A Possible US-led Campaign Against Iraq: Key Factors and an Assessment*. In: Dodge T & Simon S (eds), *Iraq at the Crossroads: State and Society in the Shadow of Regime Change*. IISS Adelphi Paper 354. Oxford University Press. January 2003.
[627] Minute PS/CDI to APS2/SofS [MOD], 28 February 2003, 'Iraq Red Team – Regional responses to conflict in Iraq and the Aftermath' attaching Paper, DIS Red Team, 'Regional Responses to Conflict in Iraq and the Aftermath'.

1422. In February 2002, Mr Sawers identified a number of questions that would need asking of the US if the UK associated itself with a policy of regime change, including: "How would we keep the Iranians from meddling?" [628]

1423. On 5 August, the JIC assessed that, after a US attack began, "Iran would probably boost its support for Shia groups working against Saddam". The Islamic Revolutionary Guard Corps (IRGC) "would be likely to work directly to undermine US influence, eg by manipulating Iraqi groups through propaganda and the selective provision of money and arms, although it would not provoke anything that would provoke US military retaliation". [629]

1424. In September, Mr Chaplin wrote in an internal FCO minute that the job of the Coalition would be to ensure stability, including "preventing interference from neighbours, especially Iran". [630]

1425. The FCO paper 'Scenarios for the future of Iraq after Saddam', sent to No.10 on 26 September, judged that Iraq's neighbours might find it difficult not to get sucked in, and included an explicit reference to Iran as the neighbour most likely to become involved. [631]

1426. Mr Hoon's advice to Mr Blair on 16 January 2003 stated that the UK military plan would need further development to address a number of specific challenges, including "handling Iran". [632]

1427. The 19 February JIC Assessment 'Southern Iraq: What's in Store?' stated that Iran might support small-scale cross-border interventions by armed groups and that the IRGC would "continue to meddle in southern Iraq". Iranian reactions to a Coalition presence in southern Iraq were unclear, but "unlikely to be aggressive". [633] Iran's aims in response to a Coalition presence in Iraq included ensuring a leading role for its allies among the Iraqi Shia (the Supreme Council for an Islamic Revolution in Iraq (SCIRI) and its armed wing the Badr Corps).

1428. In response to a request from Mr Blair for advice on the implications of the JIC Assessment and the Adelphi Paper, the FCO advised that the key to preventing a Shia uprising would be:

> "... to assure the varied Shia communities that they will be fairly represented in future Iraq ... Much will also depend on the length of a Coalition 'occupation'.

---

[628] Teleletter Sawers to Jay, 21 February 2002, 'Iraq: Policy'.

[629] JIC Assessment, 5 August 2002, 'Iraq: Regional Attitudes and Impact of Military Action'.

[630] Minute Chaplin to Gray, 13 September 2002, 'Iraq: Post-Saddam Issues'.

[631] Letter McDonald to Manning, 26 September 2002, 'Scenarios for the future of Iraq after Saddam' attaching Paper FCO, 'Scenarios for the future of Iraq after Saddam'.

[632] Letter Hoon to Blair, 16 January 2003, 'Iraq: UK Land Contribution'.

[633] JIC Assessment, 19 February 2003, 'Southern Iraq: What's in Store?'

If they see Western control becoming quasi-permanent, this too may arouse opposition, probably encouraged by neighbours like Iran."[634]

The failure to plan or prepare for known risks

1429. The information on Iraq available to the UK Government before the invasion provided a clear indication of the potential scale of the post-conflict task.

1430. It showed that, in order to achieve the UK's desired end state, any post-conflict administration would need to:

- restore infrastructure that had deteriorated significantly in the decade since 1991, to the point where it was not capable of meeting the needs of the Iraqi people;
- administer a state where the upper echelons of a regime that had been in power since 1968 had been abruptly removed and in which the capabilities of the wider civil administration, many of whose employees were members of the ruling party, were difficult to assess; and
- provide security in a country faced with a number of potential threats, including:
  - internecine violence;
  - terrorism; and
  - Iranian interference.

1431. In December 2002, the MOD described the post-conflict phase of operations as "strategically decisive".[635] But when the invasion began, the UK Government was not in a position to conclude that satisfactory plans had been drawn up and preparations made to meet known post-conflict challenges and risks in Iraq and to mitigate the risk of strategic failure.

1432. Throughout the planning process, the UK assumed that the US would be responsible for preparing the post-conflict plan, that post-conflict activity would be authorised by the UN Security Council, that agreement would be reached on a significant post-conflict role for the UN and that international partners would step forward to share the post-conflict burden.

---

[634] Letter Sinclair to Rycroft, 25 February 2003, 'Iraq: Political and Military Questions'.
[635] Paper [SPG], 13 December 2002, 'UK Military Strategic Thinking on Iraq'.

1433. On that basis, the UK planned to reduce its military contribution in Iraq to medium scale within four months of the start of the invasion[636] and expected not to have to make a substantial commitment to post-conflict administration.[637]

1434. Achieving that outcome depended on the UK's ability to persuade the US of the merits of a significant post-conflict role for the UN.

1435. The UK could not be certain at any stage in the year before the invasion that it would succeed in that aim.

1436. In January 2003, the UK sought to persuade the US of the benefits of UN leadership of Iraq's interim post-conflict civil administration.[638] Officials warned that, if the UK failed to persuade the US, it risked "being drawn into a huge commitment of UK resources for a highly complex task of administration and law and order for an uncertain period".

1437. By March 2003, having failed to persuade the US of the advantages of a UN-led interim administration, the UK had set the less ambitious goal of persuading the US to accept UN authorisation of a Coalition-led interim administration and an international presence that would include the UN.[639]

1438. On 19 March, Mr Blair stated in Parliament that discussions were taking place with the US, UN and others on the role of the UN and post-conflict issues.[640]

1439. Discussions continued, but, as the invasion began:

- The UK had not secured US agreement to a Security Council resolution authorising post-conflict administration and could not be sure when, or on what terms, agreement would be possible.

- The extent of the UN's preparations, which had been hindered by the absence of agreement on post-conflict arrangements, remained uncertain. Mr Annan emphasised to Ms Short the need for clarity on US thinking so that UN planning could proceed[641] and told Sir Jeremy Greenstock that he "would not wish to see any arrangement subjugating UN activity to Coalition activity".[642]

---

[636] Minute CDS to CJO, 18 March 2003, 'Op TELIC: Authorisation for Military Operations in Iraq' attaching Paper CDS, 'Chief of Defence Staff Execute Directive to the Joint Commander for Operation TELIC (Phases 3 and 4)'.
[637] Minute Straw and Hoon to Prime Minister, 19 March 2003, 'Iraq: UK Military Contribution to post-conflict Iraq'.
[638] Minute Ricketts to Private Secretary [FCO], 7 February 2003, 'Iraq Strategy'.
[639] Paper Iraq Planning Unit, 25 March 2003, 'Iraq: Phase IV: Authorising UNSCR'.
[640] House of Commons, *Official Report*, 19 March 2003, columns 931-932.
[641] Telegram 501 UKMIS New York to FCO London, 21 March 2003, 'Iraq Humanitarian/Reconstruction: Clare Short's Visit to New York'.
[642] Telegram 526 UKMIS New York to FCO London, 25 March 2003, 'Iraq Phase IV: UN Dynamics'.

- Potential international partners for reconstruction and additional Coalition partners to provide security continued to make their post-conflict contributions conditional on UN authorisation for Phase IV.[643]

1440. Despite being aware of the shortcomings of the US plan,[644] strong US resistance to a leading role for the UN,[645] indications that the UN did not want the administration of Iraq to become its responsibility[646] and a warning about the tainted image of the UN in Iraq,[647] at no stage did the UK Government formally consider other policy options, including the possibility of making participation in military action conditional on a satisfactory plan for the post-conflict period, or how to mitigate the known risk that the UK could find itself drawn into a "huge commitment of UK resources" for which no contingency preparations had been made.

The planning process and decision-making

1441. As a junior partner in the Coalition, the UK worked within a planning framework established by the US. It had limited influence over a process dominated increasingly by the US military.

1442. The creation of the AHGI in September 2002 and the IPU in February 2003 improved co-ordination across government at official level, but neither body carried sufficient authority to establish a unified planning process across the four principal departments involved – the FCO, the MOD, DFID and the Treasury – or between military and civilian planners.

1443. Important material, including in the DFID reviews of northern and southern Iraq, and significant pieces of analysis, including the series of SPG papers on military strategic thinking, were either not shared outside the originating department, or, as appears to have been the case with the SPG papers, were not routinely available to all those with a direct interest in the contents.

1444. Some risks were identified, but departmental ownership of those risks, and responsibility for analysis and mitigation, were not clearly established.

1445. When the need to plan and prepare for the worst case was raised, including by MOD officials in advice to Mr Hoon on 6 March 2003,[648] Lt Gen Reith in his paper for the Chiefs of Staff on 21 March[649] and in Treasury advice to Mr Brown

---

[643] Paper FCO, 25 March 2003, 'Iraq: Phase IV Issues'.
[644] Minute Drummond to Rycroft, 19 March 2003, 'Iraq Ministerial Meeting'.
[645] Minute Ricketts to Private Secretary [FCO], 7 February 2003, 'Iraq Strategy'.
[646] Public hearing, 15 December 2009, page 5.
[647] Paper Middle East Department, 12 December 2002, 'Interim Administrations in Iraq: Why a UN-led Interim Administration would be in the US interest'.
[648] Minute Sec(O)4 to PS/Secretary of State [MOD], 6 March 2003, 'Iraq: Aftermath – Medium to Long Term UK Military Commitment'.
[649] Minute Reith to COSSEC, 21 March 2003, 'Phase IV Planning – Taking Stock'.

on 24 March,[650] there is no evidence that any department or individual assumed ownership or was assigned responsibility for analysis or mitigation. No action ensued.

1446. In April 2003, Mr Blair set up the Ad Hoc Ministerial Group on Iraq Rehabilitation (AHMGIR), chaired by Mr Straw, to oversee the UK contribution to post-conflict reconstruction (see Section 10.1).

1447. Until the creation of the AHMGIR, Mr Straw, Mr Hoon and Ms Short remained jointly responsible for directing post-conflict planning and preparation.

1448. In the absence of a single person responsible for overseeing all aspects of planning and preparation, departments pursued complementary, but separate, objectives. Gaps in UK capabilities were overlooked.

1449. The FCO, which focused on policy-making and negotiation, was not equipped by past experience or practice, or by its limited human and financial resources, to prepare for nation-building of the scale required in Iraq, and did not expect to do so.

1450. DFID's focus on poverty reduction and the channelling of assistance through multilateral institutions instilled a reluctance, before the invasion, to engage on anything other than the immediate humanitarian response to conflict.

1451. When military planners advised of the need to consider the civilian component as an integral part of the UK's post-conflict deployment, the Government was not equipped to respond. Neither the FCO nor DFID took responsibility for the issue.

1452. The shortage of expertise in reconstruction and stabilisation was a constraint on the planning process and on the contribution the UK was able to make to the administration and reconstruction of post-conflict Iraq.

1453. The UK Government's post-invasion response to the shortage of deployable experts in stabilisation and post-conflict reconstruction is addressed in Section 10.3.

1454. Constraints on UK military capacity are addressed in Sections 6.1 and 6.2.

1455. The UK contribution to the post-conflict humanitarian response is assessed in Section 10.1.

1456. At no stage did Ministers or senior officials commission the systematic evaluation of different options, incorporating detailed analysis of risk and UK capabilities, military and civilian, which should have been required before the UK committed to any course of action in Iraq.

---

[650] Minute Dodds to Chancellor, 24 March 2003, 'Iraq: UK Military Contribution to Post-Conflict Iraq'.

1457. Where policy recommendations were supported by untested assumptions, those assumptions were seldom challenged. When they were, the issue was not always followed through.

1458. It was the responsibility of officials to identify, analyse and advise on risk and Ministers' responsibility to ensure that measures to mitigate identifiable risks, including a range of policy options, had been considered before significant decisions were taken on the direction of UK policy.

1459. Occasions when that would have been appropriate included:

- after Mr Blair's meeting with Mr Hoon, Mr Straw and others on 23 July 2002;
- after the adoption of resolution 1441;
- before or immediately after the decision to deploy troops in January 2003;
- after the Rock Drill in February 2003; and
- after Mr Blair's meeting on post-conflict issues on 6 March 2003.

1460. There is no indication of formal risk analysis or formal consideration of options associated with any of those events.

1461. In his statement to the Inquiry, Mr Blair said:

"... with hindsight, we now see that the military campaign to defeat Saddam was relatively easy; it was the aftermath that was hard. At the time, of course, we could not know that and a prime focus throughout was the military campaign itself ..."[651]

1462. The conclusions reached by Mr Blair after the invasion did not require the benefit of hindsight.

1463. Mr Blair's long-standing conviction that successful international intervention required long-term commitment had been clearly expressed in his Chicago speech in 1999.

1464. That conviction was echoed, in the context of Iraq, in frequent advice to Mr Blair from Ministers and officials.

1465. Between early 2002 and the invasion of Iraq in March 2003, Mr Blair received warnings about:

- the significance of the post-conflict phase as the "strategically decisive" phase of the engagement in Iraq (in the SPG paper of 13 December 2002[652])

---

[651] Statement, 14 January 2011, page 14.
[652] Paper [SPG], 13 December 2002, 'UK Military Strategic Thinking on Iraq'.

and the risk that a badly handled aftermath would make intervention a "net failure" (in Mr Watkins' letter to Sir David Manning of 19 November 2002[653]);

- the likelihood of internal conflict in Iraq (including from Mr Powell on 26 September 2002, who warned of the need to stop "a terrible bloodletting of revenge after Saddam goes. Traditional in Iraq after conflict"[654]);

- the potential scale of the political, social, economic and security challenge (including from Sir Christopher Meyer on 6 September 2002: "it will probably make pacifying Afghanistan look like child's play"[655]);

- the need for an analysis of whether the benefits of military action outweighed the risk of a protracted and costly nation-building exercise (including from Mr Straw on 8 July 2002: the US "must also understand that we are serious about our conditions for UK involvement"[656]);

- the absence of credible US plans for the immediate post-conflict period and the subsequent reconstruction of Iraq (including from the British Embassy Washington after the Rock Drill on 21 and 22 February 2003: "The inter-agency rehearsal for Phase IV … exposes the enormous scale of the task … Overall, planning is at a very rudimentary stage"[657]);

- the need to agree with the US the nature of the UK contribution to those plans (including in the letter from Mr Hoon's Private Office to Sir David Manning on 28 February 2003: it was "absolutely clear" that the US expected the UK to take leadership of the South-East sector. The UK was "currently at risk of taking on a very substantial commitment that we will have great difficulty in sustaining beyond the immediate conclusion of conflict"[658]); and

- the importance (including in the 'UK overall plan for Phase IV', shown to Mr Blair on 7 March 2003[659]) of:

  ○ UN authorisation for the military occupation of Iraq, without which there would be no legal cover for certain post-conflict tasks; and

  ○ a UN framework for the administration and reconstruction of Iraq during the transition to Iraqi self-government.

---

[653] Letter Watkins to Manning, 19 November 2002, 'Iraq: Military Planning after UNSCR 1441'.
[654] Manuscript comment Powell to Manning on Letter McDonald to Manning, 26 September 2002, 'Scenarios for the future of Iraq after Saddam'.
[655] Telegram 1140 Washington to FCO London, 6 September 2002, 'PM's visit to Camp David: Iraq'.
[656] Letter Straw to Prime Minister, 8 July 2002, 'Iraq: Contingency Planning'.
[657] Telegram 235 Washington to FCO London, 24 February 2003, 'Iraq: Day After: Rehearsal of Office of Reconstruction and Humanitarian Assistance'.
[658] Letter Williams to Manning, 28 February 2003, 'Iraq: Military Planning and Preparation' attaching Paper [unattributed], 28 February 2003, 'Iraq: Military Planning Update – 28 February 2003'.
[659] Paper Iraq Planning Unit, 7 March 2003, 'The UK overall plan for Phase IV'.

1466. Mr Blair told the Chiefs of Staff on 15 January 2003 that "the 'Issue' was aftermath – the Coalition must prevent anarchy and internecine fighting breaking out".[660]

1467. In his evidence to the House of Commons Liaison Committee on 21 January 2003, Mr Blair emphasised the importance of the post-conflict phase:

"You do not engage in military conflict that may produce regime change unless you are prepared to follow through and work in the aftermath of that regime change to ensure the country is stable and the people are properly looked after."[661]

1468. On 24 January 2003, Mr Blair told President Bush that the biggest risk they faced was internecine fighting, and that delay would allow time for working up more coherent post-conflict plans.[662]

1469. Yet when Mr Blair set out the UK's vision for the future of Iraq in the House of Commons on 18 March 2003, no assessment had been made of whether that vision was achievable, no agreement had been reached with the US on a workable post-conflict plan, UN authorisation had not yet been secured, and there had been no decision on the UN's role in post-conflict Iraq.

1470. UK policy rested on the assumption that:

- the US would provide effective leadership of the immediate post-conflict effort in Iraq;
- the conditions would soon be in place for UK military withdrawal;
- after a short period of US-led, UN-authorised military occupation, the UN would administer and provide a framework for the reconstruction of post-conflict Iraq;
- substantial international support would follow UN authorisation; and
- reconstruction and the political transition to Iraqi rule would proceed in a secure environment.

1471. Mr Blair was already aware that those assumptions concealed significant risks:

- UK officials assessed that ORHA, the US body that would assume responsibility for the immediate post-invasion administration of Iraq, was not up to the task.

---

[660] Minute MA/DCJO to MA/CJO, 15 January 2003, 'Briefing to Prime Minister'.
[661] Liaison Committee, Session 2002-2003, Minutes of Evidence Taken Before the Liaison Committee Tuesday 21 January 2003, Q 117.
[662] Letter Manning to Rice, 24 January 2003, [untitled] attaching 'Note'.

- Significant differences remained between UK and US positions on UN involvement, and between the UK and the UN.

- International partners were scarce and thought to be unlikely to come forward in the absence of UN authorisation.

- UK officials recognised that occupying forces would not remain welcome for long and threats to security could quickly escalate.

1472. In the year before the invasion, Mr Blair:

- stated his belief in the importance of post-conflict planning on several occasions, including in Cabinet, in Parliament and with President Bush;

- requested advice on aspects of post-conflict Iraq (including for his summer reading pack in July 2002, for his meeting with President Bush on 31 January 2003, and twice in February 2003 after reading the JIC Assessment of southern Iraq and the Adelphi Paper *Iraq at the Crossroads*);

- at the meeting with Mr Hoon and the Chiefs of Staff on 15 January 2003, asked the MOD to consider the "big 'what ifs'" in the specific context of the UK military plan;

- convened a Ministerial meeting on post-conflict issues on 6 March 2003;

- raised concerns about the state of planning with President Bush; and

- succeeded in the narrow goal of securing President Bush's agreement that the UN should be "heavily involved" in "the post-conflict situation", a loose formulation that appeared to bridge the gap between US and UK positions on UN authorisation and the post-conflict role of the UN, but did not address the substantive issues.

1473. Mr Blair did not:

- establish clear Ministerial oversight of post-conflict strategy, planning and preparation;

- ensure that Ministers took the decisions needed to prepare a flexible, realistic and fully resourced plan integrating UK military and civilian contributions;

- seek adequate assurances that the UK was in a position to meet its likely obligations in Iraq;

- insist that the UK's strategic objectives for Iraq were tested against anything other than the best case: a well-planned and executed US-led and UN-authorised post-conflict operation in a relatively benign security environment;

- press President Bush for definitive assurances about US post-conflict plans or set out clearly to him the strategic risk in underestimating the post-conflict challenge and failing adequately to prepare for the task; or

- consider, or seek advice on whether the absence of a satisfactory plan was a sufficient threat to UK strategic objectives to require a reassessment of the terms of the UK engagement in Iraq. Despite concerns about the state of US planning, he did not make agreement on a satisfactory post-conflict plan a condition of UK participation in military action.

1474. In the weeks immediately following the invasion, Mr Blair's omissions made it more difficult for the UK Government to take an informed decision on the establishment of the UK's post-conflict Area of Responsibility (AOR) in southern Iraq (addressed in more detail in Section 8).

1475. In the short to medium term, his omissions increased the risk that the UK would be unable to respond to the unexpected in Iraq.

1476. In the longer term, they reduced the likelihood of achieving the UK's strategic objectives in Iraq.

SECTION 7

CONCLUSIONS: PRE-CONFLICT STRATEGY AND PLANNING

Contents

Conclusions

1. After the attacks on the US on 11 September 2001 and the fall of the Taliban regime in Afghanistan in November, the US Administration turned its attention to regime change in Iraq as part of the second phase of what it called the Global War on Terror.

2. The UK Government sought to influence the decisions of the US Administration and avoid unilateral US military action on Iraq by offering partnership to the US and seeking to build international support for the position that Iraq was a threat with which it was necessary to deal.

3. In Mr Blair's view, the decision to stand "shoulder to shoulder" with the US was an essential demonstration of solidarity with the UK's principal ally as well as being in the UK's long-term national interests.

4. To do so required the UK to reconcile its objective of disarming Iraq, if possible by peaceful means, with the US goal of regime change. That was achieved by the development of an ultimatum strategy threatening the use of force if Saddam Hussein did not comply with the demands of the international community, and by seeking to persuade the US to adopt that strategy and pursue it through the UN.

5. President Bush's decision, in September 2002, to challenge the UN to deal with Iraq, and the subsequent successful negotiation of resolution 1441 giving Iraq a final opportunity to comply with its disarmament obligations or face serious consequences if it did not, was perceived to be a major success for Mr Blair's strategy and his influence on President Bush.

6. But US willingness to act through the UN was limited. Following the Iraqi declaration of 7 December 2002, the UK perceived that President Bush had decided that the US would take military action in early 2003 if Saddam Hussein had not been disarmed and was still in power.

7. The timing of military action was entirely driven by the US Administration.

8. At the end of January 2003, Mr Blair accepted the US timetable for military action by mid-March. President Bush agreed to support a second resolution to help Mr Blair.

9. The UK Government's efforts to secure a second resolution faced opposition from those countries, notably France, Germany and Russia, which believed that the inspections process could continue. The inspectors reported that Iraqi co-operation, while far from perfect, was improving.

10. By early March, the US Administration was not prepared to allow inspections to continue or give Mr Blair more time to try to achieve support for action. The attempt to gain support for a second resolution was abandoned.

11. In the Inquiry's view, the diplomatic options had not at that stage been exhausted. Military action was therefore not a last resort.

12. In mid-March, Mr Blair's determination to stand alongside the US left the UK with a stark choice. It could act with the US but without the support of the majority of the Security Council in taking military action if Saddam Hussein did not accept the US ultimatum giving him 48 hours to leave. Or it could choose not to join US-led military action.

13. Led by Mr Blair, the UK Government chose to support military action.

14. Mr Blair asked Parliament to endorse a decision to invade and occupy a sovereign nation, without the support of a Security Council resolution explicitly authorising the use of force. Parliament endorsed that choice.

15. This Section sets out how the choices made by the UK Government resulted in that outcome.

The UK decision to support US military action

16. President Bush decided at the end of 2001 to pursue a policy of regime change in Iraq.

17. The UK shared the broad objective of finding a way to deal with Saddam Hussein's defiance of UN Security Council resolutions and his assumed weapons of mass destruction (WMD) programmes. However, based on consistent legal advice, the UK could not share the US objective of regime change. The UK Government therefore set as its objective the disarmament of Iraq in accordance with the obligations imposed in a series of Security Council resolutions.

UK policy before 9/11

18. Before the attacks on the US on 11 September 2001 (9/11), the UK was pursuing a strategy of containment based on a new sanctions regime to improve international support and incentivise Iraq's co-operation, narrowing and deepening the sanctions regime to focus only on prohibited items and at the same time improving financial controls to reduce the flow of illicit funds to Saddam Hussein.

19. When UK policy towards Iraq was formally reviewed and agreed by the Ministerial Committee on Defence and Overseas Policy (DOP) in May 1999, the objectives towards Iraq were defined as:

"... in the short term, to reduce the threat Saddam [Hussein] poses to the region including by eliminating his weapons of mass destruction (WMD) programmes;

and, in the longer term, to reintegrate a territorially intact Iraq as a law-abiding member of the international community."[1]

20. The policy of containment was seen as the "only viable way" to pursue those objectives. A "policy of trying to topple Saddam would command no useful international support". Iraq was unlikely to accept the package immediately but "might be persuaded to acquiesce eventually".

21. After prolonged discussion about the way ahead, the UN Security Council adopted resolution 1284 in December 1999, although China, France and Russia abstained.[2]

22. The resolution established:

- a new inspectorate, the United Nations Monitoring, Verification and Inspection Commission (UNMOVIC) (which Dr Hans Blix was subsequently appointed to lead);
- a timetable to identify and agree a work programme; and
- and the principle that, if the inspectors reported co-operation in key areas, that would lead to the suspension of economic sanctions.[3]

23. Resolution 1284 described Iraq's obligations to comply with the disarmament standards of resolution 687 and other related resolutions as the "governing standard of Iraqi compliance"; and provided that the Security Council would decide what was required of Iraq for the implementation of each task and that it should be "clearly defined and precise".

24. The resolution was also a deliberate compromise which changed the criterion for the suspension, and eventual lifting, of sanctions from complete disarmament to tests which would be based on judgements by UNMOVIC on the progress made in completing identified tasks.

25. Iraq refused to accept the provisions of resolution 1284, including the re-admission of weapons inspectors. Concerns about Iraq's activities in the absence of inspectors increased.

26. The US Presidential election in November 2000 prompted a further UK review of the operation of the containment policy (see Section 1.2). There were concerns about how long the policy could be sustained and what it could achieve.

27. There were also concerns over both the continued legal basis for operations in the No-Fly Zones (NFZs) and the conduct of individual operations.[4]

---

[1] Joint Memorandum by the Secretary of State for Foreign and Commonwealth Affairs and the Secretary of State for Defence, 17 May 1999, 'Iraq Future Strategy'.
[2] UN Security Council Press Release, 17 December 1999, *Security Council Establishes New Monitoring Commission For Iraq Adopting Resolution 1284 (1999) By Vote of 11-0-4* (SC/6775).
[3] UN Security Council, '4084th Meeting Friday 17 December 1999' (S/PV.4084).
[4] Letter Goulty to McKane, 20 October 2000, 'Iraq'.

28. In an Assessment on 1 November, the Joint Intelligence Committee (JIC) judged that Saddam Hussein felt "**little pressure to negotiate** over … resolution 1284 because the proceeds of oil smuggling and illicit trade have increased significantly this year, and more countries are increasing diplomatic contacts and trade with Iraq".[5]

29. The JIC also judged:

"Saddam would only contemplate co-operation with [resolution] 1284, and the return of inspectors … if it could be portrayed as a victory. He will not agree to co-operate unless:

- there is a **UN-agreed timetable for the lifting of sanctions**. Saddam suspects that the US would not agree to sanctions lift while he remained in power;

- **he is able to negotiate with the UN in advance to weaken the inspection provisions**. His ambitions to rebuild Iraq's weapons of mass destruction programmes makes him hostile to intrusive inspections or any other constraints likely to be effective.

"Before accepting 1284, Saddam will try to obtain the abolition of the No-Fly Zones. He is also likely to demand that the US should abandon its stated aim to topple the Iraqi regime."

30. In November 2000, Mr Blair's "preferred option" was described as the implementation of 1284, enabling inspectors to return and sanctions to be suspended.[6]

31. In December 2000, the British Embassy Washington reported growing pressure to change course from containment to military action to oust Saddam Hussein, but no decision to change policy or to begin military planning had been taken by President Clinton.[7]

32. The Key Judgements of a JIC Assessment in February 2001 included:

- There was "broad international consensus to **maintain the arms embargo at least as long as Saddam remains in power. Saddam faces no economic pressure to accept** … [resolution] **1284 because he is successfully undermining the economic sanctions regime**."

- "Through abuse of the UN Oil-for-Food [OFF] programme and smuggling of oil and other goods" it was estimated that Saddam Hussein would "**be able to appropriate in the region of $1.5bn to $1.8bn in cash and goods in 2001**", and there was "scope for earning even more".

---

[5] JIC Assessment, 1 November 2000, 'Iraq: Prospects for Co-operation with UNSCR 1284'.
[6] Letter Sawers to Cowper-Coles, 27 November 2000, 'Iraq'.
[7] Letter Barrow to Sawers, 15 December 2000, 'Iraq'.

- "**Iranian** interdiction efforts" had "**significantly reduced smuggling down the Gulf**", but Saddam Hussein had "compensated by **exploiting land routes** to Turkey and Syria".

- "**Most countries**" believed that economic sanctions were "**ineffective, counterproductive and should now be lifted**. Without active enforcement, the economic sanctions regime" would "continue to erode".[8]

33. The Assessment also stated:

- Saddam Hussein needed funds "to maintain his military and security apparatus and secure its loyalty".

- Despite the availability of funds, Iraq had been slow to comply with UN recommendations on food allocation. Saddam needed "**the Iraqi people to suffer to underpin his campaign against sanctions**".

- Encouraged by the success of Iraq's border trade agreement with Turkey, "**front-line states**" were "**not enforcing sanctions**".

- There had been a "**significant increase in the erosion of sanctions** over the past six months".

34. When Mr Blair had his first meeting with President Bush at Camp David in late February 2001, the US and UK agreed on the need for a policy which was more widely supported in the Middle East region.[9] Mr Blair had concluded that public presentation needed to be improved. He suggested that the approach should be presented as a "deal" comprising four elements:

- do the right thing by the Iraqi people, with whom we have no quarrel;
- tighten weapons controls on Saddam Hussein;
- retain financial control on Saddam Hussein; and
- retain our ability to strike.

35. The stated position of the UK Government in February 2001 was that containment had been broadly successful.[10]

36. During the summer of 2001, the UK had been exploring the way forward with the US, Russia and France on a draft Security Council resolution to put in place a "smart sanctions" regime.[11] But there was no agreement on the way ahead between the UK, the US, China, France and Russia, the five Permanent Members of the UN Security Council.

---

[8] JIC Assessment, 14 February 2001, 'Iraq: Economic Sanctions Eroding'.
[9] Letter Sawers to Cowper-Coles, 24 February 2001, 'Prime Minister's Talks with President Bush, Camp David, 23 February 2001'.
[10] House of Commons, *Official Report*, 26 February 2001, column 620.
[11] Minute McKane to Manning, 18 September 2001, 'Iraq Stocktake'.

37. Mr Blair told the Inquiry that, until 11 September 2001, the UK had a policy of containment, but sanctions were eroding.[12] The policy was "partially successful", but it did not mean that Saddam Hussein was "not still developing his [prohibited] programmes".

The impact of 9/11

38. The attacks on the US on 11 September 2001 changed perceptions about the severity and likelihood of the threat from international terrorism. They showed that attacks intended to cause large-scale civilian casualties could be mounted anywhere in the world.

39. In response to that perception of a greater threat, governments felt a responsibility to act to anticipate and reduce risks before they turned into a threat. That was described to the Inquiry by a number of witnesses as a change to the "calculus of risk" after 9/11.

40. In the wake of the attacks, Mr Blair declared that the UK would stand "shoulder to shoulder" with the US to defeat and eradicate international terrorism.[13]

41. The JIC assessed on 18 September that the attacks on the US had "set a new benchmark for terrorist atrocity", and that terrorists seeking comparable impact might try to use chemical, biological, radiological or nuclear devices.[14] Only Islamic extremists such as those who shared Usama Bin Laden's agenda had the motivation to pursue attacks with the deliberate aim of causing maximum casualties.

42. Throughout the autumn of 2001, Mr Blair took an active and leading role in building a coalition to act against that threat, including military action against Al Qaida and the Taliban regime in Afghanistan. He also emphasised the potential risk of terrorists acquiring and using nuclear, biological or chemical weapons, and the dangers of inaction.

43. In November 2001, the JIC assessed that Iraq had played no role in the 9/11 attacks on the US and that practical co-operation between Iraq and Al Qaida was "unlikely".[15] There was no "credible evidence of covert transfers of WMD-related technology and expertise to terrorist groups". It was possible that Iraq might use WMD in terrorist attacks, but only if the regime was under serious and imminent threat of collapse.

44. The UK continued actively to pursue a strengthened policy of containing Iraq, through a revised and more targeted sanctions regime and seeking Iraq's agreement to the return of inspectors as required by resolution 1284 (1999).

---

[12] Public hearing, 21 January 2011, page 8.
[13] The National Archives, 11 September 2001, *September 11 attacks: Prime Minister's statement*.
[14] JIC Assessment, 18 September 2001, 'UK Vulnerability to Major Terrorist Attack'.
[15] JIC Assessment, 28 November 2001, 'Iraq after September 11 – The Terrorist Threat'.

45. The adoption on 29 November 2001 of resolution 1382 went some way towards that objective. But support for economic sanctions was eroding and whether Iraq would ever agree to re-admit weapons inspectors and allow them to operate without obstruction was in doubt.

46. Although there was no evidence of links between Iraq and Al Qaida, Mr Blair encouraged President Bush to address the issue of Iraq in the context of a wider strategy to confront terrorism after the attacks of 9/11. He sought to prevent precipitate military action by the US which he considered would undermine the success of the coalition which had been established for action against international terrorism.

47. President Bush's remarks[16] on 26 November renewed UK concerns that US attention was turning towards military action in Iraq.

48. Following a discussion with President Bush on 3 December, Mr Blair sent him a paper on a second phase of the war against terrorism.[17]

49. On Iraq, Mr Blair suggested a strategy for regime change in Iraq. This would build over time until the point was reached where "military action could be taken if necessary", without losing international support.

50. The strategy was based on the premise that Iraq was a threat which had to be dealt with and it had multiple diplomatic strands. It entailed renewed demands for Iraq to comply with the obligations imposed by the Security Council and for the re-admission of weapons inspectors, and a readiness to respond firmly if Saddam Hussein failed to comply.

51. Mr Blair did not, at that stage, have a ground invasion of Iraq or immediate military action of any sort in mind. The strategy included mounting covert operations in support of those "with the ability to topple Saddam". But Mr Blair did state that, when a rebellion occurred, the US and UK should "back it militarily".

52. That was the first step towards a policy of possible intervention in Iraq.

53. A number of issues, including the legal basis for any military action, would need to be resolved as part of developing the strategy.

54. The UK Government does not appear to have had any knowledge at that stage that President Bush had asked General Tommy Franks, Commander in Chief, US Central Command, to review the military options for removing Saddam Hussein, including options for a conventional ground invasion.

55. Mr Blair also emphasised the threat which Iraq might pose in the future. That remained a key part of his position in the months that followed.

---

[16] The White House, 26 November 2001, *The President Welcomes Aid Workers Rescued from Afghanistan*.
[17] Paper [Blair to Bush], 4 December 2001, 'The War against Terrorism: The Second Phase'.

56. In his annual State of the Union speech on 29 January 2002, President Bush described the regimes in North Korea and Iran as "sponsors of terrorism".[18] He added that Iraq had continued to:

"... flaunt its hostility towards America and to support terror ... The Iraqi regime has plotted to develop anthrax, and nerve gas, and nuclear weapons for over a decade. This is a regime that has already used poison gas to murder thousands of its own citizens ... This is a regime that agreed to international inspections – then kicked out the inspectors. This is a regime that has something to hide from the civilized world."

57. President Bush stated:

"States like these [North Korea, Iran and Iraq], and their terrorist allies, constitute an axis of evil, arming to threaten the peace of the world. By seeking weapons of mass destruction these regimes pose a grave and growing danger."

58. From late February 2002, Mr Blair and Mr Straw began publicly to argue that Iraq was a threat which had to be dealt with. Iraq needed to disarm or be disarmed.

59. The urgency and certainty with which the position was stated reflected the ingrained belief that Saddam Hussein's regime retained chemical and biological warfare capabilities, was determined to preserve and if possible enhance its capabilities, including at some point in the future a nuclear capability, and was pursuing an active policy of deception and concealment. It also reflected the wider context in which the policy was being discussed with the US.

60. On 26 February 2002, Sir Richard Dearlove, the Chief of the Secret Intelligence Service, advised that the US Administration had concluded that containment would not work, was drawing up plans for a military campaign later in the year, and was considering presenting Saddam Hussein with an ultimatum for the return of inspectors while setting the bar "so high that Saddam Hussein would be unable to comply".[19]

61. The following day the JIC assessed that Saddam Hussein feared a US military attack on the scale of the 1991 military campaign to liberate Kuwait but did not regard such an attack as inevitable; and that Iraqi opposition groups would not act without "visible and sustained US military support on the ground".[20]

62. At Cabinet on 7 March, Mr Blair and Mr Straw emphasised that no decisions to launch further military action had been taken and any action taken would be in accordance with international law.

---

[18] The White House, 29 January 2002, *The President's State of the Union Address*.
[19] Letter C to Manning, 26 February 2002, 'US Policy on Iraq'.
[20] JIC Assessment, 27 February 2002, 'Iraq: Saddam Under the Spotlight'.

63. The discussion in Cabinet was couched in terms of Iraq's need to comply with its obligations, and future choices by the international community on how to respond to the threat which Iraq represented.

64. Cabinet endorsed the conclusion that Iraq's WMD programmes posed a threat to peace and endorsed a strategy of engaging closely with the US Government in order to shape policy and its presentation. It did not discuss how that might be achieved.

65. Mr Blair sought and was given information on a range of issues before his meeting with President Bush at Crawford on 5 and 6 April. But no formal and agreed analysis of the issues and options was sought or produced, and there was no collective consideration of such advice.

66. Mr Straw's advice of 25 March proposed that the US and UK should seek an ultimatum to Saddam Hussein to re-admit weapons inspectors.[21] That would provide a route for the UK to align itself with the US without adopting the US objective of regime change. This reflected advice that regime change would be unlawful.

67. At Crawford, Mr Blair offered President Bush a partnership in dealing urgently with the threat posed by Saddam Hussein. He proposed that the UK and the US should pursue a strategy based on an ultimatum calling on Iraq to permit the return of weapons inspectors or face the consequences.[22]

68. President Bush agreed to consider the idea but there was no decision until September 2002.

69. In the subsequent press conference on 6 April, Mr Blair stated that "doing nothing" was not an option: the threat of WMD was real and had to be dealt with.[23] The lesson of 11 September was to ensure that "groups" were not allowed to develop a capability they might use.

70. In his memoir, Mr Blair characterised the message that he and President Bush had delivered to Saddam Hussein as "change the regime attitude on WMD inspections or face the prospect of changing regime".[24]

71. Documents written between April and July 2002 reported that, in the discussion with President Bush at Crawford, Mr Blair had set out a number of considerations in relation to the development of policy on Iraq. These were variously described as:

- The UN inspectors needed to be given every chance of success.
- The US should take action within a multilateral framework with international support, not unilateral action.

---

[21] Minute Straw to Prime Minister, 25 March 2002, 'Crawford/Iraq'.
[22] Letter Manning to McDonald, 8 April 2002, 'Prime Minister's Visit to the United States: 5-7 April'.
[23] The White House, 6 April 2002, *President Bush, Prime Minister Blair Hold Press Conference*.
[24] Blair T. *A Journey*. Hutchinson, 2010.

- A public information campaign should be mounted to explain the nature of Saddam Hussein's regime and the threat he posed.
- Any military action would need to be within the framework of international law.
- The military strategy would need to ensure Saddam Hussein could be removed quickly and successfully.
- A convincing "blueprint" was needed for a post-Saddam Hussein Iraq which would be acceptable to both Iraq's population and its neighbours.
- The US should advance the Middle East Peace Process in order to improve the chances of gaining broad support in the Middle East for military action against Iraq; and to pre-empt accusations of double standards.
- Action should enhance rather than diminish regional stability.
- Success would be needed in Afghanistan to demonstrate the benefits of regime change.

72. Mr Blair considered that he was seeking to influence US policy by describing the key elements for a successful strategy to secure international support for any military action against Iraq.

73. Key Ministers and some of their most senior advisers thought these were the conditions that would need to be met if the UK was to participate in US-led military action.

74. By July, no progress had been made on the ultimatum strategy and Iraq was still refusing to admit weapons inspectors as required by resolution 1284 (1999).

75. The UK Government was concerned that the US Administration was contemplating military action in circumstances where it would be very difficult for the UK to participate in or, conceivably, to support that action.

76. To provide the basis for a discussion with the US, a Cabinet Office paper of 19 July, 'Iraq: Conditions for Military Action', identified the conditions which would be necessary before military action would be justified and the UK could participate in such action.[25]

77. The Cabinet Office paper stated that Mr Blair had said at Crawford:

"… that the UK would support military action to bring about regime change, provided that certain conditions were met:

- efforts had been made to construct a coalition/shape public opinion,
- the Israel-Palestine Crisis was quiescent, and
- the options for action to eliminate Iraq's WMD through the UN weapons inspectors had been exhausted."

---

[25] Paper Cabinet Office, 19 July 2002, 'Iraq: Conditions for Military Action'.

78. The Cabinet Office paper also identified the need to address the issue of whether the benefits of military action would outweigh the risks.

79. The potential mismatch between the timetable and work programme for UNMOVIC stipulated in resolution 1284 (1999) and the US plans for military action was recognised by officials during the preparation of the Cabinet Office paper, 'Iraq: Conditions for Military Action' for Mr Blair's meeting of 23 July.[26]

80. The issue was not addressed in the final paper submitted to Ministers on 19 July.[27]

81. Sir Richard Dearlove reported that he had been told that the US had already taken a decision on action – "the question was only how and when"; and that he had been told it intended to set the threshold on weapons inspections so high that Iraq would not be able to hold up US policy.[28]

82. Mr Blair's meeting with Ministerial colleagues and senior officials on 23 July was not seen by those involved as having taken decisions.[29]

83. Further advice and background material were commissioned, including on the possibility of a UN ultimatum to Iraq and the legal basis for action. The record stated:

> "We should work on the assumption that the UK would take part in any military action. But we needed a fuller picture of US planning before we could take any firm decisions. CDS [the Chief of the Defence Staff, Admiral Sir Michael Boyce] should tell the US military that we were considering a range of options."

84. Mr Blair was advised that there would be "formidable obstacles" to securing a new UN resolution incorporating an ultimatum without convincing evidence of a greatly increased threat from Iraq.[30] A great deal more work would be needed to clarify what the UK was seeking and how its objective might best be achieved.

85. Mr Blair's Note to President Bush of 28 July sought to persuade President Bush to use the UN to build a coalition for action by seeking a partnership between the UK and the US and setting out a framework for action.[31]

86. The Note began:

> "I will be with you, whatever. But this is the moment to assess bluntly the difficulties. The planning on this and the strategy are the toughest yet. This is not Kosovo. This is not Afghanistan. It is not even the Gulf War.

---

[26] Paper [Draft] Cabinet Office, 'Iraq: Conditions for Military Action' attached to Minute McKane to Bowen, 16 July 2002, 'Iraq'.
[27] Paper Cabinet Office, 19 July 2002, 'Iraq: Conditions for Military Action'.
[28] Report, 22 July 2002, 'Iraq [C's account of discussions with Dr Rice]'.
[29] Minute Rycroft to Manning, 23 July 2002, 'Iraq: Prime Minister's Meeting, 23 July'.
[30] Letter McDonald to Rycroft, 26 July 2002, 'Iraq: Ultimatum' attaching Paper 'Elements which might be incorporated in an SCR embodying an ultimatum to Iraq'.
[31] Note Blair [to Bush], 28 July 2002, 'Note on Iraq'.

"The military part of this is hazardous but I will concentrate mainly on the political context for success."

87. Mr Blair stated that getting rid of Saddam Hussein was:

"… the right thing to do. He is a potential threat. He could be contained.
But containment … is always risky. His departure would free up the region.
And his regime is … brutal and inhumane …"

88. Mr Blair told President Bush that the UN was the simplest way to encapsulate a "casus belli" in some defining way, with an ultimatum to Iraq once military forces started to build up in October. That might be backed by a UN resolution.

89. Mr Blair thought it unlikely that Saddam Hussein intended to allow inspectors to return. If he did, the JIC had advised that Iraq would obstruct the work of the inspectors. That could result in a material breach of the obligations imposed by the UN.

90. A workable military plan to ensure the collapse of the regime would be required.

91. The Note reflected Mr Blair's own views. The proposals had not been discussed or agreed with his colleagues.

Decision to take the UN route

92. Sir David Manning, Mr Blair's Foreign Policy Adviser, told President Bush that it would be impossible for the UK to take part in any action against Iraq unless it went through the UN.

93. When Mr Blair spoke to President Bush on 31 July the "central issue of a casus belli" and the need for further work on the optimal route to achieve that was discussed.[32] Mr Blair said that he wanted to explore whether the UN was the right route to set an ultimatum or whether it would be an obstacle.

94. In late August, the FCO proposed a strategy of coercion, using a UN resolution to issue an ultimatum to Iraq to admit the weapons inspectors and disarm. The UK was seeking a commitment from the Security Council to take action in the event that Saddam Hussein refused or subsequently obstructed the inspectors.

95. Reflecting the level of public debate and concern, Mr Blair decided in early September that an explanation of why action was needed to deal with Iraq should be published.

96. In his press conference at Sedgefield on 3 September, Mr Blair indicated that time and patience were running out and that there were difficulties with the existing policy of containment.[33] He also announced the publication of the Iraq dossier, stating that:

---

[32] Rycroft to McDonald, 31 July 2002, 'Iraq: Prime Minister's Phone Call with President Bush, 31 July'.
[33] The National Archives, 3 September 2002, *PM press conference* [at Sedgefield].

"… people will see that there is no doubt at all the United Nations resolutions that Saddam is in breach of are there for a purpose. He [Saddam Hussein] is without any question, still trying to develop that chemical, biological, potentially nuclear capability and to allow him to do so without any let or hindrance, just to say, we [sic] can carry on and do it, I think would be irresponsible."

97. President Bush decided in the meeting of the National Security Council on 7 September to take the issue of Iraq back to the UN.

98. The UK was a key ally whose support was highly desirable for the US. The US Administration had been left in no doubt that the UK Government needed the issue of Iraq to be taken back to the Security Council before it would be able to participate in military action in Iraq.

99. The objective of the subsequent discussions between President Bush and Mr Blair at Camp David was, as Mr Blair stated in the press conference before the discussions, to work out the strategy.[34]

100. Mr Blair told President Bush that he was in no doubt about the need to deal with Saddam Hussein.[35]

101. Although at that stage no decision had been taken on which military package might be offered to the US for planning purposes, Mr Blair also told President Bush that, if it came to war, the UK would take a significant military role.

102. In his speech to the General Assembly on 12 September, President Bush set out his view of the "grave and gathering danger" posed by Saddam Hussein and challenged the UN to act to address Iraq's failure to meet the obligations imposed by the Security Council since 1990.[36] He made clear that, if Iraq defied the UN, the world must hold Iraq to account and the US would "work with the UN Security Council for the necessary resolutions". But the US would not stand by and do nothing in the face of the threat.

103. Statements made by China, France and Russia in the General Assembly debate after President Bush's speech highlighted the different positions of the five Permanent Members of the Security Council, in particular about the role of the Council in deciding whether military action was justified.

104. The Government dossier on Iraq was published on 24 September.[37] It was designed to "make the case" and secure Parliamentary (and public) support for the Government's policy that action was urgently required to secure Iraq's disarmament.

---

[34] The White House, 7 September 2002, *President Bush, Prime Minister Blair Discuss Keeping the Peace*.
[35] Minute Manning to Prime Minister, 8 September 2002, 'Your Visit to Camp David on 7 September: Conversation with President Bush'.
[36] The White House, 12 September 2002, *President's Remarks to the United Nations General Assembly*.
[37] *Iraq's Weapons of Mass Destruction. The Assessment of the British Government*, 24 September 2002.

105. In his statement to Parliament on 24 September and in his answers to subsequent questions, Mr Blair presented Iraq's past, current and potential future capabilities as evidence of the severity of the potential threat from Iraq's weapons of mass destruction. He said that at some point in the future that threat would become a reality.

106. Mr Blair wrote his statement to the House of Commons himself and chose the arguments to make clear his perception of the threat and why he believed that there was an "overwhelming" case for action to disarm Iraq.[38]

107. Addressing the question of why Saddam Hussein had decided in mid-September, but not before, to admit the weapons inspectors, Mr Blair stated that the answer was in the dossier, and it was because:

"… his chemical, biological and nuclear programme is not an historic left-over from 1998. The inspectors are not needed to clean up the old remains. His weapons of mass destruction programme is active detailed and growing. The policy of containment is not working. The weapons of mass destruction programme is not shut down; it is up and running now."

108. Mr Blair posed, and addressed, three questions: "Why Saddam?"; "Why now?"; and "Why should Britain care?"

109. On the question "Why Saddam?", Mr Blair said that two things about Saddam Hussein stood out: "He had used these weapons in Iraq" and thousands had died, and he had used them during the war with Iran "in which 1 million people died"; and the regime had "no moderate elements to appeal to".

110. On the question "Why now?", Mr Blair stated:

"I agree I cannot say that this month or next, even this year or next, Saddam will use his weapons. But I can say that if the international community, having made the call for his disarmament, now, at this moment, at the point of decision, shrugs its shoulders and walks away, he will draw the conclusion dictators faced with a weakening will always draw: that the international community will talk but not act, will use diplomacy but not force. We know, again from our history, that diplomacy not backed by the threat of force has never worked with dictators and never will."

Negotiation of resolution 1441

111. There were significant differences between the US and UK positions, and between them and China, France and Russia about the substance of the strategy to be adopted, including the role of the Security Council in determining whether peaceful means had been exhausted and the use of force to secure disarmament was justified.

---

[38] House of Commons, *Official Report*, 24 September 2002, columns 1-23.

112. Those differences resulted in difficult negotiations over more than eight weeks before the unanimous adoption of resolution 1441 on 8 November 2002.

113. When President Bush made his speech on 12 September, the US and UK had agreed the broad approach, but not the substance of the proposals to be put to the UN Security Council or the tactics.

114. Dr Naji Sabri, the Iraqi Foreign Minister, wrote to Mr Kofi Annan, the UN Secretary-General, on 16 September to inform him that, following the series of talks between Iraq and the UN in New York and Vienna between March and July 2002 and the latest round in New York on 14 and 15 September, Iraq had decided "to allow the return of United Nations inspectors to Iraq without conditions".[39]

115. The US and UK immediately expressed scepticism. They had agreed that the provisions of resolution 1284 (1999) were no longer sufficient to secure the disarmament of Iraq and a strengthened inspections regime would be required.

116. A new resolution would be needed both to maintain the pressure on Iraq and to define a more intrusive inspections regime allowing the inspectors unconditional and unrestricted access to all Iraqi facilities.

117. The UK's stated objective for the negotiation of resolution 1441 was to give Saddam Hussein "one final chance to comply" with his obligations to disarm. The UK initially formulated the objective in terms of:

- a resolution setting out an ultimatum to Iraq to readmit the UN weapons inspectors and to disarm in accordance with its obligations; and
- a threat to resort to the use of force to secure disarmament if Iraq failed to comply.[40]

118. Lord Goldsmith, the Attorney General, informed Mr Blair on 22 October that, although he would not be able to give a final view until the resolution was adopted, the draft of the resolution of 19 October would not on its own authorise military action.[41]

119. Mr Blair decided on 31 October to offer significant forces for ground operations to the US for planning purposes.[42]

120. During the negotiations, France and Russia made clear their opposition to the use of force, without firm evidence of a further material breach and a further decision in the Security Council.

---

[39] UN Security Council, 16 September 2002, 'Letter dated 16 September from the Minister of Foreign Affairs of Iraq addressed to the Secretary-General', attached to 'Letter dated 16 September from the Secretary-General addressed to the President of the Security Council' (S/2002/1034).
[40] Minute Straw to Prime Minister, 14 September 2002, 'Iraq: Pursuing the UN Route'.
[41] Minute Adams to Attorney General, 22 October 2002, 'Iraq: Meeting with the Prime Minister, 22 October' attaching Briefing 'Lines to Take'.
[42] Letter Wechsberg to Watkins, 31 October 2002, 'Iraq: Military Options'.

121. The UK was successful in changing some aspects of the US position during the negotiations, in particular ensuring that the Security Council resolution was based on the disarmament of Iraq rather than wider issues as originally proposed by the US.

122. To secure consensus in the Security Council despite the different positions of the US and France and Russia (described by Sir Jeremy Greenstock, the UK Permanent Representative to the UN in New York, as "irreconcilable"), resolution 1441 was a compromise containing drafting "fixes". That created deliberate ambiguities on a number of key issues including:

- the level of non-compliance with resolution 1441 which would constitute a material breach;
- by whom that determination would be made; and
- whether there would be a second resolution explicitly authorising the use of force.

123. As the Explanations of Vote demonstrated, there were significant differences between the positions of the members of the Security Council about the circumstances and timing of recourse to military action. There were also differences about whether Member States should be entitled to report Iraqi non-compliance to the Council.

124. Mr Blair, Mr Straw and other senior UK participants in the negotiation of resolution 1441 envisaged that, in the event of a material breach of Iraq's obligations, a second resolution determining that a breach existed and authorising the use of force was likely to be tabled in the Security Council.

125. Iraq announced on 13 November that it would comply with resolution 1441.[43]

126. Iraq also re-stated its position that it had neither produced nor was in possession of weapons of mass destruction since the inspectors left in December 1998. It explicitly challenged the UK statement on 8 November that Iraq had decided to keep possession of its WMD.

The prospect of military action

127. Following Iraq's submission of the declaration on its chemical, biological, nuclear and ballistic missile programmes to the UN on 7 December, and before the inspectors had properly begun their task, the US concluded that Saddam Hussein was not going to take the final opportunity offered by resolution 1441 to comply with his obligations.

128. Mr Blair was advised on 11 December that there was impatience in the US Administration and it was looking at military action as early as mid-February 2003.[44]

---

[43] UN Security Council, 13 November 2002, 'Letter dated 13 November 2002 from the Minister for Foreign Affairs of Iraq addressed to the Secretary-General' (S/2002/1242).
[44] Minute Manning to Prime Minister, 11 December 2002, 'Iraq'.

129. Mr Blair told President Bush on 16 December that the Iraqi declaration was "patently false".[45] He was "cautiously optimistic" that the inspectors would find proof.

130. In a statement issued on 18 December, Mr Straw said that Saddam Hussein had decided to continue the pretence that Iraq had no WMD programme. If he persisted "in this obvious falsehood" it would become clear that he had "rejected the pathway to peace".[46]

131. The JIC's initial Assessment of the Iraqi declaration on 18 December stated that there had been "No serious attempt" to answer any of the unresolved questions highlighted by the UN Special Commission (UNSCOM) or to refute any of the points made in the UK dossier on Iraq's WMD programme.[47]

132. President Bush is reported to have told a meeting of the US National Security Council on 18 December 2002, at which the US response to Iraq's declaration was discussed, that the point of the 7 December declaration was to test whether Saddam Hussein would accept the "final opportunity" for peace offered by the Security Council.[48] He had summed up the discussion by stating:

"We've got what we need now, to show America that Saddam won't disarm himself."

133. Mr Colin Powell, the US Secretary of State, stated on 19 December that Iraq was "well on its way to losing its last chance", and that there was a "practical limit" to how long the inspectors could be given to complete their work.[49]

134. Mr Straw told Secretary Powell on 30 December that the US and UK should develop a clear "plan B" postponing military action on the basis that inspections plus the threat of force were containing Saddam Hussein.[50]

135. In early 2003, Mr Straw still thought a peaceful solution was more likely than military action. Mr Straw advised Mr Blair on 3 January that he had concluded that, in the potential absence of a "smoking gun", there was a need to consider a "Plan B".[51] The UK should emphasise to the US that the preferred strategy was peaceful disarmament.

136. Mr Blair took a different view. By the time he returned to the office on 4 January 2003, he had concluded that the "likelihood was war" and, if conflict could not be avoided, the right thing to do was fully to support the US.[52] He was focused on the need

---

[45] Letter Rycroft to McDonald, 16 December 2002, 'Prime Minister's Telephone Call with President Bush, 16 December'.

[46] The National Archives, 18 December 2002, *Statement by Foreign Secretary on Iraq Declaration*.

[47] JIC Assessment, 18 December 2002, 'An Initial Assessment of Iraq's WMD Declaration'.

[48] Feith DJ. *War and Decision: Inside the Pentagon at the Dawn of the War on Terrorism.* HarperCollins, 2008.

[49] US Department of State Press Release, *Press Conference Secretary of State Colin L Powell, Washington, 19 December 2002*.

[50] Letter Straw to Manning, 30 December 2002, 'Iraq: Conversation with Colin Powell, 30 December'.

[51] Minute Straw to Prime Minister, 3 January 2003, 'Iraq – Plan B'.

[52] Note Blair [to No.10 officials], 4 January 2003, [extract 'Iraq'].

to establish evidence of an Iraqi breach, to persuade opinion of the case for action and to finalise the strategy with President Bush at the end of January.

137. The UK objectives were published in a Written Ministerial Statement by Mr Straw on 7 January.[53] The "prime objective" was:

"... to rid Iraq of its weapons of mass destruction (WMD) and their associated programmes and means of delivery, including prohibited ballistic missiles ... as set out in UNSCRs [UN Security Council resolutions]. This would reduce Iraq's ability to threaten its neighbours and the region, and prevent Iraq using WMD against its own people. UNSCRs also require Iraq to renounce terrorism, and return captured Kuwaitis and property taken from Kuwait."

138. Lord Goldsmith gave Mr Blair his draft advice on 14 January that resolution 1441 would not by itself authorise the use of military force.[54]

139. Mr Blair agreed on 17 January to deploy a UK division with three combat brigades for possible operations in southern Iraq.[55]

140. There was no collective discussion of the decision by senior Ministers.

141. **In January 2003, there was a clear divergence between the UK and US Government positions over the timetable for military action, and the UK became increasingly concerned that US impatience with the inspections process would lead to a decision to take unilateral military action in the absence of support for such action in the Security Council.**

142. On 23 January, Mr Blair was advised that the US military would be ready for action in mid-February.[56]

143. In a Note to President Bush on 24 January, Mr Blair wrote that the arguments for proceeding with a second Security Council resolution, "or at the very least a clear statement" from Dr Blix which allowed the US and UK to argue that a failure to pass a second resolution was in breach of the spirit of 1441, remained in his view, overwhelming; and that inspectors should be given until the end of March or early April to carry out their task.[57]

144. Mr Blair suggested that, in the absence of a "smoking gun", Dr Blix would be able to harden up his findings on the basis of a pattern of non-co-operation from Iraq and that that would be sufficient for support for military action in the Security Council.

---

[53] House of Commons, *Official Report*, 7 January 2003, columns 4-6WS.
[54] Minute [Draft] [Goldsmith to Prime Minister], 14 January 2003, 'Iraq: Interpretation of Resolution 1441'.
[55] Letter Manning to Watkins, 17 January 2003, 'Iraq: UK Land Contribution'.
[56] Letter PS/C to Manning, 23 January 2003, [untitled].
[57] Letter Manning to Rice, 24 January 2003, [untitled], attaching Note [Blair to Bush], [undated], 'Note'.

145. The US and UK should seek to persuade others, including Dr Blix, that that was the "true view" of resolution 1441.

146. Mr Blair used an interview on *Breakfast with Frost* on 26 January to set out the position that the inspections should be given sufficient time to determine whether or not Saddam Hussein was co-operating fully.[58] If he was not, that would be a sufficient reason for military action. A find of WMD was not required.

147. Mr Blair's proposed approach to his meeting with President Bush was discussed in a meeting of Ministers before Cabinet on 30 January and then discussed in general terms in Cabinet itself.

148. In a Note prepared before his meeting with President Bush on 31 January, Mr Blair proposed seeking a UN resolution on 5 March followed by an attempt to "mobilise Arab opinion to try to force Saddam out" before military action on 15 March.[59]

149. When Mr Blair met President Bush on 31 January, it was clear that the window of opportunity before the US took military action would be very short. The military campaign could begin "around 10 March".[60]

150. President Bush agreed to seek a second resolution to help Mr Blair, but there were major reservations within the US Administration about the wisdom of that approach.

151. Mr Blair confirmed that he was "solidly with the President and ready to do whatever it took to disarm Saddam" Hussein.

152. Reporting on his visit to Washington, Mr Blair told Parliament on 3 February 2003 that Saddam Hussein was not co-operating as required by resolution 1441 and, if that continued, a second resolution should be passed to confirm such a material breach.[61]

153. Mr Blair continued to set the need for action against Iraq in the context of the need to be seen to enforce the will of the UN and to deter future threats.

The gap between the Permanent Members of the Security Council widens

154. In their reports to the Security Council on 14 February:

- **Dr Blix reported that UNMOVIC had not found any weapons of mass destruction and the items that were not accounted for might not exist, but Iraq needed to provide the evidence to answer the questions, not belittle them.**

---

[58] *BBC News*, 26 January 2003, *Breakfast with Frost*.
[59] Note [Blair to Bush], [undated], 'Countdown'.
[60] Letter Manning to McDonald, 31 January 2003, 'Iraq: Prime Minister's Conversation with President Bush on 31 January'.
[61] House of Commons, *Official Report*, 3 February 2003, columns 21-38.

- **Dr Mohamed ElBaradei, Director General of the International Atomic Energy Agency (IAEA), reported that the IAEA had found no evidence of ongoing prohibited nuclear or nuclear-related activities in Iraq although a number of issues were still under investigation.**[62]

155. In the subsequent debate, members of the Security Council voiced widely divergent views.

156. Mr Annan concluded that there were real differences on strategy and timing in the Security Council. Iraq's non-co-operation was insufficient to bring members to agree that war was justified; they would only move if they came to their own judgement that inspections were pointless.[63]

157. On 19 February, Mr Blair sent President Bush a six-page Note. He proposed focusing on the absence of full co-operation and a "simple" resolution stating that Iraq had failed to take the final opportunity, with a side statement defining tough tests of co-operation and a vote on 14 March to provide a deadline for action.[64]

158. President Bush and Mr Blair agreed to introduce a draft resolution at the UN the following week but its terms were subject to further discussion.[65]

159. On 20 February, Mr Blair told Dr Blix that he wanted to offer the US an alternative strategy which included a deadline and tests for compliance.[66] He did not think Saddam Hussein would co-operate but he would try to get Dr Blix as much time as possible. Iraq could have signalled a change of heart in the December declaration. The Americans did not think that Saddam was going to co-operate: "Nor did he. But we needed to keep the international community together."

160. Dr Blix stated that full co-operation was a nebulous concept; and a deadline of 15 April would be too early. Dr Blix commented that "perhaps there was not much WMD in Iraq after all". Mr Blair responded that "even German and French intelligence were sure that there was WMD in Iraq". Dr Blix said they seemed "unsure" about "mobile BW production facilities": "It would be paradoxical and absurd if 250,000 men were to invade Iraq and find very little."

161. Mr Blair responded that "our intelligence was clear that Saddam had reconstituted his WMD programme".

---

[62] UN Security Council, '4707th Meeting Friday 14 February 2003' (S/PV.4707).
[63] Telegram 268 UKMIS New York to FCO London, 15 February 2003, 'Foreign Secretary's Meeting with the UN Secretary-General: 14 February'.
[64] Letter Manning to Rice, 19 February 2003, 'Iraq' attaching Note [Blair to Bush], [undated], 'Note'.
[65] Letter Rycroft to McDonald, 19 February 2003, 'Iraq and MEPP: Prime Minister's Telephone Conversation with Bush, 19 February'.
[66] Letter Cannon to Owen, 20 February 2003, 'Iraq: Prime Minister's Conversation with Blix'.

162. On 24 February, the UK, US and Spain tabled a draft resolution stating that Iraq had failed to take the final opportunity offered by resolution 1441 and that the Security Council had decided to remain seized of the matter.[67] The draft failed to attract support.

163. France, Germany and Russia responded by tabling a memorandum, building on their tripartite declaration of 10 February, stating that "full and effective disarmament" remained "the imperative objective of the international community".[68] That "should be achieved peacefully through the inspection regime". The "conditions for using force" had "not been fulfilled". The Security Council "must step up its efforts to give a real chance to the peaceful settlement of the crisis".

164. On 25 February, Mr Blair told the House of Commons that the intelligence was "clear" that Saddam Hussein continued "to believe that his weapons of mass destruction programme is essential both for internal repression and for external aggression".[69] It was also "essential to his regional power". "Prior to the inspectors coming back in", Saddam Hussein "was engaged in a systematic exercise in concealment of those weapons". The inspectors had reported some co-operation on process, but had "denied progress on substance".

165. The House of Commons was asked on 26 February to reaffirm its endorsement of resolution 1441, support the Government's continuing efforts to disarm Iraq, and to call upon Iraq to recognise that this was its final opportunity to comply with its obligations.[70]

166. The Government motion was approved by 434 votes to 124; 199 MPs voted for an amendment which invited the House to "find the case for military action against Iraq as yet unproven".[71]

167. In a speech on 26 February, President Bush stated that the safety of the American people depended on ending the direct and growing threat from Iraq.[72]

168. President Bush also set out his hopes for the future of Iraq.

169. Reporting discussions in New York on 26 February, Sir Jeremy Greenstock wrote that there was "a general antipathy to having now to take decisions on this issue, and a wariness about what our underlying motives are behind the resolution".[73] Sir Jeremy concluded that the US was focused on preserving its room for manoeuvre while he was

---

[67] Telegram 302 UKMIS New York to FCO London, 25 February 2003, 'Iraq: Tabling of US/UK/Spanish Draft Resolution: Draft Resolution'.
[68] UN Security Council, 24 February 2003, 'Letter dated 24 February 2003 from the Permanent Representatives of France, Germany and the Russian Federation to the United Nations addressed to the President of the Security Council' (S/2003/214).
[69] House of Commons, *Official Report*, 25 February 2003, columns 123-126.
[70] House of Commons, *Official Report*, 26 February 2003, column 265.
[71] House of Commons, *Official Report*, 26 February 2003, columns 367-371.
[72] The White House, 26 February 2003, *President discusses the future of Iraq*.
[73] Telegram 314 UKMIS New York to FCO London, 27 February 2003, 'Iraq: 26 February'.

"concentrating on trying to win votes". It was the "middle ground" that mattered. Mexico and Chile were the "pivotal sceptics".

170. Lord Goldsmith told No.10 officials on 27 February that the safest legal course for future military action would be to secure a further Security Council resolution.[74] He had, however, reached the view that a "reasonable case" could be made that resolution 1441 was capable of reviving the authorisation to use force in resolution 678 (1990) without a further resolution, if there were strong factual grounds for concluding that Iraq had failed to take the final opportunity offered by resolution 1441.

171. Lord Goldsmith advised that, to avoid undermining the case for reliance on resolution 1441, it would be important to avoid giving any impression that the UK believed a second resolution was legally required.

172. Informal consultations in the Security Council on 27 February showed there was little support for the UK/US/Spanish draft resolution.[75]

173. An Arab League Summit on 1 March concluded that the crisis in Iraq must be resolved by peaceful means and in the framework of international legitimacy.[76]

174. Following his visit to Mexico, Sir David Manning concluded that Mexican support for a second resolution was "not impossible, but would not be easy and would almost certainly require some movement".[77]

175. During Sir David's visit to Chile, President Ricardo Lagos repeated his concerns, including the difficulty of securing nine votes or winning the presentational battle without further clarification of Iraq's non-compliance. He also suggested identifying benchmarks.[78]

176. Mr Blair wrote in his memoir that, during February, "despite his best endeavours", divisions in the Security Council had grown not reduced; and that the "dynamics of disagreement" were producing new alliances.[79] France, Germany and Russia were moving to create an alternative pole of power and influence.

177. Mr Blair thought that was "highly damaging" but "inevitable": "They felt as strongly as I did; and they weren't prepared to indulge the US, as they saw it."

---

[74] Minute Brummell, 27 February 2003, 'Iraq: Attorney General's Meeting at No. 10 on 27th February 2003'.
[75] Telegram 318 UKMIS New York to FCO London, 28 February 2003, 'Iraq: 27 February Consultations and Missiles'.
[76] Telegram 68 Cairo to FCO London, 2 March 2003, 'Arab League Summit: Final Communique'.
[77] Telegram 1 Mexico City to Cabinet Office, 1 March 2003, 'Iraq: Mexico'.
[78] Telegram 34 Santiago to FCO London, 2 March 2003, 'Chile/Iraq: Visit by Manning and Scarlett'.
[79] Blair T. *A Journey*. Hutchinson, 2010.

178. Mr Blair concluded that for moral and strategic reasons the UK should be with the US and that:

> "… [W]e should make a last ditch attempt for a peaceful solution. First to make the moral case for removing Saddam … Second, to try one more time to reunite the international community behind a clear base for action in the event of a continuing breach."

179. On 3 March, Mr Blair proposed an approach focused on setting a deadline of 17 March for Iraq to disclose evidence relating to the destruction of prohibited items and permit interviews; and an amnesty if Saddam Hussein left Iraq by 21 March.[80]

180. Mr Straw told Secretary Powell that the level of support in the UK for military action without a second resolution was palpably "very low". In that circumstance, even if a majority in the Security Council had voted for the resolution with only France exercising its veto, he was "increasingly pessimistic" about support within the Labour Party for military action.[81] The debate in the UK was:

> "… significantly defined by the tone of the debate in Washington and particularly remarks made by the President and others to the right of him, which suggested that the US would go to war whatever and was not bothered about a second resolution one way or another."

181. Following a discussion with Mr Blair, Mr Straw told Secretary Powell that Mr Blair:

> "… was concerned that, having shifted world (and British) public opinion over the months, it had now been seriously set back in recent days. We were not in the right position. The Prime Minister was considering a number of ideas which he might well put to the President."[82]

182. Mr Straw recorded that Secretary Powell had advised that, if Mr Blair wanted to make proposals, he should do so quickly. The US was not enthusiastic about the inclusion of an immunity clause for Saddam Hussein in the resolution.

183. Mr Straw reported that Secretary Powell had told President Bush that he judged a vetoed resolution would no longer be possible for the UK. Mr Straw said that without a second resolution approval for military action could be "beyond reach".

184. Mr Straw told the Foreign Affairs Committee (FAC) on 4 March that it was "a matter of fact" that Iraq had been in material breach "for some weeks" and resolution 1441 provided sufficient legal authority to justify military action against Iraq if it was "in further material breach".[83]

---

[80] Note (handwritten) [Blair], 3 March 2003, [untitled].
[81] Minute Straw to Prime Minister, 3 March 2003, 'Iraq: Second Resolution'.
[82] Letter Straw to Manning, 4 March 2003, 'Iraq: Conversation with Colin Powell, 3 March'.
[83] Minutes, Foreign Affairs Committee (House of Commons), 4 March 2003, [Evidence Session], Qs 151 and 154.

185. Mr Straw also stated that a majority of members of the Security Council had been opposed to the suggestion that resolution 1441 should state explicitly that military action could be taken only if there were a second resolution.

186. Mr Blair was informed on the evening of 4 March that US military planners were looking at 12 March as the possible start date for the military campaign; and that Mr Geoff Hoon, the Defence Secretary, was concerned about the apparent disconnect with activity in the UN.[84]

187. Baroness Amos, Minister of State, Department for International Development (DfID), advised on 4 March that Angola, Cameroon and Guinea were not yet ready to commit to a "yes vote" and had emphasised the need for P5 unity.[85]

188. Sir Christopher Hum, British Ambassador to China, advised on 4 March that, if the resolution was put to a vote that day, China would abstain.[86]

189. Sir John Holmes, British Ambassador to France, advised on 4 March that France's main aim was to "avoid being put on the spot" by influencing the undecided, preventing the US and UK mustering nine votes, and keeping alongside the Russians and Chinese; and that there was "nothing that we can now do to dissuade them from this course".[87] Sir John also advised that "nothing the French say at this stage, even privately, should be taken at face value".

190. Mr Igor Ivanov, the Russian Foreign Minister, told Mr Straw on 4 March that Russia had failed in an attempt to persuade Saddam Hussein to leave and it would veto a resolution based on the draft circulated on 24 February.[88]

191. France, Germany and Russia stated on 5 March that they would not let a resolution pass that authorised the use of force.[89] Russia and France, "as Permanent Members of the Security Council, will assume all their responsibilities on this point".

192. The British Embassy Washington reported overnight on 5/6 March that "barring a highly improbable volte face by Saddam", the US was now firmly on track for military action and would deal firmly with any efforts in the UN to slow down the timetable.[90]

193. The Embassy reported that the only event which might significantly affect the US timetable would be problems for the UK. That had been described as "huge – like trying

---

[84] Letter Watkins to Manning, 4 March 2003, 'Iraq: Timing of Military Action'.
[85] Minute Amos to Foreign Secretary, 4 March 2003, [untitled].
[86] Telegram 90 Beijing to FCO London, 4 March 2003, 'Iraq: Lobbying the Chinese'.
[87] Telegram 110 Paris to FCO London, 4 March 2003, 'Iraq: Avoiding a French Veto'.
[88] Telegram 37 FCO London to Moscow, 3 [sic] March 2003, 'Iraq: Foreign Secretary's Meetings with Russian Foreign Minister, 4 March'.
[89] *The Guardian*, 5 March 2003, *UN war doubters unite against resolution. The Guardian*, 6 March 2003, *Full text of Joint declaration*.
[90] Telegram 294 Washington to FCO London, 6 March 2003, 'Personal Iraq: UN Endgame'.

to play football without the quarterback". The US was "therefore pulling out all the stops at the UN". The US fully understood the importance of the second resolution for the UK.

194. Sir Jeremy Greenstock advised that the US would not countenance the use of benchmarks. That risked delaying the military timetable.[91]

195. Mr Blair told Cabinet on 6 March that the argument boiled down to the question of whether Saddam Hussein would ever voluntarily co-operate with the UN to disarm Iraq.[92]

196. Mr Blair concluded that it was for the Security Council to determine whether Iraq was co-operating fully.

197. In his discussions with President Lagos on 6 March, Mr Blair stated that the US would go ahead without the UN if asked to delay military action until April or May.[93]

198. **In his report to the Security Council on 7 March, Dr Blix stated that there had been an acceleration of initiatives from Iraq since the end of January, but they could not be said to constitute immediate co-operation.[94] Nor did they necessarily cover all areas of relevance; but they were nevertheless welcome. UNMOVIC was drawing up a work programme of key disarmament tasks, which would be ready later that month, for approval by the Security Council. It would take "months" to complete the programme.**

199. **Dr ElBaradei reported that there were no indications that Iraq had resumed nuclear activities since the inspectors left in December 1998 and the recently increased level of Iraqi co-operation should allow the IAEA to provide the Security Council with an assessment of Iraq's nuclear capabilities in the near future.**

200. There was unanimity in calls for Iraq to increase its co-operation. But there was a clear division between the US, UK, Spain and Bulgaria who spoke in favour of a further resolution and France, Germany, Russia and China and most other Member States who spoke in favour of continuing to pursuing disarmament through strengthened inspections.

201. The UK, US and Spain circulated a revised draft resolution deciding that Iraq would have failed to take the final opportunity offered by resolution 1441 (2002) unless the Council concluded, on or before 17 March 2003, that Iraq had demonstrated full, unconditional, immediate and active co-operation in accordance with its disarmament obligations and was yielding possession of all weapons and proscribed material to UNMOVIC and the IAEA.

---

[91] Telegram 353 UKMIS New York to FCO London, 6 March 2003, 'Iraq: 5 March'.
[92] Cabinet Conclusions, 6 March 2003.
[93] Letter Cannon to Owen, 6 March 2003, 'Iraq: Prime Minister's Conversation with President of Chile, 6 March'.
[94] UN Security Council, '4714th Meeting Friday 7 March 2003' (S/PV.4714).

202. President Putin told Mr Blair on 7 March that Russia would oppose military action.[95]

203. Mr Straw told Mr Annan that military considerations could not be allowed "to dictate policy", but the military build-up "could not be maintained for ever", and:

> "... the more he had looked into the Iraq dossier [issue] the more convinced he had become of the need for action. Reading the clusters document [a report of outstanding issues produced by UNMOVIC on 7 March] made his hair stand on end."[96]

204. Mr Straw set out the UK thinking on a deadline, stating that this was "Iraq's last chance", but the objective was disarmament and, if Saddam Hussein did what was demanded, "he could stay". In those circumstances, a "permanent and toughened inspections regime" would be needed, possibly "picking up some earlier ideas for an all-Iraq NFZ".

205. Lord Goldsmith sent his formal advice to Mr Blair on 7 March.[97]

The end of the UN route

206. When Mr Blair spoke to President Bush at 6pm on 7 March he emphasised the importance of securing nine positive votes[98] in the Security Council for Parliamentary approval for UK military action.[99]

207. Mr Blair argued that while the 17 March deadline in the draft resolution was not sufficient for Iraq to disarm fully, it was sufficient to make a judgement on whether Saddam Hussein had had a change of heart. If Iraq started to co-operate, the inspectors could have as much time as they liked.

208. In a last attempt to move opinion and secure the support of nine members of the Security Council, Mr Blair decided on 8 March to propose a short extension of the timetable beyond 17 March and to revive the idea of producing a "side statement" setting out a series of tests which would provide the basis for a judgement on Saddam Hussein's intentions.

209. The initiative was pursued through intensive diplomatic activity to lobby for support between London and the capitals of Security Council Member States.

---

[95] Letter Rycroft to McDonald, 7 March 2003, 'Iraq: Prime Minister's Conversation with President Putin, 7 March'.
[96] Telegram 366 UKMIS New York to FCO London, 7 March 2003, 'Iraq: Foreign Secretary's Meeting with UN Secretary-General, New York, 6 March'.
[97] Minute Goldsmith to Prime Minister, 7 March 2003, 'Iraq: Resolution 1441'.
[98] The number of votes required, in the absence of a veto from one or more of the five Permanent Members, for a decision to take action with the authority of the Security Council.
[99] Letter Rycroft to McDonald, 7 March 2003, 'Iraq: Prime Minister's Conversation with Bush, 7 March'.

210. Mr Blair told the Inquiry:

"It was worth having one last-ditch chance to see if you could bring people back together on the same page … [W]hat President Bush had to do was agree to table a fresh resolution. What the French had to agree was you couldn't have another resolution and another breach and no action. So my idea was define the circumstances of breach – that was the tests that we applied with Hans Blix – get the Americans to agree to the resolution, get the French to agree that you couldn't just go back to the same words of 1441 again, you had to take it a stage further."[100]

211. In a discussion on 9 March, Mr Blair told President Bush that he needed a second resolution to secure Parliamentary support for UK involvement in military action.[101] He sought President Bush's support for setting out tests in a side statement, including that the vote in the Security Council might have to be delayed "by a couple of days".

212. President Bush was unwilling to countenance delay. He was reported to have told Mr Blair that, if the second resolution failed, he would find another way to involve the UK.

213. Mr Blair told President Bush the UK would be with the US in taking action if he (Mr Blair) possibly could be.

214. Sir Jeremy Greenstock reported that Dr Blix was prepared to work with the UK on identifying tests but had reminded him that UNMOVIC still lacked clear evidence that Iraq possessed any WMD.[102]

215. Mr Blair spoke twice to President Lagos on 10 March in an attempt to find a path that President Lagos and President Vicente Fox of Mexico could support.

216. In the second conversation, Mr Blair said that he thought it "would be possible to find different wording" on the ultimatum to Iraq. Timing "would be difficult, but he would try to get some flexibility" if the first two issues "fell into place".[103]

217. Mr Straw reported that Secretary Powell thought that there were seven solid votes, and uncertainty about Mexico, Chile and Pakistan.[104] If there were fewer than nine, the second resolution should not be put to the vote.

218. Mr Straw replied that "he was increasingly coming to the view that we should not push the matter to a vote if we were going to be vetoed"; but that had not yet been agreed by Mr Blair.

---

[100] Public hearing, 29 January 2010, page 127.
[101] Letter Rycroft to McDonald, 9 March 2003, 'Iraq: Prime Minister's Conversation with Bush, 9 March'.
[102] Telegram 391 UKMIS New York to FCO London, 10 March 2003, 'Iraq: Second Resolution'.
[103] Letter Rycroft to McDonald, 10 March 2003, 'Iraq: Prime Minister's Phone Calls with Lagos, Bush and Aznar, 10 March'.
[104] Letter Straw to Manning, 11 March 2003, 'Conversation with US Secretary of State, 10 March'.

219. By 10 March, President Bush's position was hardening and he was very reluctant to delay military action.

220. When Mr Blair spoke to President Bush, they discussed the "seven solid votes" for the resolution.[105]

221. Mr Alastair Campbell, Mr Blair's Director of Communications and Strategy, wrote that Mr Blair had done most of the talking.[106] President Bush thought President Jacques Chirac of France was "trying to get us to the stage where we would not put [the resolution] to a vote because we would be so worried about losing".

222. Mr Blair had argued that if Chile and Mexico could be shifted, that would "change the weather". If France and Russia then vetoed the resolution but the "numbers were right on the UN", Mr Blair thought that he would "have a fighting chance of getting it through the Commons". Subsequently, Mr Blair suggested that a change in Chile and Mexico's position might be used to influence President Putin.

223. President Bush was "worried about rolling in more time" but Mr Blair had "held his ground", arguing that Chile and Mexico would "need to be able to point to something that they won last minute that explains why they finally supported us". President Bush "said 'Let me be frank. The second resolution is for the benefit of Great Britain. We would want it so we can go ahead together.'" President Bush's position was that the US and UK "must not retreat from 1441 and we cannot keep giving them more time"; it was "time to do this" and there should be "no more deals".

224. Sir David Manning sent the UK proposals for a revised deadline, and a side statement identifying six tests on which Saddam Hussein's intentions would be judged, to Dr Condoleezza Rice, President Bush's National Security Advisor, and to President Lagos.[107]

225. Mr Blair wrote in his memoir that President Bush and his military were concerned about delay.[108]

> "It [the proposal for tests/more time] was indeed a hard sell to George. His system was completely against it. His military were, not unreasonably, fearing that delay gave the enemy time – and time could mean a tougher struggle and more lives lost. This was also troubling my military. We had all sorts of contingency plans in place ... There was both UK and US intelligence warning us of the risk.
>
> "Nonetheless I thought it was worth a try ..."

---

[105] Letter Rycroft to McDonald, 10 March 2003, 'Iraq: Prime Minister's Phone Calls with Lagos, Bush and Aznar, 10 March'.
[106] Campbell A & Hagerty B. *The Alastair Campbell Diaries. Volume 4. The Burden of Power: Countdown to Iraq*. Hutchinson, 2012.
[107] Letter Manning to Rice, 10 March 2003, [untitled].
[108] Blair T. *A Journey*. Hutchinson, 2010.

226. Mr Blair also wrote:

"Chile and Mexico were prepared to go along, but only up to a point. Ricardo made it clear that if there was heavy opposition from France, it would be tough for them to participate in what would then be a token vote, incapable of being passed because of a veto – and what's more, a veto not by Russia, but by France.

"Unfortunately, the French position had, if anything, got harder not softer. They were starting to say they would not support military action in any circumstances, irrespective of what the inspectors found ..."

227. In a press conference on 10 March, Mr Annan reiterated the Security Council's determination to disarm Iraq, but said that every avenue for a peaceful resolution of the crisis had to be exhausted before force should be used.[109]

228. Mr Annan also warned that, if the Security Council failed to agree on a common position and action was taken without the authority of the Council, the legitimacy and support for any such action would be seriously impaired.

229. In an interview on 10 March, President Chirac stated that it was for the inspectors to advise whether they could complete their task.[110] If they reported that they were not in a position to guarantee Iraq's disarmament, it would be:

"... for the Security Council alone to decide the right thing to do. But in that case ... regrettably, the war would become inevitable. It isn't today."

230. President Chirac stated that he did not consider that the draft resolution tabled by the US, UK and Spain would attract support from nine members of the Security Council. In that case, there would be no majority for action, "So there won't be a veto problem."

231. But if there were a majority "in favour of the new resolution", France would "vote 'no'".

232. In response to a question asking, "And, this evening, this is your position in principle?", President Chirac responded:

"My position is that, regardless of the circumstances, France will vote 'no' because she considers this evening that there are no grounds for waging war in order to achieve the goal we have set ourselves, that is to disarm Iraq."

233. By 11 March, it was clear that, in the time available before the US was going to take military action, it would be difficult to secure nine votes in the

---

[109] United Nations, 10 March 2003, *Secretary-General's press conference (unofficial transcript)*.
[110] The Élysée, *Interview télévisée de Jacques Chirac, le 10 mars 2003*. A translation for HMG was produced in a Note, [unattributed and undated], 'Iraq – Interview given by M. Jacques Chirac, President of the Republic, to French TV (10 March 2003)'.

Security Council for a resolution determining that Iraq had failed to take the final opportunity offered by resolution 1441.

234. Mr Straw wrote to Mr Blair on 11 March setting out his firm conclusion that:

> "If we cannot gain nine votes and be sure of no veto, we should not push our second resolution to a vote. The political and diplomatic consequences for the UK would be significantly worse to have our … resolution defeated … than if we camp on 1441 …"[111]

235. Mr Straw set out his reasoning in some detail, including that:

- Although in earlier discussion he had "warmed to the idea" that it was worth pushing the issue to a vote "if we had nine votes and faced only a French veto", the more he "thought about this, the worse an idea it becomes".

- A veto by France only was "in practice less likely than two or even three vetoes".

- The "best, least risky way to gain a moral majority" was "by the 'Kosovo route' – essentially what I am recommending. The key to our moral legitimacy then was the matter never went to a vote – but everyone knew the reason for this was that Russia would have vetoed."

236. Mr Straw suggested that the UK should adopt a strategy based on the argument that Iraq had failed to take the final opportunity offered by resolution 1441, and that the last three meetings of the Security Council met the requirement for Security Council consideration of reports of non-compliance.

237. Mr Straw also identified the need for a "Plan B" for the UK not to participate in military action in the event that the Government failed to secure a majority in the Parliamentary Labour Party for military action.

238. Mr Straw concluded:

> "We will obviously need to discuss all this, but I thought it best to put it in your mind as event[s] could move fast. And what I propose is a great deal better than the alternatives. When Bush graciously accepted your offer to be with him all the way, he wanted you alive not dead!"

239. There was no reference in the minute to President Chirac's remarks the previous evening.

240. When Mr Blair and President Bush discussed the position late on 11 March, it was clear that President Bush was determined not to postpone the start of military action.[112] They discussed the impact of President Chirac's "veto threats". Mr Blair considered that President Chirac's remarks "gave some cover" for ending the UN route.

---

[111] Minute Straw to Prime Minister, 11 March 2003, 'Iraq: What if We Cannot Win the Second Resolution?'
[112] Letter Cannon to McDonald, 11 March 2003, 'Iraq: Prime Minister's Conversations with Bush and Lagos, 11 March'.

241. Reporting discussions in New York on 11 March on the draft resolution and details of a possible "side statement", Sir Jeremy Greenstock advised that the draft resolution tabled by the UK, US and Spain on 7 March had "no chance ... of adoption".[113]

242. When he discussed the options with Mr Straw early on 12 March, Mr Blair decided that the UK would continue to support the US.[114]

243. During Prime Minister's Questions on 12 March, Mr Blair stated:

"I hope that even now those countries that are saying they would use their veto no matter what the circumstances will reconsider and realise that by doing so they put at risk not just the disarmament of Saddam, but the unity of the United Nations."[115]

244. In a telephone call with President Bush on 12 March, Mr Blair proposed that the US and UK should continue to seek a compromise in the UN, while confirming that he knew it would not happen. He would say publicly that the French had prevented them from securing a resolution, so there would not be one.[116]

245. Mr Blair wanted to avoid a gap between the end of the negotiating process and the Parliamentary vote in which France or another member of the Security Council might table a resolution that attracted the support of a majority of the Council. That could have undermined the UK (and US) position on its legal basis for action.

246. The FCO assessed on 12 March that the votes of the three African states were reasonably secure but Pakistan's vote was not so certain. It was hoped that the six tests plus a short extension of the 17 March deadline might deliver Mexico and Chile.[117]

247. The UK circulated its draft side statement setting out the six tests to a meeting of Security Council members in New York on the evening of 12 March.[118]

248. Sir Jeremy Greenstock told Council members that the UK "non-paper" responded to an approach from the "undecided six"[119] looking for a way forward, setting out six tasks to be achieved in a 10-day timeline.[120] Sir Jeremy reported that France, Germany and Russia all said that the draft resolution without operative paragraph 3 would still authorise force. The UK had not achieved "any kind of breakthrough" and there were "serious questions about the available time", which the US would "not help us to satisfy".

---

[113] Telegram 417 UKMIS New York to FCO London, 12 March 2003, 'Personal Iraq: Side Statement and End Game Options'.

[114] Public hearing, 21 January 2010, page 105.

[115] House of Commons, *Official Report*, 12 March 2003, column 288.

[116] Letter Rycroft to McDonald, 12 March 2003, 'Iraq: Prime Minister's Telephone Conversation with President Bush, 12 March'.

[117] Telegram 33 FCO London to Riyadh, 12 March 2003, 'Personal for Heads of Mission: Iraq: The Endgame'.

[118] Telegram 429 UKMIS New York to FCO London, 13 March 2003, 'Iraq: UK Side-Statement'.

[119] Angola, Cameroon, Chile, Guinea, Mexico, Pakistan.

[120] Telegram 428 UKMIS New York to FCO London, 13 March 2003, 'Iraq: UK Circulates Side-Statement'.

249. Mr Blair told Cabinet on 13 March that work continued in the UN to obtain a second resolution and, following the French decision to veto, the outcome remained open.[121]

250. Mr Straw described President Chirac's position as "irresponsible".

251. Mr Straw told Cabinet that there was "good progress" in gaining support in the Security Council.

252. Mr Blair concluded that the French position "looked to be based on a calculation of strategic benefit". It was "in contradiction of the Security Council's earlier view that military action would follow if Iraq did not fully and unconditionally co-operate with the inspectors". The UK would "continue to show flexibility" in its efforts to achieve a second resolution and, "if France could be shown to be intransigent, the mood of the Security Council could change towards support for the British draft".

253. Mr Blair agreed the military plan later on 13 March.[122]

254. On 13 March, Mr Blair and President Bush discussed withdrawing the resolution on 17 March followed by a US ultimatum to Saddam Hussein to leave within 48 hours. There would be no US military action until after the vote in the House of Commons on 18 March.[123]

255. Mr Blair continued to press President Bush to publish the Road Map on the Middle East Peace Process because of its impact on domestic opinion in the UK as well as its strategic impact.

256. Reporting developments in New York on 13 March, Sir Jeremy Greenstock warned that the UK tests had attracted no support, and that the US might be ready to call a halt to the UN process on 15 March.[124] The main objections had included the "perceived authorisation of force in the draft resolution" and a desire to wait for UNMOVIC's own list of key tasks which would be issued early the following week.

257. President Chirac told Mr Blair on 14 March that France was "content to proceed 'in the logic of UNSCR 1441'; but it could not accept an ultimatum or any 'automaticity' of recourse to force".[125] He proposed looking at a new resolution in line with resolution 1441, "provided that it excluded these options". President Chirac "suggested that the UNMOVIC work programme might provide a way forward. France was prepared to look at reducing the 120 day timeframe it envisaged."

---

[121] Cabinet Conclusions, 13 March 2003.
[122] Letter Rycroft to Watkins, 13 March 2003, 'Iraq: Military Planning'.
[123] Letter Cannon to McDonald, 13 March 2003, 'Iraq: Military Timetable'.
[124] Telegram 438 UKMIS New York to FCO London, 14 March 2003, 'Iraq: 13 March'.
[125] Letter Cannon to Owen, 14 March 2003, 'Iraq: Prime Minister's Conversation with President Chirac, 14 March'.

258. In response to a question from President Chirac about whether it would be the inspectors or the Security Council who decided whether Saddam had co-operated, Mr Blair "insisted that it must be the Security Council".

259. President Chirac agreed, "although the Security Council should make its judgement on the basis of the inspectors' report". He "wondered whether it would be worth" Mr Straw and Mr Dominique de Villepin, the French Foreign Minister, "discussing the situation to see if we could find some flexibility"; or was it "too late"?

260. Mr Blair said, "every avenue must be explored".

261. In the subsequent conversation with President Bush about the French position and what to say when the resolution was pulled, Mr Blair proposed that they would need to show that France would not authorise the use of force in any circumstances.[126]

262. President Lagos initially informed Mr Blair on 14 March that the UK proposals did not have Chile's support and that he was working on other ideas.[127] He subsequently informed Mr Blair that he would not pursue his proposals unless Mr Blair or President Bush asked him to.

263. Mr Tony Brenton, Chargé d'Affaires, British Embassy Washington, reported that President Bush was determined to remove Saddam Hussein and to stick to the US timetable for action. The UK's "steadfastness" had been "invaluable" in bringing in other countries in support of action.[128]

264. In a declaration on 15 March, France, with Germany and Russia, attempted to secure support in the Security Council for continued inspections.[129]

265. At the Azores Summit on 16 March, President Bush, Mr Blair and Prime Minister José María Aznar of Spain agreed that, unless there was a fundamental change in the next 24 hours, the UN process would end.[130]

266. In public, the focus was on a "last chance for peace". The joint communiqué contained a final appeal to Saddam Hussein to comply with his obligations and to the Security Council to back a second resolution containing an ultimatum.

267. In his memoir, Mr Blair wrote:

> "So when I look back ... I know there was never any way Britain was not going to be with the US at that moment, once we went down the UN route and Saddam was in breach. Of course such a statement is always subject to *in extremis* correction.

[126] Letter Rycroft to McDonald, 14 March 2003, 'Iraq: Prime Minister's Conversation with Bush, 14 March'.
[127] Letter [Francis] Campbell to Owen, 14 March 2003, 'Iraq: Prime Minister's Conversation with President Lagos of Chile, 14 March'.
[128] Telegram 350 Washington to FCO London, 15 March 2003, 'Iraq'.
[129] UN Security Council, 18 March 2003, 'Letter dated 15 March 2003 from the Permanent Representative of Germany to the United Nations addressed to the President of the Security Council' (S/2003/320).
[130] Letter Manning to McDonald, 16 March 2013, 'Iraq: Summit Meeting in the Azores: 16 March'.

A crazy act of aggression? No, we would not have supported that. But given the history, you couldn't call Saddam a crazy target.

"Personally I have little doubt that at some point we would have to have dealt with him …"[131]

268. At "about 3.15pm UK time" on 17 March, Sir Jeremy Greenstock announced that the resolution would not be put to a vote, stating that the co-sponsors reserved the right to take their own steps to secure the disarmament of Iraq.[132]

269. The subsequent discussion in the Council suggested that only the UK, the US, and Spain took the view that all options other than the use of military force had been exhausted.[133]

270. A specially convened Cabinet at 1600 on 17 March 2003 endorsed the decision that the diplomatic process was now at an end and Saddam Hussein should be given an ultimatum to leave Iraq; and that the House of Commons would be asked to endorse the use of military action against Iraq to enforce compliance, if necessary.[134]

271. In his statement to the House of Commons that evening, Mr Straw said that the Government had reluctantly concluded that France's actions had put a consensus in the Security Council on a further resolution "beyond reach".[135]

272. As a result of Saddam Hussein's persistent refusal to meet the UN's demands, the Cabinet had decided to ask the House of Commons to support the UK's participation in military action, should that be necessary to achieve the disarmament of Iraq "and thereby the maintenance of the authority of the United Nations".

273. Mr Straw stated that Lord Goldsmith's Written Answer "set out the legal basis for the use of force".

274. Mr Straw drew attention to the significance of the fact that no one "in discussions in the Security Council and outside" had claimed that Iraq was in full compliance with its obligations.

275. In a statement later that evening, Mr Robin Cook, the Leader of the House of Commons, set out his doubts about the degree to which Saddam Hussein posed a "clear and present danger" and his concerns that the UK was being "pushed too quickly into conflict" by the US without the support of the UN and in the face of hostility from many of the UK's traditional allies.[136]

---

[131] Blair T. *A Journey*. Hutchinson, 2010.
[132] Telegram 465 UKMIS New York to FCO London, 18 March 2003, 'Iraq: Resolution: Statement'.
[133] Telegram 464 UKMIS New York to FCO London, 18 March 2003, 'Iraq: Resolution'.
[134] Cabinet Conclusions, 17 March 2003.
[135] House of Commons, *Official Report*, 17 March 2003, columns 703-705.
[136] House of Commons, *Official Report*, 17 March 2003, columns 726-728.

276. On 17 March, President Bush issued an ultimatum giving Saddam Hussein 48 hours to leave Iraq.

277. The French President's office issued a statement early on 18 March stating that the US ultimatum was a unilateral decision going against the will of the international community who wanted to pursue Iraqi disarmament in accordance with resolution 1441.[137] It stated:

> "… only the Security Council is authorised to legitimise the use of force. France appeals to the responsibility of all to see that international legality is respected. To disregard the legitimacy of the UN, to favour force over the law, would be to take on a heavy responsibility."

278. On the evening of 18 March, the House of Commons passed by 412 votes to 149 a motion supporting "the decision of Her Majesty's Government that the United Kingdom should use all means necessary to ensure the disarmament of Iraq's weapons of mass destruction".

279. President Bush wrote in his memoir that he convened "the entire National Security Council" on the morning of 19 March where he "gave the order to launch Operation Iraqi Freedom".[138]

280. In the Security Council debate on 19 March, the majority of members of the Security Council, including France, Russia and China, made clear that they thought the goal of disarming Iraq could be achieved by peaceful means and emphasised the primary responsibility of the Security Council for the maintenance of international peace and security.[139]

281. UNMOVIC and the IAEA had provided the work programmes required by resolution 1284. They included 12 key tasks identified by UNMOVIC where progress "could have an impact on the Council's assessment of co-operation of Iraq".

282. Shortly before midnight on 19 March, the US informed Sir David Manning that there was to be a change to the plan and US airstrikes would be launched at 0300 GMT on 20 March.[140]

283. Early on the morning of 20 March, US forces crossed into Iraq and seized the port area of Umm Qasr.[141]

284. Mr Blair continued to state that France was responsible for the impasse.

---

[137] Telegram 135 Paris to FCO London, 18 March 2003, 'Iraq: Chirac's Reaction to Ultimatum'.
[138] Bush GW. *Decision Points*. Virgin Books, 2010.
[139] UN Security Council, '4721st Meeting Wednesday 19 March 2003' (S/PV.4721).
[140] Letter Manning to McDonald, 20 March 2003, 'Iraq'.
[141] Ministry of Defence, *Operations in Iraq: Lessons for the Future*, December 2003, page 12.

285. At Cabinet on 20 March, Mr Blair concluded that the Government:

"... should lose no opportunity to propagate the reason, at every level and as widely as possible, why we had arrived at a diplomatic impasse, and why it was necessary to take action against Iraq. France had not been prepared to accept that Iraq's failure to comply with its obligations should lead to the use of force to achieve compliance."[142]

Why Iraq? Why now?

286. In his memoir, Mr Blair described his speech opening the debate on 18 March as "the most important speech I had ever made".[143]

287. Mr Blair framed the decision for the House of Commons as a "tough" and "stark" choice between "retreat" and holding firm to the course of action the Government had set. Mr Blair stated that he believed "passionately" in the latter. He deployed a wide range of arguments to explain the grounds for military action and to make a persuasive case for the Government's policy.[144]

288. In setting out his position, Mr Blair recognised the gravity of the debate and the strength of opposition in both the country and Parliament to immediate military action. In his view, the issue mattered "so much" because the outcome would not just determine the fate of the Iraqi regime and the Iraqi people but would:

"... determine the way in which Britain and the world confront the central security threat of the 21st century, the development of the United Nations, the relationship between Europe and the United States, the relations within the European Union and the way in which the United States engages with the rest of the world. So it could hardly be more important. It will determine the pattern of international politics for the next generation."

Was Iraq a serious or imminent threat?

289. On 18 March 2003, the House of Commons was asked:

- to recognise that Iraq's weapons of mass destruction and long-range missiles, and its continuing non-compliance with Security Council resolutions, posed a threat to international peace and security; and

- to support the use of all means necessary to ensure the disarmament of Iraq's weapons of mass destruction, on the basis that the United Kingdom must uphold the authority of the United Nations as set out in resolution 1441 and many resolutions preceding it.

---

[142] Cabinet Conclusions, 20 March 2003.
[143] Blair T. *A Journey*. Hutchinson, 2010.
[144] House of Commons, *Official Report*, 18 March 2003, columns 760-774.

290. In his statement, Mr Blair addressed both the threat to international peace and security presented by Iraq's defiance of the UN and its failure to comply with its disarmament obligations as set out in resolution 1441 (2002). Iraq was "the test of whether we treat the threat seriously".

291. Mr Blair rehearsed the Government's position on Iraq's past pursuit and use of weapons of mass destruction; its failures to comply with the obligations imposed by the UN Security Council between 1991 and 1998; Iraq's repeated declarations which proved to be false; and the "large quantities of weapons of mass destruction" which were "unaccounted for". He described UNSCOM's final report (in January 1999) as "a withering indictment of Saddam's lies, deception and obstruction".

292. Mr Blair cited the UNMOVIC "clusters" document issued on 7 March as "a remarkable document", detailing "all the unanswered questions about Iraq's weapons of mass destruction", listing "29 different areas in which the inspectors have been unable to obtain information".

293. He stated that, based on Iraq's false declaration, its failure to co-operate, the unanswered questions in the UNMOVIC "clusters" document, and the unaccounted for material, the Security Council should have convened and condemned Iraq as in material breach of its obligations. If Saddam Hussein continued to fail to co-operate, force should be used.

294. Addressing the wider message from the issue of Iraq, Mr Blair asked:

"... what ... would any tyrannical regime possessing weapons of mass destruction think when viewing the history of the world's diplomatic dance with Saddam over ... 12 years? That our capacity to pass firm resolutions has only been matched by our feebleness in implementing them."

295. Mr Blair acknowledged that Iraq was "not the only country with weapons of mass destruction", but declared: "back away from this confrontation now, and future conflicts will be infinitely worse and more devastating in their effects".

296. Mr Blair added:

"The real problem is that ... people dispute Iraq is a threat, dispute the link between terrorism and weapons of mass destruction, and dispute in other words, the whole basis of our assertion that the two together constitute a fundamental assault on our way of life."

297. Mr Blair also described a "threat of chaos and disorder" arising from "tyrannical regimes with weapons of mass destruction and extreme terrorist groups" prepared to use them.

298. Mr Blair set out his concerns about:

- proliferators of nuclear equipment or expertise;
- "dictatorships with highly repressive regimes" who were "desperately trying to acquire" chemical, biological or, "particularly, nuclear weapons capability" – some of those were "a short time away from having a serviceable nuclear weapon", and that activity was increasing, not diminishing; and
- the possibility of terrorist groups obtaining and using weapons of mass destruction, including a "radiological bomb".

299. Those two threats had very different motives and different origins. He accepted "fully" that the association between the two was:

"… loose – but it is hardening. The possibility of the two coming together – of terrorist groups in possession of weapons of mass destruction or even of a so called dirty radiological bomb – is now in my judgement, a real and present danger to Britain and its national security."

300. Later in his speech, Mr Blair stated that the threat which Saddam Hussein's arsenal posed:

"… to British citizens at home and abroad cannot simply be contained. Whether in the hands of his regime or in the hands of the terrorists to whom he would give his weapons, they pose a clear danger to British citizens …"

301. This fusion of long-standing concerns about proliferation with the post-9/11 concerns about mass-casualty terrorism was at the heart of the Government's case for taking action at this time against Iraq.

302. The UK assessment of Iraq's capabilities set out in Section 4 of the Report shows:

- The proliferation of nuclear, chemical and biological weapons and their delivery systems, particularly ballistic missiles, was regarded as a major threat. But Iran, North Korea and Libya were of greater concern than Iraq in terms of the risk of nuclear and missile proliferation.
- JIC Assessments, reflected in the September 2002 dossier, had consistently taken the view that, if sanctions were removed or became ineffective, it would take Iraq at least five years following the end of sanctions to produce enough fissile material for a weapon. On 7 March, the IAEA had reported to the Security Council that there was no indication that Iraq had resumed its nuclear activities.
- The September dossier stated that Iraq could produce a nuclear weapon within one to two years if it obtained fissile material and other essential components from a foreign supplier. There was no evidence that Iraq had tried to acquire fissile material and other components or – were it able to do so – that it had the technical capabilities to turn these materials into a usable weapon.

- JIC Assessments had identified the possible stocks of chemical and biological weapons which would largely have been for short-range, battlefield use by the Iraqi armed forces. The JIC had also judged in the September dossier that Iraq was producing chemical and biological agents and that there were development programmes for longer-range missiles capable of delivering them.

- Iraq's proscribed Al Samoud 2 missiles were being destroyed.

303. The UK Government did have significant concerns about the potential risks of all types of weapons of mass destruction being obtained by Islamist extremists (in particular Al Qaida) who would be prepared to use such weapons.

304. Saddam Hussein's regime had the potential to proliferate material and know-how to terrorist groups, but it was not judged likely to do so.

305. On 28 November 2001, the JIC assessed that:

- Saddam Hussein had "refused to permit any Al Qaida presence in Iraq".

- Evidence of contact between Iraq and Usama Bin Laden (UBL) was "fragmentary and uncorroborated"; including that Iraq had been in contact with Al Qaida for exploratory discussions on toxic materials in late 1988.

- "With common enemies ... there was clearly scope for collaboration."

- There was "no evidence that these contacts led to practical co-operation; we judge it unlikely ... There is no evidence UBL's organisation has ever had a presence in Iraq."

- Practical co-operation between Iraq and Al Qaida was "unlikely because of mutual mistrust".

- There was "no credible evidence of covert transfers of WMD-related technology and expertise to terrorist groups".[145]

306. On 29 January 2003, the JIC assessed that, despite the presence of terrorists in Iraq "with links to Al Qaida", there was "no intelligence of current co-operation between Iraq and Al Qaida".[146]

307. On 10 February 2003, the JIC judged that Al Qaida would "not carry out attacks under Iraqi direction".[147]

308. Sir Richard Dearlove told the Inquiry:

"... I don't think the Prime Minister ever accepted the link between Iraq and terrorism. I think it would be fair to say that the Prime Minister was very worried about the possible conjunction of terrorism and WMD, but not specifically in relation

---

[145] JIC Assessment, 28 November 2001, 'Iraq after September 11 – The Terrorist Threat'.
[146] JIC Assessment, 29 January 2003, 'Iraq: The Emerging view from Baghdad'.
[147] JIC Assessment, 10 February 2003, 'International Terrorism: War with Iraq'.

to Iraq … [I] think, one could say this is one of his primary national security concerns given the nature of Al Qaida."[148]

309. The JIC assessed that Iraq was likely to mount a terrorist attack only in response to military action and if the existence of the regime was threatened.

310. The JIC Assessment of 10 October 2002 stated that Saddam Hussein's "overriding objective" was to "avoid a US attack that would threaten his regime".[149] The JIC judged that, in the event of US-led military action against Iraq, Saddam would:

"… aim to use terrorism or the threat of it. Fearing the US response, he is likely to weigh the costs and benefits carefully in deciding the timing and circumstances in which terrorism is used. But intelligence on Iraq's capabilities and intentions in this field is limited."

311. The JIC also judged that:

- Saddam's "capability to conduct effective terrorist attacks" was "very limited".
- Iraq's "terrorism capability" was "inadequate to carry out chemical or biological attacks beyond individual assassination attempts using poisons".

312. The JIC Assessment of 29 January 2003 sustained its earlier judgements on Iraq's ability and intent to conduct terrorist operations.[150]

313. Sir David Omand, the Security and Intelligence Co-ordinator in the Cabinet Office from 2002 to 2005, told the Inquiry that, in March 2002, the Security Service judged that the "threat from terrorism from Saddam's own intelligence apparatus in the event of an intervention in Iraq … was judged to be limited and containable".[151]

314. Baroness Manningham-Buller, the Director General of the Security Service from 2002 to 2007, confirmed that position, stating that the Security Service felt there was "a pretty good intelligence picture of a threat from Iraq within the UK and to British interests".[152]

315. Baroness Manningham-Buller added that subsequent events showed the judgement that Saddam Hussein did not have the capability to do anything much in the UK, had "turned out to be the right judgement".[153]

316. While it was reasonable for the Government to be concerned about the fusion of proliferation and terrorism, there was no basis in the JIC Assessments to suggest that Iraq itself represented such a threat.

---

[148] Private hearing, 16 June 2010, pages 39-40.
[149] JIC Assessment, 10 October 2002, 'International Terrorism: The Threat from Iraq'.
[150] JIC Assessment, 29 January 2003, 'Iraq: The Emerging view from Baghdad'.
[151] Public hearing, 20 January 2010, page 37.
[152] Public hearing, 20 July 2010, page 6.
[153] Public hearing, 20 July 2010, page 9.

317. The UK Government assessed that Iraq had failed to comply with a series of UN resolutions. Instead of disarming as these resolutions had demanded, Iraq was assessed to have concealed materials from past inspections and to have taken the opportunity of the absence of inspections to revive its WMD programmes.

318. In Section 4, the Inquiry has identified the importance of the ingrained belief of the Government and the intelligence community that Saddam Hussein's regime retained chemical and biological warfare capabilities, was determined to preserve and if possible enhance its capabilities, including at some point in the future a nuclear capability, and was pursuing an active and successful policy of deception and concealment.

319. This construct remained influential despite the lack of significant finds by inspectors in the period leading up to military action in March 2003, and even after the Occupation of Iraq.

320. Challenging Saddam Hussein's "claim" that he had no weapons of mass destruction, Mr Blair said in his speech on 18 March:

- "… we are asked to believe that after seven years of obstruction and non-compliance … he [Saddam Hussein] voluntarily decided to do what he had consistently refused to do under coercion."

- "We are asked now seriously to accept that in the last few years – contrary to all history, contrary to all intelligence – Saddam decided unilaterally to destroy those weapons. I say that such a claim is palpably absurd."

- "… Iraq continues to deny that it has any weapons of mass destruction, although no serious intelligence service anywhere in the world believes it."

- "What is perfectly clear is that Saddam is playing the same old games in the same old way. Yes, there are minor concessions, but there has been no fundamental change of heart or mind."[154]

321. At no stage was the proposition that Iraq might no longer have chemical, biological or nuclear weapons or programmes identified and examined by either the JIC or the policy community.

322. Intelligence and assessments were used to prepare material to be used to support Government statements in a way which conveyed certainty without acknowledging the limitations of the intelligence.

323. Mr Blair's statement to the House of Commons on 18 March was the culmination of a series of public statements and interviews setting out the urgent need for the international community to act to bring about Iraq's disarmament in accordance with

---

[154] House of Commons, *Official Report*, 18 March 2003, columns 760-764.

those resolutions, dating back to February 2002, before his meeting with President Bush at Crawford on 5 and 6 April.

324. As Mr Cook's resignation statement on 17 March made clear, it was possible for a Minister to draw different conclusions from the same information.

325. Mr Cook set out his doubts about Saddam Hussein's ability to deliver a strategic attack and the degree to which Iraq posed a "clear and present danger" to the UK. The points Mr Cook made included:

- "… neither the international community nor the British public is persuaded that there is an urgent and compelling reason for this military action in Iraq."
- "Over the past decade that strategy [of containment] had destroyed more weapons than in the Gulf War, dismantled Iraq's nuclear weapons programme and halted Saddam's medium and long range missile programmes."
- "Iraq probably has no weapons of mass destruction in the commonly understood sense of the term – namely a credible device capable of being delivered against a strategic city target. It probably … has biological toxins and battlefield chemical munitions, but it has had them since the 1980s when US companies sold Saddam anthrax agents and the then British Government approved chemical and munitions factories. Why is it now so urgent that we should take military action to disarm a military capacity that has been there for twenty years, and which we helped to create? Why is it necessary to resort to war this week, while Saddam's ambition to complete his weapons programme is blocked by the presence of UN inspectors?"[155]

326. On 12 October 2004, announcing the withdrawal of two lines of intelligence reporting which had contributed to the pre-conflict judgements on mobile biological production facilities and the regime's intentions, Mr Straw stated that he did:

"… not accept, even with hindsight, that we were wrong to act as we did in the circumstances that we faced at the time. Even after reading all the evidence detailed by the Iraq Survey Group, it is still hard to believe that any regime could behave in so self-destructive a manner as to pretend that it had forbidden weaponry, when in fact it had not."[156]

327. Iraq had acted suspiciously over many years, which led to the inferences drawn by the Government and the intelligence community that it had been seeking to protect concealed WMD assets. When Iraq denied that it had retained any WMD capabilities, the UK Government accused it of lying.

328. This led the Government to emphasise the ability of Iraq successfully to deceive the inspectors, and cast doubt on the investigative capacity of the inspectors. The role

---

[155] House of Commons, *Official Report*, 17 March 2003, columns 726-728.
[156] House of Commons, *Official Report*, 12 October 2004, columns 151-152.

of the inspectors, however, as was often pointed out, was not to seek out assets that had been hidden, but rather to validate Iraqi claims.

329. By March 2003, however:

- The Al Samoud 2 missiles which exceeded the range permitted by the UN, were being destroyed.

- The IAEA had concluded that there was no Iraqi nuclear programme of any significance.

- The inspectors believed that they were making progress and expected to achieve more co-operation from Iraq.

- The inspectors were preparing to step up their activities with U2 flights and interviews outside Iraq.

330. When the UK sought a further Security Council resolution in March 2003, the majority of the Council's members were not persuaded that the inspections process, and the diplomatic efforts surrounding it, had reached the end of the road. They did not agree that the time had come to terminate inspections and resort to force. The UK went to war without the explicit authorisation which it had sought from the Security Council.

331. At the time of the Parliamentary vote of 18 March, diplomatic options had not been exhausted. The point had not been reached where military action was the last resort.

The predicted increase in the threat to the UK as a result of military action in Iraq

332. Mr Blair had been advised that an invasion of Iraq was expected to increase the threat to the UK and UK interests from Al Qaida and its affiliates.

333. Asked about the risk that attacking Iraq with cruise missiles would "act as a recruiting sergeant for a young generation throughout the Islamic and Arab world", Mr Blair responded that:

"… what was shocking about 11 September was not just the slaughter of innocent people but the knowledge that, had the terrorists been able, there would have been not 3,000 innocent dead, but 30,000 or 300,000 … America did not attack the Al Qaida terrorist group … [it] attacked America. They did not need to be recruited … Unless we take action against them, they will grow. That is why we should act."[157]

334. The JIC judged in October 2002 that "the greatest terrorist threat in the event of military action against Iraq will come from Al Qaida and other Islamic extremists"; and they would be "pursuing their own agenda".[158]

---

[157] House of Commons, *Official Report*, 18 March 2003, column 769.
[158] JIC Assessment, 10 October 2002, 'International Terrorism: The Threat from Iraq'.

335. The JIC Assessment of 10 February 2003 repeated previous warnings that:

- Al Qaida and associated networks would remain the greatest terrorist threat to the UK and its activity would increase at the onset of any military action against Iraq.

- In the event of imminent regime collapse, Iraqi chemical and biological material could be transferred to terrorists, including Al Qaida.[159]

336. Addressing the prospects for the future, the JIC Assessment concluded:

"... **Al Qaida and associated groups will continue to represent by far the greatest terrorist threat to Western interests, and that threat will be heightened by military action against Iraq.** The broader threat from Islamist terrorists will also increase in the event of war, reflecting intensified anti-US/anti-Western sentiment in the Muslim world, including among Muslim communities in the West. And there is a risk that the transfer of CB [chemical and biological] material or expertise, during or in the aftermath of conflict, will enhance Al Qaida's capabilities."

337. In response to a call for Muslims everywhere to take up arms in defence of Iraq issued by Usama Bin Laden on 11 February, and a further call on 16 February for "compulsory jihad" by Muslims against the West, the JIC Assessment on 19 February predicted that the upward trend in the reports of threats to the UK was likely to continue.[160]

338. The JIC continued to warn in March that the threat from Al Qaida would increase at the onset of military action against Iraq.[161]

339. The JIC also warned that:

- Al Qaida activity in northern Iraq continued.
- Al Qaida might have established sleeper cells in Baghdad, to be activated during a US occupation.

340. The warning about the risk of chemical and biological weapons becoming available to extremist groups as a result of military action in Iraq was reiterated on 19 March.[162]

341. Addressing the JIC Assessment of 10 February 2003, Mr Blair told the Intelligence and Security Committee (ISC) later that year that:

"One of the most difficult aspects of this is that there was obviously a danger that in attacking Iraq you ended up provoking the very thing you were trying to avoid. On the other hand I think you had to ask the question, 'Could you really, as a result

---

[159] JIC Assessment, 10 February 2003, 'International Terrorism: War with Iraq'.
[160] JIC Assessment, 19 February 2003, 'International Terrorism: The Current Threat from Islamic Extremists'.
[161] JIC Assessment, 12 March 2003, 'International Terrorism: War with Iraq: Update'.
[162] Note JIC, 19 March 2003, 'Saddam: The Beginning of the End'.

of that fear, leave the possibility that in time developed into a nexus between terrorism and WMD in an event?' This is where you've just got to make your judgement about this. But this is my judgement and it remains my judgement and I suppose time will tell whether it's true or it's not true."[163]

342. In its response to the ISC Report, the Government drew:

"... attention to the difficult judgement that had to be made and the factors on both sides of the argument to be taken into account."[164]

343. Baroness Manningham-Buller told the Inquiry:

"By 2003/2004 we were receiving an increasing number of leads to terrorist activity from within the UK ... our involvement in Iraq radicalised, for want of a better word ... a few among a generation ... [who] saw our involvement in Iraq, on top of our involvement in Afghanistan, as being an attack on Islam."[165]

344. Asked about the proposition that it was right to remove Saddam Hussein's regime to forestall a fusion of weapons of mass destruction and international terrorism at some point in the future, and if it had eliminated a threat of terrorism from his regime, Baroness Manningham-Buller replied:

"It eliminated the threat of terrorism from his direct regime; it didn't eliminate the threat of terrorism using unconventional methods ... So using weapons of mass destruction as a terrorist weapon is still a potential threat.

"After all Usama Bin Laden said it was the duty of members of his organisation or those in sympathy with it to acquire and use these weapons. It is interesting that ... such efforts as we have seen to get access to these sort of materials have been low-grade and not very professional, but it must be a cause of concern to my former colleagues that at some stage terrorist groups will resort to these methods. In that respect, I don't think toppling Saddam Hussein is germane to the long-term ambitions of some terrorist groups to use them."[166]

345. Asked specifically about the theory that at some point in the future Saddam Hussein would probably have brought together international terrorism and weapons of mass destruction in a threat to Western interests, Baroness Manningham-Buller responded:

"It is a hypothetical theory. It certainly wasn't of concern in either the short-term or the medium-term to my colleagues and myself."[167]

---

[163] Intelligence and Security Committee, *Iraqi Weapons of Mass Destruction – Intelligence and Assessments*, September 2003, Cm5972, paragraph 128.
[164] *Government Response to the Intelligence and Security Committee Report on Iraqi Weapons of Mass Destruction – Intelligence and Assessments, 11 September 2003*, February 2004, Cm6118, paragraph 22.
[165] Public hearing, 20 July 2010, page 19.
[166] Public hearing, 20 July 2010, pages 23-24.
[167] Public hearing, 20 July 2010, page 24.

346. Asked if "a war in Iraq would aggravate the threat from whatever source to the United Kingdom", Baroness Manningham-Buller stated that that was the view communicated by the JIC Assessments.[168]

347. Baroness Manningham-Buller subsequently added that if Ministers had read the JIC Assessments they could "have had no doubt" about that risk.[169] She said that by the time of the July 2005 attacks in London:

"... an increasing number of British-born individuals ... were attracted to the ideology of Usama Bin Laden and saw the West's activities in Iraq and Afghanistan as threatening their fellow religionists and the Muslim world."

348. Asked whether the judgement that the effect of the invasion of Iraq had increased the terrorist threat to the UK was based on hard evidence or a broader assessment, Baroness Manningham-Buller replied:

"I think we can produce evidence because of the numerical evidence of the number of plots, the number of leads, the number of people identified, and the correlation of that to Iraq and statements of people as to why they were involved ... So I think the answer to your ... question: yes."[170]

349. In its request for a statement, the Inquiry asked Mr Blair if he had read the JIC Assessment of 10 February 2002, and what weight he had given to it when he decided to take military action.[171]

350. In his statement Mr Blair wrote:

"I was aware of the JIC Assessment of 10 February that the Al Qaida threat to the UK would increase. But I took the view then and take the same view now that to have backed down because of the threat of terrorism would be completely wrong. In any event, following 9/11 and Afghanistan we were a terrorist target and, as recent events in Europe and the US show, irrespective of Iraq, there are ample justifications such terrorists will use as excuses for terrorism."[172]

The UK's relationship with the US

351. The UK's relationship with the US was a determining factor in the Government's decisions over Iraq.

352. It was the US Administration which decided in late 2001 to make dealing with the problem of Saddam Hussein's regime the second priority, after the ousting of the Taliban

---

[168] Public hearing, 20 July 2010, page 31.
[169] Public hearing, 20 July 2010, page 33.
[170] Public hearing, 20 July 2010, pages 33-34.
[171] Inquiry request for a witness statement, 13 December 2010, Qs 11c and 11d page 7.
[172] Statement, 14 January 2011, page 16.

in Afghanistan, in the "Global War on Terror". In that period, the US Administration turned against a strategy of continued containment of Iraq, which it was pursuing before the 9/11 attacks.

353. This was not, initially, the view of the UK Government. Its stated view at that time was that containment had been broadly effective, and that it could be adapted in order to remain sustainable. Containment continued to be the declared policy of the UK throughout the first half of 2002.

354. The declared objectives of the UK and the US towards Iraq up to the time of the invasion differed. The US was explicitly seeking to achieve a change of regime; the UK to achieve the disarmament of Iraq, as required by UN Security Council resolutions.

355. Most crucially, the US Administration committed itself to a timetable for military action which did not align with, and eventually overrode, the timetable and processes for inspections in Iraq which had been set by the UN Security Council. The UK wanted UNMOVIC and the IAEA to have time to complete their work, and wanted the support of the Security Council, and of the international community more widely, before any further steps were taken. This option was foreclosed by the US decision.

356. On these and other important points, including the planning for the post-conflict period and the functioning of the Coalition Provisional Authority (CPA), the UK Government decided that it was right or necessary to defer to its close ally and senior partner, the US.

357. It did so essentially for two reasons:

- Concern that vital areas of co-operation between the UK and the US could be damaged if the UK did not give the US its full support over Iraq.
- The belief that the best way to influence US policy towards the direction preferred by the UK was to commit full and unqualified support, and seek to persuade from the inside.

358. The UK Government was right to think very carefully about both of these points.

359. First, the close strategic alliance with the US has been a cornerstone of the UK's foreign and security policy under successive governments since the Second World War. Mr Blair rightly attached great importance to preserving and strengthening it.

360. After the attacks on the US on 11 September 2001, that relationship was reinforced when Mr Blair declared that the UK would stand "shoulder to shoulder" with the US to defeat and eradicate international terrorism.[173] The action that followed in Afghanistan to bring about the fall of the Taliban served to strengthen and deepen the sense of shared endeavour.

---

[173] The National Archives, 11 September 2001, *September 11 attacks: Prime Minister's statement.*

361. When the US Administration turned its attention to regime change in Iraq as part of the second phase of the "Global War on Terror", Mr Blair's immediate response was to seek to offer a partnership and to work with it to build international support for the position that Iraq was a threat which had to be dealt with.

362. In Mr Blair's view, the decision to stand alongside the US was in the UK's long-term national interests. In his speech of 18 March 2003, he argued that the handling of Iraq would:

> "… determine the way in which Britain and the world confront the central security threat of the 21st century, the development of the United Nations, the relationship between Europe and the United States, the relations within the European Union and the way in which the United States engages with the rest of the world. So it could hardly be more important. It will determine the pattern of international politics for the next generation."

363. In his memoir in 2010, Mr Blair wrote:

> "I knew in the final analysis I would be with the US, because it was right morally and strategically. But we should make a last ditch attempt for a peaceful solution. First to make the moral case for removing Saddam … Second, to try one more time to reunite the international community behind a clear base for action in the event of a continuing breach."[174]

364. Concern about the consequences, were the UK not to give full support to the US, featured prominently in policy calculations across Whitehall. Mr Hoon, for example, sought advice from Sir Kevin Tebbit, MOD Permanent Under Secretary, on the implications for the alliance of the UK's approach to Iraq.[175]

365. Although there has historically been a very close relationship between the British and American peoples and a close identity of values between our democracies, it is an alliance founded not on emotion, but on a hard-headed appreciation of mutual benefit. The benefits do not by any means flow only in one direction.

366. In his memoir, Mr Blair wrote:

> "… I agreed with the basic US analysis of Saddam as a threat; I thought he was a monster; and to break the US partnership in such circumstances, when America's key allies were all rallying round, would in my view, then (and now) have done major long-term damage to that relationship."

---

[174] Blair T. *A Journey*. Hutchinson, 2010.
[175] Minute Tebbit to Secretary of State [MOD], 14 January 2003, 'Iraq: What If?'

367. The Government was right to weigh the possible consequences for the wider alliance with the US very carefully, as previous Governments have done. A policy of direct opposition to the US would have done serious short-term damage to the relationship, but it is questionable whether it would have broken the partnership.

368. Over the past seven decades, the UK and US have adopted differing, and sometimes conflicting, positions on major issues, for example Suez, the Vietnam War, the Falklands, Grenada, Bosnia, the Arab/Israel dispute and, at times, Northern Ireland. Those differences did not fundamentally call into question the practice of close cooperation, to mutual advantage, on the overall relationship, including defence and intelligence.

369. The opposition of Germany and France to US policy in 2002 to 2003 does not appear to have had a lasting impact on the relationships of those countries with the US, despite the bitterness at the time.

370. However, a decision not to oppose does not have to be translated into unqualified support. Throughout the post-Second World War period (and, notably, during the wartime alliance), the UK's relationship with the US and the commonality of interests therein have proved strong enough to bear the weight of different approaches to international problems and not infrequent disagreements.

371. Had the UK stood by its differing position on Iraq – which was not an opposed position, but one in which the UK had identified conditions seen as vital by the UK Government – the Inquiry does not consider that this would have led to a fundamental or lasting change in the UK's relationship with the US.

372. This is a matter of judgement, and one on which Mr Blair, bearing the responsibility of leadership, took a different view.

373. The second reason for committing unqualified support was, by standing alongside and taking part in the planning, the UK would be able to influence US policy.

374. Mr Blair's stalwart support for the US after 9/11 had a significant impact in that country. Mr Blair developed a close working relationship with President Bush. He used this to compare notes and inject his views on the major issues of the day, and it is clear from the records of the discussions that President Bush encouraged that dialogue and listened to Mr Blair's opinions.

375. Mr Blair expressed his views in frequent telephone calls and in meetings with the President. There was also a very active channel between his Foreign Affairs Adviser and the President's National Security Advisor. Mr Blair also sent detailed written Notes to the President.

376. Mr Jonathan Powell, Mr Blair's Chief of Staff, told the Inquiry:

> "… the Prime Minister had a habit of writing notes, both internally and to President Clinton and to President Bush, on all sorts of subjects, because he found it better to put something in writing rather than to simply talk about it orally and get it much more concretely … in focused terms."[176]

377. Mr Blair drew on information and briefing received from Whitehall departments, but evidently drafted many or most of his Notes to the President himself, showing the drafts to his close advisers in No.10 but not (ahead of despatch) to the relevant Cabinet Ministers.

378. How best to exercise influence with the President of the United States is a matter for the tactical judgement of the Prime Minister, and will vary between Prime Ministers and Presidents. In relation to Iraq, Mr Blair's judgement, as he and others have explained, was that objectives the UK identified for a successful strategy should not be expressed as conditions for its support.

379. Mr Powell told the Inquiry that Mr Blair was offering the US a "partnership to try to get to a wide coalition" and "setting out a framework" and to try to persuade the US to move in a particular direction.[177]

380. Mr Blair undoubtedly influenced the President's decision to go to the UN Security Council in the autumn of 2002. On other critical decisions set out in the Report, he did not succeed in changing the approach determined in Washington.

The legal basis for military action and the authority of the UN

381. There was a vigorous debate in late 2002 and early 2003 about the legal effect of resolution 1441 and the question of whether military action against Iraq could be undertaken without the Security Council having first considered, and then assessed, whether or not Iraq was in breach of its terms.

382. Many distinguished jurists have expressed opinions on that question and the debate will no doubt continue. The Inquiry received many opinions from experts in international law which demonstrate the complexities of the issues.

383. The Inquiry has reviewed the debate that took place within the Government and how it reached its decision.

384. The circumstances in which it was ultimately decided that there was a legal basis for UK participation were far from satisfactory.

385. It was not until 13 March 2003 that Lord Goldsmith advised that there was, on balance, a secure legal basis for military action.

---

[176] Public hearing, 18 January 2010, page 38.
[177] Public hearing, 18 January 2010, pages 77-78.

386. In the letter of 14 March 2003 from Lord Goldsmith's office to No.10, which is addressed in Section 5 of the Report, Mr Blair was told that an essential ingredient of the legal basis was that he, himself, should be satisfied of the fact that Iraq was in breach of resolution 1441.

387. In accordance with that advice, it was Mr Blair who decided that, so far as the UK was concerned, Iraq was and remained in breach of resolution 1441.

388. Apart from No.10's response to the letter of 14 March, sent the following day, in terms that can only be described as perfunctory, no formal record was made of that decision and the precise grounds on which it was made remain unclear.

389. The Inquiry was told, and it accepts, that it would have been possible at that stage for the UK Government to have decided not to go ahead with military action if it had been necessary to make a decision to do so; or if the House of Commons on 18 March had voted against the Government.

390. Although there had been unanimous support for a rigorous inspections and monitoring regime backed by the threat of military force as the means to disarm Iraq when resolution 1441 was adopted, there was no such consensus in the Security Council in March 2003. If the matter had been left to the Security Council to decide, military action might have been postponed and, possibly, avoided.

391. The Charter of the United Nations vests responsibility for the maintenance of peace and security in the Security Council. The UK Government was claiming to act on behalf of the international community "to uphold the authority of the Security Council", knowing that it did not have a majority in the Security Council in support of its actions. In those circumstances, the UK's actions undermined the authority of the Security Council.

392. A determination by the Security Council on whether Iraq was in fact in material breach of resolution 1441 would have furthered the UK's aspiration to uphold the authority of the Council.

Decision-making

393. The way in which the policy on Iraq was developed and decisions were taken and implemented within the UK Government has been at the heart of the Inquiry's work and fundamental to its conclusions.

394. The Inquiry has set out in Section 2 of the Report the roles and responsibilities of key individuals and bodies in order to assist the reader. It is also publishing with the Report many of the documents which illuminate who took the key decisions and on what basis, including the full record of the discussion on Iraq in Cabinet on five key occasions pre-conflict, and policy advice to Ministers which is not normally disclosed.

Collective responsibility

395. Under UK constitutional conventions – in which the Prime Minister leads the Government – Cabinet is the main mechanism by which the most senior members of the Government take collective responsibility for its most important decisions. Cabinet is supported by a system of Ministerial Committees whose role is to identify, test and develop policy options; analyse and mitigate risks; and debate and hone policy proposals until they are endorsed across the Government.[178]

396. The *Ministerial Code* in place in 2003 said:

> "The Cabinet is supported by Ministerial Committees (both standing and ad hoc) which have a two-fold purpose. First, they relieve the pressure on the Cabinet itself by settling as much business as possible at a lower level or, failing that, by clarifying the issues and defining the points of disagreement. Second, they support the principle of collective responsibility by ensuring that, even though an important question may never reach the Cabinet itself, the decision will be fully considered and the final judgement will be sufficiently authoritative to ensure that the Government as a whole can properly be expected to accept responsibility for it."[179]

397. The Code also said:

> "The business of the Cabinet and Ministerial Committees consists in the main of:
>
> a. questions which significantly engage the collective responsibility of the Government because they raise major issues of policy or because they are of critical importance to the public;
>
> b. questions on which there is an unresolved argument between Departments."

398. Lord Wilson of Dinton told the Inquiry that between January 1998 and January 1999, in the run-up to and immediate aftermath of Operation Desert Fox in December 1998 (see Section 1.1), as Cabinet Secretary, he had attended and noted 21 Ministerial discussions on Iraq: 10 in Cabinet, of which seven had "some substance"; five in DOP; and six ad hoc meetings, including one JIC briefing.[180] Discussions in Cabinet or a Cabinet Committee would have been supported by the relevant part of the Cabinet Secretariat, the Overseas and Defence Secretariat (OD Sec).

399. Similarly, Lord Wilson stated that, between 11 September 2001 and January 2002, the Government's response to international terrorism and the subsequent military action against the Taliban in Afghanistan had been managed through 46 Ministerial meetings.[181]

---

[178] *Ministerial Code,* 2001, page 3.
[179] *Ministerial Code,* 2001, page 3.
[180] Public hearing, 25 January 2011, page 11.
[181] Public hearing, 25 January 2011, page 11.

400. The last meeting of DOP on Iraq before the 2003 conflict, however, took place in March 1999.[182]

401. In April 2002, the MOD clearly expected consideration of military options to be addressed through DOP. Mr Simon Webb, the MOD Policy Director, advised Mr Hoon that:

> "Even these preparatory steps would properly need a Cabinet Committee decision, based on a minute from the Defence Secretary ..."[183]

402. Most decisions on Iraq pre-conflict were taken either bilaterally between Mr Blair and the relevant Secretary of State or in meetings between Mr Blair, Mr Straw and Mr Hoon, with No.10 officials and, as appropriate, Mr John Scarlett (Chairman of the JIC), Sir Richard Dearlove and Adm Boyce. Some of those meetings were minuted; some were not.

403. As the guidance for the Cabinet Secretariat makes clear, the purpose of the minute of a meeting is to set out the conclusions reached so that those who have to take action know precisely what to do; the second purpose is to "give the reasons why the conclusions were reached".[184]

404. Lord Turnbull, Cabinet Secretary from 2002 to 2005, described Mr Blair's characteristic way of working with his Cabinet colleagues as:

> "... 'I like to move fast. I don't want to spend a lot of time in kind of conflict resolution, and, therefore, I will get the people who will make this thing move quickly and efficiently.' That was his sort of characteristic style, but it has drawbacks."[185]

405. Lord Turnbull subsequently told the Inquiry that the group described above was "a professional forum ... they had ... with one possible exception [Ms Clare Short, the International Development Secretary], the right people in the room. It wasn't the kind of sofa government in the sense of the Prime Minister and his special advisers and political cronies".[186]

406. In July 2004, Lord Butler's Report stated that his Committee was:

> "... concerned that the informality and circumscribed character of the Government's procedures which we saw in the context of policy-making towards Iraq risks reducing the scope for informed collective political judgement. Such risks are particularly significant in a field like the subject of our Review, where hard facts are inherently

---

[182] Email Cabinet Office to Secretary Iraq Inquiry, 5 July 2011, 'FOI request for joint MOD/FCO memo on Iraq Policy 1999'.
[183] Minute Webb to PS/Secretary of State, 12 April 2002, 'Bush and the War on Terrorism'.
[184] Cabinet Office, June 2001, *Guide to Minute Taking*.
[185] Public hearing, 13 January 2010, page 28.
[186] Public hearing, 13 January 2010, pages 45-46.

difficult to come by and the quality of judgement is accordingly all the more important."[187]

407. In response, Mr Blair agreed that:

"… where a small group is brought together to work on operational military planning and developing the diplomatic strategy, in future such a group will operate formally as an ad hoc Cabinet Committee."[188]

408. The Inquiry considers that where policy options include significant military deployments, particularly where they will have implications for the responsibilities of more than one Cabinet Minister, are likely to be controversial, and/or are likely to give rise to significant risks, the options should be considered by a group of Ministers meeting regularly, whether or not they are formally designated as a Cabinet Committee, so that Cabinet as a whole can be enabled to take informed collective decisions.

409. Describing the important function a Cabinet Committee can play, Mr Powell wrote:

"Most of the important decisions of the Blair Government were taken either in informal meetings of Ministers and officials or by Cabinet Committees … Unlike the full Cabinet, a Cabinet Committee has the right people present, including, for example, the military Chiefs of Staff or scientific advisers, its members are well briefed, it can take as long as it likes over its discussion on the basis of well-prepared papers, and it is independently chaired by a senior Minister with no departmental vested interest."[189]

410. The Inquiry concurs with this description of the function of a Cabinet Committee when it is working well. In particular, it recognises the important function which a Minister without departmental responsibilities for the issues under consideration can play. This can provide some external challenge from experienced members of the government and mitigate any tendency towards group-think. In the case of Iraq, for example, the inclusion of the Chancellor of the Exchequer or Deputy Prime Minister, as senior members of the Cabinet, or of Mr Cook, as a former Foreign Secretary known to have concerns about the policy, could have provided an element of challenge.

411. Mr Powell likewise recognises the importance of having written advice which can be seen before a meeting, allowing all those present to have shared information and the opportunity to digest it and seek further advice if necessary. This allows the time in meetings to be used productively.

412. The Inquiry considers that there should have been collective discussion by a Cabinet Committee or small group of Ministers on the basis of inter-departmental advice

---

[187] *Review of Intelligence on Weapons of Mass Destruction* ["The Butler Report"], 14 July 2004, HC 898.
[188] Cabinet Office, *Review on Intelligence on Weapons of Mass Destruction: Implementation of its Conclusions*, March 2005, Cm6492.
[189] Powell J. *The New Machiavelli: How to wield power in the modern world.* The Bodley Head, 2010.

agreed at a senior level between officials at a number of decision points which had a major impact on the development of UK policy before the invasion of Iraq. Those were:

- The decision at the beginning of December 2001 to offer to work with President Bush on a strategy to deal with Iraq as part of Phase 2 of the "War on Terror", despite the fact that there was no evidence of any Iraqi involvement with the attacks on the US or active links to Al Qaida.

- The adoption of the position at the end of February 2002 that Iraq was a threat which had to be dealt with, together with the assumption that the only certain means to remove Saddam Hussein and his regime was to invade Iraq and impose a new government.

- The position Mr Blair should adopt in discussions with President Bush at Crawford in April 2002. The meeting at Chequers on 2 April was given a presentation on the military options and did not explore the political and legal implications of a conflict with Iraq. There was no FCO representative at the Chequers meeting and no subsequent meeting with Mr Straw and Mr Hoon.

- The position Mr Blair should adopt in his discussion with President Bush at Camp David on 5 and 6 September 2002. Mr Blair's long Note of 28 July, telling President Bush "I will be with you, whatever", was seen, before it was sent, only by No.10 officials. A copy was sent afterwards to Mr Straw, but not to Mr Hoon. While the Note was marked "Personal" (to signal that it should have a restricted circulation), it represented an extensive statement of the UK Government's position by the Prime Minister to the President of the United States. The Foreign and Defence Secretaries should certainly have been given an opportunity to comment on the draft in advance.

- A discussion in mid-September 2002 on the need for robust post-conflict planning.

- The decision on 31 October 2002 to offer ground forces to the US for planning purposes.

- The decision on 17 January 2003 to deploy large scale ground forces for operations in southern Iraq.

- The position Mr Blair should adopt in his discussion with President Bush in Washington on 31 January 2003.

- The proposals in Mr Blair's Note to President Bush of 19 February suggesting a deadline for a vote in the Security Council of 14 March.

- A review of UK policy at the end of February 2003 when the inspectors had found no evidence of WMD and there was only limited support for the second resolution in the Security Council.

- The question of whether Iraq had committed further material breaches as specified in operative paragraph 4 of resolution 1441 (2002), as posed in Mr Brummell's letter of 14 March to Mr Rycroft.

413. In addition to providing a mechanism to probe and challenge the implications of proposals before decisions were taken, a Cabinet Committee or a more structured process might have identified some of the wider implications and risks associated with the deployment of military forces to Iraq. It might also have offered the opportunity to remedy some of the deficiencies in planning which are identified in Section 6 of the Report. There will, of course, be other policy issues which would benefit from the same approach.

414. Cabinet has a different role to that of a Cabinet Committee.

415. Mr Powell has written that:

> "... Cabinet is the right place to ratify decisions, the right place for people to raise concerns if they have not done so before, the right place for briefings by the Prime Minister and other Ministers on strategic issues, the right place to ensure political unity; but it is categorically not the right place for an informed decision on difficult and detailed policy issues."[190]

416. In 2009, in a statement explaining a Cabinet decision to veto the release of minutes of one of its meetings under the Freedom of Information Act 2000, Mr Straw explained the need for frank discussion at Cabinet very cogently:

> "Serious and controversial decisions must be taken with free, frank – even blunt deliberations between colleagues. Dialogue must be fearless. Ministers must have the confidence to challenge each other in private. They must ensure that decisions have been properly thought through, sounding out all possibilities before committing themselves to a course of action. They must not feel inhibited from advancing options that may be unpopular or controversial. They must not be deflected from expressing dissent by the fear that they may be held personally to account for views that are later cast aside."[191]

417. Mr Blair told the Inquiry that:

> "... the discussion that we had in Cabinet was substantive discussion. We had it again and again and again, and the options were very simple. The options were: a sanctions framework that was effective; alternatively, the UN inspectors doing the job; alternatively, you have to remove Saddam. Those were the options."[192]

---

[190] Powell J. *The New Machiavelli: How to wield power in the modern world*. The Bodley Head, 2010.
[191] Statement J Straw, 23 February 2009, 'Exercise of the Executive Override under section 53 of the Freedom of Information Act 2000 in respect of the decision of the Information Commissioner dated 18 February 2008 (Ref: FS50165372) as upheld by the decision of the Information Tribunal of 27 January 2009 (Ref: EA/2008/0024 and EA/2008/0029): Statement of Reasons'.
[192] Public hearing, 29 January 2010, page 22.

418. Mr Blair added:

"Nobody in the Cabinet was unaware of … what the whole issue was about. It was the thing running throughout the whole of the political mainstream at the time. There were members of the Cabinet who would challenge and disagree, but most of them agreed."[193]

419. The Inquiry has seen the minutes of 26 meetings of Cabinet between 28 February 2002 and 17 March 2003 at which Iraq was mentioned and Cabinet Secretariat notebooks. Cabinet was certainly given updates on diplomatic developments and had opportunities to discuss the general issues. The number of occasions on which there was a substantive discussion of the policy was very much more limited.

420. There were substantive discussions of the policy on Iraq, although (as the Report sets out) not necessarily of all the issues, in Cabinet on 7 March and 23 September 2002 and 16 January, 13 March and 17 March 2003. Those are the records which are being published with the Report.

421. At the Cabinet meeting on 7 March 2002, Mr Blair concluded:

"… the concerns expressed in discussion were justified. It was important that the United States did not appear to be acting unilaterally. It was critically important to reinvigorate the Middle East Peace Process. Any military action taken against President Saddam Hussein's regime had to be effective. On the other hand, the Iraqi regime was in clear breach of its obligations under several United Nations Security Council resolutions. Its WMD programmes posed a threat to peace. Iraq's neighbours regarded President Saddam Hussein as a danger. The right strategy was to engage closely with the Government of the United States in order to be in a position to shape policy and its presentation. The international community should proceed in a measured but determined way to decide how to respond to the real threat represented by the Iraqi regime. No decisions to launch military action had been taken and any action taken would be in accordance with international law.

"The Cabinet, 'Took note, with approval.'"[194]

422. Cabinet on 17 March 2003 noted Mr Blair's conclusion that "the diplomatic process was at an end; Saddam Hussein would be given an ultimatum to leave Iraq; and the House of Commons would be asked to endorse the use of military action against Iraq to enforce compliance, if necessary".

423. In Section 5 of the Report, the Inquiry concludes that Lord Goldsmith should have been asked to provide written advice which fully reflected the position on 17 March and explained the legal basis on which the UK could take military action and set out the risks of legal challenge.

---

[193] Public hearing, 29 January 2010, pages 228-229.
[194] Cabinet Conclusions, 7 March 2002.

424. There was no substantive discussion of the military options, despite promises by Mr Blair, before the meeting on 17 March.

425. In his statement for the Inquiry, Mr Hoon wrote that by the time he joined Cabinet, in 1999:

> "... the pattern of the organisation and format of Cabinet meetings was ... well established. Tony Blair was well known to be extremely concerned about leaks from Cabinet discussions ... It was my perception that, largely as a consequence of this, he did not normally expect key decisions to be made in the course of Cabinet meetings. Papers were submitted to the Cabinet Office, and in turn by the Cabinet Office to appropriate Cabinet Committees for decisions."[195]

426. Mr Hoon wrote:

> "At no time when I was serving in the Ministry of Defence were other Cabinet Ministers involved in discussions about the deployment of specific forces and the nature of their operations. Relevant details would have been circulated to 10 Downing Street or other Government departments as necessary ... I do not recall a single Cabinet level discussion of specific troop deployments and the nature of their operations."[196]

427. The Inquiry recognises that there will be operational constraints on discussion of the details of military deployments, but that would not preclude the discussion of the principles and the implications of military options.

428. In January 2006, the Cabinet discussed the proposal to deploy military forces to Helmand later that year.

429. The Inquiry also recognises that the nature of foreign policy, as the Report vividly demonstrates, requires the Prime Minister of the UK, the Foreign Secretary and their most senior officials to be involved in negotiating and agreeing policy on a day-by-day, and sometimes hour-by-hour basis.

430. It would neither be necessary nor feasible to seek a mandate from Cabinet at each stage of a discussion. That reinforces the importance of ensuring Cabinet is kept informed as strategy evolves, is given the opportunity to raise questions and is asked to endorse key decisions. Cabinet Ministers need more information than will be available from the media, especially on sensitive issues of foreign and security policy.

431. In 2009, three former Cabinet Secretaries[197] told the House of Lords Select Committee on the Constitution:

---

[195] Statement, 2 April 2015, page 1.
[196] Statement, 2 April 2015, page 2.
[197] Lord Armstrong of Ilminster, Lord Butler of Brockwell and Lord Wilson of Dinton.

"… each of us, as Secretary of the Cabinet, has been constantly conscious of his responsibility to the Cabinet collectively and of the need to have regard to the needs and responsibilities of the other members of the Cabinet (and indeed of other Ministers) as well of those of the Prime Minister. That has coloured our relationships with Number 10 as well as those with other Ministers and their departments."[198]

432. Lord Turnbull told the Inquiry that Mr Blair:

"… wanted a step change in the work on delivery and reform, which I hope I managed to give him. Now … how does the Cabinet Secretary work? You come in and you are – even with the two roles that you have, head of an organisation of half a million civil servants and in some sense co-ordinating a public sector of about five million people. You have to make choices as to where you make your effort, and I think the policy I followed was not to take an issue over from someone to whom it was delegated simply because it was big and important, but you have to make a judgement as to whether it is being handled competently, whether that particular part is, in a sense, under pressure, whether you think they are getting it wrong in some sense, or they are missing certain important things."[199]

433. The responsibility of the Cabinet Secretary to ensure that members of Cabinet are fully engaged in ways that allow them to accept collective responsibility and to meet their departmental obligations nevertheless remains.

Lessons

434. In a democratic system, public support and understanding for a major military operation are essential. It is therefore important to guard against overstating what military action might achieve and against any tendency to play down the risks. A realistic assessment of the possibilities and limitations of armed force, and of the challenges of intervening in the affairs of other States, should help any future UK Government manage expectations, including its own.

435. When the potential for military action arises, the Government should not commit to a firm political objective before it is clear that it can be achieved. Regular reassessment is essential, to ensure that the assumptions upon which policy is being made and implemented remain correct.

436. Once an issue becomes a matter for the Security Council, the UK Government cannot expect to retain control of how it is to be discussed and eventually decided unless it is able to work with the interests and agendas of other Member States. In relation to Iraq, the independent role of the inspectors was a further dimension.

---

[198] Fourth Report from the House of Lords Select Committee on the Constitution, Session 2009-10, *The Cabinet Office and the Centre of Government*, HL Paper 30.
[199] Public hearing, 13 January 2010, page 3.

437. A military timetable should not be allowed to dictate a diplomatic timetable. If a strategy of coercive diplomacy is being pursued, forces should be deployed in such a way that the threat of action can be increased or decreased according to the diplomatic situation and the policy can be sustained for as long as necessary.

438. The issue of influencing the US, both at the strategic and at the operational level, was a constant preoccupation at all levels of the UK Government.

439. Prime Ministers will always wish to exercise their own political judgement on how to handle the relationship with the US. It will depend on personal relationships as well as on the nature of the issues being addressed. On all these matters of strategy and diplomacy, the Inquiry recognises that there is no standard formula that will be appropriate in all cases.

440. Whether or not influence has been exercised can be difficult to ascertain, even in retrospect. The views of allies are most likely to make a difference when they come in one side of an internal debate, and there are a number of instances where the UK arguments did make a difference to the formation and implementation of US policy. The US and UK are close allies, but the relationship between the two is unequal.

441. The exercise of influence will always involve a combination of identifying the prerequisites for success in a shared endeavour, and a degree of bargaining to make sure that the approach meets the national interest. In situations like the run-up to the invasion of Iraq:

- If certain measures are identified as prerequisite for success then their importance should be underlined from the start. There are no prizes for sharing a failure.
- Those measures that are most important should be pursued persistently and consistently.
- If it is assumed that a consequence of making a contribution in one area is that a further contribution would not be required in another, then that should be made explicit.
- Influence should not be set as an objective in itself. The exercise of influence is a means to an end.